GARDA POWERS

Law and Practice

GARDA POWERS

Law and Practice

By

Rebecca Coen

B.C.L., LL.M. (Criminal Justice), BL

Consultant Editor

Dr Paul Anthony McDermott

B.C.L., LL.M. (Cantab), BL, Ph.D (NUI)

CLARUS PRESS

Published by
Clarus Press Ltd,
Griffith Campus,
South Circular Road,
Dublin 8.

Reprinted 2022

Typeset by
Datapage International Limited,
18 Docklands Innovation Park,
East Wall Road,
Dublin 3.

Printed by
SPRINT-print Ltd,
Dublin

ISBN
Paperback
978-1-905536-60-3

Hardback
978-1905536-57-3

Image on front cover of paperback edition reproduced with kind permission from © Julien Behal/PA Images.

For Catherine Coen and Bobby Maher

FOREWORD

This book is a very welcome addition to the growing library on Irish criminal law. In the thirty years since the enactment of the Criminal Justice Act 1984, which provided a power of detention by the Garda Síochána of suspects for a broad range of offences, the number of Garda investigative powers has increased enormously. On every front covered by this very comprehensive work there have been significant developments. The Garda Síochána now have very wide powers of detention for questioning and for significant periods, and increased powers in relation to the collection of evidence and covert policing, including surveillance. However the expansion of these powers has not been matched by a streamlining or simplification of their application. The current fragmented state of the law constitutes a daily challenge to investigators.

There are many compelling reasons why investigating Gardaí must be fully conversant with all of the requirements for the lawful exercise of these powers. Not least is what the author describes as "the stringent effects of the Irish exclusionary rule" if evidence is gathered in breach of an accused's constitutional rights. There is extensive discussion of the case law in this area including, *DPP v Kenny* [1990] 2 IR 110 which is the origin of the current exclusionary rule in Irish law.

It is therefore essential that the Garda Síochána have available to them in this book such a thorough overview of the scope and limits of their powers. There is a very detailed analysis of even the more obscure areas of operational activity for Gardaí. The book is an admirable step by step guide, referencing guidelines, regulations, caselaw and legislation in a seamless and accessible way. I believe it will be a welcome companion work to that other mainstay for Garda investigators, the *Garda Síochána Guide*.

However not alone is this work an immensely practical guide and resource for legal practitioners and investigators alike, it is also an impressive academic work drawing on a wide range of sources, with the author offering her own view on the criminal justice system as it operates in Ireland. Citing case law from other jurisdictions, and on the European Convention on Human Rights, and referencing UN human rights, the author ably demonstrates the wider context within which the Irish criminal justice system operates.

I welcome this publication which I am confident will prove very useful to both professionals within, and students of, the criminal justice system.

Claire Loftus
Director of Public Prosecutions

2 December 2013

PREFACE

"The exercise of power is determined by thousands of interactions between the world of the powerful and that of the powerless, all the more so because these worlds are never divided by a sharp line: everyone has a small part of himself in both."

- Václav Havel, *Disturbing the Peace* (1986)

Members of Ireland's national police force, An Garda Síochána, are empowered by an array of legislation and case-law to intervene in our emergencies, to investigate and prevent crimes against us, to protect the vulnerable, to maintain peace and order and to safeguard the security of the State. In order to fulfil their various functions, the gardaí are vested with an extraordinary range of powers, powers which facilitate arrest, detention, surveillance, the taking of forensic samples, photographs and fingerprints, the search of individuals, their homes and vehicles. In addition to proficiency in crime prevention and detection, intelligence-gathering, crowd-control, crime-scene management and the gathering of forensic and technical evidence, dedicated units have expertise in ballistics, in computer fraud and cyber-crime, human trafficking, domestic violence and sexual offences, immigration and juvenile justice. There is inter-agency and international cooperation in the investigation of transnational crime as well as in the investigation and prosecution of domestic offences in collaboration with agencies such as Revenue, the Competition Authority, the Health and Safety Authority, the Environmental Protection Agency, the Sea Fisheries Protection Authority, the Criminal Assets Bureau and the Department of Social Protection. Interventions are made with mentally ill persons under the Mental Health Acts; vulnerable complainants, witnesses and suspects are dealt with; children are taken into emergency care; offences perpetrated by children and against them are investigated. Each situation is complicated not only on a human level, but on a legal level also.

Garda powers are sanctioned interferences in the lives of individuals in the interests of the common good. Finely balanced against the rights of the individual to liberty, freedom of association, speech, reputation, privacy—the personal rights with which the Gardaí routinely intersect in the performance of their duties—the appropriate exercise of garda powers is essential, not only to ensure the admissibility of evidence gathered, but also for the wider objectives of the maintenance both of public confidence in policing and the preservation of the legitimacy of the criminal justice system.

As policing has become increasingly sophisticated and professionalised, layer upon layer of law has been introduced to which legislative changes are made piecemeal rather than by consolidation. Important legal principles are teased out case-by-case, while the Constitution and international human rights instruments provide the backdrop. The result is patchwork quilt of powers, neither easily identifiable nor readily accessible. This book identifies, analyses and distils garda powers, with a primary focus on the investigation of indictable offences, grounded in human rights principles and international standards. It is hoped that it will make the law and practice of policing in Ireland penetrable for gardaí, practitioners, students and citizens.

PREFACE

I am sincerely grateful for the assistance of many people, family, friends and colleagues, who have, in many varied ways, helped me as I wrote this book.

Particular thanks are owed to Claire Loftus, Director of Public Prosecutions, for taking the time from her demanding schedule to write a generous foreword. She, together with Barry Donoghue, Deputy Director of Public Prosecutions and James Hamilton, former Director of Public Prosecutions, have been unstinting in their support and encouragement from the initial stages to the final furlong.

Dr Paul Anthony McDermott of University College Dublin has been an invaluable resource as consultant editor, skilfully guiding me and sharing his insights.

Dr Liz Campbell of the University of Edinburgh has, with academic rigour and a keen critical eye, helped shape and make sense of my work.

I thank the gardaí that I have learned from, as well as my colleagues, past and present, in the Office of the Director of Public Prosecutions who have shared their experience and expertise so generously. I am especially grateful to Aisling Kelly, who is a fountain of knowledge and a great hoarder of precedents, which she very kindly shared with me.

David McCartney of Clarus Press has shown tremendous patience and understanding throughout this arduous process. The idea, which was the genesis of this book, was David's, and I thank him for offering me the opportunity to write it. I thank Dr Yvonne Daly of Dublin City University for sending David in my direction.

I am most indebted to my twin anchors, Bobby Maher and Catherine Coen, who have, with an inordinate amount of practical support and patience, carried me through the troughs and illuminated my path.

All errors are my own.

The opinions I have expressed ought not to be taken to represent the Director of Public Prosecutions or her Office.

Rebecca Coen
Dublin

2 January 2014

SHORT TABLE OF CONTENTS

Part VI
VULNERABLE COMPLAINANTS

Part VII
LANGUAGE RIGHTS

DETAILED TABLE OF CONTENTS

Part I
INTRODUCTION

Part II
THE POWER TO ARREST

Part V
THE POWER TO SURVEY AND INTERCEPT

Part VI
VULNERABLE COMPLAINANTS

Part VII
LANGUAGE RIGHTS

TABLE OF CASES

TABLE OF LEGISLATION

Constitutional Provisions

Pre-1922 Legislation

Acts of the Oireachtas

Statutory Instruments

Rules of Court

Other Jurisdictions

Belgium

International Instruments

Part I
Introduction

Introduction

MODERN POLICING AND GARDA POWERS

The work of the gardaí traverses constitutional and legal rights in overt and covert ways: powers to undertake surveillance, to take samples, to stop, arrest and search individuals and their homes are derived from a tapestry of interwoven and constantly evolving legislation and case-law. It has been said that it is the application of the legitimate use of force to a variety of situations which distinguishes the police from ordinary citizens. We vest in these designated individuals the power to intervene in our difficult situations. We assent to their use of force to do so. As Bittner put it:

> "...the police are empowered and required to impose or, as the case may be, coerce a provisional solution upon emergent problems... their competence to intervene extends to every kind of emergency ... it is on this basis that they may be required to do the work of thief-catchers and of nurses, depending on the occasion..."[1]

However, to equate policing with the application of force for problem-solving underestimates the complexity of modern criminal investigations in legal and practical terms. It is arguable that rather than by the visible display of coercive techniques, it is the unseen vesting of powers of considerably greater sophistication, to legitimately interfere in and investigate the lives of others, that is now the defining characteristic of the gardaí and of modern police forces generally.

It has been said that "the existence of police powers facilitates the exercise of generalised police power... the importance of legal powers is not so much that they are *actually* invoked frequently, but that they *could* be".[2] As a criminal accusation is the most coercive interaction with the agents of the State that any individual is likely to face, it is imperative that rights are respected and the law is adhered to. The appropriate use of garda discretion is therefore an important consideration in any discussion of garda powers, since "a power that is limited in law is not necessarily limited in action".[3]

---

1 E Bittner, "Florence Nightingale in pursuit of Willie Sutton: a theory of the police" in H Jacob (ed) *The Potential for Reform of Criminal Justice,* (Newbury Park, CA, Sage, 1974) at p 17.

2 A Sanders and R Young, "Police Powers" in T Newburn (ed.), *Handbook of Policing* (2nd ed, Willan Publishing, Cullompton, 2008) at p 281.

3 *ibid.*

Accordingly, the laws which curb garda intrusion into the lives of individuals and the oversight mechanisms of the criminal process, as well as the Garda Inspectorate and the garda Síochána Ombudsman Commission (GSOC), are indicative of the distinction between democracy and totalitarianism.

Policing is multi-faceted and has been professionalised: gardaí are required to combine technical and legal proficiency with the social skills necessary for the management of a variety of challenging situations. In addition to proficiency in crime prevention and detection, intelligence-gathering, crowd-control, crime-scene management and the gathering of forensic evidence, dedicated units have expertise in ballistics, in computer fraud and cyber-crime, human trafficking, domestic violence and sexual offences, immigration and juvenile justice. There is inter-agency and international cooperation in the investigation of transnational crime as well as in the investigation and prosecution of domestic offences in collaboration with agencies such as Revenue, the Competition Authority, the Health and Safety Authority, the Environmental Protection Agency, the Sea Fisheries Protection Authority, the Criminal Assets Bureau and the Department of Social Protection. Every day in every garda station the skills of the social worker are brought to bear on the investigation of offences perpetrated against and by children. Children are taken into emergency care on the basis of concerns for their welfare. Interventions are made with mentally ill persons under the Mental Health Acts and specialist skills are required to deal with vulnerable complainants, suspects and witnesses. Each situation is not only complicated on a human level, but on a legal level also.

THE CRIMINAL JUSTICE SYSTEM

To assess the role of the gardaí and the powers that they exercise it is important to have some understanding of the theoretical architecture of the criminal justice system and the exclusionary rule that governs the admissibility of evidence. The criminal justice system performs many functions. It aspires to the prevention, punishment and deterrence of crime, the adjudication of guilt, the exoneration of the innocent, the diversion of juveniles and appropriate adults and the management of offenders in the short, medium and long-term. In addition it falls to the criminal justice system to rehabilitate and supervise prisoners pre and post-release and to impart the retribution and censure of the community to those who have offended against members of it. The overarching objective of the system is to do justice for those who have been offended against (both the individual and the community) and for those who have offended. Their differing and occasionally competing priorities need not be mutually exclusive, but there is a delicate balancing act inherent in the process, a balancing act which is performed almost exclusively by the gardaí in the pre-trial stages of the criminal process. For this reason, though the gardaí maintain an involvement through all the stages of the criminal process, this work is concentrated on the powers exercised in investigation, crime control and the preservation of order.

The criminal justice system may be thought of as a combination of rules underpinned by principles, with broad discretion afforded the police, prosecutors, judges and juries at various points in the process.[4] There is an overarching emphasis on due process which

[4] A Ashworth, *Principles of Criminal Law,* (3rd ed, Oxford University Press, Oxford) at p 59.

is designed not to guarantee a perfect trial, but a fundamentally fair one.[5] The rights of the accused have been carved out over centuries of trials, embedded into the common law, the laws of evidence, the Constitution, and international human rights law to seek to ensure that the machinery of criminal justice is untainted, unprejudiced and just. Equality before the law, non-retroactivity of criminal legislation, due process in the determination of guilt and equity of arms between the accused and the State are therefore among the fundamental tenets of our system.

Article 38.1 of the Irish Constitution provides that "No person shall be tried on any criminal charge save in due course of law." The text is somewhat vague, so vague as to omit even reference to the presumption of innocence.[6] As such, the 1996 Report of the Constitution Review Group recommended a more explicit enunciation of what exactly "trial in due course of law" entails. In considering Article 38.1 the Review Group distilled the detailed fair trial rights which have been identified in Irish case law and in the European Convention on Human Rights, and the Covenant of Civil and Political Rights, of which the following are relevant to garda investigations:

> "i) to be presumed innocent of a criminal charge until the contrary is proven (*O'Leary v Attorney General* [1995] IR 254, Article 14(2) CCPR, Article 6(2) ECHR)
>
> ii) to be informed of the nature and cause of the charge promptly, in detail, and in a language which is understood (*The State (Buchan) v Coyne* [1936] 70 ILTR 185, *In re Haughey* [1971] IR 217, *Director of Public Prosecutions v Doyle* [1994] 2 IR 486, Article 14(3)(a) CCPR, Article 6(3)(a) ECHR)
>
> ...
>
> viii) to be given the assistance of an interpreter, where necessary (*The State (Buchan) v Coyne* [1936] 70 ILTR 185, Article 14(3)(a) CCPR, Article 6(3)(e) ECHR)
>
> ...
>
> x) not to be compelled to incriminate oneself (*Heaney v Ireland* [1994] 3 IR 593, Article 14(2) and 3(g) CCPR)
>
> xi) to be subject to fair procedures relating to arrest, detention, charging, trial, appeal and sentence, which are prescribed or permitted by law (*The People (Director of Public Prosecutions) v Healy* [1990] 2 IR 73, *Cox v Ireland* [1992] 2 IR 503, Article 14 CCPR, Article 6(1) ECHR)..."[7]

The European Convention on Human Rights provides at Article 6 that:

> "1. In the determination of his civil rights and obligations or of any criminal charge against him, everyone is entitled to a fair and public hearing within a reasonable time by an independent and impartial tribunal established by law. Judgment shall be pronounced

---

[5] See *R v Find* [2001] 1 SCR 863, 1999 DLR (4th) 193 at [28], and *R. v O'Connor* [1995] 4 SCR 863, 130 DLR (4th) 235 at [193].

[6] For an excellent critical analysis of the presumption of innocence as it currently stands in Ireland see C Hamilton, *The Presumption of Innocence and Irish Criminal Law – Whittling the Golden Thread* (Irish Academic Press, Dublin, 2007).

[7] Convention for the Protection of Human Rights and Fundamental Freedoms.

publicly but the press and public may be excluded from all or part of the trial in the interests of morals, public order or national security in a democratic society, where the interests of juveniles or the protection of the private life of the parties so require, or to the extent strictly necessary in the opinion of the court in special circumstances where publicity would prejudice the interests of justice.

2. Everyone charged with a criminal offence shall be presumed innocent until proved guilty according to law.

3. Everyone charged with a criminal offence has the following minimum rights:
   (a) to be informed promptly, in a language which he understands and in detail, of the nature and cause of the accusation against him;
   (b) to have adequate time and facilities for the preparation of his defence;
   (c) to defend himself in person or through legal assistance of his own choosing or, if he has not sufficient means to pay for legal assistance, to be given it free when the interests of justice so require;
   (d) to examine or have examined witnesses against him and to obtain the attendance and examination of witnesses on his behalf under the same conditions as witnesses against him;
   (e) to have the free assistance of an interpreter if he cannot understand or speak the language used in court."

By virtue of the European Convention on Human Rights Act 2003 every organ of the State, including the gardaí, is obliged to perform its functions in a manner compatible with the State's obligations under the Convention provisions.[8]

The duty of gardaí to protect the rights of the citizens they serve is specifically outlined in the UN Code of Conduct for Law Enforcement Officials, which provides at Article 2 that '[i]n the performance of their duty, law enforcement officials shall respect and protect human dignity and maintain and uphold the human rights of all persons.'[9]

In the Declaration of Professional Values and Ethical Standards of An Garda Síochána gardaí commit themselves to "respect the human dignity of every person,"[10] to "uphold and protect the human rights of all"[11] and to "adhere to the principle of legality and apply the law in an equitable manner".[12]

Policing is "an extremely significant manifestation of government and a very significant touchstone of the nature of the relationship between government and the governed".[13] Each citizen has ceded a degree of liberty to facilitate the exercise of the powers associated with policing, since each power intersects with a constitutional right — to liberty, autonomy, bodily integrity or inviolability of the dwelling as the case may be. Such rights are ceded on the understanding that those who have the power to infringe

[8] European Convention on Human Rights Act, s 3.

[9] UN Code of Conduct for Law Enforcement Officials, G.A. Res. 34/169 (adopted 17 December 1979).

[10] *Professional Values and Ethical Standards of An garda Síochána*, Art 1.

[11] *ibid*, Art. 2.

[12] *ibid*, Art. 4.

[13] P Neyroud, "Policing and Ethics" in *Handbook of Policing* in T Newburn ed (2nd ed, Willan Publishing, Cullompton, 2008), at p 674.

upon them do so lawfully. It is presumed, indeed expected, that the gardaí will pursue criminal investigations lawfully and without infringing upon the constitutional rights of those who they police.[14]

THE EXCLUSIONARY RULE

The exclusionary rule of evidence impacts to a very large degree on the admissibility of evidence gathered in the course of criminal investigations and applies where evidence is gathered improperly, whether in breach of a legal or constitutional right of the accused. The result can be the exclusion of evidence obtained in breach of a legal right and automatic exclusion of evidence obtained in deliberate and conscious breach of the constitutional rights of the accused, even if the breach was inadvertent.[15] Where constitutional rights have been breached the rule operates to exclude evidence where there is a causative link between the breach and the evidence gathered if there are no extraordinary excusing circumstances.[16] The delineation between illegally and unconstitutionally obtained evidence may be a somewhat artificial one — as Daly has commented:

> "the interaction between a criminal suspect and the Gardaí in the pre-trial period affects so many constitutional rights, e.g. the right to liberty, the inviolability of the dwelling, the right to silence, the right to access pre-trial legal advice and the right to bodily integrity. Therefore, there is little interaction between Gardaí and suspects in the pre-trial process, which might be classified as purely legal rather than involving at least some constitutional element."[17]

The exclusionary rule of evidence has developed with a number of principles underpinning it[18]: the deterrence of unlawful police conduct[19]; the maintenance of the integrity of the criminal justice system[20] and the vindication of the constitutional rights of the individual.[21] Exclusion of evidence which has been improperly obtained is justified on a number of grounds: that a criminal process which admits the fruits of illegality in evidence is one which undermines itself; that the police must be deterred from wrongdoing and that the rights of the individual must, if breached by the police, be vindicated by the courts.

[14] As Heffernan has commented: "In contemporary society, criminal justice presupposes that law enforcement authorities will conduct criminal investigations using exclusively lawful means", L. Heffernan, *Evidence: Cases and Materials* (Thomson Round Hall, Dublin, 2005), p 475.

[15] *People (DPP) v Kenny* [1990] IR 110.

[16] *People (DPP) v Walsh* [1980] IR 294; *People (DPP) v Shaw* [1982] IR 1.

[17] YM Daly, "Unconstitutionally Obtained Evidence in Ireland: Protectionism, Deterrence and the Winds of Change" (2009) 19(2) ICLJ 40.

[18] See D McGrath, "The Exclusionary Rule in Respect of Unconstitutionally Obtained Evidence" (2004) (11)(1) DULJ 108.

[19] This remains the rationale for the exclusionary rule in the United States. See *United States v Calandra* (1974) 414 US 338 at 348, US SC; *Stone v Powell* (1976) 428 US 465 at 486; US SC; *United States v Leon* (1983) 468 US 897 at 906, US SC.

[20] McGrath notes that this is the foundation of the exclusionary rule in Canada, citing s 24(2) of the Canadian Charter of Rights and Freedoms. This principle has also been referred to in American cases e.g. *Olmstead v United States* (1928) 277 US 438, US SC. See further D McGrath, "The Exclusionary Rule in Respect of Unconstitutionally Obtained Evidence" (2004) (11)(1) DULJ 108.

[21] *DPP v Kenny* [1990] IR 110.

It is the vindication principle which the foundation of the Irish exclusionary rule. As judges are required to uphold the constitution[22] and to protect the rights of the accused from violation, it is reasoned that the appropriate remedial action is to return the accused to the position in which he stood before the breach. In *(People) (DPP) v Kenny* Finlay CJ explained:

> "The detection of crime and the conviction of guilty persons, no matter how important they may be in relation to the ordering of society, cannot, however, in my view, outweigh the unambiguously expressed constitutional obligation ' as far as practicable to defend and vindicated the personal rights of the citizen.' "[23]

A distinction was drawn between illegally and unconstitutionally obtained evidence in the seminal case of *People (AG) v O'Brien*:

> "Where evidence is found to have been illegally obtained, i.e. in breach of the legal rights of the suspect, the inclusion or exclusion of such evidence is a matter for the discretion of the trial judge; and
>
> where evidence is deemed to have been obtained in breach of the constitutional rights of a suspect it must be automatically excluded from evidence, unless there are extraordinary excusing circumstances in existence which would justify its admission; in which case, admission or inclusion is a matter for the discretion of the trial judge."[24]

This remains the essential rule today. A deliberate and conscious breach of a constitutional right results in an automatic exclusion, whereas the infringement of a legal right — such as a failure to abide by the Custody Regulations,[25] or the flawed search of a business premises as distinct from the home of the accused — will be a matter for the trial judge, with a reported tendency towards inclusion.[26] Hogan asserts:

> "In practice, the courts almost never exclude evidence on the ground that there has been a mere illegality (as distinct from unconstitutionality) and there is nearly always a reason why such evidence should be held to be admissible in the overall public interest."[27]

In *O'Brien* evidence had been obtained following the search of a private dwelling which had been misdescribed on the search warrant: whereas the correct address was "118 Captain's Road, Crumlin" the warrant incorrectly referred to "118 Cashel Road, Crumlin." The Court found that the error had been inadvertent. Whereas Kingsmill Moore J took the view that a trial judge ought to have discretion in deciding whether or not to admit unconstitutionally obtained evidence, Walsh J held that evidence obtained

[22] *DPP v Lynch* [1982] IR 64 at 76.

[23] *People (DPP) v Kenny* [1990] 2 IR 110 at 134.

[24] *People (AG) v O'Brien* [1965] IR 142.

[25] Statutory provision has been made for the inclusion of evidence which has been obtained in breach of the Custody Regulations, with the Criminal Justice Act 1984 providing at s 7(3) that failure to observe the Custody Regulations will not of itself affect the admissibility of statements made while in custody. See also *People (DPP) v Darcy*, unreported, Court of Criminal Appeal, 29 July 1997.

[26] Gerard Hogan's Note of Dissent on the Exclusionary Rule in the *Report of the Balance in the Criminal Law Review Group*, said " 15 March 2007, p 289.

[27] *ibid.*

in deliberate and conscious breach of the constitutional rights of an accused person should be absolutely inadmissible absent extraordinary excusing circumstances, three of which were identified:

> "The courts in exercising the judicial powers of government and State must recognise the paramount position of constitutional rights and must uphold the objection of an accused person to the admissibility at his trial of evidence obtained or procured by the State or its servants or agents as a result of deliberate and conscious violation of the constitutional rights of the accused person where no extraordinary excusing circumstances exist, such as the imminent destruction of vital evidence or the need to rescue a victim in peril. A suspect has no constitutional right to destroy or dispose of evidence or to imperil the victim. I would also place in the excusable category evidence obtained by search incidental to and contemporaneous with a lawful arrest although made without a valid search warrant.
>
> In my view evidence obtained in deliberate conscious breach of the constitutional rights of an accused person should, save in the excusable circumstances outlined above, be absolutely inadmissible. It follows therefore that evidence obtained without a deliberate and conscious violation of the accused's constitutional rights is not excludable by reason only of the violation of his constitutional right."[28]

The parameters of the rule have been grappled with for decades. There having been judicial controversy and disagreement as to the meaning of the terms "conscious and deliberate"[29] the rule was revisited in *People (DPP) v Kenny*[30] where Finlay CJ delivered the majority judgment, holding:

> "the correct principle is that evidence obtained by invasion of the constitutional personal rights of a citizen must be excluded unless a court is satisfied that either the act constituting the breach of constitutional rights was committed unintentionally or accidentally, or is satisfied that there are extraordinary excusing circumstances which justify the admission of the evidence in its (the court's) discretion."[31]

The effect of *Kenny* was to hold that a deliberate and conscious breach of the constitutional right had occurred regardless of whether the breach of the right was intentional. The gardaí in *Kenny* had not realised that they were encroaching on the constitutional rights of the accused, but their actions in forcibly entering the dwelling were neither unintentional nor accidental and so the evidence obtained in the course of the search ought to have been excluded.

It was argued by the *Balance in the Criminal Law Review Group* that the effect of such a strict exclusionary rule as applies in Ireland is to fetter the discretion of the trial judge and to preclude him or her from weighing the "public interest in ensuring that constitutional rights are protected by agents of the State as against the public interest in ensuring that crime is detected and punished and that the constitutional rights of victims are vindicated

[28] *O'Brien v Attorney General* [1965] IR 142 at 170.

[29] See D *McGrath, Evidence*, (Thomson Round Hall, Dublin, 2005) at p 340, citing *People (DPP) v Shaw* [1982] IR 1 and *People (DPP) v Healy* [1990] 2 IR 73; [1990] ILRM 313.

[30] *People (DPP) v Kenny* [1990] 2 IR 110.

[31] *ibid* at 134.

by the courts".[32] The Committee argued that the objectives of the rule could be achieved as satisfactorily by a discretionary exclusionary rule as by a strict one.[33]

In the case of *People (DPP) v Mallon* the Court of Criminal Appeal attempted to temper the consequences of the strict exclusionary rule where grammatical or typographical errors on search warrants are at issue. There a search warrant was challenged on the basis that it referred to "4 Marrowbone Lane" when it ought to have recited the correct address as "4 Marrowbone Lane Close". The Court, upholding the warrant, commented:

> "The remorseless logic of the *Kenny* decision leading to the automatic exclusion of evidence sometimes as a result of quite trivial errors, has been the subject of critical comment, most notably by the former Chief Justice Keane C.J. in the foreword to McGrath, Evidence, (Dublin: Roundhall Press, 2005) and by Charleton, J. (himself a distinguished author in the field of criminal law) in the High Court decision of Director of *Public Prosecutions v Cash* [2007] IEHC 108, and that dissatisfaction is perhaps reflected in the comments of the trial judge here. However, this case does not raise the question of the admissibility of evidence obtained subsequent to an illegal and therefore, unconstitutional search. Instead it raised a logically anterior issue: in what circumstances will a warrant be considered ineffective, or invalid so as to give rise to the argument that evidence obtained should be excluded?"

The warrant was not invalidated since the error did not go to its jurisdiction, was not calculated to mislead and did not in fact mislead. The Court held:

> "It is important that a court should insist upon accuracy, particularly in addresses in relation to warrants since they authorise forcible entry of premises including dwelling homes. But invalidation of every warrant on the ground of error and description does not seem to serve any advance purpose in respect of the Constitution or even of proper grammar, usage, or clarity in communication. As the trial judge here observed, this is a mistake which is regularly made in everyday life. It is only necessary to consider the variety of texts which go through professional editing processes, such as newspapers, books, road signs, Acts of the Oireachtas and even sometimes judgments in the Official Reports, to recognise that some level of error is almost unavoidable. Furthermore, particularly in so long as Irish law maintains an almost absolute exclusionary rule for evidence obtained as a result of an illegal and therefore unconstitutional search of a dwelling house, courts should be slow to invalidate warrants on the grounds of typographical grammatical, or transcription errors, which are neither calculated to mislead, nor in truth do mislead, any reasonable reader of the words."[34]

The warrant was considered to describe the premises with the requisite clarity such that a postman, taxi-driver or garda reasonably familiar with the area could direct the reader of the warrant to the premises.

To the person attempting to discern for practical policing purposes whether an action is a trivial error, as outlined in *Mallon*, or a breach of one of the fundamental rights of the accused which will inevitably result in the exclusion of evidence, the caselaw is not

[32] Balance in the Criminal Law Review Group: Final Report, Department of Justice, Equality and Law Reform, 15 March 2007.

[33] *ibid*, at p 158 available online at: http://www.justice.ie/en/JELR/BalanceRpt.pdf/Files/BalanceRpt.pdf <accessed 7 November 2013>.

[34] *People (DPP) v Mallon* [2011] IECCA 29.

readily reconciled. Given the stringency of the exclusionary rule, and the fact that much of the work of the gardaí in criminal investigation affects constitutional rights—in search warrants, in the search and detention of suspects, in surveillance—it is essential that in the pre-trial process garda powers are exercised correctly and appropriately, within their permitted limits. The rights themselves must be the focus point from which the actions of gardaí are guided. Lord Bingham stated:

> "It cannot be too strongly emphasised that these are not the rules of a game. They are rules designed to safeguard the fairness of proceedings brought to determine whether a defendant is guilty of committing a crime or crimes conviction of which may expose him to serious penal consequences. In a criminal trial as in other activities the observance of basic rules has been shown to be the most effective safeguard against unfairness, error and abuse."[35]

Therefore the appropriate perspective from which to view garda powers is not in terms of the gardaí having an array of powers at their discretionary disposal, but rather to consider the individual as shrouded with the protection of an array of legal safeguards and rights of international and constitutional origin, including liberty, freedom of association, privacy, silence, autonomy, access to a solicitor and inviolability of the dwelling. Individual rights are the starting point. A garda ought not to exercise a power without first considering the rights at play and the justification, necessity and legitimacy of the interference which invocation of a power constitutes.

The exclusionary rule might appear to be a hurdle in an incomprehensible prosecutorial obstacle course, but that obstacle course serves an important purpose. It is grounded in the idea that the burden of proof in criminal cases rests on the prosecution, and that punishment should only take place after the State has discharged that burden to prove the case against the suspect beyond all reasonable doubt.[36] That defendants are acquitted is an indication that the system is working as intended. Were that not the case it would suffice to accuse. As Judge Hardiman, writing extra-judicially, has asked:

> "Would even the most ardent advocates of 'law and order' favour a higher conviction rate? Would ninety-nine point something per cent as in China, be more satisfactory, or is it possible that there are drawbacks to a system that so weakly scrutinises State allegations against individuals?"[37]

That our system demands adherence to the statutory provisions which permit encroachment on the rights of individuals, and particularly suspects, is to be admired rather than bemoaned. "Technicalities", on which acquittals are sometimes based, often as a direct consequence of the exclusionary rule (a detention which becomes unlawful rendering incriminating admissions inadmissible, a search warrant which is out of date resulting in the exclusion of evidence), are not inconvenient impediments to conviction, but markers of a robust and rights-oriented criminal justice system which operates as a bulwark against injustice and abuse.

---

[35] *Randall v The Queen* [2002] UKPC 19; [2002] 1 WLR 2237; [2002] 2 Cr App. R. 17 (267) at 11.

[36] In civil cases a lower "balance of probabilities" standard applies.

[37] Adrian Hardiman, Foreword to Claire Hamilton, *The Presumption of Innocence and Irish Criminal Law – Whittling the Golden Thread* (Irish Academic Press, Dublin, 2007).

LAW AND ORDER VERSUS LIBERALISM

Undoubtedly there is an inherent contradiction in the granting of coercive powers to State officials, that they might be better equipped to combat crime, in the context of an overarching philosophy committed to restricting the power of agents of the State.[38] Many would argue that recent legislative developments in Ireland represent a move from a due process model to a crime control model of criminal justice,[39] that is to say a move from the prosecutorial obstacle course to one in which the repression of crime is the primary focus, with maximum efficiency emphasised in the pursuit of pleas of guilty. Irish developments indicative of this shift include the introduction of inferences from silence[40] and mandatory sentences which may be reduced by the entry of a plea of guilty.[41] But despite the prevailing law and order *zeitgeist* liberal notions of rights retain relevance. As Campbell puts it:

> "Liberal notions of the primacy of the individual and of individual rights are being eroded by premodern calls for vengeance, and a heightened legislative concern for security has compromised liberty. Central liberal precepts such as the concept of individual rights, the rule of law, and limitation on State power have been eroded, often during times of public anxiety and perceived social peril. Nevertheless, such attrition may be stemmed by a firm commitment to legal principles grounded in constitutional theory. While convenience and justice are often not on speaking terms, adherence to traditional liberal legal precepts will ensure the protection of individual rights and liberties."[42]

Whatever the prevailing criminal justice crisis, ours is still a society in which liberty and individuality are prized and in which the ultimate punishment is liberty's denial. Accordingly, irrespective of the legislative knee-jerk responses so often favoured over measured criminal justice debate, the foundation stones of the criminal process remain, which dictate that to deny liberty with the assent of society the criminal justice system

---

[38] See S Choongh, "Police Investigative Powers" in M McConville and G Wilson (eds), *The Handbook of the Criminal Process* (Oxford University Press, Oxford, 2002) at p 47.

[39] See for instance L Campbell "From Due Process To Crime Control—The Decline Of Liberalism In The Irish Criminal Justice System" (2007) 25 ILT 281.

[40] For a discussion on the theoretical and practical aspects of inferences under the Criminal Justice Act 2007 see R Coen, "The Decline of Due Process and the Right to Silence's Demise," (2008) 18(1) ICLJ 10; T McGillicuddy, "Restrictions on the Right to Silence under the Criminal Justice Act 2007 – Part 1," (2008) 18(3) ICLJ 77 and T McGillicuddy, "Restrictions on the Right to Silence under the Criminal Justice Act 2007 – Part 2," (2008) 18(4) ICLJ 112.

[41] For instance s 15A of the Misuse of Drugs Act 1977, as inserted by s 4 of the Criminal Justice Act 1999 provides for a ten year minimum sentence (s 27(3B) as inserted by s 5 of the Criminal Justice Act 1999. However, s 29(3C) provides that the mandatory sentence need not apply "where the court is satisfied that there are exceptional and specific circumstances relating to the offence, or the person convicted of the offence, which would make a sentence of not less than 10 years imprisonment unjust in all the circumstances and for this purpose the court may have regard to any matters it considers appropriate, including—

(a) whether that person pleaded guilty to the offence and, if so,

(i) the stage at which he indicated the intention to plead guilty, and

(ii) the circumstances in which the indication was given, and

(b) whether that person materially assisted in the investigation of the offence."

[42] L Campbell, "From Due Process To Crime Control—The Decline Of Liberalism In The Irish Criminal Justice System" (2007) 25 ILT 281.

must be characterised by due process and fairness both in the investigation of crime and in the adjudication of guilt. In addition, for reasons of practicality and effectiveness which go beyond the liberal notions of fairness and equity of arms, the broader rights of the individual to a life free from undue intrusion by the agents of the State, to liberty, privacy, freedom of expression and association, freedom from torture and from arbitrary arrest and punishment, must pervade every aspect of policing. These values form the theoretical backdrop to the more concrete aims and objectives of the criminal justice system, which in the English and Welsh context have been identified as follows:

- to reduce the level of actual crime and disorder;
- to reduce the adverse impact of crime and disorder on people's lives;
- to reduce the economic costs of crime;
- to ensure just processes and just and effective outcomes;
- to deal with cases throughout the criminal justice process with appropriate speed;
- to meet the needs of victims, witnesses and jurors within the system;
- to respect the rights of defendants and treat them fairly;
- to promote confidence in the Criminal Justice System.[43]

The law provides legitimate obstacles, such as rendering inadmissible evidence obtained in breach of the fundamental rights of the individual. Yet recent Irish discourse has centred on the need to 'rebalance' the criminal law.[44] In England and Wales a similar dialogue can be seen in documents such as the 2006 "Criminal Justice System Review: Rebalancing the criminal justice system in favour of the law-abiding majority".[45] The emergence of a crime control model of criminal justice is very clearly in evidence in Ireland, both in the tenor of the debates and in the legislation which has resulted from them.[46] Notwithstanding the adoption of a raft of significant measures — including expansive inference from silence provisions, the enactment of a comprehensive surveillance Act[47] and even appeals against acquittals,[48] undoubtedly significant erosions of the

[43] *Criminal Justice: The Way Ahead, Cm 5074 (Feb 2001)*, see McConville and Wilson *The Handbook of the Criminal Justice Process* (Oxford University Press, Oxford, 2002) at p 7.

[44] See *Balance in the Law Review Group: Final Report*, Department of Justice, Equality and Law Reform, 15 March 2007, available online at: http://www.justice.ie/en/JELR/BalanceRpt.pdf/Files/BalanceRpt.pdf <accessed 7 November 2013>.

[45] *Criminal Justice System Review: Rebalancing the Criminal Justice System in Favour of the Law-Abiding Majority*, Home Office, 2006, available online at http://webarchive.nationalarchives.gov.uk/20060904182404/homeoffice.gov.uk/documents/cjs-review.pdf/ <accessed 7 November 2013 >.

[46] See for example the Criminal Justice Act 2006, Criminal Justice Act 2007, Criminal Justice (Miscellaneous Provisions) Act 2009, Criminal Justice (Surveillance) Act 2009, Criminal Justice (Amendment) 2009, Criminal Procedure Act 2010, Criminal Justice Act 2011.

[47] The Criminal Justice (Surveillance) Act 2009 was enacted to remove any potential legal obstacles to the admissibility of material gained by means of secret surveillance in cases involving arrestable offences.

[48] The Criminal Procedure Act 2010 has modified the rule against double jeopardy in order to allow a person who has been acquitted of an offence to be re-tried in circumstances where "new and compelling evidence" emerges or where the acquittal is tainted due, for example, to corruption or intimidation of witnesses or jurors or perjury and provides the Director of Public Prosecutions with a right of appeal to the Supreme Court on a "with prejudice" basis against an acquittal where the acquittal arises from an erroneous ruling by the trial court on a point of law arising during the trial or from a decision by the Court of Criminal Appeal not to order a re-trial following the quashing of a conviction.

rights of the accused — commentators frequently opine that the gardaí fight crime "with one hand tied behind their backs."[49] While these developments are mirrored in England and Wales, other methods are also being explored there such as the use of restorative justice and community sanctions as a means of delivering justice.[50] In other European jurisdictions the use of administrative measures to disrupt organised crime is a novel approach to crime reduction and arguably more effective than traditional policing.[51] This approach utilises the agencies of the State involved in the issuing of licenses, permits, planning permission — the pre-requisites for enterprise — so that legislative provisions in areas such as importation, exportation, licensing, fiscal and customs regulation which are vulnerable to abuse by organised crime groups are identified. The aim is to:

> "... try to exclude organised crime groups from participation in certain legal activities or from doing business with the government. For this purpose, special legal instruments can be developed which make it possible to exclude (organised) criminals from contracting with the government (e.g. public procurement) or from obtaining official permits or licences (e.g. building permits, the sale of financial services) from that government or public administration."[52]

The approach is based on the following premise:

> "The idea that traditional 'repressive' law enforcement bodies (police, prosecutors, courts) should have a monopoly on reactions to organised crime is under widespread revision because it is clear that alone, they are unlikely to have sufficient impact on levels of criminality."[53]

These developments augur for the continuation of the shifting sands. But as new means of combating crime are identified and explored it is worthwhile asking if the extant powers are of use, or whether they could be whittled, refined and consolidated to make them readily accessible to lawyer, garda and citizen. Often extensive criminal justice Acts serve to add amendment to amendment, and to complicate rather than clarify. Therefore announcements heralding the arrival of new garda powers ought to be critically examined for efficacy. To assert that gardaí are hampered to an unmanageable extent by the fundamental rights of

---

[49] This is a common refrain. See P Rabbitte TD, "Latest Gangland Murder Condemned," *Labour Party Press Release*, 9 July 2010, available online http://www.labour.ie/press/listing/12786867251213035.html <accessed 7 November 2013> ; Former Minister D Ahern, "Ahern calls for greater EU cooperation to combat criminal gangs," Department of Justice, Equality and Law Reform Press Release, 16 July 2009, available online: http://www.justice.ie/ga/JELR/Pages/PR09000111 <accessed 7 November 2013>.

[50] The Ministry of Justice Structural Reform Plan published in July 2010 set out a commitment to introduce a 'rehabilitation revolution' and conduct a review of sentencing policy. See 'Breaking the Cycle: Effective Punishment, Rehabilitation and Sentencing of Offenders', available online at www.justice.gov.uk/consultations/docs/breaking-the-cycle.pdf <accessed 7 November 2013>. See also the Restorative Justice Council: http://www.restorativejustice.org.uk <accessed 7 November 2013>.

[51] See C Fijnaut and L Paoli, *Organised Crime in Europe: Concepts, Patterns and Control Policies in the European Union and Beyond*, Springer, 2004; Council of Europe, *Preventative Legal Measures Against Organised Crime, Best Practice Survey No. 9*, PC-S-CO (2003) E.

[52] Council of Europe, *Preventative Legal Measures Against Organised Crime, Best Practice Survey No. 9*, PC-S-CO (2003) E, p 4.

[53] Council of Europe, *Preventative Legal Measures Against Organised Crime, Best Practice Survey No. 9*, PC-S-CO (2003) E, p 3.

citizens is to grossly over-simplify and to ignore both the potential for alternatives and the impact of under-resourcing, which is a significant policing obstacle.[54]

HUMAN-RIGHTS-BASED POLICING AND COMMUNITY POLICING

Human-rights-based and community policing are increasingly emphasised by An Garda Síochána, but are perhaps yet to be fully embraced.[55] The move within An Garda Síochána towards human-rights-based policing is by no means accidental: it coincides with the obligation imposed by incorporation of the European Convention on Human Rights into Irish law, with the requirement that "every organ of the state shall perform its functions in a manner compatible with the state's obligations under the Convention provisions".[56] It also ties in with the endorsement, at a senior level at least, of Community Based Policing as a key strategic objective of An Garda Síochána.[57] The 'reactive' or 'fire brigade' method of policing is now dated and has been seen to be ineffective in the face of overwhelming demands on the police.[58] As the role of the gardaí expands, and expectations of the service increase, there is a very practical rationale for the adoption of the community policing model, which is that the police cannot effectively address crime alone.[59]

Tilley explains community policing in simple terms:

> "Community policing stresses policing *with* and *for* the community rather than *of* the community. It aspires to improve the quality of life of communities. In improving the

---

[54] Referring to the gardaí having 'one hand behind their backs' in February 2009 Charles Flanagan pointed to the inadequacy of garda radio systems and the lack of availability of the PULSE system, saying "the garda is trapped in a technological stone age with the failure to introduce a national digital radio scheme, which has been promised for more than ten years, and now serious shortcomings with the PULSE computer system placing gardaí in the fight against crime in a position of great disadvantage." Vol. 673 No. 2 *Dáil Debates*, 3 February 2009. In 2012 the Department of Justice revealed that 40% of garda stations did not have internet access and as such did not have access to the PULSE database, nor to email, while senior gardai asked for patrol cars to be prioritised over internet access, see "No internet in 40% of garda stations", *The Irish Times*, 13 February 2012; "Plea for patrol cars over internet", *Irish Independent*, 13 February 2012.

[55] Walsh notes, in relation to the Ionann Human Rights audit of An Garda Síochána that piecemeal initiatives aimed at greater community engagement "did not trigger a concerted garda effort to implement more sustained and committed community policing methods. Subsequently, the Ionann human rights audit encountered considerable scepticism at community level over the garda commitment to meaningful engagement with local communities." Dermot Walsh, *Human Rights and Policing in Ireland: Law, Policy and Practice* (Clarus Press, Dublin, 2009) at p 376.

[56] European Convention on Human Rights Act 2003, s 3.

[57] That An Garda Síochána favours the community policing model is evidenced in the organisation's Strategy Statement for 2010 – 2012, which is entitled 'Working With Our Communities.'

[58] For an interesting discussion of community policing see N Tilley "Modern approaches to policing: community, problem-oriented and intelligence-led" in T Newburn (ed) *Handbook of Policing* (2nd ed, Willan Publishing, Cullompton, 2008) at pp 373 – 403.

[59] See N Tilley "Modern approaches to policing: community, problem-oriented and intelligence-led" in T Newburn (ed) *Handbook of Policing* (2nd ed, Willan Publishing, Cullompton, 2008) at pp 373 – 403.

> quality of life it aims to solve community problems alongside the community and as defined by the community."[60]

Referring to the launch of the National Model of Community Policing in 2009, Commissioner Murphy stated:

> "The Model builds on the success of existing good Community Policing practice and aims to create a policing environment where collaborative partnerships are fostered between An Garda Síochána and community members. I am committed to ensuring that this strong Community Policing ethos permeates throughout An Garda Síochána and I am confident that this will result in an increased level of community partnerships, a more visible Garda presence and a reduction in crime and the fear of crime in our communities."[61]

The emphasis is on garda–community partnerships and the 'pillars' of the approach include collaborative engagement, visibility, problem-solving, accessibility, enforcement and a shared responsibility for crime reduction.[62] The 2011 Policing Plan of An Garda Síochána, which, like the Strategy Statement 2010 – 2012, is entitled *Working With Our Communities*, identifies community policing as a strategic goal, a goal which is stated to acknowledge that:

> "a community based approach is a priority for An Garda Síochána, in order to build and maintain trust and confidence in the Garda service. We will deliver a service that recognises the diverse needs and priorities of all the people and communities in Ireland."[63]

Initiatives listed within the Strategy Statement 2010 – 2012 in pursuit of that goal include: fully respecting the rights of all people in contact with the garda service; building trust and confidence with diverse communities; the provision of support and protection for the most vulnerable; meaningful engagement with children and young people; meaningful support for victims of crime; accessibility; partnership based problem-solving; improved communication and crime prevention and reduction.

It is certain that the mistrust of large sections of the community significantly impedes policing. The fact that the most marginalised and disaffected are the least likely to engage positively with the gardaí, or to participate in community policing initiatives, is an obvious weakness of the model, and the clearest indicator that it is not a policing panacea. The aspirational jargon of community policing is viewed with scepticism, but there is merit in the concept.

Human-rights-based policing fits well with the community policing model. Human-rights-based policing has been seen to protect both the public and the police, to improve effectiveness and the legitimacy both of police forces and of the criminal justice system generally. As such, embedding human rights in policing is of inestimable importance in

[60] N Tilley "Modern approaches to policing: community, problem-oriented and intelligence-led" in T Newburn (ed.) *Handbook of Policing*, (2nd ed, Willan Publishing, Cullompton, 2008) at p 376.
[61] An Garda Síochána Strategy Statement 2010 – 2012: Working With Our Communities, at p 1.
[62] *ibid.*
[63] An Garda Síochána Policing Plan 2011: Working With Our Communities.

strengthening prosecutions, by providing a consistent mechanism to build the trust and confidence of the communities from which witnesses, complainants and suspects are drawn.

"HUMAN RIGHTS PROOFING" THE GARDAÍ

Nuala O'Loan, former Police Service of Northern Ireland (PSNI) Ombudsman, refers to a submission of the (UK) National Policing Improvement Agency to the Equality and Human Rights Commission that "if human rights are done right, they can have a powerful legitimising effect. They are a key part of effectiveness in policing".[64] O'Loan puts the argument for human rights based policing thus:

> "Policing has never been easy. It must deal with matters as diverse as human trafficking, murder, burglary, confrontational young people on street corners and major protests. The challenge ... is to ensure that it meets all these responsibilities... It is vital that the methods used do not alienate the population, are not counterproductive, and do not grow the very terrorism and organised crime it is striving to prevent. Policing can be effective only with the community's consent. A human rights approach is one of the best tools to ensure a secure and fair society."[65]

Human-rights-based policing supports community policing objectives and is capable of being readily implemented in every garda decision. Policing which is neither rights aware nor rights compliant is ultimately counter-productive, because to disregard the rights of the complainants on whose evidence the criminal process depends, or to encroach excessively upon the rights of suspects, is to potentially undermine not only the case under investigation, but also the broader and the of the public in the gardaí.

The 2004 Human Rights Audit of An Garda Síochána noted that "human rights are not yet embedded in and intrinsic to the culture and ethos of An Garda Síochána". The audit expressed the hope that:

> "In 2009, An Garda Síochána should be a police service where:
> - There are no critical reports from any source about excessive or disproportionate use of force in using police powers.
> - There is a flourishing network of active community support across all diverse groups.
> - A high level human rights advisory committee, a high profile human rights champion and a strong management structure for human rights work is well established.
> - User satisfaction surveys show high levels of satisfaction with An Garda Síochána across all sections of the community.
> - Systems are well established for monitoring, measuring and reporting on compliance with human rights standards across all of An Garda Síochána's work.
> - All policies and procedures have been 'human rights proofed' and published wherever possible.
> - An Garda Síochána's staff more closely reflect the communities they serve.
> - All staff put human rights observance at the heart of everything they do – and can be seen to do so."

[64] N O'Loan "My Lessons for the Police," *The Guardian*, 26 June 2009, available online: http://www.guardian.co.uk/commentisfree/2009/jun/26/human-rights-police-northern-ireland <accessed 7 November 2013>.

[65] *ibid.*

Achieving these objectives and translating the words into actions is an ongoing challenge.

The function of An Garda Síochána was statutorily defined for the first time in the Garda Síochána Act 2005, as being the provision of:

> "policing and security services for the State with the objective of
> (a) preserving peace and public order,
> (b) protecting life and property,
> (c) vindicating the human rights of each individual,
> (d) protecting the security of the State,
> (e) preventing crime,
> (f) bringing criminals to justice, including by detecting and investigating crime, and
> (g) regulating and controlling road traffic and improving road safety."[66]

The inclusion of specific reference to the vindication of human rights is important. The Strategy Statement of An Garda Síochána 2010 – 2012 includes respect "for people, their Human Rights and their needs," as a core value which Commissioner Murphy stated would "become deeply ingrained in the minds of garda members. Together with honesty, accountability and professionalism, the core values are to act as "cultural cornerstones. They are inherent and sacrosanct and can never be compromised".[67]

Those who come into contact with the gardaí are among the most vulnerable in society. The gardaí are not only expected to refrain from undue encroachment on the rights of those individuals; they are expected to vindicate their rights to the fullest possible extent. Individuals, and especially those who are accused of criminal offences, are often ignorant of their rights and entitlements in garda custody, which places an even higher onus on gardaí to vindicate those rights, to ensure that entitlements are fully explained and understood and to pro-actively provide access to legal advice, medical attention and interpretation services in custody. The European Court of Human Rights has emphasised that persons in custody are in a vulnerable position and that the authorities are under a duty to protect them.[68] As outlined by the UK Joint Committee on Human Rights:

> "...the majority of people entering custody are extremely vulnerable individuals. ... It must be recognised that by taking people into custody the state takes upon itself a particular duty of care, because of their vulnerability, and a special responsibility to ensure their protection and to uphold their human rights... The multiple vulnerabilities of the people detained, the acute need for medical treatment and drug and alcohol detoxification facilities, low educational achievement and poor communication skills, and the high rate of mental illness, are all found to a greater or lesser extent in all forms of state detention."

As the interface between the citizen and the State the gardaí play a crucial role in the protection of the rights of the individual, be that individual a victim of crime, a suspect,

---

[66] Garda Síochána Act 2005, s 7.

[67] An Garda Síochána Strategy Statement 2010 – 2012: Working With Our Communities, at p 1.

[68] See, for example, *Salman v Turkey* [GC], no. 21986/93, § 99, ECHR 2000-VII.

or a person vulnerable through mental illness, homelessness, intoxication, age or other circumstance.

Equally the gardaí are required to accommodate the rights of victims of crime, with whose needs the criminal justice system has grappled with only a limited degree of success. With increasing rights of participation being afforded to victims within the criminal process,[69] policing must ensure the privacy, dignity and protection of crime victims through the provision of meaningful support, participation and information within the process.[70]

Human-rights-based policing means that human rights thinking must pervade every operation and tour of duty, that evidence of innocence should be sought out as fervently as evidence of guilt[71] and that consideration should be given to the individual right potentially affected by garda action before a decision is made to exercise any discretionary garda powers of stop, search, arrest, detention or use of force. That, perhaps, requires a reorientation of garda focus, for instance viewing protest marches first and foremost as indicative of freedom of expression, assembly, thought and conscience, with consideration then being given to the need, if any, to curb or curtail the protest in the interest of the maintenance of order or the prevention of crime. Restraint in such situations furthers and augments consent-based and community policing. In suggesting a model for 'human-rights proofing' garda policies and procedures, Ionann suggested that the following examination be undertaken:

> " For each interference with a right
> - Is the interference legal? (Evidence with relevant legislation)
> - Is the interference necessary? (Evidence by, for example, asking does it protect the rights of others, is there a pressing social need, does it meet legitimate aims under the ECHR?)
> - Is the interference proportionate? (Are there alternative actions available? Is this the least intrusive interference possible?)
> - What safeguards exist to protect ECHR in relation to this policy?
> - Is there a remedy for the person who believes their ECHR rights have been infringed by the policy?"

[69] Victim centred initiatives have included providing rights of audience to victims of crime to give victim impact evidence at the sentencing hearing in Criminal Justice Act 1993, s 5, which has recently been expanded by the Criminal Procedure Act 2010, as well as the provision of separate legal representation afforded to complainants in rape cases in the Sex Offenders Act 2001, s 34. Ireland has also opted into Directive 2012/29/EU of 25 October 2012 establishing minimum standards on the rights, support and protection of victims of crime. The Directive must be transposed into Irish law by 16 November 2015.

[70] *The Victims' Charter and Guide to the Criminal Justice System* has recently been revised and sets out comprehensively the entitlements of victims, the service they can expect from the various State agencies involved in the criminal process and their recourse in the event that their expectations are not met.

[71] The duty to seek out and preserve evidence has been the subject of a number of significant decisions. See *Murphy v DPP* [1989] ILRM 71; *Braddish v DPP* [2001] 3 IR 127, [2002] 1 ILRM 151 and *Dunne v DPP* [2002] 2 IR 306. See also G Birmingham, "The Obligation to Seek Out and Preserve Evidence" (2004) 9 BR 86.

In addition the broader human rights implications must be considered, for family members, bystanders and members of the public.[72] A recommendation of the Human Rights Audit undertaken by Ionann in 2004 was that, by 2009, all garda policies and procedures should be 'human rights proofed' and published wherever possible in the interests of transparency. Very few policy documents have been made publicly available as yet. The abuse of power by some gardaí of the Donegal Division, which was ultimately the subject of the Morris Tribunal, unearthed a catalogue of allegations of criminal and unethical conduct by members of An Garda Síochána. Walsh has stated that:

> "It can be no exaggeration to say that these reports collectively offer the most incisive and sustained exposé of: the nature and extent of corruption, abuse and/or incompetence among gardaí in junior and managerial ranks; systemic failures in senior Garda management; and serious deficiencies in police governance, accountability and working practices."[73]

The Tribunal has been described as a "dark period in the history of a proud organisation,"[74] but it is a salutary lesson also: that it is of fundamental importance that garda powers are exercised with restraint and effective oversight, and that the rights of individuals are as important as the detection and investigation of crime. Post-Morris the force has the oversight of the Garda Inspectorate and the Garda Síochána Ombudsman Commission (GSOC) and has embarked on an extensive change and modernisation programme aimed at addressing the significant failings identified by the Morris Tribunal Reports. The high-level organisational response is strategic and includes the following initiatives: the introduction of a performance and accountability framework; the implementation of a new management system for handling covert human intelligence sources (CHIS); the establishment of a Crime Training Faculty; the introduction of extensive training programmes for Senior Investigating Officers and crime scene investigators; the appointment of specially trained forensic collision investigators; the appointment of family liaison officers and the introduction of new comprehensive Treatment of Persons in Custody records and guidelines.

It is the gardaí who are charged with the vindication of the rights of suspects in the crucial investigation period: to ensure that the requisite suspicion is present before a personal search; to clearly communicate the reasons for a search or an arrest and the legal basis for them; to obtain a warrant where necessary for entry and search of a dwelling; to provide access to a solicitor, interpreter or an appropriate adult for juveniles and mentally impaired adults in custody. It is, therefore, incumbent upon the gardaí to daily strike a balance between the public interest in the investigation and prosecution of criminal offences and the rights of the individual to liberty, freedom of association, speech, reputation, privacy — the personal rights with which the gardaí

---

[72] Ionnan Management Consultants Ltd, *Human Rights Audit of An Garda Síochána* (June 2004).

[73] D Walsh, *Human Rights and Policing in Ireland* (Clarus Press, Dublin, 2009), preface, at x.

[74] Commissioner Fachtna Murphy, Morris Tribunal Statement by the Commissioner on the 7/10/08 - 1163/08, available online http://Garda.ie/Controller.aspx?Page=2151&Lang=1 <accessed 7 November 2013>.

routinely intersect in the performance of their duties. By upholding and protecting the human rights of all the people of Ireland the actions of the gardaí are legitimised, the effectiveness of the force in securing peace and order is increased and policing is undertaken with the consent and cooperation of the community.

If the police force of a nation is not rights-aware and rights-compliant, not only is the force devoid of legitimacy and in breach of the contract by which the public have willingly forfeited a portion of their liberty and privacy to assist in the detection of crime, it is one in which victims of crime do not place their trust and confidence. The Morris Tribunal sharply illustrates that rights are abstract concepts unless they are enforced, meaningless words on a page unless they are protected, respected and vindicated.

IDENTIFYING GARDA POWERS

Identifying garda powers and thus determining the basic rules is increasingly difficult in Ireland. In England and Wales the Police and Criminal Evidence Act 1984 is accompanied by extensive PACE Codes of Conduct. There the core framework of police powers and safeguards around stop and search, arrest, detention, investigation, identification and interviewing detainees is clearly laid out. In Ireland the sands are continually shifting as new powers are incrementally introduced and even long-established rules, such as those pertaining to the exclusion of improperly obtained evidence, are refined and occasionally side-stepped. In the absence of a comprehensive criminal code those working with the criminal law must perpetually sift through layers of legal inheritance — an unwieldy array of legislation and case-law — to distil the applicable principles. The pace of legislative change in the criminal justice sphere, combined with the practice of amending Acts piecemeal rather than by consolidation, makes identification of the extent and scope of the powers of the gardaí a challenge which is grappled with by gardaí and practitioners alike. It is almost certainly impenetrable for the ordinary citizen. The codification of the basics of arrest, search and other fundamental powers would be a significant improvement. That the legislation providing a power and governing its use has been continually amended, section-by-section, by deletion, addition and substitution has a number of consequences: it means that citizens cannot have any degree of certainty as to the law and as to their rights in interacting with the gardaí; from the perspective of the gardaí it makes training difficult, provides more scope for errors and complicates matters such as detention periods and search procedures which ought to be straightforward. Perhaps most importantly, it makes the law so opaque as to hamper effective oversight of policing. Determining whether the gardaí have acted in breach of a particular power is difficult if there is unnecessary duplication of powers concerning basic procedures, without any uniformity nor guiding principles against which a critical examination of garda behaviour can be undertaken and adjudicated. This book illustrates, by no means exhaustively, the scope, extent and in many cases the overlap of garda powers. For the time being each power and piece of legislation must be scrutinized on a number of levels: for garda guidance and compliance as well as for assessment of utility and necessity.

This book attempts to identify and elucidate in detail the powers of the gardaí in the investigation of crime and the legal issues which arise in their exercise, with an emphasis on the practicalities of policing. While reference is made to certain powers under the Road Traffic Acts, the primary focus is on indictable offences as road traffic law is so voluminous as to require much greater elaboration than can be achieved in a book of this size. Where there are gaps in the Irish material the approaches of the courts and police forces of other common-law jurisdictions to particular policing questions have been considered. Insofar as is possible, best practice guidance has been incorporated, grounded in human rights principles and international standards. Each member of An Garda Síochána shares responsibility for the maintenance of public confidence in policing through consistent professionalism and stringent respect for and vindication of the rights of every person with whom they come in contact. It is hoped that this book will contribute to better understanding of the practical intersection between the gardaí and the rights of the individuals to whom they provide a policing service.

Part II

The Power to Arrest

CHAPTER 1

Arrest

PART 1: POWERS, PRINCIPLES AND FORMALITIES

PART 2: DISCRETIONARY POWERS OF ARREST

PART 3: ARREST WARRANTS

PART 1: POWERS, PRINCIPLES AND FORMALITIES

WHAT IS AN ARREST?

1–01 Arrest is a procedure whereby a person is lawfully deprived of liberty.[1] It begins the process of detention and should only occur when authorised by law.[2] The power to arrest may derive from statute, from an arrest warrant or from the common law. The validity of an arrest will depend on the existence of a warrant or a power authorising it, and the use of that power within its permitted limits.

1–02 The conceptual starting point in consideration of arrest is the liberty of the individual. Article 40.4.1° of the Constitution provides that "[n]o citizen shall be deprived of his personal liberty save in accordance with law."[3] That there should be no arrest without law is firmly established and mirrored in international human rights law: the *Universal Declaration on Human Rights* states at Article 3 that "[e]veryone has the right to life, liberty and security of person," and at Article 9 that "[n]o one shall be subjected to arbitrary arrest, detention or exile."[4]

1–03 The right to liberty enshrined by the Constitution is one which the State is obliged to protect and vindicate. It follows that gardaí are far from unfettered in the exercise of their powers. Given that arrest is an extraordinary departure from the freedom that we habitually enjoy, it is a power which must be exercised with care and restraint.

[1] Zander defines being under arrest as "being subject to restraint as to one's movements." Zander, *The Police and Criminal Evidence Act 1984* (2nd edition, Sweet & Maxwell, 1990) p 71.

[2] See Myjer, Hancock and Cowdery (Eds.), *Human Rights Manual for Prosecutors* (Wolf Legal Publishers, the Hague, 2003) p 61.

[3] "Citizen" may be read in this context as synonymous with "person", see Casey, *Constitutional Law in Ireland,* (3rd ed, Round Hall Sweet & Maxwell, Dublin, 2000), p 444 *et seq.* Professor Casey suggests "for many purposes, the supposed distinction between 'citizens' and 'persons' has no practical consequences." Nevertheless, the *Constitution Review Group* recommended that 'person' be substituted for 'citizen' in Art 40.4.1°. (*Report of the Constitution Review Group*, Stationery Office, Dublin, 1996) at pp 283-284. The review group noted, however, that non-citizens can and do avail of the enquiry procedure under Art 40.4.2°-5° and that the section does not entitle any invasion of an alien's right to liberty or to disregard that right in any way not otherwise authorised by law.

[4] Universal Declaration of Human Rights (adopted 10 December 1948) (UDHR). Similarly, the International Covenant on Civil and Political Rights provides at Art 9(1) "[E]veryone has the right to liberty and security of person. No one shall be subject to arbitrary arrest or detention. No one shall be deprived of his liberty except on such grounds and in accordance with such procedure as are established by law." International Covenant on Civil and Political Rights (adopted 16 December 1966, entered into force 23 March 1976) 999 UNTS 171 (ICCPR).

In arresting and detaining members of the community, the gardaí must act within the law: there must be a reason to arrest, a power which permits it and adherence to the conditions which attach to that power's exercise. Whether an individual can be stopped, arrested or detained, and the extent of the force that may be used in doing so, is dictated by a network of intertwined legal provisions.

THE POWERS, PRINCIPLES AND FORMALITIES OF ARREST

The powers and formalities of arrest and detention have developed piecemeal. Some have been inherited through the common law in case-by-case examination of the practical parameters of garda powers, but most are found in legislation of ever-increasing complexity.[5] In simple terms, gardaí either arrest in execution of a warrant, or without warrant (summarily), pursuant to a statutory or common law power of arrest. The power to arrest at common law has to a large extent been superseded by the myriad of statutory arrest powers now available to the gardaí. Before examining the powers themselves in detail, the formalities and practicalities of arrest must be explored, to distil the basic principles. **1–04**

Once the existence of an arrest power is established, and the statutory pre-conditions attaching to its exercise (such as reasonable suspicion) are present, there are a number of formalities of arrest which must be complied with. Those formalities are drawn from international human rights instruments, from the Irish legislation in which the powers of arrest are contained and from the case-law which has evolved in putting the legislation into practice. **1–05**

The existence of numerous overlapping arrest powers unduly over-complicates the law relating to arrest. It would be of immense practical benefit to have the kind of guidance provided in England and Wales by the Police and Criminal Evidence Act (PACE) codes of practice, clearly elucidating the appropriate steps which ought to be taken. In the absence of an Irish equivalent, we must make do with cobbling together the legislation, case-law and the principles contained in both, to discern the legality of each arrest.[6]

Communication of the Fact of and Reason for Arrest

In order to complete a valid arrest, it is not sufficient simply to take a person into custody. A form of words indicating that the person is under restraint and no longer **1–06**

[5] s 4 of the Criminal Justice Act 1984, for instance, has been amended by s 2 of the Criminal Justice (Miscellaneous, Provisions) Act 1997, s 34 of the Criminal Justice Act 1999, s 9 of the Criminal Justice Act 2006, s 24 of the Criminal Justice (Amendment) Act 2009 and s 7 of the Criminal Justice Act 2011. One amendment corrected the inadvertent substitution of a sub-section in a previous amendment. For a critical analysis, see Hunt, *The Irish Statute Book: A Guide to Irish Legislation* (First Law, Dublin, 2007).

[6] In England and Wales, the Police and Criminal Evidence Act 1984 and the PACE codes of practice provide the core framework of police powers and safeguards around stop and search, arrest, detention, investigation, identification and interviewing detainees.

at liberty is necessary.[7] It is important that it be made clear to that person that he or she is actually under arrest. While the courts have been somewhat creative in their interpretation of what constitutes communication, it seems clear that some communication of the fact of arrest is vital. Hederman J stated in the Supreme Court in *Director of Public Prosecutions v McCreesh*:

> "An arrest consists in or involves the seizure or touching of a person's body accompanied by a form of words which indicate to that person that he is under restraint. Whilst the older cases held that words alone would not suffice to constitute an arrest, nowadays words alone may amount to an arrest if, in the circumstances, they are calculated to bring, and do bring, to the person's notice that he was under restraint and he submitted to the compulsion – see eg *Alderson v Booth* [1969] 2 QB 216."[8]

1–07 Handcuffs are no substitute for communication of arrest. In *DPP v Kehoe*[9] the placing of handcuffs on the accused during the course of a shoot-out with gardaí did not amount to a formal arrest.

An individual is entitled to know the reason for his arrest, and the crime of which he is suspected. Article 9 of the International Covenant on Civil and Political Rights states in para 2:

> "Anyone who is arrested shall be informed, at the time of arrest, of the reasons for his arrest and shall be promptly informed of any charges against him."

The European Convention on Human Rights mirrors the provision, providing at Article 5(2):

> "Everyone who is arrested shall be informed promptly, in a language he understands, of the reasons for the arrest and of the charges against him."

The principle permeates the Irish caselaw. As Maguire CJ stated in *Re Ó Laighleis*:

> "the reason for the rule is not far to seek. Arrest must be for a lawful purpose; and since no one is obliged to submit to an unlawful arrest the citizen has a right before acquiescing in his arrest to know why he is being arrested".[10]

1–08 This applies whether the person is being arrested pursuant to a warrant, or without warrant under a statutory or common law power. It may raise interesting questions in the future where language barriers make communication of arrest, and the reasons for it, impractical or impossible. In *Ladent v Poland*[11] the European Court of Human Rights held that there had been a violation of the applicant's right under Article 5(2)

---

7 *DPP v McCormack* [1999] 4 IR 158, [2000] 1 ILRM 241.

8 *DPP v McCreesh* [1992] 2 IR 239 at 250.

9 *People (DPP) v Kehoe* [1985] IR 444.

10 *Re Ó Laighléis* [1960] IR 93.

11 *Ladent v Poland* (Application no 11036/03), 18 June 2008.

of the ECHR to prompt information, in a language which he understood, of the reasons for his arrest and of any charge against him. Ladent, a French national, was initially informed of the reasons for his arrest and the charges against him in Polish. He was not informed in a language which he understood as to why he had been deprived of his liberty during his arrest and ten-day detention. The Court found Article 5(2) to be an "elementary safeguard ... an integral part of the scheme of protection afforded by Article 5".[12] The explanation need not be simultaneous to the actual arrest but it must be prompt:

> "[A]ny person arrested must be told, in simple, non-technical language that he can understand, the essential legal and factual grounds for his arrest, so as to be able, if he sees fit, to apply to a court to challenge its lawfulness in accordance with paragraph 4. Whilst this information must be conveyed 'promptly' (in French: *'dans le plus court de délai'*), it need not be related in its entirety by the arresting officer at the very moment of the arrest. Whether the content and promptness of the information conveyed were sufficient is to be assessed in each case according to its special features (see *mutatis mutandis, Murray v the United Kingdom,* (1996) 22 EHRR 29 and *Conka v Belgium*, no 51564/99, § 50, ECHR 2002-I)."[13]

While it is advisable to caution a person who is being arrested, a garda in making **1–09** an arrest does not have to use technical or precise language.[14] Nor is it necessary for gardaí to cite the particular section under which a power is exercised. Provided the arrested person knows in substance why he is being arrested the arrest is valid.[15] Layman's language is perfectly acceptable. In *DPP (Cloughley) v Mooney,*[16] the explanation of the arresting garda that the suspect was being arrested for 'drunk driving' was a sufficient communication of the reason for his arrest: it told the suspect in substance why he was being arrested. That no precise form of words is necessary was affirmed in the case of *DPP v Warren.*[17] Indeed, in certain circumstances it is not even necessary to tell a suspect expressly that he is under arrest. In *Warren,* a decision which is perhaps at odds with the earlier decision of *DPP v Kehoe,*[18] the arresting garda conceded that he had not told the suspect that he was under arrest. The garda had not done so because he was off duty, and had awaited the arrival of an on-duty garda to assist him, who then expressly told the accused that he was under arrest. Having formed a suspicion that the suspect was driving under the influence of alcohol, the off-duty garda had asked the suspect to get out of his car, informed him that he was suspected of an offence contrary to s 49 of the Road Traffic Act 1961 and, when the suspect fled, the garda had chased and apprehended him, and brought

[12] *ibid* para 63.

[13] *ibid.*

[14] See *People (DPP) v Warren* [2006] IEHC 189; [2006] 8 ICLMD 40.

[15] *People (DPP) v Walsh* [1980] IR 294, *DPP (Cloughley) v Mooney* [1993] ILRM 214.

[16] *DPP (Cloughley) v Mooney* [1993] ILRM 214.

[17] *People (DPP) v Warren* [2006] IEHC 189; [2006] 8 ICLMD 40.

[18] *People (DPP) v Kehoe* [1985] IR 444.

him back to his car. It was argued that the initial detention by the off-duty garda was unlawful. Dunne J in the High Court held:

> "...the Respondent had been told to stay by the car. In that way, a form of words indicating that the person was under restraint had been used... in those circumstances the Respondent was under arrest. It is manifestly clear that the Respondent was not free to leave. His liberty had been curtailed".[19]

1–10 The decision would appear to be ECHR-compliant. In *Conka v Belgium*[20] the applicants argued that they had been given insufficient information about the reasons for their arrest. The European Court of Human Rights reiterated that, while the reason must be given promptly, it need not be related in its entirety by the arresting officer at the very moment of the arrest. At their arrival at the police station the applicants had been served with the decision ordering their arrest. The document handed to them for that purpose stated that their arrest had been ordered pursuant to s 7, first paragraph, point (2), of the Aliens Act, in view of the risk that they might seek to evade deportation. A note in the documents mentioned an appeal to the committals division of the criminal court as being an available remedy against the detention order. When the applicants were arrested at the police station, a Slovak-speaking interpreter was present for the purposes of informing them of the content of the verbal and written communications which they had received – in particular, the document ordering their arrest. The information furnished to them was held to satisfy the requirements of Article 5 (2) of the Convention. Consequently, there had been no violation of that provision.[21]

1–11 If, in the circumstances, it is entirely obvious why a person is being arrested, the garda does not have to communicate the reason for the arrest. In *People (DPP) v Walsh*,[22] O'Higgins CJ cited with approval the following dictum from the judgment of Viscount Simon in *Christie v Leachinsky*: "The requirement that the person arrested should be informed of the reason why he is seized naturally does not exist if the circumstances are such that he must know the general nature of the alleged offence for which he is detained."[23] The judgment of Viscount Simon sets out the general principles which underpin a proper arrest:

> "(1) If a policeman arrests without warrant upon reasonable suspicion of felony, or of other crime of a sort which does not require a warrant, he must in ordinary circumstances inform the person arrested of the true ground of arrest. He is not entitled to keep the reason to himself or to give a reason which is not the true reason. In other words a citizen is entitled to know on what charge or on suspicion of what crime he is seized.

---

19 *ibid.*

20 *Conka v Belgium* (2002) 34 EHRR 54.

21 *ibid* at paras 50-52.

22 *People (DPP) v Walsh* [1980] IR 294.

23 *ibid.*

(2) If the citizen is not so informed but is nevertheless seized, the policeman, apart from certain exceptions, is liable for false imprisonment.

(3) The requirement that the person arrested should be informed of the reason why he is seized naturally does not exist if the circumstances are such that he must know the general nature of the alleged offence for which he is detained.

(4) The requirement that he should be so informed does not mean that technical or precise language need be used. The matter is a matter of substance, and turns on the elementary proposition that in this country a person is, *prima facie*, entitled to his freedom and is only required to submit to restraints on his freedom if he knows in substance the reason why it is claimed that this restraint should be imposed.

(5) The person arrested cannot complain that he has not been supplied with the above information as and when he should be, if he himself produces the situation which makes it practically impossible to inform him, e.g. by immediate counter-attack or by running away. There may well be other exceptions to the above general rule in addition to those I have indicated, and the above propositions are not intended to constitute a formal or complete code, but to indicate the general principles of our law on a very important matter."[24]

To summarise: **1–12**

1) A suspect arrested without warrant is entitled to know the true reason for his arrest.
2) Generally arrest without communication of the reason for the arrest amounts to false imprisonment.
3) If, in the circumstances, it is entirely obvious why the suspect is being arrested there is no need to communicate the reason for the arrest.
4) Technical language need not be used.
5) If an arrested person makes it impossible to communicate the reason for his arrest, he cannot subsequently complain about not having been informed of the reason for his arrest.[25]

The communication with suspects who may have difficulty understanding reasons for arrest (and police proceedings generally) due to language barriers, hearing impairment or intellectual disability is considered in detail below.

Transfer to a Garda Station

An arrested person, if not already in a garda station, should be transferred to a garda station as soon as possible after arrest, whether the arrest occurs with or without warrant.[26] The arrestee should be brought before the District Court as soon as practicable thereafter.[27] **1–13**

---

[24] *Christie v Leachinsky* [1947] AC 573 at 587.

[25] However, efforts should be made to communicate the reason for the arrest as soon as is reasonably possible, though failure to give reasons at that point will not necessarily invalidate the preceding detention: *DPP v Hawkins* [1988] I WLR 1166; *Lewis v Chief Constable of the South Wales Constabulary* [1991] 1 All ER 206.

[26] Criminal Justice Act 1984, s 4(2), as amended by s 9 of the Criminal Justice Act 2006.

[27] s 15 of the Criminal Justice Act 1951, as amended by s 26 of the Criminal Justice Act 1984 and by s 18 of the Criminal Justice (Miscellaneous Provisions) Act 1997, provides:

"15 (1) A person arrested pursuant to a warrant shall on arrest be brought, as soon as practicable, before a judge of the District Court having jurisdiction to deal with the offence concerned.

Invitation to Attend Garda Station to Assist with Enquiries

1–14 An invitation to attend voluntarily at a garda station does not amount to an arrest. Persons invited to assist gardaí with their enquiries must be informed that they are not under arrest, and that they are free to leave at any time. This was outlined by Walsh J in *People (DPP) v Lynch*:

> "Generally speaking, nobody is obliged to answer any questions and, if one were to assume that everybody knows that that is the law, there would be no need for the warning; but practical experience has shown that there is a need for such a warning. In my view, the same should apply to persons who are invited to come to a Garda station for the purpose of being questioned about an offence. They should be made aware that at all times they are free to leave until the point is reached when they are in fact not free to leave. If they are arrested, then the law requires that they must be informed of the charge if they do not already know it, and they must be brought before a court ... as soon as is reasonably possible."[28]

1–15 In *People (DPP) v Conroy*, it was suggested that a person "assisting the Gardaí with their enquiries" was in fact detained if he is not informed of their right to freely leave the garda station.[29] The statutory time limits and duties imposed on gardaí in relation to detained persons post-arrest do not apply to persons who attend garda stations voluntarily.[30] Accordingly if, during the course of the voluntary attendance, a person becomes a suspect, he should be so informed, cautioned and arrested so that the statutory mechanisms and the protections pertaining to the detention come into operation. If a person is not informed of the change in status, his detention will be unlawful.[31]

Arrest and Release Without Charge

1–16 A charge is an accusation of criminal conduct. However, there is no requirement that a person must be charged immediately on arrest—it is permissible, and often preferable, to

---

(2) A person arrested without warrant shall, on being charged with an offence, be brought, as soon as practicable, before a judge of the District Court having jurisdiction to deal with the offence concerned.

(3) Where a person is arrested pursuant to a warrant later than the hour of 5 o'clock on any evening or, having been arrested without warrant, is charged after that hour and a judge of the District Court is due to sit in the District Court District in which the person was arrested not later than noon on the following day, it shall be sufficient compliance with sub-section (1) or (2) of this section, as the case may be, if he is brought before a judge of the District Court sitting in that District Court District at the commencement of the sitting.

(4) If the accused is remanded on bail and there and then finds bail, the case shall be remitted to the next sitting of the District Court

(5) In any other event, the case shall be remitted to a sitting of the District Court at a named place to be held within a period not exceeding eight days of the arrest

(6) This section is without prejudice to the provisions of any enactment relating to proceedings after arrest or charge in particular cases".

[28] *People (DPP) v Lynch* [1982] IR 64 at 86, *per* Walsh J.

[29] *People (DPP) v Conroy* [1986] IR 460, [1988] ILRM 4.

[30] See D Walsh, *Criminal Procedure* (Thomson Round Hall, Dublin, 2002) at p 153.

[31] *People (DPP) v Coffey* [1987] ILRM 727.

arrest, question and release a suspect without charge while the investigation progresses. An early arrest or charge can deprive the gardaí of an opportunity to put evidence to the suspect or to question him further if important new evidence comes to light. In the investigation of offences in which it is quite readily apparent what the primary evidence will be, such as drug offences, there is no reason to delay the questioning of the suspect pending forensic analysis of the suspected substance. However, it is prudent to refrain from questioning suspects where crucial technical evidence must first be analysed, such as computer hard drives in the investigation of crimes such as possession and production of child pornography. In certain circumstances preliminary questioning, which can be conducted on the basis of an invitation to attend at the garda station, can be undertaken, with the formal interview under arrest being conducted when the key evidence has been forensically or technically examined. In the white collar crime context—that is to say in the investigation of offences outlined in schedule 1 of the Criminal Justice Act 2011 (which include offences relating to banking, investment of funds and other financial activities, company law, money laundering, theft and fraud, bribery, corruption, consumer protection and criminal damage to data)—the suspension of detention periods under s 4 of the Criminal Justice Act 1984 for up to four months is provided for.[32] The purpose of these provisions is to allow the gardaí to follow up information obtained during questioning and, in the course of the suspension, the person is released without charge.

Reasonable Suspicion

"Reasonable cause for suspicion" is an important safeguard against arbitrary arrest. **1–17**
Whereas warrants are orders to arrest, statutory arrest provisions give individual gardaí considerable discretion in the timing and exercise of arrest, with the trigger being 'reasonable suspicion'. Where a statute requires it, 'reasonable suspicion' is an essential condition precedent to arrest.[33] Suspicion does not equate to proof, as Lord Devlin put it:

> "The circumstances of the case must be such that a reasonable man acting without passion or prejudice would fairly have suspected the person of having committed the offence ... suspicion in its ordinary meaning is a state of conjecture or surmise where proof is lacking: 'I suspect but I cannot prove'."[34]

The formulation varies according to the statute, but generally the requirement is that the garda has reasonable grounds to believe that the person in question has committed or is in the course of committing a relevant offence. Where the suspicion concerns offences scheduled under the Offences against the State Acts, the suspicion may be that a person is *about to commit* a scheduled offence, or that a person is concerned in the *intended* commission of an offence, or has in his possession documents or information relating to it. It has been suggested that the use of s 30 of the Offences against the State Act to effect an arrest before the commission of an offence—for preparatory acts,

[32] s 7 of the Criminal Justice Act 2011, which inserts new ss 3A-3F into the Criminal Justice Act 1984.
[33] *People (DPP) v Tyndall* [2005] IR 593 at 599, [2006] 1 ILRM 1.
[34] *Shaaban Bin Hussein v Chong Fook Kam* [1970] AC 942 at 948-949.

as distinct from attempted offences—may amount to preventative detention that is unconstitutional.[35] As will be seen below, there is no requirement for suspicion to be 'reasonable' under s 30 of the Offences against the State Act 1939.

1–18 Where reasonableness is a pre-requisite, i.e. in non-scheduled offences, the suspicion grounding the arrest must be personally held and be reasonable in the circumstances. If an order to arrest is given by a more senior officer to the garda who is actually to effect the arrest, the arrest will be invalid unless the arresting garda has other grounds on which his own suspicion is based. As Keane CJ put it in *Walshe v Fennessy:*

> "…the suspicion which the arresting Garda member is required to have in order to effect such an arrest must be founded on something more than a mere order of a superior to carry out that arrest. The fact that such an order is given to a Garda member by a superior officer is a fact that may be taken into account in determining whether the arresting officer had grounds for a reasonable suspicion, but there must be some other element than a bare order to carry out the arrest".[36]

In *Director of Public Prosecutions v Cash* the Supreme Court emphasised that:

> "the requirement of 'reasonable cause' is not to be overlooked. An arrest without reasonable cause or suspicion or however that requirement is expressed in a particular statute is an unlawful act and may give rise to a claim for damages".[37]

1–19 The court also held that the basis for reasonable suspicion does not equate to the test of admissibility under the rules of evidence during the hearing of a criminal trial—matters which ground suspicion do not have to satisfy the admissibility requirements of evidence, but the suspicion must be reasonable and *bona fide*. As the Privy Council held in *Shaaban Bin Hussein v Chong Fook Kam:*

> "Suspicion arises at or near the starting point of an investigation of which the obtaining of *prima facie* proof is the end… *Prima facie* proof consists of admissible evidence. Suspicion can take into account matters that could not be put in evidence at all."[38]

Discerning what constitutes "suspicion" is sometimes less than clear-cut. The presence of the requisite suspicion may be proved by direct evidence. It may also be inferred from the circumstances, but evidence must exist from which it may be inferred. In *People (DPP) v Tyndall,* Denham J held:

> "Suspicion… should be *bona fide* and not irrational. It is a fact to be proved by direct evidence, or it may be inferred from the circumstances. It is an essential proof."[39]

1–20 Accordingly suspicion can be based on a statement given by a complainant or witness, on the viewing of footage and the identification of a suspect therefrom, from forensic analysis

---

[35] D Walsh, *Human Rights and Policing in Ireland* (Clarus Press, Dublin, 2009) at p 37.

[36] *Walshe v Fennessy* [2005] 3 IR 516, at 518.

[37] *Director of Public Prosecutions v Cash* [2010] 1 IR 609 at 632; [2010] IESC 1.

[38] *Shaaban Bin Hussein v Chong Fook Kam* [1970] AC 942 at 948-949, *per* Lord Devlin.

[39] *People (DPP) v Tyndall* [2005] IR 593 at p 599, [2006] 1 ILRM 1.

or from covert policing methods such as surveillance, informants or controlled drug purchases. Suspicion can, of course, be present without specific intelligence, and mere suspicion will not inevitably mean that an arrest ought to be made. As Sanders and Young put it:

> "Clearly, police officers have to exercise discretion in deciding whether to stop and search and arrest, for all sorts of behaviour could be interpreted as suspicious... some people look less 'suspicious' than others, and multitudes of actual or likely offences have to be prioritised. Minor offenders (prostitutes, unlicensed street traders and so forth) are often simply ignored (Smith and Gray 1983)."[40]

Various suspicion formulations are used in the most frequently employed arrest provisions in relation to indictable offences (with emphasis added): **1–21**

Section 4 of the Criminal Law Act 1997:

> "(1) ... any person may arrest without warrant anyone who is or whom he or she, *with reasonable cause, suspects to be in the act of committing an arrestable offence.*
>
> (2) ... where an arrestable offence has been committed, any person may arrest without warrant anyone who is or whom he or she, *with reasonable cause, suspects to be guilty of the offence.*
>
> (3) Where a member of the Garda Síochána, with reasonable cause, suspects that an arrestable offence has been committed, he or she may arrest without warrant anyone whom the member, with reasonable cause, suspects to be guilty of the offence..."

Section 30(1) of the Offences against the State Act 1939:

> "A member of the Garda Síochána (if he is not in uniform on production of his identification card if demanded) may without warrant stop, search, interrogate, and arrest any person, or do any one or more of those things in respect of any person, whom he *suspects of having committed or being about to commit or being or having been concerned in the commission of an offence under any section or sub-section of this Act or an offence which is for the time being a scheduled offence* for the purposes of Part V of this Act *or whom he suspects of carrying a document relating to the commission or intended commission of any such offence* as aforesaid *or whom he suspects of being in possession of information relating to the commission or intended commission of any such offence* as aforesaid."

While there is no requirement in s 30 that the suspicion of the investigating garda be reasonable, in *The People (DPP) v Quilligan* it was held that the suspicion of the garda "must be *bona fide* held and not unreasonable".[41] **1–22**

Section 25(1) of the Misuse of Drugs Act 1977:

> " (1) Where *with reasonable cause* a member of the Garda Síochána suspects that an offence under s 15 of this Act has been committed and so *suspects a person of having committed the offence*, he may arrest the person without warrant."

---

40 A Sanders and R Young, "Police Powers" in *Handbook of Policing* (T Newburn ed, 2nd ed, Willan Publishing, Cullompton, 2008) at p 286.

41 *The People (DPP) v Quilligan* [1986] IR 495.

1–23 The degree of latitude afforded to police is clearly considerable, with only the amorphous 'reasonable suspicion' requirement to fetter their discretion. In England and Wales the PACE code of practice for the statutory power of arrest by police officers (Code G) outlines a requirement that the suspicion be objectively justifiable:

> "There must be some reasonable, objective grounds for the suspicion, based on known facts or information which are relevant to the likelihood the offence has been committed and the person to be questioned committed it."[42]

1–24 Walsh has commented that, in Ireland, where no such code exists and where offences are broadly drawn, garda discretion is so extensive as potentially to fall foul of the requirement in Article 5(1) of the ECHR that intrusions on the right to liberty should be "in accordance with law", such is the dearth of concrete and transparent guidance on when individual arrest powers should or should not be used.[43] The tendency in Ireland is to augment arrest and detention powers, whereas there is much to be said for simplification and streamlining, codification and consolidation. Such measures would improve intelligibility of the law both for gardaí and for those they police, ensure ECHR compliance and aid, where necessary, in the determination of the legitimacy of the exercise of garda discretion.

Necessity

1–25 An important practical consideration is whether the arrest of the person is necessary. In England and Wales, clear criteria are given by PACE Code G on the determination of necessity,[44] reflective of a legal requirement in that jurisdiction that the arresting officer must consider whether the arrest is reasonably necessary.[45] Though there is no corresponding requirement in Ireland, whether an arrest is necessary and, if so, at what point in the investigation it should be effected, is an important exercise of garda discretion. In England and Wales, an assessment of necessity is made based on the individual circumstances, taking into account "the situation of the victim, the nature of the offence, the circumstances of the suspect and the needs

---

[42] PACE Code G: code of practice for the statutory power of arrest by police officers (Home Office, 2005) p 224.

[43] D Walsh, *Human Rights and Policing in Ireland* (Clarus Press, Dublin, 2009) at p 37.

[44] PACE Code G: code of practice for the statutory power of arrest by police officers (Home Office, 2005) p 224.

[45] Police and Criminal Evidence Act 1984: s 24(4) provides that the power of summary arrest is exercisable only if the constable has reasonable grounds for believing that it is necessary to arrest the person for one of the reasons set out in s 24(5), ie (a) to enable the name of the person to be ascertained (in the case where the constable does not know, and cannot readily ascertain, the person's name, or has reasonable grounds for doubting whether a name given by the person as his name is his real name); (b) correspondingly as regards the person's address; (c) to prevent the person in question —
(i) causing physical injury to himself or any other person; (ii) suffering physical injury; (iii) causing loss of or damage to property; (iv) committing an offence against public decency (subject to sub-section (6)); or (v) causing an unlawful obstruction of the highway; (d) to protect a child or other vulnerable person from the person in question; (e) to allow the prompt and effective investigation of the offence or of the conduct of the person in question; (f) to prevent any prosecution for the offence from being hindered by the disappearance of the person in question.

of the investigative process".[46] Other factors which might be taken into account in considering whether to arrest a suspect are the potential for absconsion, the seriousness of the offence under investigation, whether there is a concern about the mental health or capacity of the person (and accordingly risks to their safety or the safety of others), the potential risk the person is thought to pose to others and (in the case of minor offences) whether the identity and address of the person has been ascertained with sufficient certainty to ensure that a summons can be delivered.

As O'Malley has pointed out, "the method adopted to secure an accused person's attendance before court should be that which is the least restrictive of the person's liberty".[47] For minor offences, a summons is a more delicate method of ensuring the appearance in court of a suspect. The option to arrest is still available if the accused person should subsequently fail to appear. **1–26**

Arrest for Investigation

Arrest is an evolving concept in Irish law. Traditionally, arrest was the culmination of an investigation, and the idea that it could be used to gather evidence was anathema.[48] However, a power of arrest for investigation has gradually developed and gained acceptance, and is now a firmly established feature of the Irish legal landscape.[49] This is well illustrated by the powers of arrest and conditional release introduced by the Criminal Justice Act 2011, which facilitates arrest for investigation while investigative avenues are explored. It clearly envisages the active participation of the suspect in that investigation. It was not always so. The jurisprudential shift to arrest for investigation is discernable by comparing the *dicta* in cases that preceded the introduction of a statutory power of post-arrest detention and those which followed it. In the 1930 case of *Dunne v Clinton*,[50] it was said that Irish law knew no "half-way house" between liberty and arrest during which a person might be questioned. Fifty years later, in *People (DPP) v Walsh*,[51] O'Higgins CJ stated: **1–27**

---

46 PACE Code G: code of practice for the statutory power of arrest by police officers (Home Office, 2005) at p 219.

47 T O'Malley, *The Criminal Process* (Round Hall Thomson Reuters, Dublin, 2009) at p 303.

48 Before the enactment of the Criminal Justice Act 1984, arrest for the purpose of interrogation was permitted only to a limited extent by the Offences against the State Act 1939, outside of which the practice was condemned by the courts. See for instance *People (DPP) v Walsh* [1980] IR 294, *People (DPP) v Higgins*, unreported, Supreme Court, 22 November 1985. See also Ryan and Magee, *The Irish Criminal Process*, 1983, and Ryan "Arrest and Detention: a Review of the Law" (2000) (1) ICLJ 2.

49 Writing in 2000, Andrea Ryan noted: "[A]rrest has moved a considerable distance from its stated purpose of ensuring the attendance at Court of the arrested person. While this undoubtedly remains one of the purposes, the lengthy periods during which a person may be detained in a Garda station signify that a fundamental purpose of arrest is an investigation of the offence by means of questioning the arrested person." (Ryan "Arrest and Detention: A Review of the Law" (2000) 1 ICLJ 2). In the UK, where arrest has similarly developed and become an investigative tool, McConville and Wilson have noted that there too there has been reticence to accept this shift: "The law and the courts were slow to recognise this change and its implications." (McConville and Wilson, *The Handbook of the Criminal Justice Process* (Oxford University Press, Oxford, 2002) p 100.

50 *Dunne v Clinton* [1930] IR 366.

51 *People (DPP) v Walsh* [1980] IR 294.

> "It has been stated many times in our courts that there is no such procedure permitted by the law as 'holding for questioning' or detaining in any pretext, except pursuant to a court order for the purpose of charging and bringing a person detained before a court. Any other purpose is unknown to the law and constitutes a flagrant and unwarranted interference with the liberty of the suspect."[52]

1–28 In contrast, in the 1995 case of *People (DPP) v Reddan and Hannon*,[53] Blayney J held:

> "It was ... submitted that a person could not be detained under s 4 of the Act of 1984 for the sole purpose of being questioned. In the view of the Court, it is not necessary to decide whether this is so or not. The section permits the detention of arrested persons for a certain period so that the offence on suspicion of which they have been arrested may be properly investigated. One of the ways of investigating the offence is to question the suspect – and if, in the particular circumstances of any case, that is the only way in which the offence can be investigated, there is no reason why because of this the right to question should be abrogated."

In 2006 in *People (DPP) v Birney*,[54] Hardiman J clarified that the passage in *Dunne v Clinton*[55] rejected the proposition that an arrested person could be held for the purpose of investigation "in the absence of any statutory provision in that behalf". With the advent of such a provision, it would appear now to be fully acceptable.

1–29 The enactment of the Criminal Justice Act 1984, with its power of detention under s 4, can be seen as the marker of the introduction of an interrogational model for garda investigations. Even at this remove, with the extension of the statutory periods of detention through various pieces of legislation subsequently,[56] there is still a reluctance to accept this new function of arrest. For instance, McGrath, citing the case of *DPP v Quilligan*, states:

> "[a]lthough it has been suggested that a person may not be arrested under [s 30 of the Offences against the State Act 1939, s 4 of the Criminal Justice Act 1984 or s 2 of the Criminal Justice (Drug Trafficking) Act 1996] simply for the purpose of questioning, this is commonly done and would seem permissible".[57]

---

52 *ibid* at 229.

53 *People (DPP) v Reddan and Hannon* [1995] 3 IR 560.

54 *People (DPP) v Birney* [2007] 1 IR 337.

55 *Dunne v Clinton* [1930] IR 366.

56 See for example the Criminal Justice (Drug Trafficking) Act 1996, s 2 and the Criminal Justice Act 2007, s 50.

57 McGrath, *Evidence* (Thomson Round Hall, Dublin, 2005), p 371. In *DPP v Quilligan,* Walsh J said: "I have dealt in some detail with the powers given by s 30 and s 52 because it appears from the learned trial judge's reference to s 30 as providing the Garda Síochána with 'patently draconian powers' and giving them the right to 'compulsorily interrogate a person suspected of crime' that he felt that ss 30 and 52 give to members of the Garda Síochána *carte blanche* both as to the manner, nature and duration of the interrogation of persons so arrested. I hope I have succeeded in showing that such is not the case and that any mistaken beliefs to the contrary wherever they reside will be dissipated. The object of the powers given by s 30 is not to permit the arrest of people simply for the purpose of subjecting them to questioning. Rather it is for the purpose of investigating the commission or suspected commission of a crime by the person already arrested

If not officially endorsed or acknowledged as such, it seems clear that what was a procedural mechanism for initiating criminal proceedings is now, in the indictable context in particular, primarily an investigative mechanism: arrest has become the starting point for questioning and forensic sampling and, as such, forms an integral part of the investigation process.[58] Post-arrest detention is strictly limited, with detention permissible only in accordance with statutory provisions which set out the parameters of that detention. The offence under investigation and the circumstances of its alleged commission will dictate which piece of legislation is used. The main powers of detention post-arrest are contained in s 4 of the Criminal Justice Act 1984 (as amended by s 2 of the Criminal Justice (Miscellaneous Provisions) Act 1997, s 34 of the Criminal Justice Act 1999, s 9 of the Criminal Justice Act 2006, s 24 of the Criminal Justice (Amendment) Act 2009 and s 7 of the Criminal Justice Act 2011); s 30 of the Offences against the State Act 1939; s 2 of the Criminal Justice (Drug Trafficking) Act 1996 (as amended by s 10 of the Criminal Justice Act 2006), and s 50 of the Criminal Justice Act 2007 (as amended by s 23 of the Criminal Justice (Amendment) Act 2009). Detention is considered in further detail below in *Chapter 5: Detention in Garda Custody.* **1–30**

PART 2: DISCRETIONARY POWERS OF ARREST

POWERS OF SUMMARY ARREST

Statutory provisions for summary arrest without warrant give gardaí considerable latitude and discretion in the exercise of their wide-ranging powers. These statutory powers have largely overtaken the common law powers of arrest and the arrest warrant procedure as a means of commencing criminal proceedings. Arrest warrants are required in certain circumstances but, as statutory arrest provisions are those most frequently employed, they will be considered first. **1–31**

Arrestable and Indictable Offences Defined

Criminal offences fall into three categories: summary offences, indictable offences and 'hybrid' offences, which are triable either summarily or on indictment. An indictable offence may be tried by a judge and jury, whereas there is no option for jury trial in respect of purely summary offences. Purely summary offences are minor offences, whereas, broadly speaking, indictable offences are non-minor, so are unsuited to summary disposal in the District Court. However, not all indictable offences are tried by **1–32**

---

and to enable that investigation to be carried on without the possibility of obstruction or other interference which might occur if the suspected person were not under arrest. s 30 is part of the statute law of the State permanently in force and it does not permit of any departure from normal police procedure save as to the obligation to bring the arrested person before a court as soon as reasonably possible." [1986] IR 495 at 509; [1987] ILRM 606 at 624.

[58] On the changing purpose of arrest, see McConville and Wilson, *The Handbook of the Criminal Justice Process* (Oxford University Press, Oxford, 2002) p 100.

jury, with some being disposed of in the District Court by a judge sitting alone, and others being tried before a panel of judges in the Special Criminal Court.

1–33 An arrestable offence is one which is punishable by imprisonment for a term of five years or more, whether by enactment or under the common law.[59] The power of arrest contained in s 4 of the Criminal Law Act 1997 also applies to attempts to commit any such offence.[60] Whether, in reality, the offence would attract such a punishment is immaterial; it is the potential term of imprisonment which is relevant. Where an offence is triable either summarily or on indictment, and the offence for which the accused was arrested is ultimately disposed of summarily, the arrest will retain its validity if the offence is potentially punishable by five years' imprisonment or a more significant penalty. For summary offences, for which a 12-month maximum penalty applies, a specific statutory power of arrest must be relied on.[61]

Section 4 Criminal Law Act 1997—Arrestable Offences

1–34 A general statutory power of arrest without warrant for serious offences is contained in s 4 of the Criminal Law Act 1997, which provides:

> "4.—(1) Subject to subsections (4) and (5), any person may arrest without warrant anyone who is or whom he or she, with reasonable cause, suspects to be in the act of committing an arrestable offence.
>
> (2) Subject to subsections (4) and (5), where an arrestable offence has been committed, any person may arrest without warrant anyone who is or whom he or she, with reasonable cause, suspects to be guilty of the offence.
>
> (3) Where a member of the Garda Síochána, with reasonable cause, suspects that an arrestable offence has been committed, he or she may arrest without warrant anyone whom the member, with reasonable cause, suspects to be guilty of the offence.
>
> (4) An arrest other than by a member of the Garda Síochána may only be effected by a person under subsection (1) or (2) where he or she, with reasonable cause, suspects that the person to be arrested by him or her would otherwise attempt to avoid, or is avoiding, arrest by a member of the Garda Síochána.

---

59 s 8 of the Criminal Justice Act 2006 amended s 2(1) of the Criminal Law Act 1997 extending the definition of "arrestable offence" by providing for the inclusion of offences punishable under the common law.

60 s 2(1) of the Criminal Law Act 1997 (as amended by s 8 of the Criminal Justice Act 2006) provides: "…'arrestable offence' means an offence for which a person of full capacity and not previously convicted may, under or by virtue of any enactment or the common law, be punished by imprisonment for a term of five years or by a more severe penalty and includes an attempt to commit any such offence; 'fixed by law', in relation to a sentence for an arrestable offence, means a sentence which the court is required by law to impose on an offender, being a person of full capacity".

61 For a comprehensive (but not exhaustive) list of offences with easy reference to the penalties they may attract, see *Offences Handbook 2010, Criminal and Road Traffic* (Thomson Round Hall, Dublin, 2010). See also Law Society of Ireland (M Butler (ed)), *Criminal Litigation* (3rd ed, Oxford University Press, Oxford, 2011) on the Road Traffic Act 2010, the Road Traffic Act 2011 and the Road Traffic (No 2) Act 2011.

> (5) A person who is arrested pursuant to this section by a person other than a member of the Garda Síochána shall be transferred into the custody of the Garda Síochána as soon as practicable.
>
> (6) This section shall not affect the operation of any enactment restricting the institution of proceedings for an offence or prejudice any power of arrest conferred by law apart from this section."

This is perhaps the most important arrest provision in Irish law. It applies only to arrestable offences. The delineation of arrestable offences by the potential punishment they attract is indicative that the power to arrest without warrant is a significant one, reserved for serious offences which would have previously constituted felonies.[62] When offences attract a more modest penalty, gardaí must rely on specific arrest provisions, such as those contained in the Criminal Justice Public Order Act 1994[63] and the Road Traffic Acts 1961-2010,[64] tying the arrest power to the offence itself. In the absence of a specific arrest provision, the only option is to proceed by way of summons. Assault *simpliciter*,[65] for instance, is not an arrestable offence, the maximum penalty being a fine or imprisonment for six months,[66] and neither is there a specific power of arrest associated with it. However assault causing harm[67] and causing serious harm,[68] attracting penalties of up to five years[69] and life imprisonment[70] respectively, are clearly arrestable offences and accordingly are subject to the general arrest power in s 4 of the Criminal Law Act 1997. Section 4 operates in tandem with other arrest powers, s 4(6) providing that the section "shall not ... prejudice any **1–35**

62 The Criminal Law Act 1997 abolished the distinction between felony and misdemeanour. Gardaí had a common law power of arrest where a felony or treason was being committed, had been committed or where it was suspected that a felony or treason was about to be committed. While the common law power in respect of felonies has been codified and replaced by the power to arrest without warrant contained in the 1997 Act, a residual common law power to arrest for breach of the peace still persists.

63 s 24(1) of the Criminal Justice (Public Order) Act 1994 provides that, where a member of the Garda Síochána finds any person committing certain public order offences, the member may arrest that person without warrant. s 24(2) provides that, where a garda is of the opinion that a public order offence has been committed, he or she may demand the name and address of any person whom the member suspects, with reasonable cause, has committed, or whom the member finds committing, such an offence, and arrest without warrant any person who fails or refuses to give his name and address when demanded, or gives a name or address which the member has reasonable grounds for believing is false or misleading.

64 The power to arrest for drink driving offences is, for instance, contained in s 4(8) of the Road Traffic Act 2010, a restatement of the original s 49 provision contained in the Road Traffic Act 1961. The restated s 4(8) provision was commenced by SI No 543 of 2011 Road Traffic Act 2010 (Certain Provisions) (Commencement) (No 2) Order 2011 on 28 October 2011; the power to arrest for dangerous driving causing death or serious bodily injury is contained in s 53(5) of the Road Traffic Act 1961 as substituted by the Road Traffic (No 2) Act 2011.

65 Non Fatal Offences against the Person Act 1997, s 2.

66 *ibid* s 2(4).

67 *ibid* s 3.

68 *ibid* s 4.

69 *ibid* s3(2)(b).

70 *ibid* s 4(2).

power of arrest conferred by law apart from this section." Therefore, where gardaí have a choice of arrest powers, either power may be used.

Garda Arrest Under Section 4 of the Criminal Law Act 1997

1–36 There are two key conditions for the exercise of the power of arrest without warrant under s 4:

i. An arrestable offence has been, or is in the process of being committed;
ii. There is reasonable cause to suspect that the person to be arrested is guilty of that offence.

Citizen's Arrest Under Section 4

1–37 Under s 4 of the Criminal Law Act 1997, *any person* may arrest without warrant anyone whom they, with reasonable cause, suspect to be in the act of committing an arrestable offence,[71] or to have committed an arrestable offence.[72] However, they can only do so where, with reasonable cause, they suspect that the person would otherwise attempt to avoid, or is avoiding, arrest by a member of the Garda Síochána. A person who has been subjected to a citizen's arrest must be transferred into the custody of the Garda Síochána as soon as practicable. This is particularly apposite in the context of detention by store detectives who may, more frequently than most citizens, encounter the commission of arrestable offences in the form of theft. There is an additional "citizen's arrest" power for the related offence of making off without payment,[73] which may arise in similar circumstances.

Arrest for Making Off Without Payment

1–38 The offence of making off without payment is designed for situations in which payment on the spot is expected and evaded. Prior to its introduction, the deception and intention elements of theft had proved problematic in circumstances in which it could be argued that the person had intended to pay at some point in the future. As the offence carries a maximum penalty of two years' imprisonment, it is not an arrestable offence under s 4 of the Criminal Law Act 1997, but a specific power of arrest is inbuilt into the provision which criminalises the offence—s 8 of the Criminal Justice (Theft and Fraud Offences) Act 2001, at subsection (3). It was envisaged as a practical power to assist hoteliers, restaurateurs and others in shops and service industries in tackling dishonesty encountered in their daily commercial dealings.[74] Like the general power of arrest in s 4 of the Criminal Law Act 1997, the citizen arresting a person for making off without payment may only exercise the power where he or she, with reasonable cause, suspects that the offender would otherwise avoid arrest by the gardaí and thereafter must hand over responsibility to the gardaí. The arrest power for citizens applies only for persons "in the act of committing an offence" under the

---

[71] Criminal Law Act 1997, s 4(1).

[72] *ibid.*

[73] Criminal Justice (Theft and Fraud Offences) Act 2001, s 8(3).

[74] See Law Reform Commission *Report on the Law Relating to Dishonesty* (LRC 43–1992) p 230.

section, whereas the gardaí are additionally empowered to arrest persons suspected, with reasonable cause, of having made off without payment.

Citizen's Arrest for Criminal Damage

Criminal damage and arson are arrestable offences for the purposes of s 4 of the Criminal Law Act 1997. However there is a dedicated power of arrest for criminal damage, contained in s 12 of the Criminal Damage Act 1991, a provision which obviously pre-dates the general arrest power under s 4.[75] The 1991 Act expanded the concept of damage to property to cover damage to a computer system, so criminal damage and its associated offences (such as threat to damage property under s 3 and possessing anything with intent to damage property under s 4) apply equally to data and to tangible property.[76] The arrest power is exercisable by anyone who encounters a person that they, with reasonable cause, suspect to be in the act of committing or to have committed an offence under the Criminal Damage Act, with the exception of the offences which are not concerned with the immediacy of the threat of or actual damage to property: unlawfully accessing data and obstructing, impeding or failing to cooperate with a garda acting under the authority of a search warrant.[77] **1–39**

The powers of the gardaí under the Act are more extensive than those which are vested in the civilian. In addition to arrest where an offence is considered to have taken place, gardaí may also arrest where it is considered that a criminal damage offence is about to be committed.[78] Also exercisable solely by gardaí is the power to arrest for obstruction under s 13(4) which, being punishable by a fine or imprisonment not exceeding 12 months, does not constitute an arrestable offence. Accordingly, it is s 12 of the Criminal Damage Act 1991 which should be invoked in arresting for obstruction, rather than s 4 of the Criminal Law Act 1997. Gardaí are also empowered under s 12 to enter and search any place to arrest a person for an offence under the Criminal Damage Act 1991, forcibly if necessary. **1–40**

Arrest Under Section 30 of the Offences against the State Act 1939—Scheduled Offences

The Offences against the State Act 1939 contains an extensive arrest (and stop, search, and interrogate) power in relation to subversive and "scheduled" offences. s 30(1) provides: **1–41**

> "A member of the Garda Síochána ... may without warrant stop, search, interrogate and arrest any person, or do any one or more of those things in respect of any person, whom he suspects of having committed or being about to commit or being or having been concerned in the commission of an offence under any section or sub-section of

---

[75] The Criminal Damage Act 1991 replaced, for the most part, the Malicious Damage Act 1861.

[76] Property is defined in s1(1) as "(a) property of a tangible nature, whether real or personal, including money and animals that are capable of being stolen, and (b) data."

[77] Criminal Damage Act 1991, s 13(4).

[78] *ibid* s 12(5).

> this Act or an offence which is for the time being a scheduled offence ... or whom he suspects of carrying a document relating to the commission or intended commission of any such offence as aforesaid or whom he suspects of being in possession of information relating to the commission or intended commission of any such offence as aforesaid."[79]

Allied with an extraordinary arrest power is an extraordinary period of detention, which is considered in detail at para [5–25] *et seq.*

Scheduled Offences

1–42 Section 36 of the Offences against the State Act 1939 permits the designation of 'scheduled offences' to which the powers of arrest and detention in s 30 apply.[80] Offences may be scheduled only if there is a government proclamation in force bringing part V of the Act into operation, declaring the need for extraordinary powers.

Offences Scheduled Under the Offences against the State Act 1939 (Scheduled Offences) Order 1972

1–43 The Offences against the State Act 1939 (Scheduled Offences) Order 1972 has been in operation since 1972, and provides that the following are scheduled offences[81]: offences

---

79 For a detailed examination of this section (and the Offences against the State legislation generally), see the Report of the Committee to Review the Offences against the State Acts 1939-1998 and Related Matters (the Hederman Report) (Dublin, 2002).

80 s 36 provides: "36(1) Whenever while this Part of this Act is in force the Government is satisfied that the ordinary courts are inadequate to secure the effective administration of justice and the preservation of public peace and order in relation to offences of any particular class or kind or under any particular enactment, the Government may by order declare that offences of that particular class or kind or under that particular enactment shall be scheduled offences for the purposes of this Part of this Act.

(2) Whenever the Government has made under the foregoing sub-section of this section any such declaration as is authorised by that sub-section, every offence of the particular class or kind or under the particular enactment to which such declaration relates shall, until otherwise provided by an order under the next following sub-section of this section, be a scheduled offence for the purposes of this Part of this Act.

(3) Whenever the Government is satisfied that the effective administration of justice and the preservation of public peace and order in relation to offences of any particular class or kind or under any particular enactment which are for the time being scheduled offences for the purposes of this Part of this Act can be secured through the medium of the ordinary courts, the Government may by order declare that offences of that particular class or kind or under that particular enactment shall, upon the making of such order, cease to be scheduled offences for the purposes of this Part of this Act."

It should be noted that s 14(3) of the Offences against the State (Amendment) Act 1998 (No 39 of 1998) provides that nothing in s 14(1) or (2) of that Act shall be construed as affecting or limiting in any particular case the exercise by the Government of any of its powers under any provision of s 36 of this Act

81 The Offences against the State Act 1939 (Scheduled Offences) (No. 2) Order 1972 added offences under s 7 of the Conspiracy and Protection of Property Act, 1875. s 7 of the 1875 Act was repealed by s 31 of the Non-Fatal Offences against the Person Act 1997.

under the Malicious Damage Act 1861,[82] offences under the Explosive Substances Act 1883, offences under the Firearms Acts 1925 to 1971 and offences under the Offences against the State Act 1939.

Offences Scheduled Under the Offences against the State (Amendment) Act 1998

The Offences against the State (Amendment) Act 1998 provides at s 14[83] for the scheduling of the following offences contained in the Act: directing an unlawful organisation,[84] possession of articles for purposes connected with certain offences,[85] unlawful collection of information,[86] withholding information[87] and training persons in the making or use of firearms.[88] **1–44**

The Offences against the State (Amendment) Act was an emergency piece of legislation enacted in the aftermath of the Omagh bombing. Its extensive powers in ss 2 – 12, the scheduling provision in s 14 and a provision relating to the forfeiture of property contained in s 17 were due to "cease to be in operation on and from the 30th day of June, 2000, unless a resolution has been passed by each House of the Oireachtas resolving that that section should continue in operation." A resolution has passed every year since.[89] **1–45**

[82] s 15 of the Criminal Damage Act 1991 repealed the Malicious Damage Act 1861 with the exception of ss 35 to 38, 40, 41, 47, 48, 58 and 72. s 35 was repealed by s 5 and schedule 1 of the Railway Safety Act 2005. The sections of the Malicious Damage Act 1861 which remain in force are s 36 (obstructing engines or carriages on railways), s 37 (injuries to electric or magnetic telegraphs), s 38 (attempt to injure such telegraph, as amended by s 14 of the Criminal Damage Act 1991), s 40 (killing or maiming cattle, as amended by s 14 of the Criminal Damage Act 1991), s 41 (killing or maiming other animals, as amended by s 14 of the Criminal Damage Act 1991), s 48 removing or concealing buoys and other sea marks, s 58 and s 72.

[83] The Offences against the State (Amendment) Act 1998 provides at s 14 "14(1) It is hereby declared that the ordinary courts are inadequate to secure the effective administration of justice and the preservation of public peace and order in relation to each offence under sections 6 to 9 and 12.

(2) Each offence under sections 6 to 9 and 12 shall be deemed to be a scheduled offence for the purposes of Part V of the Act of 1939 as if an order had been made under s 36 of that Act in relation to it and sub-section (3) of that s and s 37 of that Act shall apply to such an offence accordingly.

(3) Nothing in sub-section (1) or (2) shall be construed as affecting, or limiting in any particular case, the exercise—

(a) by the Government of any of its powers under any provision of s 35 or 36 of the Act of 1939,
(b) by the Director of Public Prosecutions of his or her power under s 45(2) of the said Act to direct that a person not be sent forward for trial by the Special Criminal Court on a particular charge, or
(c) by the Government or the Director of Public Prosecutions of any other of its or his or her powers under Part V of the said Act or by any other person of his or her powers under the said Part".

[84] Offences against the State (Amendment) Act 1998, s 6, as substituted by the Criminal Justice (Amendment) Act 2009, s 25.

[85] *ibid* s 7.

[86] *ibid* s 8.

[87] *ibid* s 9.

[88] *ibid* s 12.

[89] Confirmation of the passing of the resolution is published annually in *Iris Oifigiúil.* The 2013 resolution was passed by both houses of the Oireachtas on 19 June 2013, and provides that ss 2 to 4, 6 to

Offences Scheduled Under the Criminal Justice (Amendment) Act 2009

1–46 The Criminal Justice (Amendment) Act 2009 adds to the list of scheduled offences by making a number of "organised crime" offences in the Criminal Justice Act 2006 scheduled offences for the purpose of s 30 of the Offences against the State Act 1939. Section 8 of the Criminal Justice (Amendment) Act 2009 states broadly that "[i]t is hereby declared that the ordinary courts are inadequate to secure the effective administration of justice and the preservation of public peace and order" in relation to these offences: directing a criminal organisation,[90] participating or contributing to organised crime[91] and commission of an offence for a criminal organisation.[92] Somewhat oddly, it appears that an "organised crime" offence committed by a body corporate under Part 7 of the Criminal Justice Act 2006 is also a scheduled offence. The Criminal Justice (Amendment) Act 2009 provides at s 8 that an offence under s 76 of the Criminal Justice Act 2006 is scheduled under that section. However, s 76 does not contain an offence—it is a provision ascribing liability to company personnel where it has been proved that offences by the companies in which they are involved have been committed with their consent, connivance or approval, or are attributable to their wilful neglect. Like s 7 of the Criminal Law Act 1997, which provides that any person who aids, abets, counsels or procures the commission of an indictable offence is liable to be indicted, tried and punished as a principal offender, s 76 of the Criminal Justice Act 2006 permits the trial of company officers and personnel as principal offenders. This is an unusual and somewhat awkward manner of scheduling an offence and is lacking in clarity.

Sunset Clause

1–47 It should be noted that s 8 of the Criminal Justice (Amendment) Act 2009 contains a sunset clause at subsection (4), providing that it will cease to be in operation 12 months after the date of its passing, unless a resolution has been passed in both houses of the Oireachtas that the section should continue in operation. As with s 18 of the Offences against the State (Amendment) Act 1998, *Iris Oifigiúil* should be consulted to confirm that a resolution has been passed to provide for the continuance in operation of these sections. Similarly, the *Iris* will arguably not suffice under the Documentary

---

12, 14 and 17 of the Offences against the State (Amendment) Act 1998 shall continue in operation for the period beginning on 30 June 2013 and ending on 29 June 2014, *Iris Oifigiúil*, 5 July 2013, at p 836. *Prima facie* evidence of any proclamation, order, rule, regulation, bye-law or other official document may be given in any legal proceedings by production of a copy of the *Iris* purported to contain such matter under the Documentary Evidence Act 1925, s 4. A resolution is not included in the terms of s 4, so it is thought that the actual resolution must be exhibited for the avoidance of doubt. However, where the courts are sufficiently familiar with the statutory provision in question, judicial notice may be taken of its contents – see *State (Taylor) v Circuit Judge of Wicklow* [1951] IR 311 at p 314 and *DPP v Collins* [1981] ILRM 447 at 450-451.

[90] Contrary to s 71A of the Criminal Justice Act 2006. as inserted by s 5 of the Criminal Justice (Amendment) Act 2009.

[91] Contrary to s 72 of the Criminal Justice Act 2006, as substituted by s 6 of the Criminal Justice (Amendment) Act 2009. A new s 72A was inserted into the 2006 Act by s 9 of the Criminal Justice (Amendment) Act 2009.

[92] Contrary to s 73 of the Criminal Justice Act 2006, as amended by s 10 of the Criminal Justice (Amendment) Act 2009.

Evidence Act 1925, which provides at ss 3-4 that proof of proclamations, orders, rules, regulations, bye-laws, or other official documents may be given by the production of a copy of the *Iris Oifigiúil*. No mention is made of resolutions.[93]

Limitations of Scheduled Offences

An obvious limitation of the Offences against the State Act 1939 (Scheduled Offences) Order 1972 is its confinement to firearms offences under the Firearms Acts 1925-1971, resulting in the exclusion of offences contained in the Firearms and Offensive Weapons Act 1990. While the Acts are collectively construed and cited as the Firearms Acts 1925-2009, the 1990 Act is excluded from the schedule in the 1972 order (as the order preceded the Act), so offences which do not have their basis in the Acts of 1925-1971 are not scheduled offences for the purposes of s 30. Such offences include reckless discharge,[94] possession of a knife[95] or flick-knife,[96] possession of an offensive weapon,[97] being an armed trespasser,[98] producing a weapon in the commission of an offence or in the course of a dispute,[99] manufacturing or dealing in weapons[100] and shortening a barrel of a shotgun or rifle.[101] Arrest for these offences should be based either on s 4 of the Criminal Law Act 1997 or on s 14 of the Firearms and Offensive Weapons Act 1990, which is a specific power of arrest which applies to offences under ss 9, 10 and 11 of the 1990 Act, ie possession of knives and other articles; trespassing with a knife, weapon of offence or other article and production of article capable of inflicting serious injury. **1–48**

While the Criminal Justice (Terrorist Offences) Act 2005 extends the concept of membership of an unlawful organisation to international terrorist groups,[102] offences which have as their basis the Criminal Justice (Terrorist Offences) Act 2005 are not scheduled offences for the purposes of s 30. Accordingly persons arrested for engaging in offences created under that Act, which include terrorist activity, hostage taking, **1–49**

[93] In 2013, the requisite resolution pertaining to the Criminal Justice (Amendment) Act 2009 was passed in Dáil Éireann on 19 June and in Seanad Éireann on the same date. The resolution provides that s 8 of the 2009 Act shall continue in operation for the period beginning on 30 June 2013 and ending on 29 June 2014, *Iris Oifigiúil*, 5 July 2013, at p 836.

[94] Firearms and Offensive Weapons Act 1990, s 8.

[95] *ibid* s 9.

[96] *ibid* s 9(4).

[97] *ibid* s 9(5).

[98] *ibid* s 10.

[99] *ibid* s 11.

[100] Firearms and Offensive Weapons Act 1990, s 12.

[101] *ibid* s 12 as inserted by the Criminal Justice Act 2006, s 65, as amended by the Criminal Justice Act 2007, s 40.

[102] s 5(1) of the Criminal Justice (Terrorist Offences) Act 2005 provides that "A terrorist group that engages in, promotes, encourages or advocates the commission, in or outside the State, of a terrorist activity is an unlawful organisation within the meaning and for the purposes of the Offences against the State Acts 1939 to 1998 and s 3 of the Criminal Law Act 1976." s 5(2) provides that "for the purposes of this Act, the Offences against the State Acts 1939 to 1998 and s 3 of the Criminal Law Act 1976 apply with any necessary modifications and have effect in relation to a terrorist group referred to in sub-section (1) as if that group were an organisation referred to in s 18 of the Act of 1939."

terrorist bombing, and funding terrorist groups, should be arrested under s 4 of the Criminal Law Act 1997 rather than under s 30 of the Offences against the State Act.

It has also been remarked upon as anomalous that murder is not a scheduled offence.[103] However it would perhaps be more logical to limit, rather than extend, the parameters of scheduled offences rather than characterising every serious offence as warranting extraordinary powers.

Use of Section 30 for "Ordinary" Offences

1–50 There is no requirement in s 30(1) that the offences under investigation be motivated by subversive or political ends: the arrest power contained in s 30 applies equally to "ordinary crime" and "gangsterism"[104] as much as to political criminal activity, once the offence under investigation is scheduled. Neither is there any requirement in the section as drafted that the suspicion of the investigating garda be reasonable. However, in *People (DPP) v Quilligan* it was held that the suspicion of the garda "must be *bona fide* held and not unreasonable".[105]

1–51 Prior to the enactment of the Criminal Justice Act 1984,[106] the gardaí had no power of detention for offences which did not come within the ambit of s 30 through scheduling or subversion. In that context, s 30 was extensively (and creatively) used in arrests for murder and manslaughter involving a firearm, though neither murder nor manslaughter are scheduled offences, the use of the firearm facilitating detention for questioning.[107] Though neither murder nor manslaughter are scheduled offences, if they involved the use of a firearm they could be brought within the ambit of s 30. The practice continued after the enactment of s 4 of the Criminal Justice Act 1984, as the 48-hour detention permitted under s 30 was preferable to the 12-hour period provided for in s 4 of the 1984 Act. Section 50 of the Criminal Justice Act 2007[108] now provides

---

[103] *State (Bowes) v Fitzpatrick* [1978] ILRM 195.

[104] In *People (DPP) v Quilligan* [1986] IR 495, Walsh J stated: "It is common knowledge, and indeed was discussed in the debates in the Oireachtas leading to the enactment of the Act of 1939, that what was envisaged were cases or situations of a political nature where juries could be open to intimidation or threats of various types. However a similar situation could also arise in types of cases far removed from what one would call 'political type' offences. There could well be a grave situation in dealing with ordinary gangsterism or well financed and well organised large-scale drug dealing, or other situations where it might be believed or established that juries were for some corrupt reason, or by virtue of threats, or illegal interference, being prevented from doing justice. … I am satisfied that the learned trial judge… was in error in holding that a scheduled offence must be shown to be a 'subversive' offence as distinct from an 'ordinary' offence before the power of arrest given by s 30 can be exercised in relation to that offence." See also *Kavanagh v Ireland* [1996] 1 IR 348.

[105] *People (DPP) v Quilligan* [1986] IR 495.

[106] s 4 of the Criminal Justice Act 1984 was commenced on 1 July 1987 by the Criminal Justice Act 1984 (Commencement) Order 1987, SI No 150 of 1987.

[107] See Chapter 7 of the *Report of the Committee to Review the Offences against the State Acts 1939-1998 and Related Matters* (the Hederman Report) (Dublin, 2002).

[108] s 50 was brought into operation on 18 May 2007 by the Criminal Justice Act 2007 (Commencement) Order 2007, SI No 236 of 2007. For an excellent theoretical analysis of the provisions of the Criminal

for seven-day detention for those suspected of murder involving the use of a firearm or an explosive, murder of a garda, prison officer or head of State,[109] possession of a firearm with intent to endanger life[110] or an offence of false imprisonment involving the use of a firearm, obviating the need to resort to s 30. The detention provisions of the Criminal Justice Act 2006 have extended the maximum period of detention in custody under the Criminal Justice Act 1984 to 24 hours for other arrestable offences.

MISCELLANEOUS POWERS OF ARREST WITHOUT WARRANT

There are many other statutory arrest powers for both minor and serious offences. **1–52**
They are generally contained in the legislation that criminalises them, and it is quite common for more than one power of arrest to be available to an arresting garda, particularly in statutes which preceded the enactment of the general arrest power in s 4 of the Criminal Law Act 1997. The breadth of the remit of s 4 of the Criminal Law Act 1997 means that an arrest will be valid if the arresting member arrests under s 4, notwithstanding the existence of a distinct and specific arrest provision which is not invoked by the arresting garda. Once the offence is an arrestable one (in the sense that it is punishable by five years or more, whether by common law or statute), the requisite suspicion is present and the suspect is aware of the reason for and fact of the arrest, the arrest will be lawful.[111] Specific arrest powers must, however, be invoked in relation to minor offences, which are not arrestable for the purpose of s 4. If no such specific arrest power exists an arrest cannot be effected, no matter how desirable arrest might be. Indecency, for instance, has no associated arrest power, which poses practical difficulties for gardaí who encounter "streaking" at sporting events, a not infrequent occurrence.[112] In addition the offences of "causing scandal and injuring the morals of the community"

Justice Act 2007, see L Campbell: "The Criminal Justice Act 2007—A Theoretical Perspective" (2007) 17(3) ICLJ 8.

[109] Contrary to s 3 of the Criminal Justice Act 1990.

[110] Contrary to s 15 of the Firearms Act 1925.

[111] In *People (DPP) v Birney and others* [2007] 1 IR 337 it was argued that s 4 of the 1997 Act had no place in the statutory code governing the jurisdiction and procedures of the Special Criminal Court, and that the applicants' arrest under s 4 of the 1997 Act deprived the Special Criminal Court of jurisdiction. The Court of Criminal Appeal found that there was no justification for the proposition that a person arrested under s 4 of the 1997 Act may not be brought before the Special Criminal Court pursuant to s 47 of the Offences against the State Acts, and that the term "lawfully brought" should not be restrictively interpreted. It was not argued that the offences for which the applicants were arrested were not arrestable offences or that no *bona fide* suspicion existed to ground the arrest, or that the arrest was otherwise invalid. Where a specific offence-related power of arrest exists and ought to have been utilised, it is doubtful that an assertion that s 4 has been inappropriately used would be entertained, once the offence in question is, in fact, an arrestable offence.

[112] s 18 of the Criminal Law Amendment Act 1935, as amended by s 18 of the Criminal Law (Rape) (Amendment) Act 1990, provides that "Every person who shall commit at or near and in sight of any place along which the public habitually pass as of right or by permission, any act in such a way as to offend modesty or cause scandal or injure the morals of the community shall be guilty of an offence under this section and shall on summary conviction thereof be liable to a fine not exceeding €634.87 or at the discretion of the Court to imprisonment for any term not exceeding 6 months or to both."

as provided for in s 18 of the 1935 Act were found to be unconstitutional given that the offences were "hopelessly vague and subjective in character" in *Douglas v Director of Public Prosecutions and Others.*[113] The judgment, though it does not refer to the offence of "offending modesty" also contained within the section, casts doubt on the constitutionality of the section as a whole and further restricts the gardaí in dealing with public indecency offences. The Court in *Douglas* suggested that the Oireachtas could legislate to create new offences to address conduct of this nature in public.[114] From a practical perspective it is also essential that any replacement legislation should have an associated summary power of arrest.

Some offences which are subject to specific arrest powers are outlined below.

Drug Offences

1–53 There is a dedicated arrest power for drug offences in s 25 of the Misuse of Drugs Act 1977. Like s 4 of the Criminal Law Act 1977, "reasonable cause" is required. The power differentiates between possession of controlled drugs for sale or supply and other offences under the Misuse of Drugs Act 1977. Reasonable cause for suspicion of possession for sale or supply provides a basis for arrest, whereas for other drug offences an additional level of suspicion is required—that the person will evade or obstruct the course of justice, or a reasonable doubt as to the name, address or residency of the person in the State. Section 25 provides:

> "(1) Where with reasonable cause a member of the Garda Síochána suspects that an offence under s 15 of this Act has been committed and so suspects a person of having committed the offence, he may arrest the person without warrant.
>
> (2) Where with reasonable cause a member of the Garda Síochána,
> (a) suspects that an offence under this Act, other than an offence under s 15, has been committed or attempted, and
> (b) suspects a person of having committed the offence or having made the attempt, then if the member,
> (c) with reasonable cause suspects that the person unless he is arrested either will abscond for the purposes of evading justice or will obstruct the course of justice, or
> (d) having enquired of the person, has reasonable doubts as to the person's identity or place of abode, or
> (e) having enquired of the person, knows that the person does not ordinarily reside in the state, or has reasonable doubts as to whether the person so resides, he may arrest the person without warrant."

[113] *Douglas v Director of Public Prosecutions and Others* [2013] IEHC 343, Hogan J held at para.65: "… the offences of causing scandal and injuring the morals of the community are hopelessly vague and subjective in character and they intrinsically lend themselves to arbitrary and inconsistent application. No clear standard of the conduct which is prohibited by law is articulated thereby and s. 18 does not contain any clear principles and policies. In this respect the relevant provisions of s. 18 are manifestly unconstitutional and are inconsistent with Article 15.2.1, Article 15.5.1, Article 38.1, Article 40.1 and Article 40.4.1 of the Constitution."

[114] *ibid* at para. 68.

If the drug offence in question is arrestable, it will also come within the ambit of the general arrest power in s 4 of the Criminal Law Act 1997; if it is a minor offence, such as possession of a small quantity of cannabis for personal use, the requisite additional features outlined in s 25 (2)(c), (d) and (e) must be present before an arrest can be effected.

Theft and Fraud Offences

Most of the offences contained in the Criminal Justice (Theft and Fraud Offences) Act 2001 attract significant penalties and are arrestable, but two specific powers of arrest apply to more minor offences under the Act: making off without payment (s 8) and obstructing a garda acting under a search warrant (s 49). Arrest for making off without payment is considered in further detail at para [1 – 38] above. **1–54**

Firearms and Offensive Weapons

Most, but not all, firearms offences are scheduled under the Offences against the State Act 1939, so occasionally an arrest under s 30 of the 1939 Act will be appropriate. However, there is a specific power of arrest which applies to offensive weapons in s 14 of the Firearms and Offensive Weapons Act 1990. Section 14 provides: **1–55**

> "A member of the Garda Síochána may arrest without warrant any person who is, or whom the member, with reasonable cause, suspects to be, in the act of committing an offence under s 9, 10 or 11."

Equally, an arrest may be effected under the general arrest power contained in s 4 of the Criminal Law Act 1997, once the offence is an indictable one.

Section 14 of the Firearms and Offensive Weapons Act 1990 applies to offences under s 9 (possession of a knife, article with a blade, a pointed article, a flick-knife, an article made or adapted for use for causing injury to or incapacitating a person or a realistic imitation firearm[115]); s 10 (trespassing with a knife or any weapon of offence) or s 11 (production of an article capable of inflicting serious injury, in the course of a dispute or in the commission or apparently imminent commission of an offence, in a manner likely to unlawfully intimidate). **1–56**

Sexual Offences: Prostitution and Child Pornography

The majority of sexual offences are indictable and therefore arrestable. Section 13 of the Criminal Law (Sexual Offences) Act 1993 provides a power of arrest for a number of summary offences relating to prostitution, including soliciting or importuning for the purposes of commission of a sexual offence (s 6 of the Criminal Law (Sexual Offences) Act 1993, as substituted by s 2 of the Criminal Law (Sexual Offences) (Amendment) Act 2007); soliciting or importuning for the purposes of prostitution (s 7), failure to **1–57**

---

[115] A realistic imitation firearm is a device that appears to the ordinary observer so realistic as to make it indistinguishable from a firearm (s 9A(4) of the Firearms and Offensive Weapons Act 1990, as inserted by s 40 of the Criminal Justice (Miscellaneous Provisions) Act 2009).

obey a direction from a member of An Garda Síochána to leave when loitering for the purposes of prostitution (s 8) and obstructing a search warrant in relation to a suspected offence of living on the earnings of prostitution (s 10(3)). Gross indecency had been included in the s 13 arrest power, but gross indecency has since been repealed[116] and replaced by defilement[117] which is an arrestable offence. It is important to note that the offence of organising prostitution contained in s 9 of the Criminal Law (Sexual Offences) Act 1993 is not listed among the offences to which the arrest power in s 13 applies. It is an arrestable offence, and accordingly persons suspected of organising prostitution should be arrested under the general power of arrest contained in s 4 of the Criminal Law Act 1997.

1–58 Allied with the arrest power in relation to the offences listed, s 13 of the 1993 Act provides that, where gardaí reasonably suspect that a person has committed one of those offences they may require the suspect's name and address, and arrest the person if his name and address are not forthcoming, or if the garda reasonably suspects that the name and address given are false or misleading. A similar arrest power for non-cooperation with the gardaí applies under the Child Trafficking and Pornography Act 1998, which provides at s 7 for the arrest without warrant of anyone who obstructs or attempts to obstruct a garda acting under search warrant issued under s 7 (1), or who fails or refuses to give their name and address or who gives a false or misleading name or address.

1–59 The Child Trafficking and Pornography Act 1998 does not contain a specific arrest power for the offences of production and possession of child pornography, but the arrestable offence general power under s 4 of the Criminal Law Act 1997 can be used in the investigation of those offences. The only specific arrest power under the Child Trafficking and Pornography Act 1998 is for obstruction or attempted obstruction of a search, refusal or failure to comply with a requirement under s 7, or giving a name or address which is false or misleading. The obstruction offence is contained in s 7(4), while the arrest power is contained in s 7(5).

Criminal Damage and Cybercrime

1–60 Section 12 of the Criminal Damage Act 1991 contains a power of arrest for gardaí in relation to all offences under the Act bar one – unlawfully accessing data under s 5—whether triable summarily or on indictment. As outlined above paras 1 – 37 *et seq*, there are also certain citizen's arrest powers.

1–61 The omission of an arrest power for unlawfully accessing data is significant, given that the s 5 offence is a key cybercrime offence. Cybercrime encompasses a broad range of activities: some are traditional criminal offences recast for the modern age—the trade in child abuse images, fraud in its various forms—but others are of a different order, attacks on

---

[116] Criminal Law (Sexual Offences) Act 2006, s 8 and Schedule.

[117] *ibid*, s 3, as amended by the Criminal Law (Sexual Offences) (Amendment) Act 2007, s 5.

the information networks on which we rely for our personal affairs and those of the State, as well as cyber-attacks motivated by malice, ideology, international or industrial espionage. Cyber attacks, whether as a consequence of "hacktivism" (computer hacking and political activism combined) or organised crime, threaten the critical information infrastructure which is now vital to private individuals, corporate entities and governments. Computers are vulnerable to viruses and malicious software. These zombie computers are gathered together in networks known as botnets which can be remotely activated with considerable impact, for instance in denial of service attacks. Tracing denial of service attacks and malware back to the source computer is exceptionally difficult. Where demonstrable damage is intentionally or recklessly caused, the offence of criminal damage applies. Given the amount of personal data stored by State and private entities, hacking represents a major threat to individual privacy, and the penalties contained in s 5 of the Criminal Damage Act 1991 are undoubtedly inadequate. The offence of unlawful use of a computer, contained in s 9 of the Criminal Justice (Theft and Fraud Offences) Act 2001, criminalises the operation of a computer within the State (whether within or outside the State) with the intention of making a gain or of causing loss to another. The offence covers a wide range of criminal activity and attracts a penalty of ten years' imprisonment, and there is no requirement to prove damage.

Animal Cruelty

For over one hundred years, cruelty to animals has been governed for the most part by **1–62** the Protection of Animals Act 1911. The Act, as amended by s 48 of the Control of Horses Act 1996, provides at s 1(1):

> "(1) If any person—
>
> (a) shall cruelly beat, kick, ill-treat, over-ride, over-drive, over-load, torture, infuriate, or terrify any animal, or shall cause or procure, or, being the owner, permit any animal to be so used, or shall, by wantonly or unreasonably doing or omitting to do any act, or causing or procuring the commission or omission of any act, cause any unnecessary suffering, or, being the owner, permit any unnecessary suffering to be so caused to any animal; or
>
> (b) shall convey or carry, or cause or procure, or, being the owner, permit to be conveyed or carried, any animal in such manner or position as to cause that animal any unnecessary suffering; or
>
> (c) shall cause, procure, or assist at the fighting or baiting of any animal; or shall keep, use, manage, or act or assist in the management of, any premises or place for the purpose, or partly for the purpose, of fighting or baiting any animal, or shall permit any premises or place to be so kept, managed, or used, or shall receive, or cause or procure any person to receive, money for the admission of any person to such premises or place; or
>
> (d) shall wilfully, without any reasonable cause or excuse, administer, or cause or procure, or being the owner permit, such administration of, any poisonous or injurious drug or substance to any animal, or shall wilfully, without any reasonable cause or excuse, cause any such substance to be taken by any animal; or
>
> (e) shall subject, or cause or procure, or being the owner permit, to be subjected, any animal to any operation which is performed without due care and humanity; or
>
> (f) being the owner or having charge or control of any animal shall without reasonable cause or excuse abandon it, whether permanently or not, in

circumstances likely to cause it unnecessary suffering, or cause or procure or, being the owner, permit it to be so abandoned; such person shall be guilty of an offence of cruelty within the meaning of this Act..."

1–63 There is no arrest power in the 1911 Act for the general offence of animal cruelty. The penalties are low-level fines and imprisonment for terms not exceeding six months on summary disposal and two years' imprisonment on indictment, so the general arrest power in s 4 of the Criminal Law Act 1997 is not applicable. The Animal Health and Welfare Act 2013, which at the time of writing had not yet been commenced,[118] provides for arrest powers in the investigation of animal cruelty and represents a major advance on the existing law. The standard cruelty offence set out in the Act is as follows:

"12(1) A person shall not –
(a) do, or fail to do, anything or cause or permit anything to be done to an animal that causes unnecessary suffering to, or endangers the health or welfare of, an animal, or
(b) neglect, or be reckless, regarding the health or welfare of an animal."

1–64 The section provides at subsection 4 that the factors which can be considered in determining whether suffering is unnecessary will include whether the suffering could have reasonably have been avoided, terminated or reduced; whether the conduct was lawful in accordance with the Act or another piece of legislation, animal health and welfare regulations or a code of practice; whether the conduct was for a legitimate purpose, such as benefiting the health and welfare of the animal or protecting a person, property or other animal; whether the suffering was proportionate to the purpose of the conduct and whether the conduct was, in all the circumstances, that of a competent and humane person.

A number of other arrestable offences are set out in the Act, including failing to provide appropriate food and water for a protected animal (essentially an animal under human control for domestic, farming or sporting purposes) (s 13); involvement in or presence at animal fighting and related offences (s 15) as well as abandoning a protected animal (s 14).

The penalties for animal cruelty and other serious animal health and welfare offences under the Act are increased to a maximum of five years' imprisonment, making the Act's core offences arrestable offences for the purposes of s 4 of the Criminal Law Act 1997. Further powers to arrest are set out at s 39 for more minor offences under the Act and offences contrary to regulations made under the Act.[119]

Public Order Offences

Power to Direct Persons to 'Move On'

1–65 Gardaí are empowered to direct persons to desist from misbehaviour, and to order them to move on from the area in which they engage in it, by s 8 of the Criminal Justice

[118] The Act requires a commencement order to be made, pursuant to s 1(2).
[119] Such offences include, for instance, failure to comply with a requirement by an authorised officer in respect of animal cruelty (s 12(6)), permitting farm animals to stray (s 8(3)) and failing to keep records in relation to intensive units (s 20(4)).

(Public Order) Act 1994. The section applies when gardaí suspect, with reasonable cause, that a person is loitering in a public place in circumstances, which may include the company of other persons, that give rise to a reasonable apprehension for the safety of persons or the safety of property or for the maintenance of the public peace, or where gardaí suspect persons of behaving or having behaved in a manner contrary to ss 4, 5, 6, 7, or 9 of the Criminal Justice (Public Order) Act 1994. Failure to comply with a direction under s 8 is an offence.[120]

Such a direction to "move on" is the first port of call in defusing situations which are potentially public order incidents. The then Minister for Justice commented at the second stage of the Criminal Justice (Public Order) Bill that: **1–66**

> "A power for the Gardaí 'to move on' people where they are acting contrary to the provisions of sections 4,[121] 5[122] and 6[123] represents a sensible approach which avoids the need to deal with every difficulty which can arise from the type of behaviour involved by invoking the full rigours of the criminal law through arrest and charging. It will give the Gardaí powers to nip in the bud a potentially difficult situation and the people involved an opportunity to desist from behaviour which they may genuinely not have realised was giving rise to concern. Equally, giving the Gardaí power to 'move on' [those] who are loitering in the circumstances specified in the Bill should greatly increase the powers of the Gardaí to deal with the activities of those who stalk certain locations with a view to preying on others."[124]

In *Director of Public Prosecutions (Sheehan) v Galligan,*[125] Laffoy J held that a person in respect of whom a s 8 direction was made was entitled to be informed of his legal obligation to comply with such direction and of the penal sanction applicable in the event of non-compliance. **1–67**

> "In a prosecution for an offence contrary to s 8(2) of the Act of 1994, there should be evidence before the court of trial that the accused was informed or was aware of the fact that if he did not comply with the direction being given to him by a member of An Garda Síochána he would be committing a criminal offence; no particular form of words need be used to convey such a warning."[126]

This statement of the law was affirmed by Ó Caoimh J in *Bates v Brady.*[127]

[120] Criminal Justice (Public Order) Act 1994, s 8(2).

[121] Intoxication in a public place to such an extent as would give rise to a reasonable apprehension that a person might endanger himself or any other person in his vicinity, *ibid,* s 4.

[122] Disorderly conduct in a public place – unreasonable behaviour which, having regard to all the circumstances, is likely to cause serious offence or serious annoyance to any person who is, or might reasonably be expected to be, aware of such behaviour, *ibid,* s 5.

[123] Threatening, abusive or insulting words or behaviour in a public place with intent to provoke a breach of the peace or being reckless as to whether a breach of the peace may be occasioned, *ibid,* s 6.

[124] Máire Geoghegan Quinn, 433 Dáil Debates, cols 952–953.

[125] *Director of Public Prosecutions (Sheehan) v Galligan,* unreported, High Court, 2 November 1995 (Laffoy J).

[126] *ibid.*

[127] *Bates v Brady* [2003] 4 IR 111.

1–68 The Criminal Justice (Public Order) Act 2011 adds, in s 3, a specific power to move on in relation to begging. The Act permits gardaí to direct a person to desist and to move on if they are begging and are believed, on reasonable grounds, to be doing so in such a manner as harasses, intimidates, assaults or threatens others or obstructs their passage (such as would constitute an offence under s 2 of the 2011 Act), or gives rise to an apprehension for the safety of persons or property in the vicinity. In addition, gardaí may direct a person begging to desist and to leave the area in the following circumstances:

- where the person begging does so at or near the entrance to a dwelling, an automated teller machine, a vending machine or a night safe;
- where the begging is at the entrance to business premises during opening hours, if there are reasonable grounds to suspect that members of the public are being, or are likely to be, deterred from entering the premises.
- Where a person begs in a private place – although, if that private place is a dwelling, the consent of the owner or occupier is required.

1–69 Both begging in the proscribed manner (by intimidation, harassment or obstruction of passage) and failure to comply with a direction to desist from aggressive begging, constitute offences with an associated arrest power. Following the authorities which relate to failure to move on under s 8 of the Criminal Justice (Public Order) Act 1994, it should be made clear that both constitute offences. The relevant arrest power is contained in s 4 of the 2011 Act. Gardaí may only exercise their powers under the Act in a private dwelling with the permission of the owner or occupier of the dwelling. Section 4 provides:

> "(1) A member of the Garda Síochána may arrest without warrant any person whom he or she suspects, upon reasonable grounds, of having committed an offence under s 2 or 3 [ie begging, or failing to desist from begging on being told to move on]…
>
> …
>
> (4) A member of the Garda Síochána shall not perform functions under subsection (1) while in a dwelling unless he or she is in the dwelling with the consent of the owner or occupier of the dwelling."

1–70 An important aspect of the legislation is that begging is defined as requesting or soliciting money from another person or persons "other than in accordance with a licence, permit or authorisation (howsoever described) granted by or under an enactment".[128] It was held in *DPP v Rostas and another*[129] that:

> "The issue of licence, permit or authorisation is not a matter of legal defence. The prosecution are obliged to lead some evidence to establish a *prima facie* case that the begging took place without legal authorisation. Once this is established the burden of proof is transferred to the accused to establish a reasonable doubt as to the legality of the begging."[130]

Therefore, where it is proposed to prosecute persons for begging, gardaí must seek evidence to establish that the suspect did not have a licence, permit or authorisation to beg.

---

[128] Criminal Justice (Public Order) Act 2011, s 1(2).

[129] *DPP v Rostas and another* [2012] 1 IR 393.

[130] *ibid* at 399.

Section 24—The General Public Order Arrest Power

Section 24 of the Criminal Justice (Public Order) Act 1994 provides a summary power of arrest for certain public order offences under the 1994 Act, but there are a number of conditions which must be met before the arrest power can be exercised: **1–71**

i. the person must be found actually committing an offence to which s 24 applies (a "relevant offence") or
ii. where a garda is of the opinion that an offence has been committed to which s 24 applies, the person who is reasonably suspected of having committed it refuses to give his name and address when demanded, or gives a name or address which, on reasonable grounds, is believed to be false or misleading.

The 'relevant offences' for the purposes of arrest under s 24 are: **1–72**

- intoxication in a public place giving rise to a reasonable apprehension of a danger to self or others (s 4)
- threatening, abusive or insulting behaviour in a public place with intent to provoke a breach of the peace, or being reckless as to whether a breach of the peace may be caused (s 6),
- distribution or display in a public place of material which is threatening, abusive, insulting or obscene (s 7),
- failure to comply with a direction of a member of An Garda Síochána (s 8),
- entering a building with intent to commit an offence (s 11),
- trespassing in such a manner as is likely to cause fear in another person (s 13),
- riot (s 14),
- violent disorder (s 15),
- affray (s 16),
- blackmail, extortion and demanding money with menaces (s 17),
- assault with intent to cause bodily harm or commit an indictable offence (s 18) or assault or obstruction of a peace officer (s 19).

The offences of riot (s 14), violent disorder (s 15), affray (s 16), blackmail, extortion and demanding money with menaces (s 17), assault with intent to cause bodily harm or commit indictable offence (s 18) and assault or obstruction of a peace officer (s 19) are all also arrestable offences, in respect of which the general arrest power in s 4 of the Criminal Law Act 1997 may equally be used.

Road Traffic Offences

The most common road traffic offences contain inbuilt arrest powers. This is a formula replicated throughout the Road Traffic Acts to distinguish between arrestable and non-arrestable road traffic offences. **1–73**

The 'drink driving' arrest power in s 49(8) of the Road Traffic Act 1961 was among the most frequently employed arrest provisions, and gave rise to extensive litigation.[131] **1–74**

[131] For a detailed treatment of the law on intoxicated driving, see de Blácam, *Drunken Driving and the Law* (3rd ed, Thomson Round Hall, Dublin, 2003).

Section 49 has now been repealed, and is replaced by s 4 of the Road Traffic Act 2010. Section 4 restates the provisions relating to the prohibition on driving a vehicle while under the influence of an intoxicant. It also lowered the maximum permitted blood alcohol concentration (BAC) in relation to a person driving or attempting to drive a mechanically propelled vehicle, from 80mg to 50mg (and the equivalent levels in urine or breath) for most drivers and from 80mg to 20mg (and the equivalent levels in urine or breath) for novice and professional drivers. The arrest power, contained in s 4(8), mirrors that which was contained in s 49(8) of the Road Traffic Act, and provides that:

> "a member of the Garda Síochána may arrest without warrant a person who in the member's opinion is committing or has committed an offence under this section".

1–75 Although the requirement to explain to the person who is to be arrested the reason for and fact of the arrest is not expressly outlined in the section, the case-law which has been born out of s 49 arrests makes it clear that, in addition to forming an opinion that the person is committing or has committed an offence, the garda must tell the person that he is under arrest. The reason for the arrest must also be explained. It is not necessary to recite the statute under which the arrest is effected and, where a statute is cited incorrectly, it will not invalidate an arrest. In *DPP v O'Connell,*[132] the prosecuting garda had given evidence before the District Court of arresting the accused under s 49(8) of the Road Traffic Act 1994, when in fact he had intended to state that he had arrested him under s 49(8) of the 1961 Act. The provision which he had purportedly used did not exist. Geoghegan J stated:

> "A judge at all times takes judicial notice of the law and in my opinion there is only one inference which a judge could draw from the statutory citation given by the sergeant. It was perfectly obvious beyond any doubt at all that the Garda was referring to s 49(8) of the Road Traffic Act, 1961, as inserted by s. 10 of the Road Traffic Act, 1994, even though he clumsily and indeed incorrectly gave the citation. The District Court Judge therefore would have had to draw the conclusion that the Garda was intending to arrest under s 49(8) of the Road Traffic Act, 1961, as inserted by s 10 of the Road Traffic Act, 1994. But that is not the end of the matter, because of course the Garda's intention is only one constituent element in the validity of an arrest. *The arrested person must have knowledge of why he was being arrested.* On the facts as set out in the case stated, I am satisfied that the defendant would have known the reason for his arrest, sufficiently to render the arrest valid."[133]

1–76 Geoghegan J went on to explain the level of information which ought to be provided in a drunk-driving arrest. He stated:

> "Following *Director of Public Prosecutions v Mooney* [1992] 1 IR 548, I likewise take the view that the evidence that Sergeant Connolly informed the accused in layman's language that he was being arrested for drunk-driving was sufficient communication of the reason for the arrest and indeed I further agree with the suggestion of Blayney J that having regard to the fact that a breath test was taken and proved positive, it was not even necessary to state a reason. However, a reason which was sufficient was in fact stated."[134]

---

[132] *DPP v O'Connell* [1998] 3 IR 62.

[133] *ibid* at 66 (emphasis added).

[134] *ibid* at 67.

In *DPP v Ennis*[135] the Supreme Court considered the lawfulness of an arrest where a garda had in mind an arrest under s 49(8) of the Road Traffic Act 1961 and then explained the arrest as being for "drink driving" without reference to either the section or the Act under which the arrest was effected. Citing *Mooney,*[136] the Court held that "it is sufficient for a lawful arrest if the ground of the arrest is communicated in ordinary language. That is sufficient to dispose of the question as to the legality of the arrest".[137]

The following (non-exhaustive) road traffic offences have associated arrest powers: **1–77**

a. Failure or refusal to produce a test certificate, contrary to s 19 of the Road Traffic Act 1961[138];
b. Failure to produce a driving licence on demand, contrary to s 40 of the Road Traffic Act 1961[139];
c. Driving a mechanically-propelled vehicle while under the influence of an intoxicant, contrary to s 4 of the Road Traffic Act 2010;
d. Being in charge of a mechanically-propelled vehicle while under the influence of an intoxicant, contrary to s 5 of the Road Traffic Act 2010;
e. Driving an animal-drawn vehicle or pedal cycle while under the influence of intoxicating liquor, contrary to s 6 of the Road Traffic Act 2010[140];
f. Dangerous driving causing death or serious bodily injury to another, contrary to s 53 of the Road Traffic Act 1961[141];
g. Parking a vehicle in a dangerous position, contrary to s 55 of the Road Traffic Act 1961[142];
h. Failure or refusal to produce a certificate of insurance or exemption, contrary to s 69 of the Road Traffic Act 1961[143];
i. Non-performance of duties following an accident, ie where injury is caused to a person or property, failure to stop the vehicle, keep the vehicle at the scene, provide information and report the occurrence to the gardaí, contrary to s 106 of the Road Traffic Act 1961[144];

---

135 *DPP v Ennis* [2011] IESC 46.

136 *DPP v Mooney* [1992] 1 IR 548.

137 *DPP v Ennis* [2011] IESC 46.

138 Gardaí may also arrest for failure or refusal to give a name and address or giving a name or address which is suspected to be false or misleading when demanded under s 19.

139 As inserted by s 25 of the Road Traffic Act 1994 and amended by s18 of the Road Traffic Act 2002 and s 13 of the Road Traffic Act 2006. Gardaí may also arrest for failure or refusal to give a name and address or giving a name or address which is suspected to be false or misleading when demanded under s 40.

140 As amended by s 18 of the Road Traffic Act 2006.

141 As substituted by s 4 of the Road Traffic (No 2) Act 2011.

142 *ibid.*

143 As amended by SI No 463 of 2001, European Communities (Road Traffic) (Compulsory Insurance) (Amendment) Regulations, 2001, Art 4, s 18 of the Road Traffic Act 2006 and s 22(a) of the Road Traffic Act 2006. Gardaí may also arrest for failure or refusal to give a name and address or giving a name or address which is suspected to be false or misleading when demanded under s 69.

144 As amended by s 45 of the Road Traffic Act 1994 and s 18 of the Road Traffic Act 2006.

j. Failure or refusal to give information on demand to a member of the Garda Síochána where that member alleges or has reasonable grounds to believe that a road traffic offence has been committed, contrary to s 107 of the Road Traffic Act 1961[145];
k. Unauthorised taking of a vehicle, contrary to s 112 of the Road Traffic Act 1961[146];
l. Unauthorised interference with the mechanism of a vehicle, contrary to s 113 of the Road Traffic Act 1961[147];
m. Failure or refusal to give a breath sample, contrary to ss 9 or 10 of the Road Traffic Act 2010[148];
n. Failure to comply with the a garda who requires a breath specimen required where a garda is of the opinion that a person in charge of a mechanically propelled vehicle has (i) consumed intoxicating liquor (ii) is committing or has committed an offence under the Road Traffic Acts 1961 to 2001 or (iii) has been involved with the vehicle in an event in which injury has been caused or is claimed to have been caused, contrary to s 12(3) of the Road Traffic Act 1994 (inserted by s 2 of the Road Traffic Act 2003) as substituted by s 2 of the Road Traffic Act 2011.

1–78 There is no arrest power associated with careless driving *simpliciter*,[149] but there is an arrest power for the offence of careless driving causing death.[150]

When gardaí arrest under the Road Traffic Acts, they are empowered to remove or temporarily dispose of the vehicle of the arrested person.[151] In doing so, the general requirement of compulsory insurance does not apply to them.[152]

Obstruction

1–79 A general offence of resisting or obstructing a peace officer (or a person assisting a peace officer) in the course of their duty is contained in s 19(3) of the Criminal Justice (Public Order) Act 1994,[153] and is arrestable under s 24 of the same Act. Various other

[145] As amended by s 3 of the Road Traffic (Amendment) Act 1984, ss 46 and 49 of the Road Traffic Act 1994 and s 25 of the Road Traffic Act 2002 and s18 of the Road Traffic Act 2006.

[146] As amended by s 65 of the Road Traffic Act 1968 and s 18 of the Road Traffic Act 2006.

[147] As amended by s 6 of the Road Traffic Act 1968 and s 23 of the Road Traffic Act 2002.

[148] As amended by s 9(c) of the Road Traffic Act 2011.

[149] The offence of careless driving in s 52 of the Road Traffic Act 1961 is amended by s 23 of the Road Traffic Act 2002 and substituted by s 4 of the Road Traffic (No 2) Act 2011.

[150] Careless driving causing death is a new offence which was inserted into s 52 of the Road Traffic Act 1961 by s 4 of the Road Traffic (No 2) Act 2011.

[151] Road Traffic Act 1961, s 110 as amended by s 49 of the Road Traffic Act 1961 and by s 25 of the Road Traffic Act 2002. s 110 of the Road Traffic Act 1961 provides "Where a member of the Garda Síochána arrests under this Act without warrant a person in charge of a mechanically propelled vehicle, the member may, if the circumstances so require, take or cause to be taken such steps as he may consider proper for the temporary disposition of the vehicle".

[152] Road Traffic Act 1961, s 4(2)(c).

[153] s 19(3) of the Criminal Justice (Public Order) Act 1994 provides that

"Any person who resists or wilfully obstructs or impedes—

(a) a person providing medical services at or in a hospital, knowing that he or she is, or being reckless as to whether he or she is, a person providing medical services, or

(b) a person assisting such a person, or

statutory provisions permit the arrest of persons from whom assistance is statutorily sought and not forthcoming, and who go further and obstruct the gardaí in carrying out their duties. Obstruction can consist of non-compliance with the terms of a search warrant,[154] refusal to allow a garda to see a driving licence on request,[155] or failure to move on when directed to do so.[156]

Numerous statutory provisions permit arrest for refusal to give a name and address when requested or giving a false or misleading response.[157]

In addition, there are dedicated obstruction offences to enable gardaí to investigate, with enforced cooperation where necessary, but not all contain an inbuilt arrest power. Examples include obstruction of gardaí under s 2(9) the Criminal Justice (Forensic Evidence) Act 1990[158] and s 6(4) of the Criminal Justice Act 1984,[159] and failure or refusal to give information or giving false or misleading information to gardaí in connection with firearms or ammunition.[160] It is arguable, however, that while these provisions do not of themselves include a power to arrest, the actions impugned, being offences of obstruction, might come within the ambit of s 19(3) of the Criminal Justice (Public) Order Act 1994. If an arrest is necessary, the offence of wilfully obstructing a peace officer acting in the execution of his duty under s 19(3) might be more suitable. **1–80**

Common Law Power of Arrest—Breach of the Peace

Gardaí had a common law power of arrest where a felony or treason was being committed, had been committed or where it was suspected that a felony or treason was about to be committed. The Criminal Law Act 1997 abolished the distinction between misdemeanour and felony and, while the common law power in respect of felonies has been codified and replaced by the power to arrest without warrant in s 4 of the 1997 Act, a residual common law power to arrest for breach of the peace still remains. **1–81**

(c) a peace officer acting in the execution of a peace officer's duty, knowing that he or she is or being reckless as to whether he or she is, a peace officer so acting, or

(d) a person assisting a peace officer in the execution of his or her duty,

shall be guilty of an offence." 'Peace officers' include gardaí, prison officers, members of the defence forces, ambulance personnel, and members of the fire brigade.

[154] See s 10 of the Criminal Justice (Miscellaneous Provisions) Act 1997 as substituted by s 6(1) of the Criminal Justice Act 2006.

[155] Road Traffic Act 1961, s 40(4)(a) as substituted by s 25 of the Road Traffic Act 1994 and as amended by s 18 of the Road Traffic Act 2002 and s 13 of the Road Traffic Act 2006.

[156] Criminal Justice (Public Order) Act 1994, s 8.

[157] Such as the Road Traffic Act 1961, s 40(4)(b), as substituted by s 25 of the Road Traffic Act 1994 and as amended by s 18 of the Road Traffic Act 2002 and s 13 of the Road Traffic Act 2006; the Criminal Justice (Public Order) Act 1994, s 24(2)(b); the Criminal Assets Bureau Act 1996, s 16(1)(b).

[158] As amended by s 14 of the Criminal Justice Act 2006.

[159] As amended by s 13(a) of the Criminal Justice Act 2006. The offence refers to obstructing gardaí acting under s 6(1) of the Criminal Justice Act 1984, in taking the details of a detained person, and provides for an offence of failing to give a name and address or providing a name or address which is false or misleading. No arrest power is required here, given that the person will already be in custody

[160] Criminal Justice Act 1999, s 15(2).

1–82 Common law breach of the peace is an imprecise and curious creature: it encompasses behaviour which is serious enough to be an offence, as well as behaviour falling short, and both categories of conduct are arrestable. As Murphy J put it: "[T]here are more serious breaches of the peace which are offences under common law and others which are simply preventative in nature and not being an offence nor being susceptible to a penalty. Both are subject to a power of arrest."[161] Murphy J noted that the offence is unique in its vagueness: "It is anomalous, however, that breach of the peace is not prescribed by law, nor that there is no definition of the categories, nor of a dividing line between the serious and minor breaches."[162] Many of the offences which were traditionally breach of the peace offences have been replaced by statutory offences under the Criminal Justice (Public Order) Act 1994. A key difference between breach of the peace and public order is that the latter depends on the impugned behaviour occurring in a public place, whereas a breach of the peace may occur on private property. Even so, there is a public element to the offence of breach of the peace, so the gardaí are constrained to a large degree in dealing with disturbances in the domestic context. See further *Chapter 13: Domestic Abuse*.

1–83 It should be noted that common law breach of the peace is not an arrestable offence within the meaning of s 4 of the Criminal Law Act 1997. Rather, there is a separate common law power of arrest for breach of the peace, exercisable by gardaí and ordinary citizens. In *Thorpe v Director of Public Prosecutions*, Murphy J noted:

> "Glanville Williams: Arrest for Breach of the Peace (1954) Crim. L.R. 578 pointed out that, apart from arrest for felony, the only power of arrest at common law is in respect of breach of the peace. However, there was a surprising lack of authoritative definition of what one would suppose to be a fundamental concept in criminal law. While a breach of the peace is supposed to underlie every crime, the narrower meaning encompasses a riot or an unlawful assembly which has not yet become a riot. There may also be a breach of the peace without any general disorder where a unilateral battery or an assault is committed.
>
> Each of the instances involves some danger to the person, and it is submitted that this is the general meaning of a breach of the peace in criminal law."[163]

1–84 In *Clifford v DPP* Charleton J explored the parameters of the offence finding:

> "A breach of the peace implies conduct which goes beyond boisterousness. Instead, the offence involves a situation which imminently threatens a person, through the conduct of those involved in the breach of the peace, but not necessarily directly, of being

---

[161] See *Thorpe v Director of Public Prosecutions* [2007] 1 IR 502 at 519.

[162] *ibid* at 520.

[163] *ibid* at 512. He remarked later in the judgment: "Over 50 years after Glanville Williams' observations, the power of arrest at common law in respect of breach of the peace still lacks an authoritative definition of what one would suppose to be a fundamental concept in criminal law." Murphy J's analysis was cited with approval in the subsequent case of *Clifford v Director of Public Prosecutions* [2008] IEHC 322. The High Court decision in *Clifford* was subsequently upheld by the Supreme Court, *Clifford v DPP* [2013] IESC 43.

> harmed through an assault, an affray, a riot, an unlawful assembly or any other serious disturbance; *R v Eroll Howell* (1981) 71 Cr App r 31 per Watkins LJ ..."[164]

He concluded that

> "... breach of the peace... occurs where a person finds himself, or herself, in a situation where they reasonably fear that, if they do not withdraw from it quite promptly, they may either be assaulted or that the disturbance in respect of which the accused stands charged may create the risk of a response which is disorderly and in consequence potentially violent whereby, through direct or indirect means, bystanders may be caught up in violence. In this context, shoving, flying missiles, stampeding by a few people or a section of a crowd and fighting within a group, constitute examples of the kind of indirect violence that may ensnare the uninvolved and so constitute a breach of the peace."[165]

This passage in *Clifford* was cited with approval in *Brady v Director of Public Prosecutions*[166] as being "inferentially at least supportive of the view expressed by Murphy J in *Thorpe* that the offence of breach of the peace is indeed an offence well known and long known to Irish law."[167] In *Brady* the applicant sought a declaration that breach of the peace was not an offence known to the law and argued that *Thorpe* had been wrongly decided. Both lines of argument were rejected by Kearns P. **1–85**

Notwithstanding the clear and consistent judicial support of the offence of breach of the peace, by comparison with the available statutory offences breach of the peace is vague and incongruous. There is no specific penalty associated with it, but it has been held to be prosecutable summarily in the District Court and the penalty resultant on conviction is a matter for the District Court acting within its sentencing limits.[168] With the enactment of the Criminal Procedure Act 2010, breach of the peace has been added to the first schedule of the Criminal Justice Act 1951 to clarify that it is an indictable offence which may be dealt with summarily by the District Court.[169] **1–86**

A person may also of course be bound to the peace. It would seem that the offence's advantage lies in being a prosecutable public order-type offence, which does not have to have been committed in public. Given the amorphous nature of breach of the peace, it is submitted that it is preferable to arrest and prosecute for a statutory offence.

---

164 *ibid.*

165 *ibid.*

166 *Brady v Director of Public Prosecutions* [2010] IEHC 231.

167 *ibid, per* Kearns P.

168 It is, however an indictable offence. O'Malley points out that it is oddly omitted from the list in the first schedule of the Criminal Justice Act 1951 which outlines indictable offences triable summarily. See T O'Malley, *The Criminal Process* (Round Hall Thomson Reuters, Dublin, 2009) at p 302.

169 Criminal Procedure Act 2010, s 38. The Criminal Procedure Act 2010 came into operation on 1 September 2010, see SI No 414 of 2010, Criminal Procedure Act 2010 (Commencement) Order 2010.

Demands for Name and Address and Fixed Charges

1–87 There is nothing to prevent gardaí from approaching members of the public and seeking information from them. Gardaí in the discharge of their duties may request the names and addresses of persons they encounter, and if they do so on an informal basis, there is no legal obligation on the person who is asked for his name to comply. When the request is informal, there is no offence committed in failing to accede to it. If, however, the garda has occasion to make the request on the basis of a statutory power, the person of whom the request is made should be informed of the legal power under which the name and address demand is made, and of the fact that failure to supply an accurate name and address is an offence for which they may be arrested.

1–88 In the public order context s 24(2) of the Criminal Justice (Public Order) Act 1994 provides a formal power to demand names and addresses. Where gardaí are of the opinion that an offence has been committed under one of the specified provisions of the 1994 Act (ie ss 4, 6, 7, 8, 11, 13, 14, 15, 16, 17, 18 or 19—the offences to which a power of arrest applies under s 24(1)), they may demand the name and address of any person who is, with reasonable cause, thought to have committed, or to have been found committing, a specified offence. If there is a refusal, or there are reasonable grounds to believe that the name and address given is false or misleading, the garda may arrest that person without warrant. To arrest a person on the basis of a failure to give a correct name and address is a significant garda power, which was considered in *Director of Public Prosecutions (Ryan) v Mulligan*.[170] There the arresting garda demanded the name and address of a suspect, but she did not inform him that she made the demand pursuant to her power under s 24(2) of the Criminal Justice (Public Order) Act 1994. Neither did she inform him that he could be arrested for failing to give his name and address, nor that failure to give his name and address in the circumstances constituted an offence. Charleton J held that:

> "In many cases, a simple request for a person's name and address will be sufficient to obtain that information without any necessity for recourse to statutory powers of compulsion. However, a person who fails to comply with such an informal request commits no offence. By contrast, where a power of compulsion, enforceable by sanction, is exercised, a person should be informed of this power and also of the consequences of a refusal to comply."[171]

1–89 Charleton J emphasised that there was no requirement that the precise section be cited—what is necessary is a communication that the demand is made under a Garda power:

> "It cannot…be expected that the Gardaí should be turned into walking repositories of sections and sub-sections of various Acts of the Oireachtas. That has never been the law. A citizen is not obliged to submit to a demand pursuant to police powers unless

[170] *Director of Public Prosecutions (Ryan) v Mulligan* [2009] 1 IR 794.
[171] *ibid* at 798.

> information is provided to the citizen that such a power exists… a lawful demand for a name and address is made where a Garda specifies that he or she has a power under the Public Order Act or Criminal Justice Act to demand such particulars and that if they are not given an offence is committed."[172]

It is notable that s 5 of the Criminal Justice (Public Order) Act 1994, which proscribes disorderly conduct, is excluded from the power to demand a name and address in s 24(2), as it is from the power of arrest in s 24(1). The Criminal Justice Act 2006 amended the 1994 Act by inserting a new s 23A, to provide for so-called 'fixed charge' offences under s 5 and s 4 of the Criminal Justice (Public Order) Act 1994.[173] Rather than adding an additional power of arrest for disorderly conduct which is accompanied by a refusal to give a name and address, or a true name and address, the section provides for an on-the-spot fine for disorderly conduct. It also provides for an on-the-spot fine for intoxication under s 4, which gives gardaí discretion whether to arrest or not for that offence.[174] Under s 23A(2), a garda may request the person concerned to give his or her name and address and to verify the information given. If the garda is not satisfied with the name and address or any verification given, he or she request that the person accompany the member to a garda station for the purpose of confirming the person's name and address. Thereafter, the garda must serve on the person personally or by post a notice containing the following information: **1–90**

(a) that the person is alleged to have committed the relevant offence;
(b) when and where it is alleged to have been committed;
(c) that a prosecution for it will not be instituted if the applicable fine is paid to a specified Garda station within 28 days;
(d) that, after the expiry of the first 28-day period, the fine will increase by 50 per cent, and the suspect has a further 28 days in which to pay the increased amount;
(e) In default of payment of the fine, the person will be prosecuted for the alleged offence.

The rationale behind the introduction of fixed charge offences in this manner is to ease the administrative and time burden on the District Court by diverting trivial matters, with the advantage for the defendant of a speedy resolution of the matter and the avoidance of a court appearance and possible conviction. However, it has been noted that the trend sacrifices the independence of the various participants in the prosecutorial system and the presumption of innocence. As Spencer puts it: **1–91**

> "It is likely that many persons faced with the penalty under the section will choose to pay it rather than risk conviction in the criminal courts in a case in which the evidence ultimately boils down to their word against that of a member of the Garda Síochána. The pressures of expense and the uncertainty of running the gauntlet that face an individual in this situation are considerable. Interestingly there is no requirement that the member of the Garda Síochána has personally witnessed the offence and the section vests all of the various roles associated with a criminal trial and usually played by several different

---

172 *ibid* at 799-800.

173 Criminal Justice Act 1994, s 23A, as inserted by s 184 of the Criminal Justice Act 2006.

174 Criminal Justice Act 1994, s 23B, as inserted by s 184 of the Criminal Justice Act 2006.

> parties, in the member of the Garda Síochána. In effect, the Garda Síochána becomes the prosecutor of the offence, and is also responsible for the adjudicative and sentencing roles usually ascribed to the court. This provides members of the Garda Síochána with an extremely wide discretion in the name of executive convenience. While these fixed penalty mechanisms have been deployed in relation to regulatory offences, it is cause for concern that they are now being used in relation to public order offences which are now effectively being decided on the street by members of the Garda Síochána, rather than in the District Court by judges appointed under the Constitution."[175]

There are numerous other statutory powers to demand names and addresses. See further the consideration of stop and search powers in chapter *Chapter 7: Powers to Stop and Search*.

PART 3: ARREST WARRANTS

ARREST WARRANTS—FUNCTION AND LEGAL FRAMEWORK

1–92 An arrest warrant is a written order to arrest a specified person. Arrest warrants are issued by judges either of their own volition (such as where a person has failed to appear before the court), or on the application of gardaí, in which case the warrant is based on the sworn information of gardaí given on oath and in writing.[176]

Arrest warrants are used in the following circumstances:

- To charge a person suspected of committing an indictable offence and thereby commence legal proceedings against them[177];
- To bring an accused person before the court where they have failed to appear in answer to a summons or having been released on bail[178];
- When it is thought that an accused person remanded on bail is about to abscond or breach a condition of their recognisance;
- To initiate extradition proceedings[179];
- To bring persons directly before the Special Criminal Court;
- To arrest prisoners;
- To re-arrest persons who have already been arrested and detained for questioning.

These aspects of arrest warrants are considered in further detail below. First, some of the legal architecture and jurisprudence underpinning arrest warrants should be considered.

---

[175] Spencer, "Annotations on the Criminal Justice Act 2006", *Irish Current Law Statutes Annotated*, (Thomson Round Hall, Dublin, 2006).

[176] See Order 16 Rule 1 District Court Rules, 1997, SI No 93 of 1997.

[177] Proceedings in minor offences usually proceed by way of summons.

[178] Order 22 District Court Rules, 1997, SI No 93 & 1997. See also SI No 498 of 2008 District Court (Bench Warrants) Rules 2008.

[179] See generally M Forde, *Extradition Law in Ireland* (3rd ed, Thomson Round Hall, Dublin, 2005) and Farrell and Hanrahan, *The European Arrest Warrant in Ireland* (Clarus Press, Dublin, 2011).

A Command to Arrest, Rather than a Discretionary Power

In *Dunne v Director of Public Prosecutions*, Carney J outlined that an arrest warrant, rather than being a discretionary power, is a command to arrest which the gardaí are obliged to obey: **1–93**

> "A warrant of apprehension is a command issued to the Gardaí by a Court established under the Constitution to bring a named person before that Court to be dealt with according to law. It is not a document which merely vests a discretion in the Guards to apprehend the person named in it; it is a command to arrest that person immediately and bring him or her before the Court which issued it. That it is a command to arrest rather than merely an authority or permission to arrest can be clearly seen from the terms of the warrant..."[180]

This is mirrored in Order 26 Rule 7 of the District Court Rules 1997, which is framed in non-discretionary terms: **1–94**

> "[W]here the person against whom the warrant is issued is found... in any place for which the Superintendent or Inspector to whom the warrant is addressed acts, then such Superintendent or Inspector ... or any member of the Garda Síochána appointed by any such Superintendent or Inspector *shall* execute the warrant."[181]

A warrant then is a command to arrest which gives gardaí no discretion.[182] In *Murphy v Shields*, Carney J criticised what he viewed as a lax approach by gardaí to the execution of warrants: **1–95**

> "Under the District Court Rules, a warrant of apprehension upon being issued by a judge of the District Court is directed by him to a Garda Superintendent or Inspector who acts for the place where the warrant is issued. The officer to whom it is issued may delegate its execution to another member of An Garda Síochána. I have on more than one occasion formed the view that the guards do not have a full appreciation of the mandatory duty they are under to execute warrants and a full appreciation that warrants are commands to arrest and not merely authorities to arrest. It has seemed to me from time to time that the guards have sat on a warrant and waited for the wanted person to gratuitously fall into their laps by, for example, being arrested in relation to a further crime rather than taking any active steps to find him."[183]

Arrest warrants are issued pursuant to the District Court Rules, which in turn derive their authority from s 11 of the Petty Sessions (Ireland) Act 1851[184] and the Dublin Police Act 1842.[185]

---

180 *Dunne v Director of Public Prosecutions,* unreported, High Court, 6 June 1996.

181 Emphasis added.

182 See also *Dalton v Governor of Training Unit Glengarriff Parade,* unreported, Supreme Court, 29 February 2000.

183 *Murphy v Shields* [1998] IEHC 167.

184 14 and 15 Vict, Chapter 93. See *Dunphy v Crowley,* unreported, High Court, 17 February 1997.

185 Both Acts remain in force, unaffected by the Statute Law Revision Act 2007.

1–96 Section 11 of the Petty Sessions (Ireland) Act 1851 provides:

> "(1) In all Cases of Indictable Crimes and Offences (where an Information that any Person has committed the same shall have been taken in Writing and on Oath) the Justice shall issue a Warrant (B b.) to arrest and bring such Person before him, or some other Justice of the same County, to answer to the Complaint made in the Information (and which Warrant may be issued or executed on a Sunday as well as on any other Day): or if he shall think that the Ends of Justice would be thereby sufficiently answered, it shall be lawful for him, instead of issuing such Warrant, to issue a Summons in the first instance to such Person, requiring him to appear and answer to the said Complaint; but nothing herein contained shall prevent any Justice from issuing a Warrant for the Arrest of such Person at any Time before or after the Time mentioned in such Summons for his Appearance; and whenever such Person shall afterwards appear or be brought before any such Justice he shall proceed according to the Provisions hereinafter contained as to taking the Evidence against such Person, and committing such Person for Trial.
>
> (2) In all Cases of Summary Jurisdiction the Justice may issue his Summons directed to such Person, requiring him to appear and answer to the Complaint, and it shall not be necessary that such Justice shall be the Justice or One of the Justices by whom the Complaint shall be afterwards heard and determined; and in all Cases of Offences where such Person shall not appear at the required Time and Place, and it shall be proved on Oath either that he was personally served with such Summons or that he is keeping out of the Way of such Service, (the Complaint being in Writing and on Oath,) the Justice may issue a Warrant to arrest and bring such Person before him or some other Justice of the same County, to answer to the said Complaint; and when such Person shall afterwards be arrested under such Warrant, the Justice before whom he shall be brought may either by Warrant (E b.) commit him to Gaol, until the Hearing of the Complaint, or may discharge him upon his entering into a Recognizance (C.), with or without Sureties, at the Discretion of the Justice, conditioned for his Appearance at such Hearing:"

1–97 To summarise—a judge may issue a warrant for the arrest of a person suspected of having committed an indictable offence, or may decide to issue a summons instead. Having issued a summons, the judge may change his mind and choose to issue a warrant for his arrest after all. Summonses are used to command the appearance in court of persons accused of minor offences, unless they evade service or fail to appear, in which case a warrant will issue for their arrest to compel their appearance in court.

1–98 To complicate matters, the Petty Sessions (Ireland) Act 1851 does not apply to the Dublin Metropolitan District.[186] Warrants in Dublin are issued pursuant to powers conferred by ss 49 and 51 of the Dublin Police Act 1842. Section 49 provides:

> "And be it enacted. That upon any Information or Complaint to be laid or made before any Divisional Justice of any Matter which such Justice is authorized to hear and determine summarily, he may summon the Party charged, and if such Party shall not appear according to the Tenor of the Summons, any one of the Divisional Justices,

---

[186] s 41 of the Petty Sessions (Ireland) Act 1851 states: "[N]othing in this Act shall extend to the Police District of Dublin metropolis, or alter or affect in any Manner whatsoever any of the Provisions or Enactments contained in any Act regulating the Powers and Duties of Justices of the Peace or of the Police of the District of Dublin Metropolis, or be deemed applicable in any way to the same, save so far as relates to the backing or executing of any warrant…"

upon Proof of the Service of the Summons, may proceed, in all Cases which are not of a Criminal Nature, if no sufficient Cause shall be shown for the Non-appearance of the Party, to hear and determine the Case in the Absence of the Party, and in all Criminal Cases shall issue his Warrant for apprehending and bringing such Party before him or some other Divisional Justice, in order that the said Information or Complaint may be heard and determined."

Section 51 provides:

"And be it enacted. That every such Justice may, without issuing any Summons, forthwith issue his Warrant for the Apprehension of any Person charged with any Offence cognizable before him, whenever good Grounds for so doing shall be stated on Oath before him."

In practical terms, there is little difference between the general and Dublin provisions; **1–99**
but it should be noted that the latter requires evidence of good grounds as to why an arrest warrant is necessary. In *Judge v District Judge Scally*,[187] the High Court found that the warrant had been issued *ultra vires* the powers of the District Judge in the absence of the requisite "good grounds" to justify the issue of a warrant under s 51.

Bench Warrants

Warrants, spontaneously issued for failure to appear, are commonly referred to as **1–100**
"bench warrants".

Order 22, Rule 1 of the District Court Rules provides for the issue of a bench warrant when a suspect has failed to appear in answer to a summons or is thought to be evading service. It provides:

"Where a summons is issued requiring the appearance before the Court of a person against whom a complaint has been made or an offence has been alleged and such person fails to appear at the required time and place or at any adjourned hearing of the matter, and it is proved to the Judge there present that such person has been served with the summons, or where at any time either before or after the date on which such person is required by the summons to appear an information, in the Form 22.1, Schedule B, is made that he or she is evading service or is about to abscond or has absconded, the Judge may issue a warrant, in the Form 22.2, Schedule B, for the arrest of such person."

Order 22 Rule 2 provides for the issue of a bench warrant where a suspect fails to **1–101**
appear after release or remand on bail:

"Where—

(a) a person who has been arrested and charged with an offence is released on bail by recognisance by a member of the Garda Síochána for his or her appearance before a sitting of the Court at a time on a date and at a place specified in the recognisance or

(b) an accused person is before the Court in connection with an offence and, on being remanded, is admitted to bail by recognisance for his or her appearance before a

[187] *Judge v District Judge Scally* [2006] 1 IR 491.

subsequent sitting of the Court (either in the same or another place), and that person, having entered into the recognisance, fails to appear at a time on a date and at a place at or on which he or she was bound by the recognisance to appear, the Judge then and there sitting may, on production of the recognisance to him or her, issue a warrant, in the Form 22.3, Schedule B, for the arrest of that person."

1–102 Failure to appear in court having been released on bail is in itself an offence, unless the individual has a reasonable excuse for non-attendance.[188]

As with arrest in anticipation of absconsion or potential bail condition breach, there is no requirement that gardaí must have in their possession the bench warrant issued for failure to appear, but the warrant must be furnished to the arrestee as soon as practicable afterwards.[189]

Arrest Warrant Contents

1–103 Gardaí arresting under warrant must inform the person of the reason for his arrest and that they are acting on the authority of a warrant.[190]

1–104 The person against whom the warrant is issued must be named in the body of the warrant by his surname and first name. In the very exceptional case where the name is unknown, that must be stated and the person sufficiently described as to leave no reasonable doubt as to his identity.[191] Warrants should state the substance of the offence in ordinary language, giving reasonable information as to the nature of the complaint and must be signed by the issuing judge.[192] Unless otherwise directed by the court, a warrant should be addressed to the Superintendent or Inspector of the Garda Síochána for the district within which the person named on the warrant lives, where that information is available when the warrant is being prepared. Otherwise it should be addressed to the Superintendent or an Inspector for the District in which the warrant is issued is situated.[193]

---

[188] s 13 of the Criminal Justice Act 1984 as amended by s 23 of the Criminal Justice Act 2007 provides "(1) If a person who has been released on bail in criminal proceedings fails to appear before a court in accordance with his recognisance, he shall be guilty of an offence and shall be liable on summary conviction to a fine not exceeding €5,000 or to imprisonment for a term not exceeding 12 months or to both. (2) It shall be a defence in any proceedings for an offence under sub-section (1) for the accused to show that he had a reasonable excuse for not so appearing."

[189] s 13 of the Bail Act 1997 provides at sub-sections (4) and (5) that: "Where a person has failed to appear before a court in answer to his bail and the court has directed that a warrant be issued for the arrest of that person by reason of his failure to answer his bail, a member of the Garda Síochána may arrest such a person, notwithstanding that he does not have the warrant in his possession at the time of the arrest.

(5) Where a person is arrested pursuant to sub-section (4), the member arresting him shall as soon as practicable produce and serve on the said person the said warrant."

[190] *Christy v Leachinsky* [1947] AC 573; *R v Kulynycz* [1971] 1 QB 367, [1970] 1 All ER 881

[191] *State (Rossi and Blythe) v Bell* [1957] IR 281.

[192] Ord 16 R 2 DCR 1997, SI No 93 of 1997.

[193] Ord 26 R 2 DCR 1997, SI No 93 of 1997, as substituted by SI No 203 of 2007, District Court (Criminal Justice Act 2006) Rules 2007. s 193 of the Criminal Justice Act 2006 amended s 25(1) of

Expiry, Execution and Re-Issue

A warrant for the arrest of a person or an order of committal of a person may be executed by a member of the Garda Síochána in any part of the State.[194] An arrest warrant retains its validity until its execution.[195] It may be issued or executed on any day and at any time,[196] whereas a warrant to commit a person to prison will expire six months after its issue. **1–105**

Once expired it cannot lawfully be executed, though it may be reissued. In *Healy v Governor of Cork Prison,* O'Flaherty J remarked: **1–106**

> "Now it is quite clear that if the person to whom the warrant is addressed is in a position to execute it straightaway, and knows where the accused is, he should execute it as promptly as possible. It is his duty under the general law to make sure that orders of courts are observed. However, if he is unable to find the person against whom the warrant is issued, or has an apprehension that he may have gone abroad (which is what happened in this case), the duty of the Gardaí in those circumstances is to go back within a reasonable time, and certainly not exceeding six months, and have it reissued with the hope that it can be executed. If nothing is done within the six months, then the status of the warrant is that it is spent."[197]

A re-issued warrant has the same function as a warrant issued *de novo*.[198]

No Requirement that Arresting Garda has Possession of Warrant at the Point of Arrest

The Criminal Law Act 1997[199] provides that an arrest warrant or order of committal may be executed whether it is in a garda's possession at the time of arrest or not, once it is shown to the arrested person as soon as practicable. **1–107**

The Bail Act 1997 makes further, more specific provision that, if a warrant is issued under s 6(5) of the Bail Act 1997 (potential breach of the conditions of bail recognisance), a member of the gardaí may arrest the specified person notwithstanding that the warrant is not in his or her possession at the time of the arrest, but in those circumstances the warrant must be produced and served on the arrested person as soon as practicable.[200] They will then be brought before the court[201] and either imprisoned or further remanded.[202] **1–108**

---

the Petty Sessions (Ireland) Act 1851 by substitution. s 25(1) now provides: "[A]ll warrants (except as otherwise provided by law) in proceedings in respect of offences punishable either on indictment or summarily issued by the District Court shall be addressed to the superintendent or an inspector of the Garda Síochána of the Garda Síochána district within which the place where the warrant is issued is situated or the person named in the warrant resides"

194 Criminal Justice Act 2006, s 194.
195 Petty Sessions (Ireland) Act 1851, s 11(1).
196 Ord 16 R 4 DCR 1997 (SI No 93 of1997).
197 *Healy v Governor of Cork Prison* [1998] 2 IR 93, [1997] 2 ILRM 357.
198 See Ord 26 R 11 DCR.
199 Criminal Law Act 1997, s 5.
200 Bail Act 1997, ss 6(6) and 6(7).
201 *ibid* s 6(8).
202 *ibid* s 6(9).

1–109 Failure to appear in court having been released on bail is in itself an offence, unless the individual has a reasonable excuse for non-attendance. As with arrest in anticipation of absconsion or potential bail condition breach, there is no requirement that gardaí have in their possession the bench warrant issued for failure to appear, but the warrant must be furnished to the arrestee as soon as practicable afterwards.

1–110 European Arrest Warrants may equally be executed according to the exigencies of the moment, without physical possession of the warrant at the time of the arrest, with the distinction that the subject of the warrant must be provided with it within 24 hours of the arrest.

Why Opt for Arrest Under Warrant Where a Statutory Power Exists?

1–111 As outlined above, arrest warrants are used in numerous circumstances, the most common being to charge persons suspected of committing an indictable offence[203] and to commence legal proceedings against them[204] and to secure the appearance of accused persons in court where they have failed to appear in answer to a summons or have been released on bail.[205] While gardaí may seek a warrant for preliminary arrest or for charge for both indictable and summary offences, where a statutory power to arrest exists, it is perhaps more straightforward to use that power rather than the warrant procedure.

1–112 However, there are a number of other instances in which gardaí have no choice and in which a warrant is the only mechanism for a lawful arrest. Such situations include the re-arrest for questioning of persons who have already been arrested and detained for questioning; to arrest prisoners and to arrest suspects who have been admitted to bail where it is thought that the persons are about to abscond or breach a condition of their recognisance. Arrest warrants are also used to initiate extradition proceedings.[206] Though not required to bring an accused person before the Special Criminal Court, the Offences against the State Act 1939 also provides for the issue of arrest warrants by the Special Criminal Court. Warrants for re-arrest for further investigation are considered in detail in *Chapter 2: Re-Arrest*. The other circumstances in which arrest warrants are required are examined below at paras 1–113 to 1–120.

Potential Abscsonsion or Breach of Bail Conditions

1–113 Arrest warrants may be sought for minor offences when gardaí or sureties are concerned that an accused person who has been released on bail will abscond or otherwise contravene any of the conditions of their recognisance.[207] The Bail Act 1997 provides at s 6(5) that:

> "Where a person charged with an offence is admitted to bail by a court on his or her entering into a recognisance with or without a surety or sureties, the court may, on the application to it in that behalf by a surety or sureties of the accused person or of a

---

[203] Such warrants are based on the sworn information of gardaí given on oath and in writing. See Order 16 Rule 1 District Court Rules, 1997, SI No 93 of 1997.

[204] Proceedings in minor offences usually be by way of summons

[205] Order 22 District Court Rules, 1997, SI No 93 of 1997. See also SI No 498 of 2008 District Court (Bench Warrants) Rules 2008.

[206] See generally M Forde, *Extradition Law in Ireland* (3rd ed, Thomson Round Hall, Dublin, 2005).

[207] See Ord 20 DCR 1997 (SI No 93 of 1997).

> member of the Garda Síochána and upon information being made in writing and on oath by or on behalf of such surety or member that the accused is about to contravene any of the conditions of the recognisance, issue a warrant for the arrest of the accused person."

Section 6 of the Bail Act 1997 replaced s 33 of the Criminal Procedure Act 1967, the **1–114**
original provision for this type of arrest warrant application. The Bail Act expanded it to include all potential bail recognisance breaches. Previously a warrant could only be sought in situations where there was concern about potential absconsion "for the purpose of evading justice."

To Commence Extradition Proceedings

Where the surrender of a suspect is sought from another country an arrest warrant **1–115**
is required to ground the extradition proceedings. Section 25 of the Extradition Act 1965[208] provides that requests for extradition must be supported by the warrant of arrest in respect of the person whose extradition is sought or, in the case of convicted persons, the original or an authenticated copy of the conviction and sentence or detention order. Requests must also be supported with a statement of each offence for which extradition is requested and the details of its alleged commission; as accurate a description as possible of the person claimed, together with any other information which will help to establish his identity and nationality; and any other document required under the relevant extradition provisions.[209]

In European Arrest Warrant proceedings, the domestic warrant need not be appended **1–116**
to or incorporated in the European Arrest Warrant: the European warrant must only specify that a domestic warrant has been issued.[210] This was clarified in the case of *Minister for Justice v Altaravicius,* in which Murray CJ stated:

> "So far as the form set out in the Framework Decision [the European Council Framework Decision of 13 June 2002 on the European Arrest Warrant and the surrender procedures between member states] is concerned, it is clear that all which it envisages is that certain information is given concerning an underlying domestic warrant or enforceable judgment, as the case may be. It does not in any sense suggest that a copy of the domestic warrant or judgment in question should be part of the European Arrest Warrant."[211]

The decision illustrates the simplification of extradition procedures which the European **1–117**
Arrest Warrant regime represents, and the practical application of the principles of mutual recognition. However, as will be seen below, the surrender process is not entirely straightforward, even in the European Union context.

---

208 Extradition Act 1965, s 25, as amended by s 17 of the Extradition (European Union Conventions) Act 2001.

209 Extradition Act 1965 s 25 as amended by s 17 of the Extradition (European Union Conventions) Act 2001. See also Extradition Act 1965 (Application of Part II) Order 2000, SI No 474 of 2000; Extradition Act 1965 (Application of Part II) (Amendment) Order 2002 (SI No 173 of 2002); Extradition Act 1965 (Application of Part II) (Amendment) Order 2003 (SI No 479 of 2003);); and Extradition Act 1965 (Application of Part II) (Amendment) (No.2) Order 2003 (SI No 649 of 2003).

210 *Minister for Justice v Altaravicius* [2006] 3 IR 148; [2006] 2 ILRM 241.

211 *ibid.*

To Bring a Suspect Before the Special Criminal Court

1–118 There is provision in s 47 of the Offences against the State Act 1939 to bring a person directly before the Special Criminal Court for charge and trial if the suspect is to be charged with a scheduled offence. It can also apply to non-scheduled offences if the Director of Public Prosecutions has certified that, in his or her opinion, the ordinary courts are inadequate to secure the effective administration of justice and the preservation of public peace and order in relation to the trial of the suspect. An arrest warrant is not required to bring an accused person before the Special Criminal Court. However, s 47(3) provides that the Special Criminal Court can issue a warrant for the arrest of the suspect.[212] There is no requirement that the Court must be satisfied on information provided to it that there are reasonable grounds to suspect that the person in question has committed the offence.[213]

Arresting Prisoners

1–119 Prisoners may be arrested in relation to offences other than those for which they are imprisoned, but only on the authority of a judge of the District Court.[214] The District Court must hear sworn information from a garda not below the rank of Superintendent, be satisfied that there are reasonable grounds for suspecting that the prisoner has committed an offence or offences other than those for which he or she is imprisoned and also be satisfied that the arrest is necessary for the proper investigation of the offence or offences. The same section permits prisoners to be re-arrested for offences for which they had previously been arrested in the event of further information coming to light concerning the prisoner's suspected involvement in the alleged offence for which their re-arrest is sought.[215]

1–120 Arrested prisoners must be brought to a Garda station and detained there in accordance with s 4 of the Criminal Justice Act 1984.[216] If at any stage during the detention there are no longer reasonable grounds for suspecting the person of having committed the offence for which he or she has been arrested, or for believing that the detention is necessary, the detention in Garda custody will be terminated,[217] and the prisoner

---

[212] Offences against the State Act 1939, s 47(3). See SI 234 of 1975, Offences against the State Acts, 1939 to 1972 Special Criminal Court Rules 1975, r 17(4). As amended by SI No 536 of 2001 Offences against the State Acts, 1939 -1998 (Special Criminal Court Rules), 2001.

[213] See *McMahon v Special Criminal Court*, unreported, High Court, 30 August 1998.

[214] s 42 of the Criminal Justice Act 1999 introduced a statutory basis for the arrest of prisoners, a practice previously prohibited under s 8 of the Habeas Corpus Act 1782. s 42 has been amended by the substitution of s 42(2) by s 11 of the Criminal Justice Act 2006, and the amendment of s 42(5) to extend the remit of the arrest power to allow for the investigation of multiple offences. The form that the warrant should take is set out in SI No 448 of 2001 District Court (Criminal Justice)(No 2) Rules, 2001. It should be noted that there is a distinct power to arrest persons who are unlawfully at large, set out in s 7 of the Criminal Justice Act 1960 as follows: "A member of the Garda Síochána may arrest without warrant a person whom he suspects to be unlawfully at large and may take such person to the place in which he is required in accordance with law to be detained."

[215] Criminal Justice Act 1999, s 42(2)(c), as inserted by s 11 of the Criminal Justice Act 2006.

[216] *ibid*, s 42(3). s 42(4) provides that s 4(4), (5A) and s 10 of the Act of 1984 shall not apply to persons arrested and detained under s 42.

[217] Criminal Justice Act 1999, s 42(5).

transferred back into the custody of the governor of the prison in which he or she was imprisoned at the time of arrest.

Minor Offences Should Proceed by Summons

A warrant should not be used in circumstances when a summons is as likely to secure the appearance of the accused person. Save in circumstances where a suspect evades service of a summons or fails to appear, offences which are triable summarily should proceed only by summons. **1–121**

The District Court (Order 16) Rules 2006[218] deleted Order 16 Rule 5 of the District Court Rules, 1997 (SI No 93 of 1997) which had provided that "[w]here at common law or under any statute there is power to arrest a person without a warrant, a warrant for his or her arrest may be issued in accordance with the provisions of rule 1 of this Order." The deletion gives effect to the High Court decision in *Judge v District Judge James Scally,*[219] where the judge found that "a practice of convenience" had developed whereby warrants were applied for in the District Court to enable cases that had been struck out "to be reinstated expeditiously on a mutual, even if unexpressed, understanding that the arrest would be effected at such a time and place as to cause a minimum of inconvenience and embarrassment to the party charged so that the arrest when effected bore only the merest semblance to the execution of a warrant". Herbert J found that the practice, however expeditious and discreet it may have been, flew in the face of Article 40.4.1° of the Constitution. The case of *O'Brien v Brabner* was cited to support the proposition that there is no justification for using the warrant procedure when a summons is as likely to secure the appearance of the accused person. The relevant passage quoted is as follows: **1–122**

> "The whole of the mischief arose from the improper issue of the warrant. No doubt the information laid before the magistrate induced him to believe that the assault complained of was more serious than it turned out to be. But for all that there does not seem to have been any reason to believe that a summons would not have been equally effectual in securing the appearance of the accused person and if that really was the case the issuing of a warrant instead of a summons cannot be justified. It ought to be borne in mind that a warrant ought never to be issued when a summons will be equally effectual in procuring the appearance of the person charged, except perhaps when the charge is of a very serious nature."[220]

Holding that drink driving is a minor offence, and in the absence of any suggestion that the accused would abscond, in *Judge v District Judge James Scally*[221] the High Court concluded that there were no good grounds to justify the issue of a warrant where a summons would suffice. This accords with the view endorsed by Carroll J in *Cleary v Commissioner of the Garda Síochána*[222] that an arrest where it was intended to proceed by summons amounted to a serious neglect of the garda's duty to vindicate the right to liberty.[223] **1–123**

---

218 SI No 238 of 2006 The District Court (Order 16) Rules 2006.

219 *Judge v District Judge James Scally* [2005] IEHC 366.

220 *O'Brien v Brabner* 1885, 49 JP 227, at 228.

221 *Judge v District Judge James Scally* [2005] IEHC 366.

222 *Cleary v Commissioner of the Garda Síochána, Irish Times,* 4 March 1994.

223 The offence in question was speeding and, notwithstanding his intention to obtain a summons in respect of the offence, the probationer garda had arrested the suspect. The suspect was conveyed to

European Arrest Warrants

1–124 In the European Union,[224] the European Arrest Warrant (EAW) has replaced extradition with a surrender process in respect of suspects or convicted persons sought in one Member State for prosecution or punishment in another Member State. Under the European Arrest Warrant procedure warrants for arrest may originate from the judicial authorities of other Member States of the European Union, or third countries which have agreements with the European Union, for execution by the police forces of participating countries. In essence, the EAW system extends the European principle of free movement into the realm of criminal law, to allow for the return and transfer of persons sought by the authorities of Member States and third countries. Gardaí are frequently required to arrest persons who are wanted in other Member States,[225] and ask their European counterparts to reciprocate by arresting and surrendering persons wanted in Ireland. Implemented in Irish law by the European Arrest Warrant Act 2003,[226] the principles of mutual assistance and mutual recognition underpin the operation of the EAW procedure, whereby decisions taken in Member States and relevant third countries are accepted as valid in another on the basis of reciprocal trust and confidence in the legal systems of other European countries. The EAW is the first concrete criminal law measure implementing the principle of mutual recognition, which has been described by the European Council as the cornerstone of judicial cooperation.[227] The Act defines a European Arrest Warrant as follows:

> "a warrant, order or decision of a judicial authority of a Member State, issued under such laws as give effect to the Framework Decision[228] in that Member State, for the

---

a Garda station and given into the custody of other gardaí. The suspect subsequently alleged assault and was found not guilty of the speeding offence. An internal investigation was conducted which resulted in the dismissal of the probationer garda. He brought unfair dismissal proceedings against the Garda Commissioner, but his claim was dismissed in the High Court.

[224] The European Arrest Warrant (Application to Third Countries and Amendment) and Extradition (Amendment) Act 2012 provides in Irish law for an extension of the European Arrest Warrant regime to third countries by order of the Minister for Foreign Affairs, in consultation with the Minister for Justice and Equality, s 2. There is an agreement between the European Union and Norway and Iceland to extend the EAW surrender process to those countries. At the time of writing an order extending the Irish EAW scheme to Iceland and Norway had not been made.

[225] By March 2013, 750 orders for surrender had been executed by the Irish authorities since the European Arrest Warrant Act 2003 was enacted, with 313 requests received in 2012 (annual report for 2012 on the operation of the European Arrest Warrant Act 2003, Department of Justice and Equality, 28 March 2013).

[226] The Act implements Council Framework Decision on the European Arrest Warrant and Surrender Procedures between Member States (2002/584/JHA Official Journal L 190, 18/07/2002 P 1-20). The Framework Decision has been amended by 2009/299/JHA of 26 February 2009 amending Framework Decisions 2002/584/JHA, 2005/214/JHA, 2006/783/JHA, 2008/909/JHA and 2008/947/JHA.

[227] Council Framework Decision 2002/584/JHA of 13 June 2002 on the European Arrest Warrant and The Surrender Procedures between Member States, recital (6) of the Preamble.

[228] The Framework Decision referred to is Council Framework Decision 2002/584 on the European Arrest Warrant and Surrender Procedures between Member States. The European Arrest Warrant (Application to Third Countries and Amendment) and Extradition (Amendment) Act 2012 clarifies

> arrest and surrender by the State to that Member State of a person in respect of an offence committed or alleged to have been committed by him or her under the law of that Member State."[229]

Whereas previously extradition operated as "an exercise in political cooperation between friendly states", there now exists a "process of direct engagement between judicial authorities"[230]—a judicial authority in this context being a judge, a magistrate or other person who is authorised under the law of the Member State to issue a warrant for the arrest of a person.[231] **1–125**

The Framework Decision on which the European Arrest Warrant Act 2003 is based expressly abolishes the concept of extradition between Member States, as is outlined at recital (5) of the Preamble: **1–126**

> "The objective set for the Union to become an area of freedom, security and justice leads to abolishing extradition between Member States and replacing it by a system of surrender between judicial authorities. Further, the introduction of a new simplified system of surrender of sentenced or suspected persons for the purposes of execution or prosecution of criminal sentences makes it possible to remove the complexity and potential for delay inherent in the present extradition procedures. Traditional cooperation relations which have prevailed up till now between Member States should be replaced by a system of free movement of judicial decisions in criminal matters, covering both pre-sentence and final decisions, within an area of freedom, security and justice."[232]

As Walsh put it:

> "... it reflects a very definite and substantial movement towards the creation of a single European criminal space superimposed on distinct jurisdictional territories. Within this space, the police and judicial authorities of each territories are obliged to assist in the enforcement of each other's criminal law and procedure, even where those laws differ materially from our own."[233]

---

at s 4 that the definition of the Framework Decision has been amended by inserting: "'Council Framework Decision 2009/299/JHA' means Council Framework Decision 2009/299/JHA of 26 February 2009 amending Framework Decisions 2002/584/JHA, 2005/214/JHA, 2006/783/JHA, 2008/909/JHA and 2008/947/JHA, thereby enhancing the procedural rights of persons and fostering the application of the principle of mutual recognition to decisions rendered in the absence of the person concerned at the trial."

229 European Arrest Warrant Act 2003, s 2.

230 D Walsh: "The European Arrest Warrant", paper delivered at TCD Developments in Criminal Law and Procedure Conference, 6 December 2008. For a good overview on the law relating to European Arrest Warrants generally, see R Farrell and A Hanrahan, *The European Arrest Warrant in Ireland* (Clarus Press, 2011).

231 European Arrest Warrant Act 2003, s 2(1). The Irish High Court is the judicial authority in this jurisdiction.

232 Council Framework Decision 2002/584/JHA of 13 June 2002 on the European Arrest Warrant and the surrender procedures between Member States, which is set out in full in the schedule to the European Arrest Warrant Act 2003, at Part B.

233 D Walsh: "European Arrest Warrant", paper delivered at Criminal Law Update 2010, School of Law, Trinity College Dublin, 26 June 2010.

1–127 Indeed, the streamlining of laws concerning the surrender of citizens between Member States has not been entirely straightforward, in particular as many Member States had prohibitions in their domestic legislation on the surrender of their own nationals.[234] However, the European Court of Justice upheld the Framework Decision establishing the EAW procedure in the case of *Advocaten voor de Wererd VZW v Leden Van de Ministerraad*.[235] The Opinion of the Advocate General in the case plainly described the concept of the surrender procedure as "assistance", rather than extradition when he said:

> "No one would accord the status of extradition to legal assistance for the surrender of an accused between a court in the Land of Bavaria and a court in the Land of Lower Saxony, or between a court in the autonomous community of Catalonia and a court in the autonomous community of Andalusia, from which it follows that assistance should not be regarded as extradition where it takes place in the context of the European Union."[236]

1–128 The European Court of Justice subsequently rejected arguments about the propriety of the legal instrument used to establish the EAW procedure, and further rejected arguments that the manner in which the verification of double criminality had been dispensed with in Article 2(2) of the Framework Decision was contrary to the principle of equality and non-discrimination and the principle of legality in criminal law. It was held that the harmonisation of the laws of Member States was not the objective of the Framework Decision[237] and therefore, insofar as it dispenses with verification of double criminality in respect of the specified offences, it does not breach the principle of legality of criminal offences.[238] The Court found no factor capable of affecting the validity of the Framework Decision.[239]

---

[234] The Polish Constitutional Court held the national law transposing the Framework Decision to be unconstitutional in the *Case P 1/05 Wyrok z dnia 27 kwietnia 2005 r. Sygn. akt. P 1/05,* OTK ZU 2005, seria A, nr 4, poz. 42. No 4/A/2005 poz 42. A summary of the Polish Constitutional Tribunal judgment of 27 April 2005 is available here: http://www.trybunal.gov.pl/eng/summaries/summaries_assets/documents/P_1_05_GB.pdf <accessed 10 October 2013>. National courts in other Member States including Belgium, Germany, the Czech Republic and Cyprus also grappled with the replacement of traditional extradition measures and the Framework Decision – *Arrêt* No 124/2005, *Numéro du rôle* 3027, Cour d'Arbitrage, 13 July 2005; *Europäischer Haftbefehl*, 113 BVerfGE 273 (2005), available in English at http://www.bverfg.de/en/decisions/rs20050718_2bvr223604en.html <accessed 10 October 2013>; Decision of the Czech Constitutional Court No. Pl. ÚS 66/04, of May 3 2006; A No 294/2005 Supreme Court of Cyprus, 7 November 2005. See further: O Pollicino: "European Arrest Warrant and Constitutional Principles of the Member States: A Case Law-Based Outline in the Attempt to Strike the Right Balance between Interacting Legal Systems" 2008 German Law Journal Vol 9, No 10, 1313-1355, and D Sarmiento "European Union: The European Arrest Warrant and the Quest for Constitutional Coherence", *Int J Constitutional Law* (2008) 6(1):171-183, at p 171.

[235] Case C-303/05 *Advocaten voor de Wererd VZW v Leden Van de Ministerraad* (ECJ 3 May 2007).

[236] *ibid*, para 45, fn 40.

[237] *ibid*, para 59 (ECJ, 3 May 2007).

[238] *ibid*, para 60.

[239] *ibid*, para 61.

Though what was envisaged was a streamlined surrender process of mutual assistance, dispensing even with the need to prove double criminality for a significant array of offences, in reality the operation of the European Arrest Warrant is cumbersome. In Ireland, the EAW involves an array of agencies: the gardaí of the extradition unit which is part of the broader mutual legal assistance unit of An Garda Síochána; the Minister for Justice and Equality who acts as the Central Authority, the minister's functions in this regard being carried out by the mutual assistance and extradition division of the Department of Justice and Equality; the Attorney General, who provides legal advice to the Central Authority; the Office of the Chief State Solicitor, which provides legal services to the government; the Office of the Director of Public Prosecutions as the independent prosecution service of Ireland; the High Court which is the judicial authority that adjudicates on all endorsements and surrenders under the EAW regime; and the Supreme Court, which hears appeals on EAW matters.[240] The Act has been substantially amended by the Criminal Justice (Terrorist Offences) Act 2005, the Criminal Justice (Miscellaneous Provisions) Act 2009 and the European Arrest Warrant (Application to Third Countries and Amendment) and Extradition (Amendment) Act 2012. The foundation Framework Decision has also been amended.[241] It has been remarked that **1–129**

> "[I]n practice, the law in Ireland relating to extradition is a hybrid of criminal and civil law… it has been stated that the European Arrest Warrant Act 2003, as originally passed was unworkable, due to the complexity of the system and the lack of engagement in the legislative process by the Oireachtas at the time the Act was passed. This position has been remedied to a large extent… however there remain significant problems with the processes."[242]

The addition of third countries serves further to complicate the system, and raises questions on the status of bilateral extradition agreements with non-European third countries where agreements are in place with those third countries at a European level, for instance between the European Union and the USA[243] and between the European Union and Japan.[244] **1–130**

Countries in which the EAW is Operative

With the exception of Croatia, all countries in the European Union have now given effect to the Framework Decision[245] and, as was outlined in the preceding paragraph, **1–131**

240 See Council Document 11843/06 REV 1.

241 The Framework Decision has been amended by 2009/299/JHA of 26 February 2009 amending Framework Decisions 2002/584/JHA, 2005/214/JHA, 2006/783/JHA, 2008/909/JHA and 2008/947/JHA.

242 Law Society of Ireland (M Butler (ed)), *Criminal Litigation* (3rd ed, Oxford University Press, Oxford, 2011) p 61.

243 See Council Decision 2009/820/CFSP of 23 October 2009 on the conclusion on behalf of the European Union of the Agreement on extradition between the European Union and the United States of America and the Agreement on mutual legal assistance between the European Union and the United States of America OJ L 291, 07.11.2009 p 40 – 41.

244 See 2010/616/EU: Council Decision of 7 October 2010 on the conclusion of the Agreement between the European Union and Japan on mutual legal assistance in criminal matters (OJ L 271, 15.10.2010, p 3–3)

245 Croatia joined the European Union on 1 July 2013 and quickly became embroiled in controversy for amending domestic legislation giving effect to the European Arrest Warrant days before accession, so

there have been moves towards expansion of the surrender process to non-EU countries. Under Irish law, the European Arrest Warrant (Application to Third Countries and Amendment) and Extradition (Amendment) Act 2012 extends the application of the EAW to third countries by order of the Minister for Foreign Affairs in consultation with the Minister for Justice and Equality.[246] A "third country" is a country other than Ireland or a Member State of the European Union[247] and an order may only be made to extend the European Arrest Warrant process to non-Member States countries where an extradition agreement is in force between the third country concerned and the European Union for the surrender of persons wanted for prosecution or punishment.[248] There is currently only one such agreement in place, between the European Union and the Republic of Iceland and the Kingdom of Norway.[249] However, as the 2012 Act was progressing through the Dáil, the Minister for Justice and Equality stated that he understood that "agreements similar to the Norway and Iceland agreement are likely to be concluded by the European Union with other countries in the future."[250] It remains to be seen how this will operate in practice.

Surrender and Arrest Procedure

1–132 There is an obligation to surrender persons sought under an EAW. The European Arrest Warrant Act 2003 provides at s 10:

> "Where a judicial authority in an issuing state issues a European Arrest Warrant in respect of a person—
>
> (a) against whom that state intends to bring proceedings for an offence to which the European Arrest Warrant relates,
> (b) who is the subject of proceedings in that state for an offence to which the European Arrest Warrant relates,

---

as to preclude the application of the EAW to crimes committed before 2002. On 25 September 2013 the Croatian Minister of Justice gave an assurance that the law would be amended by 1 January 2014 at the latest. See http://euobserver.com/justice/121561 <accessed 10 October 2013>. The European Arrest Warrant Act 2003 (Designated Member States) Orders designate participant countries for the purpose of s 3 of the Act. The designated countries are Belgium, Denmark, Finland, Portugal, Spain, Sweden, UK (SI No 4 of 2004); France, Luxembourg (SI No 130 of 2004), Austria, Cyprus, Hungary, Lithuania, Poland, Slovenia (SI No 206 of 2004); Malta, the Netherlands (SI No 400 of 2004); Estonia, Greece, Latvia (SI No 449 of 2004); Germany, Slovakia (SI No 532 of 2004); Czech Republic (SI No 27 of 2005); Italy (SI No 240 of 2005); Bulgaria, Romania (SI No 59 of 2007). An order has not yet been made in respect of Croatia.

[246] European Arrest Warrant (Application to Third Countries and Amendment) and Extradition (Amendment) Act 2012, s 2.

[247] European Arrest Warrant Act 2003, s 2.

[248] European Arrest Warrant (Application To Third Countries And Amendment) And Extradition (Amendment) Act 2012, s 2(3).

[249] Council Decision of 27 June 2006 on the signing of the agreement between the European Union, the Republic of Iceland and the Kingdom of Norway on the surrender procedure between the Member States of the European Union and Iceland and Norway; OJ L292 of 21/10/2006, p 1.

[250] Minister for Justice and Equality (Deputy Shatter) 765 Dáil Debates (no. 3) col. 282 (15 May 2012).

(c) who has been convicted of, but not yet sentenced in respect of, an offence in that state to which the European Arrest Warrant relates, or
(d) on whom a sentence of imprisonment or detention has been imposed in that state in respect of an offence to which the European Arrest Warrant relates, that person shall, subject to and in accordance with the provisions of this Act be arrested and surrendered to the issuing state."[251]

The terms are non-discretionary and, like an Irish warrant, it should be considered a non-negotiable command to arrest the specified person, once the statutory procedures set out in the Act have been followed and the warrant has been endorsed by the Irish High Court.

The Central Authority[252] is the administrative contact point for transmission and receipt of mutual assistance requests, while the High Court is the executing judicial authority.[253] On receipt of a European Arrest Warrant request from a participating State, the warrant is sent to the Office of the Chief State Solicitor who will then apply to the High Court to have the warrant endorsed for execution. If the High Court is satisfied that the provisions of the Act have been complied with, it may endorse the European Arrest Warrant for execution,[254] so there is discretion in respect of endorsement where there is none in respect of execution. **1–133**

While An Garda Síochána has a dedicated extradition unit, a European Arrest Warrant can be executed by any member of the Garda Síochána in any part of the State.[255] There is no time limit within which a European Arrest Warrant must be executed.

The arrested person must be shown a copy of the European Arrest Warrant within 24 hours if it is not immediately available on his arrest,[256] and once arrested must be made **1–134**

251 European Arrest Warrant Act, s 10, as substituted by s 71 of the Criminal Justice (Terrorist Offences) Act 2005 and as amended by s 6 of the Criminal Justice (Miscellaneous Provisions) Act 2009 and s 5 of the European Arrest Warrant (Application to Third Countries and Amendment) and Extradition (Amendment) Act 2012. The most notable difference in the 2009 amendment is the deletion of a previously included reference to the person having fled from the issuing State before commencement or completion of the sentence. The 2012 amendment clarifies that the surrender process is governed by the Act, deleting the previous reference to surrender taking place "in accordance with the provisions of this Act *and the Framework decision*". Farrell states that the 2012 Act clarifies "that the framework decision as amended is not intended to be directly effective. The various references to the framework decision throughout the Act are amended. Most significantly, the reference to the obligation that surrender be effected in accordance with the Framework Decision has been excised…" Remy Farrell: "European Arrest Warrants – Recent Developments, Bar Council CPD, 25 January 2012.

252 The Irish Central Authority for the European Arrest Warrant is the Minister for Justice, Equality and Law Reform at the Department of Justice, Equality and Law Reform, 94 St Stephen's Green, Dublin 2 (s 6, European Arrest Warrant Act 2003). A European Arrest Warrant may only be transmitted to the Central Authority (s 12(1)) or issued via the Central Authority in Ireland (s 33).

253 European Arrest Warrant Act 2003, s 9.

254 *ibid*, s 13(2), as substituted by s 8(1) of the European Arrest Warrant (Application to Third Countries and Amendment) and Extradition (Amendment) Act 2012.

255 European Arrest Warrant Act 2003, s 13.

256 *ibid.*

aware of his or her rights to legal and linguistic assistance, and of the right to consent to surrender to the requesting State.[257] If the High Court is satisfied that the person arrested and brought before the court is the person to whom the warrant relates[258] the person may be remanded in custody or on bail and a date must be set for the surrender proceedings.[259]

Offences to which the European Arrest Warrant Applies

1–135 European Arrest Warrants may be issued for acts punishable by the law of the issuing member state by a custodial sentence for a maximum period of at least 12 months, or where a sentence of four months or more has been imposed.[260]

1–136 Certain core offences give rise to surrender without verification of the double criminality of the act if they are defined by the law of the issuing Member State and punishable in the issuing Member State by a custodial sentence for a maximum period of at least three years. Those offences are set out in the Framework Decision on the European Arrest Warrant which established it as follows: participation in a criminal organisation; terrorism; trafficking in human beings; sexual exploitation of children and child pornography; illicit trafficking in narcotic drugs and psychotropic substances; illicit trafficking in weapons, munitions and explosives; corruption; fraud, including that affecting the financial interests of the European Communities within the meaning of the Convention of 26 July 1995 on the protection of the European Communities' financial interests; laundering of the proceeds of crime; counterfeiting currency, including of the euro; computer-related crime; environmental crime, including illicit trafficking in endangered animal species and in endangered plant species and varieties; facilitation of unauthorised entry and residence; murder, grievous bodily injury; illicit trade in human organs and tissue; kidnapping, illegal restraint and hostage-taking; racism and xenophobia; organised or armed robbery; illicit trafficking in cultural goods, including antiques and works of art; swindling, racketeering and extortion; counterfeiting and piracy of products; forgery of administrative documents and trafficking therein; forgery of means of payment; illicit trafficking in hormonal substances and other growth promoters; illicit trafficking in nuclear or radioactive materials; trafficking in stolen vehicles; rape; arson; crimes within the jurisdiction of the International Criminal Court; unlawful seizure of aircraft/ships; sabotage.[261]

---

[257] *ibid*, s 13(5).

[258] In *Minister for Justice, Equality and Law Reform v McGrath* [2006] 1 IR 321, Macken J refused surrender on the basis that she was not satisfied that the respondent was the person in respect of whom the European Arrest Warrant was issued.

[259] *ibid.*

[260] The Council Framework Decision on the European Arrest Warrant and the Surrender Procedures between Member States (2002/584/JHA), Art 2(1). The text of the Framework Decision is set out at Part B of the Schedule to the European Arrest Warrant Act 2003.

[261] Council Framework Decision on the European Arrest Warrant and the Surrender Procedures between Member States (2002/584/JHA), Art 2(2).

The European Arrest Warrant procedure is retrospective in that it applies equally to offences which were committed before and after its coming into force.[262]

It is stipulated that a person shall not be surrendered under the European Arrest Warrant Act if the Director of Public Prosecutions or Attorney General is contemplating a prosecution but has not yet reached a decision, or if a prosecution is pending in Ireland in respect of the offence for which surrender is sought.[263] **1–137**

Where offences are not included in the provision in Art 2(2) which dispenses with the need for verification of dual criminality, Art 2(4) provides that surrender may be subject to the condition that the acts to which the European Arrest Warrant relates constitute an offence under the law of the executing State, whatever the constituent elements or however it is described. **1–138**

Form of European Arrest Warrants

The European Arrest Warrant should be set out in the form contained in the annex to the Framework Decision 2002/584/JHA as amended by Framework Decision 2009/299/JHA.[264] It must specify: **1–139**

(a) the name and nationality of the person in respect of whom it is issued,
(b) the name of the judicial authority that issued the European Arrest Warrant and the address of its principal office,
(c) the telephone number, fax number and email address (if any) of that judicial authority,
(d) the offence to which the European Arrest Warrant relates, including the nature and classification of the law of the issuing state of the offence concerned,
(e) that a conviction, sentence or detention order is immediately enforceable against the person, or that a warrant for his or her arrest, or other order of a judicial authority in the issuing State having the same effect, has been issued in respect of one of the offences to which the European Arrest Warrant relates,
(f) the circumstances in which the offence was committed or is alleged to have been committed, including the time and place of its commission or alleged commission, and the degree of involvement or alleged involvement of the person in the alleged commission of the offence and

---

262 European Arrest Warrant Act 2003, s 4(1) as amended by s 5 of the Criminal Justice (Miscellaneous Provisions) Act 2009. It should be noted that s 4(2) and 4(3) were deleted by s 5(b) of the 2009 Act

263 European Arrest Warrant Act 2003, s 42 as amended by s 82 of the Criminal Justice (Terrorist Offences) Act 2005 as amended by s 22 of the European Arrest Warrant (Application to Third Countries and Amendment) and Extradition (Amendment) Act 2012.

264 Council Framework Decision 2009/299/JHA of 26 February 2009 amending Framework Decisions 2002/584/JHA, 2005/214/JHA, 2006/783/JHA, 2008/909/JHA and 2008/947/JHA, thereby enhancing the procedural rights of persons and fostering the application of the principle of mutual recognition to decisions rendered in the absence of the person concerned at the trial, available online at http://eur-lex.europa.eu/LexUriServ/LexUriServ.do?uri=OJ:L:2009:081:0024:0036:EN:PDF <accessed 10 October 2013>.

(g) the penalties to which the person would be subject if convicted; or, where the person has been convicted but not sentenced, the penalties to which he or she is liable; or, where sentence has been imposed, the penalties of which the sentence consists.[265]

A European Arrest Warrant may be issued in respect of one or more than one offence.[266]

Arrest Under a Schengen Alert

1–140 The Schengen Information System (SIS) is an extensive database on persons and property, one of the largest of its kind worldwide, which facilitates the exchange of information as part of the Schengen *acquis* system of free movement of persons in the European Union.[267] The information sharing is designed to compensate for the removal of border controls within the European Union, and the database is accessible by police, border control, visa, customs and vehicle registration authorities. The information shared includes:

- individuals wanted for extradition;
- persons against whom a European Arrest Warrant has been issued;
- third country nationals declared ineligible to enter national territory;
- individuals who have disappeared, for example minors who have either run away or have been abducted.[268]

1–141 On 9 April 2013, Schengen II (SIS II) was launched, increasing the capabilities of the system. The second generation of the Schengen Information System allows for the entry of biometrics (fingerprints and photographs), new types of alerts (stolen aircrafts, boats, containers, means of payment), and the possibility to link different alerts (such as an alert on a person and a vehicle). SIS II will also contain copies of European Arrest Warrants (EAW) attached directly to alerts for persons wanted for arrest,

[265] European Arrest Warrant Act 2003, s 11(1A) as inserted by s 72(a) of the Criminal Justice (Terrorist Offences) Act 2005 and as amended by s 7 of the Criminal Justice (Miscellaneous Provisions) Act 2009.

[266] European Arrest Warrant Act 2003, s 11(4).

[267] By the Schengen Agreement signed on 14 June 1985, Belgium, France, Germany, Luxembourg and the Netherlands agreed gradually to remove controls at their common borders and to introduce freedom of movement for all nationals of the signatory Member States, other member states or third countries. The Schengen Convention supplements the Agreement and lays down the arrangements and safeguards for implementing freedom of movement. It was signed by the same five Member States on 19 June 1990, but did not enter into force until 1995. The Schengen Agreements have been extended over time: Italy signed them in 1990, Spain and Portugal in 1991, Greece in 1992, Austria in 1995, Finland and Sweden in 1996, Denmark also in 1996, but under a special arrangement, and the Czech Republic, Estonia, Latvia, Lithuania, Hungary, Malta, Poland, Slovenia and Slovakia in 2007. Ireland and the United Kingdom are only partial participants in the Schengen *acquis*, since their border controls have been maintained. Bulgaria, Cyprus and Romania also apply only parts of the Schengen *acquis*, as a decision of the Council of the European Union is still required before controls at their borders can be lifted. Four non-Community countries also belong to the Schengen area: Iceland and Norway since 1996 and Switzerland and Liechtenstein since 2008. Countries that are candidates for European Union membership must have accepted the whole of the Schengen *acquis* at the time of accession.

[268] See http://www.europarl.europa.eu/comparl/libe/elsj/zoom_in/25_en.htm <accessed 10 October 2013>.

surrender or extradition, making it easier and quicker for the competent authorities to ensure the necessary follow-up.[269]

Gardaí may summarily arrest a person who is the subject of a Schengen alert.[270] **1–142**
Section 27(3A) of the Extradition (European Union Conventions) Act 2001[271] provides that an alert is deemed to constitute a request for the provisional arrest of the person named. The required suspicion to ground the arrest is that the garda believes, on reasonable grounds, that person to be a person named in an alert. A number of rights are outlined in s 14 of the European Arrest Warrant Act 2003[272]: the person must be informed, in ordinary language, of the reason for his arrest and of his or her right to access legal representation and the services of an interpreter. "As soon as may be" after arrest, the person must be provided with a copy of the alert, and brought before the High Court.[273] If the High Court is satisfied of the person's identity the court must inform the person of the entitlement to legal representation, advice and interpretation and remand the person in custody or, at its discretion, on bail for up to 14 days (and for that purpose, the High Court shall have the same powers in relation to remand as it would have if the person were brought before it charged with an indictable offence) for production to the High Court of the European Arrest Warrant, on foot of which the alert was entered.[274]

---

269 See http://europa.eu/rapid/press-release_IP-13-309_en.htm?locale=en <accessed 10 October 2013>.

270 s 14 of the European Arrest Warrant Act 2003 has been substituted by s 10 of the Criminal Justice (Miscellaneous Provisions) Act 2009. s 10 of the 2009 Act was commenced on 25 August 2009 by the Criminal Justice (Miscellaneous Provisions) Act 2009 (Commencement) (No 3) Order 2009 (SI No 330 of 2009), Art 2.

271 As inserted by s 24 of the Criminal Justice (Miscellaneous Provisions) Act 2009. Note that, at the time of writing, s 24 of the 2009 Act had not been commenced.

272 European Arrest Warrant Act 2003, s 14, as substituted by s 10 of the Criminal Justice (Miscellaneous Provisions) Act 2009.

273 *ibid*, s 14(3).

274 *ibid*, s 14(3).

CHAPTER 2

Arrest and Detention in Other Contexts

INTRODUCTION

Arrest is not confined to the gardaí, nor to the criminal process. It is a mechanism employed in a number of other ways where the law provides for temporary deprivation of liberty, for example to facilitate deportation, to allow gardaí to deal with mentally ill persons, to permit intervention in suspected child abduction, to allow members of the Garda Síochána Ombudsman Commission to arrest gardaí and so on. Some of the key provisions permitting arrest outside and in the margins of the criminal context, both by gardaí and other agencies, are considered below. **2–01**

TAKING MENTALLY ILL PERSONS INTO CUSTODY

There is an alarming rate of mental illness among the Irish prison population, both among remand and sentenced prisoners.[1] The spectrum of mental illnesses involved **2–02**

[1] Linehan Duffy, Wright, Curtin, Monks, Kennedy, Psychiatric Morbidity in a Cross Sectional Sample of Male Remanded Prisoners. *Irish Journal of Psychological Medicine 2005;* 22 (4): pp 128-132, quoted by C O'Neill in "Liaison Between Criminal Justice and Psychiatric Systems: Diversion Services" *Ir J Psych Med 2006;* 23(3): pp 87-88. Dr Conor O'Neill, a forensic psychiatrist at the Central Mental Hospital, has written that "a meta-analysis of 62 international surveys found mean prevalence rates for psychosis in prisons of 3.7%. In Ireland, the six-month prevalence rate for psychosis among male remand populations is over double this, at 7.6% with 4.5% actively psychotic." O'Neill, "Liaison Between Criminal Justice and Psychiatric Systems: Diversion Services" *Ir J Psych Med 2006;* 23(3): 87-88. Dr O'Neill asserts: "Prisons are toxic and inappropriate environments in which to manage people with major mental illnesses. The mentally ill are vulnerable in such settings. Where involuntary treatment is required, this is not permissible in a prison setting… the right of the mentally ill to the best available healthcare in the least restrictive appropriate environment has been made clear by the United Nations and should apply to mentally disordered offenders 'to the fullest extent possible'."

ranges from mild to severe, from anxiety to active psychosis. It follows that gardaí frequently encounter and arrest people who are suffering from mental illness and are asked to evaluate and respond to the complex psychiatric needs of individuals in distress in the context of an under-resourced mental health system. The challenge for gardaí is multi-faceted: balancing the rights and needs of the mentally-ill suspect with the requirement that the public is protected; attempting to support families struggling with a mentally-ill family member without contributing to the stigma associated with mental illness; and dealing with people who may not have committed an offence but who must be assumed to pose a considerable threat.[2]

Lamb *et al* have noted:

> "The police are typically the first and often the sole community resource called on to respond to urgent situations involving persons with mental illness. They are responsible for either recognizing the need for treatment for an individual with mental illness and connecting the person with the proper treatment resources or making the determination that the individual's illegal activity is the primary concern and that the person should be arrested. This responsibility thrusts them into the role of primary gatekeepers who determine whether the mental health or the criminal justice system can best meet the needs of the individual with acute psychiatric problems… A major problem with having to fulfil this role is that the police have little training in performing this kind of triage… this lack of training is one of the factors that has played an important part in the criminalization of persons with mental illness."[3]

2–03 Ideally a diversion scheme would direct the mentally ill who transgress the criminal law away from the criminal justice system and into treatment, as in other jurisdictions.[4] The practical advances for the chronically mentally-ill offender in Ireland have come from psychiatrists and psychologists who operate an in-reach service to provide psychiatric services to the prison population, and are pioneering court diversion processes from Irish remand centres where appropriate.[5] The Vision for Change document[6] published

---

2 See Schizophrenia Ireland's submission to An Garda Síochána Policing Plan 2008, Joint Working Group on Police and Mental Health.

3 Lamb, Weinberger and de Cuir, "The Police and Mental Health" Psychiatr Serv 53:1266-1271, October 2002, American Psychiatric Association.

4 Mental health courts have been developed and are operating in America, Canada and Australia. The principle underlying the operation of mental health courts is a problem-solving approach to justice, with multidisciplinary and inter-agency teams working together to deal with offending behaviour while treating the underlying mental illness which is the source of the problematic behaviour, helping the mentally ill person and reducing recidivism.

5 Dr O'Neill acknowledges that diversion is not always appropriate: "There may be cogent and legal reasons for not returning mentally ill defendants to local services. Defendants may have committed more serious offences or may pose a risk to others such that a secure setting may be required. Sentenced prisoners and those for whom non-custodial disposals cannot be considered are appropriately diverted to forensic settings. At present the only designated centre for such diversions is the Central Mental Hospital, Dundrum. Diversion to local services is indicated where illness is severe and the offence minor, particularly where the *sequelae* of mental illness act as impediments to bail or other non-custodial disposal. It is inaccurate to regard diversion as a 'get out of jail free card', since diversion does not equate with discontinuation of prosecution".

6 A Vision for Change, report of the Expert Group on Mental Health, 2007.

by the Mental Health Commission recommends that specific enabling legislation be developed to facilitate the process of court diversion. In the meantime, gardaí must grapple with their duties to the community and to the mentally-ill suspect.

The ordinary approaches of gardaí to suspected offenders, including arrest and restraint, are often inappropriate when the suspect is a mentally disordered person in distress. In turn, the reaction of mentally-ill persons in crisis is often equally inappropriate – they may be delusional, paranoid or respond to gardaí aggressively. The Canadian Mental Health Association advises that, "if the situation escalates, it can result in injury, trauma, or death – usually to the person with mental illness".[7] This was graphically illustrated by the Abbeylara incident in which John Carthy was fatally injured by gardaí. The Barr Tribunal report, which examined the Abbeylara incident, identified "[t]he desirability that the training of Garda recruits (and all officers by way of refresher courses) should include basic instruction on mental illness and how a person so afflicted should be dealt with, including the need for urgent consultation with his / her medical advisor and the importance of calming the subject".[8] **2–04**

Mental disorder is an umbrella term used in the Mental Health Act 2001 to encompass mental illness, severe dementia and significant intellectual disability, primarily as criteria for involuntary admissions to approved centres under the Act. The three subcategories are further defined: 'mental illness' as meaning a state of mind of a person which affects the person's thinking, perception, emotion or judgment and which seriously impairs the mental function of the person to the extent that he or she requires care or medical treatment in his or her own interest or in the interest of other persons; 'severe dementia' means a deterioration of the brain of a person which significantly impairs the person's intellectual function, thereby affecting thought, comprehension and memory and which includes severe psychiatric or behavioural symptoms, such as physical aggression; 'significant intellectual disability' is defined as a state of arrested or incomplete development of mind, which includes significant impairment of intelligence and social functioning and abnormally aggressive or seriously irresponsible conduct by the person.[9] **2–05**

Where gardaí believe a person to be mentally disordered, as per the definition in s 3 of the Act, and that, as a consequence, there is an immediate and significant risk of serious harm to that person or to others, gardaí may take the person into custody. Though the power to take such a person into custody, in s 12 of the Mental Health Act 2001, has some of the hallmarks of an arrest power, the term arrest has been deliberately omitted from the legislation. Section 12(1) provides that: **2–06**

7 Canadian Mental Health Association "Police and Mental Illness: Models that Work," March 2005.

8 Report of the Barr Tribunal of Inquiry into the facts and circumstances surrounding the fatal shooting of John Carthy at Abbeylara, Co Longford, on 20 April, 2000; Chapter 15, Recommendation (v).

9 Mental Health Act 2001, s 3. It is of note that a different definition applies under the Criminal Law (Insanity) Act 2006, under which 'mental disorder' includes "mental illness, mental disability, dementia or any disease of the mind but does not include intoxication".

> "Where a member of the Garda Síochána has reasonable grounds for believing that a person is suffering from a mental disorder and that because of the mental disorder there is a serious likelihood of the person causing immediate and serious harm to himself or herself or to other persons, the member may either alone or with any other members of the Garda Síochána —
> (a) take the person into custody, and
> (b) enter if need be by force any dwelling or other premises or any place if he or she has reasonable grounds for believing that the person is to be found there."

2–07 The important distinction is that, rather than commencing criminal proceedings, as an arrest normally would, taking a person into custody under the Mental Health Act 2001 should lead to therapeutic intervention. Section 12(2) provides that gardaí who take a person into custody under s 12(1) should apply to a registered medical practitioner for a recommendation that the person should be involuntarily admitted to a designated centre. If the application is refused on the basis that the registered medical practitioner is not satisfied that the person is suffering from a mental disorder,[10] the person who is the subject of the application shall be released from custody immediately.[11] If a recommendation is made to hospitalise the person, a member of the garda shall remove the person to the approved centre specified in the recommendation.[12] The gardaí may also be involved in the involuntary admission of a person to a psychiatric hospital at the request of the mental health professionals involved. Section 13(3) provides:

> "Where the clinical director of the approved centre or a consultant psychiatrist acting on his or her behalf and the registered medical practitioner who made the recommendation are of opinion that there is a serious likelihood of the person concerned causing immediate and serious harm to himself or herself or to other persons, the clinical director or a consultant psychiatrist acting on his or her behalf may, if necessary, request the Garda Síochána to assist the members of the staff of the approved centre in the removal by the staff of the person to that centre and the Garda Síochána shall comply with any such request."

2–08 Section 13(4) sets out the powers of gardaí in the event of their involvement in a request under s 13(3):

> "Where a request is made to the Garda Síochána under subsection (3), a member or members of the Garda Síochána may—
> (a) enter if need be by force any dwelling or other premises where he or she has reasonable cause to believe that the person concerned may be, and
> (b) take all reasonable measures necessary for the removal of the person concerned to the approved centre including, where necessary, the detention or restraint of the person concerned."

2–09 Notwithstanding the avoidance of the term 'arrest' in the provision for taking mentally-ill persons into custody, Schizophrenia Ireland has noted:

---

10 Mental Health Act 2001, s 10.
11 *ibid*, s 12(4).
12 *ibid*, s 12(5).

> "The role of the gardaí in relation to admissions is perhaps one of the most significant issues... frequently, an involuntary admission involving the attendance of the gardaí had all the elements of arrest. In most cases, there was virtually no therapeutic element.
>
> Many families speak positively of the involvement of the gardaí during an involuntary admission. Other families, unfortunately, have a very different experience; the inappropriate use of excessive restraint, handcuffs and several marked cars are frequently reported. Even when Garda personnel have been sensitive and supportive to family members, the stigma of a uniformed presence and a marked Garda car in a residential [*sic*] is extreme. This experience is often compounded by the fact that the involuntary admission has been preceded by a period of significant disturbance in the home, often evident to neighbours and friends. The absence of community mental health or crises [*sic*] outreach services means that, when a person reaches crises [*sic*] point, involuntary admission is the only option."[13]

While the criticism concerning the use of restraints and marked cars is fairly levelled, there is a potential for violence underlying the majority of psychiatric emergencies[14] and a subgroup of persons with serious mental illness is significantly more dangerous than persons in the general population, particularly those who are psychotic, do not take their medication and are substance abusers,[15] posing a significant challenge to both the police and mental health professionals.

Involuntary Admissions

In November 2006, key provisions of the Mental Health Act 2001 came into operation,[16] **2–10**
improving safeguards for persons who are involuntarily detained because of their mental illness. In their interactions under the 2001 Act, gardaí must be mindful that mentally-ill persons are no less entitled to privacy, autonomy, bodily integrity and liberty

13 See Schizophrenia Ireland's submission to An Garda Síochána Policing Plan 2008, Joint Working Group on Police and Mental Health.

14 Lamb, Weinberger and de Cuir, "The Police and Mental Health" Psychiatr Serv 53:1266-1271, October 2002, American Psychiatric Association, citing Ellison JM, Hughes DH, White KA: An emergency psychiatry update. Hospital and Community Psychiatry 40:250-260, 1989; DE McNeil, BL Binder: Predictive validity of judgments of dangerousness in emergency civil commitment. American Journal of Psychiatry 144:197-200, 1987; JC Beck, KA White, B Gage: Emergency psychiatric assessment of violence. American Journal of Psychiatry 148:1562-1565, 1991.

15 Lamb, Weinberger and de Cuir, "The Police and Mental Health" Psychiatr Serv 53:1266-1271, October 2002, American Psychiatric Association, citing EF Torrey: Violent behavior by individuals with serious mental illness. Hospital and Community Psychiatry 45:653–662, 1994; EP Mulvey: Assessing the evidence of a link between mental illness and violence. Hospital and Community Psychiatry 45:663–668, 1994; PM Marzuk: Violence, crime, and mental illness: how strong a link? Archives of General Psychiatry 53:481–486, 1996; J Swanson, S Estroff, M Swartz, *et al*: Violence and severe mental disorder in clinical and community populations: the effects of psychotic symptoms, co-morbidity, and lack of treatment. Psychiatry 60:1–22, 1997; HJ Steadman: Risk factors for community violence among acute psychiatric inpatients: the MacArthur risk assessment project. Paper presented at the annual meeting of the American Psychiatric Association, San Diego, 20 May 1997; C Fulwiler, B Grossman, C Forbes, *et al*: Early-onset substance abuse and community violence by outpatients with chronic mental illness. Psychiatric Services 48:1181–1194, 1997.

16 See Mental Health Act 2001 (Approved Centres) Regulations 2006, SI No 551 of 2006.

than anyone else.[17] These rights are specifically referred to in s 4 of the Mental Health Act 2001, which provides that "in making a decision under this Act concerning the care or treatment of a person (including a decision to make an admission order in relation to a person), due regard shall be given to the need to respect the right of the person to dignity, bodily integrity, privacy and autonomy".

2–11 The best interests of the mentally-ill person must be the principal consideration underpinning decisions made under the Act, including a decision to make an admission order in relation to a person. However, due regard must also be given to the interests of others who may be at risk of serious harm if the decision is not made.[18] The Act sets out the procedure for involuntary detention as a psychiatric patient; in practical terms for gardaí, the process is an application to a registered medical practitioner for a recommendation that a specified person be admitted to an approved centre. Persons may only be admitted involuntarily to an approved psychiatric centre if they are suffering from a mental disorder. As outlined above, mental disorder is defined in s 3 as meaning mental illness, severe dementia or significant intellectual disability. In addition, there must be a serious likelihood that, as a consequence of the illness, disability or dementia, the person may cause immediate and serious harm to himself or herself or to other persons. Or it may be that, because of the severity of the illness, disability or dementia, the judgment of the person is so impaired that failure to admit the person to an approved centre would be likely to lead to a serious deterioration in his or her condition or would prevent the administration of appropriate treatment. In addition it must be likely that the reception, detention and treatment of the person concerned in an approved centre will benefit or alleviate the condition of that person to a material extent.

2–12 A person may not be involuntarily admitted just because he or she is suffering from a personality disorder, is socially deviant or is addicted to drugs or intoxicants, unless there is an accompanying mental disorder.[19] The exclusion of 'social deviants', addicts and the personality disordered poses practical difficulties in the absence of legislative definitions of those terms and in the absence of alternative services for such persons where necessary. As the then Mental Health Bill was debated, Senator Dermot Fitzpatrick noted:

> "I have enough experience as a general practitioner to know that one would have to be a genius to make such a clear distinction [between mental illness and the excluded categories of personality disorder, social deviance or addiction to drugs, or intoxicants] ... We would all like an explanation as to how this section will be applied with due regard to the safety of the patient and the public and the general concerns of the patient's family."[20]

2–13 However, the Mental Health Commission has defended the categories on the basis that they

---

[17] See *A Ward of Court (withholding medical treatment) (No. 2), In Re a* [1996] 2 IR 79. See also M Donnelly "Legislating for Incapacity: Developing A Rights-Based Framework" (2008) 15(1) DULJ 395.

[18] Mental Health Act 2001, s 4(1).

[19] *ibid*, s 8(2).

[20] 166 Seanad Debates, Cols 1450-1451.

> "... bring Irish mental health law into conformity with the United Nations Principles for the Protection of Persons with Mental Illness and the Improvement of Mental Health Care (1991)[21] and are an essential protection to ensure that a person's moral, social, cultural, religious or political values shall never be the sole determining factor in diagnosing mental disorder. They bring Irish legislation in line with most other countries in respect of substance abuse and addictions. The rationale generally behind having exclusion criteria is to protect against political abuse and to encourage the idea of individual responsibility."[22]

The challenge for gardaí in negotiating the competing interests of the patient and the public, and having to assess whether a person comes within the definition of mental disorder is recognised by the Mental Health Commission, noting that: **2–14**

> "Unlike a registered medical practitioner, members of the Garda Síochána cannot rely on clinical judgement to assess whether or not someone is suffering from a mental disorder. However, they are entitled to form a belief, based on their training, experience and judgement that a person is suffering from a mental disorder, so long as that belief is reasonable."[23]

There is also, of course, the danger that the gardaí will not recognise mental disorder and therefore not react appropriately, since a person who appears to be mentally ill to a mental health professional may not seem so to gardaí: mental illness may be masked by or mistaken for drug or alcohol intoxication[24] or, in the confusion of an encounter with police necessitating the use of restraint, signs of mental illness may go unnoticed.[25]

Applications for Admission

An application for admission may be made by a spouse or relative, an authorised officer, a garda or any other person.[26] An authorised officer is an officer of the Health Service Executive (HSE) area who is designated by the chief officer of the HSE area for the purposes of making such applications. An application may not be made by persons under 18 years of age, a garda or HSE authorised officer who is related to the person concerned or that person's spouse, a member of the governing body (not including a member of an HSE area) or staff of the approved centre concerned, anyone who has an interest in the payments to be made to the approved centre, any medical practitioner **2–15**

[21] The UN Principles for the Protection of Persons with Mental Illness and the Improvement of Mental Health Care, Principle 4.3 (1991).

[22] Mental Health Commission, Reference Guide Mental Health Act 2001, Part One – Adults, at p 13, available online at http://www.mhcirl.ie/Mental_Health_Act_2001/Reference_Guide_to_the_Mental_Health_Act_2001/ <accessed 13 October 2013>.

[23] Mental Health Commission, *Reference Guide Mental Health Act 2001, Part One – Adults*, at p 58, available online at http://www.mhcirl.ie/Mental_Health_Act_2001/Reference_Guide_to_the_Mental_Health_Act_2001/ <accessed 13 October 2013>.

[24] Lamb, Weinberger and de Cuir, "The Police and Mental Health" Psychiatr Serv 53:1266-1271, October 2002, American Psychiatric Association.

[25] *ibid* citing Lamb HR, Grant RW: The mentally ill in an urban county jail. Archives of general psychiatry 39:17-22, 1982.

[26] Mental Health Act 2001, s 9(1).

who provides a regular medical service to the centre, the spouse, parent, grandparent, brother, sister, uncle or aunt of any of the people specifically mentioned above.[27]

2–16 The person making the application must have observed the person whose admission is sought in the preceding 48 hours.[28] If the application is being made by a person who is neither a spouse, relative, garda nor an authorised person, the application must include a statement of the reasons why it is being made, the connection of the applicant to the person whose admission is proposed and the circumstances in which the application is made.[29] Where the application is made by gardaí, a Form 3 must be completed: *Application (to a Registered Medical Practitioner) by a member of the Garda Síochána for a recommendation for involuntary admission of an adult (to an approved centre)) (Section 9 or Section 12).*

2–17 If the application is denied, the person must be released immediately. If the application is approved, and a medical practitioner recommends the detention of the person, the applicant is responsible for the transfer of the person to an approved centre, ie a hospital or other in-patient facility for the care and treatment of persons suffering from a mental illness or mental disorder which is listed on the register of approved centres. The Mental Health Commission's Guide to the Mental Health Act 2001 states that:

> "Ordinarily the person making the application to have a person admitted involuntarily is responsible for securing his or her removal to the relevant Approved Centre. However, the assistance of the Garda Síochána may be required in circumstances where the clinical director of the Approved Centre concerned (or a consultant psychiatrist acting on his or her behalf) *and* the registered medical practitioner who made the recommendation are of the opinion that there is a serious likelihood of the person concerned causing immediate and serious harm to self or others. In such circumstances the Garda Síochána are obliged to assist members of staff of the Approved Centre in the removal of the person to the centre concerned. Members of the Garda Síochána are empowered to enter, by force if necessary, any premises where they think the person concerned may be and may, if necessary, detain or restrain the person concerned in ensuring their removal to the Approved Centre." [30]

If the person to whom it is proposed that the Mental Health Act will apply is under 18, the consent of a parent will be necessary before any psychiatric treatment can be undertaken.[31]

2–18 It is vital that a person who is to be the subject of an application for involuntary detention should be notified of the section of the Mental Health Act 2001 under which the patient

---

[27] *ibid*, s 9(2).

[28] *ibid*, s 9(4).

[29] *ibid*, s 9(5).

[30] See Mental Health Commission, *Reference Guide Mental Health Act 2001, Part One – Adults,* at p 58, available online at http://www.mhcirl.ie/Mental_Health_Act_2001/Reference_Guide_to_the_Mental_Health_Act_2001/ <accessed 13 October 2013>.

[31] Pursuant to s 23 of the Non-Fatal Offences against the Person Act 1997, psychiatric treatment requires the consent of parents of children under 18, whereas children of 16 and over may consent to medical (and dental) treatment without reference to their parent.

is being detained; that they are entitled to legal representation; a general description of the proposed treatment to be administered during the detention; that they are entitled to communicate with the Inspector of Mental Health Services; that their detention will be reviewed by a Mental Health Commission review tribunal; that they are entitled to appeal to the Circuit Court against a decision of a tribunal and that they have the right to be admitted as a voluntary patient if they wish.

Approved Centres

The register of approved centres for the purpose of detention under the Mental Health Act is kept under continuous review.[32] On 18 June 2013, the list of approved centres was as follows: **2–19**

Child and Adolescent Services

Adolescent In-patient Unit, St Vincent's Hospital, Fairview, Dublin 3 **2–20**
Child and Adolescent Mental Health In-patient Unit, Merlin Park University Hospital, Galway
Éist Linn Child and Adolescent In-patient Unit, Bessborough, Blackrock, Cork
Linn Dara Child and Adolescent In-patient Unit, St Loman's Hospital, Palmerstown, Dublin 20
Willow Grove Adolescent Unit, St Patrick's University Hospital, James's Street, Dublin 8
The Ginesa Suite, which is registered as part of St John of God Hospital Ltd, Stillorgan, Co Dublin, also provides a child and adolescent mental health in-patient service.

HSE Dublin Mid-Leinster Area

Acute Psychiatric Unit AMNCH, Tallaght, Dublin 24 **2–21**
Central Mental Hospital, Dundrum, Dublin 14
Department of Psychiatry, Midland Regional Hospital, Portlaoise, Co Laois
Elm Mount Unit, St Vincent's University Hospital, Dublin 4
Jonathan Swift Clinic, St James's Hospital, Dublin 8
Lakeview Unit, Naas General Hospital, Naas, Co Kildare
Newcastle Hospital, Greystones, Co Wicklow
St Fintan's Hospital, Portloaise, Co Laois
St Brigid's Ward and St Marie Goretti's Ward, Cluain Lir Care Centre, St Mary's Campus, Longford Road, Mullingar, Co Westmeath
St Loman's Hospital, Palmerstown, Dublin 20

HSE Dublin North East Area

Acute Psychiatric Unit, Cavan General Hospital, Cavan **2–22**
Blackwater House, St Davnet's Hospital, Armagh Road, Monaghan, Co Monaghan
Department of psychiatry, Connolly Hospital, Blanchardstown, Dublin 15

---

32 The register of approved centres may be checked on the website of the Mental Health Commission at http://www.mhcirl.ie/Registration/ACRegister <accessed 13 October 2013>.

Department of psychiatry, Our Lady's Hospital, Navan, Co Meath
Hawthorn Unit, Connolly Hospital, Blanchardstown, Dublin 15
Joyce Rooms, Fairview Community Unit, Griffith Court, Philipsburgh Avenue, Fairview, Dublin 3
O'Casey Rooms, Fairview Community Unit, Griffith Court, Philipsburgh Avenue, Fairview, Dublin 3
Phoenix Care Centre, North Circular Road, Dublin 7
St Aloysius Ward, Mater Misericordiae University Hospital, Eccles Street, Dublin 7
St Ita's Hospital – Willowbrook and Woodview Units, Portrane, Donabate, Co Dublin
St Joseph's Intellectual Disability Services, St Ita's Hospital, Portrane, Donabate, Co Dublin
St Vincent's Hospital – St Louise's, St Mary's, St Teresa's and Psychiatry of Old Age Wards, Richmond Road, Fairview, Dublin 3
Sycamore unit, Connolly Hospital, Blanchardstown, Dublin 15
Unit One and St Ita's Ward, St Brigid's Hospital, Kells Road, Ardee, Co Louth

HSE South Area

2–23 Acute Mental Health Admission Unit, Kerry General Hospital, Tralee, Co Kerry
Carraig Mór Centre, Shankiel, Cork
Centre for Mental Health Care and Recovery, Bantry General Hospital, Bantry, Co Cork
Department of Psychiatry, St Luke's Hospital, Freshford Road, Kilkenny
Department of Psychiatry, Waterford Regional Hospital, Dunmore Road, Waterford
Heywood Lodge, Heywood Road, Clonmel, Co Tipperary
Selskar House, Farnogue Residential Healthcare Unit, Old Hospital Road, Wexford, Co. Wexford
South Lee Adult Mental Health Unit, Cork University Hospital, Wilton, Cork
St Finan's Hospital, Killarney, Co Kerry
St Finbarr's Hospital, Douglas Road, Cork
St Gabriel's Ward, St Canice's Hospital, Dublin Road, Kilkenny
St Michael's Unit, Mercy University Hospital, Glenville Place, Cork
St Otteran's Hospital, John's Hill, Waterford
St Stephen's Hospital, Sarsfield Court, Glanmire, Co Cork

HSE West Area

2–24 Acute Psychiatric Unit 5B, Midwestern Regional Hospital, Dooradoyle, Limerick
Acute psychiatric Unit, Midwestern Regional Hospital, Ennis, Co Clare
Adult Mental Health Unit, Mayo General Hospital, Castlebar, Co Mayo
An Coillín, Westport Road, Castlebar, Co Mayo
Cappahard Lodge, Tulla Road, Ennis, Co Clare
Department of Psychiatry, County Hospital, Roscommon, Co Roscommon
Department of Psychiatry, Letterkenny General Hospital, Circular Road, Letterkenny, Co Donegal
Psychiatric Unit, University College Hospital Galway, Newcastle Road, Galway
Sligo/Leitrim Mental Health In-Patient Unit, Clarion Road, Ballytivnan, Sligo, Co Sligo
St Anne's Unit, Sacred Heart Hospital, Castlebar, Co Mayo
St Brigid's Hospital, Creagh, Ballinasloe, Co Galway
St Joseph's Hospital, Aurora unit, Mulgrave Street, Limerick

Teach Aisling, Westport Road, Castlebar, Co Mayo
Tearmann Ward and Curragour ward, St Camillus' Hospital, Shelbourne Road, Limerick

Independent / Private and Private Charitable Institutions

Bloomfield Hospital, Stocking Lane, Rathfarnham, Dublin 16 **2–25**
Highfield Hospital, Swords Road, Whitehall, Dublin 9
Lois Bridges, 3 Greenfield Road, Sutton, Dublin 13
St Edmundsbury Hospital, Lucan, Co Dublin
St John of God Hospital Ltd, Stillorgan, Co. Dublin
St Patrick's University Hospital, James's Street, Dublin 8

IMMIGRATION LAW ENFORCEMENT

Deportation Order Arrest and Detention

2–26 Gardaí are at the forefront of enforcement of immigration policy in that they carry out deportations, conduct border control and investigate illegal immigration and human trafficking offences. The wisdom of garda involvement in deportations is questionable, since it is counter-intuitive to the community policing model which is being pursued to have gardaí simultaneously performing the duties of immigration officers on the one hand, and the role of ethnic liaison officers on the other, if trust is to be built with minorities and immigrant communities.[33] For better or worse, it is the gardaí who arrest persons who are the subject of deportation orders. [34] Gardaí may arrest and detain persons against whom a deportation order is in force where there is reasonable cause to suspect that: the person has failed to comply with a provision of the deportation order; the person intends to leave the State and enter another country; the person has in his or her possession forged identity documents or has destroyed his or her identity documents; or that the person intends to avoid removal from the State. It is important to note that the arrest power in s 5 of the Immigration Act 1999[35] applies only to adults; children are exempted and may not be arrested.[36] However, if an immigration officer or garda has reasonable grounds to believe that the person is not in fact a minor, the person may be arrested.[37]

2–27 The Immigration Act 1999 (Deportation) Regulations 2005 provide that every Garda station is a prescribed place of detention for the purpose of s 5(1) of the Immigration Act, as are the following prisons: Castlerea Prison; Cloverhill Prison; Cork Prison;

---

[33] The human rights audit conducted by Ionann in 2004 posited among its recommendations the following: "The role of An Garda Síochána members in immigration law enforcement has sometimes brought it into conflict with some minority communities and also undermined efforts of their colleagues to develop good community relations. The Department might explore whether a separate immigration law enforcement agency would be helpful in reducing potential conflicts in relationships with minority communities." Human Rights Audit of An Garda Síochána, Ionann, 2004, at p 143. INIS, the Irish Naturalisation and Immigration Service, was established in 2005.

[34] Immigration Act 1999, s 5(1), as substituted by s 10 of the Illegal Immigrants (Trafficking) Act 2000.

[35] *ibid.*

[36] Immigration Act 1999, s 5(4)(a).

[37] *ibid*, s 5(4)(b).

Limerick Prison; The Midlands Prison; Mountjoy Prison; Saint Patrick's Institution, Dublin; The Training Unit, Glengarriff Parade, Dublin; and Wheatfield Prison, Dublin. Where an immigration officer or member of the Garda arrests a person pursuant to s 5(1) of the Act and where it is proposed that the person should be detained, the arresting immigration officer or garda must inform the member in charge of the Garda station or the governor of the prison in writing of the arrest and direct that the person be detained until further notice.[38]

Immigration Act 2004

2–28 A power in s 12 of the Immigration Act 2004, which had permitted gardaí to demand identity documents from non-nationals, was held to be unconstitutional in the case of *Dokie v Director of Public Prosecutions.*[39] The section had created an offence, with an associated arrest power under s 13, of failing to produce a passport or equivalent document establishing identity or a registration document unless a satisfactory explanation could be given of the circumstances preventing the person from so doing. Kearns P took the view that the failure to define the term 'satisfactory explanation' in s 12 of the Act gave rise to vagueness and uncertainty, with considerable potential for arbitrariness in its application by individual members of An Garda Síochána. It was noted that there was no requirement of reasonable suspicion of involvement in unlawful activity before a demand could be made of the non-national to provide a 'satisfactory' explanation for the absent documents. He held:

> "In my view, s 12 is not sufficiently precise to reasonably enable an individual to foresee the consequences of his or her acts or omissions or to anticipate what form of explanation might suffice to avoid prosecution. Furthermore, there is no requirement in the section to warn of the possible consequences of any failure to provide a 'satisfactory' explanation... while s 12 was designed as an immigration control mechanism, its vagueness is such as to fail basic requirements for the creation of a criminal offence. As drafted it gives rise to arbitrariness and legal uncertainty. It also offends the principle that a person be not obliged to incriminate himself. I find it unconstitutional for those reasons."[40]

2–29 Sections 11 and 12 have since been substituted by s 34 of the Civil Law (Miscellaneous Provisions) Act 2011 in response to the *Dokie* judgment. The reformulated sections now provide at s 11 that there is an obligation on every person landing in or embarking from the State to furnish their passport to immigration officers and to furnish them, on request with such information as the officers may reasonably require for the purposes of the performance of their functions; and at s 12 that non-nationals over 16 years of age must produce a passport or registration certificate on demand. Failure to comply with the requirements of either section is an offence[41] and the arrest power in s 13 remains.

[38] Regulation 7 of the Immigration Act 1999 (Deportation) Regulations 2005, SI No 55 of 2005.

[39] *Dokie v Director of Public Prosecutions* [2010] IEHC 110.

[40] *ibid.*

[41] The Immigration Act 2004, s 12(2)(b), as substituted by s 34 of the Civil Law (Miscellaneous Provisions) Act 2011 provides that, in any subsequent proceedings for an offence under the section, it will be a defence to prove that there was reasonable cause for non-compliance at the time of the offence.

The arrest power provided for in s 13 of the Immigration Act 2004 is exercisable in relation to all offences under the Immigration Act 2004, with the exception of offences under s 10 which relates to the maintenance of hotel registers, and s 2(1) of the Employment Permits Act 2003, which prohibits non-nationals from working without the requisite employment permit. The latter section contains an arrest power, but it only applies where a garda is obstructed. **2–30**

Section 13 was considered in the case of *Oladapo v Governor of Cloverhill Prison*,[42] in which a Nigerian national had been arrested pursuant to s 13 of the Immigration Act 2004 on suspicion of having committed offences contrary to that Act. In reality, the purpose of his arrest was not to charge him but to go through the process of denying him "permission to land" pursuant to another provision of the Act and thereby to facilitate his deportation. Murray CJ emphasised that an arrest will be unlawful if it is effected for a purpose other than that for which it is authorised: **2–31**

> "...the facts and circumstances outlined above lead me ineluctably to the conclusion that the initial arrest pursuant to s 13 was itself unlawful. It was not made for the purpose of charging the appellant with the offence for which he was purportedly arrested... What occurred in this case was a fundamental breach of the due process of law. This is not to suggest that there was malice or dishonesty on the part of Garda McGovern. Although his actions were conscious and deliberate he appears to have considered that he was properly endeavouring to apply the provisions of the Immigration Acts to a person who was unlawfully present in the State by virtue of s 5(2) of the Act of 2004. That however does not alter the position in law, namely that he deliberately effected an unlawful arrest and detention."

It is clear therefore that, if a person is arrested under a statutory power to arrest on suspicion of commission of a particular offence, it can only be used for that purpose, and that s 13 permits arrest in the immigration context only where there are reasonable grounds for suspicion that an offence under the 2004 Act has been committed.

ARREST BY MEMBERS OF THE GARDA SÍOCHÁNA OMBUDSMAN COMMISSION

The Garda Síochána Ombudsman Commission (GSOC) provides independent oversight of policing in Ireland. In that regard, GSOC directly and independently investigates complaints against members of the Garda Síochána and, even where no complaint has been made, matters where it appears that a garda may have committed an offence or behaved in a way that would justify disciplinary proceedings. The Commission was established by the Garda Síochána Act 2005, s 98 of which provides that, where directed by the Ombudsman Commission to investigate a complaint which appears to involve an offence, a designated officer has, in relation to the member of the Garda Síochána under investigation, for the purposes of the investigation "all the **2–32**

[42] *Oladapo v Governor of Cloverhill Prison* [2009] IESC 42, [2009] 2 ILRM 166.

powers, immunities and privileges conferred and all the duties imposed on any member of the Garda Síochána by or under any enactment or the common law", including powers to:

(a) Enter, search and seize evidence under warrant (with the exception of garda stations, the search of which is governed by s 99);
(b) arrest with or without warrant;
(c) charge persons;
(d) issue summonses;
(e) search, photograph, fingerprint and palmprint persons;
(f) detain and question;
(g) take bodily samples or other things from a person with a view to forensic testing.

Delay, obstruction or interference with a designated officer operating under s 98 is an offence, punishable by a fine of up to €3,000 or imprisonment for up to 12 months, or both.[43]

2–33 The search of Garda stations is dealt with in s 99. The Ombudsman Commission can authorise designated officers to search a garda station where the designated officer has reasonable cause to suspect that the garda who is under investigation may be guilty of an offence, and reasonably suspects that evidence in relation to the suspected offence or attempted offence will be found in the station or in the possession of anyonein the station. On grounds of State security, the authorisation of the minister is required for the search of certain garda stations.[44] As with the use of powers under s 98, obstruction, attempted obstruction, failure to comply, refusal to give a name or address or giving an address which is false or misleading constitute offences[45] for which designated officers may arrest without warrant.[46]

2–34 Clearly with powers of arrest, search and detention mirroring those of the gardaí, officers and investigators of the Ombudsman Commission ought to apply the same standards as gardaí do in the exercise those powers. Gardaí who are searched or arrested should be told the reason for the search or arrest, the provision under which the search or arrest is authorised and the suspicion grounding the search or arrest. Respect for and vindication of human rights should underpin all aspects of GSOC investigations.

ARREST BY MEMBERS OF THE GARDA RESERVE

2–35 The Garda Síochána Act 2005 provided for the establishment of a Garda Reserve, volunteer members who provide support to full-time members of An Garda Síochána. Section 15 of the Act provides that the Garda Commissioner may determine the range of powers to be exercised and duties to be carried out by reserve members. Subject to

---

[43] Garda Síochána Act 2005, s 98(3).
[44] *ibid*, s 99(3)-(5). The designation of such stations is dealt with in the Garda Síochána Act 2005, s 126.
[45] *ibid*, s 99(9).
[46] *ibid*, s 99(8)(b).

the determination of the Commissioner, a reserve member has, while on duty, the same powers, immunities, privileges and duties as a full-time member of An Garda Síochána.

The Garda Síochána (Reserve Members) Regulations 2006[47] set out recruitment, training and general procedures in relation to the Garda Reserve. The regulations do not refer to arrest powers, save for a reference in regulation 6 to the provision of training in relation to powers of arrest and arrestable offences. The explanatory memorandum expands on the role of reserve gardaí in arrest, stating: **2–36**

> "The Garda Commissioner has also initially determined that the powers of reserve members will be confined to the enforcement of certain aspects of the following Acts:
>
> under the Road Traffic Acts – demanding driving licences and insurance details, enforcing the wearing of seat belts etc;
>
> under the Public Order Act – dealing with the offences of intoxication, threatening behaviour, disorderly conduct and failure to comply with the direction of a member of An Garda Síochána; and
>
> under the Criminal Justice (Theft and Fraud Offences) Act – dealing with the offences of theft and burglary.
>
> Reserve members will also be given the power of arrest under the Criminal Law Act 1997, which provides powers of arrest for both members of the Garda Síochána and civilians."

The specific citizen's arrest powers outlined in Chapter 1 are also exercisable, in theory if not in practice, by members of the Garda Reserve.

ARREST BY SEA FISHERIES PROTECTION OFFICERS

The Sea-Fisheries and Maritime Jurisdiction Act 2006 was enacted to provide for the modernisation of the legislative sea-fisheries framework, the implementation of EU and national fisheries policy and to strengthen the law against illegal sea-fishing. The Act established the Sea Fisheries Protection Authority[48] and provided for the transfer of responsibility for the prosecution of sea-fisheries offences from the Attorney General to the Director of Public Prosecutions.[49] **2–37**

It is striking that the arrest powers which were included in the Act come into play only where there has been assault or obstruction of a sea-fisheries protection officer. While a vessel may be arrested and its crew detained where fisheries offences are suspected, there is no provision to allow for the arrest and detention of individual fishermen for the investigation of fisheries offences, notwithstanding the seriousness of the offences under investigation. This is an odd omission, given that the robust criminalisation of sea-fisheries offences with significant associated penalties is the kernel of the 2006 Act. As the Bill passed controversially through the Dáil, **2–38**

47 SI No 413 of 2006. The regulations came into operation on 1 August 2006.

48 Sea-Fisheries and Maritime Jurisdiction Act 2006, Ch 5, ss 40-73.

49 *ibid*, s 39. The transfer was effected on 1 August 2009 by the Sea-Fisheries (Prosecution of Offences) Order 2009, SI No 314 of 2009.

the minister referred to a small group of fishermen being involved in "systematic criminal activity".[50] There was considerable opposition to the Bill, much of it centring on the use of criminal, rather than administrative measures,[51] so perhaps it was felt that the arrest and detention of individual fishermen would have been a bridge too far. In any event, the omission of an arrest power hinders to the investigation of sea-fisheries offences, since there is no power to detain individuals for questioning as applies in the investigation of all other serious offences. Instead, it is the boat itself which is arrested and detained.

2–39 Section 18 of the Act contains a number of powers in respect of boats—boats which are underway can be ordered to be stopped, or ordered to be manoeuvred for identification or boarding.[52] Sea-fisheries protection officers can board boats and require production of all relevant documentation for inspection.[53] The master can be required to give an explanation concerning the boat or the fishing gear or equipment and any documentation on board,[54] the names and addresses of those aboard can be taken,[55] the boat can be searched[56] and any satellite or positioning equipment can be examined.[57] If there is a reasonable suspicion that an offence has been committed, the boat itself can be arrested and detained, together with the persons present on it, pending urgent applications to the District Court. Section 18(1)(i) provides that a sea-fisheries protection officer may:

> "(i) if he or she reasonably suspects that there has been a contravention by any person on board the boat of this Part, without summons, warrant or other process—
> (i) if the boat is not in a port, take or instruct that the boat and all persons on board be taken to port or order the master of the boat to take the boat directly to a specified port, and pending the taking of the steps required by section 20 or 21, as may be appropriate, detain the boat and the persons on board, or
> (ii) if the boat is in a port, detain the boat and the persons on board at the port or take it and them to a more convenient port and there detain it and them, pending (in either case) the taking of those steps."

2–40 Gardaí are included in the list of persons designated as sea-fisheries protection officers, as are officers of the Department of Marine, members of staff of the Sea-Fisheries Protection Authority, members of the Permanent Defence Forces (not below the rank of leading seaman or corporal) serving on board any ship, vessel or aircraft belonging to or employed in the service of the State, and officers of Customs and Excise authorised in that behalf by the Revenue Commissioners.[58]

---

50 Marie O'Halloran, "Fishermen Involved in Systemic Criminal Activity, Says Dempsey", *Irish Times*, 10 February 2006.
51 See, for example, the contributions of Deputy Jim O'Keeffe, 615 Dáil Debates, Col 570.
52 Sea-Fisheries and Maritime Jurisdiction Act 2006, s 18(1)(a).
53 *ibid*, s 18(1)(c).
54 *ibid*, s 18(1)(d).
55 *ibid*, s 18(1)(g).
56 *ibid*, s 18(1)(f).
57 *ibid*, s 18(1)(e).
58 *ibid*, s 16.

A wide range of powers of stop, entry and search for use in the investigation of sea-fisheries offences is provided at s 17 of the Act, including the power to stop persons believed to be conveying sea-fish[59]; to enter any premises in which sea-fish is or is believed to be sold, or kept, stored, processed or disposed of[60]; to enter fishing-related business premises, as well as piers, quays, wharves, jetties, docks or dock premises, sea-food factories or processing facilities or warehouses[61]; to board and search vessels or vehicles used for the conveyance of goods[62] as well as the premises of anyone engaged in the business of retaining documents containing information on activities relating to the Common Fisheries Policy (which could be taken to mean persons acting in a professional capacity, such as banks, accountants and solicitors).[63] Fish and fishing gear and equipment can be examined and, if necessary, taken as evidence,[64] and other forms of evidence—documentary, electronic or photographic—may also be taken.[65] In addition, sea-fisheries protection officers can request the names and addresses of the person who has custody of the fish or equipment, as well as the name and address of the owner. **2–41**

Sea-fisheries protection officers can arrest anyone who assaults a sea-fisheries protection officer in the course of their duties.[66] In addition, there is a power of arrest for obstruction of a sea-fisheries protection officer, failure or refusal to comply with their lawful directions or requirements or in the event of refusal or failure to give a name and address (or giving a name or address which is thought to be false or misleading).[67] If such an arrest is made by an officer who is not a member of An Garda Síochána, the person must be delivered into the custody of An Garda Síochána as soon as practicable. **2–42**

Search warrants may also be sought to facilitate the search of any place, including a boat, from a judge of the District Court.[68] Such warrants are grounded on information on oath of a sea-fisheries protection officer that there are reasonable grounds for suspecting that there is evidence of, or relating to, a sea-fisheries offence at the place to be searched.[69] Search warrants issued pursuant to the Sea-Fisheries and Maritime Jurisdiction Act 2006 remain in force for seven days from the date of issue, and entry may be gained by reasonable force if necessary.[70] **2–43**

Regulations concerning the Common Fisheries Policy have direct effect in Ireland, and s 11 of the 2006 Act provides that contravention of, or failure to comply with, **2–44**

59 *ibid*, s 17(1)(a).
60 *ibid*, s 17(1)(b)(i).
61 *ibid*, s 17(1)(b)(ii) and (iii).
62 *ibid*, s 17(1)(b)(iv).
63 *ibid*, s 17(1)(b)(v).
64 *ibid*, s 17(1)(c); 17(1)(e); 17(1)(f); 17(1)(g).
65 *ibid*, s 17(1)(k); 17(1)(l).
66 *ibid*, s 25.
67 *ibid*, s 24.
68 *ibid*, s 17A, as inserted by s 44 of the Criminal Justice Act 2007.
69 *ibid*, s 17A(2), as inserted by s 44 of the Criminal Justice Act 2007.
70 *ibid*, s 17A(3)(a), as inserted by s 44 of the Criminal Justice Act 2007.

a Community regulation is an offence. The section also provides for vicarious liability: where offences are committed on a fishing boat, the master and the owner of the boat each commits an offence. Equally, those involved in landing, trans-shipping, buying, handling, weighing, transporting, processing, storing, documenting or selling fish are open to prosecution where there is contravention of or non-compliance with a regulation. Penalties and forfeiture are provided for in s 28.[71]

ARREST BY AIRPORT POLICE

2–45 Gardaí and members of the Airport Police[72] have a number of powers under s 33 of the Air Navigation and Transport Act 1988, which may be exercised "in the interest of the proper operation, or the security or safety, of an airport, or the security or safety of persons, aircraft or other property thereon". The section empowers gardaí and 'authorised officers'[73] to stop, detain and search any person or vehicle at an airport, to require any person to give their name and address and evidence of identity, to state the purpose of their presence in the airport and to account for any baggage or property in their possession. If they refuse to provide the information sought, or give a name which is reasonably suspected to be fictitious, the garda or authorised officer may arrest the person without warrant or remove them from the airport. Equally, people who are reasonably suspected of not having a lawful reason for being in the airport may be removed from the airport or arrested without warrant.

2–46 The section also provides for arrest in the following situations:

a. where a person has assaulted another person or is suspected of having done so;
b. where a person is known or suspected to have stolen property in their possession;
c. where a person is known or suspected to have in their possession a dangerous article in an airport without lawful authority, ie a firearm or imitation firearm; an explosive or imitation explosive; an article made or adapted for use for causing injury to or incapacitating a person, or for damaging or destroying property or intended by a person to

---

[71] *ibid*, s 28 as amended by s 44(b) of the Criminal Justice Act 2007. See also s 28(1A) as inserted by s 44(b) of the Criminal Justice Act 2007.

[72] The powers in s 33 of the 1988 Act are vested in 'authorised officers', defined in s 2 of the Air Navigation and Transport (Amendment) Act 1998 as members of the Garda or "(b) in relation to a state airport— (i) a person, or a person belonging to a class of persons, authorised in writing by the company to perform the functions conferred on an authorised officer by or under this Act or the Act of 1988, or (ii) unless and until the Minister otherwise determines under subsection (4) of s 48, a person who immediately prior to the commencement of this section was an authorised officer within the meaning of paragraph (b) of the definition of authorised officer in s 15(1) of the [Air Navigation and Transport] Act of 1950 (as amended by s 25 of the Act of 1988), or (c) in relation to an airport in the state, other than a state airport, a person, or a person belonging to a class of persons, authorised in writing by the Minister to perform the functions conferred on an authorised officer by or under this Act or the Act of 1988".

[73] Air Navigation and Transport Act 1988, s 33(1), as amended by s 43 of the Air Navigation and Transport (Amendment) Act 1998.

be so used; or a substance (including nuclear material) which is thought to be likely to endanger persons or property.[74]

Where an arrest is effected under the section by an authorised officer, the arrested persons must be transferred into the custody of the gardaí as soon as possible.[75]

PRE-EMPTIVE DETENTION OF CHILDREN—CHILD ABDUCTION

International parental child abduction is governed by a number of international, European and domestic legal instruments.[76] The Child Abduction and Enforcement of Custody Orders Act 1991 gives effect in Irish law to the Hague and Luxembourg Conventions[77] which are designed to make the child's welfare the paramount interest in international custody disputes. The emphasis is on the speedy return of the child. A child in this context is a person who is under 16, and the Conventions apply to children who are habitually resident in a contracting State immediately before any breach of a custody or access order. The 1991 Act gives gardaí a vital power to combat potential and actual abductions: a pre-emptive power to detain a child who is thought to be imminently at risk of abduction from the State. Where there is a reasonable suspicion that a child is about to be or is being removed from the State in breach of a custody, access or care order, or an order made under the Child Abduction and Enforcement of Custody Orders Act 1991, or even when proceedings for such an order are pending or contemplated, s 37[78] may be invoked to allow gardaí to detain the child. Having been detained, the child must be returned to the custody of a person in whose favour an order has been made in relation to the child as soon as possible, unless there is reason to suspect that the person will breach the order, in which case the child should be delivered into the care of the Health Service Executive.[79] If the child has been in the care of the Health Service Executive prior to the abduction or attempted abduction, the child should be returned to the Health Service Executive.[80] **2–47**

[74] See Air Navigation and Transport Act 1988, s 19 and s 50 of the Air Navigation and Transport (Amendment) Act 1998.

[75] Air Navigation and Transport Act 1988, s 33(2).

[76] See the 1980 Hague Convention on the Civil Aspects of International Child Abduction; the 1996 Hague Convention on Jurisdiction, Applicable Law, Recognition, Enforcement and Co-operation in Respect of Parental Responsibility and Measures for the Protection of Children; the European Convention on Recognition and Enforcement of Decisions Concerning Custody of Children (the Luxembourg Convention); Council Regulation (EC) No 2201/2003. These instruments deal with the civil aspects of international child abduction.

[77] Convention on the Civil Aspects of International Child Abduction signed at The Hague on the 25th day of October, 1980, and the European Convention on Recognition and Enforcement of Decisions Concerning Custody of Children and on Restoration of Custody of Children signed at Luxembourg on the 20th day of May 1980.

[78] Child Abduction and Enforcement of Custody Orders Act 1991, s 37, as amended by the Health Act 2004, s 75 and Schedule 6, part 12.

[79] *ibid*, s 37(2)(a) and (c) as substituted by the Health Act 2004, s 75 and Schedule 6, Part 12.

[80] *ibid*, s 37(2)(b) and (c) as substituted by the Health Act 2004, s 75 and Schedule 6, Part 12.

2–48 The power to detain children is exercised in the civil realm; there is a related criminal offence in s 16 of the Non-Fatal Offences against the Person Act 1997 which applies where children are taken, sent or kept out of the State in defiance of a court order or without the consent of each parent, guardian or custodian of the child. The offence of parental abduction apples when children are taken out of the country, whereas removing children from persons in whose lawful control they ought to be is an offence when children are taken within the State.[81] The offence is punishable by up to seven years' imprisonment and is therefore arrestable. It must be established that the person who has taken the child intended to deprive the other parent or guardian of their rights to the child.

REMOVING CHILDREN TO SAFETY

2–49 Section 12 of the Child Care Act 1991 provides a power for urgent intervention by gardaí where children are seriously at risk. Where a garda has reasonable grounds for suspecting that there is an immediate and serious risk to the health or welfare of a child, and that the child would not be sufficiently protected by waiting for an application for an emergency care order to be made by the Health Service Executive, or for a warrant application under s 35 of the Child Care Act 1991, the member, accompanied by such other persons as may be necessary, may, without warrant, enter (if need be by force) any house or other place (including any building or part of a building, tent, caravan or other temporary or moveable structure, vehicle, vessel, aircraft or hovercraft) and remove the child to safety.[82] A child who has been removed under s 12 must be delivered, as soon as possible, into the care of the Health Service Executive.[83]

2–50 Gardaí have specific obligations to children under 12, set out in s 53 of the Children Act 2001. Where a child under 12 is suspected of an act which, but for their age, would amount to a criminal offence, a garda who encounters the child must endeavour to return the child to their parent or guardian[84] or, where that is not practicable, to give the child into the custody of the Health Service Executive.[85] Section 53 dovetails with the power to remove children to safety under s 12 of the Child Care Act 1991, by providing that if a garda finds a child in the circumstances outlined above, and the garda has reasonable grounds for belief that there is an immediate and serious risk to the health or welfare of the child and that waiting for an emergency care order application would not protect the child sufficiently, the garda may remove the child to safety.[86] The removal will be treated as a removal under s 12 of the Child Care Act 1991.

---

81 Non-Fatal Offences against the Person Act, 1997.

82 Child Care Act 1991, s 12(1) as amended by the Health Act 2004, s 3(1) and s 75, Sch. 7, pt 6, and as amended by the Child Care (Amendment) Act 2011, s 7.

83 Child Care Act 1991, s 12(3) as amended by the Health Act 2004, s 3(1) and s 75, Sch. 7, pt 6, as amended by the Child Care (Amendment) Act 2011, s 7.

84 Children Act 2001, s 53(1).

85 *ibid,* s 53(3).

86 *ibid,* s 53(5).

The Children Act 2001 also provides at s 254(4) for the removal of children to safety where an arrest is made under s 254 for an offence under part 12 of the Act (for instance cruelty to children,[87] begging involving children,[88] allowing a child to be in a brothel,[89] causing or encouraging a sexual offence upon a child[90]) and there are reasonable grounds to suspect that there is an immediate and serious risk to the safety, health or wellbeing of the child in circumstances where waiting for an emergency care order would not provide adequate protection. The removal will be treated as a removal under s 12 of the Child Care Act 1991. **2–51**

87 *ibid,* s 246.
88 *ibid,* s 247.
89 *ibid,* s 248.
90 *ibid,* s 249.

CHAPTER 3

Re-Arrest

3–01 There are a number of circumstances in which re-arrest is both desirable and necessary but, notwithstanding its frequent necessity, re-arrest can prove problematic.

DISTINCTION BETWEEN ARREST UPON AN ARREST AND RE-ARREST

3–02 An important distinction must be drawn between the arrest of an individual who is already in the custody of another person (be that another garda, a store detective, customs officer or private citizen), and the re-arrest for the same offence of a person who has already been lawfully arrested, detained and released. In the first context, arrest upon an arrest is generally viewed from a pragmatic perspective as a practical necessity, whereas the latter is strictly controlled to prevent an abuse of process and a mockery of the statutory time limits which apply to post-arrest detention periods.

3–03 Arrest denotes a future restriction of liberty, but liberty is not a pre-condition for arrest. Re-arrest is statutorily provided for in a number of situations[1] and even outside those confines, the practice of arrest upon arrest has received judicial approval[2] where

[1] The most obvious example is an arrest consequent upon a citizen's arrest. See s 4 of the Criminal Law Act 1997, s 8 of the Criminal Justice (Theft and Fraud Offences) Act 2001 and s 12 of the Criminal Damage Act 1991.

[2] *Re Ó Laighléis* [1960] IR 93; *People (DPP) v Kehoe* [1985] IR 444; *People (DPP) v O'Shea* [1996] 1 IR 557.

it is clear that there has been no abuse of process. In the seminal case of *Re Ó Laighléis*, the High Court held:

> "... the fallacy [in the Applicant's argument] . . . lies in regarding an arrest as essentially the determination of a pre-existing liberty. This is not, in our view, an essential or necessary feature of arrest. The essence is the restraint from liberty as from the moment of arrest, that is, the subsequent or future restraint. It is irrelevant, therefore, to the true nature of an arrest whether the person arrested was then at liberty or not".[3]

Davitt P observed:

> "In the result we do not think that there is any legal principle which prevents a person already in one custody from being arrested and taken into another custody. To put the matter another way, the transfer from one custody to another can be regarded as an arrest, in the ordinary sense of the term, by the new custodian. In ordinary language a person can be properly said to be arrested when he is taken into custody whether he is taken from a state of freedom or of previous restraint."[4]

3–04 In *DPP v Warren*[5] an off-duty garda had effectively arrested a suspected drink-driver and chased, apprehended and detained him while he awaited the arrival of an on-duty garda to arrest the suspect formally. The validity of the second arrest was challenged on the basis that the initial period of detention was unlawful. It was argued that this rendered the second arrest bad and the evidence which flowed from it inadmissible. The court found that all the elements of an arrest had been present in the initial apprehension by the off-duty garda. In effect the arrest was a single transaction, the whole purpose of which was to get the accused back to the station for a single sample-taking procedure to be performed. Thus, so long as the second arrest is a *bona fide* one and there is no unfairness or abuse of process involved, there is no reason why it should be held to be invalid. This was affirmed by the Supreme Court.[6]

In *People (DPP) v O'Shea*[7] the Court of Criminal Appeal rejected a submission that the applicant, having been arrested by customs officials after a significant amount of cannabis was found in his car, should not thereafter have been arrested by the gardaí.

It appears that the period of detention under s 4 of the Criminal Justice Act 1984 begins with the second arrest by the garda,[8] but there is perhaps scope to argue that it ought to begin with the first arrest.

---

3 *Re O'Laighléis* [1960] IR 93, *per* Davitt P, at 108.
4 *ibid.*
5 *DPP v Warren* [2006] IEHC 189; [2006] 8 ICLMD 40.
6 However no written judgment is available.
7 *People (DPP) v O'Shea* [1996] IR 557.
8 *ibid.*

An *obiter* passage in the older case of *The State (Walsh) v Maguire*,[9] suggesting that there cannot be an arrest upon an arrest, has been expressly dissented from subsequently in *Kehoe*[10] and in *O'Shea.*[11] In *The State (Walsh) v Maguire*, Henchy J said: **3–05**

> "[a]s an arrest means a physical act done with a view to detention, and since the accused was already arrested and in detention, this cannot have been an arrest in law".[12]

In *The People v Kehoe*, McCarthy J commented on Henchy J's statement thus:

> "[T]he other members of the Court in that case, O'Higgins CJ and Griffin J, expressed no view on this aspect. This Court does not share the view expressed by Henchy J if it is to be construed as meaning that where a common law arrest has been made, for instance in the course of a patent breach of the peace, that a garda officer on then discovering grounds for arrest under s 30 with the consequent statutory time for detention, is not entitled to effect a further arrest without going through the colourable manoeuvre of an apparent release from custody. Some support for this view is to be found in the judgment of Davitt P in *In Re Ó Laighléis* [1960] IR 93 at p 108."

Further, an unlawfully arrested person does not acquire immunity from a later arrest. **3–06** In *The People (Director of Public Prosecutions) v Pringle*[13] the Court of Criminal Appeal stated:

> "It is well established that a detention which may initially have been illegal can, in certain circumstances, be legalised (*Re Ó Laighléis*[14]) and there are circumstances in which a valid arrest at law can be made immediately after the release of a person from a custody which had been, for one reason or another, illegal."[15]

Arrest after a successful *habeas corpus* application is considered further below at para 3–29 *et seq*.

RE-ARREST FOR CHARGE

Gardaí may re-arrest a person in order to charge him forthwith without any difficulty.[16] **3–07** This is specifically provided for in s 10(2) of the Criminal Justice Act 1984 when the re-arrest for charge follows a standard s 4 detention. In the drug trafficking context, s 4(5) of the Criminal Justice (Drug Trafficking) Act 1996 provides for re-arrest for charge while, under the Offences against the State Act 1939, re-arrest for charge is

[9] *The State (Walsh) v Maguire* [1979] IR 372.
[10] *The People v Kehoe* [1985] IR 444.
[11] *People (DPP) v O'Shea* [1996] IR 557.
[12] *The State (Walsh) v Maguire* [1979] IR 372 at 386.
[13] *The People (Director of Public Prosecutions) v Pringle* (1981) 2 Frewen 57.
[14] *Re Ó Laighléis* [1960] IR 93.
[15] *ibid.*
[16] Criminal Justice Act 1984, s 10(2).

provided for in s 30A(3).[17] The Criminal Justice Act 2007 provides for re-arrest for charge at s 51(5) where the initial detention is pursuant to s 50 of that Act.

Persons Arrested for Charge Should be Charged Without Delay

3–08 Where persons are being re-arrested to be charged, they must be charged immediately. This was emphasised in *Massoud v Watkins and the Director of Public Prosecutions*[18] where, due to a difficulty with the PULSE charging system, two hours and 17 minutes elapsed between the arrest and the charge. As the applicant was in custody for the purpose of being charged, his detention became unlawful when he was not immediately charged. He was held to have been in unlawful custody, in breach of his constitutional right to liberty pursuant to Article 40.4.1° of the Constitution. Gilligan J held:

> "… the crucial words are 'for the purpose of charging him with that offence forthwith' … I am satisfied that this specific statutory exception has to be construed strictly and be allowed to operate only so far as is necessary to serve its statutory purpose against a background where Article 40.4.1° of the Constitution enshrines the right to personal liberty and any provision whereby a person is held without charge in police custody obviously represents an inroad into this right. Accordingly it follows that, insofar as s 10 provides for a lawful inroad into the right to personal liberty, its terms have to be construed strictly".[19]

3–09 A slight delay seems be permissible where persons are to be re-arrested for charge under s 30 of the Offences against the State Act 1939 if the delay is incurred pending access to the Special Criminal Court. Whereas under s 10(2) of the Criminal Justice Act 1984 and s 4(5) of the Criminal Justice (Drug Trafficking) Act 1996, the person rearrested must be charged "forthwith," s 30A allows re-arrest "for the purpose of charging … forthwith or bringing [the defendant] before a Special Criminal Court as soon as practicable so that he or she may be charged with that offence before that Court".[20] Section 51(5) of the Criminal Justice Act 2007 repeats the earlier formulation of charging "forthwith."

No Requirement of Release Before Re-Arrest

3–10 Where re-arrest is permissible, there may be a break between the first and second arrest, as is often the case between an arrest for investigation and a subsequent arrest for charge. However, where the suspect is in custody and a second arrest is proposed following immediately from the first, there is no requirement that the suspect should be set free in a fictional sense for the brief intervening moments between the conclusion

---

[17] As inserted by s 11 of the Offences against the State (Amendment) Act 1998 and as amended by s 187 of the Criminal Justice Act 2006.

[18] *Massoud v Watkins and the Director of Public Prosecutions* [2005] 3 IR 154.

[19] *ibid.*

[20] Offences against the State Act 1939, s 30A(3), as amended by s 187 of the Criminal Justice Act 2006.

of the first period of detention and the second arrest. As Barron J stated in *Quinlivan v Governor of Portlaoise Prison:*

> "It is significant that the challenge against this procedure is that there was no release because the applicant was not brought to the public street before he was re-arrested. The law would surely be an ass if it denied the right of the gardaí to arrest a person on private property where the person arrested had no chance of escaping arrest, in favour of permitting his arrest on the public street where he would have had the same lack of chance of escaping. But the submissions on behalf of the applicant do not stop there. It is accepted that such irregularity would have been permissible if it was necessary to ensure the arrest of the applicant. But because the irregularity could have been avoided by bringing him to the public street in the circumstances indicated, the arrest was unlawful. I cannot accede to a submission based upon such a premise."[21]

The point was reiterated in *Massoud v Watkins and the Director of Public Prosecutions*.[22] There Gilligan J stated:

> "I do not consider that there is any reality to the submission that the applicant should have been brought out onto the public street outside Swords Garda station and ought to have been advised that he was in effect free to go prior to being re-arrested against the background where he had already been advised that he was going to be re-arrested for the purpose of being charged with the offence..."[23]

A pragmatic approach is taken therefore to the re-arrest for charge procedure.

RE-ARREST FOR INVESTIGATION

If the purpose of a second arrest is further investigation, gardaí are significantly circumscribed in the exercise of their discretion and may generally only re-arrest for further investigation under judicial supervision.[24] Unless powers to split detention, set out in the Criminal Justice Act 2011 are invoked,[25] once the permitted detention period has elapsed, re-arrest for the same offence is permissible only on the authority of a warrant. The rationale for strict control of powers of re-arrest is obvious: the prevention of abuse by An Garda Síochána through repetitive detention in pursuit of the same investigation.[26] Re-arrest must therefore ordinarily be subject to judicial supervision in the form of a warrant, and be justified in accordance with statutory requirements. Re-arrest for investigation is permitted under s 10(1) of the Criminal Justice Act 1984, s 4(1) of the Criminal Justice (Drug Trafficking) Act 1996, s 30A of the Offences against the State Act 1939 and s 51 of the Criminal Justice Act 2007. **3–11**

---

21 *Quinlivan v Governor of Portlaoise Prison* [1998] 1 IR 456 at pp 462 to 463.

22 *Massoud v Watkins and the Director of Public Prosecutions* [2005] 3 IR 154.

23 *ibid.*

24 The exception to the general rule is the provision in the Criminal Justice Act 2011 for punctuated breaks in the course of the detention period during which suspects may be rearrested for continuation of their detention period, Criminal Justice Act 2011, ss 7 and 8.

25 The provisions allow for suspension of detention periods to allow for further investigation in the intervening period.

26 *O'Brien v Special Criminal Court* [2008] 4 IR 514, *per* Fennelly J.

A novel power, which allows for suspension of detention for up to four months, and for re-arrest without judicial oversight during that suspension, was introduced by the Criminal Justice Act 2011.[27] This power is termed a power to arrest and return a person for the purpose of continuation of detention. However, any subsequent re-arrest after the initial punctuated detention period has elapsed will be subject to the provisions of s 10(1) of the Criminal Justice Act 1984.[28]

Re-Arrest under Section 10(1) of the Criminal Justice Act 1984

3–12 Section 10(1) of the Criminal Justice Act 1984[29] is the standard re-arrest provision where further investigation is contemplated. The section provides that a person who has been arrested and detained under s 4 of the Criminal Justice Act 1984 cannot be arrested again in connection with the offence to which the detention related, or be arrested for any other offence which, at the time of the first arrest, the arresting garda suspected (or ought reasonably to have suspected) him of having committed, unless under the authority of a warrant issued by a judge of the District Court. The warrant must be based on sworn information from a garda of Superintendent rank or above.[30]

Requirements for Re-Arrest under Section 10

3–13 A second arrest for further questioning under s 10 can only be considered on one of two grounds:

(i) further information has come to the knowledge of the Garda Síochána since the person's release as to his suspected participation in the offence for which his arrest is sought, or
(ii) although the Garda Síochána had knowledge, prior to the person's release, of the person's suspected participation in the offence for which his arrest is sought, the questioning of the person in relation to that offence before his release would not have been in the interests of the proper investigation of the offence.

The latter, rather broad, criterion is a recent addition, having been inserted by the Criminal Justice (Amendment) Act 2009.[31] Previously, re-arrest could only be justified on the emergence of new information tending to link the person whose arrest is sought to the offence, whereas the section as re-drafted also allows for gardaí to defer questioning for essentially tactical reasons if it is deemed that questioning the suspect before his release would not be in the interests of the proper investigation of the offence.

[27] Criminal Justice Act 2011, ss 7 and 8.
[28] As substituted by s 24(3) of the Criminal Justice (Amendment) Act 2009.
[29] As substituted by the Criminal Justice (Amendment) Act 2009, s 24(3).
[30] Applications under s 10 are made in Form 31.3, Schedule B, DCR 1997, Ord 31.
[31] Criminal Justice (Amendment) Act 2009, s 24(3).

"New Information Has Come to Light"

The gardaí will have to justify the deferral, and a perfunctory recitation of either ground will not suffice. In *Larkin v O'Dea*[32] the bald statement that "since the date of release, further evidence has come into our possession and further inquiries have been made to establish the author of the alleged crime" was found to be inadequate. It was on this sworn information that the arrest warrant was based, and it was noted in the High Court that the Superintendent had made no reference to the gardaí having established that it was the applicant who had committed the offence under investigation. It was held that the judge could not have been satisfied of the accused's suspected participation in the offence for which his arrest was sought. The warrant purporting to authorise the re-arrest of the accused was bad and consequently any evidence gathered in the course of the detention which followed the second arrest had to be excluded. The order of the High Court was upheld by the Supreme Court. Though the principle was espoused in the context of a s 10 re-arrest, it would appear to have equal application where warrants are sought for second arrests under the Criminal Justice (Drug Trafficking) Act 1996 and the Offences against the State Act 1939,[33] and arguably in the context of the new ground set out in the Criminal Justice Act 2011, which allows for questioning to be deferred for operational reasons, so that further enquiries can be conducted. That 'further enquiries' were necessary may be an insufficient explanation; the specific rationale will have to be given and justified. **3–14**

Once arrested under a s 10 warrant, the arrestee will be dealt with in the ordinary way, in accordance with s 4 of the Criminal Justice Act 1984.

Section 10 Re-Arrest Warrant Applications Heard 'In Camera'

Applications for s 10 re-arrest warrants are be heard otherwise than in public[34] so as not to prejudice investigations by the disclosure of sensitive information.[35] Article 34 of the Constitution provides that "Justice shall be administered in courts established by law… and, save in such special and limited circumstances as may be prescribed by law, shall be administered in public."[36] 'Prescribed by law' in this context means by an Act of the Oireachtas and not by a lesser form of law, such as a regulation. Provision was made in the Criminal Justice (Amendment) Act 2009 for the exclusion of the public from hearings in re-arrest warrant applications.[37] Similar amendments were made in respect of search warrant applications. **3–15**

---

32 *Larkin v O'Dea* [1995] 2 IR 485.

33 *ibid* at 499-500.

34 Criminal Justice Act 1984, s 10(1A) as inserted by Criminal Justice (Amendment) Act 2009, s 24(3).

35 687 *Dáil Debates* Col 181 – 182, 3 July 2009.

36 In the context of s 10 of the Criminal Justice Act 1984, as well as s 4 of the Criminal Justice (Drug Trafficking) Act 1996, s 30A of the Offences against the State Act 1939 and s 51 of the Criminal Justice Act 2007. These provisions were set out in Part 4 of the Criminal Justice (Amendment) Act 2009 at ss 21-24.

37 Finlay CJ commented in *Irish Press v Ingersoll Publications Ltd* [1994] IR 176 at 191 that "[t]he prescription of law provided for in this constitutional provision is, of course, by enactment of the Oireachtas" [1994] IR 176 at 191.

Detention under Section 4 Not Permissible after Section 30 Arrest and Detention

3–16 Following release from arrest and custody under s 30 of the Offences against the State Act 1939, a person may not be detained under s 4 of the Criminal Justice Act 1984 for the same offence or an offence of which he was initially suspected or ought to have been suspected when arrested under s 30.[38] The provision prohibiting re-arrest, s 10(3) of the Criminal Justice Act 1984, was considered in *DPP v McKeever,*[39] where it was held that the effect of the section is that the gardaí are not entitled to re-arrest a person who has been already arrested under s 30 for any purpose other than to have him charged and brought before a court as soon as is practicable. In *McKeever*, this was what had transpired and there was, accordingly, no abuse of process.

There is nothing in s 10 to prevent an arrest under s 30 following a release from detention under s 4 of the 1984 Act, but it is arguable that the courts would not allow a re-arrest for the same offence in those circumstances if no further information linking the suspect with the offence has come to light.[40]

Re-Arrest under Section 30A of the Offences against the State Act 1939

Requirements for Re-Arrest and Detention under the Offences Against the State Act 1939

3–17 Re-arrest after an initial detention under s 30 of the Offences against the State Act 1939 is governed by s 30A of the 1939 Act.[41] Section 30A(1)[42] provides that, where a person arrested and detained under s 30 has been released without charge, he cannot be re-arrested for the same offence (or for an offence which the arresting garda ought reasonably to have suspected him of at the time of the first arrest) unless a warrant has been obtained from the District Court. The Court must be satisfied, having heard evidence on oath from a garda not below the rank of Superintendent, that either:

(i) further information has come to the knowledge of the gardaí since the person's release about his suspected participation in the offence for which his arrest is sought; or
(ii) notwithstanding that the gardaí had knowledge prior to the person's release of his suspected participation in the offence for which his arrest is sought, the questioning of the person in relation to that offence, prior to his release, would not have been in the interests of the proper investigation of the offence.[43]

---

[38] Criminal Justice Act 1984, s 10(3).

[39] *DPP v McKeever* [1994] ILRM 186.

[40] See K Boyle, Criminal Justice Act 1984, Irish Current Law Statutes Annotated and *State (Hoey) v Garda Commissioner* [1978] IR 1.

[41] Offences against the State Act 1939, s 30A, as inserted by s 11 of the Offences against the State (Amendment) Act 1998.

[42] Offences against the State Act 1939, s 30A(1), as substituted by s 21(2) of the Criminal Justice (Amendment) Act 2009.

[43] Offences against the State Act 1939, s 30A, as inserted by s 11 of the Offences against the State (Amendment) Act 1998.

Section 30A Re-arrest Warrant Applications Heard 'In Camera'

As with re-arrest under s 10 of the Criminal Justice Act 1984, the warrant application must be heard *in camera.*[44] **3–18**

A person re-arrested under s 30A will be detained and dealt with thereafter in accordance with the provisions of s 30.[45]

Questioning for Offences Other Than Those for Which the Suspect Was Originally Arrested

During a detention under s 30, the detention may be amended to allow questions to be put to a suspect concerning another scheduled offence other than that for which he was originally arrested.[46] The member seeking to alter the detention must have reasonable cause to suspect that the suspect has committed a separate offence under the Offences against the State Act 1939 or an offence which is scheduled under Part V of the Act (or a related offence), so the detention cannot be altered to allow for questioning for an 'ordinary' offence.[47] Where gardaí have information at the time of the s 30 detention concerning an 'ordinary' (that is to say a non-scheduled) offence, a warrant should be sought under s 30A for a re-arrest if necessary. If, for instance, a suspect is detained under s 30 for a scheduled offence and another garda wishes to question him about an unrelated assault offence, since s 30(3A) precludes altering a detention to question for a non-scheduled offence, and s 30A(1) prohibits the arrest without warrant of a person for an offence of which, at the time of arrest, the gardaí suspected or ought to have suspected him, the person should be released (if not charged) at the conclusion of the s 30 detention period. A warrant should be sought for the arrest of the person in order to ask him questions about the assault. A warrant in such circumstances would be justifiable on the basis of earlier questioning not having been 'in the proper interests of the investigation of the offence',[48] in that it was impermissible under the terms of s 30(3A). **3–19**

---

[44] Offences against the State Act 1939, s 30A(1A), as inserted by s 21(2) of the Criminal Justice (Amendment) Act 2009.

[45] Offences against the State Act 1939, s 30A(2), as amended by s 187 of the Criminal Justice Act 2006

[46] Offences against the State Act 1939, s 30(3A) as inserted by s 21(1)(a) of the Criminal Justice (Amendment) Act 2009.

[47] s 30(3A) of the Offences against the State Act 1939, as inserted by s 21(1)(a) of the Criminal Justice (Amendment) Act 2009, outlines that a detention may be continued in relation to an offence other than the offence to which the detention relates where the person is, with reasonable cause, suspected "of having committed an offence (the 'other offence') referred to in subsection 1 of this section, being an offence other than the offence to which the detention relates".

[48] Offences against the State Act 1939, s 30(3A)(1)(b)(ii) as inserted by s 21(1)(a) of the Criminal Justice (Amendment) Act 2009.

Where a person has his detention period altered under s 30(3A) to put further questions relating to separate scheduled offences to him, he may not be detained for any longer than the period authorised initially.[49]

Re-Arrest under Section 4(1) of the Criminal Justice (Drug Trafficking) Act 1996

3–20 Section 4 of the Criminal Justice (Drug Trafficking) Act 1996 provides for re-arrest in the context of drug trafficking investigations.[50] It applies only where the initial detention was authorise by the Criminal Justice (Drug Trafficking) Act 1996. Where a person who has been arrested under s 30 of the Act of 1939 or detained under s 4 of the Act of 1984 in connection with an offence is released without any charge against him or her, the extensive detention periods contained in s 2 of the 1996 Act do not give gardaí further opportunity to re-arrest for investigation. Accordingly, re-arrest under s 4 of the 1996 Act is not possible where the initial detention was under either the Act of 1939 or 1984.[51]

Requirements for Re-Arrest and Detention under the Criminal Justice (Drug Trafficking) Act 1996

3–21 The requirements for re-arrest and detention after an earlier detention under the Criminal Justice (Drug Trafficking) Act 1996 are contained in s 4 of the 1996 Act and mirror the provisions of s 10(1) of the Criminal Justice Act 1984, though a distinction in the 1996 Act is that the warrant may be issued by a judge of either the Circuit Court or District Court. As with the other re-arrest provisions, the issuing judge must be satisfied, on information supplied on oath by a garda not below the rank of Superintendent, that either:

(i) further information has come to the knowledge of the Garda Síochána since the person's release as to his or her suspected participation in the offence for which his or her arrest is sought; or
(ii) although the gardaí had knowledge of the person's suspected participation in the offence for which his or her arrest is sought, questioning the person in relation to that offence before release would not have been in the interests of the proper investigation of the offence.[52]

Judicial Oversight

3–22 Subsection (2) provides for greater judicial oversight than in the general re-arrest provision under s 10(1) of the 1984 Act, by providing that, when issuing the warrant, the judge may order that the person must be brought before a judge of the Circuit or District Court on arrest or at any stage during the detention that the judge may specify. If the judge is not

[49] Offences against the State Act 1939, s 30(3A) as inserted by s 21(1)(a) of the Criminal Justice (Amendment) Act 2009.
[50] Criminal Justice (Drug Trafficking) Act 1996, s 4(1), as inserted by s 22(2) of the Criminal Justice (Amendment) Act 2009.
[51] Criminal Justice (Drug Trafficking) Act 1996, s 4(6).
[52] *ibid*, s 4(1).

satisfied that person's detention is justified, the judge shall revoke the warrant and order the person's immediate release from custody.

Section 4 Re-Arrest Warrant Applications Heard in Camera

Like applications under s 10(1) of the 1984 Act, applications for re-arrest warrants under s 4(1) of the Criminal Justice (Drug Trafficking) Act 1996 are heard otherwise than in public.[53]

Detention Provisions

A person who has been re-arrested under a warrant issued in accordance with s 4(1) may be taken to and detained in a Garda station pursuant to s 2(2) of the Criminal Justice (Drug Trafficking) Act 1996.[54] Section 3 provides that persons re-arrested under the Criminal Justice (Drug Trafficking) Act 1996 are detained in accordance with s 2 of that Act with the following and any other necessary modifications: **3–23**

> "(a) Where a member of the Garda Síochána arrests a person (an "arrested person") under a warrant issued pursuant to s 4(1), the arrested person may be taken to and detained in a Garda station for a period or periods authorised by subsection (2) if the member in charge of the station to which the person is taken on arrest has at the time of the arrested person's arrival at the station reasonable grounds for believing that his or her detention is necessary for the proper investigation of the offence.[55]
>
> (b) An officer of the Garda Síochána not below the rank of chief superintendent may apply to a judge of the Circuit Court or a judge of the District Court for a warrant authorising the detention of a person detained under paragraph (b) for a further period not exceeding 24 hours if he or she has reasonable grounds for believing that such further detention is necessary for the proper investigation of the offence concerned.
>
> (c) On an application under paragraph (c) the judge concerned shall issue a warrant authorising the detention of the person to whom the application relates for a further period not exceeding 24 hours if, but only if, the judge is satisfied that such further detention is necessary for the proper investigation of the offence concerned and that the investigation is being conducted diligently and expeditiously."

Sunset Clause

Incidentally, there had originally been a 'sunset clause' in s 11 of the Criminal Justice (Drug Trafficking) Act 1996, providing for the cessation of the operation of the main provisions of the Act, pertaining *inter alia* to extensive detention periods and re-arrest. Section 11 has now been repealed and, accordingly, the sections to which it related, ie ss 2, 3, 4, 5, and 6, will continue in operation indefinitely.[56] **3–24**

---

53 Criminal Justice (Drug Trafficking) Act 1996, s 4(1A) as inserted by s 22(2) of the Criminal Justice (Amendment) Act 2009.

54 Criminal Justice (Drug Trafficking) Act 1996, s 4(3)(a), as inserted by s 10(b) of the Criminal Justice Act 2006.

55 Criminal Justice (Drug Trafficking) Act 1996, s 4(3)(a) was inserted (with paragraphs (a) and (b) renumbered as (b) and (c)) by the Criminal Justice Act 2006, s 10(b).

56 Criminal Justice (Amendment) Act 2009, s 22(4).

Re-Arrest for Continuation of Detention—The Criminal Justice Act 2011

3–25 Enacted with white collar crime and complex fraud investigations at the forefront of the legislature's mind, the Criminal Justice Act 2011 introduced a novel power to split detention periods, and thereby to effectively suspend questioning for up to four months.[57] Gardaí are permitted to suspend questioning and recall a person who is being investigated for a 'relevant offence'[58] where there are reasonable grounds for believing that the suspension is necessary to permit further enquiries to be made for the further and

[57] Criminal Justice Act 2011, s 7, which inserts subsection s (3A) – (3F) into s 4 of the Criminal Justice Act 1984. The four-month limitation period, which applies to the total period for which a person's detention may be suspended, is contained in s 4(3B)(b).

[58] Relevant offences are set out in the Criminal Justice Act 2011, Schedule 1 as follows: 1. An offence under s 58 of the Central Bank Act 1971 insofar as it relates to a contravention of s 17, 18, 23, 24 or 25 of that Act; 2. An offence under s 37 (6) or 41 (1) of the Insurance Act 1989; 3. An offence under s 20 (4) or 24 (4) of the Trustee Savings Banks Act 1989; 4. An offence under s 11 (3) or 13 (5) of the Unit Trusts Act 1990; 5. An offence under s 25 (5) or 27 (4), or subsection (7) or (8) of s 35, of the Investment Limited Partnerships Act 1994; 6. An offence under s 10 (16), 19 (1)(b), 30, 34, 35 (4), 46 (2), 54 (6), 56 (9), subsection (3), (5), (6) or (9) of s 52 or subsection (7) or (8) of s 79, of the Investment Intermediaries Act 1995; 7. An offence under s 12 (2) of the Consumer Credit Act 1995 insofar as it relates to a contravention of subsection (1) or (3) of s 97, or s 101, 102 or 127, of that Act; 8. An offence under s 29 (3), or subsection (7) or (8) of s 43 of the Investor Compensation Act 1998; 9. An offence under s 14 (3) or 15 (2) of the Investment Funds, Companies and Miscellaneous Provisions Act 2005; 10. An offence under s 5 (2) of the Markets in Financial Instruments and Miscellaneous Provisions Act 2007 insofar as it relates to— (a) a failure to discharge a duty to which a person is subject under Regulation 40(1) or 112(1) of the European Communities (Markets in Financial Instruments) Regulations 2007 (SI No 60 of 2007), or (b) a contravention of Regulation 19, 52, 159 or 187B of those Regulations; 11. An offence under Regulation 20(2), 22(4), 58(9), 59(8), 60(6), 62(4) or 76(1) of the European Communities (Reinsurance) Regulations 2006 (SI No 380 of 2006); 12. An offence under s 7 of the National Asset Management Agency Act 2009 insofar as it relates to a person other than a credit institution (within the meaning of that Act); 13. An offence under s 48 of the Central Bank Reform Act 2010; 14. An offence under s 60 (15), 295 or 297, or under paragraph (a), (d), (e), (f), (g), (i), (j), (k), (l), (m), (n), (o) or (p) of s 293 (1), of the Companies Act 1963; 15. An offence under any of the following provisions of the Companies (Amendment) Act 1986: (a) s 22(1)(a) (insofar as it relates to a failure to comply with s 5 or 16 of that Act), (b) s 22(2) (insofar as it relates to a failure to take all reasonable steps to secure compliance with the requirements of s 3 of that Act or a failure to comply with s 13 of that Act), or (c) s 22(3); 16. An offence under s 197, 202 (10), 242 or 243 (1) of the Companies Act 1990; 17. An offence under s 37 (1) of the Companies (Amendment) (No 2) Act 1999; 18. An offence under s 48 of the Investment Funds, Companies and Miscellaneous Provisions Act 2005; 19. An offence under Regulation 5 or 6 of the Market Abuse (Directive 2003/6/EC) Regulations 2005 (SI No 342 of 2005); 20. An offence under Regulation 76(4) of the Transparency (Directive 2004/109/EC) Regulations 2007 (SI No 277 of 2007); 21. An offence under s 7, 8, 9, 10, 35, 37, 38, 42 or 49 of the Criminal Justice (Money Laundering and Terrorist Financing) Act 2010; 22. An offence under s 13 of the Criminal Justice (Terrorist Offences) Act 2005; 23. An offence under s 4, 6, 7, 9, 10, 11, 15, 17, 18, 25, 26, 27, 28, 29, 33, 34, 35, 36, 37, 38, 42, 43, 44, 45 or 51 of the Criminal Justice (Theft and Fraud Offences) Act 2001; 24. Conspiracy to defraud at common law; 25. An offence under s 119 of the Registration of Title Act 1964; 26. An offence under s 17; 27. An offence under s 1 of the Prevention of Corruption Act 1906; 28. An offence under s 7 or 8 of the Prevention of Corruption (Amendment) Act 2001; 29. An offence under s 65 of the Consumer Protection Act 2007; 30. An offence under s 2, 3 or 4 of the Criminal Damage Act 1991 insofar as the offence relates to data (within the meaning of s 1 of that Act) or a storage medium in which such data are kept.

proper investigation of the offence for which he or she is detained.[59] On suspension, the suspect should be released forthwith unless his detention is separately authorised (such as by a term of imprisonment),[60] and a suspension may occur no more than twice.[61] The member in charge must give, or arrange for the person to be given, a notice in writing

(i) that his or her detention is being suspended,
(ii) of the Garda Síochána station and of the date and time on which he or she is required to return to such station for the continuation of the detention concerned, and
(iii) of the consequences of failure to return, ie that he or she may be arrested without warrant and returned to the station for continuation of the detention and that failure to return constitutes an offence punishable on summary conviction to a class A fine or to imprisonment for up to 12 months or to both.[62]

The re-arrest provision (s 4A) is inserted into s 4 of the Criminal Justice Act 1984 by s 8 of the Criminal Justice Act 2011 and, though it is effectively a re-arrest for the same offence, it does not require a warrant and operates notwithstanding s 10 of the 1984 Act. The power requires a garda to have a reasonable suspicion that a person has failed to return for the continuation of his suspended detention. Once arrested, the person must be returned to the Garda station as soon as practicable,[63] and the period between the arrest and arrival at the Garda station is excluded from calculation of the permitted detention period under s 4.[64] **3–26**

Split Detention Periods—The Experience in England and Wales

The practice of splitting detention periods in the manner set out in s 7 of the Criminal Justice Act 2011 has proved controversial in England and Wales, following the case of *R (on the application of Chief Constable of Greater Manchester Police) v Salford Magistrates' Court and Paul Hookway.*[65] A magistrate had ruled that the detention clock did not stop running when a suspect was bailed, and that ruling was upheld by the High Court. Prior to the ruling it had been common practice in England and Wales to split a suspect's detention period for weeks and even months, for which period the suspect was released on bail and could be called back so that new evidence could be gathered and put to the suspect. Under the Police and Criminal Evidence Act 1984 (PACE), detention is permitted for a maximum of 96 hours and the police had operated on the basis that only the time spent in police detention was calculable in determining the 96-hour limit and that the 'detention clock' was paused when an individual was released on police bail. Lord McCombie observed: **3–27**

> "There can be no doubt that police practice in this case has been conducted on the basis that, while any authorised period of detention remains unexpired, the suspect may be released on bail and that his detention can be reauthorised so that he can be reinterviewed at any time

---

59 Criminal Justice Act 1984, s 4(3A)(a) as inserted by s 7 of the Criminal Justice Act 2011.
60 *ibid,* s 4(3A)(b) as inserted by s 7 of the Criminal Justice Act 2011.
61 *ibid,* s 4(3B) as inserted by s 7 of the Criminal Justice Act 2011.
62 *ibid,* s 4(3C) as inserted by s 7 of the Criminal Justice Act 2011.
63 *ibid,* s 4A(2) as inserted by s 8 of the Criminal Justice Act 2011.
64 *ibid,* s 4A(3) as inserted by s 8 of the Criminal Justice Act 2011.
65 *R (on the application of Chief Constable of Greater Manchester Police) v Salford Magistrates' Court and Paul Hookway* [2011] EWHC 1578 (Admin).

> during the theoretically 'unused' period of authorised detention. Indeed in the case of serious offences where extensive investigations have to be conducted, as in this case, it is common for there to be a series of bail dates leading up to a final charging decision with or without further interview. However, on reflection it seems to me that in many such cases a suspect is bailed and only re-interviewed on a re-arrest when new evidence has come to light…"[66]

3–28 The case was appealed to the Supreme Court but withdrawn when a fast-track piece of legislation was enacted to restore the position as it had been understood prior to the case. The Act, the Police (Detention and Bail) Act 2011, received royal assent on 12 July 2011 and, interestingly, operates retrospectively. Unlike the Irish legislation, there are no limitation periods, either in terms of the time for which questioning is suspended or on the number of times a person may be recalled to the police station, once the 96-hour detention limit is not exceeded in the station.

RE-ARREST FOLLOWING SUCCESSFUL ARTICLE 40 (HABEAS CORPUS) APPLICATIONS

3–29 The law relating to re-arrest following Article 40 (*habeas corpus*) proceedings is beset with contradictory judicial *dicta*. It therefore lacks the clarity that ought to hallmark an important practical question—whether and in what circumstances a defect in the detention of suspects precludes their re-arrest.

Article 40.4.2° of the Constitution provides that

> "Upon complaint being made by or on behalf of any person to the High Court or any judge thereof alleging that such person is being unlawfully detained, the High Court and any and every judge thereof to whom such complaint is made shall forthwith enquire into the said complaint and may order the person in whose custody such person is detained to produce the body of such person before the High Court on a named day and to certify in writing the grounds of his detention, and the High Court shall, upon the body of such person being produced before that Court and after giving the person in whose custody he is detained an opportunity of justifying the detention, order the release of such person from such detention unless satisfied that he is being detained in accordance with the law."

3–30 As Hogan and Whyte put it: "Article 40.4.2° is thus the mechanism whereby the legality of a detention is most frequently challenged, and a flaw or irregularity in a detention established, with the consequent setting at liberty of the person proved to be in wrongful detention."[67] The only remedy available to litigants on a successful Article 40 enquiry is release and, when released, they are released unconditionally. The question of whether re-arrest is permissible is one which frequently arises.

3–31 The Supreme Court case of *The State (McDonagh) v Frawley*[68] is the source of much of the confusion surrounding re-arrest following an Article 40 enquiry:

---

66 *ibid*, at paras 18-19.

67 Hogan and Whyte, *JM Kelly: The Irish Constitution* (4th ed, LexisNexis Butterworths, Dublin, 2003) at p 1678.

68 *The State (McDonagh) v Frawley* [1978] IR 131.

> "... in cases where it has not been shown to the satisfaction of the court that the detention is 'in accordance with the law' in the sense indicated, the release of the detained person must be ordered and, notwithstanding judicial dicta to the contrary, the order of release *may not be coupled with an order of rearrest.* The protection of personal liberty, which Article 40, s4, is intended to ensure, would be hollow and ineffectual if the order of release was not unqualified and unconditional".[69]

The Habeas Corpus (Ireland) Act 1782 provides at s 5 that:

> "...for the prevention of unjust vexation by reiterated commitments for the same offence; ... no person... who shall be delivered or set at large upon any *habeas corpus*, shall at any time hereafter be again imprisoned, or committed for the same offence by any person or persons whatsoever, other than by the legal order or process of such court wherein he or they shall be bound by recognizance to appear, or other court having jurisdiction of the cause..."

Confusion arises because, notwithstanding the apparent impermissibility of re-arrest after release on *habeas corpus*, the prohibition is not absolute – there have been numerous examples of court sanctioned re-arrest after successful *habeas corpus* proceedings.[70] In *State (McFadden) v Governor of Mountjoy Prison (No 2)*,[71] s 5 of the Habeas Corpus (Ireland) Act 1781 was interpreted by the High Court as not precluding a re-arrest of persons in respect of the charges pending against them. Its apparent purpose was to prevent the re-committal to prison of persons awaiting trial on criminal charges who have applied to the High Court by way of *habeas corpus* and obtained bail. **3–32**

> "The prosecutor's second submission is, in my view, based upon a misinterpretation of the passage quoted from the judgment of the present Chief Justice in the case of *The State (McDonagh) v Frawley* [1978] IR 131. The learned Chief Justice does not say, in the passage quoted, that a person released on *habeas corpus* can never again be re-arrested on foot of the same charge. What he says, in my view, is that a final order of *habeas corpus*, if made at all, must be in absolute and unconditional terms and cannot be coupled with an order for the re-arrest of the prosecutor. In my view the passage quoted has no application to the circumstances of the present case."[72]

In *Hegarty v The Governor of Limerick Prison*,[73] the High Court considered the legality of a re-arrest following Article 40 proceedings. The applicant's release was occasioned when an oversight by the Department of Justice came to light, whereby a judge sitting on the Special Criminal Court had been removed from the Court without his knowledge or that of the registrar of the Court, with the result that the Court was not properly constituted and the warrant of committal that had been made in respect of the applicant was invalid. The Director of Public Prosecutions advised **3–33**

---

69 *ibid,* at 137. Emphasis added.

70 See *Hand v Governor of Mountjoy Prison (ex tempore)*, *Irish Times Law Reports*, 29 May 1989, where Lynch J "strongly emphasised his view that there was nothing to prevent the applicant from being immediately re-arrested under common law and re-charged at the conclusion of the hearing, having regard to s 10(2) of the 1984 Act".

71 *State (McFadden) v Governor of Mountjoy Prison (No 2)*[1981] ILRM 120.

72 *ibid.*

73 *Hegarty v The Governor of Limerick Prison* [1998] 1 IR 412.

the gardaí immediately to re-arrest the applicant in the event of a successful Article 40 application, and when he was released, the gardaí duly did. The applicant argued that the re-arrest was unlawful, that there were already lawful charges before the Special Criminal Court so it was an abuse of the process of that Court to re-arrest the applicant for the purpose of bringing him before the court on what were repeat charges. The Court held:

> "while there does not appear to be any direct authority on the point, it may well be that in some circumstances a re-arrest for the same charges would be an abuse of the process of the court. But the question is, was it an abuse in this case. I think not ...where a person is alleged to have committed an offence, there is nothing inherently unlawful about an officer of the Garda or indeed any other person exercising a lawful power of arrest for the purposes of having that person charged with that offence. If, however, the person is already charged with the offence before a lawful court there may be circumstances where it would be an abuse of the process of that court to effect a re-arrest. But as to whether this is so or not will depend upon intention and purpose. In this case, through no fault of the Director of Public Prosecutions, an unlawfully constituted Special Criminal Court purported to remand in custody a person being lawfully and properly prosecuted before that Court and having been originally lawfully arrested and charged and brought before that Court. Because of the unlawfully constituted Court the purported committal warrant or remand order was itself invalid and inoperative with the result that the applicant was not in lawful custody. As he was not in lawful custody, the applicant was entitled to have the unlawful custody terminated. But this could not give him an immunity from prosecution for the offences which he was alleged to have committed and for which he had been charged. The Director had a public duty and indeed a constitutional duty to proceed with the prosecutions. He therefore had to consider how best this could be done effectively. A factor that the Director was entitled to take into account was the problem of ensuring that the released men could be brought back before the Court. A person in the position of the applicant whose trial was pending in the Special Criminal Court for explosives charges would never in any circumstances be unconditionally released by that Court. He would either be remanded in custody or remanded on bail. The applicant was somebody who up to the time of the impugned order had in fact been remanded by the Special Criminal Court in custody. In these circumstances the Director, in my view, was entitled to recommence the process by arranging that the applicant, once he had been released, would be re-arrested and brought before a properly constituted Special Criminal Court and there charged with the same charges. Such a course of action would wholly regularise the position and at the same time vindicate the applicant's constitutional rights. A properly constituted Special Criminal Court would then determine whether the applicant should remain in custody or should be allowed bail if he applied for it pending the hearing of the new charges which were in effect repeat charges. It is difficult to see how that procedure, given the particular circumstances in which it was invoked, could possibly be viewed as an abuse of the process of the court. On the contrary it was a procedure which had the effect of regularising again the due process of criminal trial before that Court."

3–34 The issue was revisited, considered but not resolved, in the case of *Dunne v Governor of Cloverhill Prison,*[74] a *habeas corpus* application which arose because the applicant had been re-arrested and charged for the second time in relation to the same offence immediately after his release on an earlier successful *habeas corpus* application. He had

[74] *Dunne v Governor of Cloverhill Prison* [2008] IEHC 21 (Peart J, 15 January 2008).

argued that his detention was unlawful in the absence of evidence as to the reasons for delay in preparing a book of evidence within the 42-day period provided for in the Criminal Procedure Act 1967.[75] The second arrest and charge was the subject of a second application under Article 40.4.2°, in which Peart J found that the re-arrest of a suspect who had been previously released was not permissible. He held:

> "While I can readily understand and appreciate the desire and anxiety on the part of the prosecution to achieve the continued detention of the applicant on foot of what is clearly a very serious charge … the fact is that an order of the High Court for the applicant's release from unlawful detention was made, and that his re-arrest on 11 January 2008 in the manner in which it happened has produced a situation in which the purpose of the order of release was frustrated and set at nought, and in my view, is impermissible … a properly constituted District Court remanded the applicant in custody to 17 January 2008 pending service of a book of evidence, and that detention has been found to be unlawful by the High Court. In such circumstances the re-arrest must be seen as a device to continue the detention which had been declared unlawful."

3–35 Two separate appeals to the Supreme Court resulted, one in relation to the requirement that evidence be given before the granting an extension of time for service of the book of evidence, and another in relation to re-arrest after a successful *habeas corpus* application. The first Supreme Court appeal clarified that there is no requirement that evidence be given as to the reasons for an extension of time while the book of evidence is prepared.[76] The second appeal was found to be a moot, and the Court declined to expend "scarce judicial resources … to advance an academic analysis".[77] This is unfortunate, as the matter would have benefited from definitive clarification.

3–36 A number of commentators have opined that one of the principles governing an order for release after a successful *habeas corpus* application is that re-arrest is permissible provided the defect grounding the original complaint is not perpetuated.[78] The issue is discussed, though not formally ruled on, in the cases of *In re Paul Singer (No 2)*[79] and *The State (Gary McFadden) v The Governor of Mountjoy Prison (No 2)*.[80] Both cases seem to approve *dicta* in support of this principle from the English case of *Attorney General for Hong Kong v Kwok-a-Sing*.[81] In *Singer* Walsh J stated

> "The prosecutor next relies upon s 5 of the Irish Habeas Corpus Act (21 and 22 George III chapter II). In effect the prosecutor submits that because of the order for his release made by the Supreme Court he could not again be either arrested or detained in custody in respect of the charges upon which he was being detained at the time of his release.

---

75 *ibid.* The decision was appealed to the Supreme Court, see [2009] IESC 11 (Kearns J, 18 February 2009). Note that Peart J's judgment in *Dunne (No 2)* was delivered prior to Edwards J delivering the written judgment in the first case, so the second case is not actually called *Dunne (No 2)*.

76 *Dunne v The Governor of Cloverhill Prison* [2009] IESC 11 (Kearns J).

77 *Dunne v The Governor of Cloverhill Prison* [2009] IESC 43 (Denham J).

78 See Costello, *The Law of Habeas Corpus in Ireland* (Four Courts Press, Dublin, 2006), p 162 and Hogan and Whyte, *JM Kelly: The Irish Constitution*, p 1706.

79 *In Re Paul Singer (No 2)* (1964) 98 ILTR 112.

80 *The State (Gary McFadden) v The Governor of Mountjoy Prison (No 2)* [1981] ILRM 120.

81 *Attorney General for Hong Kong v Kwok-a-Sing* (1873) 3 LR5 PC 179.

> Such a claim, which does not take into account the reasons for the order for his release, really amounts to a claim that once a person has been released on *habeas corpus* no matter what the reason, he can never again be apprehended or detained in custody in respect of the charges which were pending against him at the time of his release. Such a proposition, if it were correct, would lead to absurd results."[82]

3–37 A key distinction is that, in *Singer* a warrant had been obtained for the suspect's second arrest, whereas in *Dunne* it would appear that the second arrest took place without warrant on the directions of the Director of Public Prosecutions.[83] Given that, in all other circumstances, a second arrest for the same offence is permissible only on the authority of a warrant, it would stand to reason that a warrant for re-arrest should be obtained where re-arrest is contemplated after a successful *habeas corpus* application also. The difficulty is that re-arrest is not statutorily provided for post-*habeas corpus*. Arguably what is proposed is a second arrest under s 10 of the Criminal Justice Act 1984, so an application should be made for a warrant in the same way, the hurdle being the requirement that new information must have come to light relating to the suspect's alleged commission of the offence. It may be that the solution ultimately arrived at in *Dunne* is the preferred course of action after a successful Article 40 enquiry: to allow the original charge to stand and to release the suspect on bail.

RE-ARREST AFTER ACQUITTAL – THE CRIMINAL PROCEDURE ACT 2010

3–38 The Criminal Procedure Act 2010 provides for a remarkable departure from the traditional prohibition of double jeopardy. Retrials are now permissible where the defendant has been acquitted but where the acquittal can be shown to have been undeserved due to the emergence of new and compelling evidence; if it can be shown that there was interference with the trial process that affected the verdict; or where the judge erred in law by, for example, excluding certain evidence. The Act permits the Director of Public Prosecutions to apply to the Court of Criminal Appeal for a re-trial following an acquittal of a number of specified offences where new and compelling evidence has emerged and where it would be in the public interest to do so. In addition, the Director may apply to the Supreme Court on a point of law on a "with prejudice" basis against an acquittal by the trial court or a decision of the Court of Criminal Appeal not to order a re-trial.[84] As such, a re-arrest power is necessary, and is provided in s 16 of the Criminal Procedure Act. Section 16 provides that a person who has been acquitted may be re-arrested on the warrant of a judge of the District Court who is satisfied by sworn information of a garda of Superintendent rank that new information has come to the

---

[82] (1964) 98 ILTR, *per* Walsh J.

[83] *Dunne v Governor of Cloverhill Prison* [2008] IEHC 21 (15 January 2008) Peart J said: "Det Sgt Kelly has clearly stated in evidence that prior to the order for release being granted, a decision had already been taken by the DPP and communicated to him that the applicant should, if ordered to be released, be re-arrested and brought back before the District Court and charged again with the same offence".

[84] Such appeals are 'with prejudice' in that there is a possibility that the appeal will result in an acquittal by a trial court or a decision of the Court of Criminal Appeal not to order a re-trial being overturned.

knowledge of the Garda Síochána since the person's acquittal of the offence, and the information is likely to reveal or confirm the existence of new and compelling evidence in relation to the person's suspected participation in the offence for which his arrest is sought. A re-arrest may be authorised only in respect of the offence in respect of which the person was acquitted. Thereafter the person will be detained in the ordinary way in accordance with s 4 of the Act of 1984, save that subsections 5 and 5A do not apply. (The detention provisions provided by other legislation, such as the Criminal Justice (Drug Trafficking) Act 1996 and the Criminal Justice Act 2007, appear not to have been contemplated).

Chapter 4

The Use of Force

INTRODUCTION

This chapter examines the law concerning the use of force by gardaí in Ireland and the available guidance which governs it.[1] **4–01**

The use of force is a key issue in policing. Gardaí are delineated from ordinary members of the community by the powers vested in them, many of which involve, or potentially involve, the use of force. Effective policing relies on, and requires the assent of, the community to the use of force by gardaí in a wide variety of situations where no other intervention will suffice However, the legitimacy of the use of force is of importance far beyond the immediate policing situation, since the exercise of restraint by (and oversight of) the police is a central tenet of a liberal democratic State. A liberal democracy derives its legitimacy in the imposition of sovereign authority when the police are credible in subduing resistance to their lawful authority, without abusing that authority.[2] Waddington and Wright have commented that: **4–02**

---

[1] Walsh has commented: "There is substantial room for improvement in the definition of the Garda power to use force, especially lethal or potentially lethal force. Not only is the power to use force not the subject of a detailed and comprehensive statutory code, but the law as currently framed suffers from an unacceptable degree of uncertainty. What, for example, is meant by the use of force in the prevention of crime? Gardaí and citizens are entitled to specific and detailed guidance on when the former can use force against the latter." D Walsh, *Human Rights and Policing in Ireland: Law, Policy and Practice* (Clarus Press, Dublin, 2009), p 255.

[2] See PAJ Waddington and M Wright "Police use of force, firearms and riot-control" in Newburn (ed.), *Handbook of Policing,* (2nd ed, Willan Publishing, Cullompton, 2008) at p 487.

> "As custodians of the state's sovereign power over its own citizens and in possession of weaponry denied to others, police officers occupy a position of supreme public trust. That trust is violated when they use force erroneously, carelessly, excessively or wilfully. It is unquestionably right for police officers to be held accountable for all their actions, especially their use of force. It is this that distinguishes liberal democracies from their authoritarian counterparts."[3]

Friedrich noted that

> "Police use of force is theoretically important because it involves the execution of perhaps the essential function of the state, and practically important because it affects the public's attitudes and behaviours towards the police and government more generally."[4]

4–03 An Garda Síochána was established as an unarmed force and, with the exception of certain units and members,[5] it remains so. Yet ASP batons and pepper spray are now standard issue, raising difficult practical, political, ethical and legal questions. Despite the questions raised and their complexity, the use of force by gardaí appears to be more closely scrutinised in the rare and exceptional cases involving lethal force, such as the fatal shooting of John Carthy at Abbeylara,[6] and of raiders at Lusk post office,[7] than in the context of day-to-day policing. Given the centrality of the appropriate use of force in governance and also the potential for the misuse of force to corrode community policing efforts, examination of the prevalence and extent of routine use of force in searches, arrests, public order policing and car-chases[8] might be of broader utility. The Garda

---

3 AJ Waddington and M Wright *"Police use of force, firearms and riot-control"* in Newburn (ed), *Handbook of Policing,* (2nd ed, Willan Publishing, Cullompton, 2008) at p 482.

4 RJ Friedrich, "Police Use of Force: Individuals, Situations and Organisations," Annals of the American Academy of Political and Social Science, (1980) 11:82-97.

5 For instance the Emergency Response Unit (ERU), Special Detective Unit (SDU) and Regional Support Unit (RSU).

6 See Report of the Tribunal of Inquiry into the Facts and Circumstances Surrounding the Fatal Shooting of John Carthy at Abbeylara, Co Longford on 20 April, 2000 (Stationery Office, Dublin, 2006).

7 The Report of the Garda Síochána Ombudsman Commission into the deaths of Eric Hopkins and Colm Griffin found that a garda who used lethal force in the course of an intercepted armed robbery was justified in the circumstances and that the garda acted in the honestly held belief that there was an immediate and real threat to life. The investigation concluded that the level of force used by the garda in the shooting of Colm Griffin and Eric Hopkins was proportionate, lawful and no more than absolutely necessary.

8 Though not immediately obvious in the context of the use of force, the pursuit by police of vehicles has been studied in a number of other jurisdictions, and it has been argued that the use of force is not confined to the application of violent methods, but extends to the high-speed pursuit of suspects (GP Alpert and LA Fridell, *Police Vehicles and Firearms: Instruments of Deadly Force* (Prospect Heights, Illinois, Waveland, 1992)). Studies have noted that vehicle pursuits that have resulted in injuries or fatalities are prompted by often minor transgressions and those killed are often the occupants of the pursued vehicle, with the efficacy of the pursuits doubtful. See M Docking, T Bucke, G Kerry, H Dady (2007) *Police Road Traffic Incidents: A Study of Cases Involving Serious and Fatal Injuries. Paper 7* (Independent Police Complaints Commission, London); D Best (2002) *Fatal Pursuit: Investigation of Road Traffic Incidents (RTIs) Involving Police Vehicles 1998 – 2001: Identifying Common Factors and Lessons to be Learned* (Police Complaints Authority, London); D Best and K Eves (2004) *Following Fatal Pursuit: A Follow-Up Assessment of Road Traffic Incidents, 2001 – 2002, Second Report into Fatal Road Traffic Incidents Involving Police Vehicles*

Code, which deals with such operational matters as the use of force, is not publicly available in Ireland,[9] whereas the policies that govern the use of force in other jurisdictions are. Walsh has argued that the guidance which exists is inadequate.[10] At a minimum, transparency in relation to the policies and procedures under which gardaí operate is necessary for accountability and to ensure that such policies are human rights-proofed.

Concerns about excessive use of force in arrest and post-arrest in Ireland have been expressed in a number of quarters. In its Human Rights Audit of An Garda Síochána (2004), Ionann Management Consultants highlighted concerns expressed by Amnesty International and by the Committee for the Prevention of Torture and Inhuman or Degrading Treatment (CPT), and said: **4–04**

> "Despite the apparent awareness of members of the importance of human rights, there is continuing public concern about public order policing, excessive use of force and oppressive questioning during detention, when lawyers are not permitted [to be present]."[11]

The CPT has consistently reported that complaints have been received of physical ill-treatment in garda custody.[12] Such ill-treatment was stated to include kicks, punches and blows with batons to various parts of the body, as well as the abusive application of handcuffs.[13] During its 2010 visit, the CPT noted that **4–05**

> "progress continues to be made in reducing ill-treatment at the hands of police officers; nevertheless, the persistence of some allegations makes clear that the Irish authorities must remain vigilant".[14]

Walsh has commented that, in Ireland:

> "The use of unnecessary force in effecting and maintaining an arrest persists as a concern in Garda practices… a further indication of the use of unnecessary and excessive force being used against arrested suspects is the steady growth of compensation awards being paid by the state in respect of assaults by gardaí."[15]

Not only does the use of a baton, pepper spray or any kind of physical force pose a threat of serious injury to suspects and to the public, but, perhaps more than any other interaction between the police and the public, it has the potential to undermine **4–06**

(Police Complaints Authority, London); G Hoffman (2003), *Police Pursuits: A Law Enforcement and Public Safety Issue for Queensland* (Crime and Misconduct Commission, Brisbane).

9 "Garda among 'most secretive' police forces", *Irish Examiner*, 3 December 2009.

10 D Walsh, *Human Rights and Policing in Ireland: Law, Policy and Practice* (Clarus Press, Dublin, 2009), p 255.

11 Ionann Management Consultants Ltd, *An Garda Síochána Human Rights Audit* (June 2004, at p 75)

12 See the Reports of the CPT - 2007 report: CPT/Inf (2007) 40; the 2011 Report: CPT/Inf (2011) 3.

13 CPT/Inf (2007) 40.

14 CPT/Inf (2011) 3 at para 15.

15 D Walsh, *Human Rights and Policing in Ireland: Law, Policy and Practice* (Clarus Press, Dublin, 2009), p 471 – 472 Walsh states that a total of almost €29 million has been paid out in awards and costs against the gardaí in respect of assaults, unlawful arrests and other claims, citing an *Irish Times* article: M O' Halloran: "Call for C&AG to inquire into settlements, *The Irish Times,* 17 November 2008.

the crucial trust and confidence of the community in their police force. In a review of police policies on the use of force by McEwen, this passage was singled out as being particularly cogent:

> "Abuse by police officers of the authority to use force violates the trust the public has given to the police, causes public indignation and erodes citizen support. Without the confidence, respect and cooperation of the community, the total police effort may be seriously handicapped. In that the unnecessary use of force is contrary to law, places the city in a position of civil liability, and the officer in jeopardy of civil and criminal liability, it is prohibited... No other area of police work is so sensitive as the use of force or as important to the implementation of the department's peace-keeping mission. In no other area is the exercise of sound judgment by the individual police officer and conformity to department policies and procedures more necessary."[16]

The appropriate and restrained use of force is indicative of policing by consent, rather than coercion. As in other areas of police work, in exercising discretion on the use of handcuffs, batons and pepper spray, garda decisions are finely balanced. Unquestionably, gardaí should err on the side of caution and use force only where it is lawful, justifiable and necessary for law enforcement or the maintenance of public order.

REASONABLE FORCE

4–07 Reasonable force may lawfully be used by gardaí and private individuals in a number of situations. Broadly speaking, the permissible occasions when reasonable force can be used are self-defence, the defence of another, the protection of property[17] or the prevention of crime.

4–08 The use of force by law enforcement officials is envisioned as the exception. rather than the rule. The European Code of Police Ethics provides that "The police may use force only when strictly necessary and only to the extent required to obtain a legitimate objective".[18] Article 3 of the UN Code of Conduct for Law Enforcement Officials is framed in similar terms: "Law enforcement officials may use force only when strictly necessary and to the extent required for the performance of their duty."[19]

The force used must not exceed that which is absolutely necessary in the circumstances.

4–09 Force is defined in Irish law in s 20(1) of the Non-Fatal Offences against the Person Act 1997 as follows:

---

16 T McEwen, "Policies on less-than-lethal force in law enforcement agencies," Policing: An International Journal of Police Strategies and Management, Volume 20(1): 21, 1 March 1997, p 47-48.

17 For defence of the dwelling, see the Criminal Law (Defence and the Dwelling) Act 2011.

18 The European Code of Police Ethics, Council of Europe Recommendation Rec (2001)10, para 37.

19 UN Code of Conduct for Law Enforcement Officials, GA Resolution 34/169 (1979).

> "(1)(a) a person uses force in relation to another person or property not only when he or she applies force to, but also where he or she causes an impact on, the body of that person or that property;
>
> (b) a person shall be treated as using force in relation to another person if—
> (i) he or she threatens that person with its use, or
> (ii) he or she detains that person without actually using it; and
>
> (c) a person shall be treated as using force in relation to property if he or she threatens a person with its use in relation to property."

Section 20(3) provides that "a threat of force may be reasonable, although the actual use of force may not be", while s 20(4) clarifies that "the fact that a person had an opportunity to retreat before using force shall be taken into account, in conjunction with other relevant evidence, in determining whether the use of force was reasonable."

Section 18(1) provides a defence where force is used in specified circumstances: **4–10**

> "The use of force by a person for any of the following purposes, if only such as is reasonable in the circumstances as he or she believes them to be, does not constitute an offence—
> (a) to protect himself or herself or a member of the family of that person or another from injury, assault or detention caused by a criminal act; or
> (b) to protect himself or herself or (with the authority of that other) another from trespass to the person; or
> (c) to protect his or her property from appropriation, destruction or damage caused by a criminal act or from trespass or infringement; or
> (d) to protect property belonging to another from appropriation, destruction or damage caused by a criminal act or (with the authority of that other) from trespass or infringement; or
> (e) to prevent crime or a breach of the peace."

Section 18(6) limits the defence, clarifying that generally the use of force cannot be justified against a member of An Garda Síochána acting in the course of duty. It states: **4–11**

> "(6) Notwithstanding subsection (1), a person who believes circumstances to exist which would justify or excuse the use of force under that subsection has no defence if he or she knows that the force is used against a member of the Garda Síochána acting in the course of the member's duty or a person so assisting such member, unless he or she believes the force to be immediately necessary to prevent harm to himself or herself or another."

The Use of Force in Effecting an Arrest

An express provision allowing the use of force in effecting an arrest or assisting in an arrest is provided in s 19 of the Non Fatal Offences against the Person Act 1997. 'Reasonableness' is determined subjectively, on the basis of the circumstances as the person using the force perceived them.[20] Section 1(2) of the 1997 Act provides that, for the purposes of s 17, 18 and 19, it is immaterial whether a belief is justified or not if it is honestly held, but the presence or absence of reasonable grounds for the belief is a **4–12**

20 Non-Fatal Offences against the Person Act 1997, s 20(5).

matter to which the court or jury is to have regard, in conjunction with other relevant matters, in considering whether the person honestly held the belief.

Gardaí are given statutory permission to use reasonable force, not only in face-to-face confrontations in the circumstances outlined above, but also in entering dwellings or other premises to effect an arrest,[21] in the execution of search warrants[22] and in the taking of fingerprints and photographs when suspects are in Garda custody.[23] However, the existence of such permission does not afford gardaí *carte blanche*: where force is used, it must always be necessary, reasonable, proportionate and justified.

The UN Basic Principles on the Use of Force and Firearms by Law Enforcement Officials

4–13 The UN Basic Principles on the Use of Force and Firearms by Law Enforcement Officials[24] provide general guidance as follows:

> "4. Law enforcement officials, in carrying out their duty, shall, as far as possible, apply non-violent means before resorting to the use of force and firearms. They may use force and firearms only if other means remain ineffective or without any promise of achieving the intended result.
>
> 5. Whenever the lawful use of force and firearms is unavoidable, law enforcement officials shall:
>
> (a) Exercise restraint in such use and act in proportion to the seriousness of the offence and the legitimate objective to be achieved;
>
> (b) Minimize damage and injury, and respect and preserve human life;
>
> (c) Ensure that assistance and medical aid are rendered to any injured or affected persons at the earliest possible moment;
>
> (d) Ensure that relatives or close friends of the injured or affected person are notified at the earliest possible moment."[25]

4–14 The same instrument refers specifically to the need to avoid force in the context of public order policing:

> "In the dispersal of assemblies that are unlawful but non-violent, law enforcement officials shall avoid the use of force or, where that is not practicable, shall restrict such force to the minimum extent necessary."[26]

And in policing persons in custody or detention:

21 Criminal Law Act 1997, s 6.

22 See, for instance, the Misuse of Drugs Act 1977, s 26(2); Criminal Justice (Theft and Fraud Offences) Act 2001, s 48(3)(a).

23 Criminal Justice Act 1984, s 6A as inserted by s 48(b) of the Criminal Justice Act 2007.

24 The UN Basic Principles on the Use of Force and Firearms by Law Enforcement Officials, adopted by the Eighth UN Congress on the Prevention of Crime and the Treatment of Offenders, Havana, 27 August-7 September 1990: Report, UN, New York, 1991 Doc A/CONF.144/28/Rev1 at 112 (1990).

25 The UN Basic Principles on the Use of Force and Firearms by Law Enforcement Officials, arts 4 and 5.

26 *ibid*, art 13.

> "Law enforcement officials, in their relations with persons in custody or detention, shall not use force, except when strictly necessary for the maintenance of security and order within the institution, or when personal safety is threatened."[27]

Garda Guidance: Recording Procedures and Guidelines relating to Children in the Care of An Garda Síochána

Article 3 of the European Convention on Human Rights contains an absolute prohibition on the use of torture and inhuman or degrading treatment or punishment. While An Garda Síochána has not made publicly available guidance on the use of force, other than in the limited case of incapacitant spray, some guidance can be garnered from the Recording Procedures and Guidelines relating to Children in the Care of An Garda Síochána: **4–15**

> "Section 3 of the European Convention on Human Rights Act 2003 (the 2003 Act) obliges An Garda Síochána, as an organ of the state, to perform its functions in a manner compatible with the state's obligations under the Convention provisions.
>
> Articles 2 and 3 of the European Convention on Human Rights (ECHR), which are incorporated into Irish law by the 2003 Act, set out the right to life and the right not to be subjected to inhuman or degrading treatment respectively. The human rights legislation applies equally to adults and to children. Every child is entitled to have these important rights upheld.
>
> (4) Gardaí are frequently required to deal with situations of conflict. The careful use of well chosen and appropriate words and the management of human interaction will resolve many situations. Others will necessarily involve the application of varying degrees of physical force. Gardaí have power under statute and common law to take action to defend themselves and others. If gardaí do not take appropriate and proportionate action to protect others from such harm, they may be violating the human rights of those others. Therefore, it is important that gardaí give due regard to the rights of individuals in how they exercise their discretion. In making these important decisions, gardaí are reminded that they are accountable through the law for their actions. Apart from the criminal law, there may follow a civil suit, complaints may be made against individual members and, in cases where death has resulted, a public inquest or other inquiry will be held by the coroner or other statutory bodies at which members of An Garda Síochána may be called to testify.
>
> Every effort should be made to resolve conflict without resorting to the use of force.
>
> Whenever it is necessary for gardaí to resort to the lawful use of force, they shall:
>
> - Exercise restraint in such use and act in proportion to the seriousness of the offence and the legitimate object to be achieved;
> - Minimise damage and injury, and respect and preserve human life;
> - Ensure that assistance and medical aid are secured to any injured person at the earliest opportunity;
> - Ensure that relatives or close friends of the injured or affected person are notified at the earliest opportunity;
> - Report the incident promptly to their supervisors.

---

[27] *ibid* art 15.

> The primary responsibility for using force rests with the individual member who is answerable ultimately to the law. Individual members are accountable and responsible for whatever force they use and must be in a position to justify their actions in the light of their legal responsibilities and powers."[28]

Specific garda guidance has been published on the use of incapacitant spray, which is considered further below.

HANDCUFFS

Garda Discretion on the Use of Handcuffs

4–16 While Irish law provides that reasonable force may be used for the purpose of arrest, handcuffs will not be necessary in every instance. In England, Wales and Northern Ireland, the Association of Chief Police Officers (ACPO) has issued useful guidance on the use of handcuffs:

> "Any intentional application of force to the person of another is an assault. The use of handcuffs amounts to such an assault and is unlawful unless it can be justified. Justification is achieved through establishing not only a legal right to use handcuffs, but also good objective grounds for doing so in order to show that what the officer or member of police staff did was a reasonable, necessary and proportionate use of force."[29]

4–17 The guidance suggests the following as criteria which may be taken into account in deciding whether to handcuff a suspect: age, gender, physical condition, respective size and apparent strength and fitness. Each of these factors may or may not support the justification of using handcuffs, depending on the circumstances. For instance, it may be both unreasonable and unnecessary to handcuff an elderly and frail suspect. The guidance emphasises that there must always be an objective basis for the decision to apply handcuffs. That objective basis may be a reasonable belief that a person may use or attempt to use violence, or may escape or attempt to escape.[30] Other factors which might be brought to bear on the decision to handcuff a suspect include the perceived potential for violence or escape or attempted escape, the need to ensure the safety of the suspect and gardaí present, and the potential for criminal damage or destruction of evidence. Handcuffs ought not to be so tight as to cause pain and the potential for injury must always be minimised. The reasonableness and practicality of the use of handcuffs will fall to be considered on a case-by-case basis.

---

[28] Recording Procedures and Guidelines relating to Children in the Care of An Garda Síochána, available online. http://www.garda.ie/Documents/User/policy%20for%20recording%20children%20in%20care%20of%20ags.pdf <accessed 13 October 2013>.

[29] Association of Chief Police Officers of England, Wales and Northern Ireland (ACPO) Guidance on the Use of Handcuffs, Version 2, 2009, at para 2.1.2. While it is, of course, not binding in Ireland, it is of use for guidance on best practice.

[30] Association of Chief Police Officers of England, Wales and Northern Ireland (ACPO) Guidance on the Use of Handcuffs, Version 2, 2009, at para 2.1.5 – 2.1.7.

In *Ward v Minister for Justice, Equality and Law Reform and others*, a refusal to allow a defendant to meet his legal advisers without handcuffs[31] was found to be reasonable in the circumstances. McGovern J held that: **4–18**

> "The Garda and the prison authorities should be allowed to exercise their power of detention or interrogation as they think fit, provided they act reasonably and in a manner which does not infringe the prisoner's legal or constitutional rights… the actions of the prison authorities in requiring the applicant to remain handcuffed even if he wished to speak with his legal advisors was not unreasonable or in breach of his legal or constitutional rights."[32]

While *Ward*[33] suggests an unwillingness by the courts to second-guess the discretionary judgements of gardaí and prison officers as to the propriety and necessity of handcuffs, there have been repeated criticisms of the unnecessary exposure of accused persons in handcuffs in public and before the media. Gardaí must take care not to expose an accused person to the media, the public or jurors in handcuffs, since: **4–19**

> "the dignity of the individual, and the perception that he is a participant in judicial proceedings with specific rights, and on a footing of equality with other participants, is inconsistent with his appearing there chained, or otherwise manifestly restrained".[34]

The Exposure of Handcuffed Accused Persons to Jurors

The Court of Criminal Appeal has condemned the exposure of an accused person to jurors while in handcuffs in a number of cases.[35] In *DPP v Davis*, the court cited numerous international instruments and said: **4–20**

> "The public depiction of any person, but particularly an unconvicted prisoner, wearing the double restraints which are now commonly used in the prison service is a depiction of him in a position of humiliation and indignity… The effect, both on the restrained person and on the public perception of him has been recognised in a number of instruments dealing with the treatment of prisoners."[36]

The Court went on to cite excerpts from the European Prison rules which provide interesting guidance on the use of handcuffs in the context of court appearances: **4–21**

---

[31] In circumstances where the accused had been afforded all reasonable access to his legal advisors and to have private consultations.

[32] *Ward v Minister for Justice, Equality and Law Reform and others* [2007] IEHC 39.

[33] *ibid.*

[34] *DPP v Davis* [2001] 1 IR 146.

[35] *DPP v Davis* [2001] 1 IR 146; *DPP v McCowen*, *Irish Times*, 1 April 2003; *DPP v O' Sullivan*, unreported, Court of Criminal Appeal, 26 November, 2003; *DPP v Collinson*, *Irish Times*, 28 January 2004; *DPP v Hourigan & anor* [2004] IECCA 8.

[36] *DPP v Davis* [2001] 1 IR 146.

> "50.1 Where prisoners are being removed to or from an institution, they shall be exposed to public view as little as possible, and proper safeguards shall be adopted to protect them from insult, curiosity and publicity in any form."[37]

Paragraph 39 provides:

> "The use of chains and irons shall be prohibited. Handcuffs, restraint-jackets and other body restraints shall never be applied as a punishment. They shall not be used except in the following circumstances:
>
> a. if necessary, as a precaution against escape during a transfer, provided that they shall be removed when the prisoner appears before a judicial or administrative authority, unless that authority decides otherwise;
> b. on medical grounds by direction and under the supervision of the medical officer;
> c. by order of the director, if other methods of control fail, in order to protect a prisoner from self-injury, injury to others or to prevent serious damage to property; in such instances the director shall at once consult the medical officer and report the higher administrative authority."

Paragraph 40 provides that "... Such instruments must not be applied for any longer time than is strictly necessary."

4–22 The Court stated that there are almost identical provisions in the United Nations Rules for Treatment of Prisoners, and pointed to the Irish Rules for the Government of Prisons, 1947, which provide at rule 17:

> "A prisoner shall be exposed to public view as little as possible while being removed from or to prison. In order to avoid exposure while passing through the public streets, he shall, if necessary, be conveyed in a closed vehicle."

4–23 The Court concluded that

> "... it has been recognised for many years, and in various jurisdictions, that the shackling of a prisoner has an adverse effect both on his dignity and subjective wellbeing and on the perception of him by the community as a whole and potential jurors in particular. There will obviously be cases where, despite these factors, restraints will be necessary, and the court is not presently concerned with the propriety of the routine application of restraints or the nature of such restraints. ... Such protection would also, at least by implication, appear to be required by persons in Garda, as opposed to prison, custody".[38]

Where court or garda station architecture does not facilitate an unseen transfer from prison van to courthouse or station, the potential for prejudice is an important factor for consideration in determining whether to handcuff a prisoner. If handcuffs are unavoidable, steps should be taken to ensure the privacy of the prisoner.

---

[37] Para 50.1, European Prison Rules, Rec(87)3. The European Prison Rules have been updated since the *Davis* judgment by Rec(2006)2, adopted by the Committee of Ministers on 11 January 2006.

[38] *DPP v Davis* [2001] 1 IR 146.

PEPPER SPRAY

Following the recommendation of the Garda Síochána Inspectorate's second report on barricade incidents, which recommended that pepper sprays should be made available to all gardaí in the interest of officer safety,[39] the Minister for Justice announced the introduction of an incapacitant spray for all operational members in October 2008. Heralded somewhat incongruously as an "important additional option for police officers committed to the human rights principle of minimum force",[40] it was not universally welcomed. The Irish Council for Civil Liberties commented that **4–24**

> "Pepper spray weapons – including their active ingredients and their chemical solvents and propellants – can have damaging short and long-term effects on a number of bodily systems and functions… These weapons are particularly dangerous if used against people whose health is impaired or on young people."[41]

Oleoresin capsicum (OC) (ie pepper spray, pepper mace, OC, capsaicin) is a noxious irritant, capable of causing extreme discomfort. When deployed, pepper spray can produce a sensation of intense burning in the skin, temporary blindness and severe pain, as well as fear and disorientation when dispersed into the eye. It is unsurprising then that it is considered to be the most effective non-lethal means of subduing resistive and combative suspects. Its use is not without its risks.[42] Pepper spray has been associated with health risks including corneal and vocal cord damage and breathing difficulties among asthmatics, and it has been suggested that it might have carcinogenic and mutagenic potential.[43] Oleoresin capsicum has been implicated as a contributing factor in a number of police deaths in custody,[44] though it has been established that factors **4–25**

---

[39] See press release on *Garda Síochána Inspectorate Status Report on the Implementation of Reports 1, 2 and 3*: "The Inspectorate remains convinced that an incapacitant spray should be issued to all gardaí on operational duties for personal safety purposes. Also, the Inspectorate believes that incapacitant spray is an important additional option for police officers committed to the human rights principle of minimum force The Inspectorate acknowledges that issuance of sprays will require the development of protocols, supervision and training to ensure appropriate use. The Inspectorate notes that the Commissioner has established a working group on the matter and is hopeful it will find that the case for incapacitant spray is already well made internationally." Full text available online at http://www.gsinsp.ie/index2.php?option=com_docman&task=doc_view&gid=19&Itemid=48 <accessed 13 October 2013>.

[40] *ibid.*

[41] Irish Council for Civil Liberties (ICCL) press release, available online: http://www.iccl.ie/news/2008/04/03/-garda-%E2%80%9Creport-cards%E2%80%9D-say-%E2%80%9Cmuch-done-more-to-do%E2%80%9D-says-the-iccl.html <accessed 13 October 2013>.

[42] See RJ Kaminski, SM Edwards, and JJ Johnson, "Assessing the incapacitative effects of pepper spray during resistive encounters with the police" Policing: An International Journal of Police Strategies & Management, Volume 22(1): 24, 1 March 1999.

[43] See M Doubet, *The Medical Implications of OC Sprays*, PPCT Management Systems, Inc, IL Millstadt, and CH Steffee, PE Lantz, LM Flanagan, RL Thompson and DR Jason, (1995) "oleoresin capsicum (pepper) spray and 'in-custody deaths'", *The American Journal of Forensic Medicine and Pathology*, vol 16 No 3, pp 185-92.

[44] See CS Petty, "Deaths in Police Confrontations When Oleoresin Capsicum is Used (a study of 63 incidents), National Institute of Justice (NIJ), February 2004, available online at http://www.ncjrs.gov/pdffiles1/nij/grants/204029.pdf <accessed 13 October 2013>.

other than pepper spray exposure, such as cocaine ingestion, positional asphyxia and pre-existing health conditions were the major contributory factors.[45] Caution should therefore be exercised before its use is ever considered.

Garda Policy on the Use of Incapacitant Spray

4–26 An Garda Síochána has made the force's policy and procedures on the use of incapacitant spray publicly available[46] and the policy contains some general guidance on the use of force generally. It provides as follows:

> "Gardaí are frequently required to deal with situations of conflict. The careful use of well chosen and appropriate words and the management of human interaction will resolve many situations. Others will necessarily involve the application of varying degrees of physical force.
>
> Gardaí have the power under statute and common law to take action to defend themselves and others. If gardaí do not take appropriate and proportionate action to protect others from such harm, they may be violating the human rights of those others. Therefore, it is important that gardaí give due regard to the rights of individuals in how they exercise their discretion.
>
> In making these important decisions, gardaí are reminded that they are accountable through the law for their actions. Apart from the criminal law, there may follow a civil suit or complaints may be made against individual members.
>
> Every effort should be made to resolve conflict without resorting to the use of incapacitant spray. Whenever it is necessary for gardaí to resort to the lawful use of incapacitant spray, they should:
>
> - Exercise restraint in such use and act in proportion to the seriousness of the offence and the legitimate object to be achieved;
> - Minimise damage and injury and respect and preserve human life;

See also ACLU of Southern California (1993), *Pepper Spray: A Magic Bullet Under Scrutiny,* American Civil Liberties Union of Southern California, Los Angeles, CA.

45 J Granfield, J Onnen, and CS Petty, (1994), *Pepper Spray and In-Custody Deaths*, International Association of Chiefs of Police, Alexandria, VA. The authors state "Research suggests that four conditions may account for the majority of custody-related deaths: positional asphyxia, cocaine intoxication, excited delirium and neuroleptic malignant syndrome." They conclude "Sudden death in custody is neither a new phenomenon nor attributable to the use of OC spray. Rather, sudden custody death can occur at any time for a variety of reasons. Any law enforcement agency may experience a sudden custody death, regardless of OC involvement. Consequently, officer awareness and recognition of risk indicators are necessary to ensure subject safety and minimize the risk of sudden custody death. These indicators generally include:
* bizarre/violent activity
* obesity – especially 'big bellies'
* drug and/or alcohol involvement
* apparent ineffectiveness of spray
Diligent observation and constant monitoring of subjects displaying any one or a combination of the indicators are procedurally warranted. Furthermore, the use of maximal, prone restraint techniques should be avoided. If prone positioning is required, subjects should be closely and continuously monitored. By implementing such procedural protocols, the potential for custody deaths may be lessened."

46 See the website of An Garda Síochána http://Garda.ie/Documents/User/Incapacitant%20Spray%20-%20Policy%20and%20Procedures.pdf <accessed 13 October 2013>.

- Ensure that assistance and medical aid are secured for any injured person at the earliest opportunity;
- Fully document the circumstances in which they found themselves and the reasons for their actions;
- Ensure that the relatives or close friends of the injured or affected person are notified at the earliest opportunity;
- Report the incident promptly to their supervisors;
- Comply with training instructions.

...

The use of incapacitant spray by members of An Garda Síochána may be necessary in some circumstances. It is essential that such use is only resorted to and applied in accordance with the law.

When gardaí are required to use incapacitant spray to achieve a lawful objective (such as to make a lawful arrest, acting in self-defence, protecting others, property, the prevention of crime or a breach of the peace), the legal basis is to be found in s 18, 19 and 20 of the Non Fatal Offences against the Person Act 1997 (the 1997 Act). The use of incapacitant spray must be 'reasonable in the circumstances' as the member of An Garda Síochána believes them to be. Section 18(5) of the 1997 Act provides that the question of whether the objective is lawful shall be defined according to the circumstances as the individual member of An Garda Síochána believes them to be...

Section 1(2) of the 1997 Act provides that having regard to the belief of the person using force, 'it is immaterial whether a belief is justified or not if it is honestly held but the presence or absence of reasonable grounds is a matter to which the court or jury is to have regard, in conjunction with any other relevant matters, in considering whether the person honestly held the belief'. Factors which may assist in establishing whether or not the use of incapacitant spray was reasonable in the circumstances are:

- Was the use of incapacitant spray lawful? - eg is the aim one of those outlined in s 18 or 19 of the 1997 Act?
- Was the degree of force used proportionate in the circumstances?
- What other options were considered? If so, what were they? Why were those options discounted? Has an adequate record of all relevant decisions been made?
- Was the use of incapacitant spray in accordance with training instructions?

Any force used must not be greater than was reasonable in the circumstances. This applies to the use of incapacitant spray. If force used is not reasonable, it may leave the member open to criminal, civil or disciplinary proceedings. Excessive use of non-lethal force by the gardaí can engage Article 3 of the ECHR and therefore it may constitute a violation of the human rights of the person against whom the force was used."[47]

Research Examining the Efficacy of Incapacitant Spray

Research has suggested that incapacitant spray may be less effective when used on those who have taken drugs, whereas it may have a greater impact on those who are intoxicated from alcohol. As Kaminski *et al* note: **4–27**

[47] See the website of An Garda Síochána http://Garda.ie/Documents/User/Incapacitant%20Spray%20-%20Policy%20and%20Procedures.pdf <accessed 13 October 2013>.

> "… there is general agreement… that OC is as effective or somewhat more effective when suspects are under the influence of alcohol. Conversely, when suspects are under the influence of drugs, OC is consistently less effective regardless of the criterion used. The results are somewhat mixed, however, for mentally disturbed suspects, with OC reportedly being less likely to ease the arrest, but slightly more likely to incapacitate mentally disturbed suspects, relative to 'other' suspects (those not mentally disturbed, on drugs or alcohol) or compared to the sample overall".[48]

They conclude:

> "Although our results suggest OC is effective generally, police frequently report fewer successes with OC during encounters with suspects thought to be mentally disturbed or under the influence of drugs or alcohol… regression analyses found consistent support for the notion that OC is less likely to affect suspects under the influence of drugs… The results indicate, then, that although officers should always be prepared to resort to alternative tactics when relying on OC spray to subdue suspects, this is especially true when suspects appear to be under the influence of drugs."

Caution should be used before a decision is taken to deploy incapacitant spray on any suspect. Whether the suspect has taken drugs or is mentally ill are important additional factors for careful consideration.

BATONS

4–28 The emphasis throughout the Policy on the use of Incapacitant Spray is on the avoidance of force. The principles apply equally to the use of batons. Studies have suggested that batons are effective in reducing the number of assaults on police officers[49]; however, there is an obvious potential for serious injury where batons are employed. A study by the Police Ombudsman for Northern Ireland examined complaints concerning police use of batons and found that:

> "While a small proportion of complainants (6%) said they had been threatened with batons or that police officers with batons had destroyed or damaged their property, the great majority (94%) claimed they had been struck… Although in a number of complaints the exact part(s) of the body struck was unspecified, a third (33%) of complainants alleged that their legs had been struck, while 31% said they had been struck on the head or neck and 30% said they had been struck on the shoulders, arms or hands. Many complainants said that they had been struck on more than one part of their bodies, while some referred to having received 'a beating', or having been 'hit all over'".[50]

---

48 See RJ Kaminski, SM Edwards, and JJ Johnson, "Assessing the incapacitative effects of pepper spray during resistive encounters with the police" *Policing: An International Journal of Police Strategies & Management*, Volume 22(1): 24, 1 March 1999, at p 15.

49 E Koch, T Kemp and B Rix "Assessing the Extendable Side-Handled Baton" (London, Police Research Group, Home Office, 1993); PCA *Striking a Balance: The Police Use of New Batons* (Police Complaints Authority, London, 1998).

50 Research Branch Office of the Police Ombudsman for Northern Ireland, *A Study of Complaints Involving the use of Batons by the Police in Northern Ireland* (March 2003).

The research considered noteworthy the manner in which batons were used, given that guidance given to police officers in Northern Ireland specified that batons were supplied to police to protect themselves and others when violently attacked, and dictated that, in using batons, police should aim at the arms or legs as in doing so they were least likely to inflict serious injury. The guidance expressly stated that baton strikes should not be aimed at the head. The high proportion of complaints alleging that complainants had been hit on the head was suggestive of poor compliance by police officers. **4–29**

It would seem to be axiomatic that batons should not be aimed at a person's head, and that their use should be restricted to self-defence or the defence of others or in public order policing as a last resort where their use may be justified on the basis of the prevention of crime.

Training is crucial on the appropriate use of batons. The UN Basic Principles on the Use of Force and Firearms provide at article 19 that: **4–30**

> "Governments and law enforcement agencies shall ensure that all law enforcement officials are provided with training and are tested in accordance with appropriate proficiency standards in the use of force. Those law enforcement officials who are required to carry firearms should be authorized to do so only upon completion of special training in their use."[51]

Article 20 dictates that:

> "In the training of law enforcement officials, Governments and law enforcement agencies shall give special attention to issues of police ethics and human rights, especially in the investigative process, to alternatives to the use of force and firearms, include uding the peaceful settlement of conflicts, the understanding of crowd behaviour, and the methods of persuasion, negotiation and mediation, as well as to technical means, with a view to limiting the use of force and firearms…"[52]

The UN Basic Principles further provide that training programmes and operational procedures should be reviewed in the light of particular incidents.[53] The principles outline that the deployment of non-lethal incapacitating weapons, such as batons and incapacitant spray, should be carefully evaluated to minimise the risk of endangering uninvolved persons, and the use of such weapons should be carefully controlled.[54] Law enforcement officials must, as far as possible, apply non-violent means before resorting to the use of force and firearms. Article 5 provides that, where force and firearms are unavoidable, law enforcement officials shall: **4–31**

> "(a) Exercise restraint in such use and act in proportion to the seriousness of the offence and the legitimate objective to be achieved;
>
> (b) Minimize damage and injury, and respect and preserve human life;

---

51 UN Basic Principles on the Use of Force and Firearms by Law Enforcement Officials, Art 20.

52 *ibid.*

53 *ibid.*

54 *ibid*, Art 3.

(c) Ensure that assistance and medical aid are rendered to any injured or affected persons at the earliest possible moment;

(d) Ensure that relatives or close friends of the injured or affected person are notified at the earliest possible moment."[55]

LETHAL FORCE

4–32 The right to life is at the apex of constitutional rights.

4–33 Article 2(1) of the European Convention on Human Rights also provides that "Everyone's right to life shall be protected by law." However, the Convention qualified this in Article 2(2) which provides that:

> "Deprivation of life shall not be regarded as inflicted in contravention of this Article when it results from the use of force which is no more than absolutely necessary:
> (a) in defence of any person from unlawful violence;
> (b) in order to effect a lawful arrest or to prevent the escape of a person lawfully detained;
> (c) in action lawfully taken for the purpose of quelling a riot or insurrection."

Given the importance of the right to life, the use of lethal force constitutes an extreme and exceptional measure.

The European Court of Human Rights has held that the taking of life must be subjected to

> "the most careful scrutiny taking into consideration not only the actions of the agents of the state who actually administer the force but also all the surrounding circumstances including such matters as the planning and control of the actions under examination."[56]

4–34 The UN Basic Principles on the Use of Force and Firearms by Law Enforcement Officials provide that firearms shall not be used against persons:

> "except in self-defence or defence of others against the imminent threat of death or serious injury, to prevent the perpetration of a particularly serious crime involving grave threat to life, to arrest a person presenting such a danger and resisting their authority, or to prevent his or her escape, and only when less extreme means are insufficient to achieve these objectives. In any event, intentional lethal use of firearms may only be made when strictly unavoidable in order to protect life".[57]

If such circumstances present themselves, law enforcement officials are obliged to:

> "identify themselves as such and give a clear warning of their intent to use firearms, with sufficient time for the warning to be observed, unless to do so would unduly place the law enforcement officials at risk or would create a risk of death or serious harm to

---

[55] UN Basic Principles on the Use of Force and Firearms by Law Enforcement Officials, Art 5.
[56] *McCann v United Kingdom* (1995) 21 EHRR 97 at para 150.
[57] UN Basic Principles on the Use of Force and Firearms by Law Enforcement Officials, Art 9.

> other persons, or would be clearly inappropriate or pointless in the circumstances of the incident."[58]

Walsh has been critical of the dearth of guidance in Irish law on the use of force, saying:

> "There is substantial room for improvement in the definition of the Garda power to use force, especially lethal or potentially lethal force. Not only is the power to use force not the subject of a detailed and comprehensive statutory code, but the law as currently framed suffers from an unacceptable degree of uncertainty… the law is framed in a manner that leaves exceptionally broad discretion in the hands of each individual member. There are no statutory provisions that control that discretion by providing more detailed guidance on when such a power to use force should be used and on what degree of force is and is not acceptable."[59]

The only substantive legal guidance in Ireland on the use of lethal force is that **4–35** contained in the Non-Fatal Offences against the Person Act 1997, and in the case-law of the European Court of Human Rights, notwithstanding the considerable attention drawn to the actions of the Emergency Response Unit in fatally shooting a mentally-ill man at Abbeylara, which was investigated by the Barr Tribunal. Though numerous failings on the part of the gardaí at the scene were identified, particularly in regard to the interaction between gardaí and John Carthy, who suffered mental illness, the tribunal found that the actions of the sergeant who killed John Carthy were not unlawful.[60] The Barr Tribunal examined police practice in relation to the use of force in a number of other jurisdictions[61] and recommended the adoption of a policing model, Project Beacon, used in the Australian jurisdiction of Victoria, which was cited as having had exceptional success. The model comprises a coordinated set of policy, procedural and training initiatives to minimise the use of force by police and to maximise community and police safety. Project Beacon established ten operational principles to inform officers' responses to every incident which may potentially involve the use of force. They are:

1. Safety first—the safety of police, the public and offenders or suspects is paramount.
2. Risk assessment—is to be applied to all incidents and operations.
3. Take charge—exercise effective command and control.
4. Planned response—take every opportunity to convert an unplanned response into a planned operation.
5. Cordon and containment—unless impractical, adopt a 'cordon and containment' approach.
6. Avoid confrontation—a violent confrontation is to be avoided.
7. Avoid force—the use of force is to be avoided.

---

58 *ibid*, Art 10.

59 D Walsh, *Human Rights and Policing in Ireland: Law, Policy and Practice* (Clarus Press, Dublin, 2009), p 255.

60 The report found that responsibility for Mr Carthy's death lay with the scene commanders and, to a lesser extent, with the ERU tactical commander.

61 Report of the Tribunal of Inquiry into the facts and circumstances surrounding the fatal shooting of John Carthy at Abbeylara, Co Longford on 20 April 2000, at chapter 12.

8. Minimum force—where use of force cannot be avoided, only use the minimum amount reasonably necessary.
9. Forced entry searches—are to be used only as a last resort.
10. Resources—it is accepted that the 'safety first' principle may require the deployment of more resources, more complex planning and more time to complete.

In Victoria, the success of an operation is primarily judged by the extent to which the use of force is avoided or minimised.[62] De-escalation is to be considered as readily as escalation in the context of potential use of lethal force.

4–36 Lethal force was more recently used during a raid at Lusk post office where two raiders, one of whom was armed, were shot dead by a garda. An investigation by the Garda Síochána Ombudsman Commission found a number of weaknesses in the planning of the Garda operation which "led to Garda A being put in a position where he was required to make a split second life and death decision".[63] The investigation found that the garda "acted in the honestly held belief that there was an immediate and real risk to life and that the use of lethal force was justified in the circumstances".[64] In both the Lusk and Abbeylara incidents, inquiries have determined that the decision to use lethal force was appropriate, but have found flaws in Garda operations which preceded the shootings. A detailed statutory framework and publicly-available guidance on the use of lethal force are required for Irish law to avoid the criticisms levelled at Greece in the case of *Makaratzis:*

> "...police officers should not be left in a vacuum when exercising their duties, whether in the context of a prepared operation or a spontaneous pursuit of a person perceived to be dangerous: a legal and administrative framework should define the limited circumstances in which law enforcement officials may use force and firearms, in the light of the international standards which have been developed in this respect".[65]

All that is clear is that Article 2 permits the defence of self and others once lethal force is necessary, proportionate and justified.

---

[62] See Review of Fatal Shootings by Victoria Police, Office of Police Integrity, November 2005, pp No 177

[63] Report of the Garda Síochána Ombudsman Commission, pursuant to s 103, Garda Síochána Act 2005, following Complaints and an Investigation arising from the Deaths of Eric Hopkins and Colm Griffin, 19 October 2011, available online at http://www.gardaombudsman.ie/docs/publications/20111019LuskReportWebFinal.pdf <accessed 13 October 2013>.

[64] Report of the Garda Síochána Ombudsman Commission, pursuant to s 103, Garda Síochána Act 2005, following Complaints and an Investigation arising from the Deaths of Eric Hopkins and Colm Griffin, 19 October 2011, available online at http://www.gardaombudsman.ie/GSOC/20111019LuskReportWebFinal.pdf <accessed 7 November 2013>.

[65] *Makaratzis v Greece* (1998) 25 EHRR 491.

Part III

The Power to Detain

CHAPTER 5

Detention in Garda Custody

INTRODUCTION

5–01 Though there is reluctance to overtly accept the shift towards an interrogatorial model of criminal investigation in Ireland,[1] the gradual expansion of periods of time for which suspects can be detained is indicative of a paradigm shift. Where previously detention was permitted only to bring a person before a court, the power to detain has been expanded piecemeal to allow for extensive periods in garda custody, such that the inescapable conclusion is that the primary purpose of detention is now interrogation. See *Chapter 1: Arrest* at para 1 – 27 *et seq*. The power to detain has become crucial to modern criminal investigation and is among the most significant powers exercised by gardaí. Liberty is temporarily suspended; privacy, the privilege against self-incrimination and the right to bodily integrity are encroached upon and suspects are questioned, sampled, fingerprinted and photographed.

5–02 To temper the statutory powers of detention which apply to all arrestable offences, a number of important safeguards apply to those in Garda custody, provided by the Constitution, the Judges' Rules, the Criminal Justice Act 1984 (Treatment Of Persons In Custody In Garda Síochána Stations) Regulations, 1987 (the Custody Regulations),[2] the European Convention on Human Rights, international human rights instruments and codes[3] as well as Irish and European case-law. Because the prospect of an indeterminate detention is oppressive, among the most important practical protections for persons in custody are stringent statutory time limits on detention periods, which vary depending on the circumstances of the case and on the detention power used.

5–03 Psychological pressure is exerted on the detained person by virtue of detention itself, but there is often also an inherent vulnerability among those who find themselves in Garda custody. Some suspects are in a weaker position than the average person owing to their age or their physical, mental or emotional condition when it comes to understanding or participating in criminal proceedings. Low educational achievement, poor communication skills, high levels of substance misuse and a high rate of mental illness are often characteristic of persons who are detained by the State.[4]

---

[1] Long after the enactment of the Criminal Justice Act 1984, there is still a reluctance to accept arrest for investigation. McGrath, citing the case of *DPP v Quilligan,* states: "[a]lthough it has been suggested that a person may not be arrested under [s 30 of the Offences against the State Act 1939, s 4 of the Criminal Justice Act 1984 or s 2 of the Criminal Justice (Drug Trafficking) Act 1996] simply for the purpose of questioning, this is commonly done and would seem permissible". If not officially endorsed or acknowledged as such, it seems clear that what was once a procedural mechanism for initiating criminal proceedings is now, in the indictable context in particular, primarily an investigative tool: arrest has become the starting point for questioning and forensic sampling, and so forms an integral part of the investigation process.

[2] SI No 119 of 1987, as amended by SI No 641 of 2006 – Criminal Justice Act 1984 (Treatment of Persons in Custody in Garda Síochána Stations) (Amendment) Regulations 2006.

[3] For example, the European Code of Police Ethics, the reports of the European Committee for the Prevention of Torture and Inhuman or Degrading Treatment of Punishment (CPT) and the *CPT Standards.*

[4] House of Lords, House of Commons Joint Committee on Human Rights, *Deaths in Custody,* Third Report of Session 2004–2005, Vol 1, The Stationery Office, 14 December 2004, HL Paper 15-I, HC 137-I, at p 7.

With vulnerability comes a greater risk of self-harm and also a higher risk of false confessions. Language barriers can also disadvantage deaf and non-English speaking suspects. This is of concern because our system places a premium on confession evidence, and because the law has provided for extensive periods of pre-charge detention as a consequence. There is a particular onus on gardaí to protect vulnerable persons in custody since, in taking people into custody, the State takes on itself a particular duty of care and a special responsibility to ensure their protection and uphold their human rights.[5]

This chapter examines the powers permitting detention by gardaí and the standards which apply as a counterbalance to them. Some aspects of the obligations placed on gardaí where vulnerable suspects are detained are also examined, with particular reference to mentally disordered and deaf detainees. **5–04**

The taking of forensic samples, fingerprints and photographs is considered separately in *Chapter 6: Forensics, Crime Scene Management and the Preservation of Evidence*.

LIBERTY AS A STARTING POINT

Detention for a period of hours or days is an extraordinary departure from the freedom which is habitually enjoyed. The Universal Declaration on Human Rights provides at Article 3 that "[e]veryone has the right to life, liberty and security of person," and at Article 9 that "[n]o one shall be subjected to arbitrary arrest, detention or exile".[6] Similarly, the International Covenant on Civil and Political Rights provides at Article 9(1) "[e]veryone has the right to liberty and security of person. No one shall be subject to arbitrary arrest or detention. No one shall be deprived of his liberty except on such grounds and in accordance with such procedure as are established by law".[7] The European Convention on Human Rights provides at Art 5(1): **5–05**

> "1. Everyone has the right to liberty and security of person. No one shall be deprived of his liberty save in the following cases and in accordance with a procedure prescribed by law:
>
> (a) the lawful detention of a person after conviction by a competent court;
> (b) the lawful arrest or detention of a person for non-compliance with the lawful order of a court or in order to secure the fulfilment of any obligation prescribed by law;
> (c) the lawful arrest or detention of a person effected for the purpose of bringing him before the competent legal authority on reasonable suspicion of having committed an offence or when it is reasonably considered necessary to prevent his committing an offence or fleeing after having done so;

---

5 *ibid.*

6 Universal Declaration of Human Rights (adopted 10 December 1948) (UDHR).

7 International Covenant on Civil and Political Rights (adopted 16 December 1966, entered into force 23 March 1976) 999 UNTS 171 (ICCPR).

(d) the detention of a minor by lawful order for the purpose of educational supervision or his lawful detention for the purpose of bringing him before the competent legal authority;
(e) the lawful detention of persons for the prevention of the spreading of infectious diseases, of persons of unsound mind, alcoholics or drug addicts or vagrants;
(f) the lawful arrest or detention of a person to prevent his effecting an unauthorised entry into the country or of a person against whom action is being taken with a view to deportation or extradition."

5–06 While there is no reference in Article 5 to ill-treatment, Article 3 of the Convention prohibits torture, inhuman and degrading treatment and has been heavily litigated in the European Court of Human Rights in the policing context.[8]

5–07 The Irish Constitution is rather more sparse in its provision that "no citizen shall be deprived of his personal liberty save in accordance with law".[9] Though the reference is to "citizen", it has been argued (and, it is thought, taken for granted) that "citizen" may be read in this context as synonymous with "person". Casey suggests "for many purposes, the supposed distinction between 'citizens' and 'persons' has no practical consequences".[10] The effect of Article 40.4.1° is that a person's freedom of movement can only be curtailed pursuant to a specific legal provision, either under the common law or statute, in line with Constitutional norms and mindful of the fundamental rights of the person whose liberty it is proposed to restrain. Article 40.4.1° thus intersects with Garda powers to stop and search, arrest and detain. It is for this reason that limitations have been placed on each of those powers, so that a person's freedom can be suspended only for a temporary and finite period prescribed by law.

DETENTION POWERS AND TIME PERIODS

5–08 The amount of time for which a person can be lawfully detained in garda custody is dictated by the seriousness of the offence under investigation. A general power of detention applies to all arrestable offences and is provided for in s 4 of

[8] See D Walsh, *Human Rights and Policing in Ireland: Law, Policy and Practice,* (Clarus Press, Dublin, 2009) chapter 4.

[9] Bunreacht na hÉireann, Article 40.4.1°. The Report of the Constitutional Review Group made only one recommendation concerning Article 40.4.1° "[t]he Review Group considers that the retention of the word 'citizen' in Article 40.4.1° would serve no purpose and accordingly recommends its replacement by the word 'person'... The Review Group is of the opinion that it would be desirable that the protection of Article 40.4 should extend to all persons, and not merely citizens... In view of the fact that the right not to be illegally detained is one of the most fundamental of rights, there would appear to be no justification for appearing to limit the benefit of this right to citizens." *Report of the Constitution Review Group* (Stationery Office, Dublin, 1996).

[10] See Casey, *Constitutional Law in Ireland,* (3rd ed, Round Hall Sweet & Maxwell, Dublin, 2000), p 444 *et seq.*

the Criminal Justice Act 1984,[11] a corollary of the general power of arrest in s 4 of the Criminal Law Act 1997. Specific detention powers apply to the investigation of other offences: s 30 of the Offences against the State Act 1939[12] is designed for the investigation of so-called "subversive" offences under the Offences against the State Acts; s 2 of the Criminal Justice (Drug Traffficking) Act 1996[13] is used only for the investigation of drug trafficking offences and s 50 of the Criminal Justice Act 2007[14] deals with certain categories of murder, offences involving firearms and organised crime. The common denominator of the latter powers is that they permit considerably longer periods of detention than is allowed under the general s 4 Criminal Justice Act 1984 provision.

The power to detain must always be approached fastidiously, since the admissibility of the vital evidence obtained in the course of a detention will depend on the lawfulness of the detention.

Section 4 of the Criminal Justice Act 1984

The most frequently employed power to detain is contained in s 4 of the Criminal Justice Act 1984. Section 4 permits detention where a person has been arrested without warrant on reasonable suspicion of having committed an arrestable offence. Before an arrestee can be detained, the member in charge of the garda station must be satisfied that the detention is necessary for the investigation of the offence. **5–09**

The initial period of detention permitted by s 4 is six hours. The detention may be extended for a further six hours on the authorisation of a garda of the rank of Superintendent or above. Again, there must be reasonable grounds for believing in the necessity of the detention before an extension can be granted. Finally, a member of the Garda Síochána not below the rank of Chief Superintendent may direct detention for a further period not exceeding 12 hours if he or she has reasonable grounds for believing that such further detention is necessary for the proper investigation of the offence. **5–10**

Rest Period from Midnight to 8 am

The Criminal Justice Act 1984 provides that detention may be suspended between midnight and 8 am if the member in charge considers that questioning should be **5–11**

---

11 As amended by s 2 of the Criminal Justice (Miscellaneous Provisions) Act 1997, s 34 of the Criminal Justice Act 1999, s 9 of the Criminal Justice Act 2006, s 24 of the Criminal Justice (Amendment) Act 2009 and s 7 of the Criminal Justice Act 2011.

12 As amended by s 10 of the Offences against the State (Amendment) Act 1998, s 187 of the Criminal Justice Act 2006 and s 21 of the Criminal Justice (Amendment) Act 2009.

13 As amended by s 10 of the Criminal Justice Act 2006.

14 As amended by s 23 of the Criminal Justice (Amendment) Act 2009.

suspended to give adequate opportunity for rest, and if the detainee consents in writing to the suspension.[15] A notice is given in writing specifying the time at which it is given

---

[15] Criminal Justice Act 1984, s 4(5A)(a). s 4(5A) was originally numbered s 4(6), and was renumbered s 4(5A) by the Criminal Justice Act 1999, s 34(b). It was deleted by s 47(a) of the Criminal Justice (Miscellaneous Provisions) Act 2009. However, s 47 of the Criminal Justice (Miscellaneous Provisions) Act 2009 was never commenced and was repealed by s 5 of the Criminal Justice Act 2011, with s 4(6) being reinstated and substituted by s 5 and s 7(c) of the Criminal Justice Act 2011. Both subsections of the 2011 Act have yet to be commenced (October 2013). The recast s 4(6) will, if commenced, provide: 4(6) (a) Subject to paragraphs (c) and (d), if a person is being detained pursuant to this section in a Garda Síochána station between midnight and 8 am—

- (i) any questioning of the person for the purpose of the investigation shall be suspended during that period,
- (ii) such period of time shall be excluded in reckoning a period of detention permitted by this section, and
- (iii) the powers conferred by section 6 shall not be exercised during the period of suspension.

(b) The member of the Garda Síochána in charge of the Garda Síochána station shall inform, or cause to be informed, the detained person that he or she may object to the suspension of questioning between midnight and 8 am.

(c) Paragraph (a) shall not have effect if the detained person objects to the suspension of questioning under that paragraph and such objection shall be recorded in writing or by electronic or other similar means.

(d) A member of the Garda Síochána in charge of a Garda Síochána station may authorise the questioning of a person detained pursuant to this section between the hours of midnight and 8 am where the member concerned has reasonable grounds for believing that to suspend the questioning would involve a risk of—

- (i) interference with, or injury to other persons,
- (ii) serious loss of, or damage to, property,
- (iii) the destruction of, or interference with, evidence,
- (iv) accomplices being alerted or the securing of their apprehension being made more difficult, or
- (v) hindering the recovery of property obtained as a result of an offence or the recovery of the value of any proceeds of an offence.

(e) If at any time during which the authorisation is in effect, the member of the Garda Síochána in charge of the Garda Síochána station believes there are no longer reasonable grounds for the authorisation, it shall be withdrawn.

(f) Where an authorisation is given under paragraph (d) it shall have effect from the time of the giving of a notice in the prescribed form under paragraph (g) until 8 am or until the time of the giving of a subsequent notice in the prescribed form under paragraph (h), as the case may be, and—

- (i) the period during which the authorisation has effect shall be included in reckoning a period of detention permitted by this section, and
- (ii) the powers conferred by section 6 shall be exercisable in respect of the person concerned.

(g) Where an authorisation is given under paragraph (d), the member of the Garda Síochána in charge of the Garda Síochána station shall give a notice in writing in the prescribed form to the detained person which shall—

- (i) state that an authorisation has been given,
- (ii) specify the time at which the authorisation was given together with the time at which the notice was given, and that member shall explain to the person orally the effect of the notice so given.

and outlining that the investigation is suspended for the period specified.[16] That period is excluded from the reckoning of a period of detention permitted by s 4 of the Criminal Justice Act 1984.[17] The effect of the suspension must be explained to the prisoner[18] and all details relating to the suspension and the notice must be recorded in the custody record.[19]

Where a suspect is detained on suspicion of drug trafficking pursuant to s 2 of the Criminal Justice (Drug Trafficking) Act 1996, there is no provision to allow for suspension of questioning from midnight to 8 am. Section 5 of the Criminal Justice (Drug Trafficking) Act 1996 provides for the application of certain provisions of the Criminal Justice Act 1984 to persons detained under s 2 of the Criminal Justice (Drug Trafficking) Act 1996 in the following terms: **5–12**

> "Sections 4(4), 4(7), 4(8), 4(8A), 4(8B), 4(11), 5,[20] 6(1) to (4), 6A, 8, 18, 19 and 19A of the Act of 1984 shall apply with any necessary modifications in relation to persons detained under section 2 as they apply to persons detained under section 4 of the Act of 1984."

Section 52 of the Criminal Justice Act 2007 is identical in its provision for the application of the same subsections of the Criminal Justice Act 1984 where suspects are detained pursuant to s 50 of the 2007 Act for the specific offences to which s 50 applies, i.e., murder involving the use of a firearm or explosive, murder to which s 3 of the Criminal Justice Act 1990 applies, possession of firearms with intent to endanger life,[21] false imprisonment involving the use of a firearm[22] or an organised crime offence.[23] Section 9 of the Criminal Justice Act 1984 provides that: **5–13**

(h) Where an authorisation is withdrawn under paragraph (e), the member of the Garda Síochána in charge of the Garda Síochána station shall give a notice in writing in the prescribed form to the detained person which shall—
  (i) state that the authorisation has been withdrawn, and
  (ii) specify the time at which the authorisation was withdrawn together with the time at which the notice was given, and that member shall explain to the person orally the effect of the notice so given.

(i) An authorisation or a withdrawal of an authorisation under this subsection may be given orally or in writing and if given orally shall be recorded in writing as soon as practicable.

(j) Nothing in paragraph (a) shall operate to prevent the powers conferred by section 6 being exercised in respect of a person who is arrested and detained between the hours of midnight and 8 am.

(k) In this subsection 'prescribed' means prescribed by the Minister in regulations made by the Minister under section 7."

16 Criminal Justice Act 1984, s 4(5A)(a).

17 *ibid*, s 4(5A)(a).

18 *ibid*, s 4(5A)(c).

19 *ibid*, s 4(5A)(d).

20 The reference here to s 5 of the Criminal Justice Act 1984 which appears in both s 5 of the Criminal Justice (Drug Trafficking) Act 1996 and s 52 of the Criminal Justice Act 2007 has been amended to refer to "5, 5A" in ss 13 and 14 of the Criminal Justice Act 2011. However, neither s 13 nor s 14 have yet been commenced (December 2013).

21 Firearms Act 1925, s 15.

22 False imprisonment is governed by s 15 of the Non Fatal Offences against the Person Act 1997

23 Under Part 7 of the Criminal Justice Act 2007.

> "Sections 4(8), 4(8A), 4(8B), 5, 6(2), 6(3), 6A, 18, 19 and 19A shall apply, with the necessary modifications, in relation to persons in custody under section 30 of the Act of 1939 and to powers conferred by section 7 of the Criminal Law Act, 1976, as they apply to persons detained under section 4 of this Act."

Section 9 of the Criminal Justice Act 1984 makes provision for the extension of s 4(8), 4(8A), 4(8B), 5, 6(2), 6(3), 6(3), 6A, 18, 19, 19A to persons detained under s 30 of the Offences against the State Act.

5–14 Given that there is no reference in s 5 of the Criminal Justice (Drug Trafficking) Act 1996, nor in s 52 of the Criminal Justice Act 2007, nor in s 9 of the Criminal Justice Act 1984 to s 4(5A) or (4(6) as the subsection was originally numbered[24]), s 4(5A) of the Act of 1984 and its provision for suspension of questioning between midnight and 8 am does not apply in the context of a detention under the Criminal Justice (Drug Trafficking) Act 1996, a s 30 detention or a detention under s 50 of the Criminal Justice Act 2007. However, it should be noted that Regulation 12 of the Custody Regulations provides that:

> "(7) (a) Except with the authority of the member in charge, an arrested person shall not be questioned between midnight and 8 a.m. in relation to an offence, which authority shall not be given unless—
> (i) he has been taken to the station during that period,
> (ii) in the case of a person detained under section 4 of the Act, he has not consented in writing to the suspension of questioning in accordance with subsection (6) of that section, or
> (iii) the member in charge has reasonable grounds for believing that to delay questioning the person would involve a risk of injury to persons, serious loss of or damage to property, destruction of or interference with evidence or escape of accomplices.
> (a) Subparagraph (a) (i) is subject to the provisions of Regulation 19 (2)."

Regulation 19(2) provides that "A person in custody shall be allowed such reasonable time for rest as is necessary."

5–15 Therefore, while the standard statutory suspension period does not apply in a drug trafficking, s 30[25] or s 50[26] detention, for compliance with the custody regulations, a suspect must have sufficient opportunity to rest, and questioning between midnight and 8 am must be authorised by the member in charge.

Medical Attention

5–16 Where medical attention is required, a detention period may be suspended to allow for medical attention. Where a garda considers that the detainee requires medical attention,

---

[24] s 4(5A) of the Criminal Justice Act 1984 was originally numbered 4(6), and was renumbered s 4(5A) by the Criminal Justice Act 1999, s 34(b). It was deleted by s 47(a) of the Criminal Justice (Miscellaneous Provisions) Act 2009. However, s 47 of the Criminal Justice (Miscellaneous Provisions) Act 2009 was never commenced and was repealed by s 5 of the Criminal Justice Act 2011, with s 4(6) being reinstated and substituted by s 7(c) of the Criminal Justice Act 2011. Both s 5 and s 7(c) of the 2011 Act have yet to be commenced (December 2013).

[25] Offences against the State Act 1939.

[26] Criminal Justice Act 2007.

or if the need for medical attention becomes apparent during the detention, and the person is taken to a hospital or elsewhere as a consequence, the period of absence from the station is excluded from the calculation of the detention period.[27] This is so whether the absence is prior to or post arrival at the garda station.[28]

Medical treatment may be required at the station, in which case a doctor may certify that, while the person does not require hospitalisation, the person is nevertheless unfit for questioning. The detainee will not be questioned during the period specified.[29] That period – which is not to exceed six hours[30] – is also excluded in the calculation of the detention period.[31] A medical certificate of suspension may only be provided once in the course of an individual's detention.[32] **5–17**

Attendance at Court

If the lawfulness of a detention under s 4 is challenged, the time spent outside the station in travelling to, from and at court is excluded from the reckoning of the permitted period of detention.[33] **5–18**

Pausing a Period of s 4 Detention under the Criminal Justice Act 2011

The Criminal Justice Act 2011 allows for the detention period under s 4 to be paused for a period not to exceed four months, to allow enquiries and investigation to be undertaken before the person is returned to custody and the fruits of those enquiries can be put to him.[34] Such a suspension may only occur twice, and the suspect is obliged to return to the garda station at a date and time notified to the suspect in writing.[35] The consequences of failure to return are arrest without warrant (whereupon the person will be returned to the station to continue the detention) and prosecution, with exposure to maximum penalties of 12 months imprisonment and a class A fine.[36] In the Dáil, the Minister for Justice and Equality, Alan Shatter, said that the period of four months was not a "magic formula," and that "[t]he figure of four months was chosen in order to ensure the suspension would not be unnecessarily extended while also giving the garda an opportunity to undertake further investigation". [37] It was felt that four months, as opposed to six or 12 months, would not unduly encroach on the rights of **5–19**

27 Criminal Justice Act 1984, s 4(8).
28 *ibid*, s 4(8).
29 *ibid*, s 4(8B)(a).
30 *ibid*, s 4(8B)(b).
31 *ibid*, s 4(8B)(a).
32 *ibid*, s 4(8B)(c).
33 *ibid*, s 4(8A).
34 *ibid*, s 4(3A), as inserted by s 7 of the Criminal Justice Act 2011.
35 *ibid*, s 4(3A)(c), as inserted by s 7 of the Criminal Justice Act 2011.
36 *ibid*, s 4(4B) and (4C), as inserted by s 8 of the Criminal Justice Act 2011. On Class A fines see the Fines Act 2010.
37 Dáil Debates, 6 July 2011.

those under investigation, and he clarified that such persons would not be restricted during the suspension in terms of travel.[38]

5–20 The rationale for the suspension period was described by the minister as being "to make more effective use of detention periods". [39] He referred to white collar crime, at which the Act is aimed, and continued:

> "The complexity of recent investigations and the volumes of documents involved have shown that it is not always possible to complete questioning and check facts in one period of detention. The suspension of detention provisions, provided for in section 7, is being applied to the 24-hour maximum detention period permitted under section 4 of the Criminal Justice Act 1984. The amendments will allow the period of detention under section 4 of the 1984 Act to be suspended and the person to be released during the period of suspension. The purpose of these provisions is to allow the garda to follow up on information obtained during questioning and to conduct further investigations during the suspension period."[40]

5–21 The Act is targeted at specified serious and complex offences attracting a penalty of at least five years' imprisonment, including offences (as well as attempts, conspiring and inciting to commit, aiding, abetting, counselling and procuring such offences) in the areas of banking and finance, company law, money laundering, fraud, corruption, competition, consumer protection and cybercrime. Relevant offences[41] for the purposes of the legislation are outlined in Schedule 1 of the Criminal Justice Act 2011 as follows:

Offences relating to banking, investment of funds and other financial activities

1. An offence under s 58 of the Central Bank Act 1971 insofar as it relates to a contravention of s 17, 18, 23, 24 or 25 of that Act.
2. An offence under s 37 (6) or 41 (1) of the Insurance Act 1989.
3. An offence under s 20 (4) or 24 (4) of the Trustee Savings Banks Act 1989.
4. An offence under s 11 (3) or 13 (5) of the Unit Trusts Act 1990.
5. An offence under s 25 (5) or 27 (4), or subsection (7) or (8) of s 35, of the Investment Limited Partnerships Act 1994.
6. An offence under s 10 (16), 19 (1)(b), 30, 34, 35 (4), 46 (2), 54 (6), 56 (9), subsection (3), (5), (6) or (9) of s 52 or subsection (7) or (8) of s 79, of the Investment Intermediaries Act 1995.
7. An offence under s 12 (2) of the Consumer Credit Act 1995 insofar as it relates to a contravention of subsection (1) or (3) of s 97, or s 101, 102 or 127, of that Act.
8. An offence under s 29 (3), or subsection (7) or (8) of s 43, of the Investor Compensation Act 1998.
9. An offence under s 14 (3) or 15 (2) of the Investment Funds, Companies and Miscellaneous Provisions Act 2005.
10. An offence under s 5 (2) of the Markets in Financial Instruments and Miscellaneous Provisions Act 2007 insofar as it relates to—

---

[38] *ibid.*

[39] Dáil Debates, 26 July 2011.

[40] *ibid.*

[41] Criminal Justice Act 2011, s 3 and schedule 1.

(a) a failure to discharge a duty to which a person is subject under Regulation 40(1) or 112(1) of the European Communities (Markets in Financial Instruments) Regulations 2007 (SI No 60 of 2007), or
(b) a contravention of Regulation 19, 52, 159 or 187B of those Regulations.

11. An offence under Regulation 20(2), 22(4), 58(9), 59(8), 60(6), 62(4) or 76(1) of the European Communities (Reinsurance) Regulations 2006 (SI No 380 of 2006).
12. An offence under s 7 of the National Asset Management Agency Act 2009 insofar as it relates to a person other than a credit institution (within the meaning of that Act).
13. An offence under s 48 of the Central Bank Reform Act 2010.

Company law offences

14. An offence under s 60 (15), 295 or 297, or under paragraph (a), (d), (e), (f), (g), (i), (j), (k), (l), (m), (n), (o) or (p) of s 293 (1), of the Companies Act 1963.
15. An offence under any of the following provisions of the Companies (Amendment) Act 1986:
    (a) s 22(1)(a) (insofar as it relates to a failure to comply with s 5 or 16 of that Act),
    (b) s 22(2) (insofar as it relates to a failure to take all reasonable steps to secure compliance with the requirements of s 3 of that Act or a failure to comply with s 13 of that Act), or
    (c) s 22(3).
16. An offence under s 197, 202 (10), 242 or 243 (1) of the Companies Act 1990.
17. An offence under s 37 (1) of the Companies (Amendment) (No 2) Act 1999.
18. An offence under s 48 of the Investment Funds, Companies and Miscellaneous Provisions Act 2005.
19. An offence under Regulation 5 or 6 of the Market Abuse (Directive 2003/6/EC) Regulations 2005 (SI No 342 of 2005).
20. An offence under Regulation 76(4) of the Transparency (Directive 2004/109/EC) Regulations 2007 (SI No 277 of 2007).

Money laundering and terrorist offences

21. An offence under s 7, 8, 9, 10, 35, 37, 38, 42 or 49 of the Criminal Justice (Money Laundering and Terrorist Financing) Act 2010.
22. An offence under s 13 of the Criminal Justice (Terrorist Offences) Act 2005.

Theft and fraud offences, etc.

23. An offence under s 4, 6, 7, 9, 10, 11, 15, 17, 18, 25, 26, 27, 28, 29, 33, 34, 35, 36, 37, 38, 42, 43, 44, 45 or 51 of the Criminal Justice (Theft and Fraud Offences) Act 2001.
24. Conspiracy to defraud at common law.
25. An offence under s 119 of the Registration of Title Act 1964.
26. An offence under s 17 of the Criminal Justice Act 2011.

Bribery and corruption offences

27. An offence under s 1 of the Prevention of Corruption Act 1906.
28. An offence under s 7 or 8 of the Prevention of Corruption (Amendment) Act 2001.

Consumer protection offences

29. An offence under s 65 of the Consumer Protection Act 2007.

Criminal damage to property offences

30. An offence under s 2, 3 or 4 of the Criminal Damage Act 1991 insofar as the offence relates to data (within the meaning of s 1 of that Act) or a storage medium in which such data are kept.

5–22 In England and Wales, the practice of pausing detention periods was scrutinised following the case of *R (on the application of Chief Constable of Greater Manchester Police) v Salford Magistrates' Court and Paul Hookway*[42] where it was held that the detention clock did not stop running when a suspect was bailed. It had been common practice prior to the decision to split a suspect's detention period for weeks and even months, during which period the suspect was released on bail and could be called back so that new evidence could be gathered and put to the suspect. Under the Police and Criminal Evidence Act 1984 (PACE), detention is permitted for a maximum of 96 hours. The police had operated on the basis that only the time spent in police detention was calculable in determining the 96-hour limit and that the 'detention clock' was paused when an individual was released on police bail. The Police (Detention and Bail) Act 2011 was enacted to restore the position as it had been understood prior to the *Hookway* decision, to provide for the clock to stop while suspects are bailed. Unlike the Irish legislation, there are no limitation periods, either in terms of the time for which questioning is suspended or on the number of times a person may be recalled to the police station, once the 96 hour detention limit is not exceeded within the station.

5–23 The Irish legislation makes the position abundantly clear:

> "For the avoidance of doubt it is hereby declared that—
> (a) where a person's detention is suspended under subsection (3A), the detention shall remain suspended until such time as it is continued under subsection (3E) and, accordingly, the period of time during which the detention remains suspended shall be excluded in reckoning a period of detention permitted by this section…"[43]

Further, an arrest for a separate offence will not in any way affect the suspension of the original detention period.[44]

5–24 Where it is proposed to suspend a detention and conditionally release the suspect, the member in charge must give (or arrange for the suspect to be given) a notice in writing[45] outlining

[42] *R (on the application of Chief Constable of Greater Manchester Police) v Salford Magistrates' Court and Paul Hookway* [2011] EWHC 1578 (Admin).

[43] Criminal Justice Act 1984, s 4(3F) as inserted by s 7 of the Criminal Justice Act 2011.

[44] *ibid*, s 4(F)(b) as inserted by s 7 of the Criminal Justice Act 2011.

[45] *ibid*, s 4(3C)(a) as inserted by s 7 of the Criminal Justice Act 2011.

(i) that his or her detention is being suspended,
(ii) the Garda Síochána station and the date and time on which he or she is required to return to the station for the continuation of the detention, and
(iii) the consequences under s 4A and 4B of failing to return in accordance with subsection (3B).

The effect of the notice must be explained when it is being given to the person.[46]

The date, time and location on which the person is expected to return to the station may be altered by a garda of Inspector rank if there are reasonable grounds to believe that the change in date, time or station is necessary for the proper investigation of the offence.[47]

Section 30 of the Offences against the State Act 1939

Section 30 of the Offences against the State Act 1939 is an extraordinary power to arrest, detain and interrogate which applies to offences which are 'scheduled' under s 36 of the Offences against the State Act 1939.[48] See further *Chapter 1: Arrest* at para 1 – 41 *et seq*. **5–25**

Section 30(1) provides: **5–26**

> "A member of the Garda Síochána ... may without warrant stop, search, interrogate and arrest any person, or do any one or more of those things in respect of any person, whom he suspects of having committed or being about to commit or being or having been concerned in the commission of an offence under any section or sub-section of this Act or an offence which is for the time being a scheduled offence ... or whom he suspects

46 Criminal Justice Act 1984, s 4(3C)(b) as inserted by s 7 of the Criminal Justice Act 2011.

47 *ibid*, s 4(3D) as inserted by s 7 of the Criminal Justice Act 2011.

48 s 36 of the Offences against the State Act 1939 provides: "36(1) Whenever while this Part of this Act is in force the Government is satisfied that the ordinary courts are inadequate to secure the effective administration of justice and the preservation of public peace and order in relation to offences of any particular class or kind or under any particular enactment, the Government may by order declare that offences of that particular class or kind or under that particular enactment shall be scheduled offences for the purposes of this Part of this Act.

(2) Whenever the Government has made under the foregoing sub-section of this section any such declaration as is authorised by that sub-section, every offence of the particular class or kind or under the particular enactment to which such declaration relates shall, until otherwise provided by an order under the next following sub-section of this section, be a scheduled offence for the purposes of this Part of this Act.

(3) Whenever the Government is satisfied that the effective administration of justice and the preservation of public peace and order in relation to offences of any particular class or kind or under any particular enactment which are for the time being scheduled offences for the purposes of this Part of this Act can be secured through the medium of the ordinary courts, the Government may by order declare that offences of that particular class or kind or under that particular enactment shall, upon the making of such order, cease to be scheduled offences for the purposes of this Part of this Act."

It should be noted that s 14(3) of the Offences against the State (Amendment) Act 1998 provides that nothing in s 14(1) or (2) of that Act shall be construed as affecting or limiting in any particular case the exercise by the Government of any of its powers under any provision of s 36 of this Act

> of carrying a document relating to the commission or intended commission of any such offence as aforesaid or whom he suspects of being in possession of information relating to the commission or intended commission of any such offence as aforesaid."[49]

5–27 Section 30(3) allows for detention for 24 hours with the potential for extension for a further 24 hours:

> "Whenever a person is arrested under this section, he may be removed to and detained in custody in a Garda station, a prison or some other convenient place for a period of twenty-four hours from the time of arrest and may, if an officer of the Garda Síochána not below the rank of Chief Superintendent so directs, be so detained for a further period of twenty-four hours."

5–28 A further 24-hour extension is possible on an application by a Superintendent to a judge of the District Court.[50] The judge must be satisfied that the further detention of the person is necessary for the proper investigation of the offence and that the investigation is being conducted diligently and expeditiously.[51]

5–29 Section 30 is unique in a number of respects: detention is permitted without the necessity of an application to the member in charge and without an offence actually having been committed. In effect, it gives a power of preventative detention for anticipated offences, since s 30(1) provides a power of arrest for persons suspected of being "about to commit" a scheduled offence or of "carrying a document relating to the commission or intended commission of any such offence..." or of "being in possession of information relating to the commission or intended commission of any such [scheduled] offence".[52] Walsh has argued that, whereas the criminalisation of an attempt is unproblematic, the arrest of a suspect who is merely at a preparatory stage may amount to an unconstitutional form of preventative detention.[53] The constitutionality and ECHR compliance of the s 30 power of arrest and detention for having documentation and/or information on the intended commission of an offence by a third party is questionable.[54] The Committee to Review the Offences against the State Acts recommended the replacement of the power to arrest where a person is "about to commit" an offence with a power to arrest "where is reasonably considered necessary to prevent the imminent commission of an offence", since the current formulation may justify detention for conduct which is not criminal, nor sufficiently proximate to an intended criminal act to amount to an attempt.[55]

---

[49] For a detailed examination of this section (and the Offences against the State legislation generally), see the *Report of the Committee to Review the Offences against the State Acts 1939–1998 and Related Matters* (the Hederman Report) (Dublin, 2002).

[50] Offences against the State Act 1939, s 30(4) as substituted by the Offences against the State (Amendment) Act 1998, s 10.

[51] *ibid,* s 30(4A) as inserted by the Offences against the State (Amendment) Act 1998, s 10.

[52] *ibid*, s 30(1).

[53] D Walsh, *Human Rights and Policing in Ireland* (Clarus Press, Dublin, 2009) at p 37.

[54] *ibid.*

[55] *Report of the Committee to Review the Offences against the State Acts 1939–1998 and Related Matters* (Stationery Office, Dublin, 2002) at paras 7.51–7.57.

Where an application is made in the District Court for the extension of a detention under s 30, the Court may direct the exclusion of all persons not directly connected with proceedings and *bona fide* representatives of the press, or may direct that the proceedings be heard otherwise than in public.[56] **5–30**

Questioning in Relation to Non-Scheduled Offences

The 72-hour detention period permitted by s 30 applies only to scheduled offences. In the course of a s 30 detention, a suspect may be questioned about related non-scheduled offences provided the scheduled offence is being genuinely investigated. The arrest for a scheduled offence may not be used as a colourable device to enable gardaí to question the suspect about a non-scheduled offence. However, where a scheduled and non-scheduled offence form part of the same transaction, the gardaí are not precluded from questioning a suspect about both.[57] In *People (DPP) v Howley*, it was held that the predominant motive for the arrest need not be the investigation of the scheduled offence; what is required is a genuine desire to pursue the scheduled offence.[58] **5–31**

Application of Provisions of the Criminal Justice Act 1984 to Persons in Section 30 Detention

Certain provisions of the Criminal Justice Act 1984 apply equally to prisoners in s 30 detention,[59] including the suspension of the period of detention for attendance at hospital[60] or when a prisoner is medically certified unfit for questioning,[61] as well as access to a solicitor and notification of the detention to a third party.[62] Inferences may also be drawn.[63] **5–32**

Section 2 of the Criminal Justice (Drug Trafficking) Act 1996

The Criminal Justice (Drug Trafficking) Act 1996 allows for detention of drug-trafficking suspects for up to seven days, and for inferences to be drawn from the silence of suspects while under questioning. **5–33**

Section 2(1) of the 1996 Act provides the threshold for detention as being "reasonable cause" for suspicion of having committed a drug-trafficking offence. A drug-trafficking offence is defined in s 3(1) of the Criminal Justice Act 1994 as meaning any of the following— **5–34**

---

[56] Offences against the State Act 1939, s 30(4BA)(a).

[57] *People (DPP) v Walsh* [1986] IR 722, [1988] ILRM 137.

[58] *People (DPP) v Howley* [1989] ILRM 629.

[59] The Criminal Justice Act 1984 provides at s 9 (as amended by s 55 of the Criminal Justice Act 2007 and s 24 of the Criminal Justice (Amendment) Act 2009) that "Sections 4(8), 4(8A), 4(8B), 5, 6(2), 6(3), 6A, 18, 19 and 19A shall apply, with the necessary modifications, in relation to persons in custody under section 30 of the Act of 1939 and to the powers conferred by section 7 of the Criminal Law Act, 1976, as they apply to persons detained pursuant to section 4 of this Act".

[60] Criminal Justice Act 1984, s 4(8).

[61] *ibid*, s 4 (8B).

[62] *ibid*, s 5.

[63] *ibid*, s 18, 19 and 19A.

(a) an offence under any regulations made under s 5 of the Misuse of Drugs Act, 1977, involving the manufacture, production, preparation, importation, exportation, supply, offering to supply, distribution or transportation of a controlled drug,[64]
(b) an offence under s 15 of that Act of possession of a controlled drug for unlawful sale or supply,
(c) an offence under s 20 of that Act (assisting in or inducing the commission outside the State of an offence punishable under a corresponding law),
(d) an offence under the Customs Acts in relation to the importation or exportation of a controlled drug or in relation to the fraudulent evasion of any prohibition, restriction or obligation in relation to such importation or exportation,
(e) an offence under s 31 of the Criminal Justice (Drug Trafficking) Act 1996 in relation to the proceeds of drug trafficking,
(f) an offence under s 33 or 34 of the Criminal Justice (Drug Trafficking) Act 1996, or
(g) an offence of aiding, abetting, counselling or procuring the commission of any of the offences mentioned in paragraphs (a) to (f) or of attempting or conspiring to commit any such offence or inciting another person to do so.

5–35 The person may be brought to a garda station where he or she may be detained if the member in charge has reasonable grounds for believing that his or her detention is necessary for the proper investigation of the offence.[65] The maximum initial period is six hours,[66] but this may be extended by a further 18 hours if an officer not below the rank of Superintendent, with reasonable grounds for believing it necessary for the proper investigation of the offence, so directs.[67] Detention may then be extended for a further 24 hours, i.e., to 48 hours in total, if a Chief Superintendent so directs on the same grounds.[68] A still further extension of up to 72 hours is possible on the application of a Chief Superintendent or officer of a higher rank to a judge of the District or Circuit Court.[69] Any such application must be predicated on the officer having reasonable grounds that such a detention is necessary for the proper investigation of the offence.[70] Finally, yet another extension may be granted for up to 48 hours, i.e., authorising detention up to a possible cumulative seven-day period, on application to a judge by such an officer on the same grounds, such further warrant to issue by reference to the same judicial test.[71]

Application of Provisions of the Criminal Justice Act 1984

5–36 The Criminal Justice (Drug Trafficking) Act 1996 provides for certain provisions of the Criminal Justice Act 1984 to apply to persons detained under s 2 of the 1996 Act.[72] Those provisions are s 4(4) (immediate release if there are no longer reasonable

[64] A controlled drug is defined by s 2 of the Misuse of Drugs Act 1977.
[65] Criminal Justice (Drug Trafficking) Act 1996, s 2(1)(a)(ii)).
[66] *ibid*, s 2(2)(a).
[67] *ibid*, s 2(2)(b).
[68] *ibid*, s 2(2)(c).
[69] *ibid*, s 2(2)(g)(i).
[70] *ibid*, s 2(2)(g)(ii).
[71] *ibid*, s 2(2)(h)(i) and (ii).
[72] *ibid*, s 5.

grounds for believing that detention is necessary for the investigation of the offence), s 4(7) (persons under 12 years of age not to be detained), s 4(8) (hospitalisation while in custody and exclusion of time in the reckoning of a period of detention), s 4(8A) (time for court applications challenging lawfulness of detention excluded in the reckoning of a period of detention), s 4(8B) (medically certified unfitness for questioning), s 4(11) (powers exercised without prejudice to other powers exercisable by gardaí), s 5 (access to solicitor and notification of detention), s 6(1) to (4) (powers to demand name, address, to search, fingerprint, photograph and seize items), s 6A (use of reasonable force for the taking of photographs, palm prints and fingerprints), s 8 (destruction of records) and s 18, s 19 and s 19A (inferences).

Procedural Aspects of Extension of Detention Applications under Section 2

The Criminal Justice Drug Trafficking Act 1996 has been amended by the Criminal Justice Act 2006 and the Criminal Justice (Amendment) Act 2009. From a procedural perspective, the important points to note are as follows: **5–37**

1. Applications for extensions of detention periods may now be made and heard *in camera*;
2. No challenge to the legality of the arrest may be made in the course of an extension application;
3. The period from the arrival in the courthouse until the final determination of the extension of detention application is not included in the calculation of the time period.[73] In a sense, time stands still once the suspect is brought before the court before the expiration of the permissible pre-application detention period.

Section 50 of the Criminal Justice Act 2007

Extensive detention periods apply under the Criminal Justice Act 2007 to certain categories of murder, firearms and organised crime offences. Suspects under investigation for such offences can be detained in Garda custody for up to 168 hours (seven days), though the detention period may amount in total to an even longer period if **5–38**

[73] s 2(7A) was inserted by the Criminal Justice Act 2006 and has since been substituted by s 22 of the Criminal Justice (Amendment) Act 2009. It now provides: "2(7A) Notwithstanding subsections (2) and (7), if—

(a) an application is to be made, or is made, under subsection (2) for a warrant authorising the detention for a further period of a person detained under that subsection, and

(b) the period of detention under that subsection has not expired at the time of the arrival of the person concerned at the court house for the purposes of the hearing of the application but would, but for this subsection, expire before, or during the hearing (including, if such should occur, any adjournment of the hearing), it shall be deemed not to expire until the final determination of the application; and, for purposes of this subsection—

(i) a certificate signed by the court clerk or registrar in attendance at the court house concerned stating the time of the arrival of the person concerned at that court house shall be evidence, until the contrary is shown, of the time of that person's arrival there;

(ii) 'court house' includes any venue at which the hearing of the application takes place."

The Criminal Justice (Amendment) Act 2009 came into operation when it was signed into law on 23 July 2009.

periods of absence for attendance at hospital or during a period of medical unfitness for interview are not included in reckoning the total detention period.[74]

5–39 The relevant offences are:

1. Murder involving the use of a firearm or an explosive (Criminal Justice Act 2007 s 50(1)(a));
2. Murder to which s 3 of the Criminal Justice Act 1990 applies, i.e.,
   (a) murder of a member of the Garda Síochána in the course of his duty,
   (b) murder of a prison officer in the course of his duty,
   (c) murder in the course or furtherance of an offence under s 6, 7, 8 or 9 of the Offences against the State Act, 1939, or in the course or furtherance of the activities of an unlawful organisation within the meaning of s 18 (other than paragraph (f)) of that Act, and
   (d) murder, committed within the state for a political motive, of the head of a foreign state or of a member of the government of, or a diplomatic officer of, a foreign state (Criminal Justice Act 2007 s 50(1)(b));
3. Possession of a firearm or ammunition with intent to endanger life or cause serious injury to property contrary to s 15 of the Firearms Act 1925[75] (Criminal Justice Act 2007 (s 50(1)(c));
4. False imprisonment involving the use of a firearm contrary to s 15 of the Non-Fatal Offences against the Person Act 1997 (Criminal Justice Act 2007, s 50(1)(d));
5. Organised crime offences under Part 7 of the Criminal Justice Act 2006,[76] i.e., conspiracy to commit a serious offence[77]; participating in, facilitating or contributing to a criminal organisation[78] and committing an offence for the benefit of, at the direction of, or in association with a criminal organisation Criminal Justice Act 2007, s 50(1)(e), as inserted by s 23 of the Criminal Justice (Amendment) Act 2009).[79]

Procedural Aspects of Extended Detention Applications under Section 50

5–40 Where there is a risk that an investigation will be compromised by public hearing, applications to extend a period of detention under s 50 may be heard *in camera*.

---

[74] Y Daly opines: "It would seem, though it is not entirely clear on the face of the [Criminal Justice] 2007 Bill, that the rest period allowable for detained suspects between midnight and 8am would not be included in the reckoning of this 168 hours, and that, accordingly, a suspect might in reality find himself confined within the Garda station for more than seven days. In fact, a suspect might conceivably find himself deprived of his liberty, in the custody of the Garda Síochána for nine or ten days." "Criminal Justice Bill, 2007: Effects on the Pre-Trial Process," Paper delivered at Criminal Justice Bill 2007: Implications for Law and Practice, Trinity College Dublin, 9 May 2007. s 52 of the Criminal Justice Act 2007 as it was eventually enacted makes no reference to the midnight to 8am rest period. There is, however, provision for suspension on medical grounds and for that time to be excluded in the reckoning of the detention period.

[75] As substituted by s 42 of the Criminal Justice Act 2006.

[76] This category of offences was brought within the remit of s 50 by s 23 of the Criminal Justice (Amendment) Act 2009, which came into effect on 23 July 2009.

[77] s 71 of the Criminal Justice Act 2006.

[78] *ibid* s 72.

[79] *ibid* s 73.

The judge hearing the application must be satisfied that the exclusion of the public is desirable to avoid a risk of prejudice to the investigation.[80] There is even provision for the exclusion of the person to whom the application relates and their legal advisers where particular evidence is to be given relating to steps that have been taken or which are to be taken in the course of the investigation.[81]

Application of Certain Provisions of the Criminal Justice Act 1984

Section 52 of the Criminal Justice Act 2007 extends provisions of the Criminal Justice Act 1984 to persons detained under s 50 of the Criminal Justice Act 2007, so that detainees can have the detention period suspended in the event of hospitalisation,[82] may be certified medically unfit for questioning[83] are entitled to access the services of a solicitor and to have a person of their choice notified of the fact of and location of their detention.[84] The same inference-drawing provisions also apply[85] and the period of suspension can also be suspended in the event of a court appearance during the detention.[86] **5–41**

THE CUSTODY REGULATIONS AND THE CPT STANDARDS

Safeguards to protect persons in custody seek to ensure that there is a degree of parity between the gardaí and the detained person, and serve a dual purpose by ensuring the quality, integrity and admissibility of evidence gathered during detention.[87] Such safeguards provide for protection from ill-treatment, cruelty and degradation as well as for the provision of adequate food, rest, medical attention, legal advice, familial contact, information, interpretation services, consular assistance and limitations on the numbers of gardaí who may be present at interview. **5–42**

Designed to provide equality of arms between the Garda and the detainee, the protections extended to prisoners in Garda custody strike a balance between the competing interests of the community in the investigation of crime and the right of the suspect to freedom from oppression and ill-treatment.[88] **5–43**

---

80 s 50(4A)(a) of the Criminal Justice Act 2007 as inserted by s 23 of the Criminal Justice (Amendment) Act 2009.

81 s 50(4A)(b) of the Criminal Justice Act 2007 as inserted by s 23 of the Criminal Justice (Amendment) Act 2009.

82 Criminal Justice Act 1984, s 4(8).

83 *ibid*, s 4(8B).

84 *ibid*, s 5.

85 s 52 of the Criminal Justice Act 2007 provides "Sections 4(4), 4(7), 4(8), 4(8A), 4(8B), 4(11), 5, 6(1) to (4), 6A, 8, 18, 19 and 19A of the Act of 1984 shall apply with any necessary modifications in relation to persons detained under section 50 as they apply to persons detained under section 4 of that Act".

86 *ibid*, s 4(8A).

87 L Campbell, S Kilcommins and C O'Sullivan, *Criminal Law in Ireland – Cases and Commentary* (Clarus Press, Dublin, 2010) at p 435.

88 *ibid* at p 435.

5–44 The primary guidelines on the treatment of persons in custody in Ireland are contained in a Statutory Instrument: the Criminal Justice Act, 1984 (Treatment Of Persons In Custody In Garda Síochána Stations) Regulations 1987,[89] which provide that gardaí shall:

> "... act with due respect for the personal rights of persons in custody and their dignity as human persons, and shall have regard for the special needs of any of them who may be under a physical or mental disability, while complying with the obligation to prevent escapes from custody and continuing to act with diligence and determination in the investigation of crime and the protection and vindication of the personal rights of other persons."[90]

5–45 The regulations outline a number of practical protective measures for detained persons: the provision of an independent member in charge to monitor the detention period; the recording of information concerning the arrested person; the details of their arrest and detention (the custody record); guidance as to the proper conduct of interviews; as well as the provision of information and medical, legal and general assistance to that person.

5–46 The Custody Regulations are not particularly expansive. Greater elaboration on best practice can be found in the CPT Standards,[91] a document published by the European Committee for the Prevention of Torture and Inhuman or Degrading Treatment or Punishment (CPT),[92] which describes some of the substantive issues which the committee pursues when carrying out visits to places of deprivation of liberty. The CPT attaches particular importance to three rights which the committee considers to be fundamental safeguards against the ill-treatment of persons detained by the police: the right of the person to have the fact of his detention notified to a third party of his choice (family member, friend, consulate); the right of access to a lawyer[93]; and the right to request a medical examination by a doctor of his choice (in addition to any medical examination carried out by a doctor called by the police authorities).[94] These rights should apply from the very outset of deprivation of liberty, i.e., from the point of arrest or apprehension. The committee emphasises the importance of the provision of information also, since rights are of little use to

---

89 SI No 119 of 1987. The regulations were amended slightly by SI No 641 of 2006, Criminal Justice Act 1984 (Treatment Of Persons In Custody In Garda Síochána Stations) (Amendment) Regulations 2006

90 *ibid*, Regulation 3.

91 European Committee for the Prevention of Torture and Inhuman or Degrading Treatment or Punishment (CPT), *CPT Standards,* CPT/Inf/E (2002) 1 - Rev. 2010.

92 The CPT organises visits to places of detention, in order to assess how persons deprived of their liberty are treated. These places include prisons, juvenile detention centres, police stations, holding centres for immigration detainees, psychiatric hospitals, social care homes, etc. After each visit, the CPT sends a detailed report to the State concerned. This report includes the CPT's findings and its recommendations, comments and requests for information. The CPT also requests a detailed response to the issues raised in its report. These reports and responses form part of the ongoing dialogue with the States concerned. See www.cpt.coe.int.

93 The right of access to a lawyer in custody has recently been the subject of a Directive, Directive 2013/48/EU of 22 October 2013 on the right of access to a lawyer in criminal proceedings and in European arrest warrant proceedings, OJ L 294, 6 November 2013. The UK, Ireland and Denmark have opted out of the Directive. See further below at paras 5 – 55 and 5 – 56.

94 *CPT Standards,* Extract from the second General Report [CPT/Inf (92) 3], para 38, p 6.

a detained person if he or she is not aware of them.[95] The CPT Standards stipulate that a person taken into police custody should be expressly informed without delay of all his rights, and that there should be no delay in assisting detained persons in the exercise of their rights.

The CPT Standards are quoted extensively in the European Code of Police Ethics, which in turn outlines the following standards for persons in police custody: **5–47**

> "54. Deprivation of liberty of persons shall be as limited as possible and conducted with regard to the dignity, vulnerability and personal needs of each detainee. A custody record shall be kept systematically for each detainee.
>
> 55. The police shall, to the extent possible according to domestic law, promptly inform persons deprived of their liberty of the reasons for the deprivation of their liberty and of any charge against them, and shall also without delay inform persons deprived of their liberty of the procedure applicable to their case.
>
> 56. The police shall provide for the safety, health, hygiene and appropriate nourishment of persons in the course of their custody. Police cells shall be of a reasonable size, have adequate lighting and ventilation and be equipped with suitable means of rest.
>
> 57. Persons deprived of their liberty by the police shall have the right to have the deprivation of their liberty notified to a third party of their choice, to have access to legal assistance and to have a medical examination by a doctor, whenever possible, of their choice.
>
> 58. The police shall, to the extent possible, separate persons deprived of their liberty under suspicion of having committed a criminal offence from those deprived of their liberty for other reasons. There shall normally be a separation between men and women as well as between adults and juveniles."

Conditions and Treatment in Custody

Regulations 19 and 20 of the Custody Regulations deal specifically with conditions and treatment in custody. They are worth setting out in full: **5–48**

> **"Conditions of custody**
> 19. (1) A person shall be kept in custody only in a station which has facilities to enable him to be treated in accordance with these Regulations for the period during which he is expected to be in custody in that station.
>
> (2) A person in custody shall be allowed such reasonable time for rest as is necessary.
>
> (3) A person in custody shall be provided with such meals as are necessary and, in any case, at least two light meals and one main meal in any twenty-four hour period. He may have meals supplied at his own expense where it is practicable for the member in charge to arrange this.

[95] The rights of suspects in the European Union to information are also set out in a European legal instrument, Directive 2012/13/EU of 22 May 2012 on the right to information in criminal proceedings. The Directive is briefly considered below at paras 5 – 53 and 5 – 54.

(4) Access to toilet facilities shall be provided for a person in custody.

(5) Where it is necessary to place persons in custody in cells, as far as practicable not more than one person shall be kept in each cell. Persons of the opposite sex shall not be placed in a cell together. A violent person shall not be placed in a cell with other persons if this can be avoided.

(6) Where a person is kept in a cell, a member shall visit him at intervals of approximately half an hour. A drunken person or a person under the influence of drugs shall be visited and spoken to and if necessary roused for this purpose at intervals of approximately a quarter of an hour for a period of two hours or longer if his condition warrants it.

(7) A member shall be accompanied when visiting a person in custody of the opposite sex who is alone in a cell.

(8) A person in custody under the age of eighteen years shall not be kept in a cell unless there is no other secure accommodation available and where practicable shall not be placed in a cell with an adult other than an adult relative.

Persons in custody not to be ill-treated.

20. (1) No member shall subject a person in custody to ill-treatment of any kind or the threat of ill-treatment(whether against the person himself, his family or any other person connected with him) or permit any other person to do so.

(2) No member shall use force against a person in custody except such reasonable force as is necessary—
(a) in self-defence,
(b) to secure compliance with lawful directions,
(c) to prevent his escape, or
(d) to restrain him from injuring himself or others, damaging property or destroying or interfering with evidence.

(3) If a member uses force which causes injury to a person in custody, he shall, if he is not the member in charge, report the circumstances to that member, who shall report the matter to the superintendent in charge of the district. If the force is used by the member in charge, he shall report the circumstances to that superintendent.

(4) If it comes to the notice of a member that there has been a contravention of paragraph (1), (2) or (3) by another member—
(a) he shall report the matter to the member in charge or (in case the contravention is by the member in charge) to the superintendent in charge of the district, and
(b) unless the matter has already been reported to that superintendent, the member in charge shall report it to him.

(5) The action taken in accordance with paragraph (3) or (4) shall be recorded.

(6) On receipt of a report under paragraph (3) or (4) by a superintendent, he shall investigate the matter without delay or cause it to be so investigated.

(7) If a person in custody makes a complaint concerning the conduct of a member (whether before or after his arrest) or, if such a complaint is made on his behalf, the fact that a complaint was made shall be recorded. Particulars of the complaint shall be recorded in a separate document, a copy of which shall be attached to and form part of the custody record. If the complaint alleges physical ill-treatment, the member in charge shall arrange for the person to be medically examined as soon as practicable unless, in

a case where the allegation relates to another member, he considers the complaint to be frivolous or vexatious."[96]

The Custody Regulations predate the establishment of the Garda Síochána Ombudsman Commission. Members must now comply with the procedures set out in the Garda Síochána Act 2005 in respect of complaints against gardaí. Complaints may be made orally or in writing, and on receipt of a complaint, the garda must

(a) record the complaint and the date and time of its receipt,
(b) provide the complainant with a written acknowledgement of its receipt, and
(c) forward to the Ombudsman Commission a copy of the complaint or, if the complaint was not made in writing, a copy of the record of the complaint.[97]

The Garda Commissioner must also be notified.[98]

Breach of the Custody Regulations

5–49 Sections 7(3) and 27 of the Criminal Justice Act 1984 provide that a breach of the Criminal Justice Act 1984 (Treatment of Persons in Custody in Garda Síochána Stations) Regulations 1987 or the Criminal Justice Act 1984 (Electronic Recording of Interviews) Regulations 1997 alone will not of itself affect the admissibility in evidence at trial of any statement made by a suspect in the pre-trial process. However, failure to comply with the Regulations may also represent a breach of the constitutional rights of the accused and as such the trial judge has a discretion to exclude evidence gathered in the course of the detention. In *DPP v Spratt*, the High Court held:

> "... [N]on-compliance with the requirements of the regulations dealing with the treatment of persons in custody in Garda Síochána stations, made under the Criminal Justice Act, 1984, or failure to give formal proof of compliance with such regulations, does not of itself invalidate the prosecution. It remains a matter for judicial discretion to decide whether the non-compliance, or failure to prove compliance, is of such a character that it should lead to the dismissal of the charge against the accused".[99]

Gannon J elaborated in the High Court in *Spratt* that:

> "...non-observance of the regulations is not to bring about automatically the exclusion from evidence of all that was done and said while the accused person was in custody. It appears to be left to the court of trial to adjudicate in every case as to the impact non-compliance with the regulations should have on the case for the prosecution".[100]

---

96 Regs 19 and 20 of SI No 119 of 1987, The Criminal Justice Act, 1984 (Treatment Of Persons In Custody In Garda Síochána Stations) Regulations, 1987.
97 Garda Síochána Act 2005, s 85(1).
98 *ibid*, s 85(2) and (3).
99 *People (DPP) v Spratt* [1995] 1 IR 585, *per* O'Hanlon J, at 589.
100 *ibid* at 591.

5–50 In *People (DPP) v Murphy*,[101] it was reiterated that non-compliance does not necessarily render the custody unlawful or statements made during detention inadmissible, but if the accused can be shown to have been prejudiced by the breach of the regulations, the trial judge may exercise discretion. The Court defined the appropriate test as follows:

> "…(a) whether a breach of regulations has taken place, and, (b) whether the accused has suffered prejudice as a consequence of the breach. This test is subject to the constitutional duty of the trial judge to ensure that the trial is fair and just".[102]

A breach of the custody regulations provides grounds for the institution of disciplinary proceedings by the Garda Commissioner.[103] It will not necessarily give rise to an action in civil law against a member of An Garda Síochána.[104]

EUROPEAN DIRECTIVES

5–51 The rights of persons in custody have been augmented on a European-wide basis with the adoption of three Directives on the rights of access to information,[105] interpretation and translation[106] and legal assistance.[107] The Directives are part of a 'Roadmap' on criminal procedural rights, agreed by the Council of the European Union in 2009,[108] setting out proposals aiming to establish common minimum standards on the rights of suspects and accused persons in criminal proceedings.

5–52 The Directive on the right to interpretation and translation in criminal proceedings[109] provides a right of access to interpretation and translation during the investigative and judicial process for suspects who do not speak or understand the language of the criminal proceedings.[110] There is an entitlement to translation of essential documents,[111] and the costs of translation and interpretation are to be borne by Member States.[112]

---

[101] *People (DPP) v Murphy*, unreported, Court of Criminal Appeal, 12 July 2001.
[102] *ibid*, at 7.
[103] Reg 7(4) of SI No 119 of 1987 – The Criminal Justice Act, 1984 (Treatment Of Persons In Custody In Garda Síochána Stations) Regulations, 1987.
[104] Criminal Justice Act 1984, s 7(3).
[105] Directive 2012/13/EU of 22 May 2012 on the right to information in criminal proceedings, OJ L 142, 1 June 2012.
[106] Directive 2010/64/EU of 20 October 2010 on the right to interpretation and translation in criminal proceedings, OJ L 280, 26 October 2010.
[107] Directive 2013/48/EU of 22 October 2013 on the right of access to a lawyer in criminal proceedings and in European arrest warrant proceedings, OJ L 294, 6 November 2013.
[108] Resolution of the Council of 30 November 2009 on a Roadmap for strengthening procedural rights of suspected or accused persons in criminal proceedings, OJ C 295, 4 December 2009.
[109] Directive 2010/64/EU of 20 October 2010 on the right to interpretation and translation in criminal proceedings, OJ L 280, 26 October 2010. The Directive sets out a transposition date of 27 October 2013.
[110] *ibid*, Article 2.
[111] *ibid*, Article 3.
[112] *ibid*, Article 4.

The Directive requires Member States to ensure that translation and interpretation are of appropriate quality, that interpreters and translators are appropriately qualified and that confidentiality is maintained.[113]

The Directive on the right to information in criminal proceedings[114] requires Member States to ensure that suspects or accused persons are provided promptly with information concerning procedural rights under national law concerning: **5–53**

(a) the right of access to a lawyer;
(b) any entitlement to free legal advice and the conditions for obtaining such advice;
(c) the right to be informed of the accusation, in accordance with Article 6 of the ECHR;
(d) the right to interpretation and translation;
(e) the right to remain silent.[115]

There is also a right of access to the materials of the case, including all material evi- **5–54**
dence.[116] A letter of rights is to be provided to all persons who are arrested or detained,[117] with a specific reference in Article 5 to persons who are arrested for the purpose of the execution of a European Arrest Warrant.[118]

Ireland has opted out[119] of the Directive on the right of access to a lawyer in criminal **5–55**
proceedings and the right to communicate on arrest, which was adopted by the Council on 7 October 2013. The Directive deals with the conditions under which suspects and accused persons can access a lawyer and includes a right to access a lawyer before the start of questioning by the police or other law enforcement authorities and also in the course of questioning. Article 4(2) provides that "the lawyer shall have the right to be present at any questioning and hearing. He shall have the right to ask questions, request clarification and make statements, which shall be recorded in accordance with national law." Article 4(3) provides:

> "the lawyer shall have the right to be present at any other investigative or evidence-gathering act at which the suspect or accused person's presence is required or permitted as a right, in accordance with national law, unless this would prejudice the acquisition of evidence."

---

113 *ibid,* Article 5.

114 Directive 2012/13/EU of 22 May 2012 on the right to information in criminal proceedings, OJ L 142, 1 June 2012.

115 *ibid,* Article 3.

116 *ibid,* Article 7.

117 *ibid,* Article 4.

118 *ibid,* Article 5.

119 The UK and Denmark have also opted out of the Directive. Under the Lisbon Treaty, Ireland and the UK negotiated an 'opt-in' protocol, Protocol 21 to the Treaty on the European Union and to the Treaty on the Functioning of the European Union. Under Article 3 of the Protocol Ireland may choose to opt into a draft measure and participate in the negotiation and adoption process. Article 4 permits Ireland to notify the acceptance of a measure after its adoption by the Council. See further E Regan (ed), *European Criminal Justice Post Lisbon: an Irish Perspective* (Institute of International and European Affairs, Dublin, 2012) available online: http://www.iiea.com/publications/european-criminal-justice-post-lisbon-an-irish-perspective <accessed 20 October 2013>.

5–56 Under the Directive access to a lawyer is unlimited in terms of duration and frequency,[120] and there is provision for access to the place where the person is detained in order to check the conditions in which the person is held. In addition the notification of third parties of the suspect's deprivation of liberty is provided for, as is the principle of confidentiality of communications between the lawyer and suspect or accused person.

THE MEMBER IN CHARGE

5–57 As a counterbalance to the power to arrest for questioning introduced by the Criminal Justice Act 1984, the concept of a "member in charge" was simultaneously introduced.

5–58 The member in charge of the station is responsible for overseeing the detention of persons in custody. The arresting garda must satisfy the member in charge that the detention of the arrestee is necessary for the proper investigation of the offence.[121] Once the member in charge is sufficiently satisfied, he or she ought thereafter to provide a degree of independent oversight of the investigation and detention and is, as far as practicable, detached from the investigation and arrest of the individual.[122]

5–59 The member in charge, whose role is statutorily outlined in s 7(2) of the 1984 Act and in the custody regulations,[123] is designed as a protective mechanism, the rationale being that there is less likelihood of ill-treatment where there is an independent monitor of the detention period. The member in charge has responsibility for overseeing the application of the custody regulations in relation to persons in custody at the station, and is required periodically to visit the person in custody for that purpose.[124] The impetus for the assignment of responsibility to a particular garda for overseeing the treatment in custody of an arrested person came from the Report of the Committee to Recommend Certain Safeguards for Persons in Custody and for Members of the Garda Síochána, under the chairmanship of Mr Justice Barra Ó Bríain which reported in April 1978 (the Barra Ó Bríain report).[125] The report recommended the appointment for each suspect of "a custodial guardian" independent of the investigation of the offence, whose duty would be to ensure humane treatment and strict compliance with the regulations, to take responsibility for the well-being of the person in custody (including assessment of medical needs), and to ensure that the rights of detainees were notified and explained to them. In addition, it would be the responsibility of such a custodial guardian to ensure that reasonable requests made by the detainee were met; to keep the detainee informed of progress as regards

---

[120] Directive on the right of access to a lawyer in criminal proceedings and on the right to communicate upon arrest, 7 October 2013 (PE-CONS 40/13).

[121] Criminal Justice Act 1984, s 4(2).

[122] Reg 4(3) of SI No 119 of 1987.

[123] The member in charge is mentioned throughout the Custody Regulations, with particular reference to his duties and responsibilities in Regs 4 and 5 of SI No 119 of 1987 – The Criminal Justice Act, 1984 (Treatment Of Persons In Custody In Garda Síochána Stations) Regulations, 1987.

[124] *ibid*, Regulations 4(1) and 5(1).

[125] *Report of the Committee to Recommend Certain Safeguards for Persons in Custody and for Members of the Garda Síochána,* (Stationery Office, Dublin, 1978).

efforts made to contact his solicitor, family or a friend; to ensure that the person is properly fed and that reasonable facilities are provided for rest and sleep.[126] The report also expressly recommended that the custodial guardian ought to intervene if any member of the force, whether senior in rank or not, should attempt to treat the person inhumanely or in contravention of the garda regulations, logging and reporting any such suspected abuse.[127]

In light of the report's recommendations, together with the recommendation made by the Tribunal of Inquiry which followed the "Kerry Babies" case,[128] the eighth report of the Dáil Select Committee on Crime, Lawlessness and Vandalism recommended that safeguards should be provided for persons in custody. This resulted in the introduction of the custody regulations and the role of the member in charge, as the person responsible for overseeing the application of the Regulations, visiting the person periodically and making any necessary enquiries. **5–60**

Walsh has argued that there has historically, and continues to be, "a tendency to see detention as a tool to expedite a criminal investigation, with the individual's right to liberty not always being afforded the full respect it deserves".[129] **5–61**

The importance of the function of the member in charge cannot be overstated. In its sixth report, the Morris Tribunal found that the failure of the member in charge to perform his duties with diligence had contributed to a cover-up for ten years. The report opined that

> "had he performed his duties as member in charge conscientiously and honestly, and had he given truthful evidence, then the entire nature of this scandal would have been uncovered earlier".[130]

Where it appears to the member in charge that a direction given or action taken by a member of higher rank is inconsistent with the proper application of the custody regulations, he is obliged to inform that member accordingly and, unless the matter is resolved, report it without delay to another member of or above the rank of Superintendent.[131] In practical terms, the appointment of a junior garda to the role of member in charge may **5–62**

---

126 *ibid* recommendation 47.

127 *ibid*, recommendation 48.

128 The "Kerry Babies Case" was the subject of a tribunal of enquiry in 1984. A baby had been found murdered on a beach, and a local woman, known by the gardaí to have been pregnant, confessed (with members of her family) to having killed the baby. They later withdrew their confessions and admitted that the baby born to the woman had been born, died shortly after birth and was buried on the family farm.

129 D Walsh, *Human Rights and Policing in Ireland: Law, Policy and Practice* (Clarus Press, Dublin, 2009), p 479.

130 Report on the Detention of 'Suspects' Following the Death of the Late Richard Barron on the 14th of October 1996 and Related Detentions and Issues, Term of Reference (b), (d) and (f), Volume 1, at p 168.

131 Reg 5(3) of SI No 119 of 1987 — the Criminal Justice Act, 1984 (Treatment Of Persons In Custody In Garda Síochána Stations) Regulations, 1987.

prove an insufficient safeguard, and the Morris Tribunal recommended that the role be performed by a garda of considerable experience, of the rank of sergeant at least. It said:

> "The Tribunal recommends that in all cases a member in charge should be a garda of considerable experience, of sergeant rank at least. The Tribunal is not satisfied, on the evidence that it has heard, that the role of a member in charge pursuant to the regulations is treated with sufficient importance, or that the member in charge is vested with sufficient authority to ensure compliance with the regulations. Thus the appointment of a junior garda as a member in charge in a station to which a suspect, arrested in respect of a serious crime, is brought, may result in a failure on the member in charge's part to act effectively in the implementation of the regulations. This may be by reason of inexperience, an apprehension on his part that representations made in order to ensure compliance with the regulations might not be viewed favourably or treated seriously by gardaí of more senior rank, or by a failure to understand the independence of his role under the Act. The role and status of the member in charge is established by statute and regulation: whether that role and status is given practical effect depends on the respect and authority given to that role in practice by other gardaí and especially those in leadership roles. It is important that the member in charge understands that he is expected to act in a proactive manner in the execution of his duties and that he is encouraged to do so by the officers of An Garda Síochána. Otherwise, the effectiveness of the role of the member in charge can be blunted in practice. The role of the member in charge, carrying out his duties under the custody regulations and the Criminal Justice Act, should be one of considerable independence from the gardaí carrying out the investigation and this may, if necessary, bring him into conflict with his colleagues and on occasion with officers of An Garda Síochána. This is a very difficult role. If it is to be carried out effectively and even-handedly the member in charge must have the support of the officers of An Garda Síochána and the encouragement to execute his duty fearlessly when required. The Tribunal is not satisfied that the role of the member in charge is in practice afforded the respect and authority contemplated by the legislation."[132]

5–63 The Regulations have continued to be the subject of comment, and the importance of the functions performed by the member in charge are thrown into sharp relief when detainees die in custody[133] or when confessions are made which are subsequently established to be false.[134] Clearly the independence envisaged by the legislation is difficult to ensure in practice where the member in charge is a colleague of the arresting member. Though a custody record is carefully kept, "this evidence is written by the members of the agency against whom it is supposed to be a protection…"[135] and applications made to the member in charge for detention are seldom refused.

[132] Report on The Detention Of 'Suspects' Following the Death of the late Richard Barron on the 14th of October 1996 and Related Detentions and Issues, Term of Reference (b), (d) and (f), Volume 3, para 16.37.

[133] High-profile examples include the deaths of Terence Wheelock (see Garda Síochána Ombudsman Commission, *The Death of Terence Wheelock: Report Pursuant to Section 103 Following Investigation*, Dublin, 10 March 2010, available online at http://www.gardaombudsman.ie/docs/publications/Section-102%284%29-Mr-Terence-Wheelock.pdf <accessed 20 October 2013>) and Peter Matthews.

[134] There are numerous examples of false confessions, including the cases of Dean Lyons, Peter Pringle and Joanne Hayes ("The Kerry Babies Case").

[135] A Sanders and R Young, "Police Powers" in *Handbook of Policing* (T Newburn ed, 2nd ed, Willan Publishing, Cullompton, 2008), at p 290.

Information to be Provided to Detainees

Regulation 8 sets out the obligation of the member in charge to inform (or cause to be informed) the arrested person without delay: **5–64**

(a) in ordinary language of the offence or other matter in respect of which they have been arrested,

(b) that they are entitled to consult a solicitor, and

(c) when the arrested person is a child, that they are entitled to have notification given of their being in custody in the station to another person reasonably named by them; that a parent or guardian (or spouse) is being told that the child is in custody in the station, and is being told of the offence or other matter in respect of which the child has been detained, of the entitlement to consult a solicitor; and that the parent, guardian or other person is being requested to attend at the station without delay.

The information must be given orally, together with a form setting out the arrested person's rights in writing, in the form C72. The form C72 sets out: **5–65**

- the role of the member in charge
- the communication of the reason for arrest
- the notification of other persons of the fact of arrest
- the opportunity for non-Irish nationals to contact diplomatic or consular representatives
- the right to communicate privately with a solicitor
- opportunities for visits from and communication with relatives, friends or other persons
- that, where searches are conducted, the reason will be explained
- that meals are provided free of charge and a meal of choice can be supplied at the detainee's own expense
- that the person may be released on station bail or, if bail is refused, there will be an opportunity to apply for it when the detainee is brought before the court
- legal aid
- examination by a doctor, including the right to be examined by a doctor of the detainee's choice
- the taking of photographs to assist in identification
- the provision under which the person has been arrested and the taking of fingerprints, palmprints, photographs and tests
- the taking of bodily samples
- inferences
- identification parades
- medical treatment for detainees who are injured, under the influence of intoxicating liquor or drugs and cannot be roused, failure to respond normally to conversation or questions (otherwise than due to the influence of intoxicating liquor alone), apparent mental illness or other apparent need for medical attention
- that the gardaí will at all times respect personal rights and the dignity of detainees as human beings and not subject them to ill-treatment of any kind.

It is of note that the Irish Translators' and Interpreters' Association asked that the right to an interpreter be added to the form C72 in its submission on the Garda Síochána corporate strategy 2007–2009. The right to interpretation and translation is also the subject of a European Directive, see para 5 – 52.

5–66 It must also be explained to the arrestee either personally by the member in charge or by another member that, if the arrestee does not wish to exercise any of his rights in custody immediately, he will not be precluded from doing so later. The fact and time that this information is given must be recorded, and the arrested person invited to sign the custody record to acknowledge receipt of the notice. Refusal to sign must be noted.

5–67 Members in charge can, and frequently do, delegate responsibility for the provision of information to other gardaí, who perform the role of gaoler or station orderly. Where the duty delegated includes visiting persons in custody and making the necessary enquiries, the delegation must be authorised in writing by the member in charge and such delegation must specify the reasons for it (such as the number of persons in custody or other circumstances) and terminate when the reasons no longer apply.[136]

The Decision to Detain

5–68 The decision to detain can only be made by the member in charge, if the member in charge is satisfied on the basis of the information provided by the arresting garda that the person's detention is necessary for the proper investigation of the offence for which he or she has been arrested.[137] Regulation 7(2) of the custody regulations provides:

> "In the case of a person who is being detained in the station pursuant to section 4 of the Act the member in charge at the time of the person's arrival at the station shall, when authorising the detention, enter in the custody record and sign the following statement:
>
> "I have reasonable grounds for believing that the detention of (insert here the name of the person detained) is necessary for the proper investigation of the offence(s) in respect of which he / she has been arrested."

5–69 The decision to detain must be based on the information given to the member in charge at the time of arrest at the station or arrival in the station,[138] and so should not be based on further evidence which becomes available subsequent to the prisoner's arrival, such as material found in the course of a search at the station tending to implicate the suspect in the offence for which he is detained. The power to detain under s 4 of the Criminal Justice Act 1984 applies only to arrestable offences, i.e., offences which are punishable by a term of imprisonment of five years or more. A person can only be detained under s 4 if they have not previously been convicted of the offence under investigation.[139] The decision taken by the member in charge to detain is not a rubber-stamping exercise: the wording

[136] Reg 5(4) of SI No 119 of 1987—the Criminal Justice Act, 1984 (Treatment Of Persons In Custody In Garda Síochána Stations) Regulations, 1987.

[137] Criminal Justice Act 1984, s 4(2), as substituted by Criminal Justice Act 2006, s 9.

[138] The formula set out in the Criminal Justice Act 1984, s 4(2) as substituted by Criminal Justice Act 2006, s 9, is that "the member of the Garda Síochána in charge of the station to which the person is taken on arrest or in which he or she is arrested has at the time of the person's arrival at the station or his or her arrest in the station, as may be appropriate, reasonable grounds for believing that his or her detention is necessary for the proper investigation of the offence".

[139] Criminal Justice Act 1984, s 4(1).

of s 4 presupposes an element of consideration by the member in charge before a decision to detain is taken.[140] In *DPP v Birney and Other* Hardiman J held that:

> "This Court is of the view that it was clearly the intention of the Oireachtas that the member in charge of a Garda station in circumstances where he is asked to detain a prisoner for the purpose of investigation of an offence pursuant to s 4 should not merely be a rubber stamp. The role of the member in charge involves both a subjective and objective element and subjectively he must believe that the applicant's detention is necessary and objectively must be satisfied that there are reasonable grounds for his belief. It is clear that the legislature, notwithstanding that s 4 of the Act of 1984 has to be construed strictly, did intend that a reasonable period would have to be allowed to the member in charge to consider his decision following the arrival at the Garda station of the arrested person…"[141]

The importance of the decision to detain being based solely on the grounds set out in the Criminal Justice Act 1984, and the protection that those grounds provide from unnecessary or unlawful detention, was illustrated in the Brian Rossiter case, in which the juvenile Brian Rossiter (who had been arrested with two other children) died in custody. The inquiry into Brian Rossiter's death disclosed that the arresting garda had sought the permission of the boys' parents to detain them in custody overnight. There was therefore no legal basis for their detention. The subsequent inquiry found that: **5–70**

> "The member-in-charge… appears to have played virtually no role whatsoever in the process whereby a decision was made to detain Brian Rossiter. He seems to have accepted with great ease the proposition that the father had consented to his son spending the night in the Garda station and made no enquiries of [the arresting garda] as to how this had come about or as to whether there was an alternative."[142]

The inquiry further commented that it was "struck by the fact that the member-in-charge played no role whatsoever in relation to the decision to detain Brian Rossiter… [the arresting garda] appears to have usurped the role of the member-in-charge, who acceded to this".[143] **5–71**

The Necessity of Detention

An important aspect of the decision to detain is the necessity and proportionality of detention having regard to the nature of the offence under investigation. In *Vasileva v Denmark*,[144] the European Court of Human rights held that the detention of a woman for 13 and a half hours arising out of a dispute over whether she had a valid bus ticket, and her subsequent refusal to give her name to the police, was a violation of Article 5 **5–72**

[140] *DPP v Birney and Others* [2007] 1 IR 337.

[141] *ibid.*

[142] *Inquiry Pursuant to the Dublin Police Act 1924 as amended by the Police Forces Amalgamation Act 1925: Summary of the Report of Mr Hugh Hartnett SC Prepared by the Department of Justice, Equality and Law Reform* (March 2008), at p 16.

[143] *ibid* at p 53.

[144] *Vasileva v Denmark* (2005) 40 EHRR 681.

of the European Convention. The deprivation of the woman's liberty for 13 and a half hours was disproportionate to the cause of her detention, and the authorities failed to strike a fair balance between the need to ensure the fulfilment of the obligation to provide personal data under Danish law and the right to liberty.

Once the necessity and proportionality of an initial period of detention have been established, the necessity of detention must be kept under continuous review.

Delay in Dealing with Persons in Custody

5–73 Regulation 3(2) of the custody regulations outlines that "there shall be no unnecessary delay in dealing with persons in custody". There should therefore be no delay on the part of the arresting garda in bringing the person who it is proposed to detain before the member in charge for a determination to be made as to the necessity of the detention. But clearly there is scope for a reasonable period to elapse to afford the member in charge appropriate time to consider the necessity of the detention.

Where There is no Available Person to Act as Member in Charge

5–74 In circumstances in which there is no available person to act as a member in charge, and if there is no period of detention proposed—for instance in a simple drink driving investigation in which the suspect is in the station for a relatively short period of time—it may not be practicable to separate the functions of investigating member and member in charge. In *DPP v Devlin*,[145] a drink-driving charge was dismissed on the basis that the arresting garda had also acted as the member in charge. The High Court found that the judge had been incorrect in dismissing the charge, as there was no detention to be authorised and the purpose of bringing the suspect to the station was to take a sample. Regulation 4 of the Custody Regulations provides that, "as far as practicable, the member in charge shall not be a member who was involved in the arrest of a person for the offence in respect of which he is in custody in the station or in the investigation of the offence". In *Devlin*, Budd J drew a distinction between the function as it applies in minor road traffic matters and its operation in the context of a s 4 detention:

> "The phrase 'as far as practicable' makes it clear that there are circumstances in which the investigating garda can also act as member in charge… in the case of detention for drunk-driving, the member in charge's role can be distinguished from that of the member in charge where an arrest is followed by a detention under Section 4 when the member in charge is required to exercise a separate discretion as to whether the detention is required. In a prosecution being brought under Section 49 of the Road Traffic Act, the accused person, having been arrested under that section, is required to attend at the Garda station for the purpose of the provision of a specimen, and it is not up to the member in charge to decide whether or not this detention is necessary."[146]

5–75 The failure of the garda to contact another member of An Garda Síochána requesting their attendance at the station did not, in the circumstances of the case, entitle the

[145] *DPP v Devlin* [1998] IEHC 139.
[146] *ibid.*

respondent to dismissal of the charge. However the court recognised that the function of the member in charge in cases of drink driving differs from the function exercised in cases where a period of detention is authorised by legislation, such as the Criminal Justice Act 1984. In the former situation, the member is performing a regulatory function whereas, in the latter, the member in charge is required to exercise a separate discretion as to the necessity and propriety of detention. Therefore, where it is proposed to detain a suspect under s 4 of the Criminal Justice Act 1984, s 2 of the Criminal Justice (Drug Trafficking) Act 1996 or s 50 of the Criminal Justice Act 2007, it will be necessary to have an independent monitor of the detention period. If no person is available at the station to act as member in charge, the prisoner should be moved to another station where an independent member is available. Section 30 of the Offences against the State Act 1939 is unique in that it permits detention for 24 hours without the necessity of the arresting garda applying to the member in charge to detain the arrestee. A member in charge is still, however, required to supervise the detention period. The detention powers are considered in detail above at para 5 – 08 *et seq*.

The Custody Record

A record must be kept in respect of each person in custody.[147] The member in charge must **5–76** ensure that all information required by the custody regulations is recorded, and each entry must be initialled by the member making it. In particular, the following must be recorded:

(a) the date, time and place of arrest and the identity of the arresting member (or other person effecting the arrest),
(b) the time of arrival at the station,
(c) the nature of the offence or other matter in respect of which he was arrested, and
(d) any relevant particulars relating to his physical or mental condition.[148]

Details of extensions of detentions, charge and all other relevant information concern- **5–77** ing the custody of the prisoner must also be recorded.[149] In the event of a transfer to another garda station, the custody record goes with the prisoner, to be given to the member in charge of the other station.[150] While each member is responsible for his or her own entries into the custody record, the member in charge bears responsibility for the accuracy and completeness of all entries made in the custody record while performing the duty of member in charge.[151]

In 2010, the Garda Síochána Ombudsman Commission's Report into the Death in Cus- **5–78** tody of Terence Wheelock[152] highlighted the necessity of accuracy in the completion

---

147 Regulation 6 of the Criminal Justice Act 1984 (Treatment of Persons in Custody) Regulations 1987, SI No 119 of 1987, sets out the requirements for maintenance of the custody record.

148 Regulation 7 of the Criminal Justice Act 1984 (Treatment of Persons in Custody) Regulations 1987.

149 *ibid.*

150 *ibid,* Regulation 6(3).

151 *ibid,* Regulation 6(4).

152 Garda Síochána Ombudsman Commission, *The Death of Terence Wheelock: Report Pursuant to Section 103 Following Investigation,* Dublin, 10 March 2010, available online at http://www.gardaombudsman.ie/docs/publications/Section-102%284%29-Mr-Terence-Wheelock.pdf <accessed 20 October 2013>.

of the custody record and recommended the introduction of a specialist role for garda members charged with the custody of prisoners:

> "This dedicated custody officer role should be given to members with the necessary experience and ability to carry out such a function. The role should only be carried out by members trained to a high standard in all areas of the custody function."[153]

In addition, first aid training for members in charge was recommended.

Errors in the Custody Record

5–79 Occasionally errors are made in the completion of the custody record. The Criminal Justice Act 1984 makes clear that an error in complying with the Regulations will not of itself affect the lawfulness of the custody or the admissibility of evidence obtained.[154] In *DPP v Clark*,[155] the offence for which the suspect was detained was incorrectly described. The charge was dismissed in the District Court and a case was stated to the High Court as to whether the District Court was correct. The error was found to be a failure to observe the custody regulations and, since the 1984 Act clearly provided that such an error ought not to be fatal, the High Court held that the District Court Judge had incorrectly dismissed the charge.[156]

RECORDING OF INTERVIEWS

5–80 Interviews with suspects must be audio-visually recorded,[157] and accurate detailed written notes must be taken. Those notes ought to be contemporaneous and be a fair record of what was actually said. The crucial aspects of the interview must be written verbatim as far as possible. In *DPP v John Diver*, the Supreme Court held unequivocally that failure to record a Garda interview "can only be regarded as a gross, deliberate and conscious breach of regulations".[158] A failure to record a "general chat" between the suspect and garda was accepted by the prosecution to have constituted a breach of Regulation 12(11) in *People (DPP) v Murphy*.[159]

Interviews are recorded on three videotapes, one of which is sealed in the presence of the suspect, retained securely and treated as an exhibit in any potential criminal proceedings. The second tape is kept by the gardaí and may be accessed by the Office of the Director of Public Prosecutions. If the accused wishes to have a copy, it is provided only on the direction of the court, with any conditions that the court may specify.[160]

---

[153] *ibid.*

[154] Criminal Justice Act 1984, s 7(3).

[155] *DPP v Clark* [2001] 5 JIC 3105.

[156] *ibid.*

[157] This is provided for in SI No 74 of 1997—Criminal Justice Act, 1984 (Electronic Recording of Interviews) Regulations, 1997.

[158] *DPP v Diver,* unreported, Supreme Court, 29 July 2005.

[159] *People (DPP) v Murphy,* unreported, Court of Criminal Appeal, 12 July 2001.

[160] Criminal Justice Act 2007, s 56.

VULNERABLE SUSPECTS

Child Suspects

Children require and are deserving of special measures for their protection in garda custody and in the criminal process generally.[161] **5–81**

The Guidelines for Prosecutors issued by the Office of the Director of Public Prosecutions state that: **5–82**

> "The long term damage which can be done to a child because of an encounter with the criminal law early in his or her life should not be underestimated and prosecution must be regarded as a severe measure with significant implications for the future development of the child concerned." [162]

Key policy documents deal with Garda interaction with children, including An Garda Síochána Youth and Children Strategy 2012–2014 and Recording Procedures and Guidelines Relating to Children in the Care of An Garda Síochána, emphasise that gardaí should ensure that the provisions of the UN Convention on the Rights of the Child are upheld at all times when members of An Garda Síochána interact with children, that the highest level of international best practice must be adhered to when dealing with children who come into conflict with the law and, in particular, that the 1985 UN Standard Minimum Rules for the Administration of Juvenile Justice (Beijing rules)[163] must be followed in the administration of juvenile justice.[164] **5–83**

Age of Criminal Responsibility

The age of criminal responsibility in Ireland is 12,[165] except in relation to murder, manslaughter, rape and aggravated sexual assault, for which children between 10 and 12 may be prosecuted.[166] Section 52(1) of the Children Act 2001 is strongly worded in its provision that, but for the above exceptions, "a child under 12 years of age shall not be charged with an offence," while charges against children under 14 can only proceed with the consent of the Director of Public Prosecutions.[167] The definition of arrestable offences in s 2(1) of the Criminal Law Act 1997[168] expressly refers to the requirement **5–84**

---

161 See D Walsh, *Juvenile Justice* (Thomson Round Hall, Dublin, 2005).

162 Office of the Director of Public Prosecutions, *Guidelines for Prosecutors,* October 2007.

163 United Nations Standard Minimum Rules for the Administration of Juvenile Justice, A/RES/40/33, 29 November 1985.

164 *An Garda Síochána Youth and Children Strategy 2009 – 2011,* p 5.

165 Children Act 2001, s 52, as substituted by s 129 of the Criminal Justice Act 2006.

166 *ibid*, s 52(2).

167 *ibid*, s 52(4).

168 s 2(1) of the Criminal Law Act 1997 (as amended by s 8 of the Criminal Justice Act 2006) provides that 'arrestable offence' means an offence for which a person *of full capacity* and not previously convicted may, under or by virtue of any enactment or the common law, be punished by imprisonment for a term of five years or by a more severe penalty and includes an attempt to commit any such offence". The requirement that an offender be of full capacity is further emphasised in the same section in the definition of "fixed by law": '"... fixed by law', in relation to a sentence for an

of an offender being of full capacity. As children under 12 cannot be charged with an arrestable offence, they should not be arrested under s 4, unless they are suspected of rape, aggravated sexual assault, murder or manslaughter.[169]

The Rights of Child Suspects

5–85 The Children Act 2001 adds to the protections set out for children in the custody regulations,[170] puts those protections on a statutory footing, and augments and modifies them. The duty of gardaí in relation to child suspects is outlined in s 55, which states:

> "In any investigation relating to the commission or possible commission of an offence by children, members of the Garda Síochána shall act with due respect for the personal rights of the children and their dignity as human persons, for their vulnerability owing to their age and level of maturity and for the special needs of any of them who may be under a physical or mental disability, while complying with the obligation to prevent escapes from custody and continuing to act with diligence and determination in the investigation of crime and the protection and vindication of the personal rights of other persons."

5–86 The section is mandatory, but the failure to refer to the need for compliance with international instruments on the rights of children in custody is of note. Notwithstanding the omission, Ireland has signed and ratified the Convention on the Rights of the Child, and accordingly it should be adhered to in the pursuit of best practice in relation to child suspects. Article 37 of the Convention is of particular importance. It provides:

> "States Parties shall ensure that:
>
> (a) No child shall be subjected to torture or other cruel, inhuman or degrading treatment or punishment. Neither capital punishment nor life imprisonment without possibility of release shall be imposed for offences committed by persons below eighteen years of age;
>
> (b) No child shall be deprived of his or her liberty unlawfully or arbitrarily. The arrest, detention or imprisonment of a child shall be in conformity with the law and shall be used only as a measure of last resort and for the shortest appropriate period of time;
>
> (c) Every child deprived of liberty shall be treated with humanity and respect for the inherent dignity of the human person, and in a manner which takes into account the needs of persons of his or her age. In particular, every child deprived of liberty shall be separated from adults unless it is considered in the child's best interest not to do so and shall have the right to maintain contact with his or her family through correspondence and visits, save in exceptional circumstances;

---

arrestable offence, means a sentence which the court is required by law to impose on an offender, being a person of *full capacity*." [emphasis added].

[169] See Walsh, *Juvenile Justice* (Dublin, Thomson Round Hall, 2005) at p 46: "Since the primary purpose of arrest is to bring a suspect before a court to answer a criminal charge or to investigate an offence, it would seem reasonable to assume that it cannot be used against a suspect who is below the age of criminal responsibility".

[170] Criminal Justice Act 1984 (Treatment of Persons in Custody in Garda Síochána Stations) Regulations 1987 (SI No 119 of 1987).

> (d) Every child deprived of his or her liberty shall have the right to prompt access to legal and other appropriate assistance, as well as the right to challenge the legality of the deprivation of his or her liberty before a court or other competent, independent and impartial authority, and to a prompt decision on any such action."

The 1985 UN Standard Minimum Rules for the Administration of Juvenile Justice (the Beijing Rules) state:

> "The juvenile justice system shall emphasise the well-being of the juvenile and shall ensure that any reaction to juvenile offenders shall always be in proportion to the circumstances of both the offender and the offence."[171]

Juvenile Diversion

While children above the age of criminal responsibility are subject to the general legislative powers of arrest and detention that apply to all citizens,[172] the question is whether they should be. Arrest is unavoidable in certain circumstances, but as outlined in Article 37(b), arrest and detention should be measures of last resort where children are concerned. The Garda Youth Diversion Project Guidelines are a suggested set of guidelines based on research carried out for the Department of Justice, Equality and Law Reform in 2003.[173] The desirability of diversion from the criminal justice system should be borne in mind in considering whether to arrest a child. If arrest is not going to lead to the commencement of criminal proceedings, its utility is questionable, especially in the context of the successful operation of the juvenile diversion programme. The diversion programme has as its objective the diversion of "any child who accepts responsibility for his or her criminal or anti-social behaviour from committing further offences or engaging in further anti-social behaviour".[174] Any children who take responsibility for their behaviour and agree to be cautioned and (where appropriate) supervised by a juvenile liaison officer, are eligible for participation in the programme, once the director of the juvenile diversion programme is satisfied that admission to the programme is appropriate, in the best interests of the child and not inconsistent with the interests of society and the victim of the offence.[175] **5–87**

If children are arrested, they have a number of entitlements: to information, to independent adult assistance, to legal advice and to segregation from adult detainees.[176] Children must be informed, in a manner and in language appropriate to the child's age and level of understanding, the offence in respect of which they have been arrested, their **5–88**

171 United Nations Standard Minimum Rules for the Administration of Juvenile Justice A/RES/40/33, 29 November 1985.

172 See M Butler (ed), *Law Society Criminal Litigation,* (Oxford University Press, Oxford, 2006), at p153.

173 L Ryan, A Warren and L Caldwell, Garda Youth Diversion Project Guidelines, 2003.

174 Children Act 2001, s 19(1), as substituted by s 124 of the Criminal Justice Act 2006.

175 *ibid,* s 23.

176 *ibid,* s 56. However, failure to observe the requirements in s 53 to 63 and 65 will not of itself render inadmissible evidence obtained during the detention. It will, however, expose the Garda involved to disciplinary proceedings. See s 66 of the Children Act 2001.

entitlement to consult a solicitor and how to do so, and that their parent or guardian is being informed of the arrest and requested to attend at the station without delay.[177] As soon as practicable on arrival in the garda station post-arrest, the member in charge must inform the child's parent or guardian that the child is in custody, explain in ordinary language the nature of the offence in respect of which the child has been arrested, that the child is entitled to consult a solicitor and the practicalities of availing of that right. The member in charge must also request the attendance of the child's parent or guardian at the station without delay.[178] If the parent or guardian is uncontactable, or indicate that they are unwilling or unable to attend the station within a reasonable time, the member in charge must inform the chid or have the child informed of the unavailability of the parent or guardian, and of the entitlement to have an adult relative or other adult requested to attend at the station in their stead.[179] Generally, unless an adult is present on the child's behalf, the child cannot be questioned or asked to make a statement.[180] Parents or guardians (or adult relatives or nominees as the case may be) may, however, be excluded from questioning in the following circumstances:

- where the parent or guardian is the victim of the offence being investigated;[181]
- where the parent or guardian has been arrested in respect of the offence under investigation[182] or where there are reasonable grounds for suspecting their complicity in the offence;[183]
- where it is thought that their presence during questioning would be likely to obstruct the course of justice or where their conduct during the taking of a written statement actually amounts to obstruction of the course of justice.[184]

In JM *(A Minor) v Member in Charge Coolock Garda Station*[185] the applicant sought an order of *habeas corpus*, arguing that the refusal by the gardaí to allow his solicitor to be present in the course of his questioning at Coolock garda station breached his constitutional right of reasonable access to a solicitor, as he was a vulnerable minor with mental health problems. It was argued that in light of his age and mental impairment, the refusal of the gardaí to allow his solicitor to be present for the interviews rendered his detention unlawful. The High Court refused to order the child's release, holding that the case of *Lavery v Member in Charge, Carrickmacross Garda Station*,[186] in which it was held that a solicitor is not entitled to be present at interviews, represents the law in this jurisdiction.

---

[177] *ibid*, s 57.

[178] *ibid*, s 58(1).

[179] Children Act 2001, s 58(2).

[180] *ibid*, s 61(1). s 61(2) provides that a child may be questioned in the absence of a parent where there are reasonable grounds for believing that to delay in questioning would involve a risk of death or injury to persons, serious loss or damage to property, destruction of or interference with evidence or escape of accomplices.

[181] *ibid*, s 61(3)(a).

[182] *ibid*, s 61(3)(a).

[183] *ibid*, s 61(3)(b).

[184] *ibid*, s 61(4).

[185] *JM (A Minor) v Member in Charge Coolock Garda Station* [2013] IEHC 251.

[186] *Lavery v Member in Charge, Carrickmacross Garda Station* [1999] 2 IR 390.

Where it is considered that the child in custody is in need of care and protection, the member in charge is obliged to inform the Health Service Executive,[187] which is obliged in turn to send a representative to the station as soon as practicable. Where appropriate, the Health Service Executive can then exercise its powers under the Child Care Act.[188] **5–89**

Under 12s

Children under the age of 12 are considered by the law to be incapable of committing a crime (except the limited offences for which children between 10 and 12 may be prosecuted, i.e., murder, manslaughter, rape, rape under s 4 of the Criminal Law (Rape) (Amendment) Act 1990 or aggravated sexual assault). Accordingly, outside those limited circumstances, they can neither be brought before the courts nor admitted to the diversion programme. **5–90**

The role of gardaí who encounter children engaging in behaviour that, but for the age of the child concerned, would constitute an offence, is limited to returning the child to its parents or to acting in a liaison capacity between the child and the Health Service Executive.[189] The Health Service Executive may be involved where the garda, on taking the child to the parent or guardian, has reasonable grounds for believing that the child is not receiving adequate care or protection.[190] If it is not practicable for the child to be taken to the parent or guardian, the garda may give the child into the custody of the Health Service Executive[191] and care proceedings may be commenced if necessary.[192] If the garda has reasonable grounds for believing that there is an immediate and serious risk to the health or welfare of the child of such urgency that the delay involved in making an application for an emergency care order cannot be risked, the garda may remove the child to safety.[193] **5–91**

The Criminal Justice Act 1984 provides at s 4(7) that the power to detain in s 4(2) of the Act shall not apply to a person below the age of 12. The prohibition on detention of under-12s does not apply if the member in charge in a station where a person is detained has reasonable grounds for believing that the person is not under 12. Section 4(7) applies to detention under s 2 of the Criminal Justice (Drug Trafficking) Act and under s 50 of the Criminal Justice Act 2007, but it is not mentioned in s 9 of the Criminal Justice Act 1984 which extends certain provisions of s 4 to detention under s 30 of the Offences against the State Act 1939. It seems therefore that, while children between 10 and 12 might be prosecuted for murder, manslaughter, rape or aggravated sexual assault, they may only be detained under s 30 of the Offences against the State Act, which is not possible if the offence under investigation is not scheduled for the **5–92**

---

[187] The section originally referred to the health board of the area concerned. The Health Act 2004 established the Health Service Executive, and provides at s 66 "references (however expressed) to a specified body in any Act passed before the establishment day, or in any instrument made before that day under an Act, are to be read as references to the Executive, unless the context otherwise requires".

[188] See Child Care Act 1991, s 3.

[189] Children Act 2001, s 53(1) as substituted by s 130 of the Criminal Justice Act 2006.

[190] *ibid*, s 53(2).

[191] *ibid*, s 53(3).

[192] *ibid*, s 53(4).

[193] *ibid*, s 53(5). In such circumstances, Part III of the Childcare Act 1991 applies as if the removal were a removal under s 12 of that Act.

purposes of the Offences against the State Act 1939. If the option of detention under s 4 of the Criminal Justice Act 1984 is unavailable, many of the powers to take samples, fingerprints, photographs and so on would be unavailable to gardaí also.

"Mentally Handicapped" Persons in Custody

5–93 Regulation 22 of the custody regulations provides that the same procedures as apply in relation to juvenile suspects apply in respect of "mentally handicapped" persons, with the proviso that, where practicable, a responsible adult contacted with a view to being present in the interview of the person shall be "a person who has experience in dealing with the mentally handicapped."[194] The term "mentally handicapped" is not defined, nor is there elaboration on the ways in which the special needs of those with physical or mental disabilities might be met in a practical sense, other than by creating an obligation for the member in charge to summon a doctor or to arrange for a person in custody to be removed to a hospital if necessary in circumstances where a person in custody:

(a) is injured,
(b) is under the influence of intoxicating liquor or drugs and cannot be roused,
(c) fails to respond normally to questions or conversation (other than owing to the presence of intoxicating liquor alone), or
(d) appears to the member in charge to be suffering from a mental illness, or
(e) otherwise appears to the member in charge to need medical attention.[195]

Mentally Ill and Substance-Using Suspects

5–94 The legislation that provides powers for gardaí to take mentally ill persons into custody is considered in detail in *Chapter 2: Arrest and Detention in Other Contexts* at para 2 – 02 *et seq.* Some considerations which arise in dealing with mentally ill suspects in garda custody are examined below.

O'Neill and McInerney have commented that:

> "The over-representation of mental illness in prison populations compared to community samples has long been recognised internationally, and is particularly true for pre-trial settings."[196]

---

[194] Criminal Justice Act 1984 (Treatment of Persons in Custody in Garda Síochána Stations) Regulations 1987, reg 22(2).

[195] *ibid*, reg 21(1). In addition, medical advice shall be sought if the person in custody claims to need medication relating to a heart condition, diabetes, epilepsy or other potentially serious medical condition or where the member in charge considers it necessary to seek such advice because the person has medication in their possession (Criminal Justice Act 1984 (Treatment of Persons in Custody in Garda Síochána Stations) Regulations 1987, reg 21(2).

[196] C McInerney and C O'Neill, Prison Psychiatric Inreach and Court Liaison Services in Ireland (2008) 8 (2) JSIJ 147.

In 1998, a police liaison scheme was established in Northern Ireland[197] under which two community mental health nurses screen custody records, carry out mental health assessments on selected individuals and liaise with appropriate agencies to arrange treatment and support, as well as providing training to police to help them understand the nature of mental disorders. Key findings from the scheme (which is still in operation) were cited in the 2006 Bamford Review of Mental Health and Learning Disability (Northern Ireland) – Forensic Services as follows: **5–95**

- 16% of custody records met one or more assessment criteria for mental disorder;
- 91% of those who underwent assessment were judged to have a mental health problem;
- typically these were single, unemployed males in their early 30s and living alone;
- two thirds had a history of having been in one or more health, social services or criminal justice institutions (47% had received inpatient care); and
- almost half had been in prison.

The most commonly recorded diagnoses were:

- depression (44%)
- substance misuse (15%);
- schizophrenia / paranoid psychosis (11%); and
- anxiety.[198]

There is no reason to believe that such figures would differ dramatically if a similar study were undertaken in the Republic of Ireland. What is clear is that mental disorders and psychiatric illnesses are prevalent among the people police regularly take into custody on suspicion of involvement of criminal activity. While it need hardly be stated that mentally ill and mentally impaired persons are deserving of additional protection in garda custody, the Dean Lyons case, in which an intellectually impaired drug user confessed to murders he had not committed, serves as a caution against complacency.[199] The incident is illustrative of research that has shown that persons with intellectual impairments or disabilities are prone to giving inaccurate or misleading statements during questioning **5–96**

---

197 Referenced in the *Bamford Review of Mental Health and Learning Disability (Northern Ireland) – Forensic Services*, October 2006, Chapter 3, pp 9–11.

198 *Bamford Review of Mental Health and Learning Disability (Northern Ireland) – Forensic Services*, October 2006, Chapter 3, pp 9–11.

199 See *Report of the Commission of Investigation (Dean Lyons Case),* Department of Justice Equality and Law Reform, 1 September 2006. Dean Lyons confessed to two murders while in Garda custody. It was subsequently established that he had no involvement in the murders. Dean Lyons was not abused or ill-treated in any way during his detention, nor was any attempt made to frame him, but he was particularly suggestible and had readily agreed to leading questions put to him by gardaí. He had acquired detailed information about the crimes from the manner in which the questions put to him were formulated. A psychological assessment outlined that he was borderline mentally handicapped, though with a memory that was better than would be expected. In addition, he was an intravenous drug user and had a track record of making up stories. An apology was printed on 24 February 2005 in the national media, stating that, following a full investigation, the gardaí were satisfied that Dean Lyons had no involvement with the Grangegorman murders.

and to acquiescence, suggestibility, compliance and confabulation.[200] Similar findings have been made in relation to substance using or addicted suspects.[201]

5–97 Research has been undertaken on the influence of drugs on the reliability of answers given during police questioning and on the adverse effects of opiates and opiate withdrawal symptoms on the validity of detainee's accounts during police questioning. The consequences of illicit and prescription drug use include disinhibition, sedation, concentration and memory disturbance.[202] In withdrawal, decision-making can be impaired, with pre-occupation with the short-term goal of stopping the distress of withdrawal. As a result, Gudjonsson states that the addict is

> "unable to consider the long-term consequences of his or her actions. This may involve their trying to expedite their release from custody by making ill-considered self-incriminating admissions, which on occasion may be false. Davison and Forshaw argue that under such circumstances the drug addict lacks the capacity for autonomy, and the confession he or she makes is likely to be unreliable unless the withdrawal symptoms are medically treated".[203]

5–98 It should therefore be borne in mind that, while the trend has been towards an interrogatorial model for criminal investigations, information elicited in interviews with suspects who are mentally ill, intellectually impaired or in substance addiction or withdrawal[204] can be lacking in reliability and result in false confessions. Such suspects may also have difficulty conveying what they mean to say, remembering events on which they are questioned, comprehending the questions that are put to them and understanding their rights in garda custody. It is interesting to note that the question of whether the right of access to a solicitor was understood by Dean Lyons was raised in the subsequent enquiry into the events surrounding his false confession. Dean's mother argued that he had not understood his entitlement to contact his mother and to have access to a solicitor, but thought that he had to opt for one or the other. Psychological

[200] See Clare and Gudjonsson "The Vulnerability of Suspects with Intellectual Disabilities During Police Interviews: A Review and Experimental Study of Decision-Making," Mental Handicap Research, Vol 8 No2 pp 110–128; Gudjonsson, Clare, Rutter and Pearse, *Persons at Risk During Interviews in Police custody: the Identification of Vulnerabilities*, Research Study No 12, The Royal Commission on Criminal Justice (HMSO, London, 1993). In relation to juvenile offenders, see O'Reilly and Hayes, "Emotional Intelligence, Mental Health and Juvenile Delinquency" (Juvenile Mental Health Matters, Cork, 2007).

[201] Lader, 1999. See also Gudjonnson, *The Psychology of Interrogations and Confessions: A Handbook* (Wiley, 2003) at p 420.

[202] Lader, 1999, cited in Gudjonnson, *The Psychology of Interrogations and Confessions: A Handbook* (Wiley, 2003) at p 420.

[203] *ibid.*

[204] See Davison and Forshaw, "Retracted Confessions: Through Opiate Withdrawal to a New Conceptual Framework," Medicine, Science and the Law 33, pp 285–290 (1993); Davison and Gossop, "The Problem of Interviewing Drug Addicts in Custody: A Study of Interrogative Suggestibility and Compliance" Psychology, Crime and Law, Volume 2, Issue 3, 1996, pp 185–195. On alcohol dependence and interrogation, see Gudjonsson *et al* "The Relationship of Alcohol Withdrawal Symptoms to Suggestibility and Compliance," Psychology Crime & Law, June 2004, Vol 10(2), pp 169–177

experts felt that this may well have been the case, but the assertion was rejected by the chairman, George Birmingham SC.[205]

Deaf Suspects

The obstacles faced by deaf defendants should not be simplistically equated with those faced by non-English speaking suspects, yet the only concession made to deaf suspects in the custody regulations is the provision of an interpreter or written questions where an interpreter is not reasonably available. Deaf people are significantly disadvantaged at every stage of the criminal justice process,[206] and the provision of an interpreter or written materials are not necessarily sufficient safeguards to remedy the inherent disadvantage faced by individuals who experience the world in a very different way to hearing people. Much has been written in the American context about the experiences of deaf defendants, raising concerns about the adequacies of explanations and the level of understanding among deaf detainees of police procedures and their rights while in custody (and indeed throughout the criminal process).[207] It has been suggested that deaf people are particularly vulnerable and are easily coerced into confessions or waiver of their rights, through a combination of communication difficulties and lack of comprehension of the legal system.[208] Twersky-Glasner has written that: **5–99**

> "Deaf people thus face tremendous challenges within the criminal justice system. Foremost among these challenges is their ability to understand what is being said to them, as well as their ability to communicate their thoughts and feelings. This inability to understand and communicate is, primarily, linguistic, which has nothing to do with overall mental status, intelligence, or competence."[209]

Providing information in written form may not be sufficient to guard against injustice:

> "It may seem logical to assume that the courts can rely on written English to provide equal access to deaf defendants... Because of the disparity in deaf educational methods, deaf people have few role models who represent their population and less access to

---

205 See *Report of the Commission of Investigation (Dean Lyons Case)*, Department of Justice Equality and Law Reform, 1 September 2006, at p 82.

206 F Vernon and K Miller "Obstacles faced by deaf people in the criminal justice system, " American Annals of the Deaf — Volume 150, No 3, Summer 2005, pp 283–291 and "Forensic pretrial police interviews of deaf suspects avoiding legal pitfalls," International Journal of Law and Psychiatry, Volume 24, Issue 1, January-February 2001, pp 43–59 The latter article posits: "Deaf people, especially those who are not well educated, are at risk for serious injustices when they enter the criminal justice system... These dangers are greatest for those who are poorly educated, read at a fourth-grade level or lower, have poor communication skills (American Sign Language and English), and lack awareness of their legal rights"

207 See for example Vernon, Raifman, Greenberg and Monteiro, "Forensic Pretrial Police Interviews of Deaf Suspects: Avoiding Legal Pitfalls" (2001); Twersky-Glasner "Miranda Warnings and Deaf Suspects: It's Not Just a Matter of Translation," 5 Crim L Bulletin 3, (2006).

208 Vernon F, Miller K "Obstacles faced by deaf people in the criminal justice system," American Annals of the Deaf, Volume 150, No 3, Summer 2005, pp 283-291.

209 Twersky-Glasner, "Miranda Warnings and Deaf Suspects: Its Not Just a Matter of Translation," 5 Crim L Bulletin 3, (2006).

academic opportunities in the educational system (Rittenhouse, Johnson, Overton, Freeman, & Jaussi, 1991; Vernon & Makowsky, 1969). Thus, for many profoundly deaf people who use sign language as a primary means of communication, written English is not an accessible format."[210]

Treatment of Persons in Custody Regulations – Deaf Arrestees

5–100 Notwithstanding the difficulties in comprehending written material outlined above, the custody regulations[211] provide:

> "(8) (a) Where an arrested person is deaf or there is doubt about his hearing ability, he shall not be questioned in relation to an offence in the absence of an interpreter, if one is reasonably available, without his written consent (and, where he is under the age of seventeen [eighteen?]years, the written consent of an appropriate adult) or in the circumstances specified in paragraph (7) (a) (iii). [ie the member in charge has reasonable grounds for believing that to delay questioning the person would involve a risk of injury to persons, serious loss of or damage to property, destruction of or interference with evidence or escape of accomplices.]
>
> (b) A consent shall be signed by the arrested person and be recorded in the custody record or a separate document.
>
> (c) Where an arrested person has requested the presence of an interpreter under subparagraph (a) and one is not reasonably available, any questions shall be put to him in writing."

It would be better practice to refrain from questioning suspects until an interpreter has been engaged. At a minimum gardaí should enquire about the suspect's comprehension of the purpose of interview before seeking the suspect's written consent to interview in the absence of an interpreter.[212]

5–101 Video recording of interviews is of the utmost importance in dealing with deaf suspects. Both the signing of the suspect and of the interpreter must be clearly visible on the recording, as the video will essentially be the deaf suspect's transcript of interview.

---

[210] Vernon F, Miller K, "Linguistic Diversity in Deaf Defendants and Due Process Rights" *Journal of Deaf Studies and Deaf Education,* 6:3, Summer 2001, pp 226-234, at p 230

[211] Criminal Justice Act 1984 (Treatment Of Persons in Custody in Garda Síochána Stations) Regulations 1987 (SI No 119 of 1987).

[212] Vernon and Miller state: "...deaf people with PPD are often asked to sign forms that they do not understand. One of their coping mechanisms in situations in which they do not fully understand what is happening is to comply with the authority figure. They will smile, nod in agreement, and sign anything put before them (Vernon, Raifman, Greenberg, & Montiero, 2001). They frequently assume that they will be released if they sign the paper. Thus, most of them sign away their basic right against self-incrimination at the time of arrest. This action can have a profoundly negative effect during a trial because it makes a substantial amount of evidence available that would otherwise never have been admissible (Vernon & Miller, 2001)". F Vernon and K Miller "Obstacles faced by deaf people in the criminal justice system," *American Annals of the Deaf*, Volume 150, No 3, Summer 2005, pp 283–291.

To summarise:

1. Deaf suspects and suspects with speech impairments are a particularly vulnerable category of accused persons;
2. Gardaí should not assume that written notices are understood by deaf detainees and, using an interpreter, should enquire as to the extent of the understanding of the suspect before proceeding to interview;
3. Interviews involving deaf suspects must be video-recorded. Care must be taken to ensure that the signing of both the suspect and the interpreter are clearly visible on the video-recording.

CONFESSIONS, THE JUDGES' RULES AND THE CONDUCT OF INTERVIEWS

There is an increasing emphasis in Irish criminal law on long periods of detention **5–102** and the invocation of inference provisions, through which the suspect is invited to account for his or her movements and advised that adverse inferences may be drawn at trial for failure to answer key questions. This is at odds with the long-standing privilege against self-incrimination, and the principle that for a confession to be admissible in evidence against its maker it must have been made voluntarily. There is a dissonance therefore in consideration of the law as it relates to the conduct of interviews which is difficult to reconcile: a right to remain silent, an emphasis on fairness, but a demand to account for movements, marks or actions with potentially adverse consequences. For gardaí, there is a practical difficulty: first to caution a suspect that he or she is not obliged to say anything, and later to withdraw that caution and advise that failure to answer material questions may lead to an inference of guilt. Inferences are considered below, but first the judges' rules must be considered.

The Judges' Rules

The judges' rules are practice guidelines which apply to the taking of police statements. **5–103** Formulated with the object of preventing confessions being improperly elicited from suspects by police officers,[213] the rules were imported into Irish law in *People (AG) v Cummins.*[214] A statement from the judgment of the Court of Appeal in *R v Voisin*[215] was cited with approval by Walsh J:

> "These rules have not the force of law; they are administrative directions the observance of which the police authorities should enforce upon their subordinates as tending to the fair administration of justice. It is important that they should do so, for statements obtained from prisoners, contrary to the spirit of these rules, may be rejected by the judge presiding at the trial."[216]

---

213 *McCarrick v Leavy* [1964] IR 225 at 231.

214 *People (AG) v Cummins* [1972] 1 IR 312.

215 *R v Voisin* [1918] 1 KB 531, at 539.

216 *People (AG) v Cummins* [1972] IR 312, at 323.

5–104 The judges' rules which apply in Ireland are as follows:

> "I. When a police officer is endeavouring to discover the author of a crime, there is no objection to his putting questions in respect thereof to any person or persons, whether suspected or not, from whom he thinks that useful information may be obtained.
>
> II. Whenever a police officer has made up his mind to charge a person with a crime, he should first caution such person before asking him any questions, or any further questions as the case may be.
>
> III. Persons in custody should not be questioned without the usual caution being first administered.
>
> IV. If the prisoner wishes to volunteer any statement, the usual caution should be administered. It is desirable that the last two words of such caution ["against you"] should be omitted, and that the caution should end with the words 'be given in evidence.'
>
> V. The caution to be administered to a prisoner when he is formally charged should therefore be in the following words:
>
> 'Do you wish to say anything in answer to the charge? You are not obliged to say anything unless you wish to do so, but whatever you say will be taken down in writing and may be given in evidence.' Care should be taken to avoid the suggestion that his answers can only be used in evidence against him, as this may prevent an innocent person making a statement which might assist to clear him of the charge.
>
> VI. A statement made by a prisoner before there is time to caution him is not rendered inadmissible in evidence merely because no caution has been given, but in such a case he should be cautioned as soon as possible.
>
> VII. A prisoner making a voluntary statement must not be cross-examined, and no questions should be put to him about it except for the purpose of removing ambiguity in what he has actually said. For instance, if he has mentioned an hour without saying whether it was morning or evening, or has given a day of the week and day of the month which do not agree, or has not made it clear to what individual or what place he intended to refer in some part of his statement, he may be questioned sufficiently to clear up the point.
>
> VIII. When two or more persons are charged with the same offence and their statements are taken separately, the police should not read these statements to the other persons charged, but each of such persons should be given by the police a copy of such statements and nothing should be said or done by the police to invite a reply. If the person charged desires to make a statement in reply, the usual caution should be administered.
>
> IX. Any statement made in accordance with the above rules should, whenever possible, be taken down in writing and signed by the person making it after it has been read to him and he has been invited to make any corrections he may wish."

5–105 In *People v Farrell*, O'Higgins CJ cautioned:

> "The Judges' Rules are not rules of law. They are rules for the guidance of persons taking statements. However they have stood the test of time and should be departed from at peril. In very rare cases, such as *R v Mills & Lemon* [1947] KB 297 a statement taken in breach may be admitted in evidence but in very exceptional circumstances. Where, however, there is a breach of the Judges' Rules, such as a failure to make a written record of the alleged confession or a failure to invite the accused to accept or reject the statements, each of such breaches calls for an adequate explanation. The breaches and

> the explanations (if any) together with the entire circumstances of the case are matters to be taken into consideration by the trial judge before exercising his judicial discretion as to whether or not he will admit such statement in evidence."[217]

Among the most important of the rules is the requirement to caution suspects before asking them to potentially incriminate themselves. This rule is grounded in the right to silence. The standard caution is as follows:

> "You are not obliged to say anything unless you wish to do so but whatever you say will be taken down in writing and may be given in evidence."

Under no circumstances should the caution add the words "against you" when advising suspects that their words may be given in evidence, since doing so may impede a person in answering questions if they feel that their account will only be used "against" them, when it might tend to exonerate them. **5–106**

Where interviews are being recorded pursuant to the Criminal Justice Act 1984 (Electronic Recording of Interviews) Regulations 1997, interviewees should be cautioned in the following way:

> "You are not obliged to say anything unless you wish to do so, but whatever you say will be taken down in writing and may be given in evidence. As you are aware, this interview is being recorded and the tape may be used in evidence."

For non-English speaking suspects, the caution should be read by the interpreter, in the language of the suspect, and a written translated copy of the caution provided.

Further procedural protections are set down in Regulation 12 of the custody regulations, which specifically dictate that interviews must be conducted in a fair and humane manner:[218] there should be provision for electronic recording, the interviewing member must identify himself and any other member present by name and by rank to the arrested person,[219] the times of interviews and the members present at each interview should be recorded[220] and there are limitations to the number of members who may be present and involved in the interview process (a maximum of two gardaí may conduct the interview, and a maximum of four may be present at any time during the interview).[221] **5–107**

Voluntariness and the Privilege Against Self-Incrimination

To be admissible in evidence, a confession must be voluntary. Voluntariness serves as a guarantee of basic fairness, as well as reliability, since a confession "forced from the **5–108**

[217] *People v Farrell* [1978] 1 IR 13 at 21.
[218] reg 12(2) of the Criminal Justice Act 1984 (Treatment of Persons in Custody) Regulations 1987
[219] *ibid* reg 12(1).
[220] *ibid* reg 12(12)(a).
[221] Regulation 12(2) of the Criminal Justice Act 1984 (Treatment of Persons in Custody) Regulations 1987

mind by the flattery of hope, or by the torture of fear, comes in so questionable a shape when it is to be considered as the evidence of guilt, that no credit ought to be given to it; and therefore it is rejected".[222] The idea that persons are entitled to refuse to answer a question when to do so would expose them to prosecution or penalty is grounded in the fair trial guarantee of Article 38 of the Constitution, and in the constitutional rights of autonomy, privacy and the freedom and dignity of the individual. It is an important aspect of the presumption of innocence and reflects the investigative, rather than interrogatorial, character of our system, since a criminal process which freely admits self-incriminating statements is one which encourages the elicitation of confessions in favour of more objective forms of evidence.[223] The accused therefore enjoys a privilege against self-incrimination, in which inheres a right to silence. This is guarded by the common law, the Constitution,[224] the United Nations Covenant on Civil and Political Rights[225] and, to a lesser extent, by the jurisprudence of the European Court of Human Rights. As Murphy J put it:

> "The privilege against compulsory self-incrimination is part of the common law of human rights. It is based on the desire to protect personal freedom and human dignity. These social values justify the impediment the privilege represents to judicial or other investigations. It protects the innocent as well as the guilty from the indignity and invasion of privacy which occurs in compulsory self-incrimination: it is society's acceptance of the inviolability of human personality."[226]

5–109 The privilege operates both in the course of the investigation and at trial: in the garda station, the accused is protected from compulsory self-incrimination by the right to silence, and at trial the accused need never rebut the evidence adduced by the prosecution against him, nor is he under compulsion to testify. The right to silence operates to ensure that evidence gatherers take pains to build a case, on the basis that the proponent of the case against an accused person bears the probative burden. The European Court of Human Rights has explained the rationale of the right to silence in the following terms:

> "Although not specifically mentioned in Article 6 of the Convention, there can be no doubt that the right to remain silent under police questioning and the privilege against self-incrimination are generally recognised international standards which lie at the heart of a notion of fair procedure under Article 6. By providing the accused with protection against improper compulsion by the authorities, these immunities contribute to avoiding miscarriages of justice and to securing the aim of Article 6."[227]

5–110 In *People (DPP) v Shaw*, Griffin J held a statement to be involuntary "if it is wrung from its maker by physical or psychological pressures, by threats or promises made by

[222] *R v Warwickshall* (1783) 1 Leach 263.

[223] See R Coen, "The Decline of Due Process and the Right to Silence's Demise" (2008) 18(1) ICLJ 10, at p 12.

[224] *Re National Irish Banks Ltd* [1999] 1 IR 145, [1999] 1 ILRM 191.

[225] United Nations Covenant on Civil and Political Rights, (1976) UNTS 171 Art 14(3)(g) provides that an accused "shall not be compelled to testify against himself or to confess guilt".

[226] *Pyneboard Pty Ltd v Trade Practices Commission* (1983) 152 CLR 328, at 346.

[227] *Murray v United Kingdom* (1996) 22 EHRR 29 at 60.

persons in authority, by the use of drugs, hypnosis, intoxicating drink, by prolonged interrogation or excessive questioning, or by any one of a diversity of methods which have in common the result or the risk that what is tendered as a voluntary statement is not the natural emanation of a rational intellect and a free will".[228]

The law in Ireland relating to confession evidence was set out succinctly in the case of *People (DPP) v Buck* as follows:

> "(1) a confession, whether made to a police officer or to any other person, will not be admitted in evidence unless it is proved beyond reasonable doubt to have been voluntarily made;
> (2) even where voluntarily made, a trial judge retains a residual discretion to exclude such a statement where it is made to a police officer otherwise than in accordance with certain procedures, accepted in Ireland as being in the English Judges' Rules;
> (3) such a statement will also be excluded where it has been obtained as a result of a conscious and deliberate violation of the accused's constitutional rights."[229]

Reliability — The Frailty of Confession Evidence

The overriding concern of the garda ought to be the reliability of any statement made, **5–111** and as such incriminating statements made in custody must be scrutinised against the available independent evidence. As George Birmingham SC (as he then was) opined in his report on the Dean Lyons case, 'interview' is something of a euphemism for interrogation in the inevitably-coercive setting that is a garda station.[230] There is an arbitrary linguistic distinction between witnesses, who are "interviewed" and suspects, who are "interrogated," perhaps on the basis that a confession is the object of the latter. Gudjonsson suggests that the more neutral term "investigative interviewing" is the appropriate phrase in respect of all persons who are questioned as part of the police investigative process with a view to gathering evidence for use in further enquiries.[231] It was said in the 1978 Ó Bríain Report[232] that "[q]uestioning within the confines of a Garda station can be a traumatic experience for all but the hardened criminal".[233] Consequently it can produce unreliable results, and this is especially so in criminal justice systems which place a premium on confession evidence.

The Dean Lyons case is illustrative of the frailty of confession evidence, particularly **5–112** when dealing with a vulnerable suspect.[234] This is not a uniquely Irish problem, nor is it a new one. Kassin *et al* posit:

---

228 *People (DPP) v Shaw* [1982] IR 1 at 60–61.
229 *People (DPP) v Buck* [2002] 2 IR 268 at 277.
230 *Report of the Commission of Investigation (Dean Lyons Case)*, p 81.
231 GH Gudjonsson, *The Psychology of Police Interrogations and Confessions: A Handbook* (Wiley, London, 2003) at pp 1-2.
232 *Report of the Committee to Recommend Certain Safeguards for Persons in Custody and for Members of the Garda Síochána,* (Stationery Office, Dublin, 1978).
233 *ibid*, recommendation 58.
234 See Report of the Commission of Investigation (Dean Lyons Case) set up pursuant to the Commissions of Investigation Act 2004, chaired by George Birmingham SC.

> "The pages of American legal history are rich in stories about false confessions. These stories date back to the Salem witch trials of 1692, during which about 50 women confessed to witchcraft... In 1989, Gary Dotson was the first wrongfully convicted individual to be proven innocent through the then-new science of DNA testing. Almost two decades later, more than 200 individuals have been exonerated by post-conviction DNA testing and released from prison, some from death row. In 15–20% of these cases, police-induced false confessions were involved (Garrett, 2008; www.innocenceproject.org) ... Post-conviction DNA tests and exonerations have offered a window into the causes of wrongful conviction... Indeed, these cases have established the leading causes of error in the criminal justice system to be eyewitness mis-identification, faulty forensic science, false informant testimony, and false confessions (Garrett, 2008)."[235]

5–113 The Council of Europe Committee for the Prevention of Torture (CPT) suggests that systems in which confessions are prized can incentivise physical or psychological coercion and therefore recommends reduced reliance on confessions and information obtained via interrogation and a focus instead on the use of other methods of investigation:

> "The questioning of criminal suspects is a specialist task which calls for specific training if it is to be performed in a satisfactory manner. First and foremost, *the precise aim of such questioning* must be made crystal clear: that aim should be to obtain accurate and reliable information in order to discover the truth about matters under investigation, not to obtain a confession from someone already presumed, in the eyes of the interviewing officers, to be guilty."[236]

5–114 In the English context, Maguire argues that traditional policing strategies, in which there was a heavy reliance (often over-reliance) on interview evidence, resulted in a tendency towards closed-minded perception among investigating officers of the interview as a vehicle for confessions, in which statements which contradicted the officers' preconceived "knowledge" of the situation were ignored. Combined with a prevailing crime control (as distinct from due process) policing culture, institutional pressures and extensive pre-PACE extensive detention periods without access to legal advice or relatives, an essentially coercive environment was created. This, he asserts, led to inbuilt risks that:

> "(1) police officers might become oppressive in their questioning; (2) people might be unfairly persuaded to make or sign self-incriminating statements (for example, in response to hints that 'co-operation' would bring quicker release); (3) some suspects (especially those with mental disabilities) might become so disoriented and vulnerable that they would make entirely false confessions to crimes mentioned by interviewers; or (4) some police officers would, in their records of interviews, distort or embellish what had been said or even invent it entirely."[237]

---

[235] SM Kassin, SA Drizin, T Grisso, GH Gudjonsson, RA Leo, AD Redlich "Police-Induced Confessions: Risk Factors and Recommendations" Law Hum Behav (2010) 34:3–38.

[236] *CPT Standards*, Extract from the 12th General Report [CPT/Inf (2002) 15], paragraph 34, p 9.

[237] M Maguire, "Criminal Investigation and Crime Control" in T Newburn (ed) *Handbook of Policing* (2nd ed, Willan Publishing, Cullompton, 2008) at pp 447-448.

Subsequent commentary on miscarriage of justice cases (in which confessions were central) from the 1970s and 1980s is cited as demonstrative of the real risks posed.[238] Research undertaken on the psychology of interrogations and confessions, including analysis of the factors at play in the Birmingham Six and Guildford Four miscarriage of justice cases, illustrates that certain people are more open to suggestibility. It is argued that even the innocent, in the face of prolonged oppressive questioning, can begin to doubt their innocence.[239] In respect of those cases, Gudjonnson says: **5–115**

> "The most striking psychological finding regarding the 'Birmingham Six' is the difference in personality scores between the two defendants who did not confess and the four that did. Thirteen years after their interrogations, the two defendants who did not make written confessions scored exceptionally low on tests of suggestibility and compliance. We have argued that this may explain why they were able to resist extensive and coercive interrogations in 1974, whilst the remaining four, who were subjected to similarly intense questioning, confessed."[240]

On beginning to believe in one's own guilt he says:

> "… there is some evidence provided from one of the 'Guildford Four' (Richardson) that 'saying may become believing'… The reason for this seems to be that after confessing for instrumental gains, the persistent questioning continues and the accused becomes increasingly confused and puzzled by the interrogators' apparent confidence in accused's guilt… Conlon (1990) describes a similar, but less striking, example of having temporarily begun to doubt his innocence during intense police interrogation."

While gardaí cannot be expected to be psychologists, the Dean Lyons case,[241] in which Dean Lyons admitted two murders he had not committed, is illustrative of the dangers of suggestibility in the Irish context. Professor Gudjonsson had been engaged by Mr Lyons' defence team and found that his scores on total suggestibility fell outside normal limits, putting him in the 5% of the population that is most suggestible. In the "Kerry Babies" case, in which Joanne Hayes and her family admitted the murder of a newborn baby, a light was also shone on the potential for coercive interrogation techniques to produce results, in the form of self-incriminating confessions, which are dangerously unreliable. Even in the absence of mistreatment or physical threats, subtle psychological pressure can be exerted in the course of interrogation which can overbear the will of suspects and lead them to confess, often (as was seen in the Kerry Babies case) **5–116**

---

238 H Fisher, *The Confait Case: Report,* (HMSO, London, 1977); J Rozenberg, "Miscarriages of Justice" in E Stockdale and S Casale (eds), *Criminal Justice Under Stress,* (Blackstone Press, London, 1992) at pp 91-117; C Walker and K Starmer, *Miscarriages of Justice,* (Blackstone, London, 1999); B Morris, "History of Criminal Investigation", in T Newburn, T Williamson and A Wright (eds), *Handbook of Criminal Investigation* (Willan Publishing Cullumpton, 2007); S Savage and B Milne, "Miscarriages of Justice" in T Newburn, T Williamson and A Wright (eds), *Handbook of Criminal Investigation,* (Willan, Cullumpton, 2007).

239 See GH Gudjonsson, *The Psychology of Police Interrogations and Confessions: A Handbook,* (Wiley, London, 2003).

240 *ibid*, p 457.

241 See *Report of the Commission of Investigation (Dean Lyons Case),* Department of Justice, Equality and Law Reform, 1 September 2006.

in great detail, falsely. Even video-recording was seen in the Dean Lyons case to be an insufficient safeguard. It is essential that the investigating garda rigorously tests the account given by the suspect in interview against that which is capable of being established independently of the suspect, and that the evidence given by the suspect is capable of being independently corroborated. As Paul O'Mahony says:

> "Police involved in criminal investigations must have some weapons at their disposal to counteract and expose the expected evasions and denials of guilty suspects. Police must be allowed to confront, contradict, undermine, pressurise and, in strictly limited ways, trick suspects. However, the need at policy level is to create structures and rules that ensure that the use of techniques of interrogation and the manipulation of the detailed suspect's environment and state of mind never amounts to the kind of psychological duress that can lead to coerced confessions of the compliant or internalized variety… there is also a strong case for a change in the law such that retracted confessions without corroborating evidence will no longer be a sufficient basis for a confession… training should alert all gardaí to the existence of suggestibility and educate them in the conscientious and legitimate use of the various subtle but powerful psychological means of persuasion. Most importantly, the force should attempt to inculcate in all its members a sense of values that sustains truth and justice as the cardinal virtues of policing and abjures all methods of investigation and interrogation that might sacrifice these virtues for the sake of seeming effectiveness."[242]

5–117 In England and Wales, there has been a shift from the traditional approach to police interviews as a mechanism for eliciting confessions to one which is primarily aimed at obtaining reliable information. This is a more ethical approach which lessens the potential for false confessions and wrongful convictions.[243] The same should apply in the Irish context. Research has highlighted the need for specialist interview training which includes equipping police officers to identify vulnerabilities in detainees which may make them more susceptible to providing an account which falsely incriminates them.[244] The approach in England and Wales is set out in nationally agreed guidelines on interviewing witnesses and suspects commonly known as the 'Peace' investigative interviewing framework. Peace stands for Preparation and Planning, Engage and Explain, Account, Closure, Evaluate:

Planning and Preparation: this includes what to consider when planning for an interview.

Engage and Explain: This describes how to cope with the special features of getting an interview started and establishing the ground rules.

Account, Clarification and Challenge: this deals with the central issue of obtaining the interviewee's account, clarifying this and, where necessary, challenging it.

---

[242] Paul O'Mahony, "The Psychology of Police Investigations: the Kerry Babies Case" in *Criminal Justice in Ireland* (O'Mahony ed), (IPA, Dublin, 2002) at pp 539-540.

[243] GH Gudjonsson, *The Psychology of Police Interrogations and Confessions: A Handbook,* (Wiley, London, 2003), at pp 55 – 56.

[244] *ibid.*

Closure: this describes the considerations before closing an interview.

Evaluation: this consists of asking questions about what was achieved during the interview and how it fits into the whole investigation. Evaluation also includes the development of an interviewer's skill level, through assessment (self, peer and manager) and feedback.

The framework operates in tandem with the comprehensive and very detailed guide to **5–118** the interview process contained in the Ministry of Justice publication Achieving Best Evidence in Criminal Proceedings: Guidance on interviewing victims and witnesses, and using special measures (March 2011).[245] The latter focuses on victims and witnesses, and in particular vulnerable witnesses, rather than suspects. The principles of investigative interviewing (revised in 2007) are a useful guide to interviewing suspects: though they are applicable only in England and Wales, they have some relevance for this jurisdiction. They are as follows:

> "i. The aim of investigative interviewing is to obtain accurate and reliable accounts from victims, witnesses or suspects about matters under police investigation.
> ii. Investigators must act fairly when questioning victims, witnesses or suspects. Vulnerable people must be treated with particular consideration at all times.
> iii. Investigative interviewing should be approached with an investigative mindset. Accounts obtained from the person who is being interviewed should always be tested against what the interviewer already knows or what can reasonably be established.
> iv. When conducting an interview, investigators are free to ask a wide range of questions in order to obtain material which may assist an investigation.
> v. Investigators should recognise the positive impact of an early admission in the context of the criminal justice system.
> vi. Investigators are not bound to accept the first answer given. Questioning is not unfair merely because it is persistent.
> vii. Even when the right of silence is exercised by a suspect, investigators have a responsibility to put questions to them."[246]

The degree to which the Garda Crime Investigation Techniques Manual addresses this **5–119** issue is unclear, and the only publicly available Irish guidance remains that which is set out in the custody regulations, with Regulation 12 providing for the conduct of interviews as follows:

> "12. (1) Before an arrested person is interviewed, the member conducting the interview shall identify himself and any other member present by name and rank to the arrested person.

[245] *Achieving best evidence in criminal proceedings: Guidance on interviewing victims and witnesses, and using special measures,* available online at http://www.justice.gov.uk/downloads/victims-and-witnesses/vulnerable-witnesses/achieving-best-evidence-criminal-proceedings.pdf <accessed 20 October 2013>.

[246] National Police Improvement Agency, *Briefing Paper: National Investigative Interviewing Strategy,* 2009, available online at http://www.acpo.police.uk/documents/crime/2009/200901CRINSI01.pdf <accessed 20 October 2013>.

(2) The interview shall be conducted in a fair and humane manner.

(3) Not more than two members shall question the arrested person at any one time and not more than four members shall be present at any one time during the interview.

(4) If an interview has lasted for four hours, it shall be either terminated or adjourned for a reasonable time.

(5) As far as practicable, interviews shall take place in rooms set aside for that purpose.

(6) Where an arrested person asks for a solicitor, he shall not be asked to make a written statement in relation to an offence until a reasonable time for the attendance of the solicitor has elapsed.

(7) (a) Except with the authority of the member in charge, an arrested person shall not be questioned between midnight and 8 am in relation to an offence, which authority shall not be given unless—

- (i) he has been taken to the station during that period,
- (ii) in the case of a person detained under s 4 of the Act, he has not consented in writing to the suspension of questioning in accordance with subsection (6) of that section, or
- (iii) the member in charge has reasonable grounds for believing that to delay questioning the person would involve a risk of injury to persons, serious loss of or damage to property, destruction of or interference with evidence or escape of accomplices.

...

(8) (a) Where an arrested person is deaf or there is doubt about his hearing ability, he shall not be questioned in relation to an offence in the absence of an interpreter, if one is reasonably available, without his written consent (and, where he is under the age of eighteen years, the written consent of an appropriate adult) or in the circumstances specified in paragraph (7) (a) (iii).

- (b) A consent shall be signed by the arrested person and be recorded in the custody record or a separate document.
- (c) Where an arrested person has requested the presence of an interpreter under subparagraph (a) and one is not reasonably available, any questions shall be put to him in writing.

(9) An arrested person who is under the influence of intoxicating liquor or drugs to the extent that he is unable to appreciate the significance of questions put to him or his answers shall not be questioned in relation to an offence while he is in that condition except with the authority of the member in charge, which authority shall not be given except in the circumstances specified in paragraph (7) (a) (iii).

(10) If, while being interviewed, an arrested person makes a complaint to a member in relation to his treatment while in custody, the member shall bring it to the attention of the member in charge, if he is not present at the interview, and record it or cause it to be recorded in the record of the interview.

(11)(a) A record shall be made of each interview either by the member conducting it or by another member who is present. It shall include particulars of the time the interview began and ended, any breaks in it, the place of the interview and the names and ranks of the members present.

- (b) Where an interview is not recorded by electronic or other similar means, the record shall—
  - (i) be made in the notebook of the member concerned or in a separate document and shall be as complete as practicable,

(ii) if it is practicable to do so and the member concerned is of opinion that it will not interfere with the conduct of the interview, be made while the interview is in progress or otherwise as soon as practicable afterwards, and

(iii) be signed by the member making it and include the date and time of signature.

(12) (a) A record shall be made of the times during which an arrested person is interviewed and the members present at each interview.

(b) Where an authority is given pursuant to this Regulation, the fact that it was given, the name and rank of the member giving the authority and the reasons for doing so shall be recorded.

c) The fact that an arrested person has consented in writing under s 4 (6) of the Act to the suspension of questioning between midnight and 8 am shall be recorded and the consent shall be attached to and form part of the custody record…."

Corroboration Warning

Concern about the reliability of confession evidence, and the potential for miscarriages of justice as a consequence, was the rationale for the introduction of a mandatory corroboration warning in s 10 of the Criminal Procedure Act 1993, which provides: **5–120**

"(1) Where at a trial of a person on indictment evidence is given of a confession made by that person and that evidence is not corroborated, the judge shall advise the jury to have due regard to the absence of corroboration.

(2) It shall not be necessary for a judge to use any particular form of words under this section."

However, the section does not alter the traditional common law position that a person may be convicted on the basis of an uncorroborated confession. It merely introduces a statutory requirement that the trial judge must advise the jury to have regard to the absence of corroboration, with the decision as to the reliability of the confession to be taken by the jury. McGrath points out that it is arguable that the section requires merely corroboration of the fact of a confession having been made, but concludes that **5–121**

"the word 'corroboration' is undoubtedly a term of art with a particular technical meaning, i.e., independent evidence that tends to implicate the accused in the commission of the offence. Thus, the use of that term indicates that the section is directed towards the risk of a miscarriage of justice that arises when the only evidence against an accused is a confession or an inculpatory statement made by him".[247]

The latter interpretation has been judicially determined to be the correct one in *People (DPP) v Connolly*[248] and *People (DPP) v Brazil*.[249]

INFERENCES

The right to silence has been described as a "bastion of human freedom from oppression from the state"[250] and yet in Ireland it has been eroded considerably, in **5–122**

[247] McGrath, *Evidence* (Thomson Round Hall, Dublin, 2005), p 451.

[248] *People (DPP) v Connolly* [2003] 2 IR 1.

[249] *People (DPP) v Brazil*, unreported, Court of Criminal Appeal, 22 March 2002.

[250] Cross and Tapper on *Evidence* (8th ed, Butterworths, 1995), p 454.

the form of criminalisation of withholding information[251] in certain circumstances and by the enactment of wide-ranging adverse inference from silence provisions.[252] Legislation allowing for adverse inferences has, like many "extraordinary" measures, been normalised by the extension of inference provisions to all arrestable offences.[253] Introduced in the Criminal Justice Act 1984,[254] inferences were subsequently legislated for in the context of drug trafficking[255] and subversive offences against the State.[256] The Criminal Justice Act 2007 repealed the earlier provisions for inferences in respect of drug trafficking and subversive offences[257] and expanded the use of inference provisions to all arrestable offences, so that persons in custody may be advised that, in criminal proceedings, evidence may be given of their failure to account for objects, substances or marks on their person or on any object, or of their failure or refusal to account for their presence at a particular place, or to mention particular facts when in the circumstances such matters "clearly call for an explanation." The court or jury may draw such inferences from the failure or refusal as appear proper. The failure or refusal may, on the basis of such inferences, be treated as, or as capable of amounting to, corroboration of any evidence in relation to which the failure or refusal is material.

5–123 The inference provisions of the Criminal Justice Act 1984 are set out at s 18,[258] s 19[259] and s 19A as follows:

18. Inferences from failure, refusal to account for objects, marks, etc

"18.(1) Where in any proceedings against a person for an arrestable offence evidence is given that the accused—

(a) at any time before he or she was charged with the offence, on being questioned by a member of the Garda Síochána in relation to the offence, or

(b) when being charged with the offence or informed by a member of the Garda Síochána that he or she might be prosecuted for it, was requested by the member to account for any object, substance or mark, or any mark on any such object, that was—

(i) on his or her person,

(ii) in or on his or her clothing or footwear,

(iii) otherwise in his or her possession, or

[251] e.g. Offences against the State (Amendment) Act 1998, s 9.

[252] Other statutes which may be said to encroach on the privilege against self incrimination include the Road Traffic Acts 1961-2011, the Customs Consolidation Act 1876, the Companies Acts 1963-2012, the Income Tax Acts, the Criminal Law Act 1976, the Bankruptcy Act 1988, the Criminal Justice (Forensic Evidence) Act 1990, the Pensions Act 1990 and the Social Welfare (Consolidation) Act 1993.

[253] An arrestable offence is an offence punishable by five years' imprisonment or more, either by statute or under the common law, Criminal Law Act 1997, s 2, as amended by the Criminal Justice Act 2006, s 8.

[254] Criminal Justice Act 1984, s 18 and 19 These sections have since been substituted and expanded by the Criminal Justice Act 2007, s 29 and 30.

[255] Criminal Justice (Drug Trafficking) Act 1996, s 7(1).

[256] Offences against the State (Amendment) Act 1998, ss 2 and 5.

[257] Criminal Justice Act 2007, Schedule 1.

[258] Criminal Justice Act 1984, s 18 as substituted by s 28(1) of the Criminal Justice Act 2007.

[259] *ibid*, s 19 as substituted by s 29(1) of the Criminal Justice Act 2007.

(iv) in any place in which he or she was during any specified period, and which the member reasonably believes may be attributable to the participation of the accused in the commission of the offence and the member informed the accused that he or she so believes, and the accused failed or refused to give an account, being an account which in the circumstances at the time clearly called for an explanation from him or her when so questioned, charged or informed, as the case may be, then, the court, in determining whether a charge should be dismissed under Part IA of the Criminal Procedure Act 1967 or whether there is a case to answer and the court (or, subject to the judge's directions, the jury) in determining whether the accused is guilty of the offence charged (or of any other offence of which he or she could lawfully be convicted on that charge) may draw such inferences from the failure or refusal as appear proper; and the failure or refusal may, on the basis of such inferences, be treated as, or as capable of amounting to, corroboration of any evidence in relation to which the failure or refusal is material.

(2) A person shall not be convicted of an offence solely or mainly on an inference drawn from a failure or refusal to account for a matter to which subsection (1) applies.

(3) Subsection (1) shall not have effect unless—
(a) the accused was told in ordinary language when being questioned, charged or informed, as the case may be, what the effect of the failure or refusal to account for a matter to which that subsection applies might be, and
(b) the accused was afforded a reasonable opportunity to consult a solicitor before such failure or refusal occurred.

(4) Nothing in this section shall, in any proceedings—
(a) prejudice the admissibility in evidence of the silence or other reaction of the accused in the face of anything said in his or her presence relating to the conduct in respect of which he or she is charged in so far as evidence thereof would be admissible apart from this section,
(b) be taken to preclude the drawing of any inference from the silence or other reaction of the accused which could properly be drawn apart from this section, or
(c) be taken to preclude the drawing of any inference from a failure or refusal to account for the presence of an object, substance or mark or for the condition of clothing or footwear which could properly be drawn apart from this section.

(5) The court (or, subject to the judge's directions, the jury) shall, for the purposes of drawing an inference under this section, have regard to whenever, if appropriate, the account of the matter concerned was first given by the accused.

(6) This section shall not apply in relation to the questioning of a person by a member of the Garda Síochána unless it is recorded by electronic or similar means or the person consents in writing to it not being so recorded.

(7) Subsection (1) shall apply to the condition of clothing or footwear as it applies to a substance or mark thereon.

(8) References in subsection (1) to evidence shall, in relation to the hearing of an application under Part IA of the Criminal Procedure Act 1967 for the dismissal of a charge, be taken to include a statement of the evidence to be given by a witness at the trial.

(9) In this section 'arrestable offence' has the meaning it has in section 2 (as amended by section 8 of the Criminal Justice Act 2006) of the Criminal Law Act 1997." [260]

[260] Criminal Justice Act 1984, s 18, as substituted by s 28(1) of the Criminal Justice Act 2007.

19. Inferences from accused's presence at a particular place

"19.(1) Where in any proceedings against a person for an arrestable offence evidence is given that the accused—

(a) at any time before he or she was charged with the offence, on being questioned by a member of the Garda Síochána in relation to the offence, or

(b) when being charged with the offence or informed by a member of the Garda Síochána that he or she might be prosecuted for it, was requested by the member to account for his or her presence at a particular place at or about the time the offence is alleged to have been committed, and the member reasonably believes that the presence of the accused at that place and at that time may be attributable to his or her participation in the commission of the offence and the member informed the accused that he or she so believes, and the accused failed or refused to give an account, being an account which in the circumstances at the time clearly called for an explanation from him or her when so questioned, charged or informed, as the case may be, then, the court, in determining whether a charge should be dismissed under Part IA of the Criminal Procedure Act 1967 or whether there is a case to answer and the court (or, subject to the judge's directions, the jury) in determining whether the accused is guilty of the offence charged (or of any other offence of which he or she could lawfully be convicted on that charge) may draw such inferences from the failure or refusal as appear proper; and the failure or refusal may, on the basis of such inferences, be treated as, or as capable of amounting to, corroboration of any evidence in relation to which the failure or refusal is material.

(2) A person shall not be convicted of an offence solely or mainly on an inference drawn from a failure or refusal to account for his or her presence at a particular place under subsection (1).

(3) Subsection (1) shall not have effect unless—

(a) the accused was told in ordinary language when being questioned, charged or informed, as the case may be, what the effect of the failure or refusal to account for his or her presence at a particular place might be, and

(b) the accused was afforded a reasonable opportunity to consult a solicitor before such failure or refusal occurred.

(4) Nothing in this section shall, in any proceedings—

(a) prejudice the admissibility in evidence of the silence or other reaction of the accused in the face of anything said in his or her presence relating to the conduct in respect of which he or she is charged in so far as evidence thereof would be admissible apart from this section,

(b) be taken to preclude the drawing of any inference from the silence or other reaction of the accused which could properly be drawn apart from this section, or

(c) be taken to preclude the drawing of any inference from the failure or refusal of a person to account for his or her presence which could properly be drawn apart from this section.

(5) The court (or, subject to the judge's directions, the jury) shall, for the purposes of drawing an inference under this section, have regard to whenever, if appropriate, the

account of his or her presence at a particular place concerned was first given by the accused.

(6) This section shall not apply in relation to the questioning of a person by a member of the Garda Síochána unless it is recorded by electronic or similar means or the person consents in writing to it not being so recorded.

(7) References in subsection (1) to evidence shall, in relation to the hearing of an application under Part IA of the Criminal Procedure Act 1967 for the dismissal of a charge, be taken to include a statement of the evidence to be given by a witness at the trial.

(8) In this section 'arrestable offence' has the meaning it has in section 2 (as amended by section 8 of the Criminal Justice Act 2006) of the Criminal Law Act 1997 ."[261]

It should be noted that s 28(2) and (3) and 29(2) and (3) of the Criminal Justice Act 2007 provide that a person shall not be convicted solely or mainly on an inference drawn from a failure or refusal to account for objects, substances or marks or from their presence at a particular place. It is also provided that inference provisions will not apply unless the accused was told in ordinary language when being questioned, charged or detained what the effect of the failure to give an account might be. The accused must have been afforded a reasonable opportunity to consult a solicitor before refusing or failing to give an account. **5–124**

Section 19A of the Criminal Justice Act 1984 as inserted by s 30(1) of the Criminal Justice Act 2007 is the most controversial of the inference provisions, since it requires a person detained to mention at interview stage anything which might later be used at trial stage in his defence. The section provides: **5–125**

19A. Inferences From Failure to Mention a Fact Later Relied on in Defence

"19A(1) Where in any proceedings against a person for an arrestable offence evidence is given that the accused—

(a) at any time before he or she was charged with the offence, on being questioned by a member of the Garda Síochána in relation to the offence, or

(b) when being charged with the offence or informed by a member of the Garda Síochána that he or she might be prosecuted for it, failed to mention any fact relied on in his or her defence in those proceedings, being a fact which in the circumstances existing at the time clearly called for an explanation from him or her when so questioned, charged or informed, as the case may be, then, the court, in determining whether a charge should be dismissed under Part IA of the Criminal Procedure Act 1967 or whether there is a case to answer and the court (or, subject to the judge's directions, the jury) in determining whether the accused is guilty of the offence charged (or of any other offence of which he or she could lawfully be convicted on that charge) may draw such inferences from the failure as appear proper; and the failure may, on the basis of such inferences, be treated as, or as

[261] Criminal Justice Act 1984, s 19, as substituted by s 29(1) of the Criminal Justice Act 2007.

capable of amounting to, corroboration of any evidence in relation to which the failure is material.

(2) A person shall not be convicted of an offence solely or mainly on an inference drawn from a failure to mention a fact to which subsection (1) applies.

(3) Subsection (1) shall not have effect unless—

(a) the accused was told in ordinary language when being questioned, charged or informed, as the case may be, what the effect of the failure to mention a fact to which that subsection applies might be, and
(b) the accused was afforded a reasonable opportunity to consult a solicitor before such failure occurred.

(4) Nothing in this section shall, in any proceedings—
(a) prejudice the admissibility in evidence of the silence or other reaction of the accused in the face of anything said in his or her presence relating to the conduct in respect of which he or she is charged in so far as evidence thereof would be admissible apart from this section, or

(b) be taken to preclude the drawing of any inference from the silence or other reaction of the accused which could properly be drawn apart from this section.

(5) The court (or, subject to the judge's directions, the jury) shall, for the purposes of drawing an inference under this section, have regard to when the fact concerned was first mentioned by the accused.

(6) This section shall not apply in relation to the questioning of a person by a member of the Garda Síochána unless it is recorded by electronic or similar means or the person consents in writing to it not being so recorded.

(7) Subject to section 7 of the Criminal Justice (Drug Trafficking) Act 1996 and section 5 of the Offences against the State (Amendment) Act 1998, this section shall not apply in relation to a failure to mention a fact if the failure occurred before the commencement of this section.

(8) References in subsection (1) to evidence shall, in relation to the hearing of an application under Part IA of the Criminal Procedure Act 1967 for the dismissal of a charge, be taken to include a statement of the evidence to be given by a witness at the trial.

(9) In this section 'arrestable offence' has the meaning it has in section 2 (as amended by section 8 of the Criminal Justice Act 2006) of the Criminal Law Act 1997 ."[262]

5–126 Though the earlier inference provisions in s 7 of the Criminal Justice (Drug Trafficking) Act 1996 and s 5 of the Offences against the State (Amendment) Act 1998 have been repealed,[263] s 2 of the Offences against the State (Amendment) Act 1998 remains. It provides that, in relation to the offence of membership of an unlawful organisation,[264] inferences may be drawn from a failure "to answer any question material to the investigation of the offence". An inference drawn under s 2 may be used as corroboration of other evidence, and no person may be convicted solely or mainly on the basis of an

262 Criminal Justice Act 1984, s 19A, as inserted by s 30(1) of the Criminal Justice Act 2007.
263 Schedule 1 of the Criminal Justice Act 2007.
264 Contrary to s 21 of the Offences against the State (Amendment) Act 1998.

inference. Ordinary language must be used to explain the effect of a failure or refusal to answer, and suspects must be afforded a reasonable opportunity to consult a solicitor. Inferences will not be drawn unless the interview has been video-recorded.

O'Malley suggests that adverse inference provisions are unobjectionable, and that the reconstituted s 18 and 19 of the Criminal Justice Act 1984 (as substituted by s 29 and 30 of the Criminal Justice Act 2007) augment the accused's protection on the basis that an accused person cannot be convicted on the basis of a refusal or failure to answer alone, gardaí must inform the accused of the consequences of failure to answer and the accused must have been afforded a reasonable opportunity to avail of legal advice before refusing or failing to answer. Video recording is also a pre-requisite before inferences can be drawn, unless the suspect has waived the right to video-recording in writing.[265] Campbell has argued on the other hand that: **5–127**

> "The right to silence, which may be regarded as overlapping with the right to the presumption of innocence, the right against self-incrimination, and the right to privacy, is a fundamental element of the principle that the prosecution must establish and prove the case against the accused … the right is underpinned by the pragmatic or consequentialist rationale of guarding against unsafe convictions through unsafe and unreliable confessions."[266]

Daly has posited that:

> "a defence to a criminal charge is a legal construct. Defences such as self-defence, provocation, duress, insanity and so on have legal meanings which may not be readily apparent to the layman. It seems harsh then to place a burden upon a suspect in the police station to mention at that point any fact which he thinks may be of relevance to a later defence. At this point, he may not be aware of what sort of a defence might be appropriate in his case and he may have no idea what sort of facts would form part of that defence".[267]

It is a contradiction in terms to speak of the right to silence and an obligation to give an account with failure to do so being capable of corroborating a suspect's guilt. Inference provisions jar with the concept of the probative burden resting with the prosecution. Their efficacy is questionable, if we accept as applicable in Ireland research conducted in the UK which found that over half of suspects who are interrogated either confess or make incriminating admissions in police custody[268] and that only two to four per cent of suspects exercise absolute silence, a further five per cent simply make flat denials, 8–15 per cent answer some questions and not others, and some suspects are silent initially but answer questions subsequently (or *vice versa*).[269] Undoubtedly, such provisions **5–128**

[265] T O'Malley, *The Criminal Process* (Round Hall, Dublin, 2009) at pp 782-783.

[266] L Campbell, *Organised Crime and the Law – A Comparative Analysis* (Oxford, Hart, 2013) at p. 105.

[267] Y Daly, "Silence and Solicitors: Lessons Learned from England and Wales?" (2007) 17(2) ICLJ 2.

[268] T Bucke, R Street and D Brown, *The Right of Silence: the Impact of the CJPO 1994, Home Office Research Study* 199, (HMSO, London, 2000).

[269] R Leng, *The Right to Silence in Police Interrogation, Royal Commission on Criminal Justice Research Study* 10, London, HMSO, 1992. See also A Sanders and R Young, "Police Powers" in T Newburn (ed), *Handbook of Policing,* (2nd ed, Willan Publishing, Cullompton, 2008) at pp 292-295.

have the capacity to increase the pressure exerted on a suspect in custody, a dissonant approach to the long-held notion that a confession must only be admitted if it has been voluntarily made. Sanders and Young have noted that the law on inferences is still being developed in England and Wales and in Europe and "is likely to remain a matter of great difficulty for lawyers, police officers and judges for some time to come. Consequently these changes have been castigated on pragmatic (for example Birch, 1999) as well as principled grounds (for example Sanders and Young 2007: 223-35)".[270]

5–129 The European Court of Human Rights has upheld the use of inference provisions, holding in *Murray v United Kingdom*[271] that the Criminal Evidence (Northern Ireland) Order 1998, which allowed adverse inferences to be drawn from the silence of a suspect, were compatible with the convention on the basis that they merely created "... a formalised system which aims to allow common sense implications to play an open role in the assessment of the evidence".[272] Recognising the contradictory nature of the right to silence, the court said:

> "On the one hand, it is self-evident that it is incompatible with the immunities under consideration to base a conviction solely or mainly on the accused's silence or on a refusal to answer a question or to give evidence himself. On the other hand, the court deems it equally obvious that these immunities cannot and should not prevent that the accused's silence, in situations which clearly call for an explanation from him, be taken into account in assessing the persuasiveness of the evidence adduced by the prosecution. Wherever the line between these two extremes is drawn, it follows from this understanding that the question whether the right is absolute must be answered in the negative."[273]

5–130 A series of Irish cases concerning legislative encroachments on the privilege against self-incrimination has found such provisions to be constitutional on the basis of proportionality,[274] and therefore compelled statements are in principle admissible, though a trial judge retains the discretion to exclude such a statement if it would be unfair to admit it.[275]

5–131 The legislation places a difficult burden not only on the suspect, but also on gardaí and defence solicitors. Interviewing gardaí must first give a caution as to the availability of the right to silence, then retract it and endeavour to explain the complex legislation permitting inferences to be drawn in layman's terms. Frequently such a warning will explain an inference as a conclusion which might be drawn from certain facts, such as

---

[270] A Sanders and R Young, "Police Powers" in T Newburn (ed), *Handbook of Policing,* (2nd ed, Willan Publishing, Cullompton, 2008) at p 295.

[271] *Murray v United Kingdom* [1996] 22 EHRR 29.

[272] *ibid*, at para 54. See also the case of *Funke v France* [1993] 16 EHRR 297.

[273] *Murray v United Kingdom* [1996] 22 EHRR 29 at pp 60-81. The European Court did, however, continue to find a violation of the accused's rights under Article 6, on the basis that the drawing of adverse inferences was reprehensible in circumstances where the accused had been denied access to a lawyer.

[274] See *Rock v Ireland* [1997] 3 IR 484, *Heaney v Ireland* [1996] IR 580 at pp 589-590, [1997] 1 ILRM 117.

[275] See D Mc Grath, *Evidence* (Thomson Round Hall, Dublin, 2005) at p 674.

a wet footpath giving rise to an inference that it must have rained. Like the inference provisions of the Offences against the State (Amendment) Act 1998, the provisions of s 18, 19 and 19A of the Criminal Justice Act 1984 require investigating gardaí to explain "in ordinary language" what the implications of a failure or refusal to mention a particular fact might be. McGillicuddy has pointed to instances in which confusion has been caused and resulted in the preclusion of the use of inferences:

> "... consider the decision of the Court of Criminal Appeal in *People (DPP) v Bowes*[276] where the caution that was administered in that case was found to be defective and the adverse inference could not be drawn in those circumstances. Indeed, the degree of confusion in that case on the appropriate caution to be given shows that this issue may arise at trials for a considerable period of time.
>
> Difficulties might also arise where different cautions are used during the course of the interrogation of a person. It is conceivable that the traditional caution may be given to the person at the outset of an interview and that, sometime thereafter, the investigating gardaí would decide to give a caution for the purposes of s19A. In those circumstances, there would have to be evidence that the traditional caution was withdrawn and an adequate explanation given that it was no longer operative. If the accused person was confused or did not understand which caution was operative during the interview it may not be possible for an adverse inference to arise from any silence that occurred".[277]

In *Bowes*, heroin had been found in the boot of the defendant's car. Following his arrest **5–132**
and detention, the accused was cautioned in the usual manner and was then told that "certain inferences can be drawn by your failure to answer some questions in relation to the amount of heroin found in your car today". The Court of Criminal Appeal held that such a formula of words did not satisfy the requirement to caution the person in relation to inferences under s 7 of the Criminal Justice (Drug Trafficking) Act 1996.

Breen and McEntee, commenting on the inference provisions in the 1998 Offences against the State legislation, said:

> "The appropriate person to advise a detained person of his legal rights and obligations is his lawyer. On the face of it there is a potential conflict of interest between those investigating an offence and a person suspected of having committed that offence or of having information in relation to it. Reference to 'ordinary language' in the sections is an implicit acceptance that the wording of the sections is arcane and needs to be interpreted. The appropriate person to advise on the meaning of arcane statutes is the solicitor of the person requiring such advice."[278]

To date it has been stated that, in Irish law, there is no right to have a lawyer present **5–133**
in the course of a garda interview, and as outlined above in para 5 – 55, Ireland has

---

276 People (DPP) v Bowes [2004] 4 IR 224 at 239.

277 T, McGillicuddy, "Restrictions on the Right to Silence under the Criminal Justice Act 2007 – Part 2" (2008) 18(4) ICLJ 112.

278 F Breen and P McEntee, "The Right to Silence in light of *Deaglan Lavery v The Member in Charge Carrickmacross Garda Station*" (1999) 5 (1) BR 6.

opted out of the Directive on the right of access to a lawyer.[279] This makes the task of advising on inferences a particularly difficult one, unlike the position in England and Wales where solicitors are present in interviews and can give effective advice as a consequence.[280] As O'Malley has noted:

> "Solicitors advising clients who are facing police questioning are now facing something of a dilemma. If they advise them to stay silent they may be leaving them at risk of having adverse inferences drawn from that silence at trial. On the other hand, advising a detained person to answer all questions might result in that person incriminating himself unfairly and perhaps beyond the extent of his factual guilt, if any."[281]

This area of Irish criminal procedure may well be informed by developments at a European level, particularly in light of the adoption of the Directive on the right of access to a lawyer.

ACCESS TO LEGAL ADVICE

5–134 The right of a person in Garda custody to reasonable access to a solicitor is constitutionally guaranteed, rather than being merely legal in origin.[282] Finlay CJ explained the rationale for the right of access to legal advice in custody in *People (DPP) v Healy,* the case which placed access to legal advice in custody on a constitutional footing:

> "The undoubted right of reasonable access to a solicitor enjoyed by a person who is in detention must be interpreted as being directed towards the vital function of ensuring that such person is aware of his rights and has the independent advice which would be appropriate in order to permit him to reach a truly free decision as to his attitude to interrogation or to the making of any statement, be it exculpatory or inculpatory. The availability of advice from a lawyer must, in my view, be seen as a contribution, at least, towards some measure of equality in the position of the detained person and his interrogators.
>
> Viewed in that light, I am driven to the conclusion that such an important and fundamental standard of fairness in the administration of justice as the right of access to a lawyer must be deemed to be constitutional in its origin, and that to classify it as merely legal would be to undermine its importance and the completeness of the protection of it which the courts are obliged to give."[283]

---

[279] *Lavery v the Member in Charge, Carrickmacross Garda Station,* unreported, Supreme Court, 23 February 1999, *per* O'Flaherty J.

[280] See F Breen and P McEntee, "The Right to Silence in light of *Deaglan Lavery v The Member in Charge Carrickmacross Garda Station*" (1999) 5 (1) BR 6.

[281] T O'Malley, *The Criminal Process* (Round Hall, Dublin, 2009) at p 790.

[282] *People (DPP) v Healy* [1990] 2 IR 73; [1990] ILRM 313. The part of the Constitution from which the right to legal advice is derived is debatable, and a point on which the courts have prevaricated. It may have its origins in Article 38 as an aspect of the right to a fair trial, in article 40.3 as an unenumerated personal right, or in Article 40.1 as an aspect of the right to liberty, see YM Daly, "Does the Buck Stop Here? An Examination Of The Pre-Trial Right To Legal Advice In Light Of *O'Brien v DPP* (2006) 13(1) DULJ 345.

[283] *People (DPP) v Healy* [1990] 2 IR 73, *per* Finlay CJ at 81.

The right to legal advice in custody was legislatively provided in the Criminal Justice Act 1984 Act and in accompanying 1987 custody regulations. It is the duty of the member in charge to ensure that persons in custody are informed of their entitlement to legal advice and that, if they do not wish to avail of the right to consult a solicitor immediately, they are free to do so at a later stage in their detention. The 1984 Act provides at s 5 that members in charge must ensure that a person detained in a Garda station is **5–135**

> "informed without delay that he is entitled to consult a solicitor and to have notification of his detention and of the station where he is being detained sent to one other person reasonably named by him..."[284]

The member in charge must "on request, cause the solicitor and the named person to be notified accordingly as soon as practicable".[285]

Regulation 9(2) of the custody regulations provides: **5–136**

> "Where an arrested person has asked for a solicitor or has asked that a person reasonably named by him should be notified of his being in custody in the station concerned—
>
> (i) the member in charge shall notify or cause to be notified the solicitor or that person accordingly as soon as practicable, and
> (ii) if the solicitor or the named person cannot be contacted within a reasonable time or if the solicitor is unable or unwilling to attend at the station, the person shall be given an opportunity to ask for another solicitor or that another person reasonably named by him should be notified as aforesaid and, if the person asks for another solicitor or asks that another person reasonably named by him should be notified as aforesaid, the member in charge shall notify or cause to be notified that other solicitor or person accordingly as soon as practicable."[286]

There is an obligation to record the fact that a solicitor was requested, as well as actions taken to fulfil the request.[287]

The right is one of "reasonable access" and private consultation. The custody regulations provide at Regulation 11 that: **5–137**

> "(1) An arrested person shall have reasonable access to a solicitor of his choice and be enabled to communicate with him privately.
> (2) Where an arrested person has not had access to a solicitor in accordance with paragraph (1) and a solicitor whose presence has not been requested by the arrested person presents himself at the station and informs the member in charge that he wishes

284 Criminal Justice Act 1984, s 5.

285 *ibid.*

286 Regulation 9 of SI No 119 of 1987 – the Criminal Justice Act, 1984 (Treatment Of Persons In Custody In Garda Síochána Stations) Regulations, 1987.

287 *ibid.*

to visit that person, the person shall be asked if he wishes to consult the solicitor and, if he does so wish, the said paragraph (1) shall apply accordingly.
(3) A consultation with a solicitor may take place in the sight but out of hearing of a member."

5–138 Despite recognition of the constitutional status of the right of access to a solicitor in custody, there are inadequate systems to ensure the vindication of the right. Gardaí do not have lists of solicitors who are likely to be available to advise suspects in custody. Unlike the position in England and Wales, there is no duty solicitor scheme in Ireland whereby a detainee is assured of legal advice, having requested it. In England and Wales, the PACE Code of Practice C provides at paragraph 3.2 that an arrested person must be told clearly on arrival at the police station that free independent legal advice is available.[288] Paragraph 6.4 provides that "No police officer should, at any time, do or say anything with the intention of dissuading a detainee from obtaining legal advice." In Ireland, while the right of access to a lawyer is guaranteed, there is no obligation to advise a detainee of his potential entitlement to *free* legal aid, but it would seem axiomatic that, if free legal advice is an entitlement of those who cannot afford to pay for it, those who are in the vulnerable position of being in Garda custody should, in order to vindicate their right, be informed of it. The Garda Station Legal Advice Scheme provides free consultations when a persons is detained in a Garda station for the purpose of the investigation of an offence under the provisions of:

- Section 30 of the Offences against the State Act 1939, as amended by the Offences against the State (Amendment) Act 1998;
- Section 4 of the Criminal Justice Act 1984;
- Section 2 of the Criminal Justice (Drug Trafficking) Act 1996; or
- Section 50 of the Criminal Justice Act 2007.

5–139 The case of *State (Healy) v O'Donoghue*[289] emphasised that every criminal trial should be conducted in accordance with the concept of justice, that the procedures applied shall be fair, and that the person accused will be given every opportunity to defend himself and this entails the provision by the State of legal aid. The right to legal aid was found to inhere in the right to a fair trial under Article 38 of the Constitution. However there is no reference to *free* legal aid in the standard C72 form given to detainees. Notwithstanding that there is no statutory obligation to do so, it is submitted that it would be best practice to advise persons detained for the investigation of an offence that, if they are recipients of social welfare or earn less than €20,316, consultations with solicitors will be paid for by the State under the Garda Station Legal Advice Scheme[290] so that they are not dissuaded by cost from availing of their right to legal advice.

[288] Under s 59 of the Police and Criminal Evidence Act 1984 and the Legal Aid Act 1988.
[289] *State (Healy) v O'Donoghue* [1976] IR 325.
[290] For details of the Garda Station Legal Aid Scheme see http://www.legalaidboard.ie/lab/publishing.nsf/content/Garda_Station_Legal_Advice_Scheme <accessed 20 October 2013>.

Refusal of Access to a Solicitor

The refusal of gardaí to accede to requests to contact a solicitor will render a suspect's detention unlawful. In *People (DPP) v Madden*, O'Higgins CJ held: **5–140**

> "This Court is satisfied that a person held in detention by the Garda Síochána, whether under the provisions of the Act of 1939 or otherwise, has got a right of reasonable access to his legal advisers and that a refusal of a request to give such reasonable access would render his detention illegal. Of course, in this context the word 'reasonable' must be construed having regard to all the circumstances of each individual case and, in particular, as to the time at which access is requested and the availability of the legal adviser or advisers sought."[291]

In *People (DPP) v Buck*,[292] the appellant was arrested on a Sunday afternoon, detained under s 4 of the Criminal Justice Act 1984 and advised of his rights including his right to consult a solicitor. In the course of his questioning the appellant requested a solicitor but questioning continued for some time afterwards, with efforts subsequently made to contact one. A number of hours elapsed before a solicitor arrived at the station. Having had a short consultation, the appellant admitted having had a role in the killing which was under investigation. It fell to the Supreme Court to consider whether incriminating admissions made by the detained person after he had requested a solicitor but before the solicitor arrived were admissible in evidence. The Supreme Court held that what had transpired did not necessarily amount to a denial of access where a detained person has requested a solicitor and is questioned pending their arrival. **5–141**

Suspension of Questioning Pending Arrival of Solicitor

In a provision which, at the time of writing, had not yet been commenced, the Criminal Justice Act 2011 inserts a new s 5A into the Criminal Justice Act 1984. The effect of the provision, if it becomes operative, will be to clarify that suspects should not be questioned pending the arrival of the solicitor.[293] The provision is strongly worded by comparison with the custody regulation which preceded it, providing that **5–142**

> "no questioning of a person detained pursuant to section 4 shall take place until such time as the person has had an opportunity to consult with a solicitor and, the period of time commencing from the time the detained person makes the request to consult a solicitor and ending upon the commencement of such a consultation, shall be excluded in reckoning a period of detention…"

Regulation 12(6) states rather more weakly that "where an arrested person asks for a solicitor, he shall not be asked to make a written statement in relation to an offence until a reasonable time for the attendance of the solicitor has elapsed".[294] However, s 5A requires a commencement order to be made under s 1 of the Criminal Justice Act 2011 if it is to come into operation. **5–143**

---

291 *People (DPP) v Madden* [1977] IR 336 at 355.

292 *People (DPP) v Buck* [2002] IR 268, [2002] 2 ILRM 454.

293 Criminal Justice Act 1984, s 5A, as inserted by s 9 of the Criminal Justice Act 2011.

294 reg 12 of SI No 119 of 1987—the Criminal Justice Act, 1984 (Treatment Of Persons In Custody In Garda Síochána Stations) Regulations, 1987.

Practical Aspects of the Right of Access to a Solicitor

5–144 The custody regulations also provide that, when an arrested person has asked for a solicitor or has asked that a person reasonably named by him should be notified of his being in custody, the member in charge must notify the solicitor or other person as soon as practicable. If the solicitor or the named person cannot be contacted within a reasonable time or if the solicitor is unable or unwilling to attend at the station, the person must be given an opportunity to ask for another solicitor or that another person reasonably named by him should be notified. If the person requests another solicitor or asks that another person reasonably named by him should be notified, the member in charge must ensure that the other solicitor or person is notified as soon as practicable.[295]

5–145 The right of access is one of "reasonable access." A legal advisor is not entitled to be present throughout a Garda interview. In *Lavery v Member-in-Charge, Carrickmacross Garda Station*,[296] it was held that, even where inference provisions are invoked, a suspect is not entitled to have his solicitor present during the interview, nor to access the contemporaneous notes of the interviews, nor to demand that that the interview be audio-visually recorded. It has been pointed out on numerous occasions that this poses significant practical difficulties for the solicitor who is called on to advise a person in custody in those circumstances. As Breen and McEntee point out, this is in marked contrast to the position in England and Wales, where solicitors are shown witness statements and a summary of the facts, can be present in the interview room, can consult their client privately to advise on the consequences of exercising the right to silence and take a copy of the transcript of interview.[297] In *JM (A Minor) v Member in Charge, Coolock Garda Station*,[298] the High Court has reiterated the position as regards the presence of solicitors during questioning, and firmly stated that the case of *Lavery v Member in Charge, Carrickmacross Garda Station*[299] represents the law in this jurisdiction. There, Sheehan J held:

> "While I agree with the applicant's submissions that the circumstances of this particular case are considerably different to those in *Lavery v Member in Charge, Carrickmacross Garda Station* [1999] 2 IR 390 and can be distinguished on that basis, I nevertheless hold that the relevant passage in *Lavery v Member in Charge, Carrickmacross Garda Station* is not an *obiter* comment made by the Supreme Court. I, therefore, agree with the submissions of the respondent in this regard that the judgment in *Lavery v Member in Charge, Carrickmacross Garda Station* represents the law in this jurisdiction concerning whether or not one is entitled to have a solicitor present when being interviewed by the gardaí while in custody."[300]

---

[295] reg 9 of SI No 119 of 1987—the Criminal Justice Act, 1984 (Treatment Of Persons In Custody In Garda Síochána Stations) Regulations, 1987.

[296] *Lavery v The Member in Charge, Carrickmacross Garda Station*, unreported, Supreme Court, of 23 February 1999.

[297] F Breen and P McEntee, "The Right to Silence in light of *Deaglan Lavery v The Member in Charge Carrickmacross Garda Station*" (1999) 5 (1) BR 6.

[298] *JM (A Minor) v Member in Charge, Coolock Garda Station* [2013] IEHC 251.

[299] *Lavery v The Member in Charge, Carrickmacross Garda Station*, unreported, Supreme Court, 23 February 1999.

[300] *JM (A Minor) v Member in Charge, Coolock Garda Station* [2013] IEHC 251 at para 24.

The case of *Cadder v Her Majesty's Advocate (Scotland)*,[301] a decision of the UK Supreme Court which applied the decision of the European Court of Human Rights in *Salduz v Turkey*[302] was opened to the Court. It was found that the European jurisprudence did not go so far as to say that there is a right to have one's solicitor present at police interviews: 5–146

> "Having considered the jurisprudence of the European Court of Human Rights which was opened to this Court, in particular *Salduz v Turkey* (2009) 49 EHRR 19 and *Panovits v. Cyprus* [2008] ECHR 1688, it is important to note that none of these judgments go so far as to say that there is a right to have one's solicitor present at police interviews. It is likewise important to note that both applicants in the case of *Salduz v Turkey* and the case of *Panovits v Cyprus*, whilst being seventeen year old minors facing serious charges, had been denied access to legal counsel prior to the initial police interviews whilst in custody. This is quite simply not the case in respect of JM In a similar vein, the reliance placed upon Cadder v Her Majesty's Advocate (Scotland) [2010] UKSC 43 [2010] 1 WLR 2601 by counsel for the applicant is similarly misconceived in respect of this applicant."[303]

As outlined above at paras 5–53 – 5–56 the Directive on the right of access to a lawyer in criminal proceedings makes clear that there is now a right, recognised across the European Union, to have lawyers present during police questioning. The notable exceptions are Ireland, the UK and Denmark who have opted-out of the Directive. 5–147

It is equally clear that, in reality, the right to pre-trial legal advice in Ireland is quite limited. The preamble to the Directive expressly states that "the United Kingdom and Ireland will not participate in the adoption of this Directive and will not be bound by or be subject to its application." Regan has expressed concern that 5–148

> "Ireland's opt-out over criminal matters has the potential to significantly hamper Ireland's effective participation in an area of core national interest... In the interests of effective detection, investigation and prosecution of serious crime it must surely be a core element of national legal policy to ensure we remain at the heart of the Union's decision-making in criminal law and policing matters."[304]

The Directive ensures the provision of practical and effective legal assistance for people in custody. It provides that a vital safeguard, the presence of a lawyer in the course of police detention, applies across the European Union, but not in Ireland. If Ireland were to opt-in to the Directive, it would significantly improve the position of Irish defendants and allow for the presence of solicitors at interview and while evidence is gathered in the course of detention in garda custody. 5–149

---

301 *Cadder v Her Majesty's Advocate (Scotland)* [2010] UKSC 43, [2010] 1 WLR 2601.

302 *Salduz v Turkey* (2009) 49 EHRR 19.

303 *JM (A Minor) v Member in Charge, Coolock Garda Station* [2013] IEHC 251 at para 27.

304 E Regan (ed), *European Criminal Justice Post Lisbon: an Irish Perspective* (Dublin, Institute of International and European Affairs, 2012), p 26, available online: http://www.iiea.com/publications/european-criminal-justice-post-lisbon-an-irish-perspective <accessed 20 October 2013>.

Part IV

The Power to Enter, Search and Sample

CHAPTER 6

Forensics, Crime Scene Management and the Preservation of Evidence

INTRODUCTION: LAW, SCIENCE AND TECHNOLOGY

Science, and the certainty associated with it, has been embraced by the criminal justice community. Where once there was a process intensely (and almost exclusively) focused on the credibility of competing accounts given by fallible human witnesses, now technologies and scientific techniques exist to put certain aspects of a criminal case beyond all doubt. The application of science and technology to criminal investigations can be seen in CCTV footage, in the use of the "Intoxilyzer" to determine levels of alcohol **6–01** in breath, in fingerprinting, in forensic collision investigations, in the retrieval of data from computers in complex fraud, child pornography and computer crime investigations, as well as in the routine analysis of DNA, drugs, ballistics, fibres and blood and urine samples by the Forensic Science Laboratory. Chemistry, biology, molecular biology, physics, analytical science and botany are brought to bear on the evidence to answer the questions presented in the course of each investigation, often in a collaborative effort between gardaí, forensic pathologists, forensic scientists, accountants, systems analysts, engineers and other professionals.[1]

6–02 Evidence gathered through the use of new technologies provides considerably greater reliability than the evidence provided by the accused or by other witnesses because science and technology can remove bias, suggestibility, and the malleability of memory from the equation. As Lord Steyn held in *R(S) v Chief Constable of South Yorkshire*:

> "[i]t is of paramount importance that law enforcement agencies should take full advantage of the available techniques of modern technology and forensic science. Such real evidence has the inestimable value of cogency and objectivity. It is in large measure not affected by the subjective defects of other testimony. It enables the guilty to be detected and the innocent to be rapidly eliminated from enquiries".[2]

6–03 There is a distinction drawn between inculpatory evidence which exists independently of an accused person, and that which is capable of being supplied in that person's oral account in a confession. A further distinction can be made between different types of real evidence—that which can be obtained without recourse to the suspect (such as CCTV footage), and that which emanates from him (such as breath, blood, hair or urine samples). CCTV footage and other sources of highly probative evidence—speed cameras, audio-recordings, mobile telecommunications data and computers—can be accessed and evidence obtained from them without the direct involvement of the individual.

6–04 By contrast, in order to make a case against an individual based on a DNA or fingerprint identification, or indeed through breath, blood or urine analysis in the investigation of intoxicant offences such as "drink driving," a sample from that individual is required and a decidedly more invasive process involved. In the taking and retention of forensic samples from suspects for comparison with those found at scenes of crime, legal and ethical issues abound, as the greater good is balanced against the privacy and bodily integrity of the individual. Compared with evidence-gathering methods such as CCTV, the taking of forensic samples by force represents a potentially humiliating and degrading intrusion. There are implications for privacy and for the privilege against self-incrimination – to force suspects to give a forensic sample on which their guilt can be determined is to force them to incriminate themselves; to retain a sample indefinitely is to encroach upon the privacy, not only of an individual, but also of his family members. Whereas devices such as CCTV and the Intoxylizer have the potential to provide proof of involvement in a single offence, DNA is considerably more sophisticated and can

---

[1] See J Donovan, 'Recent Developments in Forensic Science' in *Criminal Justice in Ireland* (P O'Mahony ed, Institute of Public Administration, Dublin, 2002) at p 480.

[2] *R(S) v Chief Constable of South Yorkshire* [2004] 39 UKHL, [2004] WLR 2196 at 2198.

offer genetic information which, for a myriad of reasons, an individual may wish to remain private. Whether evidence gathered in the investigation of crime is sourced from the account of the accused, from samples taken from him or her, or through reliance on surveillance or technology, any interference with the rights involved—of privacy, bodily integrity and the privilege against self-incrimination—must be proportionate, legitimate and minimally invasive. The dignity of suspects should be maintained and respected to the fullest extent possible, since these rights, and the rights to freedom from ill-treatment, torture or degrading treatment, go to the core of what it is to be human.

Fingerprints and forensic samples do not exist in isolation. They are harvested from the scenes of crimes and from the suspects who are considered likely to have left them there. This chapter seeks to address the legal and practical issues which arise in crime scene and exhibit management and in the gathering of evidential material from suspects. Some ethical and legal questions concerning the personal rights infringed in the taking and retention of those samples are also considered. In addition, the crucial obligations of the gardaí in seeking out, preserving, storing and maintaining items of evidential value, and subsequently proving the chain of such evidence, are discussed. **6–05**

PART 1: CRIME SCENE MANAGEMENT AND THE PRESERVATION OF EVIDENCE

THE CRIME SCENE

The crime scene is a crucial source of raw material for the investigation and prosecution of crime, "the central source and reference point for analysis of the many legal issues that are involved directly or indirectly in the field of forensic evidence".[3] Williams outlines the objective of crime scene examination for forensics as follows: **6–06**

> "...crime scene examination in particular, and forensic science support to policing in general, should be understood as the effort accountably to discern, through the rigorous examination and retention of physical traces and other information, the course of crime relevant actions and events ... forensic accomplishments can be used to direct subsequent investigatory effort (including the inculpation or exculpation of specific suspects, the structuring of interviews with witnesses, victims or suspects) as well as inform subsequent case-making against persons charged with criminal offences".[4]

While legislation has been enacted to facilitate the preservation and management of crime scenes, the term 'crime scene' itself has not been clearly defined in Ireland. The Association of Chief Police Officers (ACPO) in England and Wales uses this definition in the context of DNA retrieval: **6–07**

> "a piece of land or part of a street; a building, or a room within a building; the houses, vehicles, vessel and other property of a suspect, witness or victim; stolen or recovered

---

3 Kiely, *Forensic Evidence: Science and the Criminal Law* (2nd ed, CRC Press, Florida, 2006) at p 27.

4 R Williams "Policing and Forensic Science" in T Newburn (ed) *Handbook of Policing* (2nd ed, Willan Publishing, Cullompton, 2008) at pp 784–785.

> property; the body, personal possessions and clothing of a suspect, witness or victim; ambulances or other vehicles used to convey victims or offenders to hospital premises, police stations or mortuaries".[5]

In short, a broad perspective should be taken in the identification of possible sources of forensic (and in particular DNA) evidence.

6–08 The Irish legislation provides for useful powers of exclusion to allow for scene preservation. Thereafter the examination can begin: taking fibres; clothing or other objects on which biological clues might exist; photographing the place in which the offence has occurred to document damage to property or injuries inflicted; lifting fingermarks and footprints and swabbing visible stains.[6] The taking of samples of various kinds from suspects, for comparison with those found at crime scenes, is strictly controlled by legislation, and those provisions are considered below.

Designation and Search of Crime Scene

6–09 Frequently crime scenes are discovered on entry under the authority of a search warrant. In many instances, however, a crime scene is encountered in response to a call from a member of the public and immediate steps must be taken to preserve the integrity of the evidence which might be gleaned from it. Prior to the enactment of s 5 of the Criminal Justice Act 2006, the designation and management of crime scenes was not legislatively governed and the gardaí had no express power to search crime scenes nor to preserve, gather and retain evidence found there. Now a garda who encounters an obvious crime scene can take immediate steps to preserve it, protect it from contamination and search for and collect evidence of, or relating to, the commission of the suspected offence.

6–10 The power to designate a crime scene applies to both public and private places, though, for the latter, it is dependent on an entry which has been authorised by law or which has been based on an implied or express invitation to the garda to enter the property. If the owner or occupier of a property gives gardaí permission to designate a place a crime scene, the formalities set out in s 5 need not be complied with,[7] and gardaí can proceed to take the steps outlined in s 5(4) (of exclusion, search and so on) without the necessity of the direction of a Superintendent and the other limitations, including time limits, set out in the legislation. Investigations are, by their nature, evolving and time-consuming. Owners or occupiers might not appreciate the consequences of the designation (including exclusion from their property), and there is potential for the investigation to be compromised by the subsequent revocation of consent by the owner / occupier. Equally, where owners or occupiers are suspects, it may be arguable that they did not appreciate fully the consequences of their consent and ought to have been legally advised beforehand. Therefore it is preferable that the designation should be formalised (rather than based solely on consent) for the avoidance of doubt and to ensure the subsequent admissibility of evidence.

---

5 ACPO, *DNA Good Practice Manual* (2005), p 12.

6 See Newburn, *Handbook of Policing* (2nd ed, Willan Publishing, Cullompton, 2008), p 263.

7 Criminal Justice Act 2006, s 5(18).

6–11 The garda who seeks to designate a crime scene must have reasonable grounds for believing that an arrestable offence was, is being, or may have been committed in the place[8] or that there may be evidence of, or relating to, the commission of an arrestable offence that was or may have been committed elsewhere.[9] The garda must, as soon as reasonably practicable, arrange for a formal direction designating the crime scene by a garda of Superintendent rank or higher. In the interim, the garda may take such steps as are considered necessary to preserve the scene, pending the formal designation. The formal designation may authorise gardaí to do any or all of the following things, set out in s 5(4):

(a) delineating and segregating the area of the crime scene by notices, markings or barriers;
(b) directing a person to leave the crime scene;
(c) removing a person who fails to comply with a direction to leave the crime scene;
(d) directing a person not to enter the crime scene;
(e) preventing a person from entering the crime scene;
(f) permitting a person, authorised by a superintendent to enter a crime scene for a specified purpose under section 5(5), to enter the crime scene;
(g) preventing a person from removing anything which is, or may be, evidence or otherwise interfering with the crime scene or anything at the scene;
(h) securing the crime scene from any unauthorised intrusion or disturbance;
(i) searching the crime scene and examining the scene and anything at the scene; and
(j) photographing or otherwise recording the crime scene or anything at the scene.

6–12 The power is a significant one: it permits the exclusion of persons from their own property and for a search of a dwelling on the authorisation of gardaí. A direction in relation to private property ceases to be in force 24 hours after it is given,[10] and should not be longer than is reasonably necessary to preserve, search for and collect the evidence.[11] Applications can be made to the courts for an extension of the time period if necessary. Initially, the application is made in the District Court for an extension not to exceed 48 hours and is based on information on oath by a garda not below the rank of Superintendent. He or she must fulfil certain criteria and outline that there are reasonable grounds for believing that there is or may be evidence at the crime scene and that the continuance of the direction is necessary to preserve, search for and collect it. The gardaí must satisfy the court that the investigation is being conducted diligently and expeditiously. An application can be made in the District Court for two further 48 hour extensions.[12] In exceptional circumstances, an additional application may be made in the High Court.[13] Regardless of the court in which the extension application is made, the gardaí must (if practicable) give notice of the application to the owner or occupier, who may apply to be heard.[14]

[8] *ibid*, s 5(1)(b)(i).
[9] *ibid*, s 5(1)(b)(ii).
[10] *ibid*, s 5(7).
[11] *ibid*, s 5(6).
[12] *ibid*, s 5(10).
[13] *ibid*, s 5(11).
[14] *ibid*, s 5(12) and 5(13).

Section 5(17) provides a power of arrest for failure to comply with a direction or for obstructing a garda in the exercise of his or her powers in relation to the designated crime scene.

PROTECTION, PRESERVATION AND CHAIN OF EVIDENCE

6–13 Blackstone's Police Operational Handbook outlines the two principal objectives in managing a crime scene: the protection of the scene from contamination by others and the preservation of the integrity of everything which could be used as evidence.[15] The preservation of a crime scene and its exhibits is an aspect of the long-established onus on gardaí to seek out and preserve evidence which may have a bearing on the guilt or innocence of the accused. It is clear that the prosecution must convince the jury of the provenance, continuity and integrity of the forensic science on which it seeks to rely,[16] but also take steps, insofar as possible, to obtain and retain all the evidence which pertains to the offence. As Hardiman J held in *Braddish v DPP*[17]:

> "It is the duty of the Gardaí, arising from their unique investigative role, to seek out and preserve all evidence having a bearing or potential bearing on the issue of guilt or innocence. This is so whether the prosecution proposes to rely on the evidence or not, and regardless of whether it assists the case the prosecution is advancing or not."[18]

6–14 The Court elaborated on the extent of the burden, stating that the duty ought to be interpreted realistically on the facts of each case and that it cannot be interpreted as requiring the gardaí to engage in a disproportionate commitment of manpower or resources in an exhaustive search for every conceivable kind of evidence. In practical terms, this means that, at a minimum, each relevant piece of evidence must be sought out, seized and kept until the conclusion of the trial. Integrity is maintained not only by preventing access to the scene and by preserving the exhibits found, but also by keeping a detailed exhibits log to track each exhibit from scene to laboratory and back. Each person who has had contact with and custody of the exhibits must be recorded, so that the chain of evidence can be established and put beyond doubt in court. An outline of the expected standard is provided by Weir J in *R v Hoey,*[19] a Northern Ireland Crown Court case which concerned a challenge to the reliability of DNA evidence in a case relating to the Omagh bombing:

> "The Defence submit, correctly in my judgment, that it is for the prosecution to establish the integrity and freedom from possible contamination of each item throughout the entirety of the period between seizure and any examination relied upon. They contend, and I accept the contention, that the court must be satisfied by the prosecution witnesses and supporting documents that all dealings with each relevant exhibit have been

---

15 PNLD, I Bridges and F Sampson (eds), *Blackstone's Police Operational Handbook* (Oxford University Press, Oxford, 2006) at p 12.

16 Pattenden, "Authenticating 'things' in English law: principles for adducing tangible evidence in common law jury trials", E & P 2008, 12(4), 273-302 at p 288.

17 *Braddish v DPP* [2001] 3 IR 127.

18 *ibid.* See also *Murphy v DPP* [1989] ILRM 71.

19 *R v Hoey* [2007] NICC 49.

satisfactorily accounted for from the moment of its seizure until the moment when any evidential sample relied upon by the prosecution is taken from it and that by a method and in conditions that are shown to have been reliable. This means that each person who has dealt with the item in the intervening period must be ascertainable and be able to demonstrate by reference to some proper system of bagging, labelling, and recording that the item has been preserved at every stage free from the suspicion of interference or contamination. For this purpose they must be able to demonstrate how and when and under what conditions and with what object and by what means and in whose presence he or she examined the item. Only if all these requirements have been satisfactorily vouched can a tribunal have confidence in the reliability of any forensic findings said to have been derived from any examination of the item."[20]

In *People (DPP) v Boyce*,[21] the Irish Supreme Court held that, given the central importance of DNA in criminal investigations, there is a particular onus on the prosecution to ensure that it is conserved and its integrity maintained: **6–15**

"DNA constitutes one of the astonishing scientific advances of the age. It has already contributed greatly to the investigation of crime ... It is true that the powerful possibilities of DNA evidence place a particular burden on the prosecution to ensure the integrity of sampling, conservation of evidence and fair and balanced presentation of expert evidence. These obligations are always present but need to take account of the particular scientific characteristics of the evidence."[22]

The prosecution must therefore prove, to the criminal standard of "beyond a reasonable doubt", the continuity of evidence, given that, en route to the laboratory for examination, evidence passes through the hands of many people. This is a two-fold burden: it must be beyond doubt that swabs taken from a victim and swabs taken from a suspect are those which have been analysed and compared in the laboratory for DNA purposes. In addition, the jury must be satisfied that the chain of evidence has been maintained and thereby the scientific integrity and competence of the analyses.[23] **6–16**

LOST EVIDENCE

A raft of cases have arisen from the loss of evidence in the pre-trial period, including *Braddish v DPP*[24]; *Dunne v DPP*[25]; *Bowes v DPP, McGrath v DPP*[26]; *Scully v DPP*[27]; *McFarlane v DPP*[28] and *Ludlow v DPP*,[29] prompting Hardiman J to comment that **6–17**

"the items in question were as small as video tapes and as large as motor vehicles. From the pattern of losses it appears that An Garda Síochána have considerable difficulty in

[20] *ibid*, at para 46.
[21] *People (DPP) v Boyce* [2009] 2 IR 124.
[22] *ibid* at 161 (*per* Fennelly J).
[23] *R v Phillips* [2004] EWCA 2288, para8 (*per* May LJ).
[24] *Braddish v DPP* [2001] 3 IR 127.
[25] *Dunne v DPP* [2002] 3 IR 305.
[26] *Bowes and McGrath v DPP* [2003] 2 IR 25.
[27] *Scully v DPP* [2005] 1 IR 242.
[28] *McFarlane v DPP* [2008] 4 IR 117.
[29] *Ludlow v DPP* [2009] 1 IR 640.

retaining items of evidence in secure custody for any period of time. It is not clear, and it is not relevant, whether this difficulty arises from procedures (or the lack of them) within An Garda Síochána itself or from deficiencies in the premises and facilities provided for the Gardaí… From the fact that "lost evidence" cases continue to come before the Courts it appears that there is a serious problem at least in some units of An Garda Síochána in relation to the preservation of items of evidential significance."[30]

6–18 The judge went on to quote from *McGrath v DPP* where the Court pointed to the seriousness of the offence of dangerous driving and commented:

> "One would hope that its very seriousness would, in future cases, ensure that items of manifest evidential potential are properly preserved. These two cases tend to indicate that there may be a need for a more cohesive practise amongst the gardaí in the preservation or disposal pre-trial of evidence which is potentially relevant to the defence in the criminal proceedings. The adoption and observation of suitable guidelines might assist in avoiding pre-trial litigation of this nature".[31]

The obligation is clear. The need for the secure maintenance of items of evidence cannot be overstated. As was set out by Lynch J in *Murphy v DPP*:

> "The authorities establish that evidence relevant to guilt or innocence must insofar is necessary and practicable be kept until the conclusion of the trial. These authorities also apply to the preservation of articles which may give rise to the reasonable possibility of securing relevant evidence."[32]

6–19 Certain cases will require, as an element of fairness, that the accused is given an opportunity to examine and inspect forensic evidence. Therefore, as was outlined in *Murphy*, there is an onus on gardaí to preserve items "which may give rise to the reasonable possibility of securing relevant evidence".[33]

6–20 It is open to a defendant to seek prohibition of his trial if evidence is lost. If a trial proceeds, the loss of evidence may also be raised at trial or on appeal.[34] This ought to be borne in mind in considering whether to dispose of items of evidential value, and in decision-making regarding the return of evidence (such as motor vehicles) owned by third parties. The secure storage of physical exhibits, and careful maintenance of records concerning them, is of the utmost importance.

SECTION 35 OF THE CRIMINAL PROCEDURE ACT 2010

6–21 The Criminal Procedure Act 2010 provides at s 35 for a statutory regime for the preservation of evidence. Where property that is to be entered in evidence in a criminal trial is to be either returned to its owner or disposed of before the trial begins notice must be given by the prosecution in writing to the accused, at least 23 days before the

---

30 *ibid.*

31 *Bowes v DPP; McGrath v DPP* [2003] 2 IR 25 at 41.

32 *Murphy v DPP* [1989] ILRM 71 at 76.

33 *ibid.*

34 *People (DPP) v Christo* [2005] IECCA 3.

scheduled trial start date. The notice must give a detailed description of the property so that it is readily identifiable, and must contain a statement of the relevance of the property to the proceedings, together with one or more photographs of the property, any report intended to be entered into evidence arising from the analysis of the property and materials found on or in the property. No later than seven days after service of the prosecution notice, the defence are obliged to serve a written defence notice indicating one of the following:

(a) that the defence accepts the prosecution notice and agrees to the return or disposal of the property;
(b) that the defence wishes to provide to the prosecution a defence report of evidence;
(c) that the defence requires the property to be available as an exhibit at the trial.

Further time limits are provided for replies to be made. Written records must be kept **6–22** of the return or disposal of property and, where the property is returned to its owner, the owner must given written acknowledgement of the receipt of the property. Section 35 mirrors the provision of s 21 of the Criminal Justice Act 1984,[35] which provides for the admissibility of written statements as proof of their contents, without requiring the presence of the statement's maker to give oral evidence at trial.[36] Under the s 35 procedure, the report can provide proof of the facts stated in it. The use of reports obviates the need for the retention of the exhibit and thus the inconvenience to property owners caused by the retention of items in evidence. The Police Property Act 1897 provides a process for the return of property after the conclusion of proceedings.

PART 2: FORENSIC SAMPLING

DNA

DNA, or deoxyribonucleic acid, is contained in virtually every cell in the body. It **6–23** contains genetic information, in the form of a code which, when translated, directs all the chemical processes in the body and determines our physical characteristics.[37] It can be found in hair, saliva, semen, sweat and any other type of physiological fluid or tissue. With the exception of identical twins, it provides a unique code by which a person can be identified. Of the categories of available real evidence, DNA represents the most spectacular scientific advance in the identification and elimination of suspects. It provides a 'genetic fingerprinting' technique, which is of particular importance in the investigation of crimes of a violent and sexual nature, offences in which blood and bodily fluids are generated. Whereas fingerprints are often left at the scene of property crimes, they are less frequent in cases involving personal violence, in which there is a much greater

35 s 21 of the Criminal Justice Act 1984 as amended by s 16(4) of the Criminal Justice Act 1999.

36 See the comments of the then Minister for Justice at the committee stage of the Criminal Procedure Bill 2009, Seanad Debates, vol 199 No 1, 2 December 2009, at pp 52–53.

37 The Forensic Science Service, *Lawyer's Guide to DNA*, p 5.

likelihood that blood will be deposited on an assailant, on a weapon or other object, or in the vicinity of the attack.[38] Its use, therefore, as a tool for the identification of suspects and the evaluation of their guilt is obviously appealing. As Hardiman J put it:

> "If science or technology can provide certainty in matters of great importance which would otherwise be determined on human testimony which may be fallible or worse, who but a guilty man would not willingly invoke its aid? ... The balance has long been struck in favour of the use of technology in the search for perpetrators of crime, even when the processes involved are minimally invasive or transiently painful or undignified for innocent people. The greater good prevails. This development is due in large measure to the development of techniques of previously unimagined sophistication, from the telephoto lens and the video camera to the extraordinary precision of DNA analysis."[39]

6–24 In a DNA profile, certain parts of an individual's DNA molecule are identified and stored with some personal details. This is done by dissolving the stain or sample found at the crime scene, separating, cleaning and measuring the quality and quantity of the DNA, targeting the specific pieces of interest within the DNA molecule, producing multiple copies of the pieces of interest and sorting and measuring the pieces, in a process known as STR (Short Tandem Repeats) analysis. This results in short sequences of DNA which are repeated end-to-end, and which differ from person to person.[40] A DNA profile will itself contain very limited personal information, whereas the bodily sample from which the profile is extracted potentially contains considerably more. The Law Reform Commission has offered a concise outline of the concerns surrounding retention of genetic information, and the distinction between DNA samples and DNA profiles:

> "The distinction between the biological *sample* and DNA *profile* is important ... it is now appropriate to highlight the principal concerns which are usually voiced in relation to genetic information generally, which include that:
>
> (i) DNA testing may reveal the presence of a socially stigmatising genetic disorder or unveil behavioural traits, such as the rape or murder gene (ie behavioural genetics);
> (ii) testing may disclose information about significant future episodes and possibly shameful events, such as susceptibility to disease;
> (iii) testing may also divulge information that an individual has chosen to keep confidential, such as sexual orientation;
> (iv) As to how information of the type suggested in (i) – (iii) might be used, it might be disclosed to other government departments or even private parties, such as employers or insurance companies. The fear is that insurers or employers could use genetic information to deny cover or employment – in effect genetic discrimination;
> (v) Beyond this is the fear of the possibility that DNA testing may be misused in some way – the oft cited examples are in a degenerated eugenics movement and Nazi Germany's racial hygiene programme, a murderous genocidal 'ethnic cleansing' campaign on a massive scale."[41]

---

38 See J Donovan, 'Recent Developments in Forensic Science' Criminal Justice in Ireland (Institute of Public Administration, Dublin, 2002) at p 480.

39 *Dunne v DPP* [2002] 2 IR 305.

40 The Forensic Science Service, *Lawyer's Guide to DNA,* p 6.

41 Law Reform Commission *Consultation Paper on the Establishment of a DNA Database* (LRC CP 29 – 2004), at pp 49-50.

DNA Databases – *S and Marper v United Kingdom*

The complex questions surrounding the establishment of a DNA database have been analysed by the Law Reform Commission. Following the commission's recommendation that Ireland should follow the lead of other jurisdictions by establishing a limited DNA database, such a development seems inevitable.[42] The Law Reform Commission defined a database as follows: 6–25

> "A DNA database is a repository of DNA profiles, generated from biological samples, which can be electronically stored for comparison with profiles generated from material found at the scene of a crime. The primary aim of a DNA database is to link individuals to unsolved offences and unsolved offences to each other by means of DNA profiling."[43]

Any proposal to establish a DNA database in Ireland will have to comply with the decision *S and Marper v United Kingdom,*[44] a judgment of the European Court of Human Rights. The Court held that the UK's extensive DNA database, in which samples were indefinitely retained, violated Article 8 of the European Convention (right to respect for private and family life). Referring to a Nuffield Council on Bioethics' report entitled "The Forensic Use of Bioinformation: Ethical Issues", the Court said: 6–26

> "… the retention of fingerprints, DNA profiles and biological samples is generally more controversial than the taking of such bioinformation, and the retention of biological samples raises greater ethical concerns than digitised DNA profiles and fingerprints, given the differences in the level of information that could be revealed…"[45]

The court endorsed the report, holding: 6–27

> "The Court shares the view of the Nuffield Council as to the impact on young persons of the indefinite retention of their DNA material and notes the Council's concerns that the policies applied have led to the over-representation in the database of young persons and ethnic minorities, who have not been convicted of any crime … the Court finds that the blanket and indiscriminate nature of the powers of retention of the fingerprints, cellular samples and DNA profiles of persons suspected but not convicted of offences, as applied in the case of the present applicants, fails to strike a fair balance between the competing public and private interests and that the respondent State has overstepped any acceptable margin of appreciation in this regard."[46]

Criminal Justice (Forensic Evidence and DNA Database System) Bill 2013

On 11 September 2013 the Criminal Justice (Forensic Evidence and DNA Database System) Bill 2013 was published and, at the time of writing, was progressing through the Dáil. The 2013 Bill is influenced by the *Marper* decision and also by the lapsed 6–28

[42] A Bill, entitled "Criminal Justice (Forensic Evidence and DNA Database System) Bill 2010 had been initiated before the dissolution of the 30th Dáil on 1 February 2011.

[43] Law Reform Commission Report on the Establishment of a DNA Database (LRC 78-2005), at p 1.

[44] *S and Marper v United Kingdom* (Applications nos 30562/04 and 30566/04) 4 December 2008.

[45] *ibid*, at para 38.

[46] *ibid*, at para 124.

Criminal Justice (Forensic Evidence and DNA Database System) Bill 2010, but it differs in one key respect from its predecessor. The 2010 Bill had contained a 'default destruction period' for samples and for removal of the DNA profiles of individuals after ten years if the suspect had not had proceedings instituted against him or had been acquitted in that period, and for a shorter period where the detainee was a child or protected person.[47] The 2013 Bill, as initiated, provides for destruction of samples taken for the purpose of generating a DNA profile for the database as soon as the profile has been generated or within six months of the taking of the sample, whichever is the later. It also provides for a presumption in favour of removal from the database of the DNA profiles of suspects who are not convicted, with a power vested in the Garda Commissioner to authorise retention on the database where he determines retention necessary, with the Commissioner's decision subject to an appeal procedure in the District Court. The permitted retention periods are six years where samples are taken from adults and three years where samples are taken from children. Where samples are taken for evidential purposes it is proposed that there will be a presumption in favour of destruction of samples relating to suspects who are not convicted, subject to the Garda Commissioner having the power to authorise retention for 12 months, which will be renewable, where that is deemed is necessary, a decision which is also subject to a District Court appeal procedure.[48]

FINGERPRINTS

6–29 Fingerprints, impressions of the ridge details on the surface of the skin on our fingers, provide absolute proof of identity, as the epidermal ridges on our fingertips are arranged in unique, never replicated patterns. The information which fingerprints are capable of providing is limited to the identity of the holder of the prints. The fingerprint examiner analyses the fingerprint obtained from the scene of the crime and compares the mark with an inked fingerprint taken from the suspect to seek details common in both. The information is evaluated to ascertain if the requisite level of detail is present to conclude that the mark made at the scene of the crime and in the taken fingerprint are attributable to the same person. The findings are then verified. The best sources of crime scene fingerprints are smooth, clean and dry surfaces, as well as pieces of paper, envelopes and other movable items.[49] The impediment from an evidential standpoint is that movable objects such as bags in which drugs or weapons are found might have had a fingerprint left on them in innocuous circumstances, so their probative value is lessened if they are not matched by a fingermark on the proscribed item itself. Fingermarks left on surfaces are first powdered to develop the features of the mark before being transferred onto a 'lift'—an adhesive acetate backed by another acetate.[50]

---

47 Criminal Justice (Forensic Evidence and DNA Database System) Bill 2010, s 78.

48 See Criminal Justice (Forensic Evidence and DNA Database System) Bill 2013 as initiated. See also the comments of Minister for Justice, Alan Shatter, Dáil Debates, 9 October 2013.

49 Sampston (ed), *Blackstone's Police Operational Handbook* (Oxford University Press, Oxford, 2006).

50 T Newburn, *Handbook of Policing* (2nd ed, Willan Publishing, Cullompton, 2008) at p 763.

Heffernan notes:

> "The expert's determination of a fingerprint match, or the absence of same, may be used as an investigative tool to identify, confirm or eliminate a suspect from an investigation. The fingerprints serve an additional, evidentiary function where the expert subsequently presents his opinion at trial as to the inferences that may be drawn from the presence of the prints at the crime scene."[51]

Reliable and long-established as a detection method, fingerprinting is less sophisticated than DNA, and the results are perhaps more readily understood by virtue of the prints' visibility. However, the technique is not infallible, because ultimately it involves a finding of opinion. Heffernan cautions that: **6–30**

> "Within the realm of forensic science, the contours of fingerprinting are relatively well settled and the willingness of parties and courts to accept fingerprint evidence is reflected in a paucity of reported cases. At the same time, traditional confidence in the reliability of the predicate science should not give way to complacency. The evidence of identity offered by the fingerprint expert, based on a comparison of prints found at the crime scene with those of the accused, tends to be more subjective than that of other forensic scientists, such as the DNA analyst. Moreover, the possibility of error on the part of the fingerprint expert is not unknown and cannot be discounted."[52]

Challenges to fingerprints usually relate not to the fingerprints themselves, but to the manner in which they have been obtained and or retained.[53]

FORENSICS AND SELF-INCRIMINATION

While an accused person cannot be compelled to give an account either in the course of garda interviews or by being forced to testify at trial, there are a variety of garda powers available to take samples forcibly from suspects so that forensic analysis may be undertaken. This notwithstanding the fact that in giving a forensic sample a person may well incriminate himself—the right not to incriminate oneself is not applicable in the context of forensic sampling. In *Saunders v United Kingdom*, the European Court of Human Rights outlined that: **6–31**

> "The right not to incriminate oneself, in particular, presupposes that the prosecution in a criminal case seek to prove their case against the accused without resort to evidence obtained through methods of coercion or oppression in defiance of the will of the accused. In this sense the right is closely linked to the presumption of innocence contained in Article 6 para. 2 of the Convention (art. 6-2)... the right not to incriminate oneself is primarily concerned ... with respecting the will of an accused person to remain silent ... it does not extend to the use in criminal proceedings of material which may be obtained from the accused through the use of compulsory powers but which has an existence independent of the will of the suspect such as, *inter alia,* documents acquired pursuant to a warrant, breath, blood and urine samples and bodily tissue for the purpose of DNA testing."[54]

---

[51] L Heffernan, "The Recording Of Fingerprints: Legal Aspects" (2006) 13(1) DULJ 201.

[52] *ibid.*

[53] See for instance *DPP v Cleary* [2005] IECCA 51.

[54] *Saunders v United Kingdom* (1996) 23 EHRR 313, at paras 68-69.

In this jurisdiction, the High Court commented in the case of *DPP v Cash* that:

> "A fingerprint, in common with a blood sample or scraping for the purposes of obtaining DNA evidence, and such like, is in no way affected by the mood of a suspect giving same. Whether it is voluntary or involuntary, a fingerprint or a sample of an accused's DNA, or blood or urine for the purposes of testing for the presence of particular substances, does not change its nature. If a scraping of cells from the accused's cheek is taken by a trick, or if a hair is taken in an illegal search of his home, the later match of DNA that might be analysed in consequence to a semen sample from a rape victim will always be the same, no matter the circumstances in which it has been obtained."[55]

6–32 There is a clear distinction then, both in terms of reliability and in terms of legal treatment, between the evidence which a person's fingertips, blood, sweat or semen can provide and that which is extracted through long hours of questioning. Though the decision in *Cash* was affected by the later judgment of the Supreme Court, as was noted in *DPP v White*,[56] the Supreme Court did not disturb the above dictum. By this logic, a reference sample can be taken from the glass of water used by an accused in an interview suite, or a discarded piece of chewing gum, without the suspect's knowledge or consent. The latter circumstance resulted in a conviction in the case of *DPP v Scanlon*.[57] There the accused on arrival at the garda station for questioning asked where he might dispose of chewing gum. He was offered a bin and discarded the gum which was retrieved by the investigating gardaí and a DNA sample extracted from it was found to match DNA linked to the scene of an armed robbery.

POWERS TO TAKE FORENSIC SAMPLES

Fingerprints and Photographs

6–33 The Criminal Justice Act 1984 provides at s 6 for a number of powers in relation to persons who are detained under s 4 of the Criminal Justice Act 1984, s 2 of the Criminal Justice (Drug Trafficking) Act 1996[58] or s 50 of the Criminal Justice Act 2007.[59] Those powers permit gardaí:

i. to demand a person's name and address[60];
ii. to search him or cause him to be searched[61]

---

55 *DPP v Cash* [2007] IEHC 108.

56 *DPP v White* [2011] IECCA 78.

57 *DPP v Scanlon,* unreported, Wexford Circuit Criminal Court, October 2006. See "DNA Evidence from Chewing Gum Was Vital to Conviction," *Wexford People,* 19 October 2006, available at http://www.wexfordpeople.ie/news/dna-evidence-from-chewing-gum-was-crucial-in-conviction-977691.html <accessed 15 October 2013>.

58 The powers set out in s 6(1)-(4) of the Criminal Justice Act 1984 were extended to persons detained under s 2 of the Criminal Justice (Drug Trafficking) Act 1996 by s 5 of the 1996 Act.

59 The powers set out in s 6(1)-(4) of the Criminal Justice Act 1984 were extended to persons detained under s 50 of the Criminal Justice Act 2007 by s 52 of the 2007 Act.

60 Criminal Justice Act 1984, s 6(1)(a).

61 *ibid*, s 6(1)(b).

iii. to photograph him or cause him to be photographed[62];
iv. to take, or cause to be taken, his fingerprints and palm prints[63];
v. to seize and retain for testing anything he has in his possession.[64]

To take photographs, fingerprints and palm prints, the authorisation of a garda of the rank of Inspector is required.[65] Obstruction or attempted obstruction of a member of the Garda or any other person (such as a doctor or dentist) seeking to exercise the powers conferred by s 6(1) of the Criminal Justice Act 1984 is an offence punishable by a fine and or imprisonment for up to 12 months. The same applies to failure or refusal to give a name and address, and giving an address which is false or misleading.[66] **6–34**

Where photographs or fingerprints and palm prints, which have been taken on the statutory authority of s 6(1) are lost or damaged or are otherwise imperfect, they may be taken on a second or further occasion.[67]

Taking Fingerprints and Photographs by Force

Gardaí may use reasonable force to take the fingerprints, palm prints and photographs of detainees if they fail or refuse to allow their photograph or prints to be taken.[68] In order to take photographs, fingerprints and palm prints by force, the authorisation of a Superintendent is required[69] (which may be given orally and must be confirmed in writing as soon as practicable), and an Inspector must be present. The process must be video-recorded[70] and the detainee must be informed that it is intended to take his photograph, fingerprints and palm prints by force and that their taking has been authorised by a Superintendent. The extent of the force permissible is "such force as [the garda] reasonably considers to be necessary to take the photograph or fingerprints and palm prints". Heffernan suggests that excessive use of force in taking fingerprints could infringe a suspect's right to bodily integrity and thereby potentially warrant exclusion of the fingerprint evidence.[71] **6–35**

Criminal Law Act 1976

Gardaí have a number of powers in relation to suspects who are in custody pursuant to s 30 of the Offences against the State Act 1939, including the power to photograph **6–36**

62 *ibid*, s 6(1)(c).
63 *ibid*, s 6(1)(d).
64 *ibid*, s 6(1)(f).
65 *ibid*, s 6(2), as substituted by s 48 (a) of the Criminal Justice Act 2007. Previously the authorisation of a Superintendent was required.
66 *ibid*, s 6(4), as amended by the Criminal Justice Act 2006, s 13.
67 *ibid*, s 6(1A) as inserted by s 48(a) of the Criminal Justice Act 2007.
68 *ibid*, s 6(1A), as inserted by s 48(a) of the Criminal Justice Act 2007.
69 *ibid*, s 6A(2)(a), as inserted by s 48(a) of the Criminal Justice Act 2007.
70 *ibid*, s 6A(5), as inserted by s 48(a) of the Criminal Justice Act 2007.
71 L Heffernan, "The Recording of Fingerprints: Legal Aspects" (2006) 13(1) DULJ 201.

and fingerprint. These powers are exercised under s 7 of the Criminal Law Act 1976.[72] Section 7(1)(e) of the 1976 Act had provided for forcible testing for contact with explosive substance, but the subsection was repealed by s 6 of the Criminal Justice (Forensic Evidence) Act 1990 when a comprehensive scheme of sample taking was introduced in s 2 of the same Act to include swabs from any part of the body.

6–37 The provisions and protections of the Criminal Justice Act 1984 extend to the powers exercised under s 7 of the Criminal Law Act 1976 with a notable exception. While s 9 of the Criminal Justice Act 1984 provides that certain provisions of the Act of 1984 apply to persons in custody under s 30 of the Offences against the State Act 1939 and to the powers conferred by s 7 of the Criminal Law Act 1976 as they apply to persons detained under s 4 of the Criminal Justice Act 1984, there is no reference to s 8 of the 1984 Act having similar application. Therefore the requirement to destroy fingerprint evidence taken within a specified period did not apply to fingerprints taken under s 7 of the 1976 Act. As will be seen below, s 8 of the Criminal Justice Act 1984 has been substantially amended to provide for automatic retention of fingerprints. While the omission of s 8 leaves the 1976 Act out of the remit of the revised automatic retention regime, it would appear that there has always been an implied power to retain fingerprints taken under s 7 of the Criminal Law Act indefinitely and that the introduction of the revised scheme has not impacted on such fingerprints. Suspects cannot apply to have them destroyed if they have been taken in the course of a s 30 detention. Walsh has suggested that the "clear implication that [photographs or fingerprints] can be retained even if the suspect is released without charge, or if he is acquitted or discharged in related criminal proceedings… may raise an issue of privacy under the European Convention for the Protection of Human Rights and Fundamental Freedoms".[73]

Post-Conviction Fingerprinting

6–38 The gardaí may fingerprint, palm-print or photograph any person who has been convicted of an indictable offence or where a person has been prosecuted for an indictable offence and been dealt with under the Probation of Offenders Act 1907. The person may be fingerprinted at a convenient place within seven days of the making of the order of conviction, or may be required to attend at a specified garda station to have fingerprints, palm-prints or photographs taken.[74]

Retention of Fingerprints, Palm Prints and Photographs

6–39 Fingerprints, palm-prints and photographs taken pursuant to s 6 and 6A of the Criminal Justice Act 1984 or s 12 of the Criminal Justice Act 2006 can be retained indefinitely.[75] Prior to the enactment of the Criminal Justice Act 2007, fingerprints,

[72] Criminal Law Act 1976, s 7(1) as amended by the Criminal Justice (Forensic Evidence) Act 1990, s 6 (which repealed s 7(1)(e)).

[73] D Walsh, *Criminal Procedure* (Thomson Round Hall, Dublin, 2002), at p 342.

[74] Criminal Justice Act 1984, s 28.

[75] Criminal Justice Act 1984, s 8 as inserted by s 49 of the Criminal Justice Act 2007.

photographs and the records identifying those from whom they had been taken had to be destroyed within six months if no proceedings were brought or if the accused person was acquitted.[76] The 2007 Act replaced the earlier system of automatic destruction with a scheme of presumptive retention, with a person who is fingerprinted and photographed instead having the right to request that these items be destroyed if no proceedings are brought against them. Such a request must be made to the Garda Commissioner, with an appeals process to the District Court if the request is refused.[77] The automatic retention procedure does not apply to records taken before the commencement of the section on 18 May 2007.[78]

DNA: Taking Samples

The taking of DNA samples is governed by the Criminal Justice (Forensic Evidence) Act 1990.[79] **6–40**

The following samples may be taken from persons who are detained under s 30 of the Offences against the State Act 1939, s 4 of the Criminal Justice Act 1984, s 2 of the Criminal Justice (Drug Trafficking) Act 1996, and s 50 of the Criminal Justice Act 2007: **6–41**

- (i) blood,
- (ii) pubic hair,
- (iii) urine,
- (iv) saliva,
- (v) hair other than pubic hair,
- (vi) a nail,
- (vii) any material found under a nail,
- (viii) a swab from any part of the body including the mouth, but not from any other body orifice or a genital region,
- (ix) a swab from a body orifice, other than the mouth, or a genital region,
- (x) a dental impression,
- (xi) a footprint or similar impression of any part of the person's body other than a part of his hand.

Such samples may only be taken on the authority of a Superintendent. In the case of samples of blood, pubic hair, urine, swabs from a body orifice (other than the mouth or a genital region) or dental impressions the consent of the person from whom the sample is to be taken must be given in writing. Appropriate consent in this context is defined in s 2(10) of the 1990 Act: where the person from whom the sample is to be taken is 17 years old or over, that person's consent is required; children between the ages of 14 and 17 must **6–42**

[76] Criminal Justice (Forensic Evidence) Act 1990, s 4.

[77] Criminal Justice Act 1984, s 8 as inserted by s 49 of the Criminal Justice Act 2007.

[78] Criminal Justice Act 2007 (Commencement Order) 2007, SI No 236 of 2007.

[79] ss 2, 4 and 5 of the Criminal Justice (Forensic Evidence) Act 1990 have been significantly amended by s 14 of the Criminal Justice Act 2006.

themselves consent, as must their parent or guardian and, in the case of children under 14, a parent or guardian consents on their behalf.[80]

6–43 The authorisation of a Superintendent may only be given if the Superintendent has reasonable grounds for suspecting the detained person of involvement in the offence for which he is in custody. The Superintendent must also have reasonable grounds for believing that the sample will tend to confirm or disprove the involvement of the person from whom the sample is to be taken in the offence under investigation.[81]

6–44 Samples of blood or pubic hair may only be taken by a registered medical practitioner, and a dental impression may only be taken by a registered dentist or medical practitioner.[82] Where hair samples are taken (other than pubic hairs), the hairs may be taken by plucking with their roots and, insofar as is reasonably possible, the hairs shall be plucked singly.[83] No more hairs shall be plucked than is reasonably considered necessary to constitute a sufficient sample for the purpose of forensic testing.[84]

6–45 Before a sample is taken for forensic testing, either under s 2 of the Criminal Justice (Forensic Evidence) Act 1990 or by consent, the gardaí must inform the person from whom the sample will be taken:

(a) of the nature of the offence in which it is suspected that person has been involved;
(b) that an authorisation has been given by a garda of uperintendent rank and the grounds on which the authorisation has been given; and
(c) that the results of any tests on the sample may be given in evidence.[85]

If an authorisation is given orally, it must be committed to writing as soon as is practicable.[86]

Inferences from Refusal to Consent to Taking a Sample

6–46 The Criminal Justice (Forensic Evidence) Act 1990 provides at s 3 for such inferences as appear proper to be drawn where consent is required for the taking of a sample (ie where the sample to be taken is blood or pubic hair) and is refused without good cause. The refusal may be treated as, or as being capable of amounting to, corroboration of any evidence in relation to which the refusal is material. A person shall not, however, be convicted solely on an inference drawn from a refusal to give consent.[87] If inferences are to be drawn at trial from a refusal, the suspect must have been told in ordinary language by a member of An Garda Síochána seeking his consent that the

---

[80] See *Director of Public Prosecutions v Boyce* [2009] 2 IR 124.
[81] Criminal Justice (Forensic Evidence) Act 1990, s 2(5).
[82] *ibid*, s 2(8).
[83] *ibid*, s 2(8A)(i).
[84] *ibid*, s 2(8A)(ii).
[85] *ibid*, s 2(6).
[86] *ibid*, s 2(7).
[87] *ibid*, s 3(1).

sample was required for the purpose of forensic testing, that his consent was necessary and, if his consent was not given, the effect of his refusal.[88]

It is noteworthy that s 3(4) confirms that inferences will not be drawn in the event of consent being refused by a person under 14 years old or where consent has been refused on a child's behalf by a parent or guardian.[89]

Taking Forensic Samples from Prisoners

The same power to take forensic samples under s 2 of the Criminal Justice (Forensic **6–47**
Evidence) Act 1990 may be exercised in respect of persons who are in prison, where the sample to be taken is required in connection with an offence other than the offence for which the person is in prison (or an offence of which he could be convicted on an indictment alleging that offence), and where the sample to be taken is required in connection with an investigation of the commission of an offence under:

(a) the Offences against the State Act 1939;
(b) a scheduled offence for the purposes of Part V of that Act;
(c) an offence to which s 4 of the Criminal Justice Act 1984 applies;
(d) a drug trafficking offence within the meaning of s 3 (1) of the Criminal Justice Act 1994; or
(e) an offence to which s 50 of the Criminal Justice Act 2007 applies.

Again, the Superintendent authorising the taking of the sample must have a reasonable suspicion of the involvement of the prisoner in one of the above offences, and for believing that the sample will tend to confirm or disprove the involvement of the person from whom the sample is taken in the offence under investigation.

Destruction of DNA Records and Samples

Unlike fingerprints, which may be retained unless an application is made by an indi- **6–48**
vidual for their destruction, samples taken and the records identifying persons from whom samples have been taken under s 2 of the Criminal Justice (Forensic Evidence) Act 1990 must be destroyed within 12 months if proceedings have not been instituted against the person from whom the sample was taken.[90] The 12-month limit applies unless proceedings are not instituted as a consequence of the absconsion of the person or because the gardaí have been unable to locate the person, or unless an order has been made under s 4(5) of the 1990 Act which provides:

> "If a court is satisfied, on an application being made to it by or on behalf of the Director of Public Prosecutions or the person from whom the sample was taken, that there is good

[88] *ibid*, s 3(3).

[89] *ibid*, s 3(4).

[90] Criminal Justice (Forensic Evidence) Act 1990, s 4, as amended by s 3(b) of the Criminal Justice (Drug Trafficking) Act 1996, s 14(b) of the Criminal Justice Act 2006 and s 53(b) of the Criminal Justice Act 2007. Note however the potential for change to the retention regime in light of the Criminal Justice (Forensic Evidence and DNA Database System) Bill 2013 which was published on 11 September 2013.

reason why records and samples to which this section applies should not be destroyed under this section, it may make an order authorising the retention of such records and samples for such purpose or period as it may direct."

6–49 If proceedings are instituted within 12 months, samples and records pertaining to them must be destroyed if the person to whom the records relate is acquitted or discharged, or if the proceedings are discontinued.[91] There is also provision for the destruction of samples where the Probation of Offenders Act 1907 is applied.[92] In that event, the sample will be destroyed within three years of the making of the order, provided that the person has not been convicted during that period of an offence punishable by five years' imprisonment or more.[93]

GIVING SAMPLES BY CONSENT

6–50 There is a statutory regime governing the taking of fingerprints. Suspects may opt to voluntarily provide fingerprints, a DNA sample or to be photographed, outside the statutory regime.

6–51 Finnegan J outlined in *People (Director of Public Prosecutions) v Boyce*[94] that

> "Such consent must be freely and voluntarily given. The consent must not be obtained by trickery or unfairly or oppressively. While a discretion remains to admit evidence obtained from a detained person where he is misled or tricked such evidence, whether it be an inculpatory statement or the provision of fingerprints or DNA material, is likely to infringe the rule against self-incrimination."[95]

Regulation 18 of the custody regulations provides that:

> " (1) (a) Fingerprints, palm-prints or photographs shall not be taken of, or swabs or samples taken from, a person in custody (otherwise than pursuant to a power conferred on a member by law) except with his written consent and, where he is under the age of seventeen years, the written consent of an appropriate adult.
>
> (b) A consent shall be signed and be recorded in the custody record or a separate document.
>
> (2) The fact that fingerprints, palm-prints, photographs, swabs or samples have been taken of or from a person in custody shall be recorded.
>
> (3) Where the authority of a member of the Garda Síochána of a specified rank is required for the taking of fingerprints, palm-prints or photographs of a person in custody, the name and rank of the member giving the authority shall be recorded."

6–52 The regulation came under scrutiny in the case of *DPP v Cleary.*[96] There the desirability of a caution for persons who are giving fingerprints by consent was considered. The Court of Criminal Appeal held:

---

91 Criminal Justice (Forensic Evidence) Act 1990, s 4(3).

92 *ibid*, s 4(4).

93 *ibid*, s 4(4).

94 *Director of Public Prosecutions v Boyce* [2009] 2 IR 124.

95 *ibid.*

96 *DPP v Cleary*, [2005] IECCA 51.

> "The normal wording of the caution given on arrest, prior to interview or prior to the taking of a statement is not precisely appropriate to the situation of the taking of fingerprints, since it clearly refers to anything the suspect may 'say'. It will in general be desirable that a suspect should be informed of the purpose of taking fingerprints and of the fact that he may refuse in the first instance to undergo that procedure."[97]

In *Boyce*, the Supreme Court held that the enactment of the Criminal Justice (Forensic Evidence) Act 1990 did not limit the common law power of gardaí to take forensic samples by consent. Denham J took the view that "the common law enables a practical and efficient way to obtain samples, with consent, from the local population".[98] The Court held that samples taken by consent are outside the statutory regime, which works "in tandem with the common law" as "an alternative".[99] The significance of the judgment is that it provides for parallel systems, with in-built statutory protections (and crucially a destruction period) for those who refuse to consent to the taking of samples, and no such protections for those who cooperate and give their samples voluntarily. The reasoning of Denham J's majority judgment in *Boyce* has been remarked on by leading commentators[100] as less compelling than the minority judgment of Fennelly J. He took the view that it was anomalous that there should be a statutory regime with inbuilt safeguards which could be easily circumvented if the suspect agrees to give a sample without gardaí having to have recourse to the statutory provisions. He asked: **6–53**

> "Did the Oireachtas intend to lay down a regime which was to apply, where samples are taken by consent from persons in custody, while the Gardaí could simply ignore that regime by seeking consent based on common law? That would be absurd. It would be inherently inconsistent and potentially unfair."[101]

Campbell has commented that:

> "The co-existence of common law and statutory schemes for collecting and retaining DNA samples may lead to the latter being circumvented lawfully by the Garda' and seems to undermine the logic of having a statute in the first instance."[102]

That a parallel regime also applies to fingerprints taken by consent was confirmed in *Director of Public Prosecutions v Cash*,[103] where an aspect of the case stated concerned the propriety of the retention of fingerprints which had been given by consent. *Boyce* was decided in the intervening period between the consideration of *Cash* in the High Court and the Supreme Court. The decision in *Boyce* was applied, and counsel for the appellant accepted that "… if the blood sample taken with consent was admissible in that case, the same would apply to the fingerprints taken from the appellant while in **6–54**

[97] *ibid.*

[98] *Director of Public Prosecutions v Boyce* [2009] 2 IR 124.

[99] *ibid*, at para 63.

[100] See for instance T O'Malley, *The Criminal Process* (Round Hall, Dublin, 2009), p 342 and L Campbell "Development Of A DNA Database In Ireland—Assessing The Proposed Legislation" (2010) 7 ILT 106.

[101] *Director of Public Prosecutions v Boyce* [2009] 2 IR 124.

[102] L Campbell "Development Of A DNA Database In Ireland—Assessing The Proposed Legislation" (2010) 7 ILT 106 .

[103] *Director of Public Prosecutions v Cash* [2010] 1 IR 609.

detention in this case". The fingerprints themselves did not form part of the prosecution case, but had been used to identify the applicant and as such formed the basis for his arrest. The Supreme Court held, *obiter*, that:

> "It will be noted that the obligations to destroy applies only to prints taken under the powers conferred by s 6 of the [Criminal Justice Act 1984] and would not appear to apply if the prints were taken by consent."[104]

6–55 The law has now been amended to provide for retention of photographs, fingerprints and palm-prints as the default position, with destruction a discretionary option only exercisable on application to senior gardaí.

FORENSIC EXAMINATION OF COMPLAINANTS IN SEXUAL ASSAULT CASES

6–56 Guidance on the procedures to be followed in obtaining forensic evidence from complainants in cases in which rape or sexual assault are alleged is provided in the Rape / Sexual Assault National Guidelines on Referral and Forensic Clinical Examination in Ireland.[105] The detailed guidance dictates best practice procedures for the preservation of forensic evidence, with the proviso that medical stability always takes priority, as follows:

> "For all types of Rape / Sexual Assault
>
> - The type of seat the person sits on should have a clean plastic, leather or leatherette-type covering.
> - The person should not bathe/shower/douche.
> - If a condom was used, it should be retained.
> - The person should not consume alcohol after the assault.
>
> Vaginal and Anal Rape / Sexual Assault
>
> The person should not if possible:
> - Pass urine and/or open their bowel.
> - Wipe the genital/anal area if they have to go to the toilet.
>
> If possible:
> - Save any sanitary protection worn at the time of the assault or afterwards.
>
> Oral Rape/Sexual Assault
>
> The person should not if possible:
> - Brush their teeth or use mouthwash.
> - Take fluid or food.
> - Smoke.

[104] *ibid, per* Hardiman J in a judgment delivered separately to the majority judgment, which was delivered by Fennelly J (Murray CJ, Denham J, Geoghegan J, Macken J, Finnegan J concurring).

[105] National SATU Guidelines Development Group, *Recent Rape/Sexual Assault: National Guidelines on Referral and Forensic Clinical Examination in Ireland* (2nd edition, 2010).

Clothing

The person should if possible:

- Change out of the clothes worn at the time of the rape/sexual assault as soon as possible.
- Place the items of clothing in separate paper bags (not plastic) and label immediately.
- Underwear, worn after the incident, should also be collected and placed in a separate paper bag.

Personnel if possible:

- Do not handle clothing – if clothing is handled then it should be with gloved hands.

If clothing has to be cut:

- It should be cut along the seams of the item.
- Do not cut through any damaged areas or breaks in a garment which may be the result of the assault or bullet/knife damage.
- Do not cut through blood, semen or fluid marks.

Wounds and Blood/Saliva/Semen Stains

- Blood, saliva or semen stains should have forensic swabs taken prior to cleansing.
- If possible, forensic swabs should be taken from any wound area prior to wound cleansing.

Forensic Samples eg Weapons, Restraints, Tape, Bullets, Paint, Glass, Soil

- Do not talk, cough or sneeze over any samples.
- Do not handle samples but, if specimen must be handled, then do so with gloved hands.
- If bullets are handled, then use gloved hands – metal forceps should *not* be used.
- Package samples individually in a sealed paper bag and label immediately.

NB The continuity of evidence should be maintained."[106]

The guidelines highlight the need for a sensitive approach to be taken by gardaí in dealing with complainants in sexual offence cases, with the use of plain clothes and unmarked cars where possible. Medical assistance must be sought where necessary and the process and procedures must be explained to the complainant. Consent must be obtained for a forensic examination at a SATU (Sexual Assault Treatment Unit) from the complainant and, if he or she is under 18, from his or her parent or guardian. Contact must be made with a SATU to arrange for an early forensic examination, and an early evidence kit must be used where necessary, particularly if there is likely to be a delay in accessing the services of a SATU. Care must be taken to avoid cross-contamination, such as by ensuring the complainant is not brought to places the suspect has been, that different cars are used to transport the suspect and complainant and that neither comes in contact with the samples or clothing of the other. The guidelines operate in tandem with the Garda Síochána Policy on the Investigation of Sexual Crime, Crimes Against Children, Child Welfare (2nd edition, 2013). **6–57**

[106] This part of the guidance is referenced as follows: AP Giardino, EM Datner, JB Asher. Sexual Assault. Victimisation across the Life Span: A Clinical Guide, St Louis: GW Medical Publishing Inc, 2003: pp 85-6; S Crowley Sexual Assault: The Medical-Legal Examination. Stamford, Connecticut, Appleton & Lange, 1999; World Health Organisation. Guidelines for Medico-Legal Care for Victims of Sexual Violence (WHO, Geneva, 2003).

Chapter 7

Powers to Stop & Search

INTRODUCTION

This chapter examines the powers of gardaí to stop and search individuals summarily, without their consent. **7–01**

At issue in the search of a person or place are the rights of liberty and privacy. Neither right is absolute, but any interference must be proportionate, justified and authorised by law. Like arrest powers, stop and search powers are derived from common law and from statute and, depending on the provision utilised, are exercised with or without warrant. Some statutory powers provide for the summary search of individuals at the discretion of gardaí once certain conditions are met, whereas searches of private property generally require the authorisation of a judge or a peace commissioner in the form of a search warrant unless the property has been designated a crime scene.[1] **7–02**

---

1 Pursuant to s 5 of the Criminal Justice Act 2006 by a garda of Superintendent rank. See *Chapter 6: Forensics, Crime Scene Management and the Preservation of Evidence,* at para 6 –09 *et seq.*

7–03 The power to stop, frequently exercised in the policing of road traffic law, is a minimal interference with personal liberty in the interests of the prevention and detection of crime. However, the search of an individual and their home are among the most invasive of human experiences: a personal search impinges upon bodily integrity and privacy, while the search of a home involves the intrusion of agents of the State into a realm ordinarily considered inviolable.[2] It has been said that the power to search is less drastic in its effect than is the power to arrest,[3] and that is perhaps so, but it is arguable that the power to search is the more intrusive of the two powers. Graduated in degrees of privacy-invasion from vehicle to person to home, the power to search is subject to less stringent oversight than powers of arrest and detention are, and there is therefore an attendant potential for arbitrary or abusive exercise. Suspects can be summarily searched on the street without the supervisory protections afforded people in detention, such as audio-visual recording, notification of third parties and the presence of multiple gardaí. What is more, though 'reasonable suspicion' is the phrasing formula routinely used in both arrest and search provisions, the extent of the suspicion required to stop and search appears less onerous than that required for an arrest. Though no distinction has been expressly drawn, there is a practical difference between the hunch that a person may have a prohibited drug or weapon in his or her possession before a search, and the suspicion that an offence has actually been committed to ground an arrest.[4] Such powers are of necessity limited in their scope in law, given the conditions which attach to their exercise, but are perhaps — in the summary search context at least — less limited in their practice. These are powers of intrinsically low visibility[5] and, as Sanders and McConville have noted in the English and Welsh context:

> "...stop, search and arrest provisions are constrained only loosely by law: the powers themselves, based (at best) on reasonable suspicion, are ill-defined; and the police largely set their own priorities".[6]

7–04 Walsh has commented that powers impinging on liberty short of arrest are increasingly intrusive (such as the requirement for drivers to stop and submit to a random breath test[7] with no requirement of an underlying suspicion) and also that there is "evidence that some [powers] are being used arbitrarily or intrusively against certain categories of individual".[8] While in relation to random mandatory breath sampling,

---

[2] Article 40.5 of the Irish Constitution provides "The dwelling of every citizen is inviolable and shall not be forcibly entered save in accordance with law".

[3] *Director of Public Prosecutions v Rooney* [1992] 2 IR 7, at 10.

[4] Walsh suggests that this may be a consequence of "a police perception that stop and search is a facility for checking out a suspicion against a person with a view to determining whether to effect an arrest". Dermot Walsh *Human Rights and Policing in Ireland: Law, Policy and Practice* (Clarus Press, Dublin, 2009) at p 154, citing National Crime Council, *Public Order Offences in Ireland* (Government Publications Office, Dublin, 2003) ch 4.

[5] J Goldstein, "Police discretion not to invoke the criminal process: low visibility decisions in the administration of justice," *Yale Law Journal*, 69:543 (1960).

[6] A Sanders and R Young, "Police Powers" in *Handbook of Policing* (T Newburn ed, 2nd ed, Willan Publishing, Cullompton, 2008), at p 286.

[7] Road Traffic Act 2010, s 10(4) as amended by s 9(c) of the Road Traffic (No 2) Act 2011.

[8] Dermot Walsh, *Human Rights and Policing in Ireland: Law, Policy and Practice* (Clarus Press, Dublin, 2009) at p 147, citing National Crime Council, *Public Order Offences in Ireland* (Government Publications Office, Dublin, 2003) ch 4.

the requirement of an Inspector's authorisation to establish a checkpoint is a safeguard to prevent the targeting at will of certain persons or certain categories of persons, there can be seen, in developments such as these, a gradual dilution of the requirement of suspicion before a power is exercised, a triumph of efficiency in crime control over rights-centric due process values.[9]

Research in numerous jurisdictions is suggestive of police bias in the use of search powers.[10] There is obvious potential for misuse of powers in both summary street searches and searches under warrant, a problem which is compounded by the paradox of the law concerning searches in Ireland: that, though there are innumerable provisions providing powers to search persons and premises in many varied contexts, there is no cohesive approach to the fundamental aspects concerning the powers of search in Ireland, such as setting out who issues search warrants, the procedures governing applications for them, and the basic principles and safeguards relating to their execution. Further, there is little oversight of personal searches. The Human Rights Audit of An Garda Síochána conducted by Ionann found that the absence of detailed statutory guidance of the type that is provided by the Police and Criminal Evidence Act (PACE) in England and Wales is a barrier to complaints about unlawful arrests and searches. **7–05**

PART 1: THE POWER TO STOP

COMMON LAW POWER TO STOP INDIVIDUALS

The power to stop is the lowest in the hierarchy of intrusions in this domain, and this is reflected in the fact that gardaí have a common law power to approach and speak to a member of the public, even prior to forming an opinion that grounds exist for suspecting that such a person was committing or planned to commit an offence.[11] The effect of the decision in *DPP v Cowman*[12] is that gardaí have the right to approach members **7–06**

[9] See HL Packer, "Two Models of the Criminal Process" 113 U Penn L Rev 1 (1964) in which Packer presents two models of competing values in criminal justice, the crime control model and the due process model. The former emphasises maximum efficiency in the apprehension, trial and conviction of offenders, whereas the due process model is characterised by a comparative prosecutorial obstacle course. Under the due process model, the power of the State is recognised and curbed, mindful of potential for abuse, with controls and safeguards to protect the individual from the potency and coercive power of the State. See also D Garland, *The Culture of Control, Crime and Social Order in Contemporary Society* (Oxford University Press, Oxford, 2001).

[10] See for instance J Knowles, N Persico and P Todd, "Racial Bias In Motor Vehicle Searches: Theory And Evidence," Journal of Political Economy, 2001, v 109 (1Feb), 203-229; A Gelman, J Fagan and A Kiss, "An Analysis of the NYPD's stop-and-frisk policy in the context of claims of racial bias," Journal of the American Statistical Association, Volume 102, Issue 479, 2007, pp 813-823; VK Borooah, "Racial Disparity in Police Stop and Searches in England and Wales", J Quant Criminol (2011) 27:453-473; S Wortley and A Owusus-Bempah, "The Usual Suspects: Police Stop and Search Practices in Canada", *Policing and Society: An International Journal of Research and Policy*, Vol 21, Issue 4, 2011, pp 395-407.

[11] *Director of Public Prosecutions v Cowman* [1993] 1 IR 335, *per* O'Hanlon J.

[12] *ibid.*

of the public for the purpose of speaking to them on an informal basis. In addition to this common law power, gardaí have numerous statutory powers to stop and search in various circumstances, some of which are considered in detail below.

POWERS TO STOP VEHICLES

7–07 Perhaps the most visible exercise of the power to stop is the Garda checkpoint in which motorists are stopped at random. Gardaí have statutory and common law powers to stop vehicles, frequently exercised together.

Section 109 of the Road Traffic Act 1961 and the Common Law Power to Stop Vehicles

7–08 Though s 109 of the Road Traffic Act 1961 is often considered to provide a power for gardaí to stop motorists at random, it is in fact a section which obliges motorists to stop their vehicle when required to do so by gardaí. Failure to stop is an offence. The section provides:

> "A person driving a vehicle in a public place shall stop the vehicle on being so required by a member of the Garda Síochána and shall keep it stationary for such period as is reasonably necessary in order to enable such member to discharge his duties."

7–09 In *DPP (Stratford) v Fagan*, the power to stop under s 109 was examined, and it was concluded that gardaí have a common law power to stop motorists, and that, notwithstanding the existence of specific statutory powers, gardaí are entitled to invoke their common law powers also.[13] The two sources of powers are not mutually exclusive, but work in tandem. The Supreme Court (Finlay CJ, O'Flaherty and Blayney JJ; Egan J concurring; Denham J dissenting) held *inter alia:*

1. The gardaí are under a common law duty to detect and prevent crime. Consequently, if they find it necessary to require motorists to stop in order to adequately detect and prevent crime, they have full power to do so under common law.
2. The gardaí are under a clear duty to do everything in their power to detect and prevent the crime of drunk driving. The widespread operation of random checkpoints designed to combat this offence falls within the common law power of the gardaí to detect and prevent crime.
3. The power of the gardaí to stop a vehicle must be exercised in a *bona fide* manner. If the power were exercised in a capricious, arbitrary or improper manner it would be wholly illegal. Thus it was open to a member of the public who had been stopped and, if subsequently charged with any offence, to raise the question of the propriety of being stopped in that context.

7–10 Blayney J identified the key issue as to whether a general power to stop without suspicion exists:

> "… the issue to which the first question gives rise is whether a garda is entitled to require a motorist to stop his vehicle even though at the time the garda does not suspect that

[13] *DPP (Stratford) v Fagan* [1994] 3 IR 265; [1994] 2 ILRM 349.

any offence is being committed by the motorist. In other words, the issue is whether the gardaí are entitled to operate random checkpoints on motorists?

It seems to me that the answer to this question is to be found by considering what are the duties of the gardaí at common law. What these duties are were described as follows by Viscount Cave LJ in his speech in *Glasbook Brothers Ltd v Glamorgan County Council* [1925] AC 270 at p. 277:

No doubt there is an absolute and unconditional obligation binding the police authorities to take all steps which appear to them to be necessary for keeping the peace, for preventing crime, or for protecting property from criminal injury…

And in *Rice v Connolly* [1966] 2 QB 414, Lord Parker CJ said in his judgment at 419:

It is also in my judgment clear that it is part of the obligations and duties of a police constable to take all steps which appear to him necessary for keeping the peace, for preventing crime or for protecting property from criminal injury. There is no exhaustive definition of the powers and obligations of the police, but they are at least those, and they would further include the duty to detect crime and to bring an offender to justice.

It is clear from these statements in regard to the duties of the police at common law that part of the duties of the gardaí are to detect and prevent crime. It follows in my opinion that, in order adequately to detect and prevent crime, they find it necessary to require motorists to stop, the common law gives them full power to do so".[14]

O'Flaherty J found that: **7–11**

"At a time when crime involving motor vehicles is so rampant, it would be anomalous to suggest that while the gardaí have wide powers to stop for mundane road traffic matters (and I am of opinion that the statutory provision quoted pertains to these matters essentially) they do not have the wider power to check all motor vehicles in the performance of their duty to detect or prevent crime.

I would declare that they have this wider power. The power to stop must be exercised (like all powers) not in a capricious manner but in a constant fashion and with due civility and courtesy."[15]

On the convergence of the powers of statutory and common law origin, Finlay CJ **7–12** considered the intersection as providing a "package" which went together, the statutory powers being an indication of the intention of the legislature to set out a power in a very particular and specific manner.

The extension of the *Stratford* principle can be seen in the case of *DPP v O'Sullivan*[16] in **7–13** which a garda was found to have acted lawfully when he went onto a private driveway and opened the door of the car, the occupant of which was suspected of drink driving. That gardaí have a duty to combat drink driving was emphasised and it was held that there is an implied authority to do whatever is necessary as long as, in accordance with

[14] *DPP (Stratford) v Fagan* [1994] 2 ILRM 349.

[15] *ibid.*

[16] *DPP v O'Sullivan* [2007] IEHC 248.

DPP (Stratford) v Fagan,[17] they do not act arbitrarily, capriciously or in an unlawful manner. It was held there that:

> "[I]t would be absurd if a member of the Garda Síochána who has power to approach and speak to a member of the public, even prior to forming an opinion that grounds exist for suspecting that such person was committing or planned to commit an offence, (*Director of Public Prosecutions v. Cowman* [1993] 1 I.R. 335, per O'Hanlon J.) could not, in the circumstances to which I have adverted, lawfully open an unlocked door of that motor car for the purpose of communicating with the person believed to be in charge of the vehicle, and without using any force or acting contrary to the indicated wishes of that person."[18]

This expansion of the common law power identified in *Fagan*[19] sits awkwardly with the traditional position which prohibited curtailment of liberty short of arrest.[20]

Section 29 of the Dublin Police Act 1842

7–14 The power scrutinised in the case of *Rooney*[21] (which concerned communication of the nature of the search power) was s 29 of the Dublin Police Act 1842. Section 29 confers a power on "a constable of the Dublin police" to stop, search and detain any vessel, boat, cart or carriage, in or on which there shall be reason to suspect that anything stolen or unlawfully obtained may be found, and also any person who may be reasonably suspected of having or conveying in any manner anything stolen or unlawfully obtained.[22] The power does not apply outside Dublin.

Section 8 of the Criminal Law Act 1976

7–15 Section 8 of the Criminal Law Act 1976, as amended by s 6 of the Illegal Immigrants (Trafficking) Act 2000, is a remarkably broad stop search power, which might be considered to form part of the Offences against the State legislation.[23] Section 8 provides that gardaí may stop a vehicle where there is reasonable cause to suspect that a specified offence has been, is being or is about to be committed. The relevant offences are as follows:

(a) an offence under the Act of Offences against the State Act 1939 or a scheduled offence under Part V of that Act;
(b) an offence under s 2 or 3 of the Criminal Law (Jurisdiction) Act 1976;
(c) murder, manslaughter or an offence under s 18 of the Offences against the Person Act 1861;

---

17 *ibid.*

18 *ibid.*

19 *DPP (Stratford) v Fagan* [1994] 2 ILRM 349.

20 See *Dunne v Clinton* [1930] IR 336; *People v Walsh* [1980] IR 294 and *People v O'Loughlin* [1979] IR 85.

21 Director of Public Prosecutions v Rooney [1992] 2 IR 7.

22 See generally the Law Reform Commission *Report On Offences Under The Dublin Police Acts And Related Offences* (LRC 14 – 1985).

23 *Report of the Committee to Review the Offences against the State Acts 1939-1998 and Related Matters,* Stationery Office, 2002, at para 10.25.

(d) an offence under s 23, 23A or 23B of the Larceny Act 1916;
(e) an offence of malicious damage to property involving the use of fire or of any explosive substance (within the meaning of s 7(1)(e) of the Criminal Law Act 1976, note however that s 7(1)(e) was repealed by s 6 of the Criminal Law (Forensic Evidence) Act 1990);
(f) an offence under the Firearms Acts 1925 to 1971;
(g) escape from lawful custody;
(h) an offence under s 11 of the Air Navigation and Transport Act 1973, or under s 10 of the Criminal Law (Jurisdiction) Act 1976;
(i) an offence under the Criminal Law Act 1976;
(j) an offence under s 12 (1) of the Firearms and Offensive Weapons Act 1990;
(k) an offence under s 112 (2) of the Road Traffic Act 1961 (substituted by s 3 (7) of the Road Traffic (Amendment) Act 1984);
(l) an offence under s 2 of the Illegal Immigrants (Trafficking) Act 2000.

A garda may stop a vehicle to ascertain whether a person in the vehicle is involved in the commission or imminent commission of a relevant offence or to determine if evidence relating to the commission or intended commission of the offence by any person is in or on the vehicle or on any person in or accompanying it. There is also provision for the use of reasonable force to compel compliance with a requirement to stop a vehicle, and such force may include placing a barrier or other device in the path of vehicles.[24] Walsh has asserted that the provision "is intended to confer a power on gardaí to stop, and if necessary search cars at random as a means of preventing or detecting a relevant offence which they believe with reasonable cause has been committed".[25] He has pointed out that there is no specific obligation imposed on the occupants to answer any of the questions which might be put to them: **7–16**

> "Presumably, the member of the Garda Síochána exercising the power can ask the driver and occupants for details of their identity, movements and what, if anything, they know, about the offences in question. However, section 8 does not impose any obligation on the occupants to answer these questions. It is submitted that in the absence of any specific obligation in the section the member is confined to relying on the voluntary cooperation of the occupants, backed up by his power under the Road Traffic Acts to demand the production of the driver's licence."[26]

The power to stop under s 8 can be exercised without any suspicion having been formed as to the participation of the occupants of the vehicle in a particular offence. All that is required is suspicion, with reasonable cause, that a specified offence has been committed, is in progress or is about to be committed. A search is conducted of the vehicle to ascertain whether: **7–17**

"(a) any person in or accompanying the vehicle has committed, is committing or is about to commit the offence, or

[24] Criminal Law Act 1976, s 8(3).
[25] D Walsh, *Criminal Procedure* (Thomson Round Hall, Dublin, 2002) p 370.
[26] *ibid,* p 371.

(b) evidence relating to the commission or intended commission of the offence by any person is in the vehicle or on any person accompanying it".

If, in the course of the search of the vehicle, the garda suspects, with reasonable cause, that either of the facts outlined in (a) or (b) above exists, he or she may search any person in or accompanying the vehicle.

The Road Traffic Acts 2006 and 2010

7–18 The Road Traffic Act 2006[27] introduced a significant power for An Garda Síochána in that it provided for the first time for random checkpoints at which motorists could be breathalysed without the need for suspicion as to whether an intoxicant had been consumed. The power has been relocated and is now to be found in the Road Traffic Act 2010 at s 10(4), as amended by s 9(c) of the Road Traffic (No 2) Act 2011. It provides:

> "10(4) A member of the Garda Síochána, who is on duty at a checkpoint, may stop a vehicle at the checkpoint and, without prejudice to any other powers (including the functions under section 9) conferred bon him or her by statute or at common law, may require a person in charge of the vehicle –
> (a) to –
> (i) provide (by exhaling into an apparatus for indicating the presence of alcohol in the breath) a specimen of his or her breath, or
> (ii) accompany him or her or another member of the Garda Síochána to a place (including a vehicle) at or in the vicinity of the checkpoint and there to provide, by exhaling into such an apparatus, a specimen of his or her breath,
> or
> (b) to leave the vehicle at the place where it has been stopped, or move it to a place in the vicinity of the checkpoint, and keep or leave it there until the person has complied with a requirement made of him or her under paragraph (a)."

7–19 Checkpoints must be authorised by a garda of Inspector rank or above, with the authorisation specifying the date, place and duration of operation of the checkpoint.[28] Authorisations are recorded in writing.[29] There is a rebuttable presumption that apparatus used by gardaí in roadside breath tests is appropriate for indicating the presence of alcohol in the breath.[30] Once a checkpoint is authorised, gardaí may stop any vehicle at the checkpoint, require a breath sample and make related demands under the Road Traffic Acts. In *Weir v Director of Public Prosecutions*[31] it was noted that the new regime, colloquially referred to as "random breath testing", is in marked contrast with the system which preceded it, where gardaí were much more limited in their powers. Previously, an opinion had first to be formed that a person had consumed intoxicating liquor, with an arrest before testing for alcohol consumption, whereas random breath

---

27 Road Traffic Act 2006, s 4, repealed by the Road Traffic Act 2010, s 33(f).

28 Road Traffic Act 2010, s 10(2) and (3).

29 *ibid.*

30 Road Traffic Act 2010, s 10(8).

31 *Weir v Director of Public Prosecutions* [2008] IEHC 268.

testing has dispensed with the requirement of suspicion and as such "represented a new departure in the law governing arrest for drink driving offences".[32] As O'Neill J put it in *Weir* "[i]t authorises a garda to carry out a random breath test at a checkpoint, without the need for that garda to form any opinion about a particular driver or vehicle and to arrest or detain for that purpose".[33]

Borders, Ports and Customs

Gardaí are vested with numerous powers to search vehicles, vessels and aircraft. The Illicit Distillation (Ireland) Act 1857 confers on gardaí the powers of customs officers in the enforcement of the Customs Acts,[34] providing that all officers of the Irish Constabulary **7–20**

> "shall have, use and exercise all the Powers and Authorities, and have and possess all the Privileges, which are or may be exercised, had or possessed by any Officer of the Customs under the "Customs Consolidation Act, 1853," or any other Act now in force or hereafter to be passed, in relation to the Customs, so far as it relates to any Seizure, Detention or Prosecution which may be made or had under any such Act or Acts, and shall be deemed and considered to be Officers of Customs for such Purposes..."[35]

Section 203 of the Customs Consolidation Act 1876 provides for the search of any cart, wagon or other conveyance where there is reasonable cause for suspicion that it may contain smuggled goods. **7–21**

Section 182 of the Customs Consolidation Act 1876 provides for the search of any boat or ship within port limits for uncustomed goods or prohibited goods, whether for import or export.

Section 184 of the Customs Consolidation Act 1876 provides for the search of any person on board any ship or boat within port limits, or persons who have landed from any ship or boat, where there is good reason to suppose that such person is carrying or has any uncustomed or prohibited goods.

Gardaí and Revenue officers are empowered under s 134(2) of the Finance Act 2001 to stop any vehicle "for any purpose related to vehicle registration tax or the registration of vehicles in any of the registers established and maintained under Chapter IV of Part II of the Finance Act1992".[36] Uniformed Revenue officers may stop, examine and search vehicles[37] and sample the fuel in them[38] as well excisable products carried. **7–22**

---

[32] *ibid.*

[33] *ibid.*

[34] Illicit Distillation (Ireland) Act 1857 (20 & 21 Vict c 40).

[35] *ibid*, s 202. See also NJ Highmore, *The Customs Laws* (2nd ed, Stevens and Sons Ltd, London, 1907) at p 175. s 202 of the Illicit Distillation (Ireland) Act 1857 remains in force in Ireland pursuant to s 2(2) and Schedule 1 of the Statute Law Revision Act 2007.

[36] Finance Act 2001, s 134(2).

[37] *ibid*, s 134(1).

[38] *ibid.*

They may question occupants of the vehicle and demand information relating to the vehicle and products transported in it.[39] For the exercise of such powers, there must be reasonable grounds to believe that excisable products are being transported in the vehicle to be searched.[40]

PART 2: PERSONAL SEARCHES

RIGHTS AND ETHICS

7–23 Privacy is an unenumerated constitutional right, not expressly mentioned in *Bunreacht na hÉireann* but given judicial recognition in the case of *Kennedy v Ireland.*[41] Hamilton P in the High Court held:

> "The right to privacy is not an issue. The issue is the extent of the right 'to be let alone'. Though not specifically guaranteed by the Constitution, the right of privacy is one of the fundamental personal rights of the citizen... It is not an unqualified right. Its exercise may be restricted by the constitutional rights of others, or by the requirements of the common good, and it is subject to the requirements of public order and morality."[42]

7–24 The law concerning personal searches involves the balancing of two interests: the protection of the individual from arbitrary interference on the one hand and the legitimate interest of the State in the maintenance of public order, the detection of crime and disorder and the maintenance of public safety on the other. The power to search involves an encroachment, not only on the right to privacy, but also on the right to bodily integrity, a right also given constitutional recognition in *Ryan v Attorney General.*[43] The right to bodily integrity may be regarded as the "right to the integrity of the person".[44] A corollary of the right to bodily integrity is freedom from torture, inhuman or degrading treatment, recognised in *State (C) v Frawley.* There Finlay P said:

> "If the unspecified personal rights guaranteed by Article 40 follow in part or in whole from the Christian and democratic nature of the State, it is surely beyond argument that they include freedom from torture, and from inhuman or degrading treatment or punishment."[45]

7–25 The relevant European Convention Rights in considering personal searches are the rights to freedom from inhuman or degrading treatment (Article 3) and to respect for private life (Article 8). Just as it is beyond argument that freedom from torture inheres in the Constitution, it almost goes without saying that a person should not be degraded

---

[39] *ibid,* s 135.
[40] *ibid,* s 134.
[41] *Kennedy v Ireland* [1987] IR 587.
[42] *ibid* at 592.
[43] *Ryan v Attorney General* [1965] IR 294.
[44] This was a definition conceded by the Attorney General in *Ryan v Attorney General.*
[45] *State (C) v Frawley* [1976] IR 365 at 374.

or ill-treated in the course of a search. Care must be taken to ensure that, insofar as is possible, the dignity of the individual is respected and the search is conducted appropriately. By comparison with freedom from ill-treatment, privacy is a considerably broader and more amorphous right, capable of qualification. Article 8 of the ECHR provides:

> "1. Everyone has the right to respect for his private and family life, his home and his correspondence.
>
> 2. There shall be no interference by a public authority with the exercise of this right except such as is in accordance with the law and is necessary in a democratic society in the interests of national security, public safety or the economic well-being of the country, for the prevention of disorder or crime, for the protection of health or morals, or for the protection of the rights and freedoms of others."

To comply with Article 8, therefore, there must be a power which permits a search, and **7–26** that power must be necessary and proportionate in the pursuit of a legitimate aim. In *Colon v Netherlands*, the European Court of Human Rights considered the designation of particular areas of Amsterdam as "security risk areas" in response to a rise in violent crime. The consequence of such a designation was to empower the prosecutor to order "preventative searching": that, for a randomly selected period of 12 hours, any persons in the designated area might be subjected to a search for weapons. The applicant argued that the designation of a security risk area violated his right to privacy under Article 8 of the Convention as it enabled a public prosecutor to conduct random searches of people over an extensive period in a large area without this mandate being subject to any judicial review. The Court found that the applicant, when he was within the security risk area, could, like any member of the public, be stopped anywhere and at any time, without notice and without any choice as to whether or not to submit to a search. As such, it followed that there had been an interference with the applicant's rights under Article 8.[46] The Court referred to its well-established case-law that the wording 'in accordance with the law' requires measures to have both a basis in domestic law and to be compatible with the rule of law:

> "The law must thus be adequately accessible and foreseeable, that is, formulated with sufficient precision to enable the individual – if need be with appropriate advice – to regulate his or her conduct. For domestic law to meet these requirements, it must afford adequate legal protection against arbitrariness and accordingly indicate with sufficient clarity the scope of discretion conferred on the competent authorities and the manner of its exercise."[47]

Remarkably, in *Colon* the complaint was deemed inadmissible, *inter alia* given the **7–27** legal framework surrounding such searches and the fact that they were effective for their intended purpose. The Court found that the "domestic authorities were entitled

---

[46] The court referred to the earlier decision in *Gillan and Quinton v The United Kingdom*, no 4158/05, § 64, ECHR 2010.

[47] *Colon v the Netherlands* (dec), no 49458/06, 15 May 2012, para 72.

to consider that the public interest outweighed the subjective disadvantage which the interference with his private life caused to the applicant".[48]

7–28 The case can be contrasted with the decision in *Gillan and Quinton v The United Kingdom*[49] where the European Court found that powers to search people randomly in a particular area violated Article 8 in circumstances in which the powers of authorisation and confirmation, as well as stop and search under the legislation, were neither sufficiently circumscribed nor subject to adequate legal safeguards against abuse. They were therefore not "in accordance with the law" and Article 8 of the Convention was found to have been violated. The impugned provision provided for the authorisation of any constable in uniform to stop and search a pedestrian in any area specified by him within his jurisdiction if he "considers it expedient for the prevention of acts of terrorism". There was no requirement at the authorisation stage that the stop and search power be considered "necessary" and therefore no requirement of any assessment of the proportionality of the measure. The power was also used extensively, for purposes unconnected with the policing of terrorism, and was clearly employed in a biased manner. The Court noted:

> "The Ministry of Justice recorded a total of 33,177 searches in 2004/5, 44,545 in 2005/6, 37,000 in 2006/7 and 117,278 in 2007/8 ... In his Report into the operation of the Act in 2007, Lord Carlile noted that while arrests for other crimes had followed searches under section 44, none of the many thousands of searches had ever related to a terrorism offence; in his 2008 Report Lord Carlile noted that examples of poor and unnecessary use of section 44 abounded, there being evidence of cases where the person stopped was so obviously far from any known terrorism profile that, realistically, there was not the slightest possibility of him/her being a terrorist, and no other feature to justify the stop.
>
> 85. In the Court's view, there is a clear risk of arbitrariness in the grant of such a broad discretion to the police officer. While the present cases do not concern black applicants or those of Asian origin, the risks of the discriminatory use of the powers against such persons is a very real consideration ... The available statistics show that black and Asian persons are disproportionately affected by the powers, although the Independent Reviewer has also noted, in his most recent report, that there has also been a practice of stopping and searching white people purely to produce greater racial balance in the statistics..."[50]

7–29 In both the Dutch and British cases, the Court found the power to search persons without reasonable suspicion to be an interference with Article 8. The distinction, as a consequence of which the British scheme amounted to a violation of Article 8, was that the British scheme provided inadequate safeguards and the Court found "in the absence of any obligation on the part of the officer to show a reasonable suspicion, it is likely to be difficult if not impossible to prove that the power was improperly exercised".[51]

---

[48] *ibid*, para 95.

[49] *Gillan and Quinton v the United Kingdom*, no 4158/05, § 64, ECHR 2010.

[50] *ibid,* paras 84 and 85.

[51] *ibid*, para 86.

The European Code of Police Ethics does not expressly refer to the power to search, but provides general principles for police action and intervention of which the following are relevant in this context: police must always verify the lawfulness of their intended actions[52]; the police shall carry out their tasks in a fair manner, guided, in particular, by the principles of impartiality and non-discrimination[53]; the police shall only interfere with individual's right to privacy when strictly necessary and only to obtain a legitimate objective[54]; and police investigations shall, as a minimum, be based upon reasonable suspicion of an actual or possible offence or crime.[55] **7–30**

The following points might be considered guiding principles in stopping and searching individuals: **7–31**

1. There must be a power to permit a search;
2. The person should be told that he or she is being detained for the purpose of a search;
3. The person should be told the purpose of the search;
4. The person should be informed of the legal power under which the search is executed;
5. The garda should state clearly the suspicion grounding the search where a suspicion is required;
6. The privacy of the individual should be respected and vindicated to the greatest degree possible, if necessary by bringing the person to a garda station to conduct a search there.

Communication of the Reason for the Search and the Power which Permits It

The lawful exercise of the power to search persons without their consent, and to retain articles found thereby, is subject to the pre-condition that the suspect is informed of the reason for the search.[56] This applies whether the person searched is a suspect or an arrested person. As is the case with an arrest, a person who is to be searched is entitled to be told of the nature of the search power being exercised and the rationale for it. In *Director of Public Prosecutions v Rooney*,[57] O'Hanlon J held: **7–32**

> "Although less drastic in its effect than a power of arrest, such action on the part of the police authorities does nevertheless amount to a substantial and significant interference with the liberty of the suspect and it appears to me that the same principles which underlie the decisions in *Christy v Leachinsky* [1947] AC 573 and *The People (Attorney General) v White* [1947] IR 247 must apply with equal force in this situation also, if the constitutional guarantees of liberty of the person are to be adequately defended and vindicated… before the power of search given by s 29 of the Dublin Police Act 1842, … can now be lawfully exercised, the suspect is entitled to be informed of the nature and description of the statutory power which is being invoked."[58]

---

52 European Code of Police Ethics, para 38.
53 *ibid,* para 40.
54 *ibid*, para 41.
55 *ibid*, para 47.
56 *Christie v Leachinksy* [1947] AC 573, *Director of Public Prosecutions v Rooney* [1992] 2 IR 7.
57 *Director of Public Prosecutions v Rooney* [1992] 2 IR 7.
58 *ibid* at 10.

This is so even if the power permitting the search makes no reference to a requirement to inform the person of the reason for the search and the power that permits it. The Misuse of Drugs Act search power makes no such reference, but, in accordance with *Rooney*, the power invoked must be explained.

7–33 In *DPP v Kelly*[59] the Court of Criminal Appeal emphasised that the requirement set out in *Rooney*[60] that a person must have the search power explained applies only where a person is being searched without consent. The Court concluded that:

> "…in a case where objection is made, a Garda officer may not search a person in custody without stating clearly to the person that he proposes to do so accompanied by a simple but clear statement of the power which is being exercised. It emerges equally clearly from the same authorities that such an obligation does not exist when the person does not object."[61]

7–34 The Court highlighted the following passage from the case of *DPP v O'Donnell,* which had been cited with approval by Keane CJ in *DPP v McFadden*[62]:

> "It is only when the co-operation of the citizen is withdrawn, and it is necessary to fall back on powers of compulsion under common law or under statute, that the necessity arises for the gardaí to invoke such powers and at that stage to inform the person against whom it is sought to exercise them of the legal justification for any interference which is to take place with his or her rights under the Constitution."[63]

7–35 Of course, the crucial point is that the requisite level of suspicion should exist to allow the statutory power to be invoked. The purpose of the various powers of search is that they permit a search to take place in relevant circumstances where consent is not forthcoming. If consent is to be disregarded, there must be a clear power defined in law permitting a search, communication of the reason for the search and the power which permits it, and respect for the rights to privacy and dignity of the individual.

DRUG SEARCHES

7–36 The most commonly exercised search of the person is that which is conducted when a person is suspected of a drug offence, the search being governed by s 23 of the Misuse of Drugs Act 1977.[64]

7–37 The section does not say expressly that the suspect must have the reason for the search conveyed to him, but neither does the power in s 29 of the Dublin Police Act which was considered in the case of *Rooney*.[65] In light of *Rooney*, a suspect should be informed that he is going to be searched, that the search will be conducted under s 23 of the

---

59 *Director of Public Prosecutions v Kelly* [2012] IECCA 71.

60 *ibid.*

61 *ibid.*

62 *DPP v McFadden* [2003] 2 IR 105.

63 *DPP v O'Donnell* [1995] 3 IR 551, at para 42.

64 As amended by s 12 of the Misuse of Drugs Act 1984.

65 *Director of Public Prosecutions v Rooney* [1992] 2 IR 7.

Misuse of Drugs Act 1977 and that the search is predicated on the suspicion that the person has committed an offence under the Misuse of Drugs Act 1977 as amended.

The statutory power set out in s 23 of the Misuse of Drugs Act permits the search of persons, vehicles, vessels and aircraft.[66] In addition, s 23 provides a number of practical powers to facilitate the investigation of drug offences. The search power in s 23 may be exercised without warrant and gardaí may detain the person for as long as is reasonably necessary to conduct the search. If the search is of a vehicle, vessel or aircraft, the person in control of the vehicle, vessel or aircraft may be required to stop it and to refrain from moving it. The fruits of a successful search may be seized and retained. **7–38**

A precondition for the exercise of any of the powers contained in s 23 is a reasonable cause for suspicion that the person is in possession of a controlled drug in contravention of the Misuse of Drugs Act 1977.[67] A generalised suspicion that drugs are being sold in the vicinity will not suffice; the garda must suspect that the individual is in unlawful possession of a controlled drug. In *Director of Public Prosecutions v Farrell*,[68] a search was held to be unlawful in circumstances in which a search was conducted and justified by the garda on the basis that there was a drug problem in that particular area of Dublin. In addition, there was no evidence that the driver of the car searched was informed of the reason for the search. The High Court held: **7–39**

> "Garda Higgins could have relied on his common law powers to stop and request permission to search the car without holding any specific suspicion against the driver and had he indicated in his evidence that he had done this, then I would agree with the finding of the learned District Judge that a general awareness of a drug problem in the area was sufficient to stop and seek consent to a search the car under common law. The fact that Garda Higgins decided to do so without consent under s 23 of the Misuse of Drugs Act 1977 meant that he had to have reasonable cause for suspecting that Mr Farrell was in possession of a controlled drug. The reasonable cause to suspect Mr Farrell simply did not exist. It may have been otherwise if, having asked to search the car, Mr Farrell refused his consent. This may have given rise to a suspicion that he was concealing drugs but that was not the case here. It is therefore with some reluctance, in view of my belief that Garda Higgins had a common law power to stop and then ask to search the car, that I feel obliged to hold that the search was, in the circumstances, unlawful."[69]

---

66 As amended by s 12 of the Misuse of Drugs Act 1984.

67 In this regard, it is important to note that the possession of controlled drugs is not necessarily unlawful. Many prescription drugs are sold illegally, which is an offence contrary to s 15 of the Misuse of Drugs Act 1977, but their possession is not criminalised for the purposes of s 3(1) of the Misuse of Drugs Act 1977. The rationale for their exclusion is the frequency with which such drugs are lawfully held having been dispensed on prescription. See SI No 326 of 1988, Misuse of Drugs (Exemption) Order, 1988, which exempts a number of common medical preparations, including alprazolam (Xanax), diazepam (Valium), flurazepam (Dalmane), lorazepam (Ativan) from s 3(1) of the Misuse of Drugs Act 1977.

68 *Director of Public Prosecutions v Farrell* [2009] IEHC 368.

69 *ibid* at para 29, *per* Clark J.

7–40 Where a member of the Garda Síochána decides to search a person under s 23, he may require the person to accompany him to a garda station for the purpose of being searched there.[70]

7–41 In a vehicle, vessel or aircraft search, gardaí may require the owner or person in control of the vehicle as follows:

- not to remove any substance, article or other thing, pending the start of the search, s 23(1B)(a);
- to take the vehicle or cause it to be taken to a place which he considers suitable for such search as specified by the garda, s 23(1B)(b);
- to stay in or to accompany the vehicle, vessel or aircraft, as may be appropriate, s 23(1B)(c).

Where it is proposed to search a person or their vehicle under s 23, the search should be conducted and completed without delay.

Gardaí may arrest a person who fails to comply with a requirement made under s 23, and non-cooperation with a garda exercising his or her s 23 power constitutes an offence.

7–42 The constitutionality of s 23 was challenged and upheld in the case of *O'Callaghan v Ireland*.[71] The Supreme Court did not explore in any significant detail the practical operation of the drug search, which is regrettable, given that the section is somewhat lacking in detail as regards the practical operation of this critical search power. The Court held, however, that a person detained in a garda station for the purposes of a drug search is entitled to the rights and protections afforded an arrested person. In response to the argument that the section failed to adequately direct how the search power ought to be exercised, the Supreme Court held that the exercise of the power in an inappropriate or embarrassing manner would amount to an abuse of power and a violation of constitutional rights.

FIREARMS AND OFFENSIVE WEAPON SEARCHES

7–43 The Firearms Act 1925 provides at s 22(4) a power for gardaí to stop, search and arrest without warrant any person whom he or she "believes to be in possession of or to be using or carrying a firearm or ammunition" in contravention of the Firearms Act. A garda exercising the power, "whether arresting him or not, may seize and detain any firearm or ammunition in his possession or used or carried by him".[72] Section 22 also provides for gardaí to demand production of a firearms certificate from any person observed or believed to be in possession of or using a firearm or ammunition.[73]

[70] Misuse of Drugs Act 1984, s 23(1A).
[71] *O'Callaghan v Ireland* [1994] IR 555.
[72] Firearms Act 1925, s 22(4).
[73] *ibid*, s 22(1).

The use of the term "believes" as a pre-requisite for the exercise of the power is noteworthy, since there is no reference to the reasonableness of the belief.

Section 16 of the Firearms and Offensive Weapons Act 1990 contains an important search power which has been substantially amended and improved by the Criminal Justice (Miscellaneous Provisions) Act 2009. The power as initially drafted contained significant limitations: its exercise depended on a prerequisite congregation of people and the likelihood of a breach of the peace, either past, present or future. The section also lacked an inherent power to require a person suspected of having an offensive weapon to accompany a garda to a garda station for the purposes of a search. As possession of a knife, blade or pointed article under s 9(1) was not an arrestable offence, the gardaí were bereft of an important practical power. Offences under s 9(1) are now triable both summarily and on indictment[74] and are therefore arrestable. The re-drafted s 16, as inserted by s 41 of the Criminal Justice Act 2009, has updated the search power and provides that, if a garda suspects, with reasonable cause, that a person has an offensive weapon or a realistic imitation firearm in their possession in a public place, they can search the person and, if necessary, detain the person for as long as is reasonably necessary to conduct the search. In addition, gardaí may search any vehicle, vessel or aircraft in which they suspect that a weapon may be found and require the person in control of the vehicle to stop the vehicle or to refrain from moving it. Any weapons found may also be seized and retained as evidence. **7–44**

SECTION 30 OF THE OFFENCES AGAINST THE STATE ACT 1939

The most extensive of the stop and search powers are contained in s 30(1) of the Offences against the State Act 1939. Section 30 applies where a scheduled offence[75] past, present or future is suspected, in which case a suspect can be stopped, searched, interrogated, arrested and detained. Section 30(1) provides: **7–45**

> "A member of the Garda Síochána (if he is not in uniform on production of his identification card if demanded) may without warrant stop, search, interrogate, and arrest any person, or do any one or more of those things in respect of any person, whom he suspects of having committed or being about to commit or being or having been concerned in the commission of an offence under any section or sub-section of this Act or an offence which is for the time being a scheduled offence for the purposes of Part V of this Act or whom he suspects of carrying a document relating to the commission or intended commission of any such offence as aforesaid or whom he suspects of being in possession of information relating to the commission or intended commission of any such offence as aforesaid."

The section is a substantial departure from the norms of policing. Its noteworthy features are the absence of any need to justify a stop and search on the basis of a reasonable **7–46**

[74] As amended by s 39 of the Criminal Justice (Miscellaneous Provisions) Act 2009.

[75] s 36 of the Offences against the State Act 1939 permits the designation of 'scheduled offences' to which the powers of arrest and detention contained in s 30 apply. Offences may be scheduled only if there is a government proclamation in force bringing part V of the Act into operation, declaring the need for extraordinary powers.

suspicion and the fact that an intended, as distinct from attempted, offence will suffice, as indeed will suspected knowledge concerning an, as yet, uncommitted offence. The Committee to Review the Offences against the State Acts 1939-1998 (the Hederman Report) recommended that, although the courts have clarified that the suspicion which ought to ground the use of powers under s 30 should be "*bona fide* held and not unreasonable",[76] for the avoidance of doubt, it would be desirable in any recasting of the section to include reference to reasonable suspicion.[77] The committee grappled with the distinction between an intended offence and an attempted offence, recommending that the phrase "about to commit" should be deleted in favour of the phrase "when it is reasonably considered necessary to prevent the imminent commission of an offence".[78] Though s 30 has been added to in the years since the report was published, the formula in s 30(1) remains unchanged.

SECTION 22 OF THE CRIMINAL JUSTICE (PUBLIC ORDER) ACT 1994

7–47 The Criminal Justice (Public Order) Act 1994 provides for the erection of barriers to restrict access to events in the interests of safety or for the preservation of order.[79] This is frequently done for large-scale sporting events and concerts for which tickets are required. Where such barriers have been erected, or if it appears that a person has entered or is about to enter such an event, gardaí may search patrons if they suspect, with reasonable cause, that persons have in their possession intoxicating liquor, a disposable container or an article which could, in the circumstances, be used to cause injury.[80] The power extends to the search of any vehicle that is seeking to cross or which has crossed the barrier in erected under s 21 of the 1994. It is further provided that gardaí may refuse to allow persons entry to the event unless they surrender the item to a member of the garda. If the item is not surrendered, a garda may direct them to leave the vicinity.

CUSTOMS SEARCHES

7–48 By contrast with s 23 of the Misuse of Drugs Act 1977, s 2 of the Customs and Excise (Miscellaneous Provisions) Act 1988 provides considerably more detail on the practical aspects of a personal search undertaken by a customs official. It expressly refers to the power to undertake an intimate body search, which may be conducted by a medical practitioner at the request of the person to be searched. As will be seen below at para 7 – 55 *et seq*, an intimate search in this context does not include an internal examination. A search under s 2 of the 1988 Act can only be conducted where a Customs and Excise officer has reasonable cause to suspect that

[76] *People v Quilligan* (No1) [1986] IR 495; *People v Quilligan* (No3) [1993] 2 IR 305.

[77] *Report of the Committee to Review the Offences against the State Acts 1939 – 1998 and Related Matters*, (Dublin, 2002) at para 7.68.

[78] *ibid* at para 7.57.

[79] Criminal Justice (Public Order) Act 1994, s 21.

[80] *ibid,* s 22.

a person at or in the vicinity of any port or airport or the Northern Irish border is in possession of a controlled drug which was illegally imported, or is being, or is intended to be, illegally exported.

Where the requisite reasonable suspicion exists, the customs officer may search the person without warrant and, if necessary, detain the person for as long as is necessary to conduct the search. As with searches under the Misuse of Drugs Act, it is fundamental that the Customs officer ensures, as far as practicable, that the person understands the reason for the search and that it is conducted with due respect for the person being searched.[81] The legislation provides a number of privacy safeguards: **7–49**

- a person being detained shall not be searched by an officer or person of the opposite sex[82];
- where a search of a person being detained involves removal of clothing, other than headgear or a coat, jacket, glove or similar article of clothing, no officer or person of the opposite sex shall be present unless either that person is a designated medical practitioner or the officer considers that the presence of that person is necessary by reason of the violent conduct of the person to be searched[83];
- a search of the person may, at the request of the person to be searched or on the direction of the officer or officers present, be carried out by a medical practitioner designated by the officer or officers and may include an intimate body search. [84]

In addition, Customs officers are empowered under s 2(ii) to stop and search any vehicle, vessel or aircraft (including the contents of the vehicle, vessel or aircraft) in which it is suspected that a controlled drug may be found. The owner or person in control of the vehicle may also be instructed not to remove anything from it,[85] to move it to a place more suitable for the conduct of a search[86] or to remain in or to accompany the vehicle for as long as is necessary.[87] Customs officers may also examine (by opening or otherwise) and seize and detain anything found in the course of a search which is thought to be likely to be required as evidence in a subsequent prosecution for drug or customs offences.[88] **7–50**

A person who is the subject of a search under s 2 may also be required to accompany a Customs officer to a customs office or elsewhere to facilitate a search.[89]

---

81 Customs and Excise (Miscellaneous Provisions) Act 1988, s 2(1)(A).
82 *ibid,* s 2(1)(B).
83 *ibid,* s 2(1)(C).
84 *ibid,* s 2(1)(D).
85 *ibid,* s 2(b)(i).
86 *ibid,* s 2(b)(ii).
87 *ibid,* s (2)(b)(iii).
88 *ibid,* s 2(1)(iii).
89 *ibid,* s 2(2)(a).

7–51 Definitions are widely drawn so that 'aircraft' also includes balloons, gliders and even model airplanes.[90] The definition of a vehicle was expanded in 2005 when a significant lacuna was identified — there was no power under the original definition to search containers. Section 2(9), which was inserted by s 96 of the Finance Act 2005, now provides that 'vehicle' means a mechanically-propelled vehicle or any other conveyance, and includes any container, trailer, tank or any other thing which is or may be used for the storage of goods in the course of carriage and is designed or constructed to be placed on, in or attached to any such vehicle or other conveyance.

Failure to comply with a requirement under s 2 is an offence.

SEARCH OF AN ARRESTED PERSON

7–52 There is a common law power to search an arrested person. A member of the gardai who has effected a lawful arrest is entitled to conduct a search of the arrested person's body and to retain objects found in the course of the search, even without a search warrant.[91] Where such a search yields evidence in favour of any other criminal charge, it may be retained by the gardaí to prevent it from being removed or destroyed.[92] Section 23(1A) of the Misuse of Drugs Act 1977 provides that a garda may require a person to accompany them to a Garda station for the purpose of being searched. This is separate and distinct from both arrest and the common law power to search an arrested person.

7–53 It is standard procedure to search a person detained in a Garda station. Regulation 17(1) of the Criminal Justice Act 1984 (Treatment of Persons in Custody in Garda Síochána Stations) Regulations 1987 provides that:

> "A member conducting a search of a person in custody shall ensure, so far as practicable, that the person understands the reason for the search and that it is conducted with due respect for the person being searched."

7–54 Evidence obtained in the examination of an arrested person's wallet without his consent was found to be inadmissible by the Court of Criminal Appeal in *DPP v McFadden.*[93] The Court found that, had the garda who conducted the search informed the suspect that he was going to search his wallet to ascertain his identity, the search would have been lawful. However, in the absence of any such explanation, the search was invalid, and the evidence obtained on foot of it ought not to have been admitted in evidence by the trial judge. The applicant was at no stage told by the gardaí why he was being searched or why the contents of his wallet were being examined, nor was he informed of the power, if any, that the gardaí were relying on to justify the search. The failure of the garda in this case to give any explanation to the applicant as to why his wallet was being searched was found to be a breach of the fundamental requirement of Irish law that a police officer who is carrying out a search of a person without his

---

[90] *ibid*, s 2(8).

[91] *Dillon v O'Brien* (1887) 20 LR Ir 300; *Elias v Pasmore* [1934] 2 KB 163.

[92] *Jennings v Quinn* [1968] IR 306.

[93] *DPP v McFadden* [2003] 2 IR 105.

consent should inform that person of the legal justification for interfering with his constitutional rights. The Court endorsed as a correct statement of the law in this jurisdiction the following statement by Professor Dermot Walsh in *Criminal Procedure* (at para 4.73):

> "At common law a member of the Garda Síochána has the power to search a person whom he or she has arrested. The purpose of this search would appear to be to enable the member to take into possession anything found on the person in the nature of a dangerous weapon or which may be used to facilitate his escape from custody or any item which may be of evidentiary value. In most cases, therefore, the search will be confined to a body frisk and examination of the suspect's outer garments."[94]

As will be seen below, the legal basis for examination beyond the outer garments is not clear-cut and would benefit from legislative elaboration.

BODY SEARCHES AND "STRIP SEARCHES"

The custody regulations provide at Regulation 17 that, where practicable, a search of a person in custody involving removal of underclothing shall be carried out by a doctor.[95] Persons in custody should not be searched by a person (other than a doctor) of the opposite sex,[96] and where a search of a person in custody involves removal of clothing, other than headgear or a coat, jacket, glove or similar article of clothing, no person of the opposite sex shall be present unless either that person is a doctor or the member in charge considers that the presence of that person is necessary because of the violent conduct of the person to be searched.[97] Where clothing or footwear of a person is retained, replacements of a reasonable standard shall be provided.[98] The fact of the search must be recorded, including the name of the person conducting the search and the names of those present.[99] As with all searches, a garda conducting a search of a person in custody must ensure, so far as practicable, that the person understands the reason for the search and that it is conducted with due respect for the person being searched. **7–55**

While in other jurisdictions an intimate search is taken to include a body cavity search, Revenue Irish Tax and Customs have issued guidance to the effect that an intimate body search is a strip search, which does not include an internal examination, for which there is no legal provision in Ireland. The delineation Revenue employs is as follows: **7–56**

> "(a) Patdown Search
> This involves a search of a suspect's outer clothing but does not include the removal of clothing.

94 Walsh, *Criminal Procedure* (Round Hall, Dublin, 2002) para 4.73.

95 Criminal Justice Act 1984 (Treatment Of Persons In Custody In Garda Síochána Stations) (Amendment) Regulations 2006.
SI No 119 of 1987, Criminal Justice Act 1984 (Treatment Of Persons In Custody In Garda Síochána Stations) Regulations 1987, reg 17(4).

96 *ibid,* reg 17(2).

97 *ibid,* reg 17(3).

98 *ibid,* reg 17(5).

99 *ibid,* reg 17(6).

(b) Intimate Body Search
This means the physical examination of an undressed / stripped person by an officer or medical practitioner to verify if drugs are concealed on the suspect.

(c) Internal Body Search
Officers are reminded that they have no powers to carry out an internal body search."[100]

7–57 It is submitted that this is a correct statement of the law in Ireland and that there is no legal authority on which an internal body search may be performed. It is of note that, in the course of the Dáil debate on the Customs (Miscellaneous Provisions) Bill 1988, the Minister of State at the Department of Finance, Noel Treacy, said that "compulsory, intrusive or internal body searches are regarded by the State as an invasion of personal rights, specifically of the right to bodily integrity which is held by the courts to be one of the rights implicitly guaranteed by Article 40 of the Constitution".[101] In England and Wales, by contrast, s 65 of PACE provides expressly that an intimate search means "a search which consists of the physical examination of a person's body orifices other than the mouth". In England and Wales, intimate searches may generally only be conducted by registered doctors or nurses,[102] for whom involvement in criminal investigations can pose ethical difficulties in dealing with patients in custody who may refuse to consent to examination and treatment. The British Medical Association first published Guidelines for Doctors asked to Perform Intimate Body Searches in 1994 and has kept the guidelines under continuous revision since. The 2007 guidelines mirror the PACE definition, defining an intimate search as "a search which consists of a physical examination of a person's body orifices other than the mouth".[103] The Association advises that such searches should occur in a hospital setting and with the consent of the detainee. If consent is not forthcoming, the doctor ought to refuse to participate in the search, on the basis that "a fundamental ethical principle guiding medical practice is that no examination, diagnosis or treatment of a competent adult should be undertaken without the person's consent. The ethical obligation to seek consent applies even where this is not a legal requirement".[104]

7–58 Bearing in mind the more restrictive definition which applies to an intimate body search in this jurisdiction, Irish Revenue guidance provides that:

> "a traveller should not be subjected to an intimate body search unless:
> (i) there are grave reasons for suspecting that s/he may have drugs concealed or that the Revenue is being seriously defrauded; and

[100] Revenue, Customs Import Export Policy, Manual on the Control and Examination of Baggage, updated December 2009, paragraph 15.7. Available online: http://www.revenue.ie/en/about/foi/s16/customs/import-export-policy/baggage-control-examination.pdf <accessed 20 October 2013>.
[101] 379 Dáil Debates Cols 2142–2209, 5 May 1988.
[102] PACE, s 55.
[103] *Guidelines for Doctors asked to Perform Intimate Body Searches,* 2007.
[104] *ibid.*

> (ii) other reasonable search procedures have been completed (baggage and outer clothing)."[105]

In Ireland, the only judicial comment (beyond passing references) on intimate searches is made in the civil context. In *Devoy v Ireland and the Attorney General*,[106] the plaintiff asserted that, during a raid on a nightclub, she was searched by a female garda, as a consequence of which her breast was exposed, in view of other patrons. The plaintiff's sister gave evidence that she too had been subjected to an invasive search, that her underwear had been pulled down and her top pulled up around her neck. Relying on the same reasoning as was employed in upholding the constitutionality of s 23 of the Misuse of Drugs Act in *O'Callaghan v Ireland*,[107] the High Court in *Devoy* found that the powers of the gardaí and the rights of the citizen were appropriately balanced. Finnegan J held: **7–59**

> "The exercise of the powers in the present case clearly caused inconvenience to the patrons many of whom undoubtedly had not been in possession of a controlled drug. Their evening's entertainment was interrupted. They were exposed to the inconvenience of a search. However I am satisfied that the Oireachtas has maintained a reasonable proportionality between the evil it seeks to prevent and the interference with the constitutional rights of the citizen… In the present case I am satisfied that the Garda Síochána exercised their powers in a constitutional manner… Clearly greater privacy could have been afforded by taking one woman at a time into the women's toilet for searching but this would have extended the inconvenience to the patrons. In any event I am satisfied on the evidence that the opportunity of being searched within a cubicle within the toilet was offered and availed of on a number of occasions but that in general patrons were content to be searched in the main area of the women's toilet. I am satisfied that the manner in which the search was carried out did not impose unnecessary harassment or embarrassment or indeed inconvenience."[108]

It should be noted that, in *Devoy* the gardaí did not accept that the searches had been conducted in the manner outlined by the plaintiff. Rather it was submitted that: **7–60**

> "The search was a body search and not a strip search. At the briefing prior to the warrant being executed it was made clear to the gardaí involved in the operation that the search to be carried out was a body search and what that involves is well understood by gardaí as a result of their training. The person being searched was requested to pull out their upper garment if the same was tucked into a waistband and they were then asked to pull out the bottom of their bra so that anything concealed therein would fall to the floor. The garda would then run her hands around the back of the bra outside the outer clothing to feel for anything concealed. The waistband of trousers or skirts would then be pulled out to allow anything concealed therein to fall to the floor and if necessary a request would be made to open the waistband to achieve this. It would not be appropriate or usual to carry out a search in the manner described by the Plaintiff and so far as each of these

---

105 Revenue, Customs Import Export Policy, *Manual on the Control and Examination of Baggage*, updated December 2009, paragraph 15.7. Available online: http://www.revenue.ie/en/about/foi/s16/customs/import-export-policy/baggage-control-examination.pdf <accessed 20 October 2013>.

106 *Devoy v Ireland and the Attorney General* [2004] IEHC 404.

107 *O'Callaghan v Ireland* [1994] IR 555.

108 *Devoy v Ireland and the Attorney General* [2004] IEHC 404.

> witnesses were concerned no such search was carried out. None of the witnesses recalled the Plaintiff. None of the witnesses saw anyone's breast area being exposed."[109]

7–61 Internal searches are therefore not expressly provided for by Irish law and arguably, if introduced, would fall foul of the constitutional guarantee of bodily integrity. It would seem that the legislature favours detention to invasive search to address the issue of concealed drugs on a suspect's person, with the then Minister for Justice pragmatically commenting on the introduction of a seven-day detention period for drug trafficking offences in the Criminal Justice (Drug Trafficking) Bill 1996:

> "The seven day detention power is necessary because much of our legislation does not reflect the seriousness of the drug trafficking problem… The seven day detention period is based on sound reasoning. It will at least give the authorities an opportunity to gather evidence … It is impossible to expect the authorities to gather the necessary evidence, particularly if the case has an international dimension, in that period of time. Also, in the case of drug peddlers or traffickers who stuff or swallow drugs it is paramount that a sufficient period of time is allowed to retrieve the drugs."[110]

Such retrieval occurs in practice in a hospital setting where it is medically managed.[111]

7–62 Even in the absence of an internal examination, strip searches which do not respect, as far as possible, the dignity and privacy of the prisoner, can also amount to a breach of the European Convention on Human Rights. In *Valasinas v Lithuania*,[112] the European Court of Human Rights held that a body search of a male prisoner was degrading treatment in circumstances where the prisoner had been forced to strip naked in the presence of a female prison officer, with the intention of humiliating him. He was then ordered to squat, and his sexual organs and the food he had received were examined by guards who were not wearing gloves. The Court held:

> "117. The Court considers that, while strip-searches may be necessary on occasions to ensure prison security or to prevent disorder or crime, they must be conducted in an appropriate manner. Obliging the applicant to strip naked in the presence of a woman and then touching his sexual organs and food with bare hands showed a clear lack of respect for the applicant, and diminished in effect his human dignity. It must have left him with feelings of anguish and inferiority capable of humiliating and debasing him. The Court concludes, therefore, that the search of 7 May 1998 amounted to degrading treatment within the meaning of the Convention."

Article 3 of the ECHR, which provides that no one shall be subjected to torture or to inhuman or degrading treatment or punishment, was found to have been violated.

---

109 *ibid.*

110 Dáil Debates, Vol 467, 2 July 1996.

111 SJ Traub, RS Hoffman and CS Nelson, "Body Packing – The Internal Concealment of Illicit Drugs," N Engl J Med 2003; 349:2519-26.

112 *Valasinas v Lithuania,* Application no 44558/98, 24 July 2001.

CHAPTER 8

Powers of Entry for Arrest and Investigation

INTRODUCTION

In societies where capitalism is the overarching political ideology, the right to the unfettered enjoyment of private property is sacrosanct, save in certain limited circumstances. As Camden CJ put it in 1765, **8–01**

> "where a defendant is called upon to answer for bruising the grass and even treading upon the soil… he is bound to show, by way of justification, that some positive law has empowered or excused him".[1]

Private property encompasses land and business premises, permanent and temporary residences and the common areas of buildings to which the public may or may not have rights of access. The law provides a disjointed array of powers to empower and excuse gardaí their entry into such places in the prevention and detection of crime. There are distinctions between different categories of property and purposes of entry, with common law and statutory powers providing for entry for investigation, for arrest, for the designation of crime scenes and for the execution of search warrants. Common law **8–02**

[1] *Entick v Carrington* (1765) 19 State Trials 1030 at 1066.

powers of entry have been superseded by statutory powers.[2] Though common law powers persist,[3] given the constitutional character of the inviolability of the dwelling and the right to privacy, reliance on a clearly defined statutory power for entry is preferable. This chapter examines some of the statutory powers permitting gardaí to enter private property for arrest and criminal investigation as well as entry by express or implied permission. Entry under the authority of a search warrant is considered separately in *Chapter 9: Entry Under Search Warrant*, while crime scenes are considered in *Chapter 6: Forensics, Crime Scene Management and the Preservation of Evidence.*

The Dwelling

8–03 Article 40.5 of the Irish Constitution provides:

> "The dwelling of every citizen is inviolable and shall not be forcibly entered save in accordance with law."[4]

8–04 The constitutional inviolability of the dwellinghouse has been described as "one of the most important, clear and unqualified protections given by the Constitution to the citizen".[5] Gardaí may only enter a dwelling with a warrant, under a specific statutory authority, or by the invitation or permission of the owner, which may be express or implied. The citizen's right to the enjoyment of private property, and the extent to which the gardaí can encroach upon the dwellinghouse of an individual in the investigation of offences, will depend on whether a warrant has been obtained and, in the absence of a warrant, whether a statutory or common law power exists to override the constitutional protection of the dwelling.

8–05 In addition to the constitutional protection afforded the home, Article 8 of the European Convention on Human Rights provides:

> "1. Everyone has the right to respect for his private and family life, his home and his correspondence.
>
> 2. There shall be no interference by a public authority with the exercise of this right except such as is in accordance with the law and is necessary in a democratic society in the interests of national security, public safety or the economic well-being of the country, for the prevention of disorder or crime, for the protection of health or morals, or for the protection of the rights and freedoms of others."

---

2 The power of entry for arrest, for example, in s 6 of the Criminal Law Act 1997, has overtaken the common law power to enter to arrest a felon.

3 For instance, there is a common law power to enter private property to prevent an affray: *R v Walker* (1854) Dears CC 358; *Timothy v Simpson* (1835) 1 Cr M & R 757; *Robson v Hallett* [1967] 2 QB 939; *R v Marsden* (1925) 88 JP Jo 369.

4 Casey opines that we may presume that 'citizen' is synonymous with 'person'. J Casey, *Constitutional Law in Ireland* (Sweet and Maxwell, London, 1987).

5 Per Carney J in *DPP v Dunne* [1994] 2 IR 537.

A broad meaning is given to the term 'home' under European Convention case law. In *Bjedov v Croatia*, the European Court of Human Rights reiterated that the concept does not depend on legal ownership or occupation: 8–06

> "The Convention organs' case-law is clear on the point that the concept of "home" within the meaning of Article 8 is not limited to those premises which are lawfully occupied or which have been lawfully established. "Home" is an autonomous concept which does not depend on classification under domestic law. Whether or not a particular premises constitutes a "home" which attracts the protection of Article 8 § 1 will depend on the factual circumstances, namely, the existence of sufficient and continuous links with a specific place ... whether certain premises are to be classified as a "home" is a question of fact and does not depend on the lawfulness of the occupation under domestic law..."[6]

Squatters

In Irish law too, the term 'dwelling' is not limited to those who are legally resident in a property. It applies equally to squatters or others who are habitually resident in a place. In *DPP v Lynch*[7] the Court of Criminal Appeal found that gardaí who had searched a dwelling inhabited by a squatter on foot of an invalid warrant did so in breach of the constitutional protection provided by Article 40.5. Accordingly the fruits of the search had to be excluded, and the accused's conviction was quashed. The Court referred to the Irish text of the Constitution, which is to be preferred if there is any element of doubt as to meaning: 8–07

> "In the Irish language version, the expression corresponding to "dwelling" is "ionad cónaithe." The Court is satisfied that the question of whether a place is the "dwelling" of a person for the purpose of this provision, at least in the context of the criminal law, is one of fact, a view reinforced by the Irish language version. It is at least quite obvious that the constitutional protection would extend to a wide variety of people with dubious legal titles, such as an overholding tenant, the widow of a deceased legal owner, or a person in *bona fide* possession on foot of an invalid title."[8]

Hotel Rooms

In the case of *DPP v Yamanoha*[9] the suspect was convicted of a drug offence, the evidence of which was obtained through entry on foot of an invalid search warrant.[10] The search warrant pertained to a hotel room. Though the question of whether the hotel constituted a dwelling was not mentioned in the judgment, the case illustrated that entry even to a place of temporary residence was considered to require a search warrant. In the later case of *DPP v Cash*, Charleton J commented in the High Court that, in his view, the hotel room was certainly not a dwelling, but rather that it should be inferred that the constitutional right infringed in *Yamanoha* was that of privacy.[11] 8–08

6 *Bjedov v Croatia* (Application no 42150/09) 29 May 2012.

7 *DPP v Lynch* [2009] IECCA 31, unreported, Court of Criminal Appeal, 2 April 2009, *per* Fennelly J.

8 *ibid.*

9 *DPP v Yamanoha* [1994] 1 IR 565.

10 The key issue in the case was the swearing of the information grounding the search warrant after – rather than before – tendering the necessary evidence to the peace commissioner.

11 *DPP v Cash* [2007] IEHC 108, at para 28.

Business Premises

8–09 Though business premises open to the public may be entered by gardaí for the purpose of making enquiries in the ordinary course of their duties,[12] if they are to go further and search a premises, a warrant or a specific power is required. In *Simple Imports Ltd v Revenue Commissioners*[13] the Supreme Court endorsed the dictum of Camden CJ in *Entick v Carrington*[14] that:

> "Our law holds the property of every man so sacred, that no man can set his foot upon his neighbour's close without his leave: if he does he is a trespasser, though he does no damage at all: if he will tread upon his neighbour's ground he must justify it by law." [15]

The consequence of *Simple Imports* was to hold that protection against unjustified searches and seizures is not confined to the dwelling of the citizen: it extends to every person's private property.

Apartment Complexes

8–10 The Irish courts do not appear to have examined in depth the particular issues concerning the entry of gardaí to the common areas surrounding apartment complexes. However, the case of *Forbes*[16] (considered below) is perhaps supportive of the argument that the gardaí have an implied authority to enter, depending on the degree to which those areas are freely accessible to the public. Apartment complexes are frequently in the ownership of third parties—management companies or local authorities—whose consent for the gardaí to enter in the course of their duties might, on the basis of *Forbes,* be implied. The issue was considered in the English case of *Knox v Anderton,*[17] which concerned a prosecution for possession of an offensive weapon in a public place. The issue under consideration was whether the landing of a block of flats constituted a 'public place' within the meaning of the Prevention of Crime Act 1953. 'Public place' was defined in the Act as follows:

> "In this section 'public place' includes any highway and any other premises or place to which at the material time the public have or are permitted to have access, whether on payment or otherwise..."

8–11 In *Knox*, the area in question was local authority housing, comprising approximately 420 flats, with four floors in each block and, in each block, numerous stairways giving access to each level. It was asserted that the complex did not constitute a public place, but rather the complex was a private place, the property of the council, which gave certain limited rights of access and passage simply to tenants of the estate and their visitors.

---

[12] *Minister for Justice v Wang Zhu Jie* [1991] ILRM 823.

[13] *Simple Imports Ltd v Revenue Commissioners* [2000] 2 IR 243 at 250.

[14] *Entick v Carrington* [1765] 2 Wils 275.

[15] *ibid.*

[16] *DPP v Forbes* [1994] 2 IR 542 at 548 *per* O'Flaherty J (Finlay CJ, Egan, Blayney and Denham JJ concurring).

[17] *Knox v Anderton* (1982) 76 Cr App R 156.

The stairways and landings of the estate, it was argued, could be severed from other parts of the estate in that their sole use was to gain access to the flats, and not to any public facility. The prosecutor argued that the flats were a public place, and this submission was accepted by the Court. The defendant appealed unsuccessfully. Webster J, giving the judgment of the Court, noted:

> "There is nothing to prevent a member of the public from entering the estate, there is nothing to stop members of the public from entering the stairways of the blocks of flats, there is no barrier to prevent members of the public walking along the landings which give access to the individual flats, and there are no doors to the stairways or landings, which are open to the atmosphere. There are no notices to suggest that there is any restriction of access to the landings or stairways or to the whole estate except that there are notices on some of the buildings at the entrance to the estate which read 'Parking of vehicles above 10 cwt on the estate is Prohibited, Access is restricted to tenants and their visitors only.'"[18]

The Court held: **8–12**

> "At what point, short of the front door of the individual flats, can it be said as a matter of inevitable inference from those facts, to have ceased to have been a public place before the landings are reached? In our view there is no inevitable inference that it ceased to become a public place at any point before the landings are reached, in view of the justices' findings that there was nothing to stop members of the public from entering the stairways of the blocks, that there was no barrier to prevent members of the public walking along the landings which give access to the individual flats, that there were no doors to the stairways or landings which were open to the atmosphere and that there were no notices to suggest that there was any restriction of access to the landings and stairways or indeed to the whole estate except the notices posted on some of the buildings at the entrance to the estate to which we have already referred. For all these reasons we would, slightly rewording the question for the opinion of this court, answer it by saying that the justices have not been shown to have made any error of law in finding that the landings were a public place..."[19]

In the subsequent case in the same jurisdiction of *Heads v Chief Constable of Humberside Police*[20] the issue of whether an apartment complex is a public place was revisited. *Heads* arose out of a disturbance in the appellant's flat to which the police were called. The estate was divided into blocks of six flats, each of which had a communal entrance and then landings and stairs leading up to the floors. The entrances to the flats had aluminium doors, with glass panels and fitted locks. The lock to the door of the appellant's block was left open during the day, and usually but not always locked at night. When the police were called, they gained entry to the block without any difficulty by walking through the unlocked communal door. They arrested the appellant for public order offences, and he appealed on the ground that the complex was not a public place. His appeal was dismissed, Hirst J holding: **8–13**

---

18 *ibid*, at 160.

19 *ibid*, at 161-162.

20 *Heads v Chief Constable of Humberside Police*, unreported, Queen's Bench Division, 12 May 1986.

> "When one looks at the purpose of the statute, which is to provide a comparatively simple means of controlling disagreeable behaviour where members of the public are likely to be – and I would underline the words 'where members of the public are likely to be' – it seems perfectly reasonable to read the definition of 'public place' in the way in which the Justices did, namely, to treat it as meaning a place to which the public, unless they are forbidden, are permitted to enter as freely as they wish, subject only to the right of the owner of the premises to exclude particular individuals if he so minded. It would include a shop and a wide range of premises… there will be places where the public can be excluded, but when they are not excluded they are a 'public place' for the purposes of the definition contained in the Act."[21]

Obiter, Stocker LJ agreed, but stated

> "I would not for my part be prepared to assume that in every case a landing or staircase of a block of flats will always constitute a public place. Each case depends on its own facts."[22]

8–14 His reservation seems to suggest that, the greater the degree of exclusion of members of the public, the greater the probability that an apartment complex will be considered private property. If, for instance, there are locked gates, access codes required or locked doors impeding entry to stairs in apartment blocks, the argument that such areas constitute public places is much harder to make.

ENTRY BY CONSENT

Owners and Occupiers

8–15 Owners and occupiers may consent to the entry of gardaí to their premises. Where there are multiple occupiers, the consent of one will suffice to authorise entry.[23] Furnishing permission to the gardaí to enter creates a licence to enter. As Stone puts it: "Few problems arise as regards an express licence created verbally, except on the evidential level of what exactly was said."[24] Given the scope for disagreement subsequently on the permission given, where searches are conducted with the consent of the owner or occupier, it ought to be explained to the persons whose home is to be searched that they are under no obligation to submit to the search, and the occupier's permission to conduct the search should be recorded in writing. Signing the garda's notebook setting out the basis of the entry will suffice.

Rented Premises and Dwellings

8–16 Gardaí frequently search rented premises and dwellings. Where it is suspected that the tenants are engaged in criminal activity, the consent of the owner or landlord will be of questionable validity in the absence of a search warrant, or the consent of the lawful occupier or tenant. While the straightforward consent of a landlord might be easier to

---

21 *Heads v Chief Constable of Humberside Police,* unreported, Queen's Bench Division, 12 May 1986.

22 *ibid.*

23 *DPP v McCloskey,* unreported, High Court, 6 February 1984; *DPP v Delaney* [1996] 3 IR 556 (HC); [1997] IR 453 (SC).

24 R Stone, *The Law of Entry Search and Seizure* (4th ed, Oxford University Press, Oxford, 2005) at p 8.

obtain than a search warrant, gardaí should be mindful that the constitutional protection set out in Article 40.5 that "[t]he dwelling of every citizen is inviolable and shall not be forcibly entered save in accordance with law" is a bulwark against intrusion into the home and a significant safeguard for the individual. While it may be arguable that an apartment used as a brothel, or a house in which a cannabis factory is in advanced operation, is more accurately described as a business premises than a dwelling, in order to ensure the admissibility of any evidence found therein, a search warrant is always preferable to the consent of the landlord.

IMPLIED AUTHORITY FOR ENTRY

There is considered to be implied authority for gardaí to enter the curtilage of private property for the prevention and detection of crime, a clear delineation being drawn between the private house and the area which surrounds it. In *DPP v Forbes*[25] the Supreme Court stated: **8–17**

> "It must be regarded as axiomatic that any householder gives an implied authority to a member of the Garda to come onto the forecourt of his premises to see to the enforcement of the law or prevent a breach thereof. It will be clear that this case is not concerned with any question of entering a dwellinghouse and, therefore, there is not in the instant case any question of any form of implied waiver of any constitutional right... Further, like any implied authority, it is an implication which the evidence may, on occasion, rebut. Clearly, in this case, the Gardaí were acting in the execution of their duties. They saw a car which was driven suspiciously, to say the least; it went up a side road and into the driveway of a private dwelling. Could it be said what danger the driver of such a car might have posed for the occupants of that dwelling house? In the circumstances of this case, the Gardaí were clearly acting in the execution of their duties. This must be the acid test because they cannot be regarded as acting in the execution of their duties if they breach anyone's constitutional or legal rights (unless in an extreme situation, such as in the defence of life or limb). For them to have ignored the defendant's conduct on this occasion would have bordered on a dereliction of duty on their part. To suggest that they would be perfectly entitled to arrest the defendant if he was on the public road but not if he was on a third party's property would constitute, as was suggested in the course of the debate before us, a massive absurdity."

Opening a car door in the driveway of a suspect's home was held to be permissible in the case of *DPP v O'Sullivan*.[26] Referring to the need for gardaí to do everything in their power to combat drink driving, Herbert J held that: **8–18**

> "If the members of the Garda Síochána have, by common law, an implied authority to come onto the driveway of a private dwelling to see to the enforcement of the law or prevent a breach thereof, that authority must also entitle them to do whatever is additionally necessary on that driveway for that purpose, provided they do not act arbitrarily, capriciously or in an unlawful manner."

---

25 *DPP v Forbes* [1994] 2 IR 542 at 548 *per* O'Flaherty J (Finlay CJ, Egan, Blayney and Denham JJ concurring).

26 *DPP v O'Sullivan* [2007] IEHC 248.

8–19 The actions of the garda in opening in the car door were found not to have been arbitrary or capricious and the judge was satisfied that, in the present state of the law, the garda was not acting illegally or in breach of any constitutional right of the defendant, when she entered and remained on the driveway of the defendant's private dwelling house and when she opened the door of his car.

REFUSAL OF ENTRY

8–20 Given the private status of property, entry may be refused (unless the place has been designated a crime scene) or a statutory power to enter (for instance for arrest) is being invoked. The implied authority to enter may be revoked. In *DPP v Gaffney*[27] an arrest in a private house to which the gardaí had pursued the defendant was found by the Supreme Court to be unlawful because the owner of the house (the defendant's brother) had twice denied gardaí permission to enter the premises. In *DPP v Molloy*[28] the Supreme Court held that the arresting garda formed the opinion that the defendant was incapable of having proper control of the vehicle in a public place only when he had spoken to and observed him in his own driveway. In response to caution, the defendant told the garda that the garda could not arrest him as, having been followed onto his driveway, the arrest was unlawful. Any implied consent to the garda being on his driveway was thereby withdrawn. Accordingly, the garda was a trespasser and the arrest was unlawful. Whereas at the time the garda entered the property he was doing so on the basis of an implied authority, such authority was invalid at the time of the defendant's arrest. The case followed *DPP v McCreesh*,[29] where, in similar circumstances on being told that he was under arrest, the defendant advised the garda that he was on private property and was trespassing, and that he should leave immediately. There Hederman J had held:

> "… the defendant did not give leave or licence to the Garda to enter the driveway of his premises, the Garda was, on these authorities, undoubtedly a trespasser thereon and no other conclusion is open. Any doubt in this respect which might have arisen was put at rest when the defendant informed the Garda that he was a trespasser and should leave the premises. Applying to the facts in this case the principle stated in the passages cited from the speeches in *Morris v. Beardmore* [1981] A.C. 446, which had the approval of Henchy J. in *Director of Public Prosecutions v. Gaffney* [1987] IR 173, in my opinion the arrest of the defendant was not a lawful arrest. If it had been intended by the Oireachtas to confer on a member of the Garda the power to make inroads on the property rights of citizens which are recognised and protected by the common law, and to enter on private property against the will of the owner and there arrest the owner, express provision should have been made for such power in section 49. As the validity of the arrest is the essential question in the case, I would answer question (b) by stating that the Gardaí were trespassers on the occasion in question and the arrest of the defendant was not a valid arrest."[30]

[27] *DPP v Gaffney* [1987] IR 173.
[28] *DPP v Molloy* [2004] 3 IR 321.
[29] *DPP v McCreesh* [1992] 2 IR 239.
[30] *ibid.*

Therefore, remaining on premises where the right of entry has been refused or revoked renders gardaí trespassers and liable to be sued. Any purported exercise of powers of arrest or detention will be unlawful, unless a statutory basis for presence on the property can be established.[31] **8–21**

The question of whether gardaí are entitled to enter the dwelling of a third party to effect an arrest was considered by the High Court in the case of *DPP v Delaney*.[32] There the defendant was arrested in his brother's house on suspicion of drink driving. He had been chased by the gardaí, who accepted that they had entered the house without permission. The arresting garda formed no opinion of the commission of any offence until after entry was gained to the dwelling, which at the time of entry the gardaí believed was the defendant's house. Statutory authority to enter private property to investigate suspected offences of driving while intoxicated was at that time provided by s 39(2) of the Road Traffic Act 1994: **8–22**

> "A member of the Garda Síochána may for the purpose of arresting a person under section 49(8) or 50(10) of the Principal Act, enter without warrant (if need be by use of reasonable force) any place (including the curtilage of a dwelling, but not including a dwelling) where the person is or where the member, with reasonable cause, suspects him to be."[33]

The defendant argued that s 39 (2) did not distinguish as to the ownership of the private property and accordingly the express restriction on entering the dwelling applied whether or not the person arrested was the owner of the property. The offence in question, including the power of arrest, was governed by a statutory regime and so, if the arrest was outside that regime, the prosecution must fail. It was submitted that the obligation to give a sample under s 13 of the Road Traffic Act 1994 only arose when there was a valid arrest. The prosecution argued that the District Judge had discretion to admit the evidence, submitting that the section was widely drawn, and was intended to address the situation where the owner of the property was the person arrested. Even if the arrest was illegal, there had been no infringement of the defendant's constitutional rights, as the guarantee of the inviolability of the dwelling could only be invoked by the person whose dwelling it was. In the High Court, Ó Caoimh J held, that, while the gardaí could have effected an arrest within the curtilage of the dwelling house, having regard to the provisions of s 39(2), that power did not extend to a right to enter the dwelling. **8–23**

---

31 Such as entry for arrest pursuant to s 6 of the Criminal Law Act 1997.

32 *DPP v Delaney* [2003] 1 IR 363.

33 The section was repealed by s 33 of the Road Traffic Act 2010 and replaced by s 7 of the same Act.

STATUTORY POWERS OF ENTRY

Power of Forcible Entry for Arrest – Section 6 of the Criminal Law Act 1997

8–24 An express statutory power of forcible entry for arrest was introduced by s 6 of the Criminal Law Act 1997, which applies both to arrests under warrant and arrests without warrant for arrestable offences[34] subject to certain conditions.

8–25 Section 6(1) provides for entry where an arrest under an arrest warrant or order of committal is to be effected:

> "For the purpose of arresting a person on foot of a warrant of arrest or an order of committal, a member of the Garda Síochána may enter (if need be, by use of reasonable force) and search any premises (including a dwelling) where the person is or where the member, with reasonable cause, suspects that person to be…"

A warrant for the arrest of a person or an order of committal may be executed by a member of the Garda Síochána, notwithstanding that it is not in the member's possession at the time, but the warrant or order must be shown to him or her as soon as practicable.[35]

8–26 Section 6(2) provides for entry for the purpose of arrest for an arrestable offence:

> "For the purpose of arresting a person without a warrant for an arrestable offence, a member of the Garda Síochána may enter (if need be, by use of reasonable force) and search any premises (including a dwelling) where that person is or where the member, with reasonable cause, suspects that person to be, and where the premises is a dwelling the member shall not, unless acting with the consent of an occupier of the dwelling or other person who appears to the member to be in charge of the dwelling, enter that dwelling unless—
> (a) he or she or another such member has observed the person within or entering the dwelling, or
> (b) he or she, with reasonable cause, suspects that before a warrant of arrest could be obtained the person will either abscond for the purpose of avoiding justice or will obstruct the course of justice, or
> (c) he or she, with reasonable cause, suspects that before a warrant of arrest could be obtained the person would commit an arrestable offence, or
> (d) the person ordinarily resides at that dwelling."

8–27 If it is intended to arrest an occupier of the house, at the outset gardaí must clearly inform the owner that they are seeking to gain entry on that basis. In *The People (DPP) v Laide and Ryan*,[36] gardaí were not subsequently able to rely on their statutory

[34] An arrestable offence is defined in s 1 of the Criminal Law Act 1997 as being "an offence for which a person of full capacity and not previously convicted may, under or by virtue of any enactment, be punished by imprisonment for a term of five years or by a more severe penalty and includes an attempt to commit any such offence".

[35] Criminal Law Act 1997, s 5.

[36] *The People (DPP) v Laide and Ryan* [2005] 1 IR 209.

power of forced entry to remedy a defect which rendered their original entry on foot of a search warrant invalid. The Court of Criminal Appeal held:

> "Entry was gained to the house on that morning on foot of the search warrant. No other basis of entry was proffered to the parents on arrival. The finding that the warrant was bad has therefore removed the very foundation on which the entry was made, and in the absence of the Gardaí informing the occupiers of the house that they had another purpose apart from searching, namely the arresting of the second accused, it is the view of this court that the power provided by s. 6(2) of the Act of 1997 cannot be relied upon since it was never invoked by the Gardaí at the time. The fact that the power of entry exists does not mean, in the view of this court, that the purpose of entry, namely the arrest of somebody who resides in the house, does not have to be explained before entry is forced on foot of the power. The inviolability of a citizen's dwelling is an important constitutional right and it cannot be trespassed upon without explanation in clear and unambiguous terms. It has been recognised that where the restriction of a constitutional right is permitted by law, it must be restricted to the least extent necessary for the achievement of the desired objective."[37]

Section 6 of the Criminal Law Act 1997 operates without prejudice to other powers of **8–28** search and arrest.[38] If gardaí are present in a dwelling, having been invited inside, there is nothing to preclude them from arresting a person present once the requisite conditions for the exercise of an arrest power are met.

Entry Under the Road Traffic Acts

Section 39(1) of the Road Traffic Act 1994 provides a power of entry for the arrest of a **8–29** driver suspected of a 'hit and run' causing injury, which extends even to a dwelling house:

> "A member of the Garda Síochána may for the purpose of arresting a person under section 106 (3A) (inserted by this Act) of the Principal Act, enter without warrant (if need be by use of reasonable force) any place (including a dwelling) where the person is or where the member, with reasonable cause, suspects him to be and, in case the place is a dwelling, the member shall not so enter unless he or another such member has observed the person enter the dwelling concerned."

Section 39(2) of the Road Traffic 1994 had provided a power of entry onto the curtilage **8–30** of premises for the investigation of 'drink driving' offences, but the section has been repealed[39] and replaced by s 7 of the Road Traffic Act 2010, which provides:

> "A member of the Garda Síochána for the purpose of—

---

[37] *ibid.*

[38] Criminal Law Act 1997, s 6(3).

[39] Road Traffic Act 2010, s 33.

(a) making a requirement of a person under section 9(1)[40] or 10(4),[41] or

(b) arresting a person under section 4(8),[42] 5(10)[43] or 6(4),[44] may enter without warrant (if need be by use of reasonable force) any place (including the curtilage of a dwelling

---

[40] The Road Traffic Act 2010 provides at s 9(1):
"9(1) Where a member of the Garda Síochána–
(a) is of opinion that a person in charge of a vehicle in a public place—
(i) has consumed intoxicating liquor, the member shall require, or
(ii) (I) is or has, with the vehicle, been involved in a collision, or
(II) is committing or has committed an offence under the Road Traffic Acts 1961 to 2010, the member may require,
or
(b) attends at the scene of an event which has occurred in a public place in which injury appears or is claimed to have been caused to a person of such nature as to require medical assistance for the person at the scene of the event or for the person to be brought to a hospital for medical assistance and a vehicle was involved in the event, the member shall, subject to subsection (2), require, the person in charge of the vehicle—
(i) to provide, by exhaling into an apparatus for indicating the presence of alcohol in the breath, a specimen of his or her breath in the manner indicated by the member,
(ii) to accompany him or her to a place (including a vehicle) near the scene of the collision and there to provide, by exhaling into such an apparatus, a specimen of his or her breath in the manner indicated by the member, or
(iii) where the member does not have such an apparatus with him or her, to remain at that place in his or her presence or in the presence of another member of the Garda Síochána until such an apparatus becomes available to him or her (for a period that does not exceed one hour) and to provide, by exhaling into the apparatus, a specimen of his or her breath in the manner indicated by the member."

[41] The Road Traffic Act 2010 provides at s 10(4):
"10(4) A member of the Garda Síochána, who is on duty at a checkpoint, may stop any vehicle at the checkpoint and, without prejudice to any other powers (including the powers under section 9) conferred on him or her by statute or at common law, may require a person in charge of the vehicle"
(a) to—
(i) provide (by exhaling into an apparatus for indicating the presence of alcohol in the breath) a specimen of his or her breath, or
(ii) accompany him or her or another member of the Garda Síochána to a place (including a vehicle) at or in the vicinity of the checkpoint and there to provide, by exhaling into such an apparatus, a specimen of his or her breath,
or
(b) to—
(i) leave the vehicle at the place where it has been stopped, or
(ii) move it to a place in the vicinity of the checkpoint, and keep or leave it there until the person has complied with a requirement made of him or her under paragraph (a)."

[42] The Road Traffic Act 2010 provides at s 4(8) a power of arrest without warrant for driving or attempting to drive a mechanically propelled vehicle in a public place while under the influence of an intoxicant to such an extent as to be incapable of having proper control of the vehicle.

[43] The Road Traffic Act 2010 provides at s 5(10) a power of arrest without warrant for being in charge of a mechanically propelled vehicle in a public place with intent to drive or attempt to drive the vehicle (but not driving or attempting to drive it), while under the influence of an intoxicant to such an extent as to be incapable of having proper control of the vehicle.

[44] The Road Traffic Act 2010 provides at s 6(4) a power of arrest without warrant for driving or attempting to drive an animal-drawn vehicle or a pedal cycle while under the influence of an intoxicant to such an extent as to be incapable of having proper control of the vehicle or cycle.

> but not the dwelling) where the person is or where the member, with reasonable cause, suspects him or her to be."

However it would seem clear from the decision in *DPP v Molloy*[45] that it is crucial that the garda must have formed an opinion on the intoxication of the suspect before entering the private property. The decision related to the earlier version of the power under s 39(2) of the Road Traffic Act 1994, but the reasoning would extend equally to the recast power in s 7 of the Road Traffic Act 2010. **8–31**

Entry in the Event of Fire

The Fire Services Act 1981 provides for cooperation between members of the gardaí and the fire brigade, and for the person in charge at a fire to take such actions (either personally, by a member of a fire brigade, by a member of the Garda Síochána or by another authorised person) as are considered necessary or expedient for extinguishing the fire or protecting or rescuing persons or property. Section 28 provides that they may use force if necessary and, in particular, may: **8–32**

> "(a) enter any land or building in which there is reason to believe fire has broken out or the emergency exists or any other land or building;
>
> (b) cause any land or building to be vacated by the occupants;
>
> (c) pull down or demolish any building or part of a building;
>
> (d) use any water supply, whether public or private;
>
> (e) take water from any watercourse, lake, pond or other source, whether natural or artificial;
>
> (f) remove anything from the vicinity of the fire or other emergency."

There is also a duty on gardaí to enter a dwelling to protect the right to life.[46] As O'Flaherty J put it in *DPP v Delaney*, "the safeguarding of life and limb must be more important than the inviolability of the dwelling of a citizen".[47]

Offences Relating to Animals

The Animal Health and Welfare Act 2013 will, on commencement, provide gardaí with a number of important powers in the investigation of offences relating to animal welfare and the control of animal disease. Powers of entry are vested in authorised officers under the Act, with 'authorised officer' defined to include gardaí and officers of Customs and Excise.[48] Section 38 allows for the entry and inspection of any land and premises (except a private dwelling) where there are reasonable grounds for suspecting: **8–33**

---

45 *DPP v Molloy* [2004] 3 IR 321.

46 *DPP v Delaney* [1996] 3 IR 556 (HC); [1997] 3 IR 453.

47 *ibid.*

48 Animal Health and Welfare Act 2013, s 1.

(i) that an animal, animal product or animal feed is, may be or has been present,
(ii) a record relating to an animal, animal product or animal feed is, may be or has been present, or
(iii) equipment, machinery or other thing used in connection with an animal, animal product or animal feed is, may be or has been present.

8–34 Animals and products and equipment relating to them may be examined. Persons in possession of animals or items and equipment associated with them may be required to give their names and addresses and to provide any records or documentation which may be reasonably required. There is no requirement of suspicion that an offence has actually been committed for the power of entry to be exercised. If there are reasonable grounds to believe that there is a risk of disease or that an offence is being or has been committed under the Act, authorised officers may go beyond entry and may search the land, premises, vehicle, vessel, aircraft, railway wagon, container, equipment or machinery. They may also require the person in charge of a vehicle or vessel to refrain from moving it, or to move it to a location to facilitate a search, and may require information concerning the place of departure, journey or destination. Samples may be taken, animals and associated products may be seized and detained, as may vehicles, vessels and other conveyances to permit an inspection or a search.

8–35 Section 38(5) makes the distinction between dwellings and other premises clear, providing that a private dwelling will not be searched without a search warrant (under s 45 of the Act) or the consent of the occupier, unless there are reasonable grounds to believe that, before a search warrant could be sought, any evidence of an offence under the Act is being or is likely to be disposed of or destroyed.

8–36 In addition to their powers under the Animal Health and Welfare Act 2013, gardaí may enter any premises or land to inspect, examine or test animals which are bred or kept for the production of food, wool, skin, fur or feathers or for use in, or for the purposes of, the farming of land or of animal husbandry under s 8 of the Protection of Animals Kept for Farming Purposes Act 1984. The Control of Horses Act 1996 also provides at s 34(1) for gardaí to stop vehicles and to enter and search vehicles and premises (excluding dwellings) where there is reasonable cause to suspect that an offence is being or has been committed under the Control of Horses Act 1996 in or on any premises or vehicle, or a person is causing harm to or mistreating a horse on any premises or in any vehicle.[49] Equipment may be brought onto the premises as necessary, and the gardaí may bring persons onto the premises as required to assist them in the performance of their duties.[50] A search warrant (under s 35 of the Act) is required if the premises to be entered is a dwelling, unless gardaí have obtained the consent of the occupier.[51] A horse may also be seized or detained if there is reason to suspect it is a stray, causing a nuisance, not under adequate control, posing a danger to persons or property, a threat to the health and welfare of persons or other animals, being kept in a control area

[49] Control of Horses Act 1996, s 34(1).
[50] *ibid,* s 34(2).
[51] *ibid,* s 34(3).

without a licence entitling the horse to be kept in that area, or not identifiable or capable of identification, as may be required by section 28 of the 1996 Act, or in, or being kept or ridden or driven in, an area contrary to any by-laws made under s 47 of the 1996 Act.

Other provisions which provide powers of entry and inspection in the context of animal welfare and food production include s 9 of the Slaughter of Animals Act 1935; s 54(1) of the Abattoirs Act 1988; s 5 of the Control of Bulls for Breeding Act 1985; s 17A of the Diseases of Animals Act 1966 as inserted by s 2(1) of the Diseases of Animals (Amendment) Act 2001. It should be noted, however, that the Animal Health and Welfare Act 2013 provides at s 4 and Schedule 1 for the repeal of the Slaughter of Animals Act 1935, the Control of Bulls for Breeding Act 1985 and the Diseases of Animals (Amendment) Act 2001. As outlined above, at the time of writing the 2013 Act had not yet been commenced. **8–37**

Entry to Public Dances

A key power for entering nightclubs is provided by s 13(1) of the Public Dance Halls Act 1935 which provides: **8–38**

> "13.—(1) Any member of the Gárda Síochána in uniform may enter any place in respect of which a public dancing licence is for the time being in force at any time while such place is being used for public dancing or at any other reasonable time and there make such inspection, examination, and inquiry as he shall think proper."

Obstructing or preventing a garda from exercising the entry power is an offence, as are attempts to do so.[52]

Section 13A was inserted into the 1935 Act by s 9 of the Criminal Justice (Drug Trafficking) Act 1996 to provide for entry for the detection or prevention of drug trafficking offence. Section 13A provides: **8–39**

> "13A.—(1) Any member of the Garda Síochána whether in uniform or not may enter any place in respect of which a public dancing licence is for the time being in force at any time while such place is being used for public dancing or at any other reasonable time and there make such inspection, examination and inquiry as he shall think proper for the prevention or detection of a drug trafficking offence within the meaning of section 3 (1) of the Criminal Justice Act, 1994."

As with the original power, obstruction and attempted obstruction are offences.[53]

Miscellaneous Powers of Entry for Inspection

Numerous pieces of legislation provide for gardaí to enter and examine licences, registers and records in business premises. Further entry powers include s 38 of the Gaming and Lotteries Act 1956; s 17 of the Sea Fisheries and Maritime Jurisdiction Act 2006; s 26 of the Betting Act 1931; s 46(1) of the Pawnbrokers Act 1964 and s 24 of the Misuse of Drugs Act 1977. **8–40**

---

52 Public Dance Halls Act 1935, s 13(2).

53 *ibid*, s 13A(2) as inserted by s 9 of the Criminal Justice (Drug Trafficking) Act 1996.

CHAPTER 9

Entry Under Search Warrant

INTRODUCTION

A search warrant is a document which sets out the legal basis for entry to a dwelling or other premises. It authorises entry to search for, and frequently to seize, evidence related to a particular offence under investigation, within a specified and finite period of time. Gardaí may be given consent to search private property; a search warrant entitles gardaí (or in certain circumstance other agencies) to enter, search and seize evidence without the consent of the owner or occupier. Entry without an express or implied invitation, or without a search warrant or a valid statutory basis for entry amounts to trespassing.[1] **9–01**

As is the case with many garda powers, the legal scheme underpinning search warrants is unduly complex. Writing in 1983, Ryan and Magee lamented that "it is almost impossible to schematise the conditions under which search warrants may be issued, as the empowering provisions differ so widely in their provisions".[2] The situation has not been improved in the three intervening decades. Noting that the gardaí are authorised by 100 separate Acts and almost 200 ministerial regulations to apply to the District Court for search warrants, the Law Reform Commission has provisionally **9–02**

[1] *DPP v McMahon* [1986] IR 393.
[2] Ryan and Magee, *The Irish Criminal Process* (Mercier Press, Dublin, 1983) p 148.

recommended the adoption of a framework to govern search warrants in Ireland, stating that

> "having considered the current search warrant scheme and, most notably, identifying the vast array of search warrant provisions which exist in Ireland, the Commission is of the view that a standard search warrant framework should be implemented in Ireland".[3]

9–03 Such a framework is undoubtedly necessary — both in the context of personal searches and search warrants — to give a clear elucidation of the rules, to standardise procedures and clarify the law relating to searches so as to make the law accessible for both gardaí and those who are subjected to searches. The basics ought to be set in stone, since this is a fundamental aspect of garda practice, but instead the law concerning searches is constantly evolving. A strict exclusionary rule has been combined with the piecemeal accumulation of multiple overlapping powers to search individuals and the premises they occupy. As a consequence, a large volume of complicated and occasionally incoherent and contradictory case-law has developed,[4] and therefore determining which errors invalidate a search warrant and which errors will not is far from straightforward.

9–04 Depending on the legislative provision under which they are authorised, search warrants may be issued by judges, peace commissioners or senior members of An Garda Síochána. There is no uniformity in the duration of a warrant, nor in relation to the rank of the garda who may apply for a warrant. They are not of a standard format. Given that that is the case, it is intended to focus in detail here on only the most frequently used search warrant provisions. Before the provisions permitting search warrants are examined, the basic aspects of the application for, issue and execution of search warrants are considered. Errors in search warrants are considered, as the exclusionary rule is most often seen to operate where, as a consequence of its application, the evidence obtained on foot of an invalid search warrant is excluded at trial.

The Exclusionary Rule and Errors in Search Warrants

9–05 It is in this area of garda practice that the stringent effects of the Irish exclusionary rule are most keenly felt, when evidence gathered under a search warrant is excluded at trial on the basis that it was obtained in breach of the constitutional rights of the accused — in this context, the constitutionally protected inviolability of the dwelling. Put briefly, the exclusionary rule will apply to exclude evidence where (a) there has been a breach of the constitutional rights of the accused; (b) there is a causative link between the breach and the evidence gathered, that is to say that the evidence would not have been obtained if the right in question had not been breached; and (c) there are no extraordinary excusing circumstances. The prosecution bears the burden of establishing that the

---

[3] Law Reform Commission, *Consultation Paper on Search Warrants and Bench Warrants* (LRC, Dublin, CP 58 – 2009), December 2009, at p 37.

[4] See T O'Malley, *The Criminal Process* (Round Hall, Dublin, 2009) at p 352.

evidence which is sought to be adduced is admissible,[5] that a breach of constitutional rights has not occurred[6] or, if it has, that there were extraordinary excusing circumstances by which the breach can be justified.[7]

A distinction was drawn between illegally and unconstitutionally obtained evidence in the seminal case of *People (AG) v O'Brien*: **9–06**

> "Where evidence is found to have been illegally obtained, i.e. in breach of the legal rights of the suspect, the inclusion or exclusion of such evidence is a matter for the discretion of the trial judge; and
>
> where evidence is deemed to have been obtained in breach of the constitutional rights of a suspect it must be automatically excluded from evidence, unless there are extraordinary excusing circumstances in existence which would justify its admission; in which case, admission or inclusion is a matter for the discretion of the trial judge."[8]

This remains the essential rule today. A deliberate and conscious breach of a constitutional right results in an automatic exclusion, whereas the infringement of a legal right will be a matter for the trial judge.

In *O'Brien*, evidence had been obtained following the search of a private dwelling which had been misdescribed on the search warrant. Whereas the correct address was "118 Captain's Road, Crumlin," the warrant incorrectly referred to "118 Cashel Road, Crumlin." The Court found that the error had been inadvertent. Kingsmill Moore J took the view that a trial judge ought to have discretion in deciding whether or not to admit unconstitutionally obtained evidence, but Walsh J held that evidence obtained in deliberate and conscious breach of the constitutional rights of an accused person should be absolutely inadmissible save in extraordinary excusing circumstances: **9–07**

> "In my view evidence obtained in deliberate conscious breach of the constitutional rights of an accused person should, save in the excusable circumstances outlined above, be absolutely inadmissible. It follows therefore that evidence obtained without a deliberate and conscious violation of the accused's constitutional rights is not excludable by reason only of the violation of his constitutional right."[9]

The parameters of the rule have been grappled with for decades. There having been judicial controversy and disagreement as to the meaning of the terms "conscious and deliberate",[10] the rule was revisited in *People (DPP) v Kenny*.[11] Finlay CJ delivered the majority judgment, holding: **9–08**

---

[5] *People (DPP) v Dillon* [2003] 1 ILRM 531.

[6] *People (DPP) v Madden* [1977] IR 336.

[7] *People (DPP) v Walsh* 1980 IR 294.

[8] *People (AG) v O'Brien* [1965] IR 142.

[9] *O'Brien v Attorney General* [1965] IR 142 at 170.

[10] See D McGrath, *Evidence* (Thomson Round Hall, Dublin, 2005) at p 340, citing *People (DPP) v Shaw* [1982] IR 1 and *People (DPP) v Healy* [1990] 2 IR 73; [1990] ILRM 313.

[11] *People (DPP) v Kenny* [1990] 2 IR 110.

> "the correct principle is that evidence obtained by invasion of the constitutional personal rights of a citizen must be excluded unless a court is satisfied that either the act constituting the breach of constitutional rights was committed unintentionally or accidentally, or is satisfied that there are extraordinary excusing circumstances which justify the admission of the evidence in its (the court's) discretion".[12]

9–09 The effect of *Kenny* was to hold that a deliberate and conscious breach of the constitutional right had occurred, regardless of whether the breach of the right was intentional. The gardaí in *Kenny* had not realised that they were encroaching on the constitutional rights of the accused, but their actions in forcibly entering the dwelling were neither unintentional nor accidental, and so the evidence obtained in the course of the search ought to have been excluded.

9–10 The kinds of extraordinary excusing circumstances which might allow the admission of evidence obtained in breach of constitutional rights were stated in *O'Brien* to include the preservation of vital evidence in imminent danger of destruction, the need to rescue a victim in peril and evidence obtained by a search incidental to and contemporaneous with a lawful arrest, although made without a valid search warrant.[13]

9–11 Carney J outlined the import of search warrants and the need for an unforgiving and strict approach to their interpretation in *DPP v Dunne*,[14] holding that:

> "the constitutional protection of the inviolability of the dwellinghouse is one of the most important, clear and unqualified protections given by the Constitution to the citizen. If it is to be set aside by a printed form issued by a non-judicial personage it would appear to me to be essential that the form should be in clear, complete, accurate and unambiguous terms."

9–12 These criteria — clarity, completeness, accuracy and certainty — are the basic prerequisites for a valid search warrant. However, as the jurisprudence has evolved, a less pedantic approach to minor errors can be seen emerging. Murphy J referred to *Dunne* in the case of *The People (DPP) v Balfe*[15]:

> "While it must be recognised that the jurisprudence relating to 'the deliberate and conscious violation of constitutional rights' is still evolving, it is clear that a search warrant which innocently but vitally misdescribes premises which may be searched on foot thereof is not without operative effect. Property seized in innocent reliance thereon may be admissible in evidence on a subsequent criminal charge."[16]

---

[12] *ibid* at 134.

[13] *People (AG) v O'Brien* [1965] IR 142 at 170. See further D McGrath, *Evidence* (Thomson Round Hall, Dublin, 2005) at p 335 *et seq.*

[14] *DPP v Dunne* [1994] 2 IR 537.

[15] *The People (DPP) v Balfe* [1998] 4 IR 50.

[16] *ibid* at 59.

In *Balfe*, it was held that, where evidence has been obtained in the absence of any deliberate treachery, imposition, deceit or illegality, it is properly admitted.[17] The case muddied the waters, since in *Balfe*[18] it was found that errors did not necessarily invalidate a warrant so as to exclude evidence obtained in reliance on it. It was argued in the case of *Mallon*[19] that *Balfe* had been superseded by the decision in *DPP v Edgeworth,*[20] which concerned the signature of a peace commissioner. In *Mallon21* it was held that, while it was inappropriate for a warrant issued by a peace commissioner to bear the words "The District Court," the appearance of the words did not breach any statutory requirement as to the form of the warrant and did not mislead, where the status of the person issuing the warrant appeared clearly on its face and did not, therefore, affect the validity of the warrant. The many decisions in the area are not easily reconciled, since it is difficult to determine whether an error is an invalidating error or one of little consequence. The stringency of the *Kenny* decision has been lamented, with calls in some quarters for revision of the strict exclusionary rule it set down. A majority of the Balance in the Criminal Law Review Group regarded the rule as too strict and expressed a preference for an approach where the court would have discretion whether or not to admit evidence, "having regard to the totality of the circumstances." [22] In *The People (DPP) v Cash*, Charleton J expressed dissatisfaction with the exclusionary rule as set out in *Kenny,* noting that the rule **9–13**

> "automatically requires the exclusion of any evidence obtained through a mistake which had the accidental, and therefore unintended, result of infringing any constitutional right of one individual, namely the accused".[23]

He considered that the rule did not strike the appropriate balance between the rights of and interests of the individual and society and was of the view that "the original test, as propounded by the Supreme Court in *O'Brien* would have allowed for a balancing of the rights of parties".[24] The Supreme Court, in dealing with *Cash* on appeal, did not revisit the rule as laid down in *Kenny*.[25] **9–14**

---

[17] *ibid* at 56.

[18] *ibid.*

[19] *DPP v Mallon* [2011] 2 IR 544.

[20] *The People (DPP) v Edgeworth* [2001] 2 IR 131.

[21] *DPP v Mallon* [2011] 2 IR 544.

[22] *Balance in the Criminal Law Review Group*, Final Report (Department of Justice, Equality and Law Reform, Dublin, 2007) at p 161.

[23] *Director of Public Prosecutions v Cash* (HC) [2008] 1 ILRM 443.

[24] *ibid.*

[25] For analysis see Y Daly "Reasonable Suspicion for Arrest and Evidence at Trial: Supreme Court Excludes Consideration of Exclusionary Rule," *Human Rights in Ireland*, 19 January 2010 (http://humanrights.ie/constitution-of-ireland/reasonable-suspicion-for-arrest-and-evidence-at-trial-supreme-court-excludes-consideration-of-exclusionary-rule/ <accessed 28 October 2013>).

9–15 An attempt at clarification has been evident in the recent cases of *DPP v McCarthy*[26] (considered further below at 9–33) and *DPP v Mallon.*[27] In *Mallon*, O'Donnell J referred to criticism of the exclusionary rule:

> "5. The remorseless logic of the Kenny decision leading to the automatic exclusion of evidence sometimes as a result of quite trivial errors, has been the subject of critical comment, most notably by the former Chief Justice Keane C.J. in the foreword to McGrath, Evidence, (Dublin: Roundhall Press, 2005) and by Charleton, J. (himself a distinguished author in the field of criminal law) in the High Court decision of Director of Public Prosecutions v Cash [2007] IEHC 108, and that dissatisfaction is perhaps reflected in the comments of the trial judge here. However, this case does not raise the question of the admissibility of evidence obtained subsequent to an illegal and therefore, unconstitutional search. Instead it raised a logically anterior issue: in what circumstances will a warrant be considered ineffective, or invalid so as to give rise to the argument that evidence obtained should be excluded?
>
> 6. This is an important issue, all the more so because the consequence of any ineffectiveness or invalidity is the almost certain exclusion of the evidence in a subsequent trial. As the trial judge's ruling here shows, however, the law, even in relation to the apparently technical question of the validity of a search warrant, is far from clear. It is easy to sympathise with any trial judge confronted with the range of judgments on defective warrants which represent the current corpus of Irish law, and which perhaps, deserve the criticism applied by Tennyson to the 19th century law of England, quoted by Hardiman, J. in O'Keefe v Hickey [2009] 2 IR 302, at p. 334:
>
> > "... the lawless science of our law-
> > The codeless myriad of precedent,
> > The wilderness of single instances."[28]

9–16 In *Mallon*, a warrant had been issued in respect of "4 Marrowbone Close, Dublin 8." The correct address at which the warrant was executed, and at which diamorphine to a value of €300,000 was found, was "4 Marrowbone *Lane* Close." It was common case that there was a 4 Marrowbone Lane Close in Dublin 8 (indeed that was the premises searched) but there was no "Marrowbone Close" and consequently no 4 Marrowbone Close in Dublin 8 or elsewhere. The defence argued that the warrant had been issued for a premises which did not exist and could not, therefore, authorise the search of the premises at 4 Marrowbone Lane Close. It was accepted that this error was entirely innocent, as the garda who had sought the warrant believed that the address of the premises was 4 Marrowbone Close. That was the address he gave in the printed information and in his sworn evidence, and therefore the address for which the warrant was issued. The premises which were searched were the premises he intended to search, and which he described as 4 Marrowbone Close. It was asserted that the search was a breach of the constitutional right to inviolability of the dwelling home, which could only be entered in accordance with law. The entry was deliberate, and therefore, following the decision of the Supreme Court in *Kenny*, it constituted a deliberate and conscious violation to the breach of the constitutional right of the citizen, and accordingly the evidence

[26] *The People (DPP) v McCarthy* [2010] IECCA 89, [2011] 1 ILRM 430.
[27] *DPP v Mallon* [2011] 2 IR 544.
[28] *ibid.*

obtained must be excluded in the absence of any extraordinary excusing circumstances. Once that evidence was excluded, the charge, it was said, must be dismissed.

Distilling the myriad cases which have come before the courts concerning defective warrants, the Court praised principles which had been deduced in *McCarthy*[29]: **9–17**

> "(a) Documents, such as search warrants, must be carefully prepared having regard to the fact that they entitle Gardaí or other authorised officers to enter the property of a citizen, and in the course of so doing, to use such force as may be necessary, both to gain admission and to carry out the search and seizure authorised by the warrant;
>
> (b) This cautionary approach is particularly enjoined when the search warrant is in respect of the dwelling house of a citizen, in light of the recognition granted to such property under the Constitution;
>
> (c) Although search warrants should be prepared carefully, not every error in such a warrant will, by virtue of the same, lead automatically to the invalidation of a warrant;
>
> (d) In particular where the substance of the warrant, as opposed to its form, is not open to objection, the invalidation of the warrant will not necessarily ensue.
>
> (e) The nature of the error, or omission, must be scrutinised by the courts to see whether it is of a fundamental nature, including an error going to jurisdiction. Several factors may be taken into account, including whether the errors are mere mis-description, whether it is likely to mislead, whether it undermines the apparent jurisdiction to issue it, according to the warrant on its face, and such matters, before the courts will find, in an appropriate case, that it should be considered invalid.
>
> (f) It is not possible in relation to non-substantive errors, that is to say, errors which do not affect the substance of the legislative requirements found in the body of the warrant itself, to say that they will never lead to the invalidation of a search warrant, due to the wide variety and nature of errors which may occur."[30]

O'Donnell J concluded that: **9–18**

> "It is now clear that a mere error will not invalidate a warrant, especially one which is not calculated to mislead, or perhaps just as importantly, does not mislead. Indeed, the fact that warrants perfectly regular on their face may be invalidated if it can be demonstrated by evidence that there was no jurisdiction to issue them, demonstrates that error alone is not the critical factor. This latter fact illustrates the important feature that those warrants which have been found invalid are most clearly those where there was no jurisdiction to issue the warrant because a statutory precondition had not been fulfilled (*Byrne v Grey* [1988] IR 31, *DPP v Kenny* [1990] 1 ILRM 1) or where the warrant on its face did not show that the preconditions had been satisfied (*Simple Imports*). In such cases, the warrant has no validity in law, however, innocent the mistake (*Balfe*, *DPP v McCarthy*), and the entry on to the premises consequent on the warrants, even if permitted by the occupier, is illegal. If the entry is of a dwelling home, the entry will be unconstitutional, and any evidence obtained must be excluded absent extraordinary excusing circumstances (*DPP v Kenny*)."[31]

---

29 *ibid.*

30 *ibid* at 565, quoting *The People (DPP) v McCarthy* [2010] IECCA 89, [2011] 1 ILRM 430.

31 *ibid.*

The judgment succeeds in clarifying, to some extent, the distinction between a minor error, which will not invalidate a warrant, and one which goes to the jurisdiction of the warrant or a statutory precondition for its issue, and so is fatally flawed.

APPLICATION FOR AND ISSUE OF SEARCH WARRANTS

Sworn Information / Information on Oath

9–19 Search warrants are based on an information, which is essentially the application for a search warrant. The information lays down the grounds on which the search warrant is sought, the enactment under which the search warrant is sought, the articles or items sought and the basis for the suspicion justifying the application. The information will set out that the garda, of the appropriate rank (as dictated by the legislation under which the warrant is sought), has reasonable grounds for believing that evidence of or relating to the commission of an offence is to be found at a specified place, with the basis for such grounds identified and sworn before the court or Peace Commissioner, as the case may be.

9–20 It is indicative of the lack of uniformity in search warrant provisions that certain search warrants are grounded on sworn information, while others are based on "information on oath". Other provisions make no reference to any requirement of a declaration of the basis on which the search has been justified to the person issuing the warrant.[32] Among the provisions using the formula that the applicant should provide "information on oath" are the Misuse of Drugs Act 1977, s 26; Customs and Excise (Miscellaneous Provisions) Act 1988 ss 3 and 5; Criminal Damage Act 1991, s 13; Equal Status Act 2000, s 33; Criminal Justice (Theft and Fraud Offences) Act 2001, s 48; Company Law Enforcement Act 2001, s 30; and the Disability Act 2005, s 23. The wording "sworn information" is used in various other search warrant provisions including the Prohibition of Incitement to Hatred Act 1989, s 9; Child Trafficking and Pornography Act 1988, s 7; Immigration Act 2004, s 15. In practical terms there is little difference — the information on oath or sworn information is essentially a record of the grounds on which the search has been authorised and a declaration by the person seeking the warrant of his belief as to the veracity of the information given in the application. The sworn information should contain sufficient detail to demonstrate that the person who issued the warrant could have been objectively satisfied that there were reasonable grounds for belief or suspicion that the specified offence was being committed at the premises to be searched.

Suspicion

9–21 There is divergence in the use of the formulae "reasonable belief" and "reasonable suspicion" which are used interchangeably in the various search warrant provisions. While it may be argued that belief is firmer in conviction than suspicion,[33] what is uniform about the provisions is the requirement of reasonableness. There must be

[32] Examples include the Official Secrets Act 1963, s 16; the Criminal Justice Act 1994, ss 55 and 64; and the Sexual Offences (Jurisdiction) Act 1996, s 10.

[33] See Law Reform Commission, *Consultation Paper on Search Warrants and Bench Warrants* (LRC CP 58 – 2009), Dublin, December 2009, at p 45.

some objective basis for the belief or suspicion, generally grounded on information received from a source, observations or surveillance. A hunch, or a belief honestly held, will not suffice,[34] but equally suspicion does not equate with proof, as it was put in *Shaaban Bin Hussein v Chong Fook Kam:*

> "The circumstances of the case must be such that a reasonable man acting without passion or prejudice would fairly have suspected the person of having committed the offence ... suspicion in its ordinary meaning is a state of conjecture or surmise where proof is lacking: 'I suspect but I cannot prove'."[35]

What will be regarded as 'reasonable' will depend on all the circumstances. There must, however, be facts or information to satisfy an objective person that the person concerned may have committed the offence.[36]

Belief May be Based on Hearsay

A belief may be based on hearsay and on the account of an informant. In *The Director of Public Prosecutions v Sweeney*,[37] a warrant was issued by a Chief Superintendent under s 29 of the Offences against the State Act, the Chief Superintendent having been briefed by an Inspector on information provided by an informant. The warrant was challenged on the basis that the information was hearsay and came from a tainted source. The High Court rejected the submission that the evidence should not have been acted upon: **9–22**

> "To require that the Superintendent was entitled to form the necessary belief only on the receipt of direct evidence from the eye of a witness would make this section inoperable. I do not accept that one cannot have 'reasonable grounds for believing' that a given fact is so only by learning of this fact by direct evidence. What is required of the Chief Superintendent is that he has 'reasonable grounds for believing'. It is the function of the Chief Superintendent to exercise his judgment of whether the facts which come to his knowledge give him these reasonable grounds... It is part of the Chief Superintendent's function in deciding whether or not to issue a warrant that he should evaluate such evidence, taking into account all the factors relating to it including the fact that it has as its source an informant and if having done so, he does form the belief that the evidence is to be found on the premises then, on that basis, he is entitled to issue the warrant."[38]

In *Simple Imports v Revenue Commissioners*, the Supreme Court referred to the ministerial nature of the search warrant function exercised by a District Judge, holding: "He or she would clearly be entitled to rely on material, such as hearsay, which would not be admissible in criminal proceedings."[39]

The principle was restated in the case of *Director of Public Prosecutions v Cash*[40] where Charleton J held in the High Court: **9–23**

---

34 See *O'Hara v Chief Constable of the RUC* [1997] AC 826.

35 *Shaadban Bin Hussein v Chong Fook Kam* [1970] AC 942 at pp 948–949.

36 See *Fox v United Kingdom* (1991) 13 EHRR 157.

37 *The Director of Public Prosecutions v Sweeney,* unreported, High Court, 22 March 1996.

38 *ibid.*

39 *Simple Imports v Revenue Commissioners* [2000] 2 IR 243.

40 *Director of Public Prosecutions v Cash* (HC) [2008] 1 ILRM 443.

"12. It has never been held that what would be found a reasonable suspicion in law, requires to be based on the kind of evidence that would be admissible under the rules of evidence during the hearing of a criminal trial. On the contrary, a reasonable suspicion can be based on hearsay evidence or can be inferred from discovering that an alibi which a suspect has given to the police turns out to be false...

There is another distinction between reasonable suspicion and prima facie proof. Prima facie proof consists of admissible evidence. Suspicion can take into account matters that could not be put in evidence at all. There is a discussion about the relevance of previous convictions in the judgment of Lord Wright in McArdle v. Egan (1934) 150 L.T. 412. Suspicion can take into account also matters which, though admissible, could not form part of a prima facie case. Thus the fact that the accused has given a false alibi does not obviate the need for prima facie proof of his presence at the scene of the crime; it will become of considerable importance in the trial when such proof as there is is being weighed perhaps."[41]

The reasonableness of the suspicion or belief is therefore the crucial factor for consideration, rather than the origin or foundation for the belief on the part of the person issuing the search warrant.

Warrants Issued by District Court Judges

9–24 Most search warrants are issued by judges of the District Court; indeed, there appears in modern statutes to be a preference for confining the power to issue search warrants to District Judges, rather than Peace Commissioners.[42] The extension of powers to issue search warrants has been seen in the vesting of powers in senior gardaí,[43] a practice of which O'Malley has been critical, saying:

"In this day and age, as the Morris Tribunal has recently recommended, a warrant should always be issued by a judge. Senior police officers, for example, cannot claim to have the level of institutional independence necessary for the proper exercise of impartial judgment."[44]

9–25 Such an encroachment of constitutional rights should be attended by the utmost protection for the individual, with stringent standards to be met before a warrant can be obtained and executed. As Kinlen J put it in *Hanahoe v Hussey*:

"... in the case of a serious invasion of constitutional rights, the judge must be satisfied on the facts that the appropriate statute would apply and must seek to ensure that the

---

[41] *ibid* at 450–451.

[42] The Law Reform Commission has noted that the Firearms and Offensive Weapons Act 1990 is the most recent piece of legislation providing a new power to Peace Commissioners to issue search warrants, perhaps reflective of reticence on the part of the Oireachtas to extend the Peace Commissioner role. See Law Reform Commission, *Consultation Paper on Search Warrants and Bench Warrants* (LRC CP 58 – 2009), Dublin, December 2009, at p 77.

[43] For instance, s 29 of the Offences against the State Act 1939, as substituted by s 1 of the Criminal Justice (Search Warrants) Act 2012; s 8 of the Criminal Justice (Drug Trafficking) Act 1996 as amended by s 3 of the Criminal Justice (Search Warrants) Act 2012.

[44] T O'Malley, *The Criminal Process* (Round Hall, Dublin, 2009) at p 353.

> constitutional rights of the citizen are protected. Any diminution of these rights must be in strict accordance with the established necessity and with strict application of the relevant statutes".[45]

It falls on judges issuing search warrants to ensure compliance with the statutory conditions permitting interference with constitutional rights. In *Simple Imports v Revenue Commissioners*, Keane J (as he then was) referred to the far-reaching effects of a search warrant: **9–26**

> "Search warrants... entitle police and other officers to enter the dwellinghouse or other property of a citizen, carry out searches and ... remove material which they find on the premises and, in the course of so doing, use such force as is necessary to gain admission and carry out the search and seizure authorised by the warrant. These are powers which the police and other authorities must enjoy in defined circumstances for the protection of society, but since they authorise the forcible invasion of a person's property, the courts must always be concerned to ensure that the conditions imposed by the legislature before such powers can be validly exercised are strictly met."[46]

The power to issue search warrants having been vested in judges, with the power only exercisable once certain conditions have been met, was found to be indicative of the constitutional entitlement of the citizen to protection from unjustified searches of private property. It was held that:

> "It must be presumed that it was envisaged that the judges would, in no sense, permit themselves to be treated as ciphers, but would conscientiously satisfy themselves that the relevant preconditions had been satisfied."[47]

Applications made under any enactment to a court, or a judge of a court, for a search warrant, are made *in camera,* ie otherwise than in public.[48]

Section 32A(1) of the Courts (Supplemental Provisions) Act 1961, as inserted by s 180 of the Criminal Justice Act 2006, provides that a judge of the District Court may, in relation to a relevant district, exercise any of the following powers while anywhere in the State outside that relevant district, if, but only if, the judge would be entitled to exercise the power concerned at a sitting of the District Court in that relevant district: **9–27**

> (a) the power to issue a warrant for the arrest of a person;
>
> (b) the power to issue a warrant to a member of the Garda Síochána or, if appropriate, any other person authorising the entry to, and search of, any place or premises (including a dwelling) and, if appropriate, the search of any person found at such place or premises for all or any of the following purposes:
>
> (i) the gathering of evidence of, or relating to, the commission or attempted commission of any criminal offence;
>
> (ii) the gathering of evidence of, or relating to, the contravention in any other respect of any provision of an enactment;

[45] *Hanahoe v Hussey* [1998] 3 IR 69.

[46] *Simple Imports v Revenue Commissioners* [2000] 2 IR 243.

[47] *ibid.*

[48] Criminal Justice (Amendment) Act 2009, s 26.

(iii) ascertaining whether there is or has been compliance with any provision of an enactment;
(iv) the gathering of evidence of, or relating to, assets or proceeds deriving from criminal conduct (within the meaning of section 1(1) of the Criminal Assets Bureau Act 1996) or to their identity or whereabouts;

(c) the power to make an order, upon the application of a member of the Garda Síochána or, if appropriate, any other person, directing another person to produce, make available for inspection or to give access to any particular document, material or thing, or documents, material or things of a particular description, for the purposes of investigating—
(i) any criminal offence,
(ii) whether there is or has been a contravention in any other respect of any provision of an enactment, or
(iii) whether a person has benefited from assets or proceeds deriving from criminal conduct (within the meaning of section 1(1) of the Criminal Assets Bureau Act 1996) or is in receipt of or controls such assets or proceeds.

A "relevant district" is one to which a judge is permanently or temporarily assigned, or one in which he or she is acting in place of a permanently assigned District Court judge.

The effect of the section is to remove a territorial restriction which had previously existed.[49]

Warrants Issued by Peace Commissioners

9–28 Peace Commissioners are honorary appointees of the Minister for Justice and Law Reform vested with a number of powers and duties, including the signing of summonses and the issuing of search warrants, administering oaths and taking informations.[50] The office of Peace Commissioner was created by the District Justices (Temporary Provisions) Act 1923, s 4, and no qualifications or educational standards are required other than the person having to be of good character. One of their functions is to issue search warrants where they are statutorily permitted to do so.

9–29 The constitutionality of warrants issued by Peace Commissioners has been challenged and upheld, with the High Court endorsing the use of non-judicial warrants as a matter of practicality and convenience. It was held in *Ryan v O'Callaghan*[51] that it was in the interests of the common good to have a simple procedure whereby the gardaí could readily obtain a warrant so as to facilitate them in the investigation of crime. The issue of a search warrant was held to be an aspect of the investigative, rather than the judicial or prosecutorial, process. Further it was determined that the sworn information and the independence of the Peace Commissioner:

> "contains important elements for the protection of the public… The investigating police officer must swear an information that he has reasonable cause for suspecting that

[49] See *Creaven v Criminal Assets Bureau* [2004] 4 IR 434 and *People (DPP) v Joyce* [2009] 4 IR 656.
[50] Courts of Justice Act 1924, s 88.
[51] *Ryan v O'Callaghan,* unreported, High Court, 22 July 1987.

> stolen property is to be found at the premises to be searched and he must satisfy a peace commissioner, who is an independent person unconnected with criminal investigation per se, that it is right and proper to issue the warrant".[52]

A significant limitation of a warrant issued by a Peace Commissioner is that, unlike the warrant of a judge, it does not speak for itself. A statement is required to provide evidence as to the state of mind of the peace commissioner in issuing the warrant, ie that he or she was satisfied in issuing the warrant by the sworn information of the garda applicant that there were reasonable grounds to suspect that evidence relating to the relevant offence was to be found at the address to which the warrant relates. In the event of the death or unavailability of the Peace Commissioner to attend at trial to provide such evidence, a trial judge is entitled to rule the warrant invalid.[53] In *The People (Director of Public Prosecutions) v Owens*, Barrington J in the Supreme Court drew a distinction between warrants issued by Peace Commissioners and those issued by judges: **9–30**

> "The peace commissioner, like the Chief Superintendent, is a public officer but he is not a court of record. A search warrant is also a document which may affect constitutional right. It does not speak for itself in a criminal trial."[54]

In *Owens*, there was no reference to the earlier High Court case of *DPP v Heaphy*[55] in which the opposite conclusion had been reached. There, McGuinness J held that the presence of the Peace Commissioner in court to give evidence of his state of mind in issuing the warrant was not necessary and, provided that the Peace Commissioner had sufficient material before him to enable him to satisfy himself of the need to issue a warrant, it must be assumed that he carried out his functions properly. However, *Owens,* in which judgment was delivered by the Supreme Court one week after the High Court decision in *Heaphy,* has put beyond doubt that a Peace Commissioner's signature is not sufficient to establish the validity of a warrant and that a Peace Commissioner must be present in court to prove his state of mind and to be available, if necessary, for cross-examination by the defence. **9–31**

Peace Commissioners' search warrants are most frequently used in searches involving suspected drug offences, pursuant to s 26 of the Misuse of Drugs Act 1977 though they are statutorily authorised to issue search warrants in a limited number of other Acts. These include the Road Traffic Act 1961, s 106 (failure to remain at the scene of a road accident where injury to person or property has been caused); the Customs and Excise (Miscellaneous Provisions) Act 1988, s 3 (importation or exportation of controlled drugs); the Prohibition of Incitement to Hatred Act 1989, s 9 (possession of material or a recording or other item intended or likely to stir up hatred); the Video Recordings Act 1989, s 25 (importation of video recordings in respect of which a prohibition order **9–32**

---

52 *ibid* at 5, *per* Barr J.

53 *The People (Director of Public Prosecutions) v Owens* [1999] 2 IR 16.

54 *ibid.*

55 *DPP v Heaphy* [1999] 2 JIC 0903.

is in force); and the Firearms and Offensive Weapons Act 1990, s 15 (manufacture, importation, sale or hire of offensive weapons).

9–33 Difficulties have arisen where Peace Commissioner search warrants have been headed "The District Court." If a warrant is issued by a Peace Commissioner, it is evidently and quite obviously not issued by a judge of the District Court. In *The People (DPP) v Edgeworth*,[56] however, it was held that, while it was inappropriate for a warrant issued by a Peace Commissioner to bear the words "The District Court," the appearance of the words did not breach any statutory requirement as to the form of the warrant and did not mislead, where the status of the person issuing the warrant appeared clearly on its face and did not, therefore, affect the validity of the warrant. In *Edgeworth*, the Peace Commissioner had crossed out the printed words "Judge of the District Court" where they appeared under her signature and wrote the words "Peace Commissioner" in capital letters next to the crossed-out words. In *The People (DPP) v McCarthy*,[57] a Peace Commissioner's warrant was found to have a fundamental error where a warrant was headed "An Chúirt Dúiche" and "The District Court" combined with the signature of the peace commissioner over the printed words "Judge of the District Court assigned to the said District." "PC" had been written after the peace commisisoner's signature, but the court found that the letters were effectively blended into the signature, which was unclear. The High Court in *McCarthy* contrasted the position with that in *Edgeworth*, where it was clear that the warrant was issued by a Peace Commissioner, rather than a District Court judge. In *McCarthy*, the decision of the Circuit Court that the warrant was invalid was found to be correct because the status of the party issuing the warrant, and therefore the jurisdiction to issue the warrant, was claimed to be a judge of the District Court, and therefore no proper jurisdiction in law was disclosed. The warrant was therefore found to be wholly misleading, particularly when combined with the inclusion of the erroneous title "An Chúirt Dúiche" and "The District Court".

Warrants Issued by Gardaí

9–34 Independent and impartial supervision of the issuing of a search warrant is a bulwark against abuse. Yet legislation has provided for gardaí to issue search warrants to themselves if immediate action is necessary. Statutory provisions which provide for senior gardaí to issue search warrants or approvals for surveillance without recourse to the third party scrutiny of a District Court judge include the Official Secrets Act 1963, s 16; the Criminal Assets Bureau Act 1996, s 14; the Criminal Justice (Drug Trafficking) Act 1996, s 8; the Prevention of Corruption (Amendment) Act 2001 and the Criminal Justice (Surveillance) Act 2009, s 7.

Section 8(2) of the Criminal Justice Drug Trafficking Act 1996

9–35 Section 8(2) of the Criminal Justice (Drug Trafficking) Act 1996 permits search warrants to be issued under s 26 of the Misuse of Drugs Act 1977 by Superintendents in circumstances of urgency.

---

56 *The People (DPP) v Edgeworth* [2001] 2 IR 131.
57 *The People (DPP) v McCarthy* [2010] IECCA 89.

The Superintendent must be satisfied that the warrant is necessary for the proper investigation of a drug trafficking offence and that circumstances of urgency giving rise to the need for the immediate issue of the search warrant would render it impracticable to apply to a judge of the District Court or a Peace Commissioner for the issue of a warrant in the usual way.[58] A drug trafficking offence is defined in s 3(1) of the Criminal Justice Act 1994 as including: 9–36

> "(a) an offence under any regulations made under s 5 of the Misuse of Drugs Act, 1977, involving the manufacture, production, preparation, importation, exportation, supply, offering to supply, distribution or transportation of a controlled drug,
>
> (a) an offence under s 15 of that Act of possession of a controlled drug for unlawful sale or supply,
>
> [(bb) an offence under s 15A of that Act;][59]
>
> [(bbb) an offence under section 15B (importation of controlled drugs in excess of certain value) of that Act;][60]..."

The definition of drug trafficking offences has been broadened further to include money laundering in relation to the proceeds of drug trafficking under Part 2 of the Criminal Justice (Money Laundering and Terrorist Financing) Act 2010.[61] 9–37

Warrants issued by Superintendents under s 26 are of short duration: they cease to have effect after 24 hours.[62]

The recitation of three sources of search warrants in s 26 of the Misuse of Drugs Act 1977 does not provide a menu from which gardaí can opt for a judge, Peace Commissioner or colleague. In *DPP v Peter Byrne*, the Court of Criminal appeal held that

> "it is not the case that An Garda Síochána are free to choose whether they will apply for a warrant to a judge, to a peace commissioner or to a superintendent. They must apply to a judge or a peace commissioner unless the very limited circumstances which permit them to apply to a superintendent are present".[63]

In *Byrne*, the warrant was issued in the context of an elaborate surveillance operation of which the Chief Superintendent was aware. He was phoned and put "on call" that a warrant would be urgently required. He arrived to a place very near the house and issued a warrant without any inquiry as to the availability of a District Judge or whether any steps had been taken to contact either a judge or Peace Commissioner. The Court found this to be an incorrect approach: the gardaí must apply to a judge or Peace Commissioner unless the very limited circumstances which permit them to apply 9–38

58 Misuse of Drugs Act 1977, s 26, as amended by the Criminal Justice (Drug Trafficking) Act 1996, s 8(2).

59 Paragraph (bb) inserted by the Criminal Justice Act 1999, s 7.

60 Paragraph (bbb) inserted by the Criminal Justice Act 2006, s 86.

61 Criminal Justice Act 1994, s 3(1), paragraph (e) of "drug trafficking offence" substituted by the Criminal Justice (Money Laundering and Terrorist Financing) Act 2010, s 117(3).

62 Criminal Justice (Drug Trafficking) Act 1996, s 8(3).

63 *DPP v Byrne* [2003] 4 IR 423 at 427-428.

to a Superintendent are demonstrated. Those circumstances must be demonstrated to be present for the Superintendent's warrant to be valid. There had been time to contact the Chief Superintendent to put him "on call", there had been a long period of surveillance and so the argument that it would have been difficult to get to a Peace Commissioner or judge was difficult to justify.

9–39 The section initially made no reference to the requirement of independence of the Superintendent issuing the warrant from the investigation However, the case of *Damache v the Director of Public Prosecutions*[64] held that a member of the gardaí issuing a search warrant should be distanced from and not primarily involved in the investigation at hand. This accords with the decision of the Court of Criminal Appeal in *People (DPP) v Balfe* that the protection and vindication of rights in respect of search warrants "is achieved by the introduction of a competent, detached authority" exercising the function of determining whether a search warrant should be issued.[65] In light of *Damache*, the Criminal Justice (Search Warrants) Act 2012 was enacted and two new subsections were inserted into s 8(2) of the Criminal Justice (Drug Trafficking) Act 1996. The first subsection provides that an issuing Superintendent may only issue a search warrant under s 26 of the Misuse of Drugs Act 1977 if he or she is independent of the investigation of the offence in relation to which the search warrant is being sought, in the sense that he or she is neither involved in nor in charge of the investigation.[66] The second subsection requires that the issuing Superintendent must record in writing the grounds on which the warrant was issued, including how he or she was satisfied of the necessity for the warrant, the urgency giving rise to the immediate need for a search warrant and the impracticality of applying to a Peace Commissioner or District Judge.[67] The record should be taken either at the time the warrant is issued or as soon as reasonably practicable thereafter.

Section 29 of the Offences against the State Act 1939

9–40 The power to issue search warrants in the course of investigations into scheduled offences was found to be unconstitutional by the Supreme Court in *Damache v the Director of Public Prosecutions*[68] and accordingly the section which provided for it, s 29 of the Offences against the State Act 1939, was struck down. The Court held that the section permitted the search of the appellant's home on foot of a warrant which had not been issued by an independent person. The decision has implications for the exercise of the other statutory powers under which gardaí may issue search warrants to their colleagues, because it emphasises the imperative of independence in the authorisation of interference with the dwelling, the inviolability of which is constitutionally protected.

[64] *Damache v Director of Public Prosecutions* [2012] 2 IR 266.
[65] *People (DPP) v Balfe* [1998] 4 IR 50.
[66] Criminal Justice (Drug Trafficking) Act 1996, s 8(2A).
[67] *ibid,* s 8(2B).
[68] *Damache v Director of Public Prosecutions* [2012] 2 IR 266.

The Court held that, in addition to reasonable grounds existing that an offence has been committed and that there may be evidence to be found at the place of the search:

> "For the process of obtaining a search warrant to be meaningful, it is necessary for the person authorising the search to be able to assess the conflicting interests of the State and the individual in an impartial manner. Thus the person should be independent of the issue and act judicially… the warrant was issued by a member of a Garda Síochána investigating team which was investigating the matters. A member of An Garda Síochána who is part of an investigating team is not independent on matters related to the investigation."

A legislative response to *Damache* was required, and accordingly the Criminal Justice **9–41** (Search Warrants) Act 2012 was enacted, with a reformulated s 29. The Act provides for an application to be made for a s 29 search warrant to a judge of the District Court by a garda of sergeant rank or above and, if a Superintendent considers that a search warrant is necessary for the investigation of a limited category of offences and that "circumstances of urgency giving rise to the need for the immediate issue of the search warrant would render it impracticable to apply to a judge of the District Court under this section for the issue of the warrant", the Superintendent may issue a search warrant to a garda of sergeant rank.[69] The Superintendent issuing the warrant may only do so if he or she is independent of the investigation of the offence in relation to which the search warrant is being sought.[70] Independence is defined as not being in charge of or involved in the investigation.[71] Whereas a warrant issued by a judge under the section will allow entry for one week from the date of issue,[72] a warrant issued by a Superintendent under the section will cease to have effect 48 hours after its issue.[73]

EXECUTION

The Place to be Searched — "The Dwelling"

As is outlined in *Chapter 8:* Entry for Arrest and Investigation, the constitutional pro- **9–42** tection given to the dwelling is set out in Article 40.5 of *Bunreacht na hÉireann.* There it is stated that "The dwelling of every citizen is inviolable and shall not be forcibly entered save in accordance with law." Dwelling has been defined as follows:

> "In a case where members of a family live together in the family house, the house as a whole is for the purpose of the Constitution the dwelling of each member of the family. If a member of a family occupies a clearly defined portion of the house apart from the other members of the family, then it may well be that the part not so occupied is no

69 Offences against the State Act 1939, s 29(4)(b), as substituted by the Criminal Justice (Search Warrants) Act 2012, s 1.

70 *ibid*, s 29(5), as substituted by the Criminal Justice (Search Warrants) Act 2012, s 1.

71 *ibid*, s 29(12), as substituted by the Criminal Justice (Search Warrants) Act 2012, s 1.

72 *ibid*, s 29(6), as substituted by the Criminal Justice (Search Warrants) Act 2012, s 1.

73 *ibid*, s 29(7), as substituted by the Criminal Justice (Search Warrants) Act 2012, s 1.

longer his dwelling, as would be the case where a person not a member of the family occupied or was in possession of a clearly defined portion of the house."[74]

9–43 In *People (Director of Public Prosecutions) v Lawless*,[75] the Court of Criminal Appeal made clear that the constitutional protection given to the dwelling did not apply in circumstances where the applicant did not live at the address searched. The constitutional protection "was not the right of the applicant but of the tenant of the flat in question and persons residing with him."[76]

Squatters

9–44 However a place need not be legally occupied to be a home. In the case of *The People (DPP) v Lynch* it was held that the constitutional protection of the inviolability of a citizen's dwelling extended to a person squatting at that place, and indeed that the constitutional protection afforded the dwelling applied "to a wide variety of people with dubious legal titles, such as an overholding tenant, the widow of a deceased legal owner, or a person in *bona fide* possession on foot of an invalid title".[77] The Court looked to the Irish language version of the Constitution and the expression corresponding with dwelling which is '*ionad cónaithe*'. It found that the question of whether a place is a 'dwelling' for the purpose of a search warrant in the criminal law context is one of fact. If a person lives there, even as a trespasser, it is his dwelling and, in accordance with Article 40.5, it should not be forcibly entered without a search warrant. A warrant had been obtained in *Lynch*, but the trial judge had found it to be invalid.

Subdivided Buildings and Caravans

9–45 Where houses are subdivided, it can be difficult to determine which part of the building is the 'dwelling' for the purposes of a search warrant. Equally, a question can arise as to whether a caravan on the property in respect of which a search warrant has issued can validly be searched on the authority of the warrant, though often a warrant will refer to outbuildings and structures on the land at the relevant address. Of course, a caravan on a piece of land for which a search warrant has issued might not necessarily be a dwelling. Whether a particular location is a dwelling or not will depend very much on the facts of the case but, given the constitutional issues at play, a search warrant should be accurate and as precise as possible in describing the place to be searched. A failure to specify, for instance, a particular apartment of a number in a building may render a warrant void for ambiguity.

Rural Addresses

9–46 In rural settings, addresses may be inherently broad, with reference only to a townland and without a house number as an identifier of the particular dwelling which is to be

---

[74] *The People (Attorney General) v O'Brien* [1965] IR 142 at 169.

[75] *People (Director of Public Prosecutions) v Lawless*, unreported, Court of Criminal Appeal, 28 November 1985.

[76] *ibid.*

[77] *The People (Director of Public Prosecutions) v Lynch* [2010] 1 IR 543.

searched. Where an address cannot be cited with the requisite degree of specificity, it should be described in as much detail as possible, perhaps by reference to the ownership and tenancy or by a unique feature, because a warrant with a broad townland address would on its face purport to grant authority to search every house within that townland. The warrant itself should specify the precise house to be searched so that it is clear to the reader that the entry has been authorised.

Business Premises

Search warrants are also required if it is proposed to search a business premises. In *Simple Imports Ltd v Revenue Commissioners*, Keane J put the purpose of powers permitting searches in the following terms: **9–47**

> "Search warrants … entitle police and other officers to enter the dwelling house or other property of a citizen, carry out searches and remove material which they find on the premises and, in the course of so doing, use such force as is necessary to gain admission and carry out the search and seizure authorised by the warrant. These are powers which the police and other authorities must enjoy in defined circumstances for the protection of society, but since they authorise the forcible invasion of a person's property, the courts must always be concerned to ensure that the conditions imposed by the legislature before such powers can be validly exercised are strictly met."[78]

See further *Chapter 8:* Entry for Arrest and Investigation.

So while the constitutional right most usually associated with search warrants is that of the inviolability of the dwelling, other constitutional rights are also at play, namely the rights to privacy, property and liberty. Searches of third party premises, such as solicitor's offices, can be undertaken under s 64 of the Criminal Justice Act 1994, and in that context, the European Convention right under Article 8 comes into play.[79] **9–48**

Searches under s 64 of the Criminal Justice Act 1994 are considered below at 9–62 *et seq.*

Forcible Entry

Walsh has noted that, since search warrants permit entry by force, "it follows that the right to use force, where necessary, in order to gain access to the property is an integral element of the authority conferred by the warrant".[80] The statutory provisions permitting entry under warrant permit generally refer to the permission granted to gardaí to **9–49**

[78] *Simple Imports Ltd v Revenue Commissioners* [2000] 2 IR 243.

[79] Article 8 provides: "1. Everyone has the right to respect for his private and family life, his home and his correspondence.2. There shall be no interference by a public authority with the exercise of this right except such as is in accordance with the law and is necessary in a democratic society in the interests of national security, public safety or the economic well-being of the country, for the prevention of disorder or crime, for the protection of health or morals, or for the protection of the rights and freedoms of others."

[80] D Walsh, *Criminal Procedure* (Thomson Round Hall, Dublin, 2002) at p 414.

enter forcibly; some provisions use the formulation "by force" and others "reasonable force". The Law Reform Commission points out that necessity is a pre-condition to the use of force in the execution of search warrants and that the use of the term 'reasonable' "is another safeguard in respect of the use of force; essentially it requires any force to be used to be proportionate and not excessive."[81]

Presenting a Copy of the Search Warrant to the Occupier

9–50 There is no requirement in Irish law that gardaí give a copy of a search warrant to the owner or occupier of a dwelling to be searched. There is provision in some legislation for the occupier or owner to request to see the warrant on entry.[82] In practice, search warrants are shown to owners and occupiers on entry. The Law Reform Commission has provisionally recommended that a copy of a search warrant should be given to the owner or occupier of a property at the commencement of a search, unless doing so would be detrimental to the warrant's execution or endanger the safety of an executing officer.[83]

Search Warrant Duration and Multiple Entries

9–51 There is no uniformity in Irish search warrant provisions, and their duration is one of the aspects which changes from provision to provision. Warrants issued by Peace Commissioners or judges under s 26 of the Misuse of Drugs Act 1977 can be operative for one month. They allow entry "at any time or times" within that month, and therefore clearly envisage multiple entry. Warrants issued by District Judges for the investigation of arrestable offences under s 10 of the Criminal Justice (Miscellaneous Provisions) Act 1997 permit entry "at any time or times within one week" of the date of issue. Section 29 of the Offences against the State Act 1939[84] (considered above) repeats the formula "at any time or times within one week" in respect of warrants issued by District Judges. Shorter time periods apply where warrants are issued by gardaí (see 9–31 *et seq*).

9–52 Multiple entries may be required in a number of circumstances, particularly if there is a considerable amount of material to be seized. Noting that multiple execution search warrants are occasionally useful and necessary, the Law Reform Commission has, however, been critical of the absence of guidelines on the appropriate approach to repeated entries, remarking that "the current approach in Ireland does not sufficiently monitor

[81] Law Reform Commission, *Consultation Paper on Search Warrants and Bench Warrants* (LRC CP 58 – 2009), Dublin, December 2009, at p 125.

[82] For instance Firearms and Offensive Weapons Act 1990, s 15; Control of Horses Act 1996, s 35; Criminal Justice (Miscellaneous Provisions) Act 1997, s 10 (as substituted by s 6 of the Criminal Justice Act 2006), Safety, Health and Welfare at Work Act 2005, s 64; Employment Permits Act 2006, s 22.

[83] Law Reform Commission, *Consultation Paper on Search Warrants and Bench Warrants* (LRC CP 58 – 2009), Dublin, December 2009, at p 135.

[84] Offences against the State Act 1939, s 29, as substituted by the Criminal Justice (Search Warrants) Act 2012, s 1.

multiple executions. A more restrictive approach would help to prevent 'fishing expedition' searches or abuses of the multiple execution system."[85]

Obstruction

Search warrant provisions routinely contain powers which permit demands to be made of persons present for their name and address, with inbuilt arrest powers provided for obstruction of gardaí during the execution of search warrants. Some of those powers are considered in *Chapter 1: Arrest* at 1–79 and 1–80. **9–53**

KEY SEARCH WARRANT PROVISIONS

Drug Offences — Section 26 of the Misuse of Drugs Act 1977

The vast majority of search warrants issued and executed in Ireland relate to suspected drug offences. Section 26 of the Misuse of Drugs Act is therefore a crucial power. It provides for search warrants to be issued by judges of the District Court, Peace Commissioners and, in certain circumstances, by gardaí of Superintendent rank, where drug offences are suspected. Section 26(1) provides: **9–54**

> "(1) If a Justice of the District Court or a Peace Commissioner is satisfied by information on oath of a member of the Garda Síochána [or, if subject to the provisions of subsection (2) of section 8 of the Criminal Justice (Drug Trafficking) Act, 1996, a member of the Garda Síochána not below the rank of Superintendent is satisfied][86] that there is reasonable ground for suspecting that –
>
> (a) a person is in possession in contravention of this Act on any premises or other land of a controlled drug, a forged prescription or a duly issued prescription which has been wrongfully altered and that such drug or prescription is on a particular premises [or other land],[87] or
>
> [(aa) opium poppy, a plant of the genus *Cannabis* or a plant of the genus *Erythroxylon* is being cultivated contrary to section 17 of this Act on or in any premises or other land, or][88]
>
> (b) a document directly or indirectly relating to, or connected with, a transaction or dealing which was, or an intended transaction or dealing which would if carried out be, an offence under this Act, or in the case of a transaction or dealing carried out or intended to be carried out in a place outside the State, an offence against a provision of a corresponding law within the meaning of section 20 of this Act and in force in that place, is in the possession of a person at any premises,
>
> [such Justice, Commissioner or, as the case may be, member][89] may issue a search warrant mentioned in subsection 2 of this section."

---

85 Law Reform Commission, *Consultation Paper on Search Warrants and Bench Warrants* (LRC CP 58 – 2009), Dublin, December 2009, p 148.

86 As inserted by Criminal Justice (Drug Trafficking) Act 1996, s 8(1)(a).

87 Words inserted by Misuse of Drugs Act 1984, s 13.

88 Subsection (1)(aa) inserted by Misuse of Drugs Act 1984, s 13(b).

89 Words substituted by Criminal Justice (Drug Trafficking) Act 1996, s 8(1)(b).

9–55 Section 26(2) of the 1977 Act, as substituted by Misuse of Drugs Act 1984, s 13(c), provides the critical components of the drug search warrant: that it authorises a named member of the Garda Síochána (accompanied by such other members as necessary) to enter the specified premises at any time or times within one month of the date of issue. Force may be used to effect entry if it is required. Section 26 warrants permit the search of the premises or other land to which they apply. Land in this context includes any structure, with structure being further defined as including any building, structure or any other thing constructed, erected, placed or made on, in or under any land.[90] What is more, not only does a warrant issued under s 26 empower gardaí to search the premises, but it also allows the search of any person found there. Items may be examined, inspected and seized if they are considered to be required as evidence for potential criminal proceedings.

9–56 The circumstances in which senior gardaí may issue warrants under s 26 of the Misuse of Drugs Act 1977, and the pre-requisite conditions for the exercise of that power, are considered above at 9–35 – 9–39.

Arrestable Offences – Section 10 of the Criminal Justice (Miscellaneous Provisions) Act 1997

9–57 Though there are innumerable search warrant provisions on the Irish statutebook, an omnibus search warrant provision for arrestable offences is provided in s 10 of the Criminal Justice (Miscellaneous Provisions) Act 1997 as substituted by s 6(1)(a) of the Criminal Justice Act 2006. Where there are reasonable grounds for suspecting that evidence of or relating to an arrestable offence is to be found in a particular place, a search warrant may be sought under s 10.

Section 10(1) (as substituted) provides:

> "If a judge of the District Court is satisfied by information on oath of a member not below the rank of sergeant that there are reasonable grounds for suspecting that evidence of, or relating to, the commission of an arrestable offence is to be found in any place, the judge may issue a warrant for the search of that place and any persons found at that place."[91]

9–58 A search warrant issued under s 10 operates to authorise entry to the place named in the warrant at any time or times within one week of the date of issue. Reasonable force may be used if necessary to effect entry. The warrant is to be produced to the occupier on request. It permits the search of the place and persons present and the seizure of anything found at the place or in the possession of a person present which is reasonably believed to be evidence of or relating to the commission of an arrestable offence.

---

[90] Misuse of Drugs Act 1977, s 26(4) as inserted by Misuse of Drugs Act 1984, s 13(c).

[91] Criminal Justice (Miscellaneous Provisions) Act 1997, s 10 (1) as substituted by the Criminal Justice Act 2006, s 6(1)(a).

Theft and Fraud Offences

Since many theft and fraud offences are arrestable offences, a warrant might be sought in investigations relating to crimes of dishonesty under s 10 of the Criminal Justice (Miscellaneous Provisions) Act 1997. There is also a dedicated search warrant provision in the Criminal Justice (Theft and Fraud Offences) Act 2001 at s 48. Section 48 warrants are operative for seven days. They may only be issued by a judge of the District Court and may be issued where a judge is satisfied having received information on oath that there are reasonable grounds for suspecting that there is evidence of or relating to an arrestable offence under the Criminal Justice (Theft and Fraud Offences) Act 2001 to be found at the place it is proposed to search.[92] The warrant must specify a named garda, who may be accompanied in the execution of the warrant by others, and authorises the search of both the specified place and persons found there. Entry may be made by the use of reasonable force if necessary. **9–59**

The original formulation of s 48(2) outlined that the judge had to be satisfied "on hearing evidence on oath given by a member of the Garda Síochána". Subsection (2) was substituted by the Criminal Justice Act 2006, s 192(1)(a), to dispense with the requirement that evidence be heard. Rather it now merely requires the judge to be satisfied "by information on oath," an amendment described in the explanatory memorandum to the 2004 Criminal Justice Bill as merely technical in nature, to bring the provision into line with the language used in other statutory search warrant provisions.

Detailed guidance is provided in s 48 as to the steps which may be taken by gardaí acting on foot of a warrant issued under the section. In addition to powers to search the place and persons found there, gardaí may: **9–60**

- examine, seize and retain anything found at the place, or in the possession of a person present there at the time of the search, which is reasonably believed to be evidence of or relating to the commission of an arrestable offence under the Act[93];
- to take any other steps which may appear to the member to be necessary for preserving any such thing and preventing interference with it[94];
- make and retain a copy of any relevant document or record[95];
- seize and retain as necessary any computer or storage medium on which a record is kept[96];
- operate any computer at the place which is being searched;
- require a person present who has lawful control of a computer to divulge passwords or otherwise assist the Garda to examine the computer data, including by provision of information in a removable, visible and legible form[97];

[92] Criminal Justice (Theft and Fraud Offences) Act 2001, s 48(1). An arrestable offence is one which is punishable by five years' imprisonment or a more significant penalty.
[93] *ibid,* s 48(3)(c).
[94] *ibid,* s 48(3)(d).
[95] *ibid,* s 48(4)(a).
[96] *ibid,* s 48(4)(b).
[97] *ibid,* s 48(5).

– to seize and retain any material, other than items subject to legal privilege, which is likely to be of substantial value (whether by itself or together with other material) to the investigation for the purpose of which the warrant was issued.[98]

Child Pornography

9–61 The Child Trafficking and Pornography Act 1998 contains a number of offences relating to the sexual exploitation of children and the possession and production of images of child sexual abuse. Section 3 provides for the offences of trafficking children for sexual exploitation, sexually exploiting children and restricting the liberty of a child for that purpose[99] as well as meeting a child within or outside the State for the purpose of sexual exploitation.[100] Section 4 provides for the offence of allowing a child to be used for child pornography, s 5 provides for the offence of producing, distributing, printing, publishing, importing, exporting child pornography and s 6 covers possession of child pornography. These offences have a dedicated search power, contained in s 7, which provides that a garda of sergeant rank may apply to a judge of the District Court who must be satisfied that there are reasonable grounds for suspecting that evidence relating to an offence under s 3, 4, 5 or 6 is to be found at a specified place. If the judge is so satisfied, a warrant may be issued for the search of that place and any persons found there, and to seize any items found at the place or in the possession of persons present. Warrants issued under s 7 are operative for seven days from the date of issue.

Money Laundering and Drug Trafficking

9–62 The Criminal Justice Act 1994 is a unique piece of legislation in that it permits warrants to be executed on the premises of third parties who may be in possession of material relevant to an investigation. As was noted by Kinlen J in *Hanahoe v Hussey*:

> "The significance of the Criminal Justice Act 1994 was that it greatly extended the power to grant search warrants and obtain orders in relation to materials and documents possibly relevant to the criminal investigation and / or prosecution. Hitherto persons subject to search warrants were essentially suspects and proposed respondents in any investigation. However, the Criminal Justice Act, 1994, contemplated the obtaining of documentation from wholly innocent third parties who simply happened to have documentation or material which might be said to be relevant and might be used in evidence."[101]

In *Hanahoe v Hussey*, the premises searched was a solicitor's office in which evidence relating to suspected money laundering by a client of the firm was sought.

---

[98] *ibid,* s 48(6).

[99] Child Trafficking and Pornography Act 1998, s 3(1) and (2) as substituted by the Criminal Law (Human Trafficking) Act 2008, s 3(a).

[100] *ibid,* s 3(2A) and (2B) as inserted by the Criminal Law (Sexual Offences) (Amendment) Act 2007, s 6(a).

[101] *Hanahoe v Hussey* [1998] 3 IR 69.

The Criminal Justice Act 1994 provides at s 64(1)[102] that a member of An Garda Síochána may apply to a judge of the District Court for a warrant in relation to specified premises for the purposes of an investigation into: **9–63**

(a) drug trafficking;
(b) the commission of an offence of financing terrorism;
(c) whether a person has benefited from drug trafficking;
(d) whether a person holds funds subject to confiscation;
(e) whether a person has benefited from an offence in respect of which a confiscation order might be made under s 9 of the Criminal Justice Act 1994.

The section had previously included a reference to money laundering under s 31 of the Criminal Justice Act 1994, but s 31 has been repealed by s 4(1) of the Criminal Justice (Money Laundering and Terrorist Financing) Act 2010.[103] Money laundering is now an offence under s 7 of the 2010 Act, with provision for extra-territorial money laundering also provided in s 8. The Act has extended the definition of drug trafficking as set out in the Criminal Justice Act 1994 to include not only producing, supplying, transporting, storing importing and exporting controlled drugs, but also engaging in conduct within or outside the State in relation to property obtained directly or indirectly from anything done in relation to a controlled drug.[104] Drug trafficking offences are defined as including offences under part 2 of the 2010 Act, ie money laundering and related offences.[105] **9–64**

Warrants under s 64 of the Criminal Justice Act 1994 work in tandem with orders for production of evidential material, with production orders being governed by s 63. If a judge is satisfied that there are reasonable grounds to believe that a person has engaged in criminal conduct, that the material sought is likely to be of substantial value (whether alone or in consideration with other material) for the purposes of the investigation or proceedings and that there are reasonable grounds for believing that material should be produced or that access should be given, having regard to the benefit likely to accrue to the investigation of proceedings or any other relevant circumstances, he can issue a warrant. The order operates to require any person who appears to the judge to be in possession of the material to produce it to a named member of An Garda Síochána so that he or she may take it away, or to give the member access to it within seven days, unless a longer period for compliance is appropriate in the circumstances.[106] Reasonable force **9–65**

102 Criminal Justice Act 1994, s 64(1) as substituted by s 40(a) of the Criminal Justice (Terrorist Offences) Act 2005.

103 The Criminal Justice (Money Laundering and Terrorist Financing) Act 2010 came into operation on 15 July 2010 by virtue of the Criminal Justice (Money Laundering and Terrorist Financing) Commencement Order 2010, SI No 342 of 2010. s 4(1) of the Act repealed ss 31, 32, 32A, 57(1) to (6) and 7(a), 57A and 58(2) of the Criminal Justice Act 1994.

104 Criminal Justice Act 1994, s 3(1)(d) as substituted by s 117(2) of the Criminal Justice (Money Laundering and Terrorist Financing) Act 2010.

105 *ibid*, s 3(1), subsection (e) of "drug trafficking offence" as substituted by s 117(3) of the Criminal Justice (Money Laundering and Terrorist Financing) Act 2010.

106 *ibid*, s 63(3) as substituted by the Criminal Justice (Mutual Assistance) Act 208, s 105(g).

may be used for entry if necessary, with the power to search the place and persons present, to take away material and to take the requisite steps to preserve the material and prevent interference with it.[107] If the material sought is held on computer, the order operates to require production or access to the material in a legible or comprehensible and portable form.[108] Orders under s 63 allow for documents to be taken and copied,[109] but such orders do not confer a right to production of, or access to, any material subject to legal privilege.[110] In *Hanahoe v Hussey*[111] it was noted that the search warrant issued under s 64 was expressly worded to exclude privileged documents and it was found that, in the course of the search, "scrupulous care was taken to ensure that there would be no improper or disproportionate breach of client confidentiality".[112] The Court referred to the case law of the European Court of Human Rights and in particular the case of *Niemietz v Germany* in which the search of a lawyer's office was found to constitute a breach of Article 8 of the European Convention which provides for rights to private and family life, home and correspondence. The following passages from the *Niemietz* judgment were cited, which have particular relevance if a search warrant of a solicitor's office is contemplated:

> "58. These features of privacy are particularly strong as regards the lawyer's activities in his own law office. There he exercises domestic authority and general access by the public is excluded. Such privacy is a necessary basis for the lawyer-client relationship.
>
> 59. The Commission, having regard to these particular features of a lawyer's professional activities in his law office, finds that the search of his office amounts to an interference with his right to respect for his private life and home under Article 8(1) of the Convention.
>
> ...
>
> 74. ... The interference complained of affected the applicant in his position as a lawyer, *i.e.* as an independent organ in the administration of justice and as independent counsel of his clients, with whom he must entertain a relationship of confidentiality, ensuing the secrecy of information received from his clients and documents relating thereto. Such are also the demands of the right to a fair trial and the effective use of defence rights as envisaged by article 6(1) and (3) of the Convention in cases of representation by counsel.
>
> 75. It appears that, when the search warrant was issued against the applicant, these aspects were not taken into due consideration."[113]

9–66 In addition to the legal privilege exception, there is a diplomatic basis for refusal to produce documentation or material: if material has been supplied to a government department or other authority by or on behalf of the government of another State and an undertaking was given that the material would be used only for a particular purpose

---

107 *ibid*, s 63(3)(b) and (c) as substituted by the Criminal Justice (Mutual Assistance) Act 208, s 105(g).

108 *ibid*, s 63(4) as substituted by the Criminal Justice (Mutual Assistance) Act 208, s 105(g).

109 *ibid*, s 63(5)(a) as substituted by the Criminal Justice (Mutual Assistance) Act 208, s 105(g).

110 *ibid*, s 63(5)(b) as substituted by the Criminal Justice (Mutual Assistance) Act 208, s 105(g).

111 *Hanahoe v Hussey* [1998] 3 IR 69.

112 *ibid* at 102.

113 *Niemietz v Germany* (1993) 16 EHRR 97, cited in *Hanahoe v Hussey* [1998] 3 IR 69 at pp 101 and 102

or purposes, an order will not require production of the document without the consent of that government.[114]

Subject to the exceptions of legal privilege and undertakings having been given to a foreign government, orders will have effect notwithstanding any other obligation about secrecy or other obligations as to disclosure imposed by statute or otherwise.[115] **9–67**

There is no reference in either s 63 or s 64 to the usual grounding sworn information or information on oath: the sections respectively provide for an order and a warrant to be granted on the basis of an application by a garda to a judge of the District Court. **9–68**

Warrants under s 64 authorise a specified garda to enter a premises, by force if necessary, and to search the premises if the judge is satisfied that an order for production of material under s 63 has not been complied with or that certain conditions are fulfilled: that there are reasonable grounds for suspecting that a specified person has carried on drug trafficking (which now includes money laundering offences under Part 2 of the Criminal Justice (Money Laundering and Terrorist Financing) Act 2010), has committed an offence of financing terrorism, has benefited from drug trafficking, holds funds subject to confiscation or has benefited from an offence in respect of which a confiscation order might be made under s 9 of the Criminal Justice Act 1994. Section 9 provides for confiscation orders to apply post-conviction on indictment for offences other than drug trafficking or financing terrorism offences. **9–69**

114 Criminal Justice Act 1994, s 63(10) as substituted by the Criminal Justice (Mutual Assistance) Act 2008, s 105(g).

115 *ibid*, s 63(5)(c) as substituted by the Criminal Justice (Mutual Assistance) Act 208, s 105(g).

CHAPTER 10

Powers of Seizure

INTRODUCTION

Closely related to the power to search is the power to seize, since the purpose of an entry for search is to gather evidence.[1] A decision to seize property ought to be underpinned by consideration of the rights of the owner to enjoyment of the property, identification of a power prescribed by law permitting the seizure of the particular property, and a determination as to the necessity and proportionality of seizing the property in all the circumstances. **10–01**

The Irish Constitution pledges in Article 40.3.2° to "by its laws protect as best it may from unjust attack and, in the case of injustice done, vindicate the … property rights of every citizen". Article 43 addresses property directly, providing: **10–02**

> "1. 1° The State acknowledges that man, in virtue of his rational being, has the natural right, antecedent to positive law, to the private ownership of external goods.
>
> 2° The State accordingly guarantees to pass no law attempting to abolish the right of private ownership or the general right to transfer, bequeath, and inherit property.
>
> 2. 1° The State recognises, however, that the exercise of the rights mentioned in the foregoing provisions of this Article ought, in civil society, to be regulated by the principles of social justice.
>
> 2° The State, accordingly, may as occasion requires delimit by law the exercise of the said rights with a view to reconciling their exercise with the exigencies of the common good."

---

1 The common law power of gardaí to seize and retain the property of others as evidence was recently affirmed by the Supreme Court in *McLaughlin v Aviva* [2011] IESC 42, where O'Donnell J held that "[i]t is very well established that the police can retain items against their true owner if they are required for the investigation and prosecution of criminal offences."

10–03 When powers of seizure are exercised, the property rights of the individual are circumscribed for the benefit of the community, since the common good is served by the investigation and prosecution of criminal offences. Given that the right to enjoyment of property is constitutional in origin, any interference with or limitation of property rights must be provided for and permitted by law. Accordingly, seizure must serve a legitimate purpose and must not be exercised arbitrarily.

10–04 Gardaí most frequently exercise their power to seize items of potential evidential value in the execution of search warrants, which specifically refer to the authority given by the warrant for the seizure of items of evidence found at a particular place. There are less obvious powers of seizure vested in gardaí which arise in a variety of circumstances—from the finding of an unexplained sum of cash[2] to the seizure of uninsured vehicles[3] and detection devices which might interfere with archaeological artefacts.[4] Sometimes seizure will involve temporarily depriving the owner of legitimately-owned property which is required as evidence in criminal proceedings, but seizure may also serve as the focus of enquiries as to the legitimacy or otherwise of the origins of property. Depending on the outcome of such enquiries, ill-gotten gains may be forfeited to the State, since it is long-established that there is no legal right to derive benefit from crime. As was remarked in *Cleaver v Mutual Reserve Fund Life Association:*

> "No system of jurisprudence can, with reason, include amongst the rights which it enforces, rights directly resulting to the person asserting them from the crime of that person."[5]

Murphy has argued that the state may seek restitution on behalf of the people:

> "[t]hat claim is asserted by the State against criminals on the basis that their assets represent the proceeds of crime obtained as a result of the violation of the public law of the State."[6]

---

2 See consideration of the Criminal Justice Act 1994, s 38, at paras 10–21 to 10–24.

3 See consideration of the Road Traffic Act 1994, s 41, at paras 10–16 to 10–18.

4 The National Monuments (Amendment) Act 1994 provides at s 7(1) that gardaí may seize and detain

> "(a) a detection device found in, at the site of or in the vicinity of, a monument referred to in section 2 (1) (a) (i) or (iv) (inserted by the National Monuments (Amendment) Act, 1994) of the National Monuments (Amendment) Act of 1987, or found in, or in the vicinity of, the areas referred to in section 2 (1) (a) (ii) or (iii) of the Act of 1987, unless the person in possession of the said device is in possession of a consent in respect of that device issued under section 2 (2) (a) of the Act of 1987, (b) any equipment (being equipment of a kind capable of being used in a contravention of section 3 of the Act of 1987) which he reasonably believes is being used in the commission of an offence under the said section, found in, at or in the vicinity of— (i) the site of a wreck, or (ii) an archaeological object that is lying on, in or under the sea bed or on land covered by water, and where such wreck or object is in, or in the vicinity of, an area to which this paragraph applies".

5 *Cleaver v Mutual Reserve Fund Life Association* [1892] 1 QB 147 at 156.

6 S Murphy, "Tracing the proceeds of crime: Legal and constitutional implications" in JP McCutcheon and D Walsh (eds) *The Confiscation of Criminal Assets* (Round Hall, Dublin, 1999) at p 36.

There are therefore two primary objectives in the vesting of powers of seizure in gardaí: first to gather and retain evidence for the prosecution, and secondly to facilitate the return to the exchequer of the proceeds of crime. This chapter will explore the law governing the seizure of property by gardaí in the investigation of criminal offences.[7] **10–05**

SEIZURE OF PROPERTY FROM ARRESTED PERSONS

In *Jennings v Quinn*[8] the Supreme Court stated definitively that property seized at the time of arrest may be retained as evidence by the gardaí. O' Keeffe J held: **10–06**

> "In my opinion the public interest requires that the police, when effecting a lawful arrest, may seize, without a search warrant, property in the possession or custody of the person arrested when they believe it necessary to do so to avoid the abstraction or destruction of that property and when that property is:
>
> (a) evidence in support of the criminal charge upon which the arrest is made, or
> (b) evidence in support of any other criminal charge against that person then in contemplation, or
> (c) reasonably believed to be stolen property or to be property unlawfully in the possession of that person;
>
> and that they may retain such property for use at the trial of the person arrested, or of any other person or persons, on any criminal charge in which the property is to be used as evidence in support of the charge or charges; and thereafter they should return the property to the person from whom it was seized, unless the disposal of the property otherwise has been directed by a court of competent jurisdiction.

---

7 The Proceeds of Crime Act 1996, as amended by the Proceeds of Crime (Amendment) Act 2005, provides a civil process of asset confiscation and forfeiture undertaken by the Criminal Assets Bureau. Under the proceeds of crime legislation, no conviction is required for the confiscation of assets which the High Court believes may directly or indirectly constitute the proceeds of crime. The statutory scheme established under the 1996 Act was summarised by Keane CJ in *Murphy v GM* [2001] 4 IR 113, at para 74: "The applicant, who must be a senior Garda officer, may obtain on an *ex parte* application to the High Court an order prohibiting a person who is in possession or control of specified property an expression which would obviously include the owner of the property from disposing [of] or dealing with the property if it is shown to the satisfaction of the Court that it constitutes, either directly or indirectly, the proceeds of crime. That order remains in effect for no longer than 21 days unless, before the expiration of that period, an application for a further order is made. This application must be made on notice to the person against whom the *ex parte* order was made or anyone else claiming to be the owner of the property. Again, the Court, if satisfied that the property constitutes, directly or indirectly, the proceeds of crime, may make an order to the same effect as the interim order, unless it is satisfied that there would be a 'serious risk of injustice'. That order then remains in force and, where it has been in force for at least seven years, the Court may make, on the application of the Garda officer, a 'disposal order' transferring the property to the Minister for Finance or such other person as the Court may determine." The applicable burden of proof is borrowed from the civil realm: the balance of probability standard is applied, and an onus is placed on the person who has had property taken to prove that the property was legitimately acquired. On the civil forfeiture regime, see JP McCutcheon and D Walsh (eds), *The Confiscation of Criminal Assets* (Round Hall, Dublin, 1999). See also S Horan, *Corporate Crime* (Bloomsbury Professional, Dublin, 2011) Chapters 20-22.

8 *Jennings v Quinn* [1968] IR 305.

> In so far as the property seized at the time of the arrest of the plaintiff might be required by police officers as material evidence in any charge brought against the plaintiff in this jurisdiction, their taking and retention of that property, in my view, would clearly be excused."[9]

10–07 The Court had endorsed the earlier decision in *Dillon v O'Brien and Davis*[10] where it was held that:

> "... the interest of the State in the person charged being brought to trial in due course necessarily extends as well to the preservation of material evidence of his guilt or innocence... his custody is of no value if the law is powerless to prevent the abstraction or destruction of this evidence..."[11]

For further consideration of the power to search arrested persons, see *Chapter 7: Stop and Search* at para 7–52 *et seq*.

SEIZURE OF ITEMS NOT INITIALLY SOUGHT UNDER A WARRANT

10–08 Seizing items which are sought under the authority of a warrant is unproblematic. However, questions have arisen, particularly in cases involving warrants directed at specific offences, as to whether items of potential evidential value in unrelated offences can be simultaneously seized. In the execution of a search warrant under s 26 of the Misuse of Drugs Act 1977, the decision as to whether to seize a suspected controlled drug or mixing agent is an entirely uncomplicated one; but what of a solicitor's letter containing legally privileged material? What of evidence unconnected with a drug investigation, but potentially relevant in the investigation of an unrelated and entirely different offence? In *Mc Nulty v DPP*[12] a search warrant was challenged[13] on the basis that it was issued under the Criminal Justice (Miscellaneous Provisions) Act 1997 for the investigation of the offence of rape, and the applicant was prosecuted for the possession of controlled drugs found during that search. The High Court held that a search warrant is generally issued, not just for the purpose of furthering a Garda investigation, but also to secure evidence for the prosecution. The court pointed to statutory provisions which allow searches in relation to controlled drugs, and found that it was clear that the warrant issued in *McNulty* was issued under s 10 of the Criminal Justice (Miscellaneous Provisions) Act 1997 (see further *Chapter 9: Entry Under Search Warrant*, at paras 9–57 and 9–58) and the seizure of the drugs was incidental to that power. In any event, s 9 of the Criminal Law Act 1976 permits gardaí to seize items which are believed to be evidence of any offence or suspected offence in the course of the exercise of a search power.

---

9 *ibid*, at 309.

10 *Dillon v O'Brien and Davis* [1887] 20 LR Ir 300 at 317.

11 *ibid*, cited in *Jennings v Quinn* [1968] IR 305 at 308.

12 *Mc Nulty v DPP* [2006] IEHC 74.

13 The warrant in *Mc Nulty v DPP* was challenged by judicial review. The High Court found that it was inappropriate that the matters raised be dealt with by judicial review. A date was fixed for the trial on 8 March 2004, and the matters could have been dealt with more properly, and certainly more expeditiously, by the trial judge, *Mc Nulty v DPP* [2006] IEHC 74. A subsequent appeal to the Supreme Court was dismissed, see *McNulty v DPP* [2009] IESC 12.

Section 9 of the Criminal Law Act 1976

Section 9 of the Criminal Law Act 1976 provides: **10–09**

> "(1) Where in the course of exercising any powers under this Act or in the course of a search carried out under any other power, a member of the Garda Síochána, a prison officer or a member of the Defence Forces finds or comes into possession of anything which he believes to be evidence of any offence or suspected offence, it may be seized and retained for use as evidence in any criminal proceedings, or in any proceedings in relation to a breach of prison discipline, for such period from the date of seizure as is reasonable or, if proceedings are commenced in which the thing so seized is required for use in evidence, until the conclusion of the proceedings, and thereafter the Police (Property) Act, 1897, shall apply to the thing so seized in the same manner as that Act applies to property which has come into the possession of the Garda Síochána in the circumstances mentioned in that Act.
>
> (2) If it is represented or appears to a person proposing to seize or retain a document under this section that the document was, or may have been, made for the purpose of obtaining, giving or communicating legal advice from or by a barrister or solicitor, that person shall not seize or retain the document unless he suspects with reasonable cause that the document was not made, or is not intended, solely for any of the purposes aforesaid."

Section 9 circumvents the difficulty which might arise if a warrant has been obtained for **10–10** the investigation of a narrow category of offences. Whereas s 10 of the Criminal Justice (Miscellaneous Provisions) Act 1997 (as substituted by s 6 of the Criminal Justice Act 2006) provides for search warrants to seek evidence of, or relating to, the commission of any arrestable offence, and for the seizure of anything found at that place, or in the possession of a person present which is reasonably believed to be evidence of, or relating to, the commission of an arrestable offence, other provisions are more limited. For instance, s 26 of the Misuse of Drugs Act 1977 provides for seizure of items potentially required as evidence of an offence under the Misuse of Drugs Act 1977 only. If gardaí had encountered the converse situation to that encountered in *McNulty*—ie if, in the execution of a s 26 Misuse of Drugs warrant, evidence relating to an offence of rape was found, s 9 of the Criminal Law Act 1976 could have been invoked to seize that evidence once the gardaí were present on foot of a valid search warrant and exercising their powers under the Misuse of Drugs Act 1977. Any limitation in search warrant provisions concerning the category of items which can be seized can therefore be ignored in light of s 9 of the Criminal Law Act 1976 As Ryan and Magee commented, the section "seems to render otiose the words in individual statutes which purport to limit the property which may be seized in the course of a search executed by a warrant issued thereunder".[14]

GENERAL STATUTORY POWER OF SEIZURE – SECTION 7 OF THE CRIMINAL JUSTICE ACT 2006

There is a statutory power in s 7 of the Criminal Justice Act 2006 to seize items which **10–11** may be evidence of an arrestable offence at any place where gardaí are present under a

---

14 E Ryan and P Magee, *The Irish Criminal Process* (Mercier Press Ltd, Dublin, 1983) at p 153.

power of entry authorised by law, or by invitation or by express or implied permission. So if, for instance, gardaí are in a private dwelling on the invitation of the householder and encounter evidence of drug cultivation, they can seize any item which is reasonably believed to be evidence of that offence without the necessity of a warrant. The general statutory power of seizure as set out in s 7 of the Criminal Justice Act 2006 is as follows:

> "(1) Where a member of the Garda Síochána who is in—
>
> (a) a public place, or
> (b) any other place under a power of entry authorised by law or to which or in which he or she was expressly or impliedly invited or permitted to be, finds or comes into possession of any thing, and he or she has reasonable grounds for believing that it is evidence of, or relating to, the commission of an arrestable offence, he or she may seize and retain the thing for use as evidence in any criminal proceedings for such period from the date of seizure as is reasonable or, if proceedings are commenced in which the thing so seized is required for use in evidence, until the conclusion of the proceedings, and thereafter the Police (Property) Act 1897 shall apply to the thing so seized in the same manner as that Act applies to property which has come into the possession of the Garda Síochána in the circumstances mentioned in that Act.
>
> (2) If it is represented or appears to a member of the Garda Síochána proposing to seize or retain a document under this section that the document was, or may have been, made for the purpose of obtaining, giving or communicating legal advice from or by a barrister or solicitor, the member shall not seize or retain the document unless he or she suspects with reasonable cause that the document was not made, or is not intended, solely for any of the purposes aforesaid.
>
> (3) The power under this section to seize and retain evidence is without prejudice to any other power conferred by statute or otherwise exercisable by a member of the Garda Síochána to seize and retain evidence of, or relating to, the commission or attempted commission of an offence."

10–12 Section 7 provides an extremely broad power of seizure of any property reasonably believed to provide evidence of an arrestable offence, howsoever it comes into the possession of the gardaí. Crucially, it also provides that that evidence can be retained, so that forensic testing or other relevant investigations can be conducted. A distinction between the power in s 7 of the Criminal Justice Act 2006 and s 9 of the Criminal Law Act 1976 is that, in the case of the latter power, there is no requirement of reasonableness. Once a warrant has been issued, any item believed to relate to an offence or suspected offence may be seized.

SEIZURE OF LEGALLY PRIVILEGED MATERIAL

10–13 Legal professional privilege operates to protect the privacy of communications between a client and legal advisor.[15] It is vital that a solicitor or barrister can advise a client on legal matters in confidence. Communications made in the furtherance of criminal

---

[15] For a detailed discussion of legal professional privilege, see D McGrath, *Evidence* (Thomson Round Hall, Dublin, 2005) ch 10.

conduct, fraud[16] or injurious to the interests of justice[17] do not attract legal privilege, but determining whether or not the veil of privilege is pierced because of the content of the communication is not entirely straightforward. Privilege is not necessarily lost because a lawyer has been consulted before the commission of a crime or fraud.[18] In recognition of the protection given to legally privileged material, it may not generally be seized. The provisions of s 9(1) of the Criminal Law Act 1976 and s 7(2) of the Criminal Justice Act 2006 both deal specifically with the question of legally privileged material, with a prohibition on the seizure or retention of any document made or potentially made for the purpose of giving or obtaining legal advice. In order to seize a document, the garda must have reasonable cause to believe that it was neither made nor intended solely for the purpose of obtaining, giving or communicating legal advice.

Some search warrant provisions expressly preclude the seizure of legally privileged **10–14** material in the execution of warrants issued under their terms, including the Criminal Assets Bureau Act 1996,[19] the Criminal Justice (Theft and Fraud Offences) Act 2001,[20] the Sea-Fisheries and Maritime Jurisdiction Act 2006[21] and the Criminal Justice (Mutual Assistance) Act 2008.[22]

In practice, particularly in cases involving large amounts of documentary evidence, it will **10–15** be difficult for gardaí conducting searches to distinguish between documents and to determine which, if any, of the documents it is proposed to seize are potentially privileged. Where computers are seized for examination and contain electronic communications between a solicitor or barrister and client, the task will be even more onerous. It is noteworthy that the Law Reform Commission has provisionally recommended that a system should be implemented to provide for the possibility of assertions of legal privilege, with material over which privilege is claimed in the course of a search warrant execution to be securely sealed and removed from the course of the search for assessment by a higher authority, such as a judge of the District Court, to determine if the material is legally privileged and therefore exempt from seizure under the search warrant.[23] Such a scheme might be of particular relevance in the investigation of white collar crime, and need not interfere unduly with the questioning of suspects, given the provision for pausing a detention under s 4 of the Criminal Justice Act 1984 introduced by the Criminal Justice Act 2011.[24] See further *Chapter 3: Re-Arrest* at para 3 – 25 *et seq* and *Chapter 5: Detention in Garda Custody*, at para 5 – 19 *et seq*.

---

16 *Annesley v Earl of Anglesea* (1743) 17 How St Tr 1229.

17 *Murphy v Kirwan* [1993] 3 IR 501.

18 *R. v Campbell* [1999] 1 SCR 565; (1999) 171 DLR (4th) 193.

19 Criminal Assets Bureau Act 1996, s 14(4) as amended by the Proceeds of Crime (Amendment) Act 2005, s 16(b).

20 Criminal Justice (Theft and Fraud Offences) Act 2001, s 48(6).

21 Sea-Fisheries and Maritime Jurisdiction Act 2006, s 17A as inserted by the Criminal Justice Act 2007, s 44.

22 Criminal Justice (Mutual Assistance) Act 2008, s 74.

23 Law Reform Commission, *Consultation Paper: Search Warrants and Bench Warrants* (CP 58 – 2009, LRC, Dublin, 2009).

24 Criminal Justice Act 1984, s 4(3A), as inserted by s 7 of the Criminal Justice Act 2011.

SEIZURE OF VEHICLES

10–16 A frequently invoked power of seizure in the road traffic law context is s 41 of the Road Traffic Act 1994. It provides for the detention of vehicles:

- where there is a failure to produce a driving licence or learner permit and the garda is of the opinion that the person driving is not old enough to hold a licence or permit;
- where the garda is of the opinion that the person is disqualified from driving;
- where it is reasonable to believe that the vehicle is being driven uninsured, without road tax or without an NCT certificate or, in the case of commercial vehicles, a certificate of roadworthiness.

10–17 Section 41 has been amended substantially. It is worth setting out in full:

> "(1) The Minister may, after consultation with the Minister for Justice, make regulations authorising and providing for the detention, removal, storage and subsequent release or disposal of a mechanically propelled vehicle in use in a public place where—
>
> [(a) the person driving the vehicle—
>
> (i) refuses or fails to produce there and then a driving licence or learner permit then having effect and licensing him or her to drive the vehicle, when production of such a licence is demanded of him or her by a member of the Garda Síochána under section 40 of the Principal Act or section 61 of the Road Traffic Act 2010 and the member is of opinion that the person is by reason of his or her age ineligible to hold a driving licence or learner permit licensing him or her to drive the vehicle,
>
> (ii) has had a driving licence or learner permit seized from him or her under section 60 of the Road Traffic Act 2010, or
>
> (iii) is, in the opinion of a member of the Garda Síochána, disqualified for holding a driving licence or learner permit,][25]
>
> [(b) the vehicle is, or a member of the Garda Síochána reasonably believes it to be, in the State and the member is of the opinion that the vehicle is, being so used in contravention of section 56(1) of the Principal Act,][26]
>
> (c) a member of the Garda Síochána is of opinion that any excise duty payable under section 1 of the Finance (Excise Duties) (Vehicles) Act, 1952, in respect of the vehicle, being a vehicle which is or which the member reasonably believes to be registered in the State, has not been paid in respect of a continuous period of [2 months][27] or more immediately prior to such use,
>
> [(d) the vehicle is, or a member of the Garda Síochána is of the opinion that the vehicle is, being so used in contravention of section 18(1) of the Principal Act,
>
> (e) the vehicle is, or a member of the Garda Síochána is of the opinion that the vehicle is, being so used in contravention of Regulation 19(1) of the European Communities

[25] Road Traffic Act 1994 s 41(a) as substituted by s 60(7) of the Road Traffic Act 2010.

[26] *ibid*, s 41(b) as substituted by s 19(a) of the Road Traffic Act 2006. s 56 of the Road Traffic Act 1961 sets out the obligation to insure mechanically propelled vehicles used in public places.

[27] Road Traffic Act 1994, s 41(c) as amended by s 19(b) of the Road Traffic Act 2006.

> (Vehicle Testing) Regulations 2004 (S.I. No. 771 of 2004) [or section 6 (1) of the Road Safety Authority (Commercial Vehicle Roadworthiness) Act 2012][28]
>
> (f) in the case of a vehicle registered in another Member State, the vehicle is, or a member of the Garda Síochána is of the opinion that it is, being so used without a proof of passing a roadworthiness test in accordance with Council Directive 96/96/EC of 20 December 1996 or [Directive 2009/40/EC of the European Parliament and of the Council of 6 May 2009][29] which is for the time being in force in respect of the vehicle.][30]

The Road Traffic Act 1994 (Detention of Vehicles) Regulations 2011 (SI No 460 of 2011) gives practical effect to s 41, providing for retention, storage, disposal and release of vehicles seized under s 41. **10–18**

THE SEIZURE OF CASH

The Criminal Justice Act 1994 introduced the offence of money-laundering into Irish law and also provided for conviction-based asset confiscation, whereby the trial court can, on the application of the Director of Public Prosecutions, investigate the profit that a person convicted on indictment has made in the case of a drug trafficking offence.[31] The legislation also provided for the restraint of property pending criminal trial, to facilitate a confiscation order in the event of a subsequent conviction.[32] 'Drug trafficking' and 'drug trafficking offences' are broadly defined to include not only drug offences[33] but also money laundering of the proceeds of drug trafficking under Part 2 of the of the Criminal Justice (Money Laundering and Terrorist Financing) Act 2010.[34] The Act further provides for post-conviction forfeiture of property which has been lawfully seized or was in the defendant's possession or under his control at the time of his apprehension for an offence if the court is satisfied that the property (i) has been used for the purpose of committing, or facilitating the commission of, any offence, or (ii) was intended by him to be used for that purpose.[35] **10–19**

---

28 Road Traffic Act 1994, s 41(d) to (f) were inserted by s 19(c) of the Road Traffic Act 2006. A further insertion was made in s 41(f) by s 45(b) of the Road Safety Authority (Commercial Vehicle Roadworthiness) Act 2012.

29 Road Traffic Act 1994, s 41(d) to (f) were inserted by s 19(c) of the Road Traffic Act 2006. A further insertion was made in s 41(f) by s 45(b) of the Road Safety Authority (Commercial Vehicle Roadworthiness) Act 2012.

30 Road Traffic Act 1994, s 41(d) to (e) were inserted by s 19(c) of the Road Traffic Act 2006.

31 Criminal Justice Act 1994, s 4.

32 *ibid*, s 23.

33 Paragraph (bbb) inserted by the Criminal Justice Act 2006, s 86.

34 Criminal Justice Act 1994, s 3(1) includes reference to "(a) an offence under any regulations made under section 5 of the Misuse of Drugs Act, 1977, involving the manufacture, production, preparation, importation, exportation, supply, offering to supply, distribution or transportation of a controlled drug, (b) an offence under section 15 of that Act of possession of a controlled drug for unlawful sale or supply, [(bb) an offence under section 15A of that Act;] [(bbb) an offence under section 15B (importation of controlled drugs in excess of certain value) of that Act;]..." (paragraph (e) of 'drug trafficking offence' substituted by the Criminal Justice (Money Laundering and Terrorist Financing) Act 2010, s 117(3)).

35 Criminal Justice Act 1994, s 61.

10–20 Powers of seizure are among the most important of the Act's provisions and, in seizing cash under the Act at the investigative stage, there is no requirement that the cash be linked with a drug offence, but merely that it is suspected to constitute, directly or indirectly, the proceeds of crime or that it is intended for use in connection with any criminal conduct.

10–21 Section 38(1) of the Criminal Justice Act 1994 as substituted by s 20(a) of the Proceeds of Crime (Amendment) Act 2005 provides the power to search for cash:

> "(1) A member of the Garda Síochána or an officer of customs and excise may search a person if the member or officer has reasonable grounds for suspecting that —
>
> (a) the person is importing or exporting, or intends or is about to import or export, an amount of cash which is not less than the prescribed sum, and
> (b) the cash directly or indirectly represents the proceeds of crime or is intended by any person for use in connection with any criminal conduct."

The prescribed sum is £5,000 or €6,348.69.[36]

10–22 The power of seizure is set out in s 38(1A)[37] and may be exercised not only when it is suspected that the cash found is intended for export or import, but in any case where the cash exceeds £5,000 and there are reasonable grounds for suspecting that it directly or indirectly represents the proceeds of crime or is intended by anyone for use in any criminal conduct. Section 38(1A) provides:

> "(1A) A member of the Garda Síochána or an officer of the Revenue Commissioners may seize and in accordance with this section detain any cash (including cash found during a search under subsection (1)) if—
> (a) its amount is not less than the prescribed sum, and
> (b) he or she has reasonable grounds for suspecting that it directly or indirectly represents the proceeds of crime or is intended by any person for use in any criminal conduct."

10–23 Cash seized by virtue of s 38 may be detained initially for 48 hours, unless its detention beyond 48 hours is authorised by a judge of the District Court. No such order shall be made unless the judge is satisfied that there are reasonable grounds for the suspicion and that detention of the cash beyond 48 hours is justified while its origin or derivation is further investigated or consideration is given to the institution (whether in the State or elsewhere) of criminal proceedings against any person for an offence with which the cash is connected.[38] A District Judge may order the continuing retention of the cash every three months up to a maximum of two years.[39] Thereafter the State may apply for the confiscation of the cash under s 39 of the Act.

---

[36] The prescribed sum is set out in SI No 167 of 1996, Criminal Justice Act, 1994 (Section 44) Regulations, 1996.

[37] Criminal Justice Act 1994, s 38(1A) as inserted by the Proceeds of Crime (Amendment) Act 2005, s 20(a).

[38] Criminal Justice Act 1994, s 38(2).

[39] *ibid*, s 38(3).

It was argued in the case of *K v Taaffe and others* that there was a lacuna in the legislation permitting detention of cash, since s 38(2) refers only to the judge having to be satisfied that there are reasonable grounds for the suspicion mentioned in s 38(1) — there is no reference to s 38(1A) since that sub-section was inserted into the section by s 20 of the Proceeds of Crime (Amendment) Act 2005. O'Neill J rejected the submission, holding: **10–24**

> "I am satisfied that what is at issue here is the process of substitution i.e. removing one provision and replacing it with another. The insertion of new text into s. 38(1) of the Act of 1994, by the virtue of s. 20 of the Act of 2005, creates the situation that the reference in s. 38(2) to the power under s. 38(1) continues the connection between s. 38(2) and the substituted provision. As is readily apparent, this substitution is achieved seamlessly without creating any textual awkwardness let alone requiring any straining of interpretation and manifestly, in my opinion, preserves the functioning of s. 38(2)... I am quite satisfied that the amending provision is fully integrated into the original Act, thus maintaining the connection between s. 38(2) and the amended s. 38(1A)."[40]

For the purposes of s 38 of the Criminal Justice Act 1994, 'cash' is defined as including any notes and coins in any currency, postal orders, cheques (including travellers cheques), bank drafts, bearer bonds and bearer shares.[41]

---

40 *K v Taaffe and others* [2009] IEHC 243, at paras 3.5-3.6.

41 Criminal Justice Act 1994, s 43(1), as amended by the Proceeds of Crime (Amendment) Act 2005, s 22.

Part V

The Power to Survey and Intercept

Chapter 11

Covert Policing

INTRODUCTION

In covert policing, whether by surveillance, interception, the use of informers or in test purchases, police officers are in an unusual position. In undercover operations, they find themselves observing and encouraging, and occasionally even participating in criminal offences.[1] In doing so, they may skirt close to the limits of legality,[2] and in Ireland they do so with limited and complicated legislative guidance. **11–01**

There are obvious advantages to covert operations from a policing perspective: the evidence gathered in covert operations is reliable and often incontrovertible. Covert operations can be more effective and less resource-intensive than traditional approaches. Reflective of the move towards proactive rather than reactive policing, covert methods allow police to operate in a less-regulated environment with the potential to gather high-quality evidence and to do so relatively quickly.[3] A window is opened on the inner workings and hierarchy of criminal organisations with the potential to detect and disrupt organised and drug-related crime in which participants are complicit and accordingly **11–02**

1 See A Sanders and R Young, "Police Powers" in T Newburn (ed), *Handbook of Policing* (2nd ed, Willan Publishing, Cullompton, 2008) at p 299.

2 L Campbell, "Informers in Ireland: a Lack of Law?" *Human Rights in Ireland,* 10 May 2013 http://humanrights.ie/uncategorized/informers-in-ireland-a-lack-of-law/ <accessed 28 October 2013>.

3 See N Taylor, "Policing, Privacy and Proportionality," EHRLR, 2003, Special Issue, 86, referenced in D Clark, *Bevan and Lidstone's The Investigation of Crime: A Guide to the Law of Criminal Investigation* (3rd ed, LexisNexis, Suffolk, 2004) at p 573.

unwilling witnesses.[4] In the detection of drug-trafficking offences, for instance, harm can be prevented if covert investigative methods allow police intervention at a point before the distribution to users, thereby minimising the harm caused.[5] There is also an increasing reluctance among members of the public to give evidence, particularly in the context of organised crime and terrorism, necessitating enhancement of investigative capabilities.[6]

11–03 Covert policing brings to mind the targeted tactics of traditional or electronic surveillance and communication interception. It includes the use of covert human intelligence sources (CHIS) and other intrusive or deceptive investigative measures, but it has broadened, facilitated by the continuous collection and storage of data on everything from our medical histories to the content of our shopping trolleys.[7] Information concerning the movements, communications, internet searches, associations and activities of individuals is gathered, managed and kept, both by gardaí and by various organisations, including telecommunications companies, with which individuals come into contact.

11–04 Given the vast amount of personal and telecommunications data now routinely stored on public and private databases and the "Panopticon"[8] which has been created by

---

4 See generally C Harfield and K Harfield, *Covert Investigation* (3rd ed., Oxford University Press, Oxford, 2012).

5 *ibid*, ch 1.

6 D Clark, Bevan and Lidstone's *The Investigation of Crime: A Guide to the Law of Criminal Investigation* (3rd ed, LexisNexis, 2004) at p 573. See also "One Step Ahead: a 21st Century Response to Organised Crime" (Home Office, London, 2004).

7 See H Nissenbaum, "Protecting Privacy in an Information Age: the Problem of Privacy in Public, *Law and Philosophy*, 17: pp 559-596, 1998.

8 The legal theorist Jeremy Bentham designed the Panopticon as a model prison in which surveillance could be constant, the design ensuring that no prisoner could ever see the prison guard who conducted surveillance from a central location within the radial configuration. The uncertainty in the mind of the prisoner, who could never know when he was being observed, would provide a means of discipline. As Foucault put it: "[h]ence the major effect of the Panopticon: to induce in the inmate a state of conscious and permanent visibility that assures the automatic functioning of power. So to arrange things that the surveillance is permanent in its effects, even if it is discontinuous in its action; that the perfection of power should tend to render its actual exercise unnecessary; that this architectural apparatus should be a machine for creating and sustaining a power relation independent of the person who exercises it; in short, that the inmates should be caught up in a power situation of which they are themselves the bearers. To achieve this, it is at once too much and too little that the prisoner should be constantly observed by an inspector: too little, for what matters is that he knows himself to be observed; too much, because he has no need in fact of being so. In view of this, Bentham laid down the principle that power should be visible and unverifiable. Visible: the inmate will constantly have before his eyes the tall outline of the central tower from which he is spied upon. Unverifiable: the inmate must never know whether he is being looked at at any one moment; but he must be sure that he may always be so. In order to make the presence or absence of the inspector unverifiable, so that the prisoners, in their cells, cannot even see a shadow, Bentham envisaged not only venetian blinds on the windows of the central observation hall, but, on the inside, partitions that intersected the hall at right angles and, in order to pass from one quarter to the other, not doors but zig-zag openings; for the slightest noise, a gleam of light, a brightness in a half-opened door would betray the presence of the guardian. The Panopticon is a machine for dissociating the see / being seen dyad: in the peripheric ring, one is totally seen, without ever seeing; in the central tower, one sees everything without ever being seen." M. Foucault, *Discipline and Punish: The Birth of the Prison,* (Vintage Books, New York, 1995) pp 195–228.

the absorption of closed circuit television cameras in shops, workplaces, transport systems and public spaces, technology provides opportunities for more systematic and invasive approaches[9] to criminal investigation. The sophisticated machinery of modern investigation[10] impinges on non-suspect and suspect citizens alike, with a wide-angle lens engaged, akin to dragnet trawling, in which the activities of many non-suspects are consequentially caught and recorded. There is a discernible dilution of heretofore understood notions of privacy. In principle, privacy ought not to be sacrificed for safety, as individuals enjoy a right to both,[11] but in the electronic age, privacy is continuously challenged: it is estimated that in London in a single day, a citizen could expect to be filmed by over 300 cameras on more than 30 separate CCTV systems.[12] Whereas a search must be predicated on a prior suspicion, surveillance cameras record associations, movements, intimate and non-intimate interactions. Those movements and actions, whether immediately relevant for law-enforcement purposes or not, are captured, recorded, stored and retained, with significant implications for privacy. Cell site analysis, by which the location of a mobile phone user at a given time is determined by reference to its proximity to the mast from which it receives its signal, has proven to be an effective and powerful tool in criminal investigations,[13] but it also means that mobile phones provide a continuous record of their owners' communications and their whereabouts. Marx has referred to the phenomenon of "surveillance creep" in which the boundaries of legal acceptability are pushed, with each individual shift in practice being relatively insignificant in and of itself, but producing the cumulative effect of steadily eroding rights which were once taken for granted.[14]

The starting point in covert policing, as with other areas of police work, is the right to **11–05**
privacy of the individual. The Law Reform Commission has explained the importance of privacy in the following terms:

> "Why is privacy so important? .... Privacy is not merely instrumental[15] to the achievement of other goals but is a basic human right that applies to all persons in virtue of their status as human beings. It is not possible to overstate just how fundamental privacy is in a developed and civilised legal system. A sense of its importance can be gleaned by rehearsing briefly some of the many important overlapping values that are served by it.[16] First, privacy

9 L Campbell, *Organised Crime and the Law: A Comparative Analysis* (Oxford, Hart, 2013) at p 75.

10 A sample of the devices now available for covert surveillance is contained in the Law Reform Commission Report *Privacy: Surveillance and the Interception of Communications* (LRC 57–1998) pp 5–7.

11 See S Davies 'CCTV: a new battleground for privacy' in C Norris, J Moran and G Armstrong (eds), *Surveillance, Closed Circuit Television and Social Control* (Ashgate, Aldershot, 1998), 243 at p 246.

12 C Norris and G Armstrong, *The Maximum Surveillance Society: the Rise of CCTV* (Oxford, Berg, 1999) at p 42. See also L Hempel and E Töpfer, Urbaneye: CCTV in Europe Final Report, Working Paper No 15, Centre for Technology and Society Technical University, Berlin, August 2004.

13 In Ireland, the case of Joe O'Reilly brought the use of such evidence to the forefront of the public mind, while in the UK, such evidence was used in the investigation and prosecution of Ian Huntley for the so-called 'Soham murders'.

14 G Marx, *Police Surveillance in America* (University of California Press, Berkeley, 1988).

15 See generally Charles Fried, "Privacy", 77 Yale LJ 475 (1968).

16 For a compendium of the most significant works in the field, see the International Library of Essays in Law & Legal Theory, Vols I & II, Raymond Wacks (ed), *Privacy* (Dartmouth, 1993). See also

is closely connected to notions of inherent human dignity. The intimacies of private life go to the very core of what it means to be human. Privacy is therefore worthwhile in itself in protecting human personality or the inherent dignity of the person[17] ... Secondly, privacy is closely related to human freedom, autonomy and self-determination... The pursuit of private goals will often involve the formation of voluntary relations with others of varying degrees of intimacy. As the European Commission pointed out, privacy therefore entails the right to establish and to develop relationships with other human beings, especially in the emotional field for the development and fulfilment of one's own personality[18]. Another way of looking at this is that privacy is necessary to give efficacy to the exercise of many different liberty interests, including freedom of association...."[19]

11–06 The Commission added that privacy is "an organising principle of civil society" and "closely connected to the democratic life of the polity".[20] The Commission concluded that "[p]rivacy is important for all these reasons and is therefore indispensable to the full flourishing of the human personality in a free society".[21] Gillane has commented that, in the context of the 2009 surveillance legislation, the language used by the Law Reform Commission "almost seems quaint".[22] The right continues to be protected by the Constitution[23] and by the European Convention on Human Rights,[24] but in the context of surveillance it can be difficult to identify the outer borders of the realm of privacy—the extent of the right to be left alone[25]—since those borders are not always immediately apparent or entirely clear.

11–07 In the United Kingdom, the House of Lords Select Committee on the Constitution has commented that:

"Surveillance is an inescapable part of life in the UK. Every time we make a telephone call, send an email, browse the internet, or even walk down our local high street, our actions may be monitored and recorded. To respond to crime, combat the threat

Ferdinand Schoeman (ed), *Philosophical Dimensions of Privacy: An Anthology* (Cambridge University Press, Cambridge, 1984); and Julie C Innes, *Privacy, Intimacy and Isolation* (Oxford University Press, 1992). For an evaluation of the relative merits of the theories of *privacy*, see J Wagner DeCew, *In Pursuit of Privacy: Law, Ethics and the Rise of Technology*, (Cornell U Press, New York, 1997).

17 See generally Hyman Gross, *The Concept of Privacy*, 42 NYU Law Rev 34 (1967).

18 *X v Iceland*, Decision of the European Commission on admissibility, 5 DR, 86 at p 87.

19 Law Reform Commission Report *Privacy: Surveillance and the Interception of Communications* (LRC 57–1998) at pp 1–3.

20 *ibid* at p 3.

21 *ibid* at p 3.

22 S Gillane "Criminal Justice (Surveillance) Bill 2009" – Paper presented at the 10th National Prosecutors' Conference, 23 May 2009, at p 2.

23 *Bunreacht na hÉireann,* Art 40.

24 Article 8 of the European Convention on Human Rights provides:

"1. Everyone has the right to respect for his private and family life, his home and correspondence. 2. There shall be no interference by a public authority with the exercise of this right except such as is in accordance with the law and is necessary in a democratic society in the interests of national security, public safety or the economic well-being of the country, for the prevention of disorder or crime, for the protection of health or morals, or for the protection of the rights and freedoms of others."

25 See *Kennedy v Ireland* [1987] IR 587, [1988] ILRM 472.

> of terrorism, and improve administrative efficiency, successive UK governments have gradually constructed one of the most extensive and technologically advanced surveillance systems in the world. At the same time, similar developments in the private sector have contributed to a profound change in the character of life in this country. The development of electronic surveillance and the collection and processing of personal information have become pervasive, routine, and almost taken for granted. Many of these surveillance practices are unknown to most people, and their potential consequences are not fully appreciated."[26]

As a consequence of the technological revolution, a societal shift is discernable: the veil of privacy is thinly drawn and there are continual demands to pierce it. The tools of surveillance are freely available to police and private citizen alike, and there is a growing demand for, and interest in, the acquisition of information about others.[27] It is against this backdrop that covert policing, and the Irish legislation which governs aspects of it, falls to be considered. **11–08**

The other key right in this sphere, albeit of indirect application, is the right to fairness in pre-trial proceedings, guaranteed by Article 6 of the European Convention on Human Rights, which is not limited to the trial process but also includes the pre-trial period and the manner in which evidence is gathered.[28] **11–09**

Prior to the enactment of the Criminal Justice (Surveillance) Act 2009, covert policing activities in Ireland were largely unregulated. Even with the advent of the Criminal Justice (Surveillance) Act 2009, gardaí engage in covert policing with very limited legislative guidance and, to a large extent, without the visibility (and attendant accountability) of overt policing methods.[29] Though the enactment of the Criminal Justice (Surveillance) Act 2009 represents an advance, providing legislation to underpin certain forms of surveillance where there was none, the practical and ethical questions involved remain unanswered in Ireland. For example when are covert policing methods appropriately employed? To what degree can information gathered for other means be used in investigations? What constitutes legitimate justification for intrusion? And what occurs when information is gathered as intelligence without a specific criminal investigation as its focus? **11–10**

This chapter will examine surveillance, the interception of communications, entrapment and the use of Covert Human Intelligence Sources (CHIS). To comply with ECHR standards, practices which interfere with the right to privacy should be lawful, justifiable **11–11**

---

26 House of Lords Select Committee on the Constitution, 2nd report of 2008-2009, *Surveillance: Citizens and the State,* HL Paper 18-1, at p 5.

27 See Law Reform Commission Report *Privacy: Surveillance and the Interception of Communications,* (LRC 57–1998), p 5–7.

28 See *Teixeira de Castro v Portugal* (1999) 28 EHRR 101; *Imbrioscia v Switzerland*, 24 November 1993, Series A no 275, p 13, § 36; *Brennan – United Kingdom*,16 October 2001, appl no 39846/98), §45.

29 Harfield and Harfield have noted that "[t]he secrecy of covert investigation limits the ways in which investigators can be managed and held to account." C Harfield and K Harfield, *Covert Investigation* (3rd ed, Oxford University Press, Oxford, 2012) at p 7.

by reference to a legitimate aim, necessary and proportionate.[30] As will be seen, the Irish legislative regime governing covert policing is not comprehensive, and consequential question marks hang over areas of covert policing in Ireland in terms of ECHR compliance since, for every interference with a Convention right, there must be a basis in law which is, in key aspects of this area of garda practice, conspicuously absent.

CCTV

11–12 CCTV has to some degree displaced the public and informers in alerting the police to crime and providing evidence of it, but the corollary is monitoring of public places, with the result that a wealth of information on suspects, criminal activity and the public at large is available to the gardaí.[31] CCTV footage and other sources of highly probative evidence—speed cameras, audio recordings, mobile telecommunications data and computers—can be obtained without the direct involvement of the individual and, as such, would appear not to be perceived as objectionably intrusive interferences, notwithstanding their considerable intelligence-gathering potential. As regards CCTV in particular, the governance of the footage by the Data Protection Act 1988, as well as public knowledge of the use of CCTV recording systems, means that CCTV effectively falls outside the scope of covert policing. CCTV was omitted from the definition of surveillance in the Criminal Justice (Surveillance) Act 2009.

The Garda Síochána Act 2005 provides that CCTV has as its "sole or primary purpose ... securing public order and safety in public places by facilitating the deterrence, prevention, detection and prosecution of offences".[32]

11–13 A detailed explanation of the basis for the section was given by the then Minister for Justice, Michael McDowell:

> "At present there is no legislative basis for the operation by the Garda or local communities of CCTV. The issue of evidence derived from Garda CCTV has been raised in criminal trials but the legality of Garda CCTV does not seem to have been challenged or been the subject of any adverse finding. Judgments could be regarded as implicitly supportive of CCTV such as that in the case of *Mitchell v The Director of Public Prosecutions*, which was reported in 2000 in the Irish Law Reports Monthly. Footage from non-Garda CCTV has also featured in recent Supreme Court decisions, *Braddish v DPP* and *Dunne v DPP*. In April this year, my Department sought advice from the Attorney General as to whether legislation is required to regulate the use of CCTV in public places by the Garda and community groups ... The Attorney General advised that, subject to confirmation with the Office of the Data Protection Commissioner, the Garda Síochána and local authorities-in the case of local community groups-are data controllers for the purpose of the Data Protection Act 1988 and are therefore the subject of section 13 which allows for codes of practice to be agreed with the Data Protection Commissioner

[30] See AA Gillespie, "Covert Surveillance, Human Rights and the Law" (2009) 19(3) ICLJ 71.

[31] See BJ Goold, *CCTV and Policing: Public Area Surveillance and Police Practices in Britain* (Oxford University Press, Oxford, 2004) p 3.

[32] s 38 allows the Garda Commissioner to authorise the installation and operation of CCTV in specified areas.

> and for their elevation to the status of Statutory Instruments. These codes of practice will regulate working with CCTV but would not authorise CCTV themselves. The Office of the Data Protection Commissioner subsequently confirmed this position and supported the proposal to place the operation of CCTV on a statutory footing. In addition, in order to satisfy the requirements of Article 8 of the European Convention on Human Rights that the interference with the rights of privacy of individuals recorded by CCTV is in accordance with law, it was necessary to provide in legislation for the conditions and circumstances in which CCTV might be put in place. Failure to do so would mean it could be regarded as a disproportionate and unlimited power. As the operation of surveillance for the purposes of crime prevention, investigation and prosecution is an executive function of the State, in order for it to be carried out on the authority of the Government, legislation should provide for the delegation of the function and for an authorisation system which would enable the Garda Síochána to supervise the operation of the system and to withdraw such authorisations as necessary. In the latter regard, the aim would be to prevent those private parties, be they community groups or otherwise, who have inadequate controls in place or who breach an individual's right to privacy from continuing to record image data. The provisions in this new section give effect to this advice and have been inserted as a new section into chapter 4 of the Bill which has been re-titled 'Co-operation with Local Authorities and Security in Public Places'. Subsection (3)(c) of the new s 38, as it applies to local community-based CCTV systems, links in with the joint policing committees provided for in s 35."[33]

CCTV captures recognisable images and occasionally sounds and, as such, the images captured constitute 'personal data' within the meaning of the Data Protection Acts 1988–2003. There 'personal data' is defined as "data relating to a living individual who is or can be identified either from the data or from the data in conjunction with other information that is in, or is likely to come into, the possession of the data controller".[34] A data controller must be in a position to justify obtaining and using personal data by means of a CCTV system. A distinction is drawn by the Data Commissioner: **11–14**

> "[a] system used to control the perimeter of a building for security purposes will usually be easy to justify. The use of CCTV systems in other circumstances – for example, to constantly monitor employees, customers or students – can be more difficult to justify and could involve a breach of the Data Protection Acts".[35]

The Data Protection Act 1988 provides certain safeguards at s 2(c) (as amended by s 3 of the Data Protection (Amendment) Act 2003) which apply to information gathered by the gardaí generally, as well as in the recording of CCTV: the data must have been obtained only for one or more specified, explicit and legitimate purposes; it must not be further processed in a manner incompatible with the original purpose or purposes; and it must be proportionate, adequate and relevant to the purpose. Crucially, it must be retained for no longer than is necessary. The Data Protection Commissioner suggests that "[f]or a normal security system, it would be difficult to justify retention beyond a **11–15**

33 180 *Seanad Debates* Cols 2196–2197.

34 Data Protection Act 1988, s 1(a)(iv) as amended by s 2 of the Data Protection (Amendment) Act 2003

35 See the website of the Data Protection Commissioner http://www.dataprotection.ie/viewdoc.asp?m=m&fn=/documents/guidance/cctv.htm.

month, except where the images identify an issue – such as a break-in or theft – and is retained specifically in the context of an investigation of that issue".[36]

THE CRIMINAL JUSTICE (SURVEILLANCE) ACT 2009

11–16 The Criminal Justice (Surveillance) Act 2009 was enacted "to provide for surveillance in connection with the investigation of arrestable offences, the prevention of suspected arrestable offences and the safeguarding of the State against subversive and terrorist threats".[37] Surveillance had been undertaken prior to 2009, but the gardaí had operated in a legal vacuum in the absence of a legislative scheme to govern and underpin the use of intrusive surveillance methods, apart from telephone tapping. As the explanatory memorandum made clear when the then Criminal Justice (Surveillance) Bill was introduced:

> "It is has not been the practice to use the material gained by means of secret surveillance as evidence for legal and operational reasons. In regulating this area by law the Bill ensures that any possible legal obstacles to the admissibility of such material in criminal trials are removed in cases involving arrestable offences. A key section in the Bill deals with the admissibility of evidence gained by surveillance."

Gillane has wryly commentated:

> "It seems in reality that the [Criminal Justice (Surveillance)] Bill is attempting in this context to do two things: firstly, it sets out a statutory framework through which members of An Garda Síochána can legitimately monitor and retain details of personal conversations and communications; and secondly, acknowledges that there never has been a right to be left alone, merely you had a right not to have such invasions of your privacy as existed used against you in a court of law."[38]

11–17 There is an implicit recognition that "secret surveillance" has long been conducted, but to say that the Act served to regulate the law is something of an overstatement as, even after its introduction, there are considerable gaps in the legislative regime concerning surveillance. The Criminal Justice (Surveillance) Act was introduced with the critique of the Law Reform Commission in mind and in the wake of the Morris Tribunal. In its 1998 Report on Privacy: Surveillance and the Interception of Communications,[39] the Commission noted that a privacy problem arose out of surveillance which was grave enough to warrant a legislative response. The Commission reported that:

> "… notwithstanding the existence of a substantial volume of domestic positive law which, in some cases by design, but more often by default, addresses problems arising in the sphere of privacy – the law is at present inadequate to afford protection for privacy

---

[36] See the website of the Data Protection Commissioner http://www.dataprotection.ie/viewdoc.asp?m=m&fn=/documents/guidance/cctv.htm <accessed 28 October 2013>.

[37] Criminal Justice (Surveillance) Act 2009, long title.

[38] S Gillane "Criminal Justice (Surveillance) Bill 2009"—Paper presented at the 10th National Prosecutors' Conference, 23 May 2009, at p 2.

[39] Law Reform Commission, *Report on Privacy: Surveillance and the Interception of Communications* (LRC 57–1998).

> against unjustifiable acts of surveillance. Nor is it adequate or comprehensive enough to provide the needed ancillary protection against the dissemination or publication of any information that results from privacy-invasive surveillance."[40]

The existing law was described as providing a "patchwork quilt" of "haphazard and uncertain protection" and the Commission's recommendation was for a new law against privacy-invasive surveillance.[41] The Commission drew attention to the gap between constitutional protection for the right of privacy and practical legal provision for an effective means of redress[42] and also to the requirement to comply with the European Convention on Human Rights. **11–18**

The Law Reform Commission took the view that it was arguable that: **11–19**

> "covert police surveillance (using electronic means) amounts to an 'interference' with private life, especially the more remote it is from a specific crime. If so, some sort of legal basis is necessary to allow it to occur in a manner compatible with Article 8 … adequate guidance should be given in the law as to the scope of covert surveillance, its duration, the grounds on which an application may be made, the nature of the competent authorities permitting, executing and supervising the acts and the remedies available. What seems particularly important is the presence of some independent element in the process of supervising the implementation of such regime."[43]

The recommendations were ignored and further criticism was levelled at the inadequate guidance given to gardaí undertaking surveillance in the report of the Morris Tribunal. The tribunal commented: **11–20**

> "It became obvious during the course of the Tribunal's hearings that there is little or no, legal or ethical, guidance given to An Garda Síochána by statute or statutory instrument, or in the Garda Síochána Code, concerning covert surveillance whether by Gardaí in person or by means of audio or audio/visual electronic devices or recorders…
>
> The Tribunal was disturbed and dismayed at the extent to which covert taping was conducted by the Gardaí, not alone of conversations with civilians, but of conversations between Gardaí supposedly working together. This issue also involves the right to privacy as guaranteed under Article 40.3 of the Constitution. In the course of the examination of the allegations of bugging of interview rooms in Letterkenny Garda Station made against other Gardaí by Detective Sergeant White, the Tribunal heard evidence of a documented case of covert eavesdropping and audio recording of a conversation between two prisoners in a cell at Ballinasloe Garda Station some years previously…
>
> Having regard to the surveillance contemplated against Frank McBrearty Senior, repeated tape recording of conversations by the Gardaí, and the other evidence described

[40] *ibid*, at p 61.

[41] *ibid* at p 61.

[42] The commission noted: "[T]here is a palpable need to move beyond general constitutional protection to create effective means of redress in positive law. Irish positive law fails to deliver a comprehensive and effective means of protection at present. The glaring gap between high constitutional promise and practical legal provision needs to be closed." Law Reform Commission Report on *Privacy: Surveillance and the Interception of Communications* (LRC 57–1998) at pp 42-43.

[43] *ibid* at p 201.

in Chapter 14, the Tribunal is concerned that this area remains unregulated by statute or statutory instrument. In this regard, the Tribunal recommends that the Law Reform Commission Report on Privacy: Surveillance and the interception of Communications (June 1998) be reviewed with a view to implementing the extensive recommendations in that report concerning regulatory provisions in respect of certain forms of surveillance by An Garda Síochána and others. It is entirely wrong that the Gardaí should be recording persons, including their colleagues and senior officers, at will and/or contemplating or carrying out covert surveillance using electronic devices without any statutory guidance or regulation and without any internal Garda guidelines."[44]

11–21 The Act defines surveillance as "monitoring, observing, listening to or making a recording of a particular person or group of persons or their movements, activities and communications" or "monitoring or making a recording of places or things, by or with the assistance of surveillance devices".[45] Surveillance devices are defined as apparatuses designed or adapted for use in surveillance, although CCTV, cameras and night vision devices are specifically excluded from the definition. Here, the narrow focus of the legislation can be seen, with significant aspects of surveillance remaining unregulated. As McIntyre has noted: "[I]t does not apply to covert following or observation without such devices, which will continue to go essentially unregulated, subject only to the judicial guidance given in *Kane v Governor of Mountjoy Prison* [1988] 1 IR 757."[46] In *Kane*, the applicant had been subjected to intense overt surveillance by members of the garda and army and he argued that the degree of intrusion was excessive. In the High Court, Egan J refused to release him and outlined the crux of his argument:

> "The authorities call it 'surveillance'. The applicant is reluctant to accept the concept of legal surveillance and argues that there is no right to require a person to submit to surveillance. He contends that if there is any degree of intrusion to be tolerated it must be kept to a minimum of what is required. It is contended that the intrusion in this case was grossly excessive."[47]

11–22 Kane had argued that the degree of surveillance amounted to a continuation of his detention, an argument which was rejected. The Supreme Court upheld the decision, finding that surveillance is permissible if it can be justified. Finlay CJ held:

> "... if overt surveillance of the general type proved in this case were applied to an individual without a basis to justify it, it would be objectionable, and I would add, clearly unlawful. Overt surveillance including a number of Gardaí on foot closely following a pedestrian, and a number of Garda cars, marked as well as unmarked, tailing a driver or passenger in a motor car would, it seems to me, require specific justification arising from all the circumstances of a particular case and the nature and importance of the particular police duty being discharged."[48]

---

44 Report on the Detention of 'Suspects' Following the Death of the Late Richard Barron on the 14th of October 1996 and Related Detentions and Issues, Vol 3, pp 1249–1252.

45 Criminal Justice (Surveillance) Act 2009, s 1.

46 TJ McIntyre, "Annotations on the Criminal Justice (Surveillance) Act 2009", *Irish Current Law Statutes Annotated* (Round Hall, Dublin, 2009) 09-19.01.

47 *Kane v Governor of Mountjoy Prison* [1988] 1 IR 757 at 762.

48 *ibid* at 768.

The Law Reform Commission has commented that, while the case clarifies that justification is a pre-requisite for surveillance, it would be preferable "to provide a basis in positive law for such police action, especially where it involves covert surveillance. The need for a positive legal basis for such official action is in fact required under Article 8 of the European Convention".[49] **11–23**

Application for Authorisation

The Criminal Justice (Surveillance) Act 2009 provides that surveillance can only be carried out by a member of the Gardaí, Defence Forces or an officer of the Revenue Commissioners in accordance with a valid authorisation granted by a judge of the District Court.[50] In certain circumstances, considered at para 11–28, a superior officer can approve surveillance without an authorisation. **11–24**

A superior officer of An Garda Síochána, that is to say not below the rank of Superintendent, may apply for an authorisation where he or she has reasonable grounds for believing that: **11–25**

(a) as part of an operation or investigation being conducted by the Garda Síochána concerning an arrestable offence, the surveillance being sought to be authorised is necessary for the purposes of obtaining information as to whether the offence has been committed or as to the circumstances relating to the commission of the offence, or obtaining evidence for the purposes of proceedings in relation to the offence,
(b) the surveillance being sought to be authorised is necessary for the purpose of preventing the commission of arrestable offences, or
(c) the surveillance being sought to be authorised is necessary for the purpose of maintaining the security of the State.[51]

Provision is also made for applications to be made by senior officials of the Revenue Commissioners and the Defence Forces. In any case in which an application is made, the applicant officer must have reasonable grounds for believing that the surveillance being sought to be authorised is: **11–26**

(a) the least intrusive means available, having regard to its objectives and other relevant considerations,
(b) proportionate to its objectives, having regard to all the circumstances including its likely impact on the rights of any person, and
(c) of a duration that is reasonably required to achieve its objectives.[52]

An authorisation permits entry to any place for the purposes of initiating or carrying out the authorised surveillance, and withdrawing the authorised surveillance device, without the consent of the owner or occupier.[53]

---

49 Law Reform Commission Report on *Privacy: Surveillance and the Interception of Communications* (LRC 57–1998) at p 46.
50 Criminal Justice (Surveillance) Act 2009, s 3.
51 *ibid*, s 4(1).
52 *ibid*, s 4(5).
53 *ibid*, s 5(7).

11–27 Applications for authorisations may be made to a judge assigned to any District Court district, and the initial application and any further application to vary or renew an authorisation will be made *ex parte* and otherwise than in public.[54] A judge issuing an authorisation must be satisfied that the conditions for an application have been fulfilled and that the issuing of an authorisation is justified in all the circumstances.[55]

Authorisations are set out in writing and must specify:

(a) particulars of the surveillance device that is authorised to be used,
(b) the person who, or the place or thing that, is to be the subject of the surveillance,
(c) the name of the superior officer to whom it is issued,
(d) the conditions (if any) subject to which the authorisation is issued, and
(e) the date of expiry of the authorisation.[56]

The authorisation will expire not later than three months after the date of issue,[57] subject to the possibility of renewal for a further three months.[58]

Circumstances of Urgency

11–28 In circumstances of urgency, surveillance can be conducted on the basis of an approval from a superior officer, rather than a District Court authorisation. Like an authorisation, an approval permits entry, if necessary by use of reasonable force, to any place, without consent, for the purpose of conducting or initiating surveillance and withdrawing the surveillance device.[59] In order to conduct surveillance under an approval, the conditions for an authorisation must be fulfilled but, before an authorisation can be issued, the applicant must show that:

(a) it is likely that a person would abscond for the purpose of avoiding justice, obstruct the course of justice or commit an arrestable offence or a revenue offence, as the case may be,
(b) information or evidence in relation to the commission of an arrestable offence or a revenue offence, as the case may be, is likely to be destroyed, lost or otherwise become unavailable, or
(c) the security of the State would be likely to be compromised.[60]

The details of the approval must be committed to writing as soon as practicable and not later than eight hours after the surveillance has been approved.[61] Urgent approvals are operative for surveillance for 72 hours only.

---

54 *ibid*, s 5(1). Variations and renewals of authorisations are provided for in s 6.
55 Criminal Justice (Surveillance) Act 2009, s 5(2).
56 *ibid*, s 5(6).
57 *ibid*, s 5(8).
58 *ibid*, s 6(1).
59 *ibid*, s 7(5).
60 *ibid*, s 7(2).
61 *ibid*, s 7(6).

Communications Protected by Privilege

A judge is precluded from issuing an authorisation if he or she is satisfied that the surveillance which is sought to be authorised is likely to relate primarily to communications protected by privilege.[62] 11–29

Gillane has been stridently critical of this short subsection, which does not delineate between categories of privilege or elaborate on the circumstances in which privileged communications can be the subject of surveillance: 11–30

> "The nature of the privilege contemplated is not specified. This is a matter of tremendous practical importance and a problem of no little difficulty scarcely addressed by the terse subsection dealing with it. It might be remembered that the question of surveillance was raised in the Morris Tribunal in the context of suggested bugging of rooms where solicitors and clients consulted in Garda stations. An application to bug a solicitor's office might admit of an easy answer. But what of communications to a legal adviser from a house or mobile phone, the subject of an authorisation, which might ordinarily be regarded as privileged? Do we expect the Gardaí to stick their fingers in their ears or in the case of preservation are privileged portions of communications to be destroyed? They will have to be listened to in order for a determination to be made in any event. Is there a duty to disclose that a privileged communication has been captured and to whom should this be communicated? Will the need for secrecy trump that duty, if it exists at all? The fact that the captured communication is privileged does not itself affect the validity of the authorisation and in this respect the Act could not be plainer: evidence obtained as a result of surveillance carried out under an authorisation is admissible in criminal proceedings. What of the vestigial remains of marital privilege? While that concept has been substantially eroded marital privacy still has considerable constitutional protection."[63]

Skirting over privilege in such a cursory way provides more questions than guidance. The thin veil of protection that the legislation affords the individual from intrusion into a relationship protected by privilege is suggestive of an expansive, rather than restrictive, approach to surveillance. It is unclear how s 14, which permits the admissibility in evidence of the fruits of surveillance, will dovetail with existing laws of evidence concerning privilege. It has long been established that legal privilege cannot be invoked to protect communications in furtherance of crime.[64] As this has been the position—that "professional privilege cannot and must not be applied so as to be injurious to the interests of justice and to those in the administration of justice"[65]—the fruits of a recorded meeting with a legal advisor in the furtherance of illegal activity would already be admissible in evidence. But what of legal advice? As Gillane points out, the precise position in respect of marital privilege is difficult to determine given the Constitutional position of marital privacy. 11–31

[62] *ibid*, s 5(4).

[63] S Gillane "Criminal Justice (Surveillance) Bill 2009"—Paper presented at the 10th National Prosecutors' Conference, 23 May 2009, at p 7.

[64] *Annesley v Earl of Anglesea* (1743) 17 How St Tr 1229; *Kelly v Jackson* (1849) 1 Ir Jur 233; *R. v Cox and Railton* (1884) 14 QBD 153; *Bullivant v AG for Victoria* [1901] AC 196 at 201; *R. v Smith* (1915) 84 LJ KB 2153. See generally D McGrath *Evidence* (Thomson Round Hall, Dublin, 2005), at p 550 *et seq*

[65] *Murphy v Kirwan* [1993] 3 IR 501 at 511.

11–32 In England and Wales, the equivalent legislation, the Regulation of Investigatory Powers Act 2000, known as RIPA, does not prohibit the interception of communications likely to contain legally privileged material, nor does it prohibit interception of communications concerning confidential personal information, nor confidential journalistic material. However, additional criteria must be fulfilled in applications for warrants to intercept such communications. Extensive RIPA codes of practice assist public authorities in assessing and understanding whether and in what circumstances the use of covert techniques is appropriate and also provide guidance on the procedures to be followed in each case. The code of practice concerning the interception of communications deals at length with the forms of privilege mentioned, with oversight provided by the Interception of Communications Commissioner. Similar codes of practice and levels of oversight would be of benefit in this jurisdiction also, given the dearth of guidance in the legislation on how sensitive communications are to be dealt with.

Tracking Devices

11–33 Tracking devices may be used to monitor movements of persons or vehicles on the basis of an approval granted by a superior officer, without recourse to a judicial authorisation. For approval of a tracking device, the same criteria of necessity must be fulfilled as apply in an application for an authorisation, except that the use of a tracking device is considered sufficient to obtain the information or evidence sought, and that the information or evidence sought could reasonably be obtained by the use of a tracking device for a specified period that is as short as practicable to allow the information or evidence to be obtained.[66] A GPS tracking device may therefore be fitted to and removed from a vehicle[67] without any judicial oversight.

11–34 The rationale for a less stringent oversight method is a perception that GPS tracking is "a less intrusive form of surveillance",[68] a view reiterated by the European Court of Human Rights which held in the case of *Uzun v Germany* that:

> "GPS surveillance is by its very nature to be distinguished from other methods of visual or acoustical surveillance which are, as a rule, more susceptible of interfering with a person's right to respect for private life, because they disclose more information on a person's conduct, opinions or feelings."[69]

11–35 Campbell has argued that the perception of GPS tracking as a relatively innocuous form of surveillance is misconceived and that:

> "By regarding GPS in a benign manner, the authorisation requirements are less onerous, thus prioritising the demands of crime control over due process. This misinterprets the extent and breadth of GPS tracking, which is a burgeoning form of surveillance, and is one of considerable investigative importance, given its ability to reveal patterns of

---

[66] Criminal Justice (Surveillance) Act 2009, s 8(2).

[67] *ibid*, s 8(5).

[68] Explanatory memorandum to the Criminal Justice (Surveillance) Bill 2009.

[69] *Uzun v Germany* (2011) 53 EHRR 24, para 52.

> movement and presence at particular places… Keeping the approval of GPS monitoring in the administrative realm is a clear representation of the crime control model, where judicial oversight is circumvented, and the most efficient means of initiating and carrying out this mechanism is adopted."[70]

Murphy submits that the Strasbourg Court has underestimated the potential for tracking devices to interfere with Article 8 rights, but considers that, in light of the judgment in *Uzun,* the Irish legislation providing for tracking devices is apparently ECHR compliant.[71]

INTERCEPTION

Wiretapping and the interception of communications are effectively electronic searches.[72] While the inviolability of the dwelling is protected in Article 40.5, and the protection afforded the family implies freedom from intrusion in marital relationships, privacy itself—in the broader sense—is not expressly provided for in the Irish Constitution. Rather it has been recognised as an unenumerated right under Article 40.3.1° and was first successfully invoked in a case concerning wiretapping, *Kennedy v Ireland.*[73] The plaintiffs were journalists, and argued that the tapping of their telephones by State agents amounted to an unjustified and unlawful interference with their right to privacy. Hamilton P held: **11–36**

> "The right to privacy is not an issue, the issue is the extent of that right or the extent of the right 'to be let alone'. Though not specifically guaranteed by the Constitution, the right of privacy is one of the fundamental personal rights of the citizen which flow from the Christian and democratic nature of the State. It is not an unqualified right. Its exercise may be restricted by the constitutional rights of others, or by the requirements of the common good, and it is subject to the requirements of public order and morality … the nature of the right to privacy must be such as to ensure the freedom and dignity of an individual in the type of society envisaged by the Constitution, namely, a sovereign, independent and democratic society. The dignity and freedom of an individual cannot be ensured if his communications of a private nature, be they written or telephonic, are deliberately, consciously and unjustifiably intruded upon and interfered with. I emphasise the words 'deliberately, consciously and unjustifiably' because an individual must accept the risk of accidental interference with his communications and the fact that in certain circumstances the exigencies of the common good may require and justify such intrusion and interference. No such circumstances exist in this case."[74]

The European Court of Human Rights is not opposed to the use of covert surveillance methods *per se,* but there must be countervailing protective measures legislatively set out, with the measures themselves to be scrutinised to determine the degree of protection provided from arbitrary interference by State authorities.[75] The European Court upheld the validity of interception which was legislatively authorised in the case of **11–37**

---

70 L Campbell, *Organised Crime and the Law: A Comparative Analysis* (Hart, Oxford, 2013) at p 80.

71 MH Murphy, "Investigative Use of GPS Tracking Devices and the European Court of Human Rights ICLJ 2012, 22(1), pp 8–12.

72 A Sanders and R Young, *Criminal Justice* (3rd ed, Oxford University Press, Oxford, 2007) p 291.

73 *Kennedy v Ireland* [1987] IR 587, [1988] ILRM 472.

74 *ibid,* at 476.

75 See A Whelan, "Are They Watching You? – The Criminal Justice (Surveillance) Act 2009," (2010) 15 (1) BR 1.

Klass v Germany,[76] on the grounds that (i) the interceptions were "in accordance with law" within the meaning of Article 8 of the Convention and (ii) the interceptions had been shown to be "in the interests of national security [and] for the prevention of disorder or crime" within the meaning of the exception to Article 8(2). In *Klass* it was held that:

> "the Contracting State may not, in the name of the struggle against espionage and terrorism, adopt whatever measures they deem appropriate... [T]he Court must be satisfied that, whatever system of surveillance is adopted, there exist adequate and effective guarantees against abuse. The assessment has only a relative character: it depends on all the circumstances of the case, such as the nature, scope and duration of the possible measures, the grounds required for ordering such measures, the authorities competent to permit, carry out and supervise such measures, and the kind of remedy provided by the national law."[77]

11–38 In the later case of *Malone v United Kingdom*[78] the Court reached a different conclusion. There, the Court held that the British administrative scheme permitting interceptions was "not in accordance with law", since the law in England and Wales was "somewhat obscure and open to differing interpretations" and hence did not indicate "with sufficient clarity the scope and manner of exercise of the reasonable discretion conferred on the public authorities". Accordingly, "the minimum degree of legal protection to which citizens are entitled under the rule of law" was absent. The United Kingdom had argued that the scheme which fell within the permitted exception in Article 8(2) permitting interference with privacy if it is "in the interest of national security or for the prevention of disorder or crime". The European Court of Human Rights emphasised that it was the absence of any independent safeguards in the system which prevented the United Kingdom from relying on this exception.

Interception of Postal Packets and Telecommunications Messages (Regulation) Act 1993

11–39 A regulatory structure for ministerially authorised interception of communications was established in Ireland by the Interception of Postal Packets and Telecommunications Messages (Regulation) Act 1993. In contrast with surveillance under the Criminal Justice (Surveillance) Act 2009, the interception of postal and telecommunications messages is governed by executive, rather than judicial, approval.[79] The use of executive rather than judicial oversight has been the subject of some criticism. Campbell, while acknowledging the restrictive nature of the interception scheme in Ireland given the seniority of officers seeking interceptions, argues that interception warrants should be issued by the judiciary to ensure adherence to due process values.[80]

11–40 The Act provides that interception may be authorised by the minister for the purpose of criminal investigations concerning "serious offences" or in the interests of the security

[76] *Klass v Germany* [1979] 2 EHRR 214.
[77] *ibid*, at paras 48–50.
[78] *Malone v United Kingdom* [1984] 7 EHRR 14.
[79] L Campbell, *Organised Crime and the Law: A Comparative Analysis* (Hart, Oxford, 2013) at p 84.
[80] *ibid* at p 84–85.

of the State. A serious offence is defined as an offence "for which a person aged 21 years or over, of full capacity and not previously convicted"[81] may be punished by a period of imprisonment of five years or more and an offence:

> "(i) that involves loss of human life, serious personal injury or serious loss of or damage to property or a serious risk of any such loss, injury or damage,
>
> (ii) that results or is likely to result in substantial gain, or
>
> (iii) the facts and circumstances of which are such as to render it a specially serious case of its kind; and includes an act or omission done or made outside the State that would be a serious offence if done or made in the State:
>
> Provided, however, that an offence consisting of an attempt, conspiracy or incitement to commit an offence shall not be a serious offence unless the offence which is the subject of the attempt, conspiracy or incitement is itself a serious offence."[82]

If the interception is sought for criminal investigation, the minister must be satisfied **11–41**
that:

> "(I) investigations are being carried out by the Garda Síochána, or another public authority charged with the investigation of offences of the kind in question, concerning a serious offence or a suspected serious offence,
> (II) investigations not involving interception have failed, or are likely to fail, to produce, or to produce sufficiently quickly, either or, as the case may be, both of the following, that is to say:
> (A) information such as to show whether the offence has been committed or as to the facts relating to it,
> (B) evidence for the purpose of criminal proceedings in relation to the offence,
>
> and
>
> (III) there is a reasonable prospect that the interception of postal packets sent to a particular postal address or of telecommunications messages sent to or from a particular telecommunications address would be of material assistance (by itself or in conjunction with other information or evidence) in providing information, or evidence, such as aforesaid,
>
> or
>
> (ii) that—
>
> (I) in the case of a serious offence that is apprehended but has not been committed, investigations are being carried out, for the purpose of preventing the commission of the offence or of enabling it to be detected, if it is committed, by the Garda Síochána or another public authority charged with the prevention or investigation of offences of the kind in question,
>
> (II) investigations not involving interception have failed, or are likely to fail, to produce, or to produce sufficiently quickly, information as to the perpetrators, the time, the place, and the other circumstances, of the offence that would enable the offence to be prevented or detected, as the case may be, and

81 Interception of Postal Packets and Telecommunications Messages (Regulation) Act 1993, s 1.
82 *ibid.*

> (III) there is a reasonable prospect that the interception of postal packets sent to a particular postal address or of telecommunications messages sent to or from a particular telecommunications address would be of material assistance (by itself or in conjunction with other information) in preventing or detecting the offence, as the case may be,
>
> and
>
> (b) that the importance of obtaining the information or evidence concerned is, having regard to all the circumstances and notwithstanding the importance of preserving the privacy of postal packets and telecommunications messages, sufficient to justify the interception."[83]

11–42 If an interception is sought on the basis of a threat to the security of the State, the minister must be satisfied:

> (a) that there are reasonable grounds for believing that particular activities that are endangering or likely to endanger the security of the State are being carried on or are proposed to be carried on,
>
> (b) that investigations are being carried out by or on behalf of the person applying for the authorisation concerned to ascertain whether activities of the kind aforesaid are in fact being carried on or proposed to be carried on and, if so, by whom and their nature and extent,
>
> (c) that investigations not involving interception have failed, or are likely to fail, to produce, or to produce sufficiently quickly, information that would show whether the activities are being carried on or proposed to be carried on and, if so, by whom and their nature and extent,
>
> (d) that there is a reasonable prospect that the interception of postal packets sent to a particular postal address or of telecommunications messages sent to or from a particular telecommunications address would be of material assistance (by itself or in conjunction with other information) in providing information such as aforesaid, and
>
> (e) that the importance of obtaining the information concerned is, having regard to all the circumstances and notwithstanding the importance of preserving the privacy of postal packets and telecommunications messages, sufficient to justify the interception."[84]

11–43 Applications for authorisations to intercept must be made in writing by the Commissioner of An Garda Síochána and must be sufficiently detailed to allow the minister to determine if the statutory preconditions have been fulfilled.[85] There is provision for judicial oversight (in that the minister may consult a specified High Court judge who oversees the operation of the scheme from a distance),[86] and for a complaints procedure,[87] as well as for restriction of disclosure of the existence of authorisations and of the material disclosed.[88]

11–44 A warrant for interception under the 1993 Act can remain in force for a period of three months from the date of issue,[89] with potential to extend the period for a further three months.[90] If an interception is no longer deemed necessary, the nominated officer

---

[83] *ibid*, s 4.
[84] *ibid*, s 5.
[85] *ibid*, s 6.
[86] *ibid*, s 8.
[87] *ibid*, s 9.
[88] *ibid*, s 12.
[89] *ibid*, s 2(5).
[90] *ibid*, s 2(6).

and the person to whom the warrant is addressed must be informed without delay and the authorisation will cease to be in force.[91]

DATA AND TELECOMMUNICATIONS RECORDS

There is little case-law on the operation of the Interception of Postal Packets and Telecommunications Messages (Regulation) Act 1993.[92] Unlike the Criminal Justice (Surveillance) Act 2009, in which the focus is on the admissibility in evidence of the fruits of surveillance under the Act,[93] the 1993 Act has State security and intelligence (as distinct from evidence) gathering as its thrust. Yet the cases in which digital evidence have come to the fore have by and large been those in which telecommunications records have provided evidence of contact between persons and individual movements, without recourse to interception. That telephone records could be used in criminal investigations was established in *DPP v Murphy*.[94] There the applicant argued that adducing and admitting his phone records amounted to an invasion of his privacy. The Court of Criminal Appeal held that: **11–45**

> "the right to privacy is not absolute. It may be superseded by the public interest (see Desmond v. Glackin (No. 2) [1993] 3 I.R. 67), and also may be curtailed by the exigencies of the common good; (see Kennedy v. Ireland [1987] I.R. 587 at 592). Authors Hogan and Whyte, (Kelly on the Constitution, 4th Edition, p. 1441 at fn 254) also specifically draw attention to the right of the authorities legitimately to intercept telephone conversations and postal communications pursuant to the Interception of Postal Packets and Telecommunication Messages (Regulation) Act, 1993."[95]

McIntyre has commented that the prosecution of Joe O'Reilly for the murder of his wife, Rachel, is noteworthy because: **11–46**

> "the trial revealed the extensive digital footprints we leave behind in our day to day activities. In a first for the Irish courts, the prosecution case was built for the most part on digital evidence – including CCTV footage, mobile phone location data, details of calls and text messages and the content of emails".[96]

---

91 *ibid*, s 7.

92 One of the few cases dealing with the legislation is *People (DPP) v Dillon* [2002] 4 IR 501, where it was held that the actions of an Inspector in confiscating and listening to a conversation on a mobile phone was an unlawful interception pursuant to s 98 of the Postal and Telecommunications Services Act 1983. There the gardaí had entirely bypassed the regime for legal interception provided by the Interception of Postal Packets and Telecommunications Messages (Regulation) Act 1993. The Court of Criminal Appeal held that an interception which is unlawful cannot become lawful because of the content of the conversation overheard; if that were permissible it would "set at nought the detailed and specific statutory provisions relating to interception…".

93 The Criminal Justice (Surveillance) Act 2009, provides at s 14(1): "Evidence obtained as a result of surveillance carried out under an authorisation or under an approval granted in accordance with s 7 or 8 may be admitted as evidence in criminal proceedings."

94 *DPP v Murphy* [2005] 2 IR 125.

95 *ibid.*

96 TJ McIntyre, "The New Surveillance", written for the Irish Security Industry's *Risk Manager Magazine* and reproduced on his blog on 19 August 2007. See http://www.tjmcintyre.com/2007/08/new-surveillance-in-ireland.html <accessed 28 October 2013>.

11–47 Indeed, issue was not taken with the surveillance which underpinned the prosecution in the applicant's subsequent unsuccessful appeal to the Court of Criminal Appeal. Though three of the grounds advanced by the applicant concerned electronic evidence—the telecommunications evidence, CCTV and emails—the substantive issue of privacy was sidestepped by the Court which said that it was unnecessary to consider arguments advanced concerning an individual's right to privacy (including the right in relation to his or her telephone records, versus the power of the gardaí to investigate crime and seek material evidence) on the basis that there was evidence that the relevant telecommunications licence existed and that therefore the gardaí were entitled to obtain the telephone records pursuant to their statutory powers. The Court therefore found it unnecessary to consider the privacy arguments.[97]

11–48 Telecommunications providers operating in Ireland are obliged to retain data concerning communications (though not the content of communications) and data concerning phone and mobile traffic data for two years, while internet communications must be retained for one year.[98] The potential for access to that information and to use it against the data subject reveals most acutely the power imbalance between the State and the individual. The 2011 Act gives effect to the European Data Retention Directive. Previously the retention period was three years, pursuant to Part 7 of the Criminal Justice (Terrorist Offences) Act 2005. Before its repeal by s 13 of the Communications (Retention of Data) Act 2011, that Act had provided that the Garda Commissioner could request a service provider to retain traffic and location data for a period of three years for the prevention, detection, investigation or prosecution of crime (including, but not limited to, terrorist offences) or the safeguarding of the security of the State.

Retention and Disclosure of Telecommunications Data

11–49 Under the Communications (Retention of Data) Act 2011, a garda of at least Superintendent rank may request data from a service provider where the garda is satisfied that the data are required for:

(a) the prevention, detection, investigation or prosecution of a serious offence,
(b) the safeguarding of the security of the State,
(c) the saving of human life.[99]

11–50 A serious offence is defined in s 1 of the Act as one which is punishable by five years' imprisonment or more, as well as the offences set out in Schedule 1 of the Act which are offences contrary to:

---

[97] *DPP v O'Reilly* [2009] IECCA 18, *per* Murray CJ.

[98] Communications (Retention of Data) Act 2011.

[99] *ibid,* s 6(1). Like the Interception of Postal Packets and Telecommunications Messages (Regulation) Act 1993, requests may also be made by senior members of the Revenue Commissioners (of principal officer grade) or the Defence Forces (officers of colonel rank).

1. s 11 and s 12 of the Criminal Assets Bureau Act 1996;
2. s 6 of the Criminal Evidence Act 1992;
3. s 12 of the Non-Fatal Offences against the Person Act 1997;
4. s 1 of the Prevention of Corruption Act 1889 to 1995;
5. s 5 of the Protections for Persons Reporting Child Abuse Act 1998.

Disclosure requests are written, except in cases of exceptional urgency, in which case requests may be made orally, by telephone or otherwise.[100] Compliance with the request is obligatory: there is no scope for refusal on the part of the service provider.[101] As with interception under the Interception of Postal Packets and Telecommunications Messages (Regulation) Act 1993, there is provision for *ex post facto* supervision by a High Court judge who is tasked with keeping the operation of the legislation under review and monitor compliance.[102] There is also a complaints procedure.[103] **11–51**

COVERT HUMAN INTELLIGENCE SOURCES (CHIS)

The use of Covert Human Intelligence Sources (CHIS) is unregulated by legislation in Ireland. In the wake of the Morris Tribunal, which was highly critical of informer management,[104] a code of practice was drawn up for the management and use of covert human intelligence sources.[105] However there is no statutory framework to guide the actions of gardaí in this realm.[106] There is no Irish statutory definition of what constitutes a CHIS. In announcing an Irish code of practice for An Garda Síochána, the Commissioner used the following definition: **11–52**

> "The terms 'informant', 'informer' or 'source' are ones that are widely understood both within policing circles and the wider public. A more common term now in usage in many jurisdictions is 'Covert Human Intelligence Source'. This term, or its acronym, CHIS … is sufficiently all embracing to incorporate three distinctly separate but related categories of person who provide information to police, ie – casual contacts, informants and agents."[107]

The code of practice itself is not publicly available. The code includes a registration system for informants, subject to authorisation on the basis of a detailed assessment of the proposed informant, including a background check, risk assessment and, in certain circumstances, an interview. Recording is emphasised, with a complete record pertaining to the informant to be maintained outlining all dealings with the informant by gardaí to **11–53**

---

100 Communications (Retention of Data) Act 2011, s 6(4). A request made orally must be confirmed in writing within two days (s 6(5)).

101 Communications (Retention of Data) Act 2011, s 7.

102 *ibid*, s 11.

103 *ibid*, s 10.

104 *Report of the Tribunal of Inquiry into Certain Gardaí in the Donegal Division: Report on Explosives 'Finds' in Donegal* (Dublin, 2004) at paras 13.26 and 13.92.

105 Commissioner of An Garda Síochána *Public Statement by the Commissioner of An Garda Síochána on the Management and Use of Covert Human Intelligence Sources,* (Dublin, An Garda Síochána, 2006).

106 L Campbell, "Informers in Ireland: a Lack of Law?" *Human Rights in Ireland,* 10 May 2013 http://humanrights.ie/uncategorized/informers-in-ireland-a-lack-of-law/ <accessed 28 October 2013>.

107 Commissioner of An Garda Síochána *Public Statement by the Commissioner of An Garda Síochána on the Management and Use of Covert Human Intelligence Sources,* (An Garda Síochána, Dublin, 2006).

include any "assessments, comments, directions given, review of the relationship, policy decisions, evaluations and any other relevant information emanating from supervisors, controllers or crime and security personnel".[108] The announcement by the Garda Commissioner concerning the management and use of covert human intelligence sources claims that the "effective collection of intelligence on criminals and their organisations enables investigation to be accurately targeted with minimum interference to the lives and liberties of individual citizens".[109] He emphasised the duty for gardaí to protect the identities of CHIS,[110] whose recruitment, handling and management would only be authorised by the Assistant Commissioner for Crime and Security.[111]

11–54 Campbell has been critical of the Irish code, stating:

> "The Code states that CHIS handlers and controllers will be trained to 'approved standards', and the use of CHIS will be subject to 'appropriate reviews.' These terms are not defined anywhere, and embody the opacity of the policing of organised crime in Ireland. The genesis of the Code after a scathing Tribunal report further exemplifies the crisis-driven and *ad hoc* approach to development of policy."[112]

11–55 She further argues that the CHIS system which applies in Ireland, ungoverned as it is by legislation, is not ECHR-compliant:

> "[W]hile the Garda Code is claimed to be 'in line with best international practice' the lack of legislation in Ireland is worrying from a due process perspective and is unlikely to be compliant with the requirements of the ECHR... given that the expression 'in accordance with the law' in Article 8(2) requires that the measure has 'some basis in domestic law' and 'refers to the quality of this law, demanding that it should be accessible to the person concerned, who must moreover be able to foresee its consequences for him of her, and compatible with the rule of law'."[113,114]

11–56 The Garda Síochána Ombudsman Commission has also been critical of the CHIS system, and has publicly recorded its belief that the deficiencies of the original system have not been fully remedied, with the risk that information could continue to be collected by informants in an *ad hoc* manner outside of stated informant handling policies and in the absence of any formal registration process.[115] The Commission has further criticised the fact that the crucial issue of permitted levels of criminality within the CHIS system is unregulated, and has pointed to inconsistencies in levels of access to sensitive intelligence and inappropriate distribution or dissemination of sensitive intelligence.

---

[108] An Garda Síochána, *Communiqué,* March 2008 at p 16.

[109] Commissioner of An Garda Síochána *Public Statement by the Commissioner of An Garda Síochána on the Management and Use of Covert Human Intelligence Sources* (An Garda Síochána, Dublin, 2006).

[110] *ibid.*

[111] *ibid.*

[112] L Campbell, *Organised Crime and the Law: A Comparative Analysis* (Hart, Oxford, 2013) at p 94.

[113] *Malone v United Kingdom* (1984) 7 EHRR 14; *Kruslin v France* Series A no 176-B (1990) 2 EHRR 547; *Huvig v France* Series A no 176-B (1990) 12 EHRR 52.

[114] L Campbell, *Organised Crime and the Law: A Comparative Analysis* (Hart, Oxford, 2013) at p 94.

[115] Special Report by the Garda Síochána Ombudsman Commission to the Minister for Justice, Equality and Defence, 9 May 2013, at p 6.

The Commission recommended that any conduct of an informant which might potentially be viewed as participating in an offence with the knowledge of a State agency should be subject to the utmost scrutiny, such scrutiny to be "intrusive, robust and meticulously recorded".[116] In addition, independent scrutiny of the operation of the CHIS system was recommended, to be conducted independently of the authorities involved in the activity of the informant.[117]

Harfield and Harfield have set out a checklist of key issues when considering whether or not to deploy a CHIS, of which the following are equally relevant in the Irish context: **11–57**

"

- What evidence or intelligence is sought?
- How is it relevant to the operation under consideration?
- What is the least intrusive means of securing such evidence or information?
- Has the least intrusive means of securing the evidence or information been attempted? If not, why not?
- What is the risk of collateral intrusion against the privacy of persons not being investigated? How will collateral intrusion be prevented (or if not, minimized) and how will the product of collateral intrusion be managed?

...

- What are the risks of the CHIS being compromised by another person?
- What are the risks of the CHIS compromising him or herself?

...

- What are the risks to the public or specific third parties, including family and friends of the CHIS, when such tactics are deployed?
- What are the risks to the subject of the investigation?
- Will such methods breach Article 8(1)?
- Is there justification provided for doing so provided by Article 8(2)?
- How is the legality test met?
- How is the legitimacy test met?
- How is the proportionality test met?
- Is the proposed CHIS a juvenile? If so, have the appropriate safeguards been put in place?
- Is the proposed CHIS a vulnerable person? If so, have the appropriate safeguards been put in place?

...

- How will the product of the surveillance be managed?

...

- How are the methods by which the evidence / intelligence will be obtained to be protected at trial?"[118]

---

116 *ibid* at p 9.

117 *ibid.*

118 C Harfield and K Harfield, *Covert Investigation* (3rd ed, Oxford University Press, Oxford 2012), at pp 149–151.

11–58 Legislation is notable by its absence, given the ethical dexterity required of gardaí working with covert human intelligence sources. Walsh has identified issues arising in this context as including the credibility of information provided, the propriety of incentives such as payment or prosecutorial immunity, transparency and accountability in informer management and the exposure of the informer to potential harm.[119] There is, he says, scope for denial of the suspect's due process and privacy rights, jeopardy to the safety and life of the informer and an equally serious risk of damage to "the general public interest in the integrity and transparency of the criminal process".[120] In England and Wales, an extensive code of practice applies to the use of Covert Human Intelligence Sources, including examples of relationships established or maintained for covert purposes, general rules and special considerations concerning authorisations for the use of covert human intelligence sources, record-keeping, management of covert human intelligence sources and handling of material. Walsh has cited the code as an example of transparency in that the basic scheme and guidelines for recruitment are available in a public document, and he points out that the code and the legislation on which it is based "positively embrace Article 8 ECHR and the principle of proportionality in the recruitment and use of an informer".[121]

ENTRAPMENT, AGENTS PROVOCATEURS AND TEST PURCHASES

11–59 There is a fine line between inciting and facilitating crime; the precise point at which unexceptional opportunity ends and inducement begins can be difficult to delineate. The area is a legally complex one, since "... entrapment is not a matter going only to the blameworthiness or culpability of the defendant ... [e]ntrapment goes to the propriety of there being a prosecution at all for the relevant offence, having regard to the State's involvement in the circumstances in which it was committed".[122] An *agent provocateur* was defined in the English case of *R. v Mealy and Sheridan* as "a person who entices another to commit an express breach of the law which he would otherwise not have committed and then proceeds or informs against him in respect of such an offence".[123] There is an inherent unfairness in such an approach. There is very little case-law on the issue in Ireland. In *Dental Board v O'Callaghan*[124] Butler J referred to the use of agents provocateurs as distasteful, but he accepted their necessity in the investigation of "private and clandestine" transactions. It was held that the evidence of a person employed by an official body to secure evidence of the commission of an offence, which is the duty of that body to investigate with a view to prosecution, ought not to be treated as the evidence of an accomplice which requires corroboration.[125] Guidance may be gleaned from the House of Lords case of *R v Loosely* where the Court considered the nature and extent of police participation in the crime, holding:

---

[119] D Walsh, *Human Rights and Policing in Ireland: Law, Policy and Practice* (Clarus Press, Dublin, 2009) at p 162.
[120] *ibid* at p 162.
[121] *ibid* at p 177.
[122] *R v Loosely* [2001] UKHL 53.
[123] *R v Mealy and Sheridan* [1974] 60 Cr App R 59 at 61.
[124] *Dental Board v O'Callaghan* [1969] IR 181.
[125] *ibid*, at 185.

> "The greater the inducement held out by the police, and the more forceful or persistent the police overtures, the more readily may a court conclude that the police overstepped the boundary: their conduct might well have brought about commission of a crime by a person who would normally avoid crime of that kind."[126]

It was suggested that a useful guide was to "consider whether the police did no more than present the defendant with an unexceptional opportunity to commit a crime".[127]

The European Court of Human rights has indicated that the fairness guaranteed by Article 6 of the Convention is not confined to the trial process but also includes the pre-trial period and the manner in which evidence is gathered. In *Teixeira de Castro v Portugal*,[128] the applicant complained that he had not had a fair trial in that he had been incited by plain-clothes police officers to supply them with the heroin which was the basis of his conviction. He maintained that he had no previous convictions and would never have committed the offence had it not been for the intervention of those "*agents provocateurs*". In addition, the police officers had acted on their own initiative without any supervision by the courts and without any preliminary investigation. It was held that the actions of the police officers went beyond those of undercover agents because they instigated the offence and there was nothing to suggest that without their intervention it would have been committed. That intervention and its use in the subsequent criminal proceedings meant that, from the outset, the applicant was definitively deprived of a fair trial. Consequently, there had been a violation of Article 6(1). On the admissibility of evidence, the Strasbourg Court highlighted the absence of safeguards to ensure fairness and drew a distinction between passive actions of undercover agents and the exertion of influence on the suspect, such as to incite the commission of the offence: **11–60**

> "The Court reiterates that the admissibility of evidence is primarily a matter for regulation by national law and as a general rule it is for the national courts to assess the evidence before them ...
>
> [However, the] use of undercover agents must be restricted and safeguards put in place even in cases concerning the fight against drug-trafficking. While the rise in organised crime undoubtedly requires that appropriate measures be taken, the right to a fair administration of justice nevertheless holds such a prominent place (see the Delcourt v Belgium judgment of 17 January 1970, Series A no 11, at 15, § 25) that it cannot be sacrificed for the sake of expedience. The general requirements of fairness embodied in Article 6 apply to proceedings concerning all types of criminal offence, from the most straightforward to the most complex. The public interest cannot justify the use of evidence obtained as a result of police incitement."[129]

Particular emphasis was placed on the absence of suspicion of the suspect's involvement **11–61**
in drug-trafficking. He had no criminal record, he was not part of any preliminary

---

126 *R v Loosley* [2001] UKHL 53.

127 *ibid.*

128 *Teixeira de Castro v Portugal* (1999) 28 EHRR 101.

129 *ibid.*

investigation or any authorised anti-drug-trafficking operation and he was found only with the quantity of heroin requested by the police officers.

11–62 In Ireland, the defence of entrapment as it operates in the United States was found not to exist in *Syon v Hewitt & McTiernan*,[130] which concerned the use of 'test purchases' in the context of investigations into the breach of tobacco control legislation, ie the offence of selling tobacco to minors. In a consultative case stated, the High Court considered whether a substantive defence of entrapment arose out of the use of the test purchase procedure, and whether courts had discretion to exclude such evidence. It was held that the courts have no discretion to exclude evidence obtained by means of test purchases, other than through the application of the ordinary rules of evidence. The High Court referred to the necessity of test purchases, given the difficulties inherent in the investigation of offences committed by persons involved in 'consensual crime' and found that, in that context, it is both permissible and the function of the Office of Tobacco Control to do so. The use of children in such procedures was also found not to contravene public policy, but rather it was deemed necessary for the protection of children themselves. Crucially, however, the Office of Tobacco Control had operated a protocol for the test purchase procedure as was envisaged in the case of *Teixeira de Castro v Portugal.*[131] McDermott and Murphy assert that the judgment may amount to:

> "an endorsement of *Teixeira's* requirement of some legislative or formal framework on which entrapment-like police practices can be hung. The non-statutory protocol, adopted by a statutory body, was sufficient in *Syon*. It gave guidance on how test purchases were supposed to operate and ensured the state authorities were not at large to try roping unsuspecting individuals into criminal conduct".[132]

11–63 No such guidance is publicly available to govern the use of gardaí in test purchases of drugs. It is unclear if such operations are included in the garda code of practice for the management and use of covert human intelligence sources.

---

[130] *Syon Hewitt v McTiernan* [2008] 1 IR 168.

[131] *ibid.*

[132] PA McDermott and MW Murphy " No Revolution: The Impact of the ECHR Act 2003 on Irish Criminal Law", (2008) 15(1) DULJ 1.

Part VI

Vulnerable Complainants

CHAPTER 12

Victims

INTRODUCTION

This chapter will examine victim vulnerability, factors influencing complainant withdrawal from the criminal process, the 2012 EU Victims Directive and existing guidance documents and garda policies concerning victims of crime. **12–01**

The interventions of the criminal process are made not for the individual but for the general welfare of the State: irrespective of the gravity of the offence, the violence involved or the damage caused to an individual, the offence is an offence against society first. Whereas victims of crime once sought their own justice, the State has long assumed responsibility for the investigation and prosecution of crimes. That is not to say that the victim is excluded from consideration in garda and prosecutorial decision-making, but that investigations must be impartial. Prosecutions must be initiated only when the evidence is of the requisite strength and where it would be in the interests of justice, rather than in the interests of any one individual, to do so.[1] **12–02**

Though in many respects imperfect, the modern criminal process is undoubtedly preferable to the regime it replaced: the revenge and retaliation of the individual who has been offended against in search of reparation, often brutally meted out in the absence of the dispassionate safeguards now provided by due process, substantive law and criminal procedure in the determination of guilt and appropriate penalty.[2] The historical displacement of the victim was accompanied by a rise in the rehabilitative ideal and penal welfarism, which has in turn been overtaken by a more retributive, **12–03**

1 See J Hamilton, "The Prosecutor and the Victim," CCJHR 4th annual conference, 11 June 2010

2 See M Foucault, *Discipline and Punish: the Birth of the Prison* (Random House, New York, 1975). See also R Coen, "The Rise of the Victim – a Path to Punitiveness?" (2006) 16(3) ICLJ 10.

punitive, politicised and victim-oriented approach in penal policy.[3] Amidst a sense that the victim had been ousted from their own case, resigned to a peripheral role as a supplier of evidence to help the State make *its* case against a suspect, victim-centric legislation has been enacted[4] and measures adopted[5] to improve the standing of the victim in the criminal process. The purist black-letter lawyer's view of the victim as a one-dimensional witness has been displaced, and it is now recognised that victims have rights to information, protection and thorough, effective and competent investigation. There is also increasing interest in, and concern about, the reluctance of victims to engage with the criminal process, as well as the attrition of complainants, particularly in sexual offences.[6]

12–04 The accommodation of the victim into a process which is designed around fair procedures for the defendant has challenged the fundamental tenets of the criminal process as a dispassionate forum for the adjudication of guilt. The participation of victims in the sentencing process via victim impact evidence is an illustrative example: questions arise as to whether two offences falling into broadly the same category of gravity are treated differently, depending on the comparative extent of the emotional recovery of the victim; whether a well constructed and conveyed victim impact statement will persuade a sentencing judge to impose a harsher sentence than might be imposed in a case of similar circumstances in which the victim chooses not to give victim impact evidence, or does so in a less eloquent or expressive way; how to deal with prejudicial or unproven allegations in impact evidence and so on.[7]

---

[3] See generally D Garland, *The Culture of Control: Crime and Social Order in Contemporary Society*, (University of Chicago Press, Chicago, 2001).

[4] Such legislative provisions include victim impact statements (Criminal Justice Act 1993, s 5 as substituted by s 4 of the Criminal Procedure Act 2010); compensation orders for injured parties (Criminal Justice Act 1993, s 6); separate legal representation for victims of rape (s 4A of the Criminal Law (Rape) Act 1981 as inserted by the Sex Offenders Act 2001, s 34); the Framework Decision on victims' rights, Council Framework Decision 2001/220/JHA of 15 March 2001 on the standing of victims in criminal proceedings, OJ L 82 of 22 March 2001 and Directive 2012/29/EU of 25 October 2012 establishing minimum standards on the rights, support and protection of victims of crime.

[5] For example the establishment of agencies and initiatives such as the Criminal Injuries Compensation Tribunal (1974); The Victims Charter (1999); the Commission for the Support of Victims of Crime (2005); the Crime Victims Helpline (2005); COSC (The National Office for the Prevention of Domestic, Sexual and Gender-based Violence)(2007); and the decision of the Director of Public Prosecutions to commence a pilot project on the release of decisions not to prosecute in fatal cases to the family members of the deceased (2008).

[6] See for instance J Temkin, *Rape and the Legal Process* (2nd ed, Oxford University Press, Oxford 2002) and C Hanly, D Healy and S Scriver, *Rape and Justice in Ireland* (The Liffey Press, Dublin, 2009). Attrition in this context refers to the process by which cases 'fall out' of the criminal justice system (Gregory and Leas, 1996; Lea *et al*, 2003).

[7] The legislation which provides for victim impact evidence attempts to limit the damage which might potentially be caused to an accused person when a victim impact statement strays into prejudicial territory. The section, as revised in 2010, now provides that the court may order that information given in a victim impact statement may not be published or broadcast, with contravention of the

There is provision for separate legal representation in the trial process for victims of rape.[8] Representative groups argue that, for rape victims, the trial process is an additional violation. Yet victims of homicide frequently have their character assassinated at trial, and neither they nor their families are separately legally represented. Thus some categories of victims can be presented as more deserving of a voice in the criminal process than others, and the accommodation of those victims can be seen to challenge such long-held precepts as equality before the law, impartiality and the trial process as a confined forum in which to test fact and evidence. **12–05**

A number of victim-centred procedural, practical and legislative reforms have increased rights of participation and information for victims, and have created obligations which are designed to vindicate victims' rights, redress the perceived imbalance between victim and accused and prevent or limit what is termed 'secondary victimisation' — the harm caused by the process itself.[9] The standing of victims in criminal proceedings is considerably strengthened, on paper at least, by the 2012 Directive establishing minimum standards on the rights, support and protection of victims of crime.[10] It remains to be seen whether the agencies responsible for interacting with victims will be adequately resourced to give full effect to the Directive so that the rights it sets out are vindicated by effective access to information and special measures of protection for the victims who need them. **12–06**

VULNERABLE VICTIMS

Practical, emotional and cultural obstacles may inhibit some complainants from accessing the services of An Garda Síochána. The type of offence to which a person has been subjected may of itself leave the victim in a position of temporary or permanent vulnerability. However, there are others who are disadvantaged in accessing and participating in the criminal justice process because of their age, intellectual capacity, mental illness, disability or by virtue of their relationship to or with the person by whom they have been victimised. They may have waited many years before disclosing and reporting the offences which have been committed against them. They may be members of the travelling community, immigrants present in Ireland legally or illegally, with language and cultural barriers precluding them from accessing the criminal justice **12–07**

---

order amounting to an offence. Criminal Justice Act 1993, s 5(5) as substituted by the Criminal Procedure Act 2010, s 4.

8 Criminal Law (Rape) Act 1981, s 4A, as inserted by s 34 of the Sex Offenders Act 2001. The section allows for legal representation when it is proposed to adduce evidence of previous sexual history.

9 Legislative provisions include victim impact statements (Criminal Justice Act 1993, s 5 as substituted by s 4 of the Criminal Procedure Act 2010); compensation orders for injured parties (Criminal Justice Act 1993, s 6), separate legal representation for victims of rape (s 4A of the Criminal Law (Rape) Act 1981 as inserted by the Sex Offenders Act 2001, s 34), the Framework Decision on victims' rights, Council Framework Decision 2001/220/JHA of 15 March 2001 on the standing of victims in criminal proceedings, OJ L 82 of 22 March 2001, Directive 2012/29/EU of 25 October 2012 establishing minimum standards on the rights, support and protection of victims of crime.

10 Directive 2012/29/EU of 25 October 2012 establishing minimum standards on the rights, support and protection of victims of crime.

system, or they may for a variety of reasons be distrustful of An Garda Síochána.[11] They may be targets of intimidation because of their engagement with the gardaí. Particular supportive measures are required to facilitate such victims. The European Code of Police Ethics provides:

> "Police investigations shall be objective and fair. They shall be sensitive and adaptable to the special needs of persons, such as children, juveniles, women, minorities including ethnic minorities and vulnerable persons... The police shall be aware of the special needs of witnesses and shall be guided by rules for their protection and support during investigation, in particular where there is a risk of intimidation of witnesses."[12]

In addition, European police forces are obliged to "provide the necessary support, assistance and information to victims of crime, without discrimination",[13] including translation and interpretation services.[14]

12–08 While the Garda Victim Liaison Office, specialist victim interviewers and family liaison offices have specialised roles in that regard, all gardaí should be aware of the factors which give rise to inherent victim vulnerability and the potential effects of an adverse experience on future participation in the criminal process. Specific obligations are outlined in the 2012 Victims Directive.

DECISIONS TO REPORT AND COMPLAINANT WITHDRAWAL

12–09 The quality of interactions between gardaí and those who have been victimised can affect complainant withdrawal and the decision to report crime in the first place. A 2010 survey showed that slightly more than one in five respondents did not report a crime to the gardaí. The authors noted:

> "As has been documented in other studies, decisions on whether or not to report a crime to law enforcement authorities are influenced by a variety of factors, including views about the law enforcement authorities and their effectiveness, perceived seriousness of the offence, perceptions about the likely success of criminal proceedings and the severity of sentence, the ease with which reports can be made, issues of insurance, feelings of shame and weakness,[15] whether the victim believed that the matter could be 'sorted out'

---

[11] Walker has noted "... Traveller/Ethnic Minority survey results show that Travellers are significantly less satisfied with the Garda service than the broad spectrum of the public, migrants and refugees... For Travellers in the Traveller/Ethnic Minority survey, only one in two found the local gardaí approachable, whereas nearly nine out of ten migrants and refugees found the gardaí approachable." *Public Attitudes Survey & Traveller/Ethnic Minority Communities Attitudes Survey to the Garda Síochána,* Garda Research Unit, Templemore (2007).

[12] European Code of Police Ethics, paras 49 and 51.

[13] *ibid*, para 52.

[14] *ibid*, para 53.

[15] Hanly *et al* (2009: 362) noted for example in their study of rape victims that the most common reasons given by participants for not making a report included: "psychological factors, such as not feeling strong enough to re-tell their experiences, social considerations, including concern at how making a report might affect their families, and concerns about the criminal justice system, especially the fear of not being believed."

at a local or individual level, the fear of reprisal, the need to prevent family distress, the fear of prejudice or not being taken seriously (i.e. homophobic crime is often under reported),[16] and the fear of being implicated in the crime." [17,18]

They advised:

> "Though many of the reasons for non-reporting are beyond the direct control of the Gardaí ... it is important that the Gardaí ensure as far as possible that an environment is created where victims are in a position to make a report at a time which is convenient to them, that when reporting their account of events they will be treated seriously, that at all times they will be treated with dignity and respect, and that they will not be judged or prejudiced in giving that account."[19]

An earlier study entitled *Sexual Abuse and Violence in Ireland (SAVI)* (2002) found **12–10** strikingly low levels of reporting of sexual violence to the gardaí, at 6%.[20] The subsequent *Rape and Justice in Ireland* study (2009) found that 34% of participants had not reported to the gardaí and, while concerns about the criminal justice system featured prominently, the overriding stated concern was a desire not to have others know what had happened. The study identified a significant withdrawal rate of over 25% after a report had been made, and found that over 40% of those who made a report seriously considered withdrawing their complaint, with the primary reason given as a poor reaction from the gardaí.[21] The quality of the garda response at first instance therefore has a very real impact on the retention of complainants, at least in the context of sexual offences. It was noted in the same study that poor communication following the initial report contributes to negative complainant experiences with the reporting process. The authors suggested that "compassion, sensitivity and good communication" would give victims "a sense of ownership over their own experience and ... support and validation."[22]

THE VICTIMS' CHARTER

The Victims' Charter and Guide to the Criminal Justice System has recently been revised **12–11** and sets out the entitlements of victims, the service they can expect from the various state agencies involved in the criminal process and their avenues of recourse if their expectations are not met. The charter gives a number of undertakings on the provision of information. It provides that gardaí should give victims the name, telephone number and station of the investigating garda and the PULSE incident number; that gardaí will explain the process and keep victims of crime informed, including writing to inform them if a suspect has been charged, summonsed or cautioned in relation to

---

16 See 'Massive fall in homophobic crime sparks fear of under-reporting', *Sunday Tribune,* 26 July 2009.

17 On the reasons for non-reporting, see O'Connell (2000: 7). See also Breen and Rottman (1985) and CSO (2007).

18 Commission for the Support of Victims of Crime, *The Needs and Concerns of Victims of Crime in Ireland,* October 2010, at p 31.

19 *ibid*, at p 33.

20 H McGee, R Garavan, M de Barra, J Byrne, R Conroy, *The SAVI Report: Sexual Abuse and Violence in Ireland* (Liffey Press, Dublin, 2002).

21 C Hanly *et al*, *Rape and Justice in Ireland* (Liffey Press, Dublin, 2009) at p 160.

22 *ibid* at p 207.

their incident; that written information will be given concerning the Crime Victims' Helpline and other support services, as well as details concerning a prosecution, including whether the suspect is being held in custody or on bail, together with any bail conditions; the time, date and location of the court hearing; prosecution and court procedures, including provision for victim impact evidence where applicable; court expenses and the outcome of the criminal trial.

12–12 Specific categories of victim are identified who, as well as being referred to specialist support organisations, are to be shown special sensitivity by the gardaí. Victims to whom special sensitivity ought to be shown include complainants in sexual offences (who will have the assistance of a garda of the same gender) and families of murder victims or victims of other unlawful killings (with whom the local Superintendent will personally keep in contact. Contact will also be maintained by the investigating garda through a named family liaison officer from the investigation team); victims of domestic violence; older people; people with special needs; those who do not speak fluent English or Irish (for whom a free translation service will be provided); members of the lesbian, gay, bisexual and transgender communities; victims of racist incidents and victims of crimes committed by young people.

12–13 The charter is lacking in detail and, as Walsh points out, it contains neither a right to have access to material on the garda investigation file nor a right to have the offence in question investigated professionally, thoroughly and competently.[23] Neither is there any reference to the level of protection which can be expected or offered if victims are subjected to intimidation. The charter will require revision once the Victims Directive is transposed into Irish law in November 2015.

CHILD COMPLAINANTS AND COMPLAINANTS WITH SPECIAL NEEDS

12–14 Children and persons who are intellectually impaired are a particularly vulnerable category of victim, since they rely on others for their basic needs to be met and are frequently offended against by the very people in whose trust they have been placed.

Specialist Victim Interviewers

12–15 The Garda Síochána Policy on Sexual Crime, Crimes Against Children and Child Welfare (2nd edition, 2013) provides guidance on the approach to child complainants. Child complainants in offences of a violent or sexual nature who are under 14 must, unless in urgent exceptional circumstances, be interviewed by specialist victim interviewers who have undergone training to equip them to deal with all victims of serious offences, including people under 14 and adults with intellectual disabilities. Such interviewers must prioritise the interview of those children over any other duty.[24]

---

[23] D Walsh, *Human Rights and Policing in Ireland: Law, Policy and Practice* (Clarus Press, Dublin, 2009) at pp 724–725.

[24] The Garda Síochána Policy on Sexual Crime, Crimes Against Children and Child Welfare (2nd edition, 2013), para 34.3.4.

The policy provides:

> "There is an absolute obligation on investigating members to refer the interviewing of such complainants to trained Specialist Interviewers. Specialist Interviewers have undergone intensive training and are deemed competent to interview such complainants. Members (who are not trained Specialist Interviewers) will not attempt to take a statement from a person who is under 14 years of age or a person with intellectual disability who complains of a sexual offence or an offence involving violence or threats of violence, except in exceptional urgent circumstances."[25]

Interviews should be conducted in plain clothes[26] and officers who undertake specialist interviews will not be involved in interviewing suspects in the same case.[27] Dedicated interview suites, located away from Garda stations and specially equipped for the purpose and for the electronic recording of interviews, should be used for specialist interviews. Section 16(1)(b) of the Criminal Evidence Act 1992 provides for the video-recording of interviews with child complainants and the policy dictates: **12–16**

> "It is essential that all complainants ... are dealt with in accordance with the provisions of section 16(1)(b) to ensure that they are afforded the protections as envisaged by those provisions (i.e. not being required to give live evidence in criminal proceedings, unless otherwise directed by the Court)."[28]

It is vital that, in cases involving children, investigative procedures are completed as expeditiously as possible. The video-recording of interviews with children serves an important practical purpose: it allows jurors to see the children as they were at the date the complaint was made, rather than on the date of the trial a number of years subsequently when they have changed considerably both in terms of maturity and appearance. The video is the child or mentally impaired complainant's statement of complaint and is admissible at trial as evidence of any fact stated of which direct evidence would be admissible.[29] **12–17**

'Children First' National Guidelines on the Protection and Welfare of Children

Gardaí have obligations under the '*Children First' National Guidelines on the Protection and Welfare of Children*,[30] which set out the following principles as representing best practice principles on child protection: **12–18**

(i) The welfare of children is of paramount importance.
(ii) A proper balance must be struck between protecting children and respecting the rights and needs of parents / carers and families; but where there is conflict, the child's welfare must come first.

---

25 The Garda Síochána Policy on Sexual Crime, Crimes Against Children and Child Welfare (2nd edition, 2013), para 33.5.
26 *ibid*, para 34.3.7.
27 *ibid,* para 34.3.5.
28 *ibid*, para 33.6.
29 Criminal Evidence Act 1992, s 16(1)(b) as amended by s 4 of the Criminal Law (Human Trafficking Act 2013.
30 *Children First National Guidelines on the Protection and Welfare of Children* (Stationery Office, Dublin, September 1999).

(iii) Children have a right to be heard, listened to and to be taken seriously. Taking account of their age and understanding, they should be consulted and involved in all matters and decisions which may affect their lives.

(iv) Early intervention and support should be available to promote the welfare of children and families, particularly where they are vulnerable or at risk of not receiving adequate care or protection.

(v) Parents/carers have a right to respect and should be consulted and involved in matters which concern their family.

(vi) Actions taken to protect a child, including assessment, should not in themselves be abusive or cause the child unnecessary distress. Every action and procedure should consider the overall needs of the child.

(vii) Intervention should not deal with the child in isolation; the child must be seen in a family setting.

(viii) The criminal dimension of any action cannot be ignored.

(ix) Children should only be separated from parents/carers when all alternative means of protecting them have been exhausted. Re-union should always be considered.

(x) Agencies or individuals taking protective action should consider factors such as the child's gender, age, stage of development, religion, culture or race.

(xi) Effective prevention, detection and treatment of child abuse or neglect requires a co-ordinated multi-disciplinary approach to child care work and effective inter-agency management of individual cases. All agencies and disciplines concerned with the protection and welfare of children must work co-operatively in the best interests of children and their families.

(xii) In practice, effective child protection requires compulsory training and clarity of responsibility for personnel involved in organisations working with children.[31]

HSE Notification

12–19 The *Children First* guidelines also set out the circumstances in which the Health Service Executive (HSE) ought to refer cases of suspected neglect or abuse to the gardaí, including cases in which emergency intervention is required and cases in which informal concerns are raised, to enable the agencies to work together for chid safety. The gardaí are in turn obliged to refer cases of suspected abuse or neglect to the HSE, paragraph 9.7.1 providing:

> "Where An Garda Síochána suspect that a child has been the victim of emotional, physical or sexual abuse or neglect (whether wilful or unintentional), the health board must be formally notified. It is not necessary for An Garda Síochána to have sufficient evidence to support a criminal prosecution before notifying the health board."

12–20 The subsequent paragraphs clarify that the gardaí need not notify the health board of cases of physical or sexual assaults against children involving issues of law enforcement only; for example, cases involving the assault of a child by a stranger. The need for notification arises only when cases give rise to child protection issues, such as when the suspected abuser has ongoing contact with other children. In cases in which such considerations do

[31] *Children First National Guidelines on the Protection and Welfare of Children* (Stationery Office, Dublin, September 1999).

not apply, An Garda Síochána should contact the health board where there is need for appropriate counselling and other support services for the victims of assaults.

VICTIMS OF SEXUAL OFFENCES

Detailed practical and legal guidance on the appropriate approach to the investigation of sexual offences is provided in the Garda Síochána Policy on the Investigation of Sexual Crime, Crimes Against Children and Child Welfare (2nd edition, 2013). The policy covers such matters as the demeanour which should be adopted by investigating officers, the use of anonymous interview suites so that members of the public cannot deduce or ascertain the purpose of the complainant's meeting with the gardaí, the requisite level of detail in a complainant statement, procedures for the gathering of oral and forensic evidence, as well as the legal instruments which criminalise sexual crimes and crimes against children. The sensitivity which is referred to in the victims charter is expanded upon, with gardaí advised of the embarrassment which may be felt at having to recount details of the incident(s), the possibility that a victim of a sexual offence may be suffering from post-traumatic stress and the need for victims to be allowed to tell their stories without interruption. By the same token, the requirement that the fullest and most detailed statement possible must be taken is emphasised. At paragraph 2.4.6, the policy provides: **12–21**

> "From the beginning, the investigating member will keep in mind the emotional and physical pain the victim may be suffering, while ensuring that all available evidence regarding any reported offence is obtained."

At paragraph 2.4.7, gardaí are cautioned to "use positive language at all times, avoiding negative terminology as 'alleged' or 'allegation' and instead use such words as 'complaint' or 'account', etc." **12–22**

The policy outlines that, in the investigation of sexual offences, the privacy of the complainant is paramount: **12–23**

> "The interview of the injured party should be conducted by two members at the earliest opportunity and in a suitable location for the complainant and Gardaí. This location may be a suitable room in a Garda Station, the home of the complainant or a friend/relative, a private area in a hospital, a specialist interview suite or other carefully selected location where the injured party feels comfortable. Suspect interview rooms in Garda Stations should not be used in this regard. If the interview is to take place in a Garda station, privacy should be ensured."[32]

It is emphasised that complainants of rape or sexual assault should be interviewed as soon as possible after the occurrence and the gender of the interviewing garda should be decided by the complainant, unless this is not practicable.[33] An interview should not take place in the presence of a potential witness.[34]

---

32 Garda Síochána Policy on the Investigation of Sexual Crime, Crimes Against Children and Child Welfare, (2nd ed, 2013), para 2.43.

33 *ibid*, at para 2.7.4.

34 *ibid*, at para 2.4.12.

12–24 The policy notes that "victims of sexual crime vary. All victims both male and female, irrespective of relationship type, will have their complaint of sexual crime investigated without bias or discrimination".[35] The need for cases to be dealt with professionally is stated to be vital both for the victim and for the court system, with victims to be informed of the services available to them. Paragraph 15.3 outlines that:

> "Investigating members should be aware that research has shown that a complainant is more likely to make a statement of complaint and remain committed to the investigation and any subsequent prosecution when:
> - s/he has been supported by a victims group
> - there is a substantial investigative effort, including the early taking of a detailed statement of complaint
> - s/he has been dealt with in a sympathetic, supportive and compassionate manner, and
> - investigating Garda(í) reassure the complainant that her/his complaint will be fully investigated
> - s/he is kept fully and regularly informed of the progress of the investigation/prosecution."[36]

12–25 The need for referral to the available orders under the Domestic Violence Act 1996 is highlighted for cases involving cohabiting couples.[37] Consistency in the garda member involved is also highlighted as being of particular importance:

> "It is vital that a continued liaison is maintained with the complainant throughout the investigation and prosecution by the same member of An Garda Síochána. If this is not possible, a formal introduction of the new liaison member will take place and contact details provided. The new nominated member will continue to interact regularly with the complainant."[38]

12–26 The Policy on the Investigation of Sexual Crime, Crimes Against Children and Child Welfare operates in tandem with the Recent Rape / Sexual Assault National Guidelines on Referral and Forensic Clinical Examination in Ireland.[39] The processes for forensic examination of complainants are considered at *Chapter 6: Forensics, Crime Scene Management and the Preservation of Evidence* at para 6 – 56.

THE VICTIMS DIRECTIVE

12–27 The 2001 Framework Decision on the Standing of Victims in Criminal Proceedings[40] set out general minimum standards to address the rights and needs of victims. In 2012, it was replaced with a Directive establishing minimum standards on the rights, support and protection of victims of crime.[41] A key aspect of the 2001 Framework Decision was

---

35 *ibid*, at para 15.1.

36 *ibid*, at para 15.3.

37 *ibid*, at para 15.6.

38 *ibid*, at para 15.7.

39 National SATU Guidelines Development Group, Recent Rape/Sexual Assault: National Guidelines on Referral and Forensic Clinical Examination in Ireland, (2nd ed, 2010).

40 Council Framework Decision 2001/220/JHA of 15 March 2001 on the standing of victims in criminal proceedings, OJ L 82 of 22 March 2001.

41 Directive 2012/29/EU of the European Parliament and of the Council of 25 October 2012 establishing minimum standards on the rights, support and protection of victims of crime, and replacing Council Framework Decision 2001/220/JHA.

the provision of information with an obligation on Member States to ensure that victims have access from their first contact with law enforcement agencies "to information of relevance to their particular interests".[42] Information is crucial to maintaining victim engagement and reducing alienation from the criminal process. The SAVI Report found that a lack of information from gardaí was a major source of dissatisfaction, with gardaí reported to have given inadequate explanations of procedures being undertaken.[43] The former Director of Public Prosecutions has stated that:

> "... a person who has personally suffered as the victim of a crime and who is central to the trial process has the right to as much information about the criminal process as is consistent with the prosecutor's obligation to the interests of justice and the law."[44]

The 2012 Victims Directive outlines in detail the entitlements of victims to information, which has potential to radically alter the standing of victims in Ireland and to increase considerably the administrative burden on gardaí. 'Victim' is defined in the Directive as: **12–28**

(i) a natural person who has suffered harm, including physical, mental or emotional harm or economic loss which was directly caused by a criminal offence;
(ii) family members of a person whose death was directly caused by a criminal offence and who have suffered harm as a result of that person's death.

'Family members' are defined to mean "the spouse, the person who is living with the victim in a committed intimate relationship, in a joint household and on a stable and continuous basis, the relatives in direct line, the siblings and the dependants of the victim."[45] **12–29**

Rights to Information

In relation to information, a number of articles set out extensive obligations: **12–30**

> "Article 4
>
> Right to receive information from the first contact with a competent authority
>
> 1. Member States shall ensure that victims are offered the following information, without unnecessary delay, from their first contact with a competent authority in order to enable them to access the rights set out in this Directive:
> (a) the type of support they can obtain and from whom, including, where relevant, basic information about access to medical support, any specialist support, including psychological support, and alternative accommodation;
> (b) the procedures for making complaints with regard to a criminal offence and their role in connection with such procedures;

42 Council Framework Decision 2001/220/JHA of 15 March 2001 on the standing of victims in criminal proceedings, OJ L 82 of 22 March 2001, Art 4.

43 H McGee, R Garavan, M de Barra, J Byrne, R Conroy, The SAVI Report: Sexual Abuse and Violence in Ireland (Liffey Press, Dublin, 2002).

44 J Hamilton "*The Prosecutor and the Victim*" paper delivered at the CCJHR 4th annual conference, University College Cork, 11 June 2010.

45 Directive 2012/29/EU of the European Parliament and of the Council of 25 October 2012 establishing minimum standards on the rights, support and protection of victims of crime, and replacing Council Framework Decision 2001/220/JHA, at Article 1.

(c) how and under what conditions they can obtain protection, including protection measures;
(d) how and under what conditions they can access legal advice, legal aid and any other sort of advice;
(e) how and under what conditions they can access compensation;
(f) how and under what conditions they are entitled to interpretation and translation;
(g) if they are resident in a Member State other than that where the criminal offence was committed, any special measures, procedures or arrangements, which are available to protect their interests in the Member State where the first contact with the competent authority is made;
(h) the available procedures for making complaints where their rights are not respected by the competent authority operating within the context of criminal proceedings;
(i) the contact details for communications about their case;
(j) the available restorative justice services;
(k) how and under what conditions expenses incurred as a result of their participation in the criminal proceedings can be reimbursed.

2. The extent or detail of information referred to in paragraph 1 may vary depending on the specific needs and personal circumstances of the victim and the type or nature of the crime. Additional details may also be provided at later stages depending on the needs of the victim and the relevance, at each stage of proceedings, of such details.

Article 5

Right of victims when making a complaint

1. Member States shall ensure that victims receive written acknowledgement of their formal complaint made by them to the competent authority of a Member State, stating the basic elements of the criminal offence concerned.

2. Member States shall ensure that victims who wish to make a complaint with regard to a criminal offence and who do not understand or speak the language of the competent authority be enabled to make the complaint in a language that they understand or by receiving the necessary linguistic assistance.

3. Member States shall ensure that victims who do not understand or speak the language of the competent authority, receive translation, free of charge, of the written acknowledgement of their complaint provided for in paragraph 1, if they so request, in a language that they understand.

Article 6

Right to receive information about their case

1. Member States shall ensure that victims are notified without unnecessary delay of their right to receive the following information about the criminal proceedings instituted as a result of the complaint with regard to a criminal offence suffered by the victim and that, upon request, they receive such information:
(a) any decision not to proceed with or to end an investigation or not to prosecute the offender;
(b) the time and place of the trial, and the nature of the charges against the offender.

2. Member States shall ensure that, in accordance with their role in the relevant criminal justice system, victims are notified without unnecessary delay of their right to receive the following information about the criminal proceedings instituted as a result of

the complaint with regard to a criminal offence suffered by them and that, upon request, they receive such information:

(a) any final judgment in a trial;
(b) information enabling the victim to know about the state of the criminal proceedings, unless in exceptional cases the proper handling of the case may be adversely affected by such notification.

3. Information provided for under paragraph 1(a) and paragraph 2(a) shall include reasons or a brief summary of reasons for the decision concerned, except in the case of a jury decision or a decision where the reasons are confidential in which cases the reasons are not provided as a matter of national law.

4. The wish of victims as to whether or not to receive information shall bind the competent authority, unless that information must be provided due to the entitlement of the victim to active participation in the criminal proceedings. Member States shall allow victims to modify their wish at any moment, and shall take such modification into account.

5. Member States shall ensure that victims are offered the opportunity to be notified, without unnecessary delay, when the person remanded in custody, prosecuted or sentenced for criminal offences concerning them is released from or has escaped detention. Furthermore, Member States shall ensure that victims are informed of any relevant measures issued for their protection in case of release or escape of the offender.

6. Victims shall, upon request, receive the information provided for in paragraph 5 at least in cases where there is a danger or an identified risk of harm to them, unless there is an identified risk of harm to the offender which would result from the notification."[46]

It is unclear as yet how the obligations will be fulfilled in practical terms, since a 2010 Commission for the Support of Victims of Crime Report on the Needs and Concerns of Victims of Crime in Ireland noted a failure on the part of An Garda Síochána to adequately provide information under the existing victims charter: **12–31**

"In the initial stages, particularly after a crime is reported, victims require information from the Gardaí about the investigation (such as the contact name and details of the investigating Garda, and an incident number), the names of relevant support organisations, information on what happens when a crime is reported, and on their role and their opportunities to participate in the criminal justice process. The findings from this study would suggest however that victims are not receiving enough basic information from the Gardaí immediately after reporting the crime. 1 in 5 respondents noted that they did not receive the contact details of the investigating Garda and more than 1 in 2 of the respondents who reported a crime indicated that they did not receive the Pulse Incident Number. This information deficit can result in secondary victimisation, intensifying the harms caused by the crime and aggravating the trauma experienced by the victim. Given that the Gardaí are often one of the initial contacts following a crime, it is vital that they provide victims with relevant information on the investigation of the crime including the name and contact details of the investigating Garda and the Pulse Incident number. The findings from the research also suggest that the Gardaí do not systematically advise victims on the support services available to them at either national or local level. More than 1 in every 2 respondents who reported a crime did not receive a contact number for

[46] Directive 2012/29/EU of the European Parliament and of the Council of 25 October 2012 establishing minimum standards on the rights, support and protection of victims of crime, and replacing Council Framework Decision 2001/220/JHA, Articles 4–6.

a support group from the Gardaí and 6 out of every 10 respondents who reported a crime did not receive the Crime Victims Helpline number from them."[47]

12–32 The Office of the Director of Public Prosecution was also criticised for standards of communication with victims:

> "It is clear from this study that communication between the DPP's office and victims, particularly on decisions not to prosecute or to charge a lesser offence, needs to be improved. Overall most participants in the research concluded that contact with the office of the DPP was not relevant to them (i.e. the offence was not reported, the case did not go to trial, it was a minor offence tried in the District Court). Though the majority of relevant respondents to the questionnaire indicated that they were satisfied with the DPP's office, a significant minority expressed dissatisfaction for reasons such as the downgrading of charges, the absence of a prosecutor at the sentencing hearing, the failure to give reasons for a decision not to prosecute, and poor standards of communication with victims."[48]

Transposition and Additional Rights

12–33 The Directive replaces a 2001 Framework Decision and must be transposed into Irish law by 16 November 2015.[49] The provision of information and advice to victims of crime is resource-intensive: in other jurisdictions there are dedicated divisions within the prosecution service to undertake the work associated with victim engagement—examples include the Victim Information and Advice (VIA) service of the Crown Office and Procurator Fiscal Service in Scotland and the Witness Assistance Service operated by the DPP of New South Wales.

The 2012 Directive provides a number of other rights for victims including:

- the right to be heard in criminal proceedings (Article 10);
- the right to a review of decisions not to prosecute (Article 11);
- the right to safeguards in the context of restorative justice services (Article 12);
- the right to legal aid where victims are parties to criminal proceedings (Article 13);
- the right to reimbursement of expenses incurred as a result of active participation in criminal proceedings (Article 14);
- the right to the return of property seized if it is no longer required for criminal proceedings (Article 15);
- the right to a decision on compensation from the offender (Article 16);
- rights where victims are resident in other Member States to minimise the difficulties experienced (Article 17);
- rights to protection from secondary and repeat victimisation, from intimidation and retaliation and to protection during questioning and testimony (Article 18);
- the right to avoid contact between victim and offender, with separate waiting areas for victims (Article 19);

---

47 Commission for the Support of Victims of Crime, *Needs and Concerns of Victims of Crime in Ireland,* October 2010, at p 175–176.

48 *ibid.*

49 Directive 2012/29/EU of 25 October 2012, Art 27.

- the right to protection during criminal investigations, with interviews of victims to be concluded without unjustified delay and the number of interviews to be kept to a minimum and carried out only where strictly necessary (Article 20);
- the right to the protection of privacy (Article 21).

Assessment of Specific Needs

The Directive also provides at Article 22 for the provision of an individual assessment to identify victims' specific protection needs and to determine whether and to what extent they would benefit from special measures in the course of criminal proceedings. Such assessments will, in particular, take into account the personal characteristics of the victim, and the type or nature and circumstances of the crime. Particular attention is to be paid to victims who have suffered considerable harm due to the severity of the crime. It is noted that victims who have suffered a crime committed with a bias or discriminatory motive, which could be related to their personal characteristics (for example gender or sexual orientation) and victims whose relationship to, and dependence on, the offender make them particularly vulnerable. Child victims are presumed to have specific protection needs due to their vulnerability to secondary and repeat victimisation, to intimidation and to retaliation. The special measures to be provided for victims with specific needs are set out at Article 23 and delineated between measures at investigation stage and trial stage. During the investigation phase: **12–34**

(a) interviews with the victim should be carried out in premises designed or adapted for that purpose;
(b) interviews with the victim should be carried out by or through professionals trained for that purpose;
(c) all interviews with the victim should be conducted by the same persons unless this is contrary to the good administration of justice;
(d) all interviews with victims of sexual violence, gender-based violence or violence in close relationships, unless conducted by a prosecutor or a judge, should be conducted by a person of the same sex as the victim, if the victim so wishes, provided that the course of the criminal proceedings will not be prejudiced.

During court proceedings victims who have been assessed to have specific protection needs will be afforded: **12–35**

(a) measures to avoid visual contact between victims and offenders, including during the giving of evidence, by appropriate means including the use of communication technology;
(b) measures to ensure that the victim may be heard in the courtroom without being present, in particular through the use of appropriate communication technology;
(c) measures to avoid unnecessary questioning concerning the victim's private life not related to the criminal offence; and
(d) measures allowing a hearing to take place without the presence of the public.

Children are given additional protection in Article 24 with provision for the audiovisual recording of interviews with child victims, with such recordings admissible as evidence; the appointment of a special representative where there is a conflict of interest between **12–36** the child and its parents; the right to legal advice and representation in proceedings where there is, or could be, a conflict of interest between the child victim and holders of parental responsibility.

12–37 It is noteworthy that the language used throughout the Directive refers to 'victims' and 'offenders', rather than the more neutral terms 'complainant' and 'suspect / defendant / accused'. In the preamble to the Directive, it is said that:

> "The rights set out in this Directive are without prejudice to the rights of the offender. The term "offender" refers to a person who has been convicted of a crime. However, for the purposes of this Directive, it also refers to a suspected or accused person before any acknowledgement of guilt or conviction, and it is without prejudice to the presumption of innocence."

12–38 While reference to a 'victim' rather than complainant is less objectionable, since the fact of an injury, damage to property or other criminal event is rarely disputed, the use of the term 'offender' leads to an inevitable presupposition of guilt, despite the assertions of the preamble to the contrary. Sensitivity and special protective measures can be implemented and utilised with the potential to improve victim experiences of the criminal process in a very tangible way, but such measures need not — and ought not — to affect the impartiality and objectivity of the criminal process and its emphasis on *suspects* and *accused persons*.

CHAPTER 13

Domestic Abuse

INTRODUCTION

Dealing with domestic abuse requires delicacy in practical and legal terms. Equally, a robust policing response is often both appropriate and necessary. This is a complex crime, the consequences of which can be fatal.[1] As such, it requires victim-centred policing, mindful of the various cultural factors at play and of the inherent difficulties associated with the economic, emotional and social dependence, shared children and social isolation which often characterise domestic abuse victims.[2] By comparison with complainants in other cases, those who have been victimised may not wish for the perpetrator to be prosecuted, or indeed arrested, but rather for an immediate intervention to bring an end to the incident without legal consequences.[3] **13–01**

---

1 Women's Aid have noted that between 1996 and September 2013, 194 women have been murdered in Ireland, 117 of whom (61%) were killed in their own homes. In the resolved cases, 75 women (53%) were killed by a partner or ex-partner (Women's Aid Female Homicide Media Watch September 2013). In the US, it is estimated that four women are killed every day as a result of domestic violence (Stout, 1989, quoted in LG Mills, "Mandatory Arrest and Prosecution Policies for Domestic Violence, A Critical Literature Review and the Case for More Research to Test Victim Empowerment Approaches." *Criminal Justice and Behavior,* 1998 25: 306).

2 See L Richards, S Letchford and S Stratton, *Policing Domestic Violence – Blackstone's Practical Policing* (Oxford University Press, Oxford, 2008) at p 20.

3 C Hoyle, *Negotiating Domestic Violence* (Blackwell, Oxford, 1998) p 214.

13–02 It is not intended to explore the civil orders available under the Domestic Violence Acts 1996 and 2002 in detail here. The chapter will instead examine the policy of An Garda Síochána on domestic violence, a policy which is unapologetically pro-arrest. The emphasis is therefore on the offences for which arrest might be contemplated in the domestic abuse context, including offences relating to the breach of orders made under the Domestic Violence Acts 1996 and 2002.

DEFINING DOMESTIC ABUSE

13–03 There has been a linguistic shift in the categorisation of offences concerning intimidation in intimate relationships, with a move towards the term 'domestic abuse', rather than 'domestic violence', given that a person may be terrorised in an intimate or familial relationship without ever having actually been subjected to physical violence. The term 'domestic violence' remains the more prominent descriptor, notwithstanding increased acceptance that behaviour which constitutes 'domestic violence' may take more subtle forms of oppressive and psychologically-damaging emotional abuse and conduct.

The Garda Síochána Policy on Domestic Violence uses the following definition:

> "'Domestic violence' includes the physical, sexual, emotional or mental abuse of one partner by another partner in a relationship which may or may not be one of marriage or cohabitation and includes abuse by any family member against whom a safety or barring order may be obtained by another family member."[4]

13–04 The policy notes that domestic violence "crosses class, gender, race and religious belief," with a diverse range of victims. Categories of persons who may be affected by domestic violence are outlined as including those involved in heterosexual and lesbian, gay, bisexual or transgender (LGBT) relationships and people with disabilities or older people by their spouses, children, relatives or carers—commonly known as "elder abuse". A broad definition is therefore given to both what constitutes 'domestic' and 'violence'.[5]

13–05 The National Office for the Prevention of Domestic, Sexual and Gender-based Violence, COSC, outlines the behaviours involved in greater detail:

> "Three different dimensions of abuse characterise domestic violence: physical, sexual and emotional abuse. Behaviours that commonly occur in situations of domestic violence include various forms of physical violence such as kicking, punching, slapping, smothering or choking, biting, throwing and threatening with an object. The use of isolation can be a key device, for example where the abuser restricts communication between the victim-survivor and those who are close to the person. Domestic violence often includes the use and abuse of children, as well as economic abuse. Controlling and intimidating behaviour,

---

4 An Garda Síochána Policy on Domestic Violence http://www.garda.ie/Documents/User/Domestic Violence policy 23.11.10.pdf <accessed 28 October 2013>.

5 See R Bryant and S Bryant (eds), *Student Police Officer Handbook 2010* (4th ed, Oxford University Press, Oxford, 2009) at pp 156–157.

> including threats and blaming the victim, are common forms of emotional abuse. Older people can experience abuse by carers and by those in a position of trust."[6]

As will be seen below, the emphasis on 'violence' in the classification of domestic abuse is perhaps an impediment to its effective policing, since domestic abuse often includes assault or behaviour which is threatening and or abusive, but which does not have an associated arrest power. Gardaí are thus considerably constrained in reacting to it from a policing, as distinct from a mediating, perspective if there are no civil orders under the Domestic Violence Acts 1996 and 2002 in force. **13–06**

GARDA SÍOCHÁNA POLICY ON DOMESTIC VIOLENCE

The Garda Síochána Policy on Domestic Violence notes that "inappropriate action by the Garda Síochána can often confirm the aggressor's perception of invulnerability which can in turn lead to further violence".[7] The initial response a victim receives from An Garda Síochána is therefore critical in determining their continued interaction with the criminal justice system.[8] The response of the gardaí is also crucial in determining the future behaviour of the aggressor. **13–07**

Some key provisions of the policy are: **13–08**

- if a safety / barring / interim barring / protection order is in existence, the gardaí will always arrest where there is a reasonable cause for believing that the order has been contravened;
- on receipt of a complaint of domestic violence, the investigating officer should deal with the matter promptly and on the basis that s/he is dealing with a crime and that life and property may well be at risk;
- station bail should not be granted to the accused, as the likelihood of intimidation to the injured party is extremely high;
- the victim should be provided with information on the civil remedies available;
- the investigating garda should give the complainant his/her name in writing, along with the name of the station and telephone number. The garda should call back to the victim at least once in the following month.

The policy emphasises the need for a compassionate approach, but also the need for evidence to be gathered: **13–09**

> "From the outset, the investigating member will keep in mind the emotional and physical pain the victim may be suffering while ensuring that all available evidence regarding any alleged assault is obtained. To this end the investigating member will take note of the following:
>
> (a) Day, date, time and place of the incident;

6 COSC National Strategy on Domestic, Sexual and Gender-Based Violence 2010–2014.

7 An Garda Síochána Policy on Domestic Violence, para 1.2.

8 Summary of submissions to COSC on the *National Strategy on Domestic, Sexual and Gender-Based Violence*, October 2008, at p 25.

(b) Detailed description of the occurrence, including injuries, with indications of corroboration, if any;
(c) Name and address of the complainant/victim and alleged offender and relationship between both;
(d) The existence or otherwise of a Safety/Barring / Interim Barring/Protection Order;
(e) Name and address of any witness;
(f) Physical and emotional condition of alleged victim and alleged offender;
(g) Physical and emotional condition of any children present;
(h) Condition of premises."[9]

13–10 An inter-agency approach is considered to be best placed to provide victim-centred support,[10] so gardaí should endeavour to work and collaborate with the Health Service Executive, non-governmental organisations such as Free Legal Advice Centres (FLAC) and advise victims of the existence of the various services available.

Pro-Arrest Policy

13–11 The Garda Síochána Policy on Domestic Violence specifies that a 'pro-arrest' approach should be adopted where an arrestable offence has occurred,[11] outlining that:

> "The Garda Síochána will take a pro-active approach towards arresting and charging where there are reasonable grounds to believe that a suspect has committed an offence and a power of arrest exists."[12]

13–12 The policy expressly states that the attitude of the victim will not be the determining factor in respect of the exercise of powers of arrest in this context, and the victim should not be asked if the abuser should be arrested. There has been considerable debate in other jurisdictions about the benefits of a pro-arrest policy (which is advocated in the UK and in some US States) and its efficacy in reducing subsequent victimisation. A pro-arrest response has been favoured, as it is thought that there is "a consistent reduction in the incidents of victimization due to arrest," providing support for "the continued use of arrests as a preferred law enforcement response for reducing subsequent victimization of women by their intimate partners."[13] Maxwell, Garner and Fagan found that "a majority of suspects discontinued their aggressive behaviors even without an arrest",[14] so the utility and cost benefit of mandatory arrest policies are questioned. Their research has also

---

[9] An Garda Síochána Policy on Domestic Violence, para 2.6.

[10] "Stopping Domestic Violence: What Works?" COSC Conference Report, 28–30 May 2008.

[11] An Garda Síochána Policy on Domestic Violence, para 3.1.

[12] *ibid* at para 3.1.

[13] C Maxwell, J Garner and J Fagan, "The Preventative Effects of Arrest on Intimate Partner Violence: Research, Policy and Theory," 2002 *Criminology and Public Policy* 2(1): 51 – 80, quoted in F Heidensohn "Gender and Policing" in T Newburn (ed) *Handbook of Policing* (2nd ed, Willan Publishing, Cullompton, 2008) at p 661.

[14] C Maxwell, J Garner and J Fagan "The Effects of Arrest on Intimate Partner Violence: New Evidence From the Spouse Assault Replication Program" *National Institute of Justice Research In Brief*, July 2001, at p 13.

shown that some perpetrators of domestic abuse are undeterred and continue to commit domestic violence, regardless of the intervention they have received.[15]

POWERS OF ARREST FOR CONSIDERATION

In determining whether a power of arrest exists, the Garda policy suggests that members may have recourse to the following legislation: **13–13**

(a) Domestic Violence Act 1996 (as amended by the Domestic Violence (Amendment) Act 2002);
(b) Criminal Damage Act 1991;
(c) Non Fatal Offences against the Person Act 1997;
(d) Criminal Law (Rape) (Amendment) Act 1990;
(e) Criminal Justice (Public Order) Act 1994;
(f) Children Act 2001, s 254 (Offences Against Children);
(g) Breach of the peace at common law.[16]

If there is evidence of a sexual assault,[17] a threat to kill,[18] false imprisonment,[19] a visible physical injury[20] or damage to property[21] (which does not belong to the suspect), there are ample powers of arrest.[22] As these are offences attracting penalties of five years' imprisonment or more, there is also a power to enter property to effect an arrest pursuant to s 6(2) of the Criminal Law Act 1997, see further *Chapter 8: Entry for Arrest and Investigation* at paras 8–24 – 8–28. **13–14**

However, much of the behaviour complained of in domestic abuse does not have an associated arrest power where it consists of threatening or intimidating behaviour or assaults without physical harm.

Breach of Orders made under the Domestic Violence Acts 1996 and 2002

Where there are no grounds for belief that an arrestable offence has been committed, orders under the Domestic Violence Act 1996 are crucial in providing gardaí with a clear power of arrest for acts which, of themselves, would fall short of an arrestable offence. However, having regard to the order in place, such acts amount to a breach and therefore an offence **13–15**

---

15 Maxwell, Garner and Fagan have noted: "While arrest reduced the proportion of suspects who reoffended and the frequency with which they reoffended, arrest did not prevent all batterers from continuing their violence against their intimate partners. In fact, we found a small number of victims who have chronically aggressive intimate partners." C Maxwell, J Garner and J Fagan "The Effects of Arrest on Intimate Partner Violence: New Evidence From the Spouse Assault Replication Program", *National Institute of Justice Research In Brief*, July 2001, at p 13.

16 An Garda Síochána Policy on Domestic Violence, para 3.2.

17 Criminal Law (Rape) (Amendment) Act 1990, s 2.

18 Non-Fatal Offences against the Person Act 1997, s 5.

19 *ibid*, s 15.

20 *ibid*, s 3.

21 Criminal Damage Act 1991, s 2.

22 Under s 4 of the Criminal Law Act 1997.

for which arrest can be effected. The 1996 Act provides for four types of protective civil orders: safety orders,[23] protection orders,[24] interim barring orders[25] and barring orders.[26]

Protection Order – Section 5 of the Domestic Violence Act 1996

13–16 A protection order directs the respondent to an application for a barring order or safety order to refrain from using violence or threatening to use violence, or molesting or putting the applicant or dependent persons in fear. If the respondent is not living with the applicant, the order may further direct that the respondent does not watch or beset the place where the applicant or a dependent person resides.[27] Applications for protection orders can be made *ex parte*[28] and remain in force until the court has determined the application for a barring or safety order.[29]

Safety Order – Section 2 of the Domestic Violence Act 1996

13–17 A safety order may be granted where the court is of the opinion that there are reasonable grounds to believe that the safety of the applicant or a dependent person requires an order directing the respondent to the application (a) not to use or threaten to use violence against, molest or put in fear the applicant or that dependent person, and (b) if he or she is residing at a place other than the place where the applicant or that dependent person resides, not to watch or beset that place.[30] A safety order may remain in place for a period of up to five years if granted by the District Court or the Circuit Court on appeal from the District Court.[31] There is no limitation period in the legislation if the order is made by the Circuit Court or High Court *ab initio.*

13–18 The following categories of person may apply for a safety order:

- the spouse of the respondent[32];
- the civil partner of the respondent, or a person who was a party to a civil partnership with the respondent that has been dissolved[33];
- a person who is neither a spouse or civil partner and is not related to the respondent within the prohibited degrees of relationship, but lived with the respondent in an intimate and committed relationship prior to the application for the safety order[34];

---

[23] Domestic Violence Act 1996, s 2.

[24] *ibid*, s 5.

[25] *ibid*, s 4 as amended by s 1 of the Domestic Violence (Amendment) Act 2002. See *DK v Judge Timothy Crowley and the Attorney General*, unreported, Supreme Court, 9 October 2002.

[26] Domestic Violence Act 1996, s 3.

[27] *ibid*, s 5(1).

[28] *ibid*, s 5(4), as substituted by s 1(b) of the Domestic Violence (Amendment) Act 2002

[29] Domestic Violence Act 1996, s 5(5).

[30] *ibid*, s 2.

[31] *ibid*, s 2(5).

[32] *ibid*, s 2(1)(a)(i).

[33] *ibid*, s 2(1)(a)(ia), as inserted by s 92 of the Civil Partnership and Certain Rights and Obligations of Cohabitants Act 2010.

[34] Domestic Violence Act 1996, s 2(1)(a)(ii), as substituted by s 60(a) of the Civil Law (Miscellaneous Provisions) Act 2011.

- a parent of the respondent if the respondent is a person of full age and not dependent;
- an adult who lives with the respondent in a relationship the basis of which is not primarily contractual;
- a parent of a child whose other parent is the respondent.[35]

Barring Orders

Barring orders have the effect of prohibiting a person from entering a property, even if they are a part owner of the property. A barring order may be sought by a spouse, parent, civil partner or ex-civil partner[36] or a cohabitant who has lived with the respondent in an intimate and committed relationship for at least six months in aggregate during the nine months immediately prior to the application for the barring order.[37] **13–19**

Gardaí are furnished with copies of orders that have been made, pursuant to s 11 of the 1996 Act. The orders provide that persons to whom they are directed: **13–20**

> "shall not use or threaten to use violence against, molest or put in fear the applicant or that dependent person"

and

> "if he or she is residing at a place other than the place where the applicant or that dependent person resides, shall not watch or beset the place where the applicant or that dependent person resides."

There is no requirement that violence actually be used; it may merely be threatened to amount to a breach of the order.

Arrest for Breach of Orders

Breach of a safety, barring, interim barring or protection order is an offence under s 17 of the Domestic Violence Acts 1996 and 2002. Though the offence is only triable summarily, the gardaí are provided with a power of arrest, and a power of entry for arrest in s 18. The section is phrased interestingly, in that the power to arrest would appear to be dependent on there being a complaint from the person to whom the order relates, or on the request of another person on the applicant's behalf, as well as on the assessment of the garda evaluating the situation. Section 18(1)(a) provides: **13–21**

> "Where a member of the Garda Síochána has reasonable cause for believing that, in respect of an order under this Act, an offence is being or has been committed under

---

35 Domestic Violence Act 1996, s 2(1)(a)(ii), as inserted by s 60(a) of the Civil Law (Miscellaneous Provisions) Act 2011.

36 Domestic Violence Act 1996, s 3(1)(aa), as inserted by s 93 of the Civil Partnership and Certain Rights and Obligations of Cohabitants Act 2010.

37 Domestic Violence Act 1996, s 3(1)(b), as amended by s 60(b) of the Civil Law (Miscellaneous Provisions) Act 2011.

> section 17 the member may, *on complaint being made to him or her by or on behalf of the person who was the applicant to which the order relates,* arrest the respondent concerned without warrant."[38]

The Garda Síochána Policy on Domestic Violence points out that:

> "... a Barring Order is not made void where the respondent has been allowed back, even for an extended period, by the applicant, into the premises from which he / she has been barred. The fact that some Courts may regard this action by the applicant as inconsistent does not affect the validity of the order and consequently the power of arrest."[39]

13–22 The second sub-section of s 18 had provided for a power of arrest where persons are not protected by the Domestic Violence Act orders, but might potentially be. However, failure to amend the section to take account of the Non-Fatal Offences against the Person Act 1997 means that the power of arrest originally contained in the sub-section is now defunct. The power in s 18(2) had provided an entry and arrest power where a garda had reasonable cause for believing that a person was committing or had committed an assault occasioning actual bodily harm or an offence under s 20 of the Offences against the Person Act 1861, in circumstances which, in the opinion of the garda, could give rise to an application for a safety order or a barring order. Section 20 of the 1861 Act has now been repealed by the schedule to the Non-Fatal Offences against the Person Act 1997, and the offence of assault occasioning actual bodily harm has been abolished by s 28(1)(b) of the 1997 Act. The failure to amend this section to substitute the offence of assault causing harm may have been an oversight or omission, or perhaps such an amendment was considered unnecessary in light of the power of entry provided by the Criminal Law Act 1997 for arrestable offences. An amendment to the section to include the offence of assault *simpliciter* contrary to s 2 of the Non-Fatal Offences against the Person Act 1997 would be a worthwhile reform, to allow for arrest in domestic disturbances where there has not been harm *per se*, but where harm is apprehended or anticipated, or where a less serious assault has occurred in the domestic context.

Orders Made under the Family Law (Protection of Spouses and Children) Act 1981

13–23 Before the enactment of the Domestic Violence Act 1996, civil domestic violence orders were made under the Family Law (Protection of Spouses and Children) Act 1981. Some such orders may still be in force, since orders of unlimited duration were made under that legislation. In the event of a breach, it may therefore fall to be considered as to whether a power of arrest under s 18 of the Domestic Violence Act 1996 exists, as the power of arrest is contained in the newer legislation.

13–24 Sections 2 and 3 of the Family Law (Protection of Spouses and Children) Act 1981 provided for protection and barring orders until the 1996 Act came into force. The 1996 Act repealed (replaced and made redundant) the 1981 Act, but provided for

[38] Domestic Violence Act 1996, s 18(1).

[39] An Garda Síochána Policy on Domestic Violence, para 4.2.

transitional provisions, ie orders made under the 1981 Act were to be treated as having been made under the 1996 Act, so that the orders would continue to have effect.

Section 23 of the Domestic Violence Act 1996 provides:

> " (1) The Family Law (Protection of Spouses and Children) Act, 1981 (in this section referred to as "the Act of 1981"), is hereby repealed.
>
> (2) (a) Subject to paragraph (b), this Act shall apply to a barring order made under the Act of 1981 and which is in force, or stayed by virtue of section 10 of that Act, at the commencement of this Act as if it were an order made under section 3.
>
> ...
>
> (4) This Act shall apply to a protection order made under the Act of 1981 and which is in force at the commencement of this Act as if it were an order made under section 5."

Therefore, a barring order made under the 1981 Act and in existence at the coming into force of the 1996 Act is deemed to be a barring order made under s 3 of the 1996 Act. There is reference in the 1996 Act to the expiry of orders within a specific period if they were made by the District Court or the Circuit Court on appeal from the District Court,[40] but if the order was made by the Circuit Court or High Court in the first instance, it may be of unlimited duration. **13–25**

It would therefore appear that, once an order under the 1981 Act has been made by the Circuit Court or High Court, it remains in force and ought to be treated as equivalent to an order under the 1996 Act and that there is therefore a power to arrest for its breach pursuant to s 18 of the Domestic Violence Act 1996. **13–26**

Threatening and Abusive Behaviour

The kind of behaviour frequently encountered in domestic abuse would, if it occurred in public, come within the ambit of s 6 of the Criminal Justice (Public Order) Act 1994, which prohibits threatening, abusive and insulting behaviour. However, two necessary elements for a s 6 offence are missing in the domestic abuse context: the behaviour will generally not have taken place in public and the requisite intention or recklessness—to provoke a breach of the peace—will be absent. In that regard, gardaí are faced with a significant practical drawback, as they are devoid of an arrest power for threatening or abusive behaviour in the home which falls short of an assault causing harm. **13–27**

Assault

The offence of assault *simpliciter* contrary to s 2 of the Non-Fatal Offences against the Person Act 1997 has no associated power of arrest, so gardaí encountering a suspected assault can only exercise the power of arrest if harm has been caused, so as to bring the offence within the ambit of s 3 of the Non-Fatal Offences against the Person Act 1997. **13–28**

---

[40] Domestic Violence Act 1996, s 23.

Breach of the Peace

13–29 Breach of the peace is a common law offence with an associated common law arrest power. The advantage is that the common law power of arrest which attaches to breach of the peace can be used even if the peace has not yet been broken. Gardaí or private citizens may arrest if a breach of the peace is thought to be immediately imminent. It is also possible for breach of the peace to occur on private property. However, the concept of a breach of the peace, applied in a private home, is often artificial since there is a public element to breach of the peace, a pre-requisite which is rarely satisfied in the context of domestic abuse.

13–30 In *Clifford v DPP*, Charleton J examined the offence of breach of the peace:

> "A breach of the peace implies conduct which goes beyond boisterousness. Instead, the offence involves a situation which imminently threatens a person, through the conduct of those involved in the breach of the peace, but not necessarily directly, of being harmed through an assault, an affray, a riot, an unlawful assembly or any other serious disturbance; R v Eroll Howell (1981) 71 Cr App R 31 per Watkins LJ…"[41]

He concluded that

> "… breach of the peace… occurs where a person finds himself, or herself, in a situation where they reasonably fear that if they do not withdraw from it quite promptly, they may either be assaulted or that the disturbance in respect of which the accused stands charged may create the risk of a response which is disorderly and in consequence potentially violent whereby, through direct or indirect means, bystanders may be caught up in violence. In this context, shoving, flying missiles, stampeding by a few people or a section of a crowd, and fighting within a group, constitute examples of the kind of indirect violence that may ensnare the uninvolved and so constitute a breach of the peace."[42]

If these are the parameters of the offence they are seldom satisfied in a private home. Such behaviour, in which bystanders might be caught up in violence, is not characteristic of domestic abuse, which is an inherently private – and often hidden – experience. Breach of the peace is discussed in further detail in *Chapter 1: Arrest*, at para 1 – 81 *et seq*.

Criminal Damage

13–31 Section 2 of the Criminal Damage Act 1991 provides:

> "(1) A person who without lawful excuse damages any property belonging to another intending to damage any such property or being reckless as to whether any such property would be damaged shall be guilty of an offence.
>
> (2) A person who without lawful excuse damages any property, whether belonging to himself or another—
>
> (a) intending to damage any property or being reckless as to whether any property would be damaged, and

---

[41] *Clifford v DPP* [2008] IEHC 322. The High Court decision in *Clifford* was subsequently upheld by the Supreme Court, *Clifford v DPP* [2013] IESC 43.

[42] *ibid.*

(b) intending by the damage to endanger the life of another or being reckless as to whether the life of another would be thereby endangered, shall be guilty of an offence.

(3) A person who damages any property, whether belonging to himself or another, with intent to defraud shall be guilty of an offence.

(4) An offence committed under this section by damaging property by fire shall be charged as arson…"

In the domestic abuse context, in determining whether an arrest for criminal damage is appropriate, it can be difficult to decipher the ownership of property which has been damaged, particularly in a shared home. Notwithstanding extensive damage to property, it might not be readily apparent that an offence contrary to s 2 has been committed. As is clear from s 2, for it to be an offence for a person to damage his own property the damage must be caused with intention or recklessness as to whether the life of another person would be endangered, or with an intention to defraud. **13–32**

Threats to damage the property of others, and threats to damage one's own property in a manner likely to endanger life, both provided for by s 3 of the Criminal Damage Act 1991, are also relevant arrestable offences in domestic abuse investigations.

Harassment

Harassment is an offence which frequently involves people who are or have been intimately connected with each other. Section 10(1) and (2) of the Non Fatal Offences against the Person Act 1997 provides: **13–33**

"(1) Any person who, without lawful authority or reasonable excuse, by any means including by use of the telephone, harasses another by persistently following, watching, pestering, besetting or communicating with him or her, shall be guilty of an offence.

(2) For the purposes of this section a person harasses another where—

(a) he or she, by his or her acts intentionally or recklessly, seriously interferes with the other's peace and privacy or causes alarm, distress or harm to the other, and

(b) his or her acts are such that a reasonable person would realise that the acts would seriously interfere with the other's peace and privacy or cause alarm, distress or harm to the other."

The offence is punishable by imprisonment for a period of up to seven years and is accordingly arrestable. The impugned actions are widely drawn to encompass a wide array of behaviour that adversely affects the life of another causing alarm and fear. Where persistent distress has been caused, it is an appropriate offence for consideration. An isolated incident will not amount to harassment, since the requirement of persistence in the statutory definition clearly envisages a course of conduct, rather than a one-off incident. **13–34**

Threat to Kill or Cause Serious Harm

The Non Fatal Offences against the Person Act provides at s 5: **13–35**

"(1) A person who, without lawful excuse, makes to another a threat, by any means intending the other to believe it will be carried out, to kill or cause serious harm to that other or a third person shall be guilty of an offence"

The penalty is imprisonment for up to ten years, and the offence is therefore arrestable. Serious harm is defined in s 1 of the 1997 Act as "injury which creates a substantial risk of death or which causes serious disfigurement or substantial loss or impairment of the mobility of the body as a whole or of the function of any particular bodily member or organ". The words themselves will not suffice to establish the offence; there must also be an intention on the part of the maker of the threat that the person to whom it is addressed should consider the threat to be credible.

Threats by Phone or Text Message

13–36 Threats which are made by phone or by text message may amount to an offence contrary to s 13 of the Post Office (Amendment) Act, as substituted by s 4 and Schedule 1 of the Communications Regulation (Amendment) Act 2007 provides:

> "(1) Any person who –
> (a) sends by telephone any message that is grossly offensive, or is indecent, obscene or menacing, or
> (b) for the purpose of causing annoyance, inconvenience or needless anxiety to another person –
> (i) sends by telephone any message that the sender knows to be false, or,
> (ii) persistently makes telephone calls to another person without reasonable cause, commits an offence."

The offence is triable both summarily and on indictment and carries a penalty on indictment of imprisonment for a period of up to five years. It is therefore an arrestable offence.

Weapon Offences

13–37 Offences contrary to s 9(1), s 9(4) and s 9(5) of the Firearms and Offensive Weapons Act 1990 are only capable of commission in a public place. However, the offence of producing an article capable of inflicting serious injury in the course of a dispute in a manner likely unlawfully to intimidate another person can occur in private, as well as in public. Section 11 of the Firearms and Offensive Weapons Act 1990 is therefore an important offence to bear in mind if attending domestic disturbances.

Intervention under the Mental Health Act 2001

13–38 If gardaí are called to an incident resembling a public order offence on private property, and it appears that the person causing the disturbance may be suffering from a mental disorder, as a result of which he or she poses an immediate and serious risk to himself or herself or to others, gardaí may take the person into custody under s 12 of the Mental Health Act 2001, which is discussed in *Chapter 2: Arrest and Detention in Other Contexts*, at para 2 – 02 *et seq*.

EVIDENCE GATHERING IN DOMESTIC ABUSE CASES

13–39 Victims in domestic abuse cases are vulnerable to attrition in the criminal process: that is to say that, for a variety of reasons, they may not wish to pursue a criminal prosecution. Given the intimacy and complexity of the relationships involved, complainant withdrawal is entirely understandable.

13–40 Given the potential for complainants to be reluctant witnesses, effective evidence gathering is crucial: photographs taken at the scene and of any injuries, the recording and transcripts of 999 calls, the accounts of any independent witnesses and the account of the suspect given in a memorandum of interview either voluntarily or under arrest, can potentially enable a prosecution to proceed, notwithstanding the withdrawal of a complaint. In the UK, Harfield has outlined a checklist for actions on arrival at a domestic abuse complaint. Many are of application in this jurisdiction for the effective investigation of domestic abuse incidents:

> **"Checklist – actions on arrival at the scene**
>
> To ensure the safety of victims and children and to preserve evidence, officers should:
>
> - Reassess victim and officer safety, including immediate risk, particularly in respect of access to or use of weapons;
> - Make an immediate assessment of the need for first aid or other medical assistance, such as an ambulance (this should include the needs of the victim, any children, any other persons and the suspect);
> - Separate parties, including any children;
> - Confirm the identity of the suspect (or, if they are no longer at the scene, immediately circulate a full description);
> - Establish who is or was at the scene, including any children;
> - Request appropriate checks on the suspect and household (including warrants, bail conditions, civil orders and child protection register… firearms licence, or intelligence reports linking suspect to weapons) if not already done;
> - Make accurate records of everything said by the suspect, victim and any witnesses, including children;
> - Consider taking photographs and / or using a video camera to record evidence;
>
> …
>
> - Secure the safety of victims in their home—if this is not possible, consideration should be given to taking them to another place of safety, eg the home of a relative or a refuge…
>
> Obtain an interview of what has occurred, taking into account the established risk factors associated with DA."[43]

13–41 There is a public interest in prosecuting the perpetrators of domestic violence. It must be recalled that gardaí intervene, not for an individual victim, but for the State, and that the State has a clear interest in ensuring the safety of all members of the community.

43 C Harfield, *Blackstone's Police Operational Handbook* (Oxford University Press, Oxford, 2009) at p 850–851.

Part VII
Language Rights

CHAPTER 14

Non-English Speaking Suspects

INTRODUCTION

To the greatest extent possible, gardaí must ensure that the members of the public who are subject to their powers have their rights respected in real and practical terms.[1] Undoubtedly non-English speaking suspects and defendants are at a significant disadvantage.[2] They are ill-equipped to participate in a system in which oral evidence is central, and may not fully understand their rights within that system. **14–01**

The dramatic demographic change which has taken place in Ireland over the last two decades presents the gardaí with significant challenges, not least in terms of communications. Non-nationals now comprise approximately ten percent of the population, and it is estimated that more than 160 languages are now spoken in the State.[3] **14–02**

The submission of the National Consultative Committee on Racism and Interculturalism to An Garda Síochána Policing Plan 2005 drew on the UK experience of policing a multicultural society and pointed to the juxtaposition in that jurisdiction of the over-representation of minorities within the criminal justice system, with a marked under-representation of minorities as employees in the agencies of criminal justice and law enforcement. **14–03**

> "Policing intercultural societies presents challenges for all democratic states. Attention has focused on these challenges in recent years, given increasing global mobility; and a

---

1 See JBL Chan, *Changing Police Culture: Policing in a Multicultural Society,* (Cambridge University Press, Cambridge, 1997).

2 See I Nakane "Problems in Communicating the Suspect's Rights in Interpreted Police Interviews" *Applied Linguistics*, 2007; 28: pp 87-112.

3 *Report of the Garda Inspectorate, Policing in Ireland – Looking Forward,* August 2007 at p 18, available online at http://www.justice.ie/en/JELR/rGI05%20GI_Policing%20V2.pdf/Files/rGI05%20GI_Policing%20V2.pdf <accessed 3 November 2013>.

> recognition that respect for cultural and ethnic diversity should underpin all aspect[s] of state policy.
>
> It is clear that minority ethnic groups suffer from specific disadvantages in relating to the criminal justice system. Evidence from the UK has long demonstrated that people from ethnic communities are: more likely to have worse experiences in the criminal justice system; are over-represented in all stages of the criminal justice system and under-represented as employees of criminal justice services and agencies; and lack confidence in the police."[4]

14–04 It it is far from clear that minority groups are similarly over-represented as defendants in the Irish criminal justice system, but undoubtedly minority groups are under-represented as employees in the organisations central to the Irish criminal process. The degree to which non-English speaking suspects are accommodated in the Irish criminal process is debatable. Though the National Consultative Committee on Racism and Interculturalism has praised An Garda Síochána for initiatives reflecting the challenges of policing a multicultural society — the establishment of the Garda Racial and Intercultural Office (GRIO)[5]; the ethical framework developed by the Garda Human Rights Office; the development of diversity and anti-racism training and the appointment of Ethnic Liaison Officers (ELO)[6] — more needs to be done in practical terms to accommodate suspects who have an inadequate command of the English language, and to address the difficulties encountered by gardaí in policing multi-ethnic and minority communities. Holdaway argues that, rather than having expertise in dealing with minorities compartmentalised in specialist units, the focus should be on equipping every member of the force with the requisite skills to police a multicultural society.[7] With an emphasis on combating racist crime and increasing

---

4 National Consultative Committee on Racism and Interculturalism Submission to An Garda Síochána Policing Plan 2005, November 2004, at p 5. See also E Erez, J Finckenauer and P Ibarra, "Policing a Multicultural Society" *Police and Society, 2003, Issue no 7, pp 5–12,* and S Holdaway, "Police Race Relations in England and Wales: Theory, Policy and Practice", *Police and Society*, 2003, Issue no 7, pp 49–74.

5 The Garda Racial and Intercultural Office is responsible for advising, monitoring and co-ordinating police activity in Ireland around racial, ethnic, religious and cultural diversity. It has recently been renamed the Garda Racial, Intercultural and Diversity Office.

6 National Consultative Committee on Racism and Interculturalism Submission to An Garda Síochána Policing Plan 2005, November 2004.

7 S Holdaway, "Police Race Relations in England and Wales: Theory, Policy and Practice" *Police and Society*, 2003, Issue no 7, pp 49–74, at pp 53–54. "Until the early 1980s, the police took the widely accepted view that immigrants would gradually assimilate into our apparently homogeneous culture. The initial task for police was to understand different immigrant cultures and for people from those cultures to understand the traditions of English policing. When a problem of "police immigrant relations" (the term used) was identified, it was understood as a difficulty of communication across cultural barriers (Dear, 1972). The solution lay in better forms of communication, in the skills of officers working in specialist, police community relations departments, and through the provision of adequate information about immigrant cultures. This approach had two main effects. It located police race relations within specialist departments, not within routine policing. The problems of policing "those people" became the concern of specialist officers who understood immigrants and their cultures. The work of the rank and file was largely unaffected by police community relations policies. Further, because immigrants were thought to have distinct cultures, the idea that they

the cultural diversity of the force itself, practical initiatives aimed at addressing the day-to-day realities of dealing with non-national suspects and witnesses are perhaps less evident.

This chapter will examine some legal aspects of policing non-English speaking suspects, including rights to interpretative assistance and the policing of persons who wish to communicate in the Irish language. **14–05**

INTERPRETATION AND TRANSLATION RIGHTS

Interpretation and Translation as a Facet of Natural Justice

Interpretation and translation rights have long been recognised as a facet of natural justice at common law.[8] In *Attorney General v Joyce and Walsh*[9] Kennedy CJ held that: **14–06**

> "It would seem to me to be a requisite of natural justice, particularly in a criminal trial, that a witness should be allowed to give evidence in the language which is his or her vernacular language, whether that language be Irish or English or any foreign language; and it would follow, if the language used should not be a language known to the members of the court, that means of interpreting the language to the court (judge and jury), and also in the case of evidence against a prisoner, that means of interpreting it to the prisoner should be provided."[10]

In *State (Buchan) v Coyne,*[11] in which a District Judge had refused to order the interpretation into English of police evidence tendered in Irish, in circumstances where the defendant spoke only English, Sullivan CJ held: **14–07**

> "it is obvious that in this case one of the fundamental principles of the administration of criminal justice has been disregarded and that a conviction obtained in it could not possibly stand in any court of law."[12]

Citing the case, Hogan and Whyte state that:

> "[I]t is obviously part of the concept of natural justice that a party affected by criminal (or other legal) proceedings should be told of the case against him in a language he understands."

---

were really different from the English was emphasized. They needed to and would mould their very different cultures into the mainstream culture of English society. Immigrants were therefore not citizens in the same sense as white people were citizens. Within this framework of understanding, race relations were of little relevance to a local police commander and his officers."

8 *R v Lee Kun* (1915) 11 Cr App R 293 at 300.

9 *Attorney General v Joyce and Walsh* [1929] IR 526.

10 *ibid* at 581.

11 *State (Buchan) v Coyne* (1936) 70 ILTR 185.

12 *ibid.*

14–08 The Canadian Supreme Court has given what is considered to be the leading modern authority on the assistance of an interpreter[13] in the case of *R v Tran.*[14] Considering the purpose of a right to interpretation, the Court held:

> "It is clear that the right to the assistance of an interpreter of an accused who cannot communicate or be understood for language reasons is based on the fundamental notion that no person should be subject to a Kafkaesque trial which may result in loss of liberty. An accused has the right to know in full detail, and contemporaneously, what is taking place in the proceedings which will decide his or her fate. This is basic fairness. Even if a trial is objectively a model of fairness, if an accused operating under a language handicap is not given full and contemporaneous interpretation of the proceedings, he or she will not be able to assess this for him or herself. The very legitimacy of the justice system in the eyes of those who are subject to it is dependent on their being able to comprehend and communicate in the language in which the proceedings are taking place."[15]

14–09 There has been a shift in Irish criminal proceedings from the court to the garda station, with detention for questioning firmly embedded in the legal landscape and the gradual extension of periods of detention. The expansion of provisions for adverse inferences from silence[16] illustrates the premium placed on oral evidence in our system and underlines the importance of linguistic assistance in the garda station and through all stages of the criminal process. The requirement that interpretation and translation services be provided from the point of arrest onwards is more than a cosmopolitan reflection of our new found multiculturalism: it goes to the heart of the fairness of criminal proceedings.

European Convention on Human Rights

14–10 The European Convention for the Protection of Human Rights and Fundamental Freedoms provides for language assistance from the point of arrest onwards, and the European Convention on Human Rights Act 2003, which gives the Convention effect in Irish law, in turn requires that every organ of the State shall perform its functions in a manner compatible with the State's obligations under the Convention provisions.[17]

---

[13] See T O'Malley, *The Criminal Process* (Round Hall, Dublin, 2009) at p 206.

[14] *R v Tran* [1994] 2 SCR 951.

[15] *ibid* at 975.

[16] Adverse inferences provisions were originally contained in ss 18–19 of the Criminal Justice Act 1984; s 3 of the Criminal Justice (Forensic Evidence) Act 1990; s 7 of the Criminal Justice (Drug Trafficking) Act 1996; and ss 2 and 5 of the Offences Against the State (Amendment) Act 1998. The Criminal Justice Act 2007 repealed s 7 of the Criminal Justice (Drug Trafficking) Act 1996 and s 5 of the Offences Against the State (Amendment) Act 1998, and replaced them with significantly expanded inference provisions in Part 4 of the Criminal Justice Act 2007. There is now potential for inferences to be drawn from silence in the case of all arrestable offences, so that failure to account for various facts and assertions put to the accused during Garda questioning will result in the court being able to "... draw such inferences from the failure as appear proper; and the failure may, on the basis of such inferences, be treated as, or as capable of amounting to, corroboration of any evidence in relation to which the failure is material".

[17] European Convention on Human Rights Act 2003, s 3. The Irish Human Rights Commission points out in relation to s 3 that "[t]herefore, all public bodies, including An Garda Síochána, are

The Convention provides at Article 5(2):

> "Everyone who is arrested shall be informed promptly, in a language which he understands, of the reasons for his arrest and of any charge against him."

It is of note that the requirement is that the information be conveyed in a language which is understood, not necessarily the first language of the suspect. Enquiries should therefore be made to ascertain what languages are spoken and understood by the suspect, rather than making assumptions based on nationality. **14–11**

Article 6(3) of the Convention states that everyone charged with a criminal offence has among their minimum rights: **14–12**

> "(a) to be informed promptly, in a language which he understands and in detail, of the nature and cause of the accusation against him;
> (b) to have adequate time and facilities for the preparation of his defence;
> (c) to defend himself in person or through legal assistance of his own choosing or, if he has not sufficient means to pay for legal assistance, to be given it free when the interests of justice so require;
> (d) to examine or have examined witnesses against him and to obtain the attendance and examination of witnesses on his behalf under the same conditions as witnesses against him;
> (e) to have the free assistance of an interpreter if he cannot understand or speak the language used in court."

In *Kamasinski v Austria*, inadequate interpretation and translation facilities were held to constitute a violation of Article 6 of the European Convention on Human Rights, and the right to interpretation and translation was found to extend to pre-trial proceedings. The European Court of Human Rights held: **14–13**

> "The right, stated in paragraph 3 (e) of Article 6 (art 6-3-e), to the free assistance of an interpreter applies not only to oral statements made at the trial hearing but also to documentary material and the pre-trial proceedings… However, paragraph 3 (e) (art. 6-3-e) does not go so far as to require a written translation of all items of written evidence or official documents in the procedure. The interpretation assistance provided should be such as to enable the defendant to have knowledge of the case against him and to defend himself, notably by being able to put before the court his version of the events…. In view of the need for the right guaranteed by paragraph 3 (e) (art. 6-3-e) to be practical and effective, the obligation of the competent authorities is not limited to the appointment of an interpreter but, if they are put on notice in the particular circumstances, may also extend to a degree of subsequent control over the adequacy of the interpretation provided (see, mutatis mutandis, the *Artico* judgment previously cited, Series A no 37, pp 16 and 18, §§ 33 and 36…"[18]

---

under a specific statutory obligation to perform their functions in an ECHR compliant manner." ICHR Policy Statement: *Human Rights Compliance of An Garda Síochána* (Irish Human Rights Commission, Dublin, 2009), at p 30.

[18] *Kamasinski v Austria* (App no 9783/82) ECHR 19 December 1989, para 74, p 30.

The right to interpretation and translation has been put on a firmer footing across the European Union with the adoption of a Directive on interpretation and translation rights.

Directive on the Right to Interpretation and Translation in Criminal Proceedings

14–14 Reflective of the centrality of interpretation and translation rights as an aspect of the right to a fair trial, a European Directive on the right to interpretation and translation in criminal proceedings[19] was adopted in 2010. It provides a right of access to interpretation and translation during the investigative and judicial process for suspects who do not speak or understand the language of the criminal proceedings.[20] There is an entitlement to translation of essential documents,[21] and the costs of translation and interpretation are to be borne by Member States.[22] The Directive requires Member States to ensure that translation and interpretation are of appropriate quality, that interpreters and translators are appropriately qualified and that confidentiality is maintained.[23]

Appropriately Qualified Interpreters

14–15 When investigating offences involving non-English speaking suspects, every effort must be made to ensure that the reasons for the arrest are communicated and understood, and, where an interpreter is required, one should be sought as soon as possible. The use of friends and family members is potentially problematic and should be avoided wherever possible. Chan points to the unreliability or untruthfulness of translations, inadequate knowledge on the part of the interpreter and the use of children to interpret as problems identified in a survey of policing in New South Wales.[24] The Irish Translators' and Interpreters' Association (ITIA) maintains a register of members[25] who translate and interpret in multiple language combinations, including British and Irish sign language. The manner in which translators and interpreters are employed for An Garda Síochána has been strongly criticised, with a motion at the 2009 Garda Representative Association (GRA) annual delegate conference calling for minimum standards for interpreters used by An Garda Síochána "in view of the inadequate vetting and complete absence of accreditation at present".[26] Writing in the *Garda Review*, Detective Garda Tom O'Sullivan highlights practical and operational problems in the provision of interpretation services:

---

[19] Directive 2010/64/EU of 20 October 2010 on the right to interpretation and translation in criminal proceedings, OJ L 280, 26 October 2010. The Directive sets out a transposition date of 27 October 2013.

[20] *ibid,* Article 2.

[21] *ibid,* Article 3.

[22] *ibid,* Article 4.

[23] *ibid,* Article 5.

[24] See Chan, *Changing Police Culture: Policing in a Multicultural Society* (Cambridge University Press, 1997).

[25] Available online at http://translatorsassociation.ie.

[26] *Garda Review* Vol 37, No 3, April 2009, at p 9.

> "There are several difficulties experienced in the interaction between Gardaí and interpreters including the lack of academic checks on interpreters to ensure that they are professionally competent to do the work. More worryingly there is an abject failure to carry out criminal record security vetting on interpreters used by police. Pragmatically there are problems in sourcing interpreters outside office hours."[27]

He argues that An Garda Síochána should compile a list of competent, professionally accredited interpreters and translators whose immigration status, security clearance and criminal record have been checked, and to replace the scheme in operation currently whereby the agency contracted to undertake translation for An Garda Síochána is entrusted with verification of the qualifications and suitability of interpreters. His comments are pertinent in the context of the Directive on the right to interpretation and translation in criminal proceedings and its requirement that interpreters are appropriately qualified and that the services they provide are of the appropriate quality.[28] **14–16**

Intercultural Ireland – Your Changing Community[29] is one of two booklets published in 2002 by the Garda Racial and Intercultural Office. The second booklet, *Your Police Service in Intercultural Ireland*[30] aims to provide information for minority groups to facilitate an understanding of the role of An Garda Síochána. *Intercultural Ireland – Your Changing Community* is intended to help members of the Garda to improve understanding and delivery of policing services to people of diverse cultural, ethnic and religious backgrounds.[31] It contains an excerpt from the Garda Manual of Crime Investigation Techniques (1994): **14–17**

> "When a person who does not understand either the Irish or English language is to be questioned, it will be necessary to secure the service of an interpreter. The following procedures should be observed:
>
> 1. The person should be questioned through the interpreter who should record the statement in the language in which it is made.
>
> 2. A verbal translation should be made as the statement is taken so that any ambiguities can be rectified at the time.
>
> 3. All statements should be read over to the person making the statement and signed.

---

27 T O'Sullivan, "Lost in Translation", *Garda Review*, Vol 36, No 9, November 2008 pp 4–7.

28 Directive 2010/64/EU of 20 October 2010 on the right to interpretation and translation in criminal proceedings, OJ L 280, 26 October 2010, Article 5.

29 An Garda Síochána (2002) *Intercultural Ireland –Your Changing Community*, (Garda Racial and Intercultural Office, Dublin).

30 An Garda Síochána (2002) *Your Police Service in Intercultural Ireland*, (Garda Racial and Intercultural Office, Dublin).

31 See National Consultative Committee on Racism and Interculturalism Response by Ireland to the OSCE *Notes Verbales* Regarding Tolerance and Non-Discrimination: hate crime, including violent manifestation of racism, xenophobia, discrimination and anti-Semitism, Ireland, October 2004. See also Mary Phelan "Interpreting, Translation and Public Bodies in Ireland: The Need for Policy and Training", *National Consultative Committee on Racism and Interculturalism Advocacy Paper*, Number 5, February 2007.

> 4. An official Irish or English translation should then be made and proved by the interpreter, as an exhibit with the original statement."[32]

14–18 Mary Phelan of the Irish Translators' and Interpreters' Association states that:

> "In Garda stations, despite the above guidelines, the practice is to take the statement in English, have the translation read aloud in the foreign language by the interpreter and then the witness signs the statement if s/he is satisfied that it is accurate."[33]

14–19 Accuracy is obviously crucial in this context, and gaps in procedure provide scope for error and for potentially serious evidential difficulties. The Directive on the right to interpretation and translation in criminal proceedings does not prescribe the manner in which interpretation should be conducted, but provides at Article 2:

> "1. Member States shall ensure that suspected or accused persons who do not speak or understand the language of the criminal proceedings concerned are provided, without delay, with interpretation during criminal proceedings before investigative and judicial authorities, including during police questioning, all court hearings and any necessary interim hearings.
>
> 2. Member States shall ensure that, where necessary for the purpose of safeguarding the fairness of the proceedings, interpretation is available for communication between suspected or accused persons and their legal counsel in direct connection with any questioning or hearing during the proceedings or with the lodging of an appeal or other procedural applications.
>
> 3. The right to interpretation under paragraphs 1 and 2 includes appropriate assistance for persons with hearing or speech impediments.
>
> 4. Member States shall ensure that a procedure or mechanism is in place to ascertain whether suspected or accused persons speak and understand the language of the criminal proceedings and whether they need the assistance of an interpreter.
>
> 5. Member States shall ensure that, in accordance with procedures in national law, suspected or accused persons have the right to challenge a decision finding that there is no need for interpretation and, when interpretation has been provided, the possibility to complain that the quality of the interpretation is not sufficient to safeguard the fairness of the proceedings.
>
> 6. Where appropriate, communication technology such as videoconferencing, telephone or the Internet may be used, unless the physical presence of the interpreter is required in order to safeguard the fairness of the proceedings.
>
> 7. In proceedings for the execution of a European arrest warrant, the executing Member State shall ensure that its competent authorities provide persons subject to

---

[32] An Garda Síochána (2002) *Intercultural Ireland – Your Changing Community*, (Garda Racial and Intercultural Office, Dublin).

[33] See also Mary Phelan "Interpreting, Translation and Public Bodies in Ireland: The Need for Policy and Training", *National Consultative Committee on Racism and Interculturalism Advocacy Paper*, Number 5, February 2007.

> such proceedings who do not speak or understand the language of the proceedings with interpretation in accordance with this Article.
>
> 8. Interpretation provided under this Article shall be of a quality sufficient to safeguard the fairness of the proceedings, in particular by ensuring that suspected or accused persons have knowledge of the case against them and are able to exercise their right of defence."

The right to an interpreter applies when a suspect or witness actually needs an interpreter to give evidence or to defend himself, rather than being a matter of preference in the language chosen or in order to make a political statement.[34] However, there is a constitutional aspect to the use of the Irish language, so slightly different considerations apply. **14–20**

COMMUNICATING REASONS FOR ARREST TO NON-ENGLISH-SPEAKING SUSPECTS

The extent to which an arresting garda is required to ensure that the reasons for an arrest are understood by non-English speaking (or deaf) arrestees has yet to be definitively clarified in Irish law. Clearly there is an entitlement to know the reason for an arrest before a suspect is required to submit to it, and there is significant scope for misunderstanding and distress when the language spoken by the police authorities is not understood. While it seems that the right to understand is clearly fundamental in the pre-trial period and at trial, the extent of the level of understanding required for fairness at the point of arrest (and during the time between arrest and conveyance to the garda station) is potentially more problematic. **14–21**

The custody regulations are limited in their guidance,[35] and no distinction is made between English speaking and non-English speaking arrestees. Regulation 8(1) provides: **14–22**

> "The member in charge shall without delay inform an arrested person or cause him to be informed—
> (a) in ordinary language of the offence or other matter in respect of which he has been arrested,
> (b) that he is entitled to consult a solicitor… "

The High Court has found that the duty of a member in charge under the custody regulations is limited to ensuring that a person in custody has been informed of his rights under the regulations, and that there is no duty to ensure that those rights are understood: **14–23**

---

34 T O'Malley, *The Criminal Process* (Round Hall, Dublin, 2009) at p 209.

35 Reg 14 of the Criminal Justice Act 1984 (Treatment Of Persons in Custody in Garda Síochána Stations) Regulations 1987 (SI No 119 of 1987), imposes a duty on the member in charge to inform a foreign national that he may communicate with his consul and receive a visit from a consular representative.

> "What the Regulations require is that certain information must be given to an accused person on his arrest, and he must be given a written document setting out his rights by the member in charge of the relevant Garda station. Counsel for the Respondent submitted that this imposed an onerous duty on the member in charge, and that he must be satisfied that the accused understood his rights, as the purpose of the Regulations is to ensure that the accused is aware of his rights. I do not accept that this is a correct analysis of the situation. The Regulations require that the accused be informed of his rights, whether he understands them or not, and the essential proof at the hearing is that he was so informed. In my opinion, all that is required is that the relevant information is given to the accused, and the relevant notice is handed to him."[36]

14–24 However a distinction must be drawn between the defendant in *O'Kelly*, who spoke English, and a suspect who does not — a suspect cannot be said to have been meaningfully informed if he has been 'informed' of his rights in a language he does not understand.

14–25 Failure to communicate the reason for an arrest is not necessarily fatal, and can be subsequently rectified. The requirement under Article 5(1) of the European Convention that an arrestee be informed "promptly in a language he understands" of the reason for his or her arrest clearly envisages that it will not always be possible to do so immediately. It has been suggested that, if there is a question mark over the validity of an arrest for want of the arrestee's understanding of the reason for it, the arrest will become valid at the point at which the reason has been conveyed in a language the suspect understands. Walsh opines that:

> "If the arrest is unlawful for a failure to satisfy one or other of the formalities at the time of the arrest, the subsequent detention will become unlawful. However, if the formalities are fulfilled at some point during the suspect's detention, his custody will become lawful from that point… it would appear that the court will treat the giving of the real reason for the detention as the beginning of a valid arrest. Moreover it is not necessary to release the suspect from custody before the subsequent lawful arrest and detention can be effected."[37]

14–26 In Australasia *A Multilingual Communication Guide for Police*[38] has been developed by the Police Multicultural Advisory Bureau,[39] to provide a practical support for police with eight simple standard questions translated into 34 languages[40]:

- What is your given name and surname?

---

[36] *People (DPP) v Ivan O'Kelly*, unreported, High Court, 10 February 1998.

[37] D Walsh, *Criminal Procedure* (Butterworths, Dublin, 2002), p 185, citing the cases of *People v Shaw* [1982] IR 1 and *R v Kulyncz* [1971] 1 QB 367.

[38] The guide is available online at http://www.apmab.gov.au/guide/multilingual/guide.pdf .

[39] The Bureau, formerly known as the National Police Ethnic Advisory Bureau, promotes harmonious policing and multicultural community relations in Australasia and aims to be internationally recognised as a leading agency in the area of police management of cultural and linguistic diversity.

[40] The languages are: Amharic, Arabic, Bosnian, Cambodian, Chinese, Croatian, Czech, Filipino, French, German, Greek, Hmong, Hungarian, Indonesian, Italian, Japanese, Korean, Kurdish, Laotian, Macedonian, Maltese, Persian, Polish, Romanian, Russian, Samoan, Serbian, Somali, Spanish, Tetum, Tongan, Turkish and Vietnamese.

- What is your address and contact number?
- What is your date of birth?
- Please show me your driver's licence or other identification.
- Thank you, you may go now.
- You are not under arrest, I just want to find out more about what happened.
- Please accompany me to the police station and I will contact an interpreter.
- Please wait, I will find an interpreter to assist us.

Similar measures would be of benefit in Ireland to put the lawfulness of arrests of non-English speaking suspects on a firmer footing, to assist gardaí in investigating offences and to build trust for community policing in non-native Irish communities.

PERSONS WHO WISH TO COMMUNICATE IN THE IRISH LANGUAGE

The Irish Constitution provides at Article 8 that the Irish language, as the national language, is the first official language of the State, with English recognised as the second official language. Article 8.3 provides: **14–27**

> "[P]rovision may be made by law for the exclusive use of either of the said languages for any one or more official purposes, either throughout the State or in any part thereof."

While the Official Languages Act 2003 seeks to promote the use of the Irish language in State business (by providing for the use of Irish in the Oireachtas, for simultaneous publication of legislation in both languages, and for the provision of services by public bodies through Irish), to date no provision has been made for the *exclusive* use of either of the official languages for official purposes.[41] The Act obliges public bodies, of which An Garda Síochána is one,[42] to publish official documents, such as annual reports, in both languages and specifies that: **14–28**

> "where a person communicates in writing or by electronic mail in an official language with a public body, the public body shall reply in the same language."[43]

Communications in writing or by e-mail with the general public or a class of the general public must be in Irish or bilingual.[44]

In relation to court proceedings, the Official Languages Act 2003 provides at s 8 that: **14–29**

> "(1) A person may use either of the official languages in, or in any pleading in or document issuing from, any court.

[41] Hogan and Whyte, *JM Kelly: the Irish Constitution* (4th ed, LexisNexis Butterworths, Dublin, 2003) at p 156. See also *Ó Beoláin v Fahy* [2001] 2 IR 279.

[42] Official Languages Act 2003, First Schedule.

[43] *ibid*, s 9(2).

[44] *ibid*, s 9(3).

(2) Every court has, in any proceedings before it, the duty to ensure that any person appearing in or giving evidence before it may be heard in the official language of his or her choice, and that in being so heard the person will not be placed at a disadvantage by not being heard in the other official language.

(3) For the purposes of ensuring that no person is placed at a disadvantage as aforesaid, the court may cause such facilities to be made available, as it considers appropriate, for the simultaneous or consecutive interpretation of proceedings from one official language into the other.

(4) Where the State or a public body is a party to civil proceedings before a court—
- (a) the State or the public body shall use in the proceedings, the official language chosen by the other party, and
- (b) if two or more persons (other than the State or a public body) are party to the proceedings and they fail to choose or agree on the official language to be used in the proceedings, the State or, as appropriate, the public body shall use in the proceedings such official language as appears to it to be reasonable, having regard to the circumstances.

(5) Notwithstanding any other provision of this section, a person shall not be compelled to give evidence in a particular official language in any proceedings.

(6) In choosing to use a particular official language in any proceedings before a court, a person shall not be put by the court or a public body to any inconvenience or expense over and above that which would have been incurred had he or she chosen to use the other official language."

14–30 The duties of gardaí under the Constitution and under the statutory scheme provided by the Official Languages Act may be summarised as follows:

- there is an obligation on An Garda Síochána to ensure that its publications, stationery, signage and recorded messages are bilingual;
- persons who wish to communicate in the Irish language in their dealings with gardaí must be facilitated in doing so.

14–31 There is no requirement that gardaí dealing with an exclusively Irish-speaking person communicate in Irish but, as is the position with all non-English-speaking suspects, there is an obligation to ensure that the person has the requisite facilities and interpretative assistance to enable them to understand the proceedings and to communicate and participate effectively in the pre-trial process. In the Irish language context, this is a right which is not only based in the common law and in the European Convention, but is also constitutional in character.

INDEX

[Reader Note: The majority of entries in this index refer to paragraph numbers however there are some entries which are prefixed with a 'p' or 'pp' to denote page number(s)]